Toyota Corolla
Owners Workshop Manual

Martynn Randall

(4286 - 288)

Models covered
Saloon, Hatchback, Liftback & Estate, including special/limited editions
1.3 litre (1332cc), 1.4 litre (1398cc) & 1.6 litre (1587cc & 1598cc) petrol

Does NOT cover models with 1.8 litre (1762cc) petrol engine, diesel engines, or 4-wheel-drive
Does NOT cover new Corolla range introduced January 2002

© Haynes Publishing 2006

A book in the **Haynes Service and Repair Manual Series**

All rights reserved. No part of this book may be reproduced or transmitted in any form or by any means, electronic or mechanical, including photocopying, recording or by any information storage or retrieval system, without permission in writing from the copyright holder.

ISBN 1 84425 286 8

British Library Cataloguing in Publication Data
A catalogue record for this book is available from the British Library.

ABCDE
FGHIJ
KLMNO
PQRST

Printed in the USA

Haynes Publishing
Sparkford, Yeovil, Somerset BA22 7JJ, England

Haynes North America, Inc
861 Lawrence Drive, Newbury Park, California 91320, USA

Editions Haynes
4, Rue de l'Abreuvoir
92415 COURBEVOIE CEDEX, France

Haynes Publishing Nordiska AB
Box 1504, 751 45 UPPSALA, Sverige

Contents

LIVING WITH YOUR TOYOTA COROLLA

Safety first!	Page	0•5
Introduction	Page	0•6

Roadside repairs

Introduction	Page	0•7
If your car won't start	Page	0•7
Jump starting	Page	0•8
Wheel changing	Page	0•9
Identifying leaks	Page	0•10
Towing	Page	0•10

Weekly checks

Introduction	Page	0•11
Underbonnet check points	Page	0•11
Engine oil level	Page	0•12
Coolant level	Page	0•12
Brake and clutch fluid level	Page	0•13
Washer fluid level	Page	0•13
Tyre condition and pressure	Page	0•14
Power steering fluid level	Page	0•15
Wiper blades	Page	0•15
Battery	Page	0•16
Bulbs and fuses	Page	0•16

Lubricants and fluids

	Page	0•17

Tyre pressures

	Page	0•17

MAINTENANCE

Routine maintenance and servicing

Servicing specifications	Page	1•2
Maintenance schedule	Page	1•4
Maintenance procedures	Page	1•8

Illegal Copying

It is the policy of Haynes Publishing to actively protect its Copyrights and Trade Marks. Legal action will be taken against anyone who unlawfully copies the cover or contents of this Manual. This includes all forms of unauthorised copying including digital, mechanical, and electronic in any form. Authorisation from Haynes Publishing will only be provided expressly and in writing. Illegal copying will also be reported to the appropriate statutory authorities.

Contents

REPAIRS & OVERHAUL

Engine and associated systems

Engine in-car repair procedures	Page 2A•1
Engine removal and overhaul procedures	Page 2B•1
Cooling, heating and air conditioning systems	Page 3•1
Fuel and exhaust systems	Page 4A•1
Emission control systems	Page 4B•1
Starting and charging systems	Page 5A•1
Ignition systems	Page 5B•1

Transmission

Clutch	Page 6•1
Manual transmission	Page 7A•1
Automatic transmission	Page 7B•1
Driveshafts	Page 8•1

Brakes and suspension

Braking system	Page 9•1
Suspension and steering	Page 10•1

Body equipment

Bodywork and fittings	Page 11•1
Body electrical system	Page 12•1

Wiring diagrams

	Page 12•20

REFERENCE

Dimensions and weights	Page REF•1
Conversion factors	Page REF•2
Buying spare parts	Page REF•3
Vehicle identification	Page REF•3
General repair procedures	Page REF•4
Jacking and vehicle support	Page REF•5
Tools and working facilities	Page REF•6
MOT test checks	Page REF•8
Fault finding	Page REF•12
Glossary of technical terms	Page REF•22

Index

	Page REF•27

Advanced driving

Many people see the words 'advanced driving' and believe that it won't interest them or that it is a style of driving beyond their own abilities. Nothing could be further from the truth. Advanced driving is straightforward safe, sensible driving - the sort of driving we should all do every time we get behind the wheel.

An average of 10 people are killed every day on UK roads and 870 more are injured, some seriously. Lives are ruined daily, usually because somebody did something stupid. Something like 95% of all accidents are due to human error, mostly driver failure. Sometimes we make genuine mistakes - everyone does. Sometimes we have lapses of concentration. Sometimes we deliberately take risks.

For many people, the process of 'learning to drive' doesn't go much further than learning how to pass the driving test because of a common belief that good drivers are made by 'experience'.

Learning to drive by 'experience' teaches three driving skills:

☐ Quick reactions. (Whoops, that was close!)
☐ Good handling skills. (Horn, swerve, brake, horn).
☐ Reliance on vehicle technology. (Great stuff this ABS, stop in no distance even in the wet...)

Drivers whose skills are 'experience based' generally have a lot of near misses and the odd accident. The results can be seen every day in our courts and our hospital casualty departments.

Advanced drivers have learnt to control the risks by controlling the position and speed of their vehicle. They avoid accidents and near misses, even if the drivers around them make mistakes.

The key skills of advanced driving are **concentration,** effective all-round **observation, anticipation** and **planning.** When **good vehicle handling** is added to these skills, all driving situations can be approached and negotiated in a safe, methodical way, leaving nothing to chance.

Concentration means applying your mind to safe driving, completely excluding anything that's not relevant. Driving is usually the most dangerous activity that most of us undertake in our daily routines. It deserves our full attention.

Observation means not just looking, but seeing and seeking out the information found in the driving environment.

Anticipation means asking yourself what is happening, what you can reasonably expect to happen and what could happen unexpectedly. (One of the commonest words used in compiling accident reports is 'suddenly'.)

Planning is the link between seeing something and taking the appropriate action. For many drivers, planning is the missing link.

If you want to become a safer and more skilful driver and you want to enjoy your driving more, contact the Institute of Advanced Motorists at www.iam.org.uk, phone 0208 996 9600, or write to IAM House, 510 Chiswick High Road, London W4 5RG for an information pack.

Safety First! 0•5

Working on your car can be dangerous. This page shows just some of the potential risks and hazards, with the aim of creating a safety-conscious attitude.

General hazards

Scalding
• Don't remove the radiator or expansion tank cap while the engine is hot.
• Engine oil, automatic transmission fluid or power steering fluid may also be dangerously hot if the engine has recently been running.

Burning
• Beware of burns from the exhaust system and from any part of the engine. Brake discs and drums can also be extremely hot immediately after use.

Crushing
• When working under or near a raised vehicle, always supplement the jack with axle stands, or use drive-on ramps. *Never venture under a car which is only supported by a jack.* 
• Take care if loosening or tightening high-torque nuts when the vehicle is on stands. Initial loosening and final tightening should be done with the wheels on the ground.

Fire
• Fuel is highly flammable; fuel vapour is explosive.
• Don't let fuel spill onto a hot engine.
• Do not smoke or allow naked lights (including pilot lights) anywhere near a vehicle being worked on. Also beware of creating sparks (electrically or by use of tools).
• Fuel vapour is heavier than air, so don't work on the fuel system with the vehicle over an inspection pit.
• Another cause of fire is an electrical overload or short-circuit. Take care when repairing or modifying the vehicle wiring.
• Keep a fire extinguisher handy, of a type suitable for use on fuel and electrical fires.

Electric shock
• Ignition HT voltage can be dangerous, especially to people with heart problems or a pacemaker. Don't work on or near the ignition system with the engine running or the ignition switched on. 
• Mains voltage is also dangerous. Make sure that any mains-operated equipment is correctly earthed. Mains power points should be protected by a residual current device (RCD) circuit breaker.

Fume or gas intoxication
• Exhaust fumes are poisonous; they often contain carbon monoxide, which is rapidly fatal if inhaled. Never run the engine in a confined space such as a garage with the doors shut. 
• Fuel vapour is also poisonous, as are the vapours from some cleaning solvents and paint thinners.

Poisonous or irritant substances
• Avoid skin contact with battery acid and with any fuel, fluid or lubricant, especially antifreeze, brake hydraulic fluid and Diesel fuel. Don't syphon them by mouth. If such a substance is swallowed or gets into the eyes, seek medical advice.
• Prolonged contact with used engine oil can cause skin cancer. Wear gloves or use a barrier cream if necessary. Change out of oil-soaked clothes and do not keep oily rags in your pocket.
• Air conditioning refrigerant forms a poisonous gas if exposed to a naked flame (including a cigarette). It can also cause skin burns on contact.

Asbestos
• Asbestos dust can cause cancer if inhaled or swallowed. Asbestos may be found in gaskets and in brake and clutch linings. When dealing with such components it is safest to assume that they contain asbestos.

Special hazards

Hydrofluoric acid
• This extremely corrosive acid is formed when certain types of synthetic rubber, found in some O-rings, oil seals, fuel hoses etc, are exposed to temperatures above 400°C. The rubber changes into a charred or sticky substance containing the acid. *Once formed, the acid remains dangerous for years. If it gets onto the skin, it may be necessary to amputate the limb concerned.*
• When dealing with a vehicle which has suffered a fire, or with components salvaged from such a vehicle, wear protective gloves and discard them after use.

The battery
• Batteries contain sulphuric acid, which attacks clothing, eyes and skin. Take care when topping-up or carrying the battery.
• The hydrogen gas given off by the battery is highly explosive. Never cause a spark or allow a naked light nearby. Be careful when connecting and disconnecting battery chargers or jump leads.

Air bags
• Air bags can cause injury if they go off accidentally. Take care when removing the steering wheel and/or facia. Special storage instructions may apply.

Diesel injection equipment
• Diesel injection pumps supply fuel at very high pressure. Take care when working on the fuel injectors and fuel pipes.

⚠️ *Warning: Never expose the hands, face or any other part of the body to injector spray; the fuel can penetrate the skin with potentially fatal results.*

Remember...

DO
• Do use eye protection when using power tools, and when working under the vehicle.
• Do wear gloves or use barrier cream to protect your hands when necessary.
• Do get someone to check periodically that all is well when working alone on the vehicle.
• Do keep loose clothing and long hair well out of the way of moving mechanical parts.
• Do remove rings, wristwatch etc, before working on the vehicle – especially the electrical system.
• Do ensure that any lifting or jacking equipment has a safe working load rating adequate for the job.

DON'T
• Don't attempt to lift a heavy component which may be beyond your capability – get assistance.
• Don't rush to finish a job, or take unverified short cuts.
• Don't use ill-fitting tools which may slip and cause injury.
• Don't leave tools or parts lying around where someone can trip over them. Mop up oil and fuel spills at once.
• Don't allow children or pets to play in or near a vehicle being worked on.

Introduction

Toyota Corolla 3-door Hatchback

Continuing the tradition of the 'World's best-selling car', the range of Corolla models covered by this manual offers a wide range of body styles and engines, with the emphasis on proven, solid engineering, further reinforcing Toyota's deserved reputation for outstanding reliability. Introduced in June 1997, the Corolla was available as a 3-door Hatchback, 5-door Liftback, 4-door Saloon and a 5-door Estate, with a 5-door Hatchback version introduced in October 1998. In October 1999, the range underwent a facelift, with cosmetic revisions to the front bumper, headlights, bonnet and front grille. To coincide with the facelift, a new range of petrol engines, with variable intake camshaft timing, was introduced, replacing the existing units.

The petrol engines are all fuel injected, in-line, four-cylinder units of 1332 cc, 1398 cc, 1587 cc or 1598 cc displacement with double overhead camshaft and 16 valves. All engines are normally aspirated, with the 1.4 litre and 1.6 litre VVT-i engines (October 1999-on), incorporating an hydraulically controlled mechanism on the intake camshaft which varies the valve timing. This facility improves the driveability, efficiency and emissions of the engines. All engines feature a comprehensive engine management system with extensive emission control equipment. Although two diesel engines were available, neither are covered in this manual.

5- or 6-speed manual transmissions were available, along with 3- or 4-speed automatic options. Although a four-wheel-drive model was available in some markets, only the front-wheel-drive versions are covered by this manual.

Braking is by discs at the front, and by drums or discs at the rear. Hydraulically operated power-assisted steering is standard on all models, with ABS available as an option.

A wide range of standard and optional equipment is available within the range to suit virtually all tastes. Both a driver's and passenger's airbag were fitted as standard, with side airbags, incorporated into the front seats, and front seat belt pretensioners, available as an option on some models after the October 1999 facelift.

Provided that regular servicing is carried out in accordance with the manufacturer's recommendations, the Toyota Corolla will provide the enviable reliability for which this marque is famous. The engine compartment is relatively spacious, and most of the items requiring frequent attention are easily accessible.

Your Toyota manual

The aim of this manual is to help you get the best value from your vehicle. It can do so in several ways. It can help you decide what work must be done (even should you choose to get it done by a garage). It will also provide information on routine maintenance and servicing, and give a logical course of action and diagnosis when random faults occur. However, it is hoped that you will use the manual by tackling the work yourself. On simpler jobs it may even be quicker than booking the car into a garage and going there twice, to leave and collect it. Perhaps most important, a lot of money can be saved by avoiding the costs a garage must charge to cover its labour and overheads.

The manual has drawings and descriptions to show the function of the various components so that their layout can be understood. Tasks are described and photographed in a clear step-by-step sequence. The illustrations are numbered by the Section number and paragraph number to which they relate – if there is more than one illustration per paragraph, the sequence is denoted alphabetically.

References to the 'left' or 'right' of the vehicle are in the sense of a person in the driver's seat, facing forwards.

Acknowledgements

Thanks are due to Draper Tools Limited, who provided some of the workshop tools, and to all those people at Sparkford who helped in the production of this manual. **We take great pride in the accuracy of information given in this manual, but vehicle manufacturers make alterations and design changes during the production run of a particular vehicle of which they do not inform us. No liability can be accepted by the authors or publishers for loss, damage or injury caused by any errors in, or omissions from the information given.**

Toyota Corolla 5-door Liftback

Roadside repairs

The following pages are intended to help in dealing with common roadside emergencies and breakdowns. You will find more detailed fault finding information at the back of the manual, and repair information in the main chapters.

If your car won't start and the starter motor doesn't turn

- [ ] If it's a model with automatic transmission, make sure the selector is in P or N.
- [ ] Open the bonnet and make sure that the battery terminals are clean and tight.
- [ ] Switch on the headlights and try to start the engine. If the headlights go very dim when you're trying to start, the battery is probably flat. Get out of trouble by jump starting (see next page) using a friend's car.

If your car won't start even though the starter motor turns as normal

- [ ] Is there fuel in the tank?
- [ ] Is there moisture on electrical components under the bonnet? Switch off the ignition, then wipe off any obvious dampness with a dry cloth. Spray a water-repellent aerosol product (WD-40 or equivalent) on ignition and fuel system electrical connectors like those shown in the photos.

A Check the security of the ignition coil(s) electrical connectors.

B Check the security of the airflow meter wiring plug.

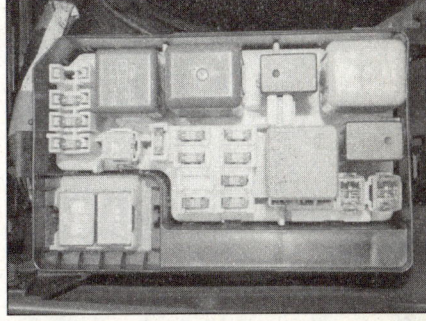

C Check that all fuses are still in good condition and none have blown.

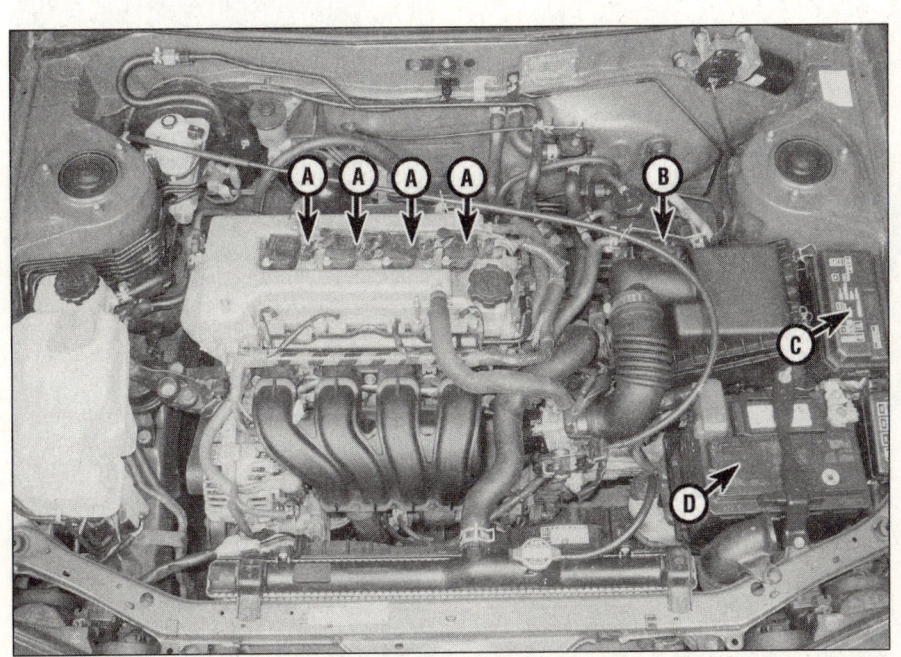

Check that electrical connections are secure (with the ignition switched off) and spray them with a water-dispersant spray like WD-40 if you suspect a problem due to damp

D Check the security and condition of the battery connections.

E Check the security of the HT leads (non-VVT-i engines).

0•8 Roadside repairs

Jump starting

When jump-starting a car using a booster battery, observe the following precautions:

✔ Before connecting the booster battery, make sure that the ignition is switched off.

✔ Ensure that all electrical equipment (lights, heater, wipers, etc) is switched off.

✔ Take note of any special precautions printed on the battery case.

✔ Make sure that the booster battery is the same voltage as the discharged one in the vehicle.

✔ If the battery is being jump-started from the battery in another vehicle, the two vehicles MUST NOT TOUCH each other.

✔ Make sure that the transmission is in neutral (or PARK, in the case of automatic transmission).

HAYNES HiNT
Jump starting will get you out of trouble, but you must correct whatever made the battery go flat in the first place. There are three possibilities:

1 The battery has been drained by repeated attempts to start, or by leaving the lights on.

2 The charging system is not working properly (alternator drivebelt slack or broken, alternator wiring fault or alternator itself faulty).

3 The battery itself is at fault (electrolyte low, or battery worn out).

1 Connect one end of the red jump lead to the positive (+) terminal of the flat battery

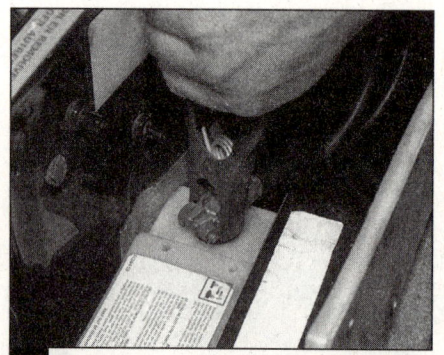

2 Connect the other end of the red lead to the positive (+) terminal of the booster battery.

3 Connect one end of the black jump lead to the negative (-) terminal of the booster battery

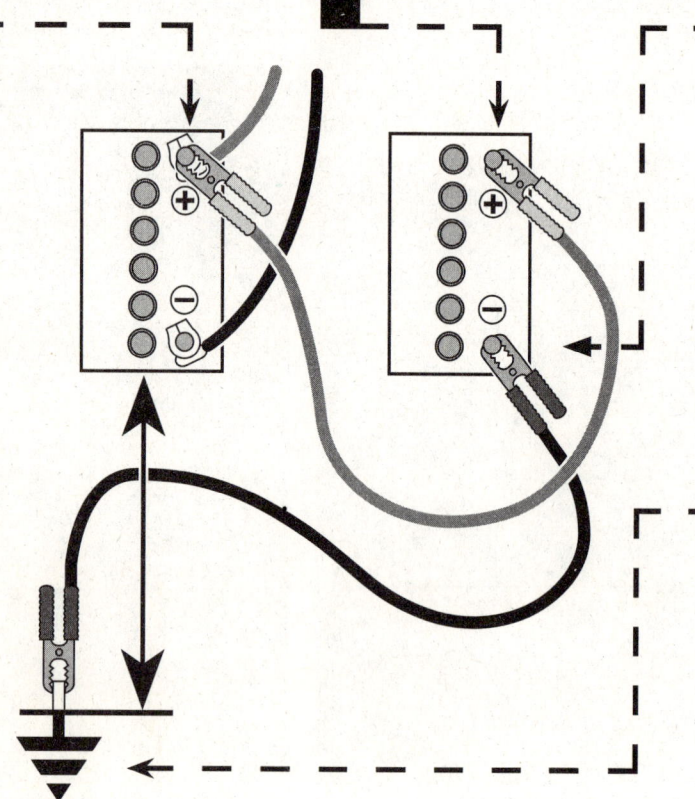

4 Connect the other end of the black jump lead to a bolt or bracket on the engine on the vehicle to be started.

5 Make sure that the jump leads will not come into contact with the cooling fan, drivebelts or other moving parts of the engine.

6 Start the engine using the booster battery and run it at idle speed. Switch on the lights, rear window demister and heater blower motor, then disconnect the jump leads in the reverse order of connection. Turn off the lights etc.

Roadside repairs 0•9

Wheel changing

⚠️ *Warning: Do not change a wheel in a situation where you risk being hit by other traffic. On busy roads, try to stop in a lay-by or a gateway. Be wary of passing traffic while changing the wheel – it is easy to become distracted by the job in hand.*

Preparation

- [ ] When a puncture occurs, stop as soon as it is safe to do so.
- [ ] Park on firm level ground, if possible, and well out of the way of other traffic.
- [ ] Use hazard warning lights if necessary.
- [ ] If you have one, use a warning triangle to alert other drivers of your presence.
- [ ] Apply the handbrake and engage first or reverse gear (or Park on models with automatic transmission).
- [ ] Chock the wheel diagonally opposite the one being removed – a couple of large stones will do for this.
- [ ] If the ground is soft, use a flat piece of wood to spread the load under the jack.

Changing the wheel

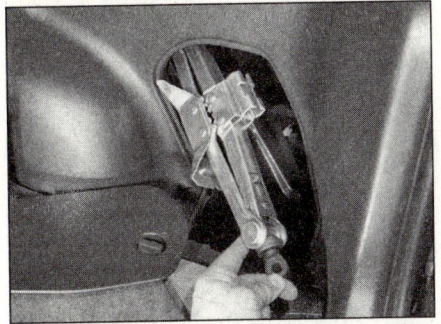

1 From inside the luggage compartment, remove the trim panel and remove the jack . . .

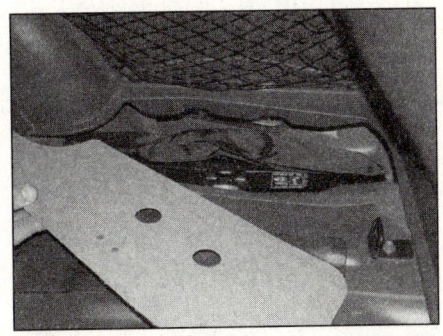

2 . . . or lift the panel in the luggage compartment floor. On some models the tools are stored with the spare wheel.

3 Lift the carpet then unscrew the spare wheel retainer from the centre of the wheel and lift out the wheel.

4 Prise off the wheel trim (where fitted), then slacken each wheel nut by a half turn, using the wheelbrace. If the nuts are too tight, DON'T stand on the brace to undo them – call for assistance. On models with alloy wheels, a Toyota socket may be needed to remove the security nut – the socket should be in the glovebox or toolkit.

5 Engage the jack head with the reinforced bracket located at the end of the sill (don't jack the vehicle at any other point of the sill).

6 Turn the handle clockwise until the wheel is raised clear of the ground, then unscrew the wheel bolts and remove the wheel.

Finally . . .

- [ ] Remove the wheel chocks.
- [ ] Stow the jack and tools back in the car.
- [ ] Check the tyre pressure on the wheel just fitted. If it is low, or if you don't have a pressure gauge with you, drive slowly to the nearest garage and inflate the tyre to the correct pressure.

7 Fit the spare wheel, then fit and screw on the nuts. Lightly tighten the nuts with the wheelbrace, then lower the vehicle to the ground. Securely tighten the wheel nuts in the sequence shown, then refit the wheel trim or hub cap, as applicable. The wheel nuts should be slackened and retightened to the specified torque (103 Nm) at the earliest possible opportunity.

Note: *Some models are supplied with a special lightweight 'space-saver' spare wheel, the tyre being narrower than standard, and marked TEMPORARY USE ONLY. The space-saver spare wheel is intended only for temporary use, and* **must** *be replaced with a standard wheel as soon as possible. Drive with particular care with this wheel fitted, especially through corners and when braking – Toyota recommend a maximum speed of 50 mph (80 km/h) when the special spare wheel is in use.*

0•10 Roadside repairs

Identifying leaks

Puddles on the garage floor or drive, or obvious wetness under the bonnet or underneath the car, suggest a leak that needs investigating. It can sometimes be difficult to decide where the leak is coming from, especially if the engine bay is very dirty already. Leaking oil or fluid can also be blown rearwards by the passage of air under the car, giving a false impression of where the problem lies.

⚠ **Warning: Most automotive oils and fluids are poisonous. Wash them off skin, and change out of contaminated clothing, without delay.**

HAYNES HiNT *The smell of a fluid leaking from the car may provide a clue to what's leaking. Some fluids are distinctively coloured. It may help to clean the car carefully and to park it over some clean paper overnight as an aid to locating the source of the leak. Remember that some leaks may only occur while the engine is running.*

Sump oil

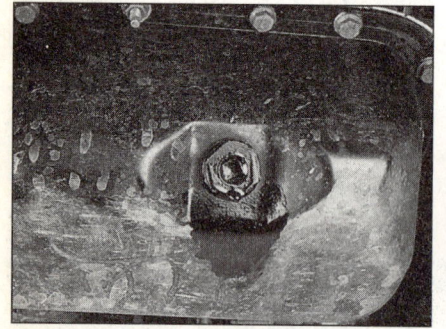

Engine oil may leak from the drain plug...

Oil from filter

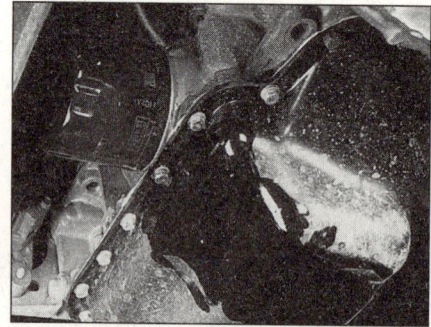

...or from the base of the oil filter.

Gearbox oil

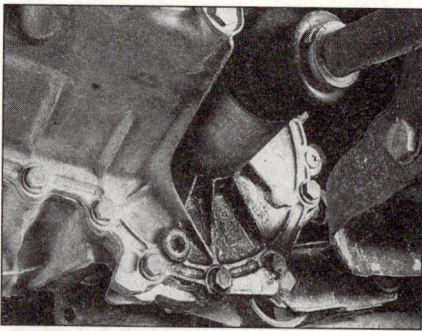

Gearbox oil can leak from the seals at the inboard ends of the driveshafts.

Antifreeze

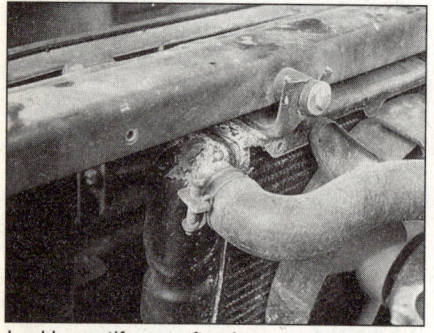

Leaking antifreeze often leaves a crystalline deposit like this.

Brake fluid

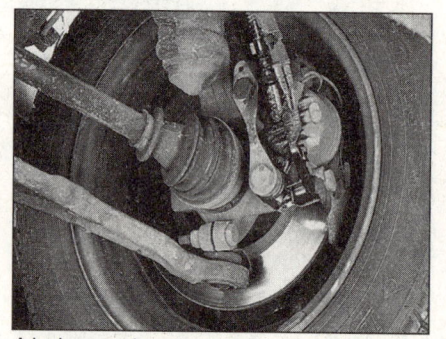

A leak occurring at a wheel is almost certainly brake fluid.

Power steering fluid

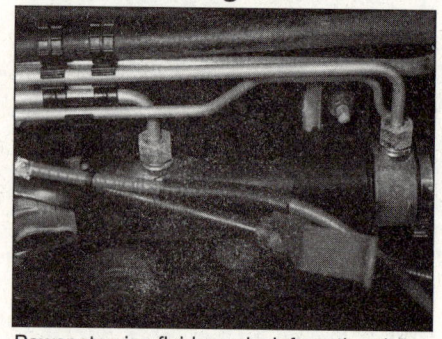

Power steering fluid may leak from the pipe connectors on the steering rack.

Towing

When all else fails, you may find yourself having to get a tow home – or of course you may be helping somebody else. Long-distance recovery should only be done by a garage or breakdown service. For shorter distances, DIY towing using another car is easy enough, but observe the following points:

☐ Use a proper tow-rope – they are not expensive. The vehicle being towed must display an ON TOW sign in its rear window.
☐ Always turn the ignition key to the 'on' position when the vehicle is being towed, so that the steering lock is released, and the direction indicator and brake lights work.
☐ A towing eye is provided below each bumper.
☐ Before being towed, release the handbrake and select neutral on the transmission. Toyota advise that automatic transmission models should only be towed for 'short distances at low speed'.
☐ Note that greater-than-usual pedal pressure will be required to operate the brakes, since the vacuum servo unit is only operational with the engine running.
☐ Because the power steering will not be operational, greater-than-usual steering effort will also be required.
☐ The driver of the car being towed must keep the tow-rope taut at all times to avoid snatching.
☐ Make sure that both drivers know the route before setting off.
☐ Only drive at moderate speeds and keep the distance towed to a minimum. Drive smoothly and allow plenty of time for slowing down at junctions.

Weekly checks 0•11

Introduction

There are some very simple checks which need only take a few minutes to carry out, but which could save you a lot of inconvenience and expense.

These *Weekly checks* require no great skill or special tools, and the small amount of time they take to perform could prove to be very well spent, for example:

☐ Keeping an eye on tyre condition and pressures, will not only help to stop them wearing out prematurely, but could also save your life.

☐ Many breakdowns are caused by electrical problems. Battery-related faults are particularly common, and a quick check on a regular basis will often prevent the majority of these.

☐ If your car develops a brake fluid leak, the first time you might know about it is when your brakes don't work properly. Checking the level regularly will give advance warning of this kind of problem.

☐ If the oil or coolant levels run low, the cost of repairing any engine damage will be far greater than fixing the leak, for example.

Underbonnet check points

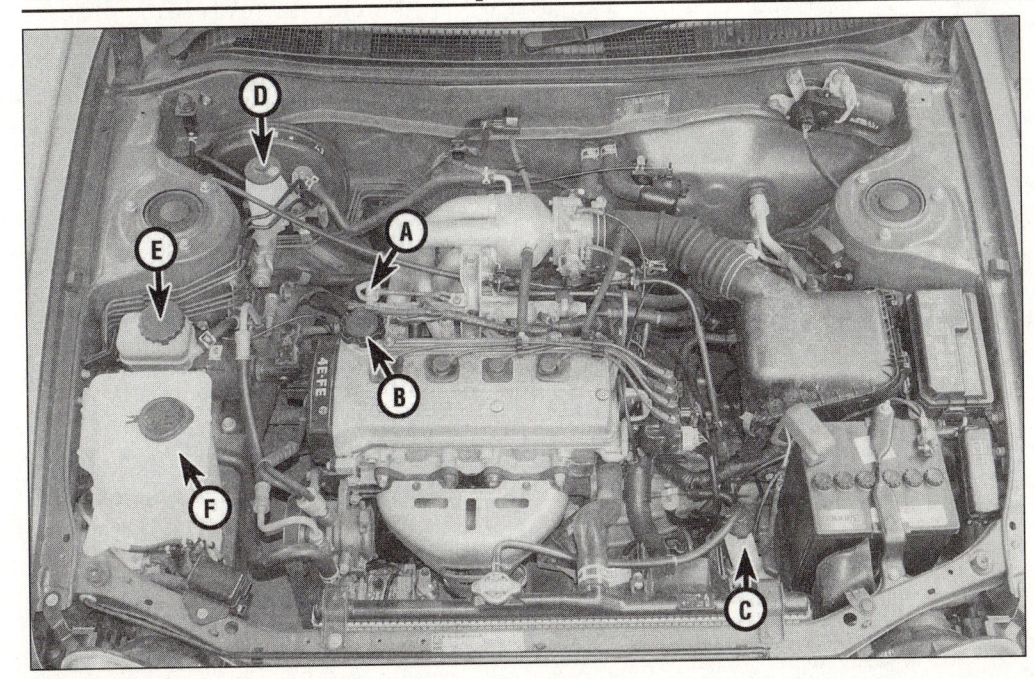

◀ **1.3 litre 4E-FE (non-VVT-i) engine (others similar)**

A Engine oil level dipstick
B Engine oil filler cap
C Coolant expansion tank
D Brake fluid reservoir
E Power steering fluid reservoir
F Screen washer fluid reservoir

◀ **1.4 litre 4ZZ-FE (VVT-i) engine (others similar)**

A Engine oil level dipstick
B Engine oil filler cap
C Coolant expansion tank
D Brake fluid reservoir
E Power steering fluid reservoir
F Screen washer fluid reservoir
G Clutch fluid reservoir

0•12 Weekly checks

Engine oil level

Before you start

✔ Make sure that your car is on level ground.
✔ Check the oil level before the car is driven, or at least 5 minutes after the engine has been switched off.

HAYNES HiNT *If the oil is checked immediately after driving the vehicle, some of the oil will remain in the upper engine components, resulting in an inaccurate reading on the dipstick.*

The correct oil

Modern engines place great demands on their oil. It is very important that the correct oil for your car is used (see *Lubricants and fluids*).

Car care

● If you have to add oil frequently, you should check whether you have any oil leaks. Place some clean paper under the car overnight, and check for stains in the morning. If there are no leaks, then the engine may be burning oil.
● Always maintain the level between the upper and lower dipstick marks. If the level is too low, severe engine damage may occur. Oil seal failure may result if the engine is overfilled by adding too much oil.

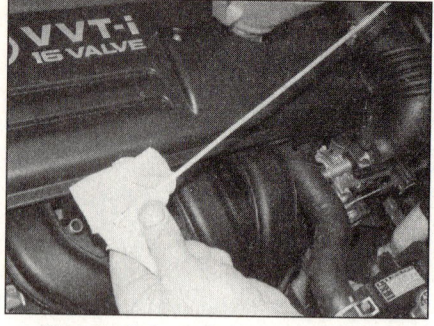

1 The dipstick top is brightly coloured for easy identification (see *Underbonnet check points* for exact location). Withdraw the dipstick, and using a clean rag or paper towel remove all oil from the dipstick. Insert the clean dipstick into the tube as far as it will go, then withdraw it again.

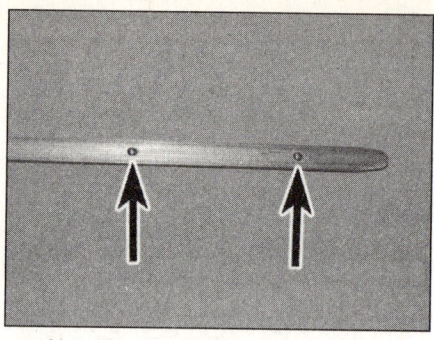

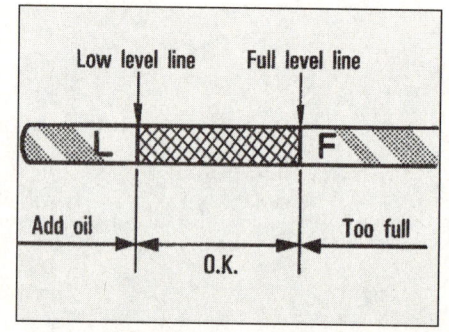

3 ... or in the hatched area indicating MAX and MIN between the upper (F) mark and lower (L) mark. Approximately 1.0 litre of oil will raise the level from the lower mark to the upper mark.

2 Note the oil level on the end of the dipstick, which should be between the maximum and minimum marks (arrowed) . . .

4 Oil is added through the filler cap. Unscrew the cap and top-up the level; a funnel may help to reduce spillage. Add the oil slowly, checking the level on the dipstick often. Don't overfill (see *Car care*).

Coolant level

⚠ **Warning: Do not attempt to remove the radiator pressure cap or expansion tank cap when the engine is hot, as there is a very great risk of scalding. Do not leave open containers of coolant about, as it is poisonous.**

Car Care

● With a sealed-type cooling system, adding coolant should not be necessary on a regular basis. If frequent topping-up is required, it is likely there is a leak. Check the radiator, all hoses and joint faces for signs of staining or wetness, and rectify as necessary.

● It is important that antifreeze is used in the cooling system all year round, not just during the winter months. Don't top up with water alone, as the antifreeze will become diluted.

1 The coolant reservoir is located on the left-hand side of the engine compartment. The coolant level is visible through the reservoir.

2 If topping-up is necessary, wait until the engine is cold and remove the cap from the reservoir. Add a mixture of water and antifreeze to the reservoir until the coolant is at the correct level. Refit the cap and tighten it securely.

Weekly checks 0•13

Brake and clutch* fluid level

Manual transmission models only.

⚠️ **Warning:** Brake fluid can harm your eyes and damage painted surfaces, so use extreme caution when handling and pouring it. Do not use fluid which has been standing open for some time, as it absorbs moisture from the air, which can cause a dangerous loss of braking effectiveness.

Before you start

✔ Make sure that the car is on level ground.

HAYNES HINT: *The fluid level in the brake reservoir will drop slightly as the brake pads wear down, but the fluid level must never be allowed to drop below the MIN mark.*

Safety first!

● If the reservoir(s) require repeated topping-up, this is an indication of a fluid leak somewhere in the system, which should be investigated immediately.
● If a leak is suspected, the car should not be driven until the braking system has been checked. Never take any risks where brakes are concerned.

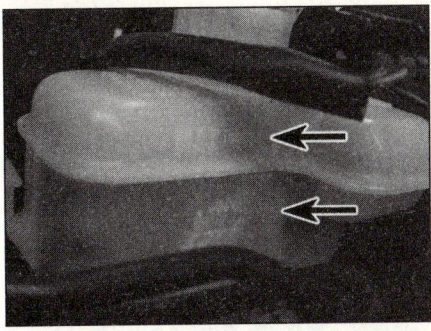

1 The MAX and MIN marks are indicated on the reservoirs. The brake fluid reservoir (MAX and MIN marks arrowed) is located in the right-hand rear corner of the engine compartment . . .

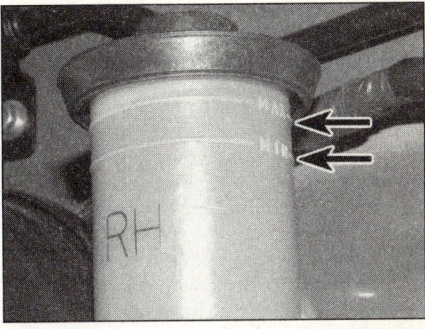

2 . . . and the clutch reservoir is adjacent to it. The fluid level must be kept between the marks (arrowed) at all times. If topping-up is necessary, first wipe clean the area around the filler cap to prevent dirt entering the hydraulic system.

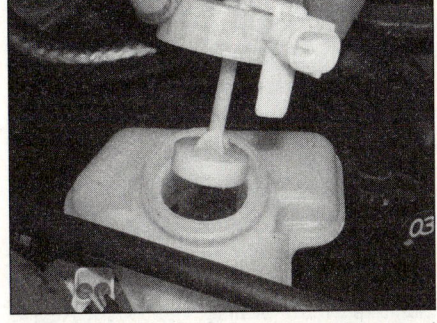

3 Unscrew the brake fluid reservoir cap and carefully lift it out of position. The clutch fluid reservoir cap peels off. Inspect the reservoir, if the fluid is dirty, the hydraulic system should be drained and refilled (see Chapter 1 or 6).

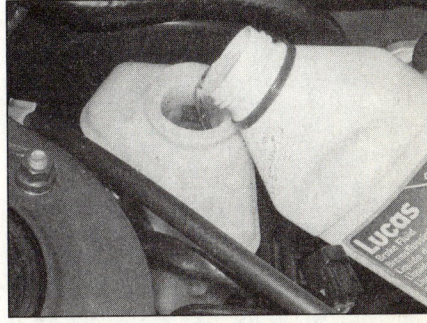

4 Carefully add fluid, taking care not to spill it onto the surrounding components. Use only the specified fluid; mixing different types can cause damage to the system. After topping-up to the correct level, securely refit the cap and wipe off any spilt fluid. Reconnect the fluid level wiring connector.

Washer fluid level

● On models so equipped, the screen washer fluid is also used to clean the tailgate rear window.
● Screenwash additives not only keep the windscreen clean during bad weather, they also prevent the washer system freezing in cold weather – which is when you are likely to need it most. Don't top-up using plain water, as the screenwash will become diluted, and will freeze in cold weather.

Caution: *On no account use engine coolant antifreeze in the screen washer system – this may damage the paintwork.*

1 The washer fluid reservoir filler is located at the front right-hand side of the engine compartment.

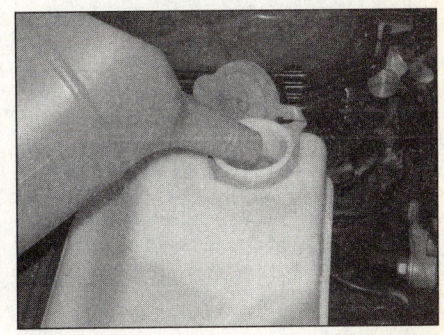

2 Release the cap and top-up the reservoir, a screenwash additive should be added in the quantities recommended on the bottle.

Weekly checks

Tyre condition and pressure

It is very important that tyres are in good condition, and at the correct pressure - having a tyre failure at any speed is highly dangerous. Tyre wear is influenced by driving style - harsh braking and acceleration, or fast cornering, will all produce more rapid tyre wear. As a general rule, the front tyres wear out faster than the rears. Interchanging the tyres from front to rear ("rotating" the tyres) may result in more even wear. However, if this is completely effective, you may have the expense of replacing all four tyres at once!

Remove any nails or stones embedded in the tread before they penetrate the tyre to cause deflation. If removal of a nail does reveal that the tyre has been punctured, refit the nail so that its point of penetration is marked. Then immediately change the wheel, and have the tyre repaired by a tyre dealer.

Regularly check the tyres for damage in the form of cuts or bulges, especially in the sidewalls. Periodically remove the wheels, and clean any dirt or mud from the inside and outside surfaces. Examine the wheel rims for signs of rusting, corrosion or other damage. Light alloy wheels are easily damaged by "kerbing" whilst parking; steel wheels may also become dented or buckled. A new wheel is very often the only way to overcome severe damage.

New tyres should be balanced when they are fitted, but it may become necessary to re-balance them as they wear, or if the balance weights fitted to the wheel rim should fall off. Unbalanced tyres will wear more quickly, as will the steering and suspension components. Wheel imbalance is normally signified by vibration, particularly at a certain speed (typically around 50 mph). If this vibration is felt only through the steering, then it is likely that just the front wheels need balancing. If, however, the vibration is felt through the whole car, the rear wheels could be out of balance. Wheel balancing should be carried out by a tyre dealer or garage.

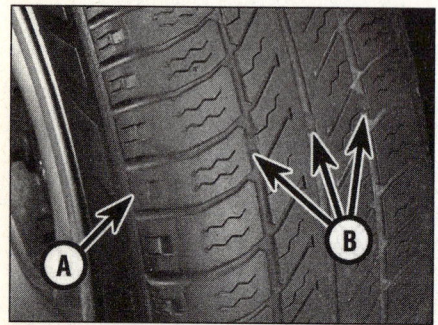

1 Tread Depth - visual check
The original tyres have tread wear safety bands (B), which will appear when the tread depth reaches approximately 1.6 mm. The band positions are indicated by a triangular mark on the tyre sidewall (A).

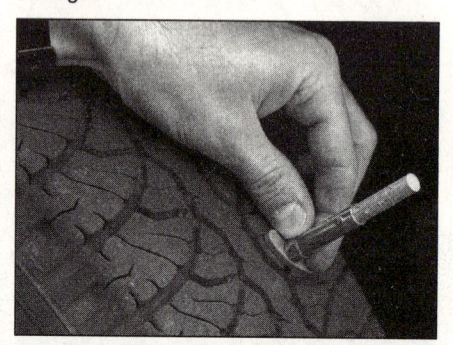

2 Tread Depth - manual check
Alternatively, tread wear can be monitored with a simple, inexpensive device known as a tread depth indicator gauge.

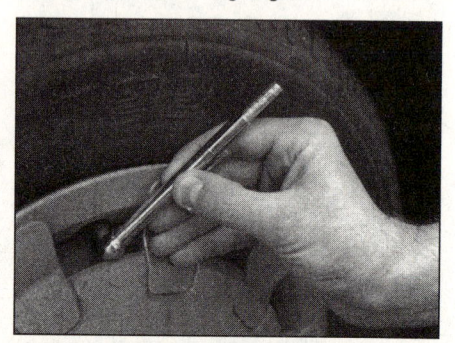

3 Tyre Pressure Check
Check the tyre pressures regularly with the tyres cold. Do not adjust the tyre pressures immediately after the vehicle has been used, or an inaccurate setting will result.

Tyre tread wear patterns

Shoulder Wear

Underinflation (wear on both sides)
Under-inflation will cause overheating of the tyre, because the tyre will flex too much, and the tread will not sit correctly on the road surface. This will cause a loss of grip and excessive wear, not to mention the danger of sudden tyre failure due to heat build-up.
Check and adjust pressures
Incorrect wheel camber (wear on one side)
Repair or renew suspension parts
Hard cornering
Reduce speed!

Centre Wear

Overinflation
Over-inflation will cause rapid wear of the centre part of the tyre tread, coupled with reduced grip, harsher ride, and the danger of shock damage occurring in the tyre casing.
Check and adjust pressures

If you sometimes have to inflate your car's tyres to the higher pressures specified for maximum load or sustained high speed, don't forget to reduce the pressures to normal afterwards.

Uneven Wear

Front tyres may wear unevenly as a result of wheel misalignment. Most tyre dealers and garages can check and adjust the wheel alignment (or "tracking") for a modest charge.
Incorrect camber or castor
Repair or renew suspension parts
Malfunctioning suspension
Repair or renew suspension parts
Unbalanced wheel
Balance tyres
Incorrect toe setting
Adjust front wheel alignment
Note: *The feathered edge of the tread which typifies toe wear is best checked by feel.*

Weekly checks 0•15

Power steering fluid level

Before you start
✔ Make sure that the car is on level ground.
✔ Set the steering wheel straight-ahead.
✔ The engine should be turned off.

Safety first!
● The need for frequent topping-up indicates a leak, which should be investigated immediately.

HAYNES HiNT *For the check to be accurate, the steering must not be turned once the engine has been stopped.*

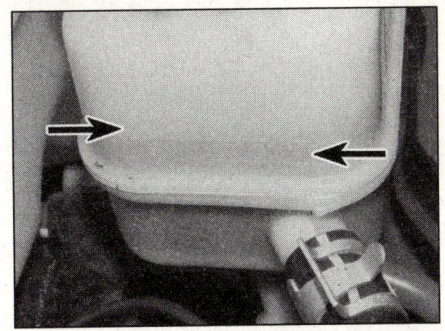

1 The reservoir is mounted on the right-hand side of the engine compartment. The HOT and COLD levels are marked on the reservoir (arrowed) . . .

2 . . . whilst on others, it's necessary to unscrew the cap/dipstick from the reservoir. Wipe clean the area around the reservoir filler neck, before unscrewing the filler cap/dipstick from the reservoir.

3 With the engine stopped check the level through the side of the reservoir, or dip the fluid with the reservoir cap/dipstick by screwing it fully back into place. When the engine is cold, the fluid level should be between the between the COLD marks; when hot it should be between the HOT marks. Add fluid if necessary.

4 When topping-up, use the specified type of fluid – do not overfill the reservoir. When the level is correct, securely refit the cap.

Wiper blades

Note: *Fitting details for wiper blades vary according to model, and according to whether genuine Toyota wiper blades have been fitted. Use the procedures and illustrations shown as a guide for your car.*

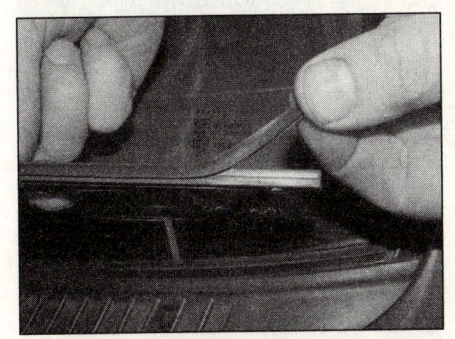

1 Check the condition of the wiper blades; if they are cracked or show any signs of deterioration, or if the glass swept area is smeared, renew them. Wiper blades should be renewed annually.

2 To remove a windscreen wiper blade, lift the wiper arm, rotate the blade on the arm and press the retaining clip (arrowed) towards the arm.

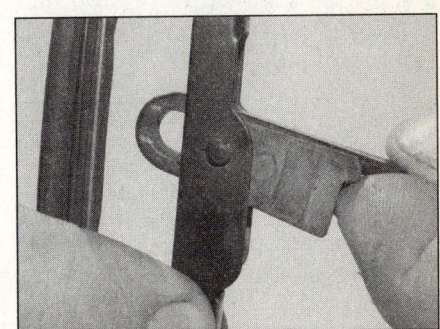

3 Slide the blade down the wiper arm and remove it from the vehicle, taking care not to allow the arm to damage the windscreen.

0•16 Weekly checks

Battery

Caution: *Before carrying out any work on the vehicle battery, read the precautions given in 'Safety first!' at the start of this manual.*

✔ Make sure that the battery tray is in good condition, and that the clamp is tight. Corrosion on the tray, retaining clamp and the battery itself can be removed with a solution of water and baking soda. Thoroughly rinse all cleaned areas with water. Any metal parts damaged by corrosion should be covered with a zinc-based primer, then painted.

✔ Periodically (approximately every three months), check the charge condition of the battery as described in Chapter 5A.

✔ If the battery is flat, and you need to jump start your vehicle, see *Roadside Repairs*.

1 Open the bonnet and lift the small cover over the battery positive terminal (arrowed). The exterior of the battery should be inspected periodically for damage such as a cracked case or cover.

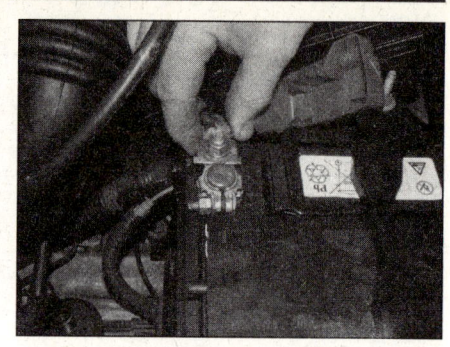

2 Check the tightness of battery clamps to ensure good electrical connections. You should not be able to move them. Also check each cable for cracks and frayed conductors.

HAYNES HiNT
Battery corrosion can be kept to a minimum by applying a layer of petroleum jelly to the clamps and terminals after they are reconnected.

3 If corrosion (white, fluffy deposits) is evident, remove the cables from the battery terminals, clean them with a small wire brush, then refit them. Automotive stores sell a tool for cleaning the battery post . . .

4 . . . as well as the battery cable clamps.

Bulbs and fuses

✔ Check all external lights and the horn. Refer to the appropriate Sections of Chapter 12 for details if any of the circuits are found to be inoperative.

✔ Visually check all accessible wiring connectors, harnesses and retaining clips for security, and for signs of chafing or damage.

HAYNES HiNT
If you need to check your brake lights and indicators unaided, back up to a wall or garage door and operate the lights. The reflected light should show if they are working properly.

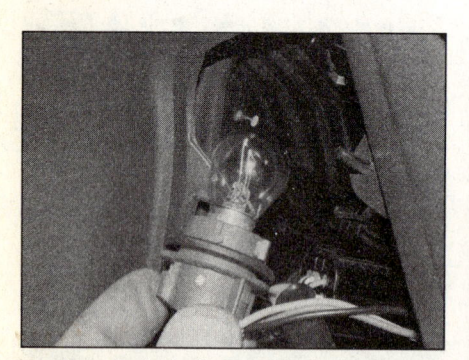

1 If a single indicator light, stop-light or headlight has failed, it is likely that a bulb has blown and will need to be renewed. Refer to Chapter 12 for details. If both stop-lights have failed, it is possible that the stop-light switch is faulty (see Chapter 9).

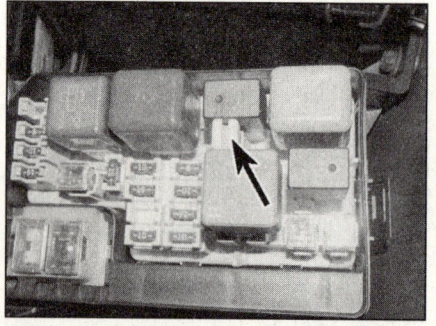

2 If more than one indicator light or headlight has failed, it is likely that either a fuse has blown or that there is a fault in the circuit (see Chapter 12). The fuses are located in the fusebox situated in the engine compartment on the passenger's side (fuse pulling tweezers arrowed).

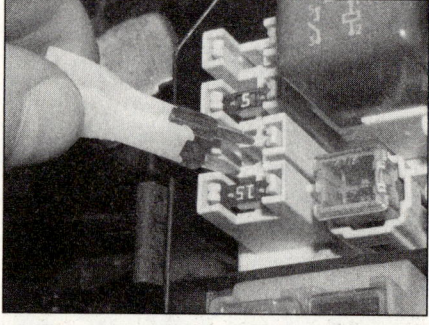

3 To renew a blown fuse, simply pull it out using the plastic tweezers provided. Fit a new fuse of the same rating (see Chapter 12). If the fuse blows again, it is important that you find out why – a complete checking procedure is given in Chapter 12.

Lubricants, fluids and tyre pressures 0•17

Lubricants and fluids

Engine*
 1.3 litre and 1.6 litre non-VVT-i engines............. Multigrade engine oil, viscosity SAE 10W/30 or 15W/30
 1.4 litre and 1.6 litre VVT-i engines .... Multigrade engine oil, viscosity 5W/30
Cooling system.................................. Toyota long life coolant
Manual transmission .... SAE 75W/90 GL4 or GL5
Automatic transmission......................... ATF Dexron II or III
Automatic transmission differential .... ATF Dexron II or III
Braking system................................. Brake and clutch fluid to DOT 3 or 4
Clutch system.................................. Brake and clutch fluid to DOT 3 or 4
Power steering .... Dexron II or III

* Certain models have a decal in the engine compartment which details the engine oil specification. Where no decal is fitted, follow the above recommendations.

Tyre pressures

All models (typical)	Front	Rear
165/70 R14 tyres	32 psi	32 psi
175/65 R14 tyres	32 psi	32 psi
185/65 R14 tyres	32 psi	32 psi
Space-saver tyre	60 psi	60 psi

Notes

Chapter 1
Routine maintenance and servicing

Contents

	Section number		Section number
Air filter element check	10	Handbrake check and adjustment	11
Automatic transmission/differential fluid level check	7	Hinge and lock lubrication	6
Auxiliary drivebelt check, adjustment and renewal	9	Hose and fluid leak check	4
Brake fluid renewal	21	Manual transmission fluid level check and renewal	8
Brake drum and shoe check	13	Pollen filter check	18
Brake pad check	12	Remote control battery renewal	16
Clutch pedal check and adjustment	17	Road test	19
Coolant renewal	23	Routine maintenance	2
Driveshaft gaiter and CV joints check	5	Spark plug renewal	22
Engine oil and filter renewal	3	Steering and suspension check	15
Exhaust system and mountings check	14	Timing belt renewal	See Chapter 2A
Fuel filter renewal	20	Valve clearance check and adjustment	24
General information	1		

Degrees of difficulty

Easy, suitable for novice with little experience

Fairly easy, suitable for beginner with some experience

Fairly difficult, suitable for competent DIY mechanic

Difficult, suitable for experienced DIY mechanic

Very difficult, suitable for expert DIY or professional

Servicing specifications

Lubricants and fluids.................................... Refer to *Weekly checks* on page 0•17

Capacities

Engine oil
Including filter:
  Non-VVT-i engines:
    1.3 litre 4E-FE engine .... 2.8 litres
    1.6 litre 4A-FE engine .... 3.2 litres
  VVT-i engines .... 3.7 litres

Cooling system (approximate):
Non-VVT-i engines:
  1.3 litre 4E-FE engine .... 5.2 litres
  1.6 litre 4A-FE engine .... 5.2 litres
VVT-i engines:
  1.4 litre 4ZZ-FE engine .... 6.0 litres
  1.6 litre 3ZZ-FE engine .... 6.0 litres

Transmission
Manual:
  5-speed transmissions .... 1.9 litres
  6-speed transmissions .... 2.1 litres
Automatic:
  Refilling after draining:
    3-speed transmissions .... 2.5 litres
    4-speed transmissions .... 3.1 litres

Fuel tank .... 50 litres

Cooling system

Frost and corrosion protection................................ Refer to antifreeze manufacturer's concentration recommendations

Engine

Engine codes:
  1.3 litre (1332 cc) non-VVT-i engine 4E-FE
  1.4 litre (1398 cc) VVT-i engine 4ZZ-FE
  1.6 litre (1587 cc) non-VVT-i engine 4A-FE
  1.6 litre (1598 cc) VVT-i engine 3ZZ-FE
Valve clearances (engine cold):
  Intake valve... 0.15 to 0.25 mm
  Exhaust valve:
    1.3 litre 4E-FE engine .... 0.31 to 0.41 mm
    All other engines.. 0.25 to 0.35 mm

Servicing specifications 1•3

Ignition system
Spark plugs:
   1.3 litre 4E-FE engine . . . . NGK BKR5EKB11
      Electrode gap . . . . 1.1 mm
   1.4 litre 4ZZ-FE engine . . . . Bosch FR8KCU
      Electrode gap . . . . 1.0 mm
   1.6 litre 4A-FE engine . . . . NGK BKR6EYA
      Electrode gap . . . . 0.8 mm
   1.6 litre 3ZZ-FE engine . . . . NGK BKR5EYA11
      Electrode gap . . . . 1.1 mm

Brakes
Brake pad friction material minimum thickness . . . . 1.0 mm
Brake shoe lining minimum thickness . . . . 1.0 mm

Torque wrench settings

	Nm	lbf ft
Automatic transmission:		
Filler plug	24	18
Level plug	24	18
Drain plug:		
3-speed transmissions	49	36
4-speed transmissions	17	13
Cylinder block drain plug	25	18
Ignition coil-to-cylinder head:		
VVT-i engines	7	5
Manual transmission:		
Filler/level plug:		
5-speed transmissions	39	29
6-speed transmissions	49	36
Drain plug:		
5-speed transmissions	39	29
6-speed transmissions	49	36
Roadwheel nuts	103	76
Spark plugs:		
Non-VVT-i engines	18	13
VVT-i engines	25	18
Sump drain plug:		
Non-VVT-i engines:		
1.3 litre 4E-FE engine	25	18
1.6 litre 4A-FE engine	44	32
VVT-i engines	37	27

1•4 Maintenance schedule

The maintenance intervals in this manual are provided with the assumption that you, not the dealer, will be doing the work. These are the minimum maintenance intervals recommended by the factory for vehicles that are driven daily. If you wish to keep your vehicle in peak condition at all times, you may wish to perform some of these procedures even more often. Because frequent maintenance enhances the efficiency, performance and resale value of your car, we encourage you to do so. If you drive in dusty areas, tow a trailer, idle or drive at low speeds for extended periods or drive for short distances (less than four miles) in below freezing temperatures, shorter intervals are also recommended.

When your vehicle is new, it should be serviced by a factory authorised dealer service department to protect the factory warranty. In many cases, the initial maintenance check is done at no cost to the owner.

Two maintenance schedules are given below. One for non-VVT-i models (1.3 litre 4E-FE and 1.6 litre 4A-FE engines) from 1997 to Oct '99, and one for VVT-i models (1.4 litre 4ZZ-FE and 1.6 litre 3ZZ-FE engines) from Oct '99 onwards.

1.3 and 1.6 litre non-VVT-i models

Every 250 miles (400 km) or weekly
☐ Refer to *Weekly checks*

Every 4500 miles (7000 km) or 6 months – whichever comes sooner
☐ Renew the engine oil and filter (Section 3).
Note: *Frequent oil and filter changes are good for the engine. We recommend changing the oil at the mileage specified here, or at least twice a year if the mileage covered is a less.*

Every 9000 miles (15 000 km) or 12 months – whichever comes sooner
☐ Check all underbonnet components or fluid leaks (Section 4).
☐ Check the condition of the driveshaft rubber gaiters and CV joints (Section 5).
☐ Lubricate all hinges and locks (Section 6).
☐ Check the transmission fluid level (Section 7 or 8).
☐ Check the condition of the auxiliary drivebelt (Section 9).
☐ Check the condition of the air filter element (Section 10).
☐ Check the operation of the handbrake (Section 11).
☐ Check the condition of the brake pads (Section 12).
☐ Check the condition of the brake drums and shoes (Section 13).
☐ Check the condition of the exhaust system and mountings (Section 14).
☐ Inspect the suspension and steering components (Section 15).
☐ Renew remote alarm/locking handset battery (Section 16).
☐ Check the clutch pedal adjustment (Section 17).
☐ Check the condition of the pollen filter (Section 18).
☐ Carry out a road test (Section 19).

Every 18 000 miles (30 000 km) or 2 years – whichever comes sooner
☐ Renew the air filter element (Section 10).
☐ Renew the fuel filter (Section 20).
☐ Renew the brake fluid (Section 21).
☐ Renew the spark plugs (Section 22).

Every 36 000 miles (60 000 km) or 4 years – whichever comes sooner
☐ Renew the transmission fluid (Section 7 or 8).
☐ Renew the coolant (Section 23).

Every 54 000 miles (90 000 km) or 6 years – whichever comes sooner
☐ Renew the timing belt (See Chapter 2A).
Note: *Although the normal interval for timing belt renewal is 63 000 miles (100 000 km), it is strongly recommended that the interval is reduced to 54 000 miles (90 000 km), especially on vehicles which are subjected to intensive use, ie, mainly short journeys or a lot of stop-start driving. The actual belt renewal interval is therefore very much up to the individual owner, but bear in mind that severe engine damage will result if the belt breaks.*
☐ Check and adjust the valve clearances (Section 24).

Maintenance schedule 1•5

1.4 and 1.6 litre VVT-i models

Every 250 miles (400 km) or weekly
☐ Refer to *Weekly checks*

Every 5000 miles (8000 km) or 6 months – whichever comes sooner
☐ Renew the engine oil and filter (Section 3).
Note: *Frequent oil and filter changes are good for the engine. We recommend changing the oil at the mileage specified here, or at least twice a year if the mileage covered is a less.*

Every 10 000 miles (16 000 km) or 12 months – whichever comes sooner
☐ Check all underbonnet components or fluid leaks (Section 4).
☐ Check the condition of the driveshaft rubber gaiters and CV joints (Section 5).
☐ Lubricate all hinges and locks (Section 6).
☐ Check the transmission fluid level* (Section 7 or 8).
☐ Check the condition of the auxiliary drivebelt (Section 9).
☐ Check the condition of the air filter element (Section 10).
☐ Check the operation of the handbrake (Section 11).
☐ Check the condition of the brake pads (Section 12).
☐ Check the condition of the exhaust system and mountings (Section 14).
☐ Inspect the suspension and steering components (Section 15).
☐ Check the clutch pedal adjustment (Section 17).
☐ Check the condition of the pollen filter (Section 18).
☐ Carry out a road test (Section 19).
** **Note:** Toyota do not specify an interval for checking the manual transmission fluid level.*

Every 20 000 miles (32 000 km) or 2 years – whichever comes sooner
☐ Check the condition of the brake drums and shoes (Section 13).
☐ Renew remote alarm/locking handset battery (Section 16).
☐ Renew the brake fluid (Section 21).

Every 40 000 miles (64 000 km) or 3 years – whichever comes sooner
☐ Renew the coolant (Section 23).

Every 40 000 miles (64 000 km) or 4 years – whichever comes sooner
☐ Renew the transmission fluid* (Section 7 or 8).
☐ Renew the air filter element (Section 10).
☐ Renew the spark plugs (Section 22).
** **Note:** Toyota do not specify an interval for renewing the automatic transmission fluid.*

Every 60 000 miles (96 000 km) or 6 years – whichever comes sooner
☐ Renew the auxiliary drivebelt (Section 9).
☐ Check and adjust the valve clearances (Section 24).

1•6 Maintenance - component location

Front underbonnet view of a 1.3 litre model

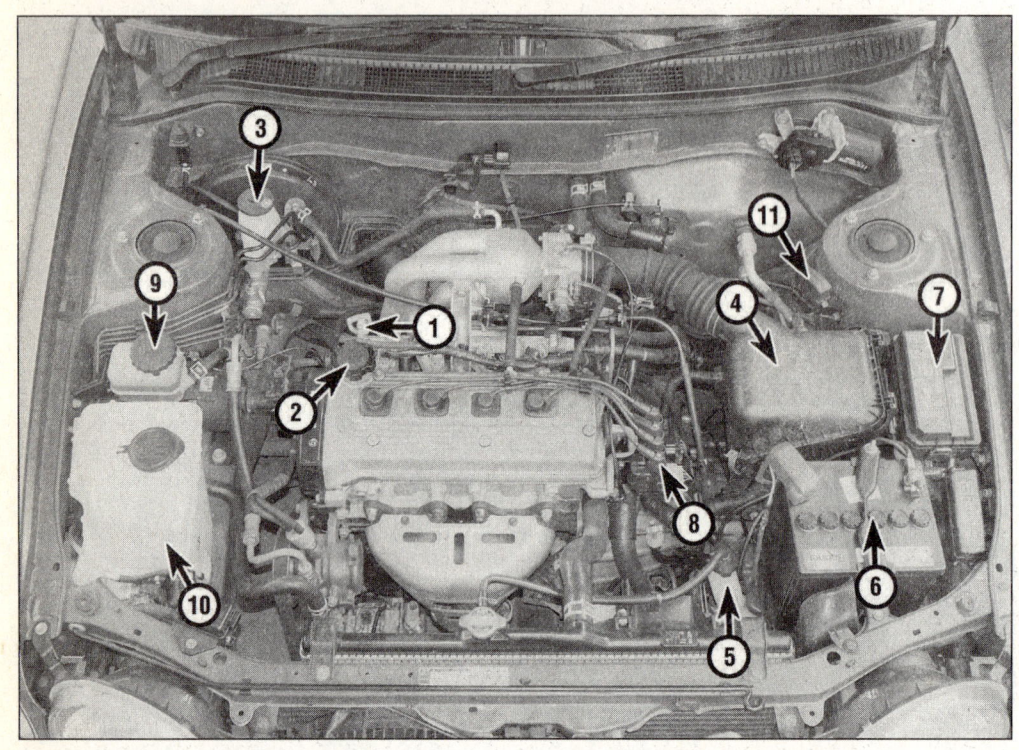

1. Oil level dipstick
2. Engine oil filler cap
3. Brake fluid reservoir
4. Air cleaner housing
5. Coolant reservoir
6. Battery
7. Fuse/relay box
8. Ignition coils
9. Power steering reservoir
10. Washer fluid reservoir
11. Test socket

Front underbonnet view of a 1.4 litre VVT-i model

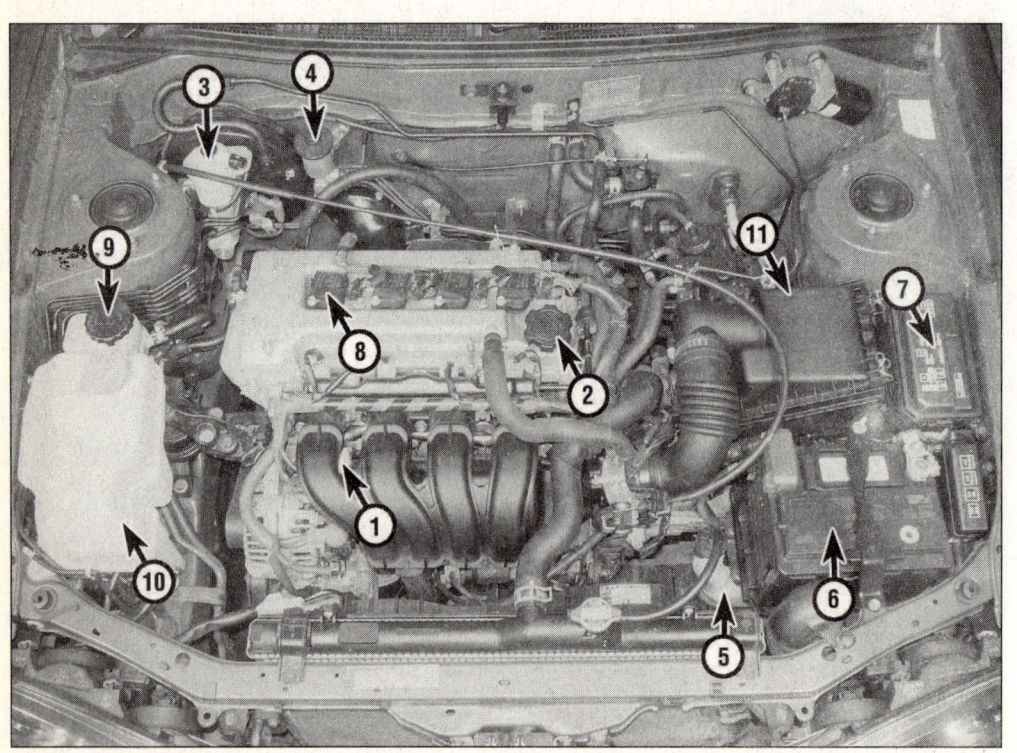

1. Oil level dipstick
2. Engine oil filler cap
3. Brake fluid reservoir
4. Clutch fluid reservoir
5. Coolant reservoir
6. Battery
7. Fuse/relay box
8. Ignition coils
9. Power steering reservoir
10. Washer fluid reservoir
11. Air cleaner housing

Maintenance - component location 1•7

Front underbody view (VVT-i model shown – other models similar)

1 Oil filter
2 Engine oil drain plug
3 Coolant reservoir
4 Right-hand driveshaft
5 Anti-roll bar
6 Suspension control arm
7 Track rod end
8 Catalytic converter
9 Radiator drain tap

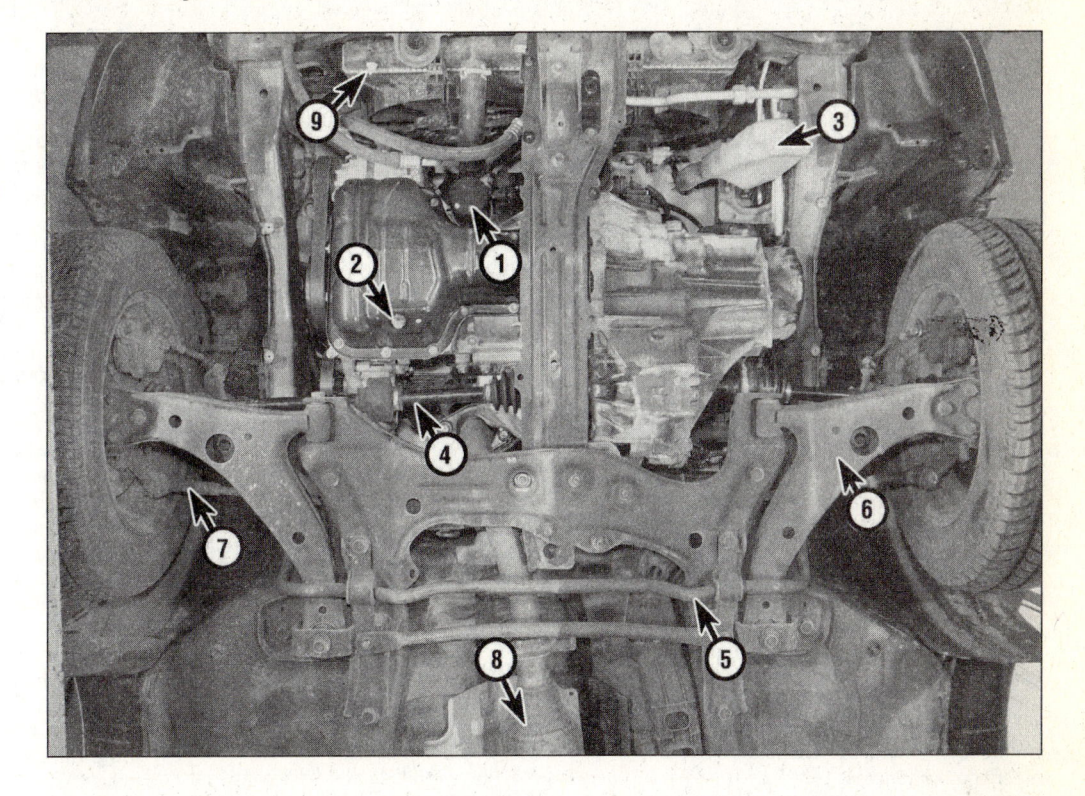

Rear underbody view

1 Fuel tank
2 Exhaust rear silencer
3 Strut rod
4 No 1 suspension arm
5 No 2 suspension arm
6 Handbrake cable
7 Anti-roll bar

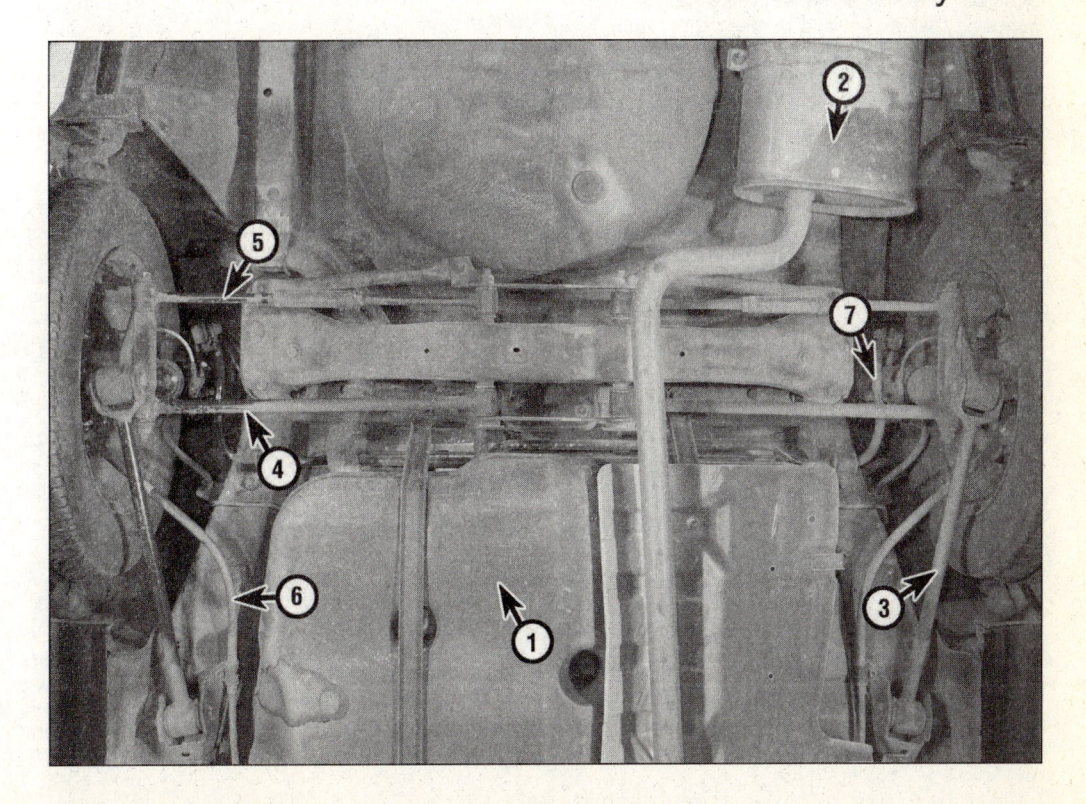

1•8 Maintenance procedures

1 General information

1 This Chapter is designed to help the home mechanic maintain his/her vehicle for safety, economy, long life and peak performance.
2 The Chapter contains master maintenance schedules, followed by Sections dealing specifically with each task in the schedule. Visual checks, adjustments, component renewal and other helpful items are included. Refer to the accompanying illustrations of the engine compartment and the underside of the vehicle for the locations of the various components.
3 Servicing your vehicle in accordance with the mileage/time maintenance schedule and the following Sections will provide a planned maintenance programme, which should result in a long and reliable service life. This is a comprehensive plan, so maintaining some items but not others at the specified service intervals will not produce the same results.
4 As you service your vehicle, you will discover that many of the procedures can – and should – be grouped together, because of the particular procedure being performed, or because of the close proximity of two otherwise-unrelated components to one another. For example, if the vehicle is raised for any reason, the exhaust can be inspected at the same time as the suspension and steering components.
5 The first step in this maintenance programme is to prepare yourself before the actual work begins. Read through all the Sections relevant to the work to be carried out, then make a list and gather together all the parts and tools required. If a problem is encountered, seek advice from a parts specialist, or a dealer service department.

2 Routine maintenance

1 If, from the time the vehicle is new, the routine maintenance schedule is followed closely, and frequent checks are made of fluid levels and high-wear items, as suggested throughout this manual, the engine will be kept in relatively good running condition, and the need for additional work will be minimised.
2 It is possible that there will be times when the engine is running poorly due to the lack of regular maintenance. This is even more likely if a used vehicle, which has not received regular and frequent maintenance checks, is purchased. In such cases, additional work may need to be carried out, outside of the regular maintenance intervals.
3 If engine wear is suspected, a compression test (refer to Chapter 2A) will provide valuable information regarding the overall performance of the main internal components. Such a test can be used as a basis to decide on the extent of the work to be carried out. If, for example, a compression test indicates serious internal engine wear, conventional maintenance as described in this Chapter will not greatly improve the performance of the engine, and may prove a waste of time and money, unless extensive overhaul work (Chapter 2B) is carried out first.
4 The following series of operations are those often required to improve the performance of a generally poor-running engine:

Primary operations

a) Clean, inspect and test the battery (See 'Weekly checks').
b) Check all the engine-related fluids (See 'Weekly checks').
c) Check the condition and tension of the auxiliary drivebelt (Section 9).
d) Renew the spark plugs (Section 22).
e) Check the condition of the air cleaner filter element, and renew if necessary (Section 10).
f) Renew the fuel filter – non-VVT-i engine models only (Section 20).
g) Check the condition of all hoses, and check for fluid leaks (Section 4).

5 If the above operations do not prove fully effective, carry out the following operations:

Secondary operations

All items listed under *Primary operations*, plus the following:
a) Check the charging system (Chapter 5A).
b) Check the ignition system (Chapter 5B).
c) Check the fuel system (Chapter 4A).

3 Engine oil and filter renewal

**Non-VVT-i models –
every 4500 miles or 6 months**

**VVT-i models –
every 5000 miles or 6 months**

1 Frequent oil and filter changes are the most important preventative maintenance procedures which can be undertaken by the DIY owner. As engine oil ages, it becomes diluted and contaminated, which leads to premature engine wear.
2 Before starting this procedure, gather together all the necessary tools and materials. Also make sure that you have plenty of clean rags and newspapers handy, to mop-up any spills. Ideally, the engine oil should be warm, as it will drain better, and more built-up sludge will be removed with it. Take care, however, not to touch the exhaust or any other hot parts of the engine when working under the vehicle. To avoid any possibility of scalding, and to protect yourself from possible skin irritants and other harmful contaminants in used engine oils, it is advisable to wear gloves when carrying out this work. Access to the underside of the vehicle will be greatly improved if it can be raised on a lift, driven onto ramps, or jacked up and supported on axle stands (see *Jacking and vehicle support*). Whichever method is chosen, make sure that the vehicle remains level, or if it is at an angle, that the drain plug is at the lowest point.
3 Although not strictly necessary, to improve access, undo the screws and remove the right-hand engine undershield – where fitted **(see illustration)**.
4 Slacken the drain plug about half a turn **(see illustration)**. Position the draining container under the drain plug, then remove the plug completely. If possible, try to keep the plug pressed into the sump while unscrewing it by hand the last couple of turns **(see Haynes Hint)**. Recover the sealing ring from the drain plug.

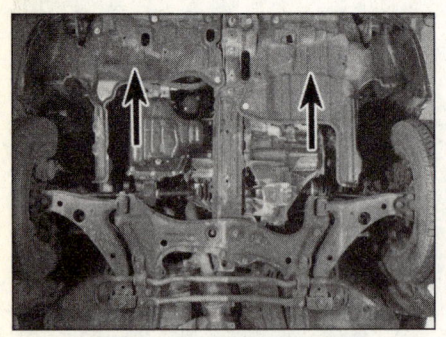

3.3 Left- and right-hand engine undershields (arrowed)

3.4 Slacken the engine oil drain plug (arrowed)

HAYNES HiNT

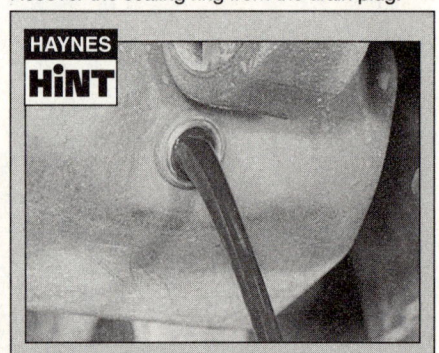

As the drain plug releases from the sump threads, move it away sharply, so the stream of oil issuing from the sump runs into the container, not up your sleeve.

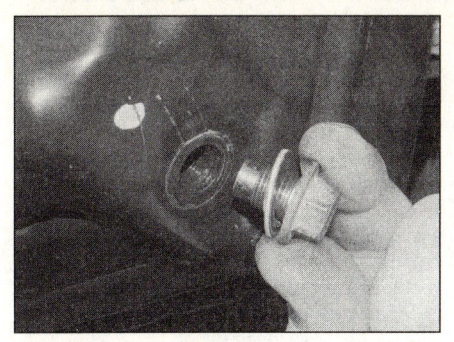

Maintenance procedures 1•9

3.6 Fit a new sealing washer to the drain plug

3.8a Oil filter – non-VVT-i engines

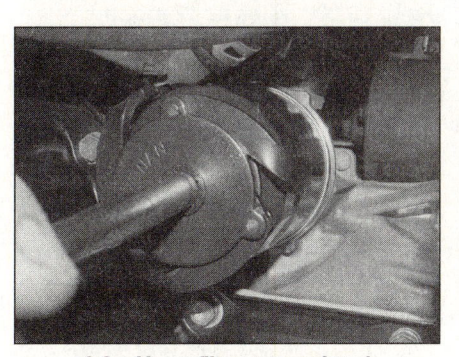

3.8b Oil filter – VVT-i engines (arrowed)

3.8c Use a filter removal tool

3.10 Apply a little clean oil to the filter sealing ring

5 Allow some time for the old oil to drain, noting that it may be necessary to reposition the container as the oil flow slows to a trickle.

6 After all the oil has drained, wipe off the drain plug with a clean rag, and fit a new sealing washer **(see illustration)**. Clean the area around the drain plug opening, and refit the plug, tightening it to the specified torque.

7 Move the container into position under the oil filter, which is located on the front of the cylinder block.

8 Using an oil filter removal tool if necessary, slacken the filter initially, then unscrew it by hand the rest of the way **(see illustrations)**. Empty the oil in the old filter into the container.

9 Use a clean rag to remove all oil, dirt and sludge from the filter sealing area on the engine. Check the old filter to make sure that the rubber sealing ring hasn't stuck to the engine. If it has, carefully remove it.

10 Apply a light coating of clean engine oil to the sealing ring on the new filter, then screw it into position on the engine **(see illustration)**. Tighten the filter firmly by hand only – **do not use any tools**.

11 Remove the old oil and all tools from under the car, then lower the car to the ground (if applicable).

12 Remove the dipstick, then unscrew the oil filler cap from the cylinder head cover. Fill the engine, using the correct grade and type of oil (see Weekly checks). An oil can spout or funnel may help to reduce spillage. Pour in half the specified quantity of oil first, then wait a few minutes for the oil to run to the sump. Continue adding oil a small quantity at a time until the level is up to the lower mark on the dipstick. Adding approximately 1 litre will bring the level up to the upper mark on the dipstick. Refit the filler cap.

13 Start the engine and run it for a few minutes; check for leaks around the oil filter seal and the sump drain plug. Note that there may be a delay of a few seconds before the oil pressure warning light goes out when the engine is first started, as the oil circulates through the engine oil galleries and the new oil filter before the pressure builds-up.

14 Refit the engine undershield (where applicable), and secure it in place with the screw fasteners.

15 Switch off the engine, and wait a few minutes for the oil to settle in the sump once more. With the new oil circulated and the filter completely full, recheck the level on the dipstick, and add more oil as necessary.

16 Dispose of the used engine oil safely, with reference to *General repair procedures*.

4 Hose and fluid leak check

Non-VVT-i models – every 9000 miles or 12 months

VVT-i models – every 10 000 miles or 12 months

1 Visually inspect the engine joint faces, gaskets and seals for any signs of water or oil leaks. Pay particular attention to the areas around the cylinder head cover, cylinder head, oil filter and sump joint faces. Bear in mind that, over a period of time, some very slight seepage from these areas is to be expected – what you are really looking for is any indication of a serious leak. Should a leak be found, renew the offending gasket or oil seal by referring to the appropriate Chapters in this manual.

2 Also check the security and condition of all the engine-related pipes and hoses. Ensure that all cable ties or securing clips are in place, and in good condition. Clips which are broken or missing can lead to chafing of the hoses, pipes or wiring, which could cause more serious problems in the future.

3 Carefully check the radiator hoses and heater hoses along their entire length. Renew any hose which is cracked, swollen or deteriorated. Cracks will show up better if the hose is squeezed. Pay close attention to the hose clips that secure the hoses to the cooling system components. Hose clips can pinch and puncture hoses, resulting in cooling system leaks. If crimped-type hose clips are used, it may be a good idea to use standard worm-drive clips.

4 Inspect all the cooling system components (hoses, joint faces, etc) for leaks **(see Haynes Hint)**.

5 Where any problems are found on system components, renew the component or gasket with reference to Chapter 3.

6 Where applicable, inspect the automatic

HAYNES HINT

A leak in the cooling system will usually show up as white- or rust-coloured deposits on the area adjoining the leak.

1•10 Maintenance procedures

5.1 Check the driveshaft gaiters for signs of damage or deterioration

transmission fluid cooler hoses for leaks or deterioration.

7 With the vehicle raised, inspect the petrol tank and filler neck for punctures, cracks and other damage. The connection between the filler neck and tank is especially critical. Sometimes a rubber filler neck or connecting hose will leak due to loose retaining clamps or deteriorated rubber.

8 Carefully check all rubber hoses and fuel pipes leading away from the petrol tank. Check for loose connections, deteriorated hoses, crimped lines, and other damage. Pay particular attention to the vent pipes and hoses, which often loop up around the filler neck and can become blocked or crimped. Follow the pipes to the front of the vehicle, carefully inspecting them all the way. Renew damaged sections as necessary.

9 From within the engine compartment, check the security of all fuel pipe attachments and unions, and inspect the fuel pipes and vacuum hoses for kinks, chafing and deterioration.

10 Where applicable, check the condition of the power steering fluid hoses and pipes.

5 Driveshaft gaiter and CV joints check

Non-VVT-i models –
every 9000 miles or 12 months

VVT-i models –
every 10 000 miles or 12 months

1 With the vehicle raised and securely supported on stands (see *Jacking and vehicle support*), turn the steering onto full lock, then slowly rotate the roadwheel. Inspect the condition of the outer constant velocity (CV) joint gaiters, squeezing the gaiters to open out the folds **(see illustration)**. Check for signs of cracking, splits or deterioration of the gaiter, which may allow the grease to escape, and lead to water and grit entry into the joint. Also check the security and condition of the retaining clips. Repeat these checks on the inner CV joints. If any damage or deterioration is found, the gaiters should be renewed (see Chapter 8).

2 At the same time, check the general condition of the CV joints themselves by first holding the driveshaft and attempting to rotate the wheel. Repeat this check by holding the inner joint and attempting to rotate the driveshaft. Any appreciable movement indicates wear in the joints, wear in the driveshaft splines, or a loose driveshaft retaining nut.

6 Hinge and lock lubrication

Non-VVT-i models –
every 9000 miles or 12 months

VVT-i models –
every 10 000 miles or 12 months

1 Work around the vehicle, and lubricate the hinges of the bonnet, doors and tailgate with a small amount of general-purpose oil.

2 Lightly lubricate the bonnet release mechanism and exposed section of inner cable with a smear of grease.

3 Check carefully the security and operation of all hinges, latches and locks, adjusting them where required. Check the operation of the central locking system (if fitted).

4 Check the condition and operation of the tailgate struts, renewing them if either is leaking or no longer able to support the tailgate securely when raised.

7 Automatic transmission/differential fluid level check

Non-VVT-i models –
every 9000 miles or 12 months

VVT-i models –
every 10 000 miles or 12 months

Automatic transmission

1 The transmission should be at normal operating temperature. Set the selector lever in the Park position, making sure the vehicle is parked on a level surface.

2 Start the engine and allow it to idle. With your foot on the brake pedal, move the selector lever through all the positions, then return to Park.

3 Pull out the transmission oil level dipstick, and wipe it clean **(see illustration)**.

4 Fully insert the dipstick, then pull it out again. The level should be within the two notches either side of the HOT mark on the dipstick **(see illustration)**. If not, add fluid and check again.

5 Check the condition of the fluid. If it smells burnt or is blackened, the fluid must be renewed as follows.

6 Stop the engine, jack up the front of the vehicle and support it securely on axle stands (see *Jacking and vehicle support*). Place a suitable container under the transmission drain plug.

7 Using an Allen (hexagonal) key, unscrew the drain plug and allow the fluid to drain into the container **(see illustration)**. When all the fluid has drained, refit the plug, tightening it to the specified torque.

8 Fill the transmission through the dipstick aperture with the correct quantity of specified fluid, and check the level as previously described.

Differential

9 The three-speed automatic transmission differential has a separate lubricant supply with a check/filler plug which must be removed to check the level.

10 Remove the filler plug from the front of the differential **(see illustration)**.

11 Use your finger as a dipstick to make sure the lubricant level is even with the bottom of

7.3 Automatic transmission oil level dipstick (arrowed)

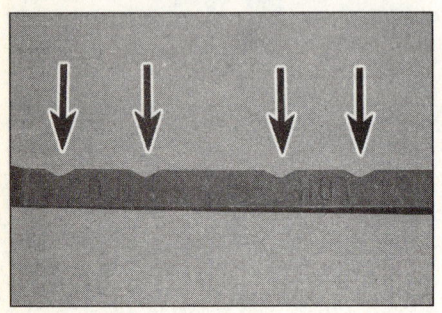

7.4 HOT max and min marks are the right-hand arrows, the COOL max and min marks are on the left

7.7 Automatic transmission drain plug (arrowed)

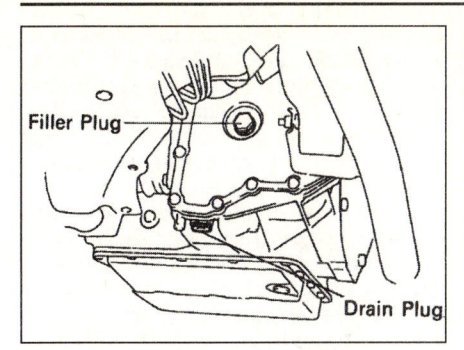

Maintenance procedures 1•11

7.10 Differential filler and drain plug details (three-speed automatic transmission)

8.2 Manual transmission fluid level plug (arrowed)

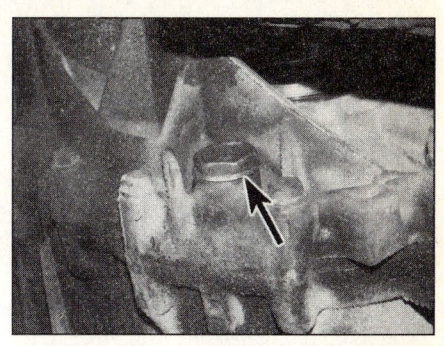

8.7 Manual transmission fluid drain plug (arrowed)

the plug hole. If not, use a syringe or a gear oil pump to add the recommended lubricant until it just starts to run out of the hole. Refit the plug and tighten it securely.

12 To renew the differential fluid, position a container under the differential fluid drain plug, remove the plug and allow the fluid to drain. Tighten the plug securely.

13 Refill the differential as described in paragraphs 9 to 11.

8 Manual transmission fluid level check

**Non-VVT-i models –
every 9000 miles or 12 months**

**VVT-i models –
every 10 000 miles or 12 months**

Level check

1 The manual transmission does not have a dipstick. To check the fluid level, raise the vehicle and support it securely on axle stands (see *Jacking and vehicle support*). Undo the screws and remove the left-hand side engine undershield (where fitted).

2 On the lower front side of the transmission housing, you will see a plug **(see illustration)**. Remove it. If the lubricant level is correct, it should be up to the lower edge of the hole.

3 If the transmission needs more lubricant (if the level is not up to the hole), use a syringe or a gear oil pump to add more. Stop filling the transmission when the lubricant begins to run out the hole.

4 Refit the plug and tighten it to the specified torque. Drive the vehicle a short distance, then check for leaks.

Fluid renewal

5 Take the vehicle for a drive of sufficient length to warm-up the transmission fluid. Although this is not essential, it does help to ensure all the fluid is drained, along with any contaminants.

6 Raise the vehicle, and remove the left-hand engine undershield as described in paragraph 1.

7 The fluid drain plug is located on the underside of the transmission casing **(see illustration)**. Position a suitable container, and undo the drain plug. Recover the drain plug sealing washer. Renew it if it shows any sign of damage, wear, or deformity.

8 Once the fluid has finished draining, refit the drain plug (with a new washer where necessary), and tighten it to the specified torque.

9 Remove the filler plug and refill the transmission as described in paragraphs 2, 3 and 4.

9 Auxiliary drivebelt check, adjustment and renewal

**Non-VVT-i models –
every 9000 miles or 12 months**

**VVT-i models –
every 10 000 miles or 12 months**

Check

1 The alternator, power steering pump, coolant pump (VVT-i engines) and air conditioning compressor drivebelt(s), also referred to as simply 'fan' belts, are located at the right end of the engine. The good condition and proper adjustment of the belts is critical to the operation of the engine. Because of their composition and the high stresses to which they are subjected, drivebelts stretch and deteriorate as they get older. They must therefore be periodically inspected.

2 The number of belts used on a particular vehicle depends on the engine type and accessories installed. On non-VVT-i engines, one belt transmits power from the crankshaft to the coolant pump and alternator. If the vehicle is equipped with power steering and/or air conditioning, a separate belt (or two separate belts) drive these components. On VVT-i engines one belt is used to drive all the pulleys.

3 With the engine stopped, open the bonnet and locate the drivebelt(s). With a torch, check each belt for separation of the adhesive rubber on both sides of the core, core separation from the belt side, a severed core, separation of the ribs from the adhesive rubber, cracking or separation of the ribs, and torn or worn ribs or cracks in the inner ridges of the ribs **(see illustration)**. Also check for fraying and glazing, which gives the belt a shiny appearance. Both sides of the belt should be inspected, which means you will have to twist the belt to check the underside. Use your fingers to feel the belt where you can't see it. If any of the above conditions are evident, renew the belt.

4 On non-VVT-i engines only, to check the tension of each belt, the following rule of thumb method is recommended: Push firmly on the belt with your thumb at a distance halfway between the pulleys and note how far the belt can be pushed (deflected). Measure this deflection with a ruler **(see illustration)**. The belt should deflect approximately 6.0 mm if the distance from pulley centre to pulley centre is between 200 to 300 mm; the belt should deflect approximately 12 mm if the distance from pulley centre to pulley centre is between 300 and 400 mm. **Note:** *On VVT-i engines, the tension of the belt is maintained by an automatic tensioner mechanism.*

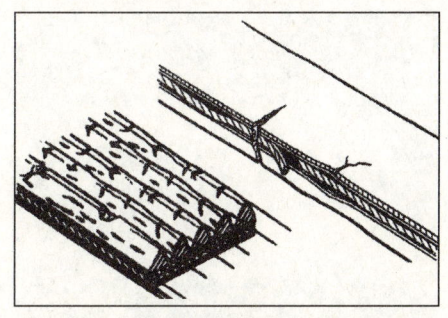

9.3 Check the multi-ribbed belt for signs of wear like these – if the belt looks worn, renew it

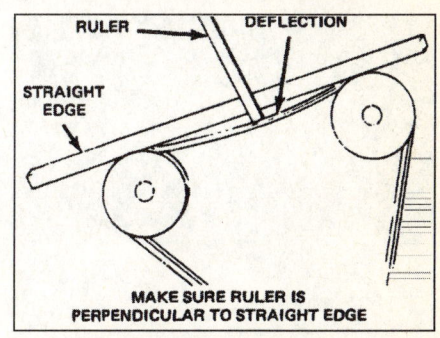

9.4 Measure the drivebelt deflection with a straight-edge and ruler

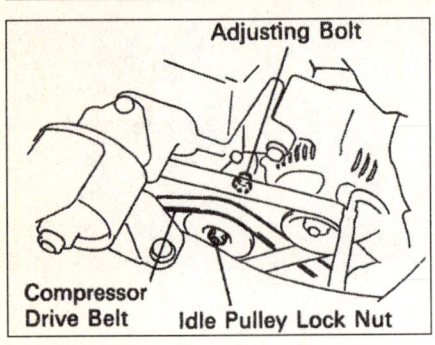

Maintenance procedures

9.5 After slackening the idler pulley locknut, turn the adjusting bolt

(Adjusting Bolt / Compressor Drive Belt / Idle Pulley Lock Nut)

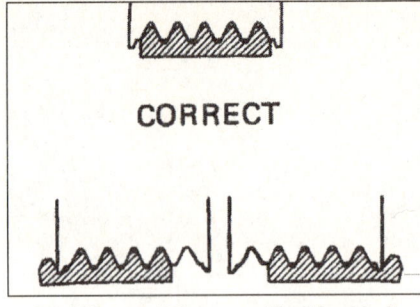

9.8 When refitting a multi-ribbed belt, ensure it is centred – it must not overlap either edge of the pulleys

(CORRECT)

9.10 Use a spanner on the hexagonal section (arrowed) of the auxiliary drivebelt tensioner

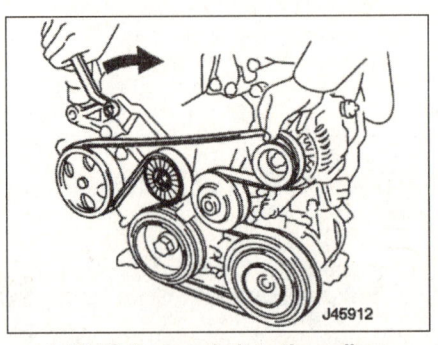

9.12 Fit the new belt to the pulleys

Adjustment

Note: The following procedure applies only to the non-VVT-i engines.

5 Two adjustment methods are used for the drivebelts according to their arrangement. On all models, the alternator drivebelt is adjusted by loosening the mounting and adjustment/lockbolts then moving the alternator either by hand, or by turning the adjuster bolt, as necessary, while checking the tension in accordance with one of the above methods. Tighten the mounting and adjustment/lockbolts when the tension is correct. To adjust the tension of the other belts, first check to see if an idler pulley is used in the belt arrangement. If an idler pulley is fitted, loosen the idler pulley locknut and turn the adjusting bolt **(see illustration)**. Measure the belt tension in accordance with one of the above methods. Repeat this step until the drivebelt is adjusted correctly then tighten the idler pulley locknut. If an idler pulley is not fitted, adjustment is carried out at the power steering pump. Loosen the adjustment bolt that secures the pump to the slotted bracket and pivot the pump (away from the engine to tighten the belt, toward it to loosen it). Repeat the procedure until the drivebelt tension is correct and tighten the bolt.

Renewal

Non-VVT-i engines

6 To renew a belt, follow the above procedures for drivebelt adjustment but slip the belt off the relevant pulleys and remove it. Depending on which belt you are renewing, it will probably be necessary to remove an outer belt first because of the way they are arranged on the pulleys. Because of this, and because belts tend to wear out more or less together, it is a good idea to renew all the belts at the same time. Mark each belt and its appropriate pulley groove so the new belts can be installed in their proper positions.

7 Take the old belts to the parts store in order to make a direct comparison for length, width and design.

8 After renewing the drivebelt, make sure that it fits properly in the ribbed grooves in the pulleys **(see illustration)**. It is essential that the belt be properly centred.

9 Adjust the belt(s) in accordance with the procedure outlined above.

VVT-i engines

10 Using a spanner on the hexagonal section, rotate the tensioner clockwise to relieve the tension on the belt **(see illustration)**.

11 Lift the belt from the pulleys.

12 Fit the new belt to the pulleys then, holding the tensioner clockwise, fit the belt around the tensioner pulley, and gently release the tensioner **(see illustration)**. If better access is required, undo the screws and remove the right-hand side engine undershield.

10 Air filter element check

10.2a Release the clips (arrowed) ...

10.2b ... lift off the cover and the air filter element (non-VVT-i engines)

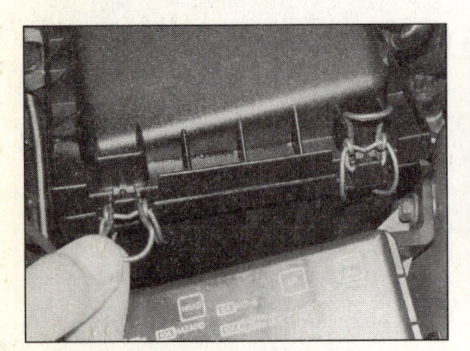

10.2c Release the spring clips ...

10.2d ... then lift out the air filter element (VVT-i engines)

Non-VVT-i models – every 9000 miles or 12 months

VVT-i models – every 10 000 miles or 12 months

1 The air filter is located inside a housing at the left side of the engine compartment.

2 To remove the air filter, release the spring clips that keep the two halves of the air cleaner housing together, then lift the cover

Maintenance procedures 1•13

up and remove the air filter element **(see illustrations)**.

3 Inspect the outer surface of the filter element. If it is dirty, renew it. If it is only moderately dusty, it can be re-used by blowing it clean from the back to the front surface with compressed air. Because it is a pleated paper type filter, it cannot be washed or oiled. If it cannot be cleaned satisfactorily with compressed air, discard and renew it. While the cover is off, be careful not to drop anything down into the housing.

Caution: Never drive the vehicle with the air cleaner removed. Excessive engine wear could result and backfiring could even cause a fire under the bonnet.

4 Wipe out the inside of the air cleaner housing.

5 Place the new filter into the air cleaner housing, making sure it seats properly.

6 Refitting of the cover is the reverse of removal.

11 Handbrake check and adjustment

Non-VVT-i models –
every 9000 miles or 12 months

VVT-i models –
every 10 000 miles or 12 months

1 To check the handbrake adjustment, applying normal moderate pressure, pull the handbrake lever to the fully-applied position, counting the number of clicks emitted from the handbrake ratchet mechanism. If adjustment is correct, the handbrake should be fully applied after 4 to 7 (rear drum brake models) or 5 to 8 (rear disc models) clicks have been emitted. If this is not the case, adjust the handbrake as described in Chapter 9.

12 Brake pad check

Non-VVT-i models –
every 9000 miles or 12 months

VVT-i models –
every 10 000 miles or 12 months

1 Slacken the front roadwheel bolts. Firmly apply the handbrake, then jack up the front of the car and support it securely on axle stands (see *Jacking and vehicle support*). Remove the front roadwheels.

2 For a quick check, the pad thickness can be carried out via the inspection hole on the front caliper **(see Haynes Hint)**. Using a steel rule, measure the thickness of the pad friction material. This must not be less than the specified minimum given in the Specifications.

3 For a comprehensive check, the brake pads should be removed and cleaned. The operation of the caliper can then be checked, and the brake disc itself can be fully examined on both sides. Refer to Chapter 9 for details.

4 If any pad's friction material is worn to the specified minimum thickness or less, all four pads must be renewed as a set. Refer to Chapter 9 for details.

5 On completion, refit the roadwheels then lower the vehicle to the ground and tighten the wheel bolts to the specified torque.

6 Slacken the rear roadwheel bolts. Jack up the rear of the car and support it securely on axle stands. Remove the rear roadwheels. Repeat the procedure described in Paragraphs 2 to 5 on the rear brake pads.

13 Brake drum and shoe check

Non-VVT-i models –
every 9000 miles or 12 months

VVT-i models –
every 20 000 miles or 2 years

⚠️ *Warning: Brake dust produced by lining wear and deposited on brake components may contain asbestos, which is hazardous to your health. DO NOT blow it out with compressed air and DO NOT inhale it. DO NOT use petrol or solvents to remove the dust. Brake system cleaner should be used to flush the dust into a drain pan. After the brake components are wiped clean with a damp rag, dispose of the contaminated rag(s) and solvent in a covered and labelled container. Try to use non-asbestos parts whenever possible.*

1 Refer to Chapter 9 and remove the rear brake drums.

2 Note the thickness of the lining material on the rear brake shoes **(see illustration)** and look for signs of contamination by brake fluid and grease.

3 If the lining material is within 1.0 mm of the recessed rivets or metal shoes, renew the brake shoes. The shoes should also be renewed if they are cracked, glazed (shiny lining surfaces) or contaminated with brake fluid or grease. See Chapter 9 for the renewal procedure.

4 Check the shoe return and hold-down springs and the adjusting mechanism to make sure they're installed correctly and in good condition. Deteriorated or distorted springs, if not renewed, could allow the linings to drag and wear prematurely.

5 Check the wheel cylinders for leakage by carefully peeling back the rubber boots **(see illustration)**. If brake fluid is noted behind the boots, the wheel cylinders must be renewed (see Chapter 9).

6 Check the drums for cracks, score marks, deep scratches and hard spots, which will appear as small discoloured areas. If imperfections cannot be removed with emery cloth, the drums must be resurfaced by an automotive engineering workshop (see Chapter 9 for more detailed information).

7 Refit the brake drums (see Chapter 9).

8 Refit the wheels and nuts.

9 Remove the axle stands and lower the vehicle.

10 Tighten the wheel nuts to the specified torque.

14 Exhaust system and mountings check

Non-VVT-i models –
every 9000 miles or 12 months

VVT-i models –
every 10 000 miles or 12 months

1 With the engine cold (at least an hour after

HAYNES HINT

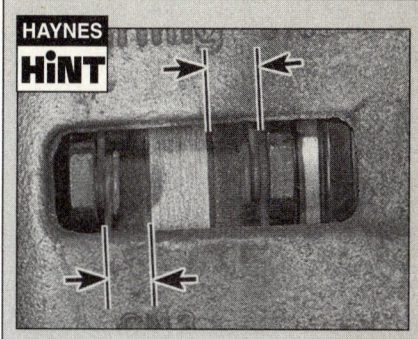

For a quick check, then thickness of the friction material on each brake pad can be measured through the aperture in the caliper body.

13.2 Measure the thickness of the brake shoe friction material

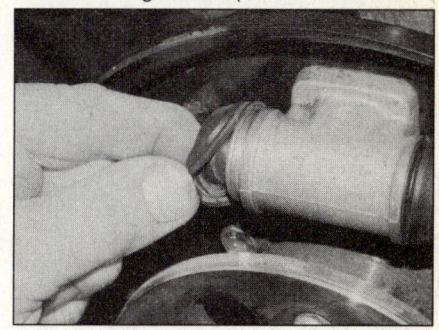

13.5 Peel back the wheel cylinder rubber boots and check for leaks

1•14 Maintenance procedures

the car has been driven), check the complete exhaust system from the engine to the end of the tailpipe. The exhaust system is most easily checked with the car raised on a hoist, or suitably-supported on axle stands, so that the exhaust components are readily visible and accessible.

2 Check the exhaust pipes and connections for evidence of leaks, severe corrosion and damage. Make sure that all brackets and mountings are in good condition, and that all relevant nuts and bolts are tight (see illustration). Leakage at any of the joints or in other parts of the system will usually show up as a black sooty stain in the vicinity of the leak.

3 Rattles and other noises can often be traced to the exhaust system, especially the brackets and mountings. Try to move the pipes and silencers. If the components are able to come into contact with the body or suspension parts, secure the system with new mountings. Otherwise separate the joints (if possible) and twist the pipes as necessary to provide additional clearance.

15 Steering and suspension check

**Non-VVT-i models –
every 9000 miles or 12 months**

**VVT-i models –
every 10 000 miles or 12 months**

Front suspension and steering

1 Raise the front of the vehicle, and securely support it on axle stands (see *Jacking and vehicle support*).

2 Visually inspect the balljoint dust covers and the steering gear gaiters for splits, chafing or deterioration. Any wear of these components will cause loss of lubricant, together with dirt and water entry, resulting in rapid deterioration of the balljoints or steering gear.

3 Check the power steering fluid pipes/hoses for chafing or deterioration, and the pipe and hose unions for fluid leaks. Also check for signs of fluid leakage under pressure from the steering gear rubber gaiters, which would

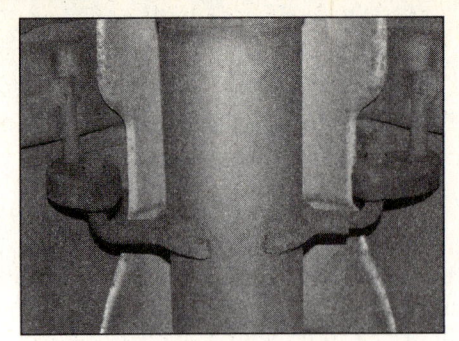

14.2 Check the condition of the exhaust rubber mountings

indicate failed fluid seals within the steering gear.

4 Grasp the roadwheel at the 12 o'clock and 6 o'clock positions, and try to rock it (see illustration). Very slight free play may be felt, but if the movement is appreciable, further investigation is necessary to determine the source. Continue rocking the wheel while an assistant depresses the footbrake. If the movement is now eliminated or significantly reduced, it is likely that the hub bearings are at fault. If the free play is still evident with the footbrake depressed, then there is wear in the suspension joints or mountings.

5 Now grasp the wheel at the 9 o'clock and 3 o'clock positions, and try to rock it as before. Any movement felt now may again be caused by wear in the hub bearings or the steering track rod balljoints. If the inner or outer balljoint is worn, the visual movement will be obvious.

6 Using a large screwdriver or flat bar, check for wear in the suspension mounting bushes by levering between the relevant suspension component and its attachment point. Some movement is to be expected as the mountings are made of rubber, but excessive wear should be obvious. Also check the condition of any visible rubber bushes, looking for splits, cracks or contamination of the rubber.

7 With the car standing on its wheels, have an assistant turn the steering wheel back-and-forth about an eighth of a turn each way. There should be very little, if any, lost movement between the steering wheel and roadwheels. If this is not the case, closely observe the joints and mountings previously described, but in addition, check the steering column universal joints for wear, and the steering gear itself.

Strut/shock absorber

8 Check for any signs of fluid leakage around the suspension strut/shock absorber body, or from the rubber gaiter around the piston rod. Should any fluid be noticed, the suspension strut/shock absorber is defective internally, and should be renewed. **Note:** *Suspension struts/shock absorbers should always be renewed in pairs on the same axle, or the handling of the vehicle will be adversely affected.*

9 The efficiency of the suspension strut/shock absorber may be checked by bouncing the vehicle at each corner. Generally speaking, the body will return to its normal position and stop after being depressed. If it rises and returns on a rebound, the suspension strut/shock absorber is probably suspect. Examine also the suspension strut/shock absorber upper and lower mountings for any signs of wear.

16 Remote control battery renewal

**Non-VVT-i models –
every 9000 miles or 12 months**

**VVT-i models –
every 20 000 miles or 2 years**

Non-VVT-i models

1 Using a screwdriver or coin, prise open the cover from the remote control unit (see illustration).

2 Note how the batteries are fitted (positive side away from the buttons), then carefully remove them from the contacts.

3 Fit the new battery (CR2016) and refit the cover making sure that it clips fully onto the base (see illustration).

VVT-i models

4 Undo the small screw and lift the cover from the remote control unit (see illustration).

5 Lift the module from the unit, then remove the battery case cover (see illustration).

15.4 Check for wear in the hub bearings by grasping the wheel and trying to rock it

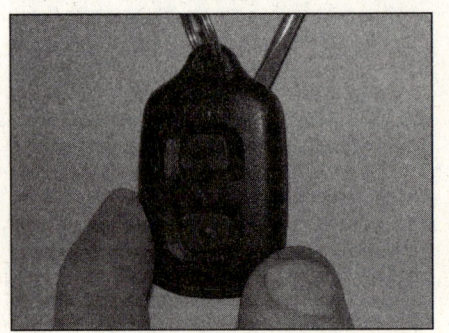

16.1 Prise open the remote control cover

16.3 The positive side of the battery faces away from the buttons

Maintenance procedures 1•15

16.4 Undo the small screw and lift the remote control cover

16.5 Prise open the battery case cover

16.6 The battery is fitted positive side upwards

6 Note how it's fitted (positive side upwards) and remove the battery (CR2016) **(see illustration)**.
7 Refitting is a reversal of removal.

17 Clutch pedal check and adjustment

**Non-VVT-i models –
every 9000 miles or 12 months**

**VVT-i models –
every 10 000 miles or 12 months**

1 Press down lightly on the clutch pedal and, with a small steel ruler, measure the distance that it moves freely before the clutch resistance is felt **(see illustration)**. The freeplay should be 1.0 to 5.0 mm. If it isn't proceed as follows:
2 Slacken the locknut on the pedal end of the clutch pushrod **(see illustration)**.
3 Turn the pushrod until the pedal freeplay is correct, then tighten the locknut.
4 After adjusting the freeplay, check the pedal height from the centre of the pedal pad to the footwell metal floor. The distance should be 141.1 to 151.1 mm.
5 If the pedal height is incorrect, slacken the locknut and turn the stop bolt until the height is correct. Tighten the locknut.

18 Pollen filter check

**Non-VVT-i models –
every 9000 miles or 12 months**

**VVT-i models –
every 10 000 miles or 12 months**

1 Reach under the passenger's side of the facia, remove the retaining clips and remove the cover over the filter **(see illustration)**.
2 Pull the tab downwards, and pull the filter from the housing **(see illustration)**. The filter is designed to fold as it's withdrawn.
3 Check the condition of the filter, and renew it if dirty.
4 Wipe clean the inside of the housing and fit the pollen filter element, making sure that it is correctly seated.

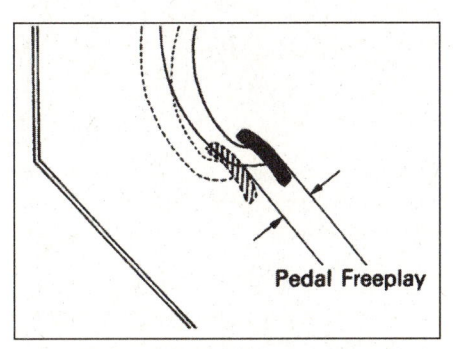

17.1 To check the clutch pedal free play, measure the distance between the natural resting place of the pedal and point where you encounter resistance

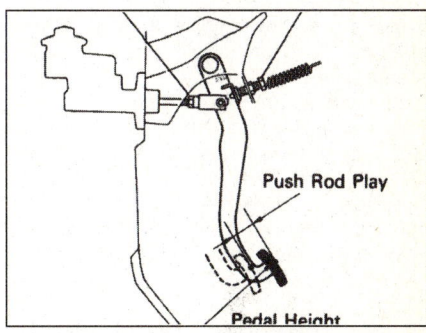

5 Refit the pollen filter cover and secure it in place with the clips.

19 Road test

**Non-VVT-i models –
every 9000 miles or 12 months**

**VVT-i models –
every 10 000 miles or 12 months**

Instruments and electrical equipment

1 Check the operation of all instruments and electrical equipment.
2 Make sure that all instruments read correctly,

18.1 Pull out the clips (arrowed) and remove the pollen filter cover

17.2 The clutch pedal pushrod play, pedal height and free play adjustments are made by slackening the locknut and turning the threaded adjuster

and switch on all electrical equipment in turn to check it functions properly.

Steering and suspension

3 Check for any abnormalities in the steering, suspension, handling or road 'feel'.
4 Drive the vehicle, and check that there are no unusual vibrations or noises.
5 Check that the steering feels positive, with no excessive 'sloppiness', or roughness, and check for any suspension noises when cornering, or when driving over bumps.

Drivetrain

6 Check the performance of the engine, clutch, transmission and driveshafts.
7 Listen for any unusual noises from the engine, clutch and transmission.

18.2 Pull the filter downwards from the housing

1•16 Maintenance procedures

20.3a Using a second spanner, remove the banjo bolt at the top of the fuel filter

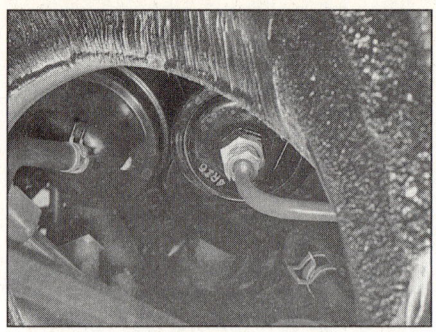

20.3b Slacken the fitting at the bottom of the filter (viewed through the wheel arch)

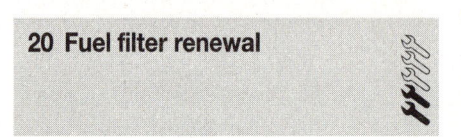

8 Make sure the engine idles smoothly, and that there is no hesitation when accelerating.
9 Check that the clutch action is smooth and progressive, that the drive is taken up smoothly, and that the pedal travel is not excessive. Also listen for any noises when the clutch pedal is depressed.
10 Check that all gears can be engaged smoothly, without noise, and that the gear lever action is smooth and not vague or 'notchy'.
11 On automatic transmission models, make sure that all gearchanges occur smoothly, without snatching, and without an increase in engine speed between changes. Check that all the gear positions can be selected with the vehicle at rest. If any problems are found, they should be referred to a Toyota dealer.
12 Listen for a metallic clicking sound from the front of the vehicle, as the vehicle is driven slowly in a circle with the steering on full lock. Carry out this check in both directions. If a clicking noise is heard, this indicates wear in a driveshaft joint, in which case, the complete driveshaft must be renewed (see Chapter 8).

Braking system

13 Make sure that the vehicle does not pull to one side when braking, and that the wheels do not lock when braking hard.
14 Check that there is no vibration through the steering when braking.
15 Check that the handbrake operates correctly, without excessive movement of the lever, and that it holds the vehicle on a slope.
16 Test the operation of the brake servo unit as follows. With the engine off, depress the footbrake four or five times to exhaust the vacuum. Start the engine, holding the brake pedal depressed. As the engine starts, there should be a noticeable 'give' in the brake pedal as vacuum builds-up. Allow the engine to run for at least two minutes, and then switch it off. If the brake pedal is depressed now, it should be possible to detect a hiss from the servo as the pedal is depressed. After about four or five applications, no further hissing should be heard, and the pedal should feel considerably firmer.

20 Fuel filter renewal

**Non-VVT-i models –
every 18 000 miles or 2 years**

Note: This procedure applies only to the non-VVT-i engine models

1 The canister filter is mounted in a bracket on the engine compartment bulkhead near the left side of the car.
2 Remove any components that would interfere with access to the top of the filter.
3 Using a second spanner to steady the filter, remove the threaded banjo bolt at the top and loosen the fitting at the bottom of the fuel filter **(see illustrations)**.
4 Remove both bracket bolts from the bulkhead and remove the old filter and the filter support bracket assembly.
5 Note that the inlet and outlet pipes are clearly labelled on their respective ends of the filter and that the flanged end of the filter faces down. Make sure the new filter is installed so that it's facing the proper direction as noted above. When correctly installed, the filter should be installed so that the outlet pipe faces up and the inlet pipe faces down.
6 Using the new crush washers provided by the filter manufacturer, install the inlet and outlet fittings and tighten them securely.
7 The remainder of installation is the reverse of the removal procedure.

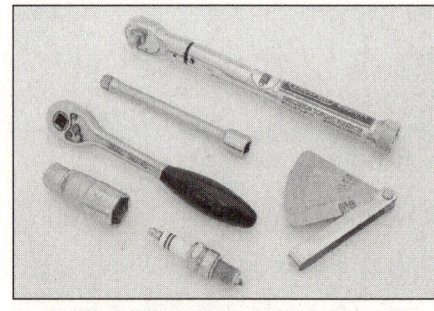

22.1 To change the spark plugs you'll need a torque wrench, extension, ratchet, socket and a set of feeler gauges

21 Brake fluid renewal

**Non-VVT-i models –
every 18 000 miles or 2 years**

**VVT-i models –
every 20 000 miles or 2 years**

⚠ *Warning: Brake hydraulic fluid can harm your eyes and damage painted surfaces, so use extreme caution when handling and pouring it. Do not use fluid that has been standing open for some time, as it absorbs moisture from the air. Excess moisture can cause a dangerous loss of braking effectiveness.*

1 The procedure is similar to that for the bleeding of the hydraulic system as described in Chapter 9, except that the brake fluid reservoir should be emptied by syphoning, using a clean ladle or similar before starting, and allowance should be made for the old fluid to be expelled when bleeding a section of the circuit.
2 Working as described in Chapter 9, open the first bleed screw in the sequence, and pump the brake pedal gently until nearly all the old fluid has been emptied from the master cylinder reservoir.

> **HAYNES HiNT** *Old hydraulic fluid is invariably much darker in colour than the new, making it easy to distinguish the two.*

3 Top-up to the MAX level with new fluid, and continue pumping until only the new fluid remains in the reservoir, and new fluid can be seen emerging from the bleed screw. Tighten the screw, and top the reservoir level up to the MAX level line.
4 Work through all the remaining bleed screws in the sequence until new fluid can be seen at all of them. Be careful to keep the master cylinder reservoir topped-up to above the MIN level at all times, or air may enter the system and increase the length of the task.
5 When the operation is complete, check that all bleed screws are securely tightened, and that their dust caps are refitted. Wash off all traces of spilt fluid, and recheck the master cylinder reservoir fluid level.
6 Check the operation of the brakes before taking the car on the road.

22 Spark plug renewal

**Non-VVT-i models –
every 18 000 miles or 2 years**

**VVT-i models –
every 40 000 miles or 4 years**

1 Spark plug renewal requires a spark plug socket which fits onto a ratchet. This socket

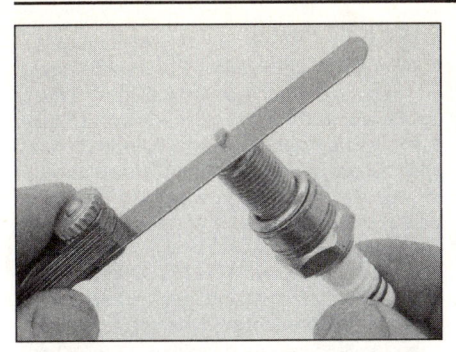

Maintenance procedures 1•17

22.4 Measure the spark plug electrode gap with a feeler gauge

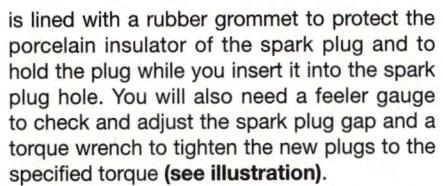

22.6 When removing the spark plug HT leads, pull only on the boot and use a twisting/pulling motion

22.8 Use a spark plug socket with a long extension to unscrew the spark plug

is lined with a rubber grommet to protect the porcelain insulator of the spark plug and to hold the plug while you insert it into the spark plug hole. You will also need a feeler gauge to check and adjust the spark plug gap and a torque wrench to tighten the new plugs to the specified torque **(see illustration)**.

2 If you are renewing the plugs, purchase the new plugs, adjust them to the proper gap and then fit each plug one at a time. **Note:** *When buying new spark plugs, it's essential that you obtain the correct plugs for your specific vehicle. This information can be found in the Specifications Section at the beginning of this Chapter, or in the owner's handbook.*

3 Inspect each of the new plugs for defects. If there are any signs of cracks in the porcelain insulator of a plug, don't use it.

4 Check the electrode gaps of the new plugs. Check the gap by inserting the feeler gauge of the proper thickness between the electrodes at the tip of the plug **(see illustration)**. The gap between the electrodes should be identical to that listed in this Chapter's Specifications. If the gap is incorrect, carefully bend the curved side electrode slightly.

Caution: *Some plugs are supplied with the gap preset. There is no need to adjust them.*

5 If the side electrode is not exactly over the centre electrode, align them.

Removal

Non-VVT-i engines

6 To prevent the possibility of mixing up spark plug leads, work on one spark plug at a time. Remove the HT lead and boot from one spark plug. Grasp the boot – not the lead – as shown, give it a half twisting motion and pull straight up **(see illustration)**.

7 If compressed air is available, blow any dirt or foreign material away from the spark plug area before proceeding (a common bicycle pump will also work).

8 Remove the spark plug **(see illustration)**. Examination of the spark plugs will give a good indication of the condition of the engine. If the insulator nose of the spark plug is clean and white, with no deposits, this is indicative of a weak mixture or too hot a plug (a hot plug transfers heat away from the electrode slowly, a cold plug transfers heat away quickly).

9 If the tip and insulator nose are covered with hard black-looking deposits, then this is indicative that the mixture is too rich. Should the plug be black and oily, then it is likely that the engine is fairly worn, as well as the mixture being too rich. If the insulator nose is covered with light tan to greyish-brown deposits, then the mixture is correct and it is likely that the engine is in good condition.

VVT-i engines

10 Undo the two nuts, prise out the two plastic fasteners at the rear, then lift off the plastic cover on top of the engine **(see illustrations)**.

11 Disconnect the wiring plugs from the ignition coils.

12 Undo the bolts and pull the ignition coils from the top of the spark plugs **(see illustration)**. Recover the dust seal (where fitted).

13 If compressed air is available, blow any dirt or foreign material away from the spark plug area before proceeding (a common bicycle pump will also work).

14 Remove the spark plug. Examination of the spark plugs will give a good indication of the condition of the engine. If the insulator nose of the spark plug is clean and white, with no deposits, this is indicative of a weak mixture or too hot a plug (a hot plug transfers heat away from the electrode slowly, a cold plug transfers heat away quickly).

15 If the tip and insulator nose are covered with hard black-looking deposits, then this is indicative that the mixture is too rich. Should the plug be black and oily, then it is likely that the engine is fairly worn, as well as the mixture being too rich. If the insulator nose is covered with light tan to greyish-brown deposits, then the mixture is correct and it is likely that the engine is in good condition.

Refitting

16 Prior to installation, it's a good idea to coat the spark plug threads with anti-seize compound **(see illustration)**. Also, it's often difficult to insert spark plugs into their holes without cross-threading them. To avoid this possibility, fit a short piece of 8 mm internal diameter rubber hose over the end of the spark plug **(see illustration)**. The flexible hose acts as a universal joint to help align the plug with the plug hole. Should the plug begin to cross-thread, the hose will slip on the spark

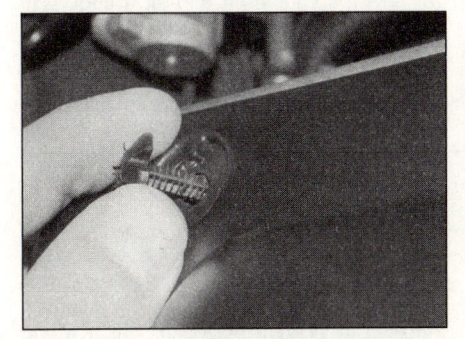

22.10a Prise out the fasteners at the rear of the plastic cover . . .

22.10b . . . then lift the cover from place

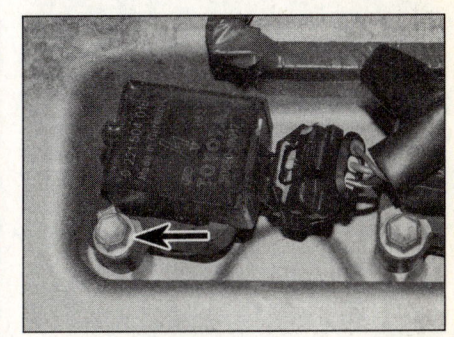

22.12 Undo the screw (arrowed) and lift out the ignition coil

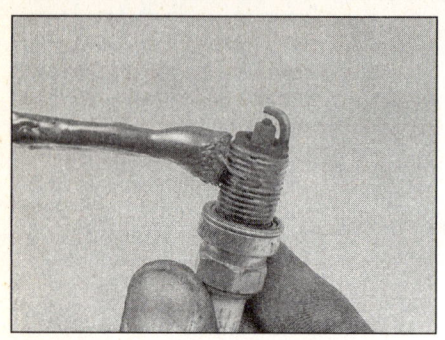

1•18 Maintenance procedures

22.16a Apply a thin coat of anti-seize compound to the spark plug threads

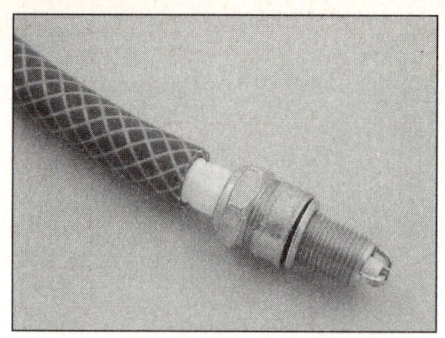

22.16b A length of 8 mm ID rubber hose will save time and prevent damaged threads when installing the spark plugs

plug, preventing thread damage. Tighten the plug to the torque listed in this Chapter's Specifications.

Non-VVT-i engines

17 Attach the plug lead to the new spark plug, again using a twisting motion on the boot until it is firmly seated on the end of the spark plug.
18 Follow the above procedure for the remaining spark plugs, renewing them one at a time to prevent mixing up the spark plug leads.

VVT-i engines

19 Refit the coils to the top of each spark plug, ensuring the dust seal (where fitted) is correctly located. Tighten the ignition coil bolts to the specified torque.

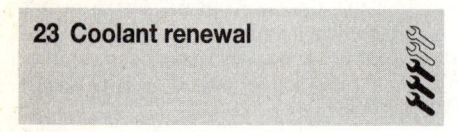

23 Coolant renewal

**Non-VVT-i models –
every 36 000 miles or 4 years**

**VVT-i models –
every 40 000 miles or 3 years**

⚠️ *Warning: Wait until the engine is cold before starting this procedure. Do not allow antifreeze to come in contact with your skin, or with the painted surfaces of the vehicle. Rinse off spills immediately with plenty of water. Never leave antifreeze lying around in an open container, or in a puddle in the driveway or on the garage floor. Children and pets are attracted by its sweet smell, but antifreeze can be fatal if ingested.*

Cooling system draining

1 With the engine completely cold, unscrew the radiator pressure cap.
2 Undo the screws and remove the right-hand engine undershield (where fitted) **(see illustration 3.3)**.
3 Position a suitable container beneath the coolant drain tap at the lower right-hand side of the radiator, then open the drain tap, and allow the coolant to drain into the container **(see illustration)**. When the coolant has finished draining, close the tap.
4 Move the container to under the rear of the engine block, then open the block drain tap and drain the coolant into the container **(see illustration)**. Once the coolant has finished draining, close the tap.

Cooling system flushing

5 If coolant renewal has been neglected, or if the antifreeze mixture has become diluted, then in time, the cooling system may gradually lose efficiency, as the coolant passages become restricted due to rust, scale deposits, and other sediment. The cooling system efficiency can be restored by flushing the system clean.
6 The radiator should be flushed separately from the engine, to avoid excess contamination.

23.3 Radiator drain tap (arrowed)

23.4 There is a coolant drain tap on the rear of the engine block

Radiator flushing

7 Disconnect the top and bottom hoses and any other relevant hoses from the radiator (see Chapter 3).
8 Insert a garden hose into the radiator top inlet. Direct a flow of clean water through the radiator, and continue flushing until clean water emerges from the radiator bottom outlet.
9 If after a reasonable period, the water still does not run clear, the radiator can be flushed with a good proprietary cleaning agent. It is important that their manufacturer's instructions are followed carefully. If the contamination is particularly bad, insert the hose in the radiator bottom outlet, and reverse-flush the radiator.

Engine flushing

10 To flush the engine, remove the thermostat (see Chapter 3).
11 With the bottom hose disconnected from the radiator, insert a garden hose into the coolant housing. Direct a clean flow of water through the engine, and continue flushing until clean water emerges from the radiator bottom hose.
12 When flushing is complete, refit the thermostat and reconnect the hoses (see Chapter 3).

Cooling system filling

13 Before attempting to fill the cooling system, make sure that all hoses and clips are in good condition, and that the clips are tight. Note that an antifreeze mixture must be used all year round, to prevent corrosion of the engine components (see following sub-Section).
14 Remove the radiator pressure cap, and ensure all drain taps/plugs are secured.
15 Place the heater temperature control in the maximum heat position.
16 Slowly add new coolant (50/50 mix of antifreeze and coolant) to the radiator until it's full. Add coolant to the reservoir up to the lower mark. Note that Toyota genuine antifreeze is normally supplied premixed.
17 Leave the radiator cap off, and run the engine in a well-ventilated area until the thermostat opens (coolant will begin flowing through the radiator and the upper hose will become hot).
18 Turn the engine off and let it cool. Add more coolant mixture to bring the level back to the lip of the radiator filler neck.
19 Squeeze the upper radiator hose to expel air, then add more coolant mixture if necessary. Refit the filler cap.
20 Start the engine, allow it to reach normal operating temperature and check for leaks.

Antifreeze mixture

21 The antifreeze should always be renewed at the specified intervals. This is necessary not only to maintain the antifreeze properties, but also to prevent corrosion which would otherwise occur as the corrosion inhibitors become progressively less effective.

Maintenance procedures 1•19

22 Always use an ethylene-glycol based antifreeze which is suitable for use in mixed-metal cooling systems.

23 Before adding antifreeze, the cooling system should be completely drained, preferably flushed, and all hoses checked for condition and security.

24 After filling with antifreeze, a label should be attached to the expansion tank, stating the type and concentration of antifreeze used, and the date installed. Any subsequent topping-up should be made with the same type and concentration of antifreeze.

25 Do not use engine antifreeze in the windscreen/tailgate washer system, as it will damage the vehicle paintwork. A screenwash additive should be added to the washer system in the quantities stated on the bottle.

24 Valve clearance check and adjustment

**Non-VVT-i models –
every 54 000 miles or 6 years**

**VVT-i models –
every 60 000 miles or 6 years**

Non-VVT-i engines

Note: *The following procedure requires the use of a special tool (Toyota No 09248-55020) which compresses the cam follower a little to enable the removal of the adjustment shim. Without the tool, it will be necessary to remove the camshaft(s) as described in Chapter 2A.*

1 Remove the cylinder head cover as described in Chapter 2A..

2 Remove the spark plugs (see Section 20).

3 Refer to Chapter 2A and position the number 1 piston at TDC on the compression stroke.

4 Measure the clearances of the indicated valves with feeler gauges **(see illustrations)**. Record the measurements for those which are out of specification. They will be used later to determine the required shims.

5 Turn the crankshaft one complete revolution and realign the crankshaft timing marks. Measure the remaining valves **(see illustration)**.

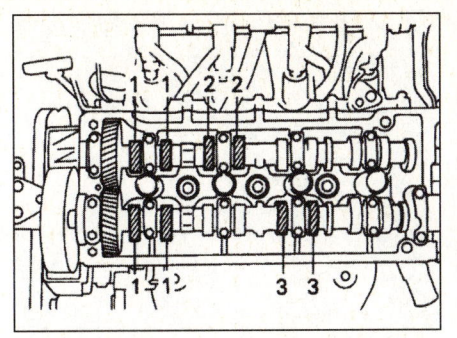

24.4a When the No 1 piston is at TDC on the compression stroke, the valve clearance for the No 1 and No 3 cylinder exhaust valves and the No 1 and No 2 intake valves can be measured

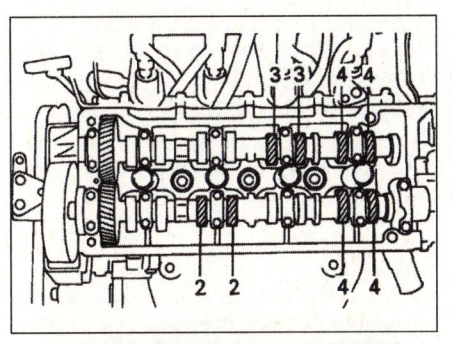

24.5 When the No 4 piston is at TDC on the compression stroke, the valve clearances for the No 2 and No 4 exhaust valves and the No 3 and No 4 intake valves can be checked

With Toyota tool No 09248-55020

6 After all the valves have been measured, turn the crankshaft pulley until the camshaft lobe above the first valve which you intend to adjust is pointing upward, away from the shim.

7 Position the notch in the cam follower toward the spark plug. Then depress the cam follower with the Toyota special tools (see note at the start of this Section) **(see illustration)**. Place the special cam follower tool in position as shown, with the longer jaw of the tool gripping the lower edge of the cast follower boss and the upper, shorter jaw gripping the upper edge of the follower itself. Depress the cam follower

24.7b Keep pressure on the cam follower with the smaller tool and remove the shim with a small screwdriver . . .

24.7c . . . a pair of tweezers or a magnet as shown

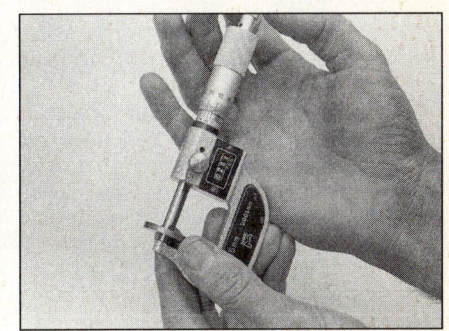

24.4b Check the clearance for each valve with a feeler gauge of the specified thickness – if the clearance is correct, you should feel a slight drag on the gauge as you pull it out

24.7a Install the cam follower tool as shown and squeeze the handles together to depress the cam follower, then hold the follower down with the smaller tool so the shim can be removed

by squeezing the handles of the cam follower tool together, then hold the cam follower down with the smaller tool and remove the larger one. Remove the adjusting shim with a small screwdriver or a pair of tweezers **(see illustrations)**. Note that the wire hook on the end of some cam follower tool handles can be used to clamp both handles together to keep the cam follower depressed while the shim is removed.

8 Measure the thickness of the shim with a micrometer **(see illustration)**. To calculate the correct thickness of a new shim that will place the valve clearance within the specified value, use the following formula:

24.8 Measure the shim thickness with a micrometer

1•20 Maintenance procedures

Shim No.	Thickness	Shim No.	Thickness
1	2.55 (0.1004)	9	2.95 (0.1161)
2	2.60 (0.1024)	10	3.00 (0.1181)
3	2.65 (0.1043)	11	3.05 (0.1201)
4	2.70 (0.1063)	12	3.10 (0.1220)
5	2.75 (0.1083)	13	3.15 (0.1240)
6	2.80 (0.1102)	14	3.20 (0.1260)
7	2.85 (0.1122)	15	3.25 (0.1280)
8	2.90 (0.1142)	16	3.30 (0.1299)

New shim thickness mm (in.)

24.9 Valve adjusting shim thickness chart

$N = T + (A − V)$.
A = Valve clearance measured.
N = Thickness of the new shim.
T = Thickness of the old shim.
V = Desired valve clearance (see this Chapter's Specifications).

9 Select a shim with a thickness as close as possible to the valve clearance calculated. Shims, which are available in 17 sizes in increments of 0.050 mm, range in size from 2.500 mm to 3.300 mm **(see illustration)**.
Note: *Through careful analysis of the shim sizes needed to bring the out-of-specification valve clearance within specification, it is often possible to simply move a shim that has to come out anyway to another cam follower requiring a shim of that particular size, thereby reducing the number of new shims that must be purchased.*
Caution: The engine must not be rotated with any shims missing.
10 Place the special cam follower tool in position **(see illustration 22.9a)**, with the longer jaw of the tool gripping the lower edge of the cast follower boss and the upper, shorter jaw gripping the upper edge of the follower itself, press down the cam follower by squeezing the handles of the cam follower tool together and install the new adjusting shim (note that the wire hook on the end of one cam follower tool handle can be used to clamp the handles together to keep the lifter depressed while the shim is inserted. Measure the clearance with a feeler gauge to make sure that your calculations are correct.

24.18 Measure the clearance between the camshaft lobe and the cam follower

11 Repeat this procedure until all the valves which are out of clearance have been corrected.
12 Installation of the spark plugs, cylinder cover, spark plug leads and boots, etc. is the reverse of removal.

Without the Toyota tool

13 After all the valve clearances have been measured, if any require adjustment, remove the camshafts as described in Chapter 2A.
14 Use a small flat-bladed screwdriver to carefully prise the relevant shim from the cam follower.
15 Select the required shim as described in paragraphs 8 and 9, then place the shim on the top of the relevant cam follower.
16 Once all the necessary shims have been changed, refit the camshafts as described in Chapter 2A.

VVT-i engines

17 Remove the cylinder head cover and position the engine at TDC for No 1 cylinder, as described in Chapter 2A.
18 Using feeler gauges, measure the clearance between the camshaft lobes and the cam followers of the intake valves for cylinders 1 and 2, and the exhaust valves for cylinders 1 and 3. No 1 cylinder is at the timing chain end of the engine. Record the measurements obtained **(see illustration)**.
19 Turn the crankshaft *one* complete revolution (360°).
20 Using feeler gauges, measure the

24.22 Measure the thickness of the cam follower using a micrometer

clearance between the camshaft lobes and the cam followers of the intake valves for cylinders 3 and 4, and the exhaust valves for cylinders 2 and 4. Record the measurements obtained.
21 Compare the measurements obtained with those given in the Specifications. If any measure is outside the specified range, remove the camshafts as described in Chapter 2A.
22 With the camshafts removed, use a magnet to lift the relevant cam follower(s) from place, then measure and record the thickness of the follower using a micrometer **(see illustration)**.
23 Determine the required thickness of the new follower using the following formula:
Intake followers: $N = T + (A − 0.20$ mm$)$.
Exhaust followers: $N = T + (A − 0.30$ mm$)$.
A = Measured valve clearance.
N = Thickness of new follower.
T = Thickness of the used follower.
24 Select a follower with a thickness as close as possible to the valve clearance calculated. Followers, which are available in 35 sizes in increments of 0.020 mm, range in size from 5.060 mm to 5.740 mm.
25 With all the followers in their correct locations, refit the camshafts as described in Chapter 2A. Before refitting the cylinder head cover, recheck the valve clearances as previously described, and, if necessary, remove the camshafts again and change followers as necessary.

Chapter 2 Part A:
Engine in-car repair procedures

Contents

	Section number
Auxiliary drivebelt – check, adjustment and renewal	See Chapter 1
Camshaft oil seal – renewal	9
Camshafts and followers – removal, inspection, and refitting	10
Crankshaft oil seal – renewal	8
Cylinder compression check	2
Cylinder head – removal and refitting	11
Cylinder head cover – removal and refitting	4
Engine mountings – check and renewal	17
Engine oil and filter change	See Chapter 1
Flywheel/driveplate – removal and refitting	15
General information	1
Main oil seal – renewal	16

	Section number
Oil pressure switch – renewal	14
Oil pump – removal, inspection and refitting	13
Oil sump – removal and refitting	12
Repair operations possible with the engine in the vehicle	2
Spark plug renewal	See Chapter 1
Timing belt and sprockets – removal, inspection and refitting	5
Timing chain and sprockets – removal, inspection and refitting	6
Top Dead Centre (TDC) for number one piston – locating	3
Valve clearance	See Chapter 1
VVT-i (Variable Valve Timing) components – removal, inspection and refitting	7

Degrees of difficulty

Easy, suitable for novice with little experience

Fairly easy, suitable for beginner with some experience

Fairly difficult, suitable for competent DIY mechanic

Difficult, suitable for experienced DIY mechanic

Very difficult, suitable for expert DIY or professional

Specifications

General
Engine type	DOHC, in-line four-cylinder, four valves per cylinder
Cylinder numbers (timing belt/chain end to transmission end)	1-2-3-4
Firing order	1-3-4-2
Engine codes:	
1.3 litre (1332 cc) non-VVT-i engine	4E-FE
1.4 litre (1398 cc) VVT-i engine	4ZZ-FE
1.6 litre (1587 cc) non-VVT-i engine	4A-FE
1.6 litre (1598 cc) VVT-i engine	3ZZ-FE
Compression pressure:	
Minimum	10.0 bar
Difference between cylinders (maximum)	1.0 bar

Oil pump

	Standard	Service limit
Rotor-to-body clearance		
Non-VVT-i engines:		
1.3 litre engine	0.100 to 0.210 mm	0.25 mm
1.6 litre engine	0.025 to 0.075 mm	0.10 mm
VVT-i engines	0.260 to 0.350 mm	0.325 mm
Rotor tip clearance:		
Non-VVT-i engines:		
1.3 litre engine	0.060 to 0.150 mm	0.20 mm
1.6 litre engine	0.060 to 0.180 mm	0.35 mm
VVT-i engines	0.040 to 0.160 mm	0.160 mm
Rotor-to-cover clearance:		
Non-VVT-i engines:		
1.3 litre engine	2.91 to 2.97 mm	2.90 mm
1.6 litre engine	0.080 to 0.180 mm	0.20 mm
VVT-i engines	0.025 to 0.071 mm	0.071 mm
Oil pressure:		
Non-VVT-i engines:		
At idle speed	0.29 bar min	
At 3000 rpm	2.45 to 4.9 bar	
VVT-i engines:		
At idle speed	0.29 bar min	
At 3000 rpm	2.94 to 5.39 bar	

Timing belt

Tensioner spring free length:
- 1.3 litre engine .... 38.4 mm
- 1.6 litre engine .... 36.9 mm

Timing belt deflection .... 5.0 to 6.0 mm @ 20 N

Timing chain and sprockets

Maximum chain length at 16 pins (see text) .... 122.7 mm
Crankshaft sprocket minimum diameter (with chain) .... 51.6 mm
Camshaft sprocket minimum diameter (with chain) .... 97.3 mm

Camshaft thrust clearance (endfloat)

	Intake camshaft	Exhaust camshaft
Non-VVT-i engines:		
1.3 litre engine:		
Standard	0.045 to 0.100 mm	0.045 to 0.100 mm
Service limit, maximum	0.12 mm	0.12 mm
1.6 litre engine:		
Standard	0.030 to 0.085 mm	0.035 to 0.090 mm
Service limit, maximum	0.11 mm	0.11 mm
VVT-i engines:		
Standard	0.040 to 0.095 mm	0.040 to 0.095 mm
Service limit, maximum	0.11 mm	0.11 mm

Cylinder head bolt length

VVT-i engines:
- Standard .... 156.0 to 159.0 mm
- Maximum .... 159.5 mm

Torque wrench settings

	Nm	lbf ft
Non-VVT-i engines		
Camshaft bearing cap bolts	13	10
Camshaft sprocket bolt:		
1.3 litre engine	51	38
1.6 litre engine	59	44
Centre chassis brace bolts	60	44
Connecting rod (big-end)*:		
1.3 litre engine	39	29
1.6 litre engine:		
Stage 1	29	21
Stage 2	Angle tighten a further 90°	
Crankshaft oil seal retainer bolts:		
1.3 litre engine	7	5
1.6 litre engine	10	7
Crankshaft pulley-to-crankshaft bolt:		
1.3 litre engine	155	114
1.6 litre engine	118	87
Cylinder head bolts:		
1.3 litre engine:		
Stage 1	30	22
Stage 2	45	33
Stage 3	Angle tighten a further 90°	
1.6 litre engine:		
Stage 1	29	21
Stage 2	Angle tighten a further 90°	
Stage 3	Angle tighten a further 90°	
Cylinder head cover	7	5
Engine/transmission stiffener bolts (1.6 litre engine)	22	17
Exhaust manifold brace bolts (1.6 litre engine)	59	44
Exhaust manifold nuts/bolts:		
1.3 litre engine	48	35
1.6 litre engine	34	25
Flywheel/driveplate bolts:		
1.3 litre engine	90	66
1.6 litre engine:		
Flywheel (manual transmission)	78	58
Driveplate (automatic transmission)	64	47

Torque wrench settings (continued)

	Nm	lbf ft
Non-VVT-i engines (continued)		
Idler pulley bolts:		
1.3 litre engine:		
Upper pulley to cylinder head	19	14
Lower pulley to cylinder block	28	21
1.6 litre engine	37	27
Intake air chamber (plenum) cover (1.6 litre engine)	19	14
Intake manifold bolts	19	14
Main bearing cap bolts	58	43
Oil pump bolts:		
1.3 litre engine	8	6
1.6 litre engine	21	15
Oil pick-up/strainer nuts/bolts:		
1.3 litre engine	11	8
1.6 litre engine	10	7
Oil pressure switch	13	10
Oil sump bolts:		
1.3 litre engine	13	10
1.6 litre engine	5	4
VVT-i engines		
Auxiliary belt tensioner:		
Bolt	69	51
Nut	29	21
Camshaft bearing cap:		
No 1 (right-hand) bearing cap	23	17
All other bearing caps	13	10
Camshaft position sensor	9	7
Camshaft sprocket bolts	54	40
Connecting rod (big-end) bolts*:		
Stage 1	20	15
Stage 2	Angle tighten a further 90°	
Coolant pump	10	7
Crankshaft pulley bolt	138	102
Cylinder head bolts:		
Stage 1	49	36
Stage 2	Angle tighten a further 90°	
Cylinder head cover	9	7
Driveplate	83	61
Flywheel:		
Stage 1	49	36
Stage 2	Angle tighten a further 90°	
Ignition coil to cylinder head	9	7
Main bearing ladder bolts:		
M8	19	14
M10:		
Stage 1	44	32
Stage 2	Angle tighten a further 90°	
Oil control valve	9	7
Oil control valve filter	30	22
Oil drain plug	37	27
Oil pick-up strainer	9	7
Oil pressure relief valve plug	37	27
Oil pressure switch	13	10
Oil pump	9	7
Oil pump cover screws	10	7
Oil sump	9	7
Timing chain cover:		
10 mm head	13	10
12 mm head	19	14
Timing chain guide bolts	9	7
Timing chain tensioner housing	9	7
Timing chain tensioner slipper bolts	19	14

Do not re-use

1 General information

How to use this Chapter

This Part of Chapter 2 is devoted to in-vehicle engine repair procedures. All information concerning engine removal and refitting, and engine block and cylinder head overhaul can be found in Part B of this Chapter.

The following repair procedures are based on the assumption that the engine is installed in the vehicle. If the engine has been removed from the vehicle and mounted on a stand, many of the steps outlined in this Part of Chapter 2 will not apply.

The Specifications included in this Part of Chapter 2 apply only to the procedures contained in this Part. Part B of Chapter 2 contains the Specifications necessary for cylinder head and engine block rebuilding.

Engine description

Whilst all the engines covered by this manual are four cylinder, double overhead camshaft (DOHC) 16-valve units, they can be split into two categories: Those without variable valve timing, and those with (VVT-i).

The 1.3 litre 4E-FE and 1.6 litre 4A-FE engines fitted from 1997 to 2000 have fixed valve timing and a timing belt which drives the exhaust camshaft, which is geared to the intake camshaft.

The 1.4 litre 4ZZ-FE and 1.6 litre 3ZZ-FE engines fitted from 2000 have a variable valve timing unit fitted to the intake camshaft sprocket, and a timing chain driving both the camshafts. The engine management system adjusts the timing of the camshaft via a hydraulic control system (using engine oil as the hydraulic fluid). The timing is varied according to engine speed and load – retarding the timing at low and high engine speeds to improve low speed driveability and maximum power respectively. At medium engine speeds, the timings are advanced (the valves open earlier) to increase mid-range torque and to improve exhaust emissions.

On non-VVT-i engines, the valve clearances are adjusted by interchangeable steel shims fitted to the top of the camshaft followers, acting directly on the underside of their respective camshafts. On VVT-i engines no shims are fitted, and to adjust the clearances the camshaft followers themselves must be changed, necessitating the removal of the camshafts.

At the lower end of the engine, the one-piece crankshafts are supported by five plain bearings retained by traditional bearing caps on the 4E-FE and 4A-FE engines, whilst the 4ZZ-FE and 3ZZ-FE engines are fitted with a cast main bearing 'ladder' fitted between the engine block and the oil sump. A rotor-type oil pump is fitted directly over the end of and driven directly by the crankshaft (4A-FE, 4ZZ-FE and 3ZZ-FE engines) or by the timing belt (4E-FE engines).

Operations with engine in car

The following operations can be carried out without having to remove the engine from the vehicle:

a) Removal and refitting of the cylinder head.
b) Removal and refitting of the timing chain/belt and sprockets.
c) Removal and refitting of the camshafts.
d) Removal and refitting of the oil sump.
e) Removal and refitting of the oil pump.
f) Renewal of the engine/transmission mountings.
g) Removal and refitting of the flywheel/driveplate.

Although in theory, it is possible to remove the big-end bearings, connecting rods and pistons with the engine in place, for reasons of access and cleanliness it is recommended that the engine is removed.

2 Cylinder compression check

1 When engine performance is down, or if misfiring occurs which cannot be attributed to the ignition or fuel systems, a compression test can provide diagnostic clues as to the engine's condition. If the test is performed regularly, it can give warning of trouble before any other symptoms become apparent.
2 The engine must be fully warmed-up to normal operating temperature, the battery must be fully-charged. The aid of an assistant will also be required.
3 Remove the fuel pump fuse (No 10 from the engine compartment fusebox), and if possible, start the engine and allow it to run until the residual fuel in the system is exhausted. Failure to do so could result in damage to the catalytic converter.
4 Remove the spark plugs as described in Chapter 1.
5 Fit a compression tester to the No 1 cylinder spark plug hole – the type of tester which screws into the plug thread is to be preferred (see illustration).
6 Have the assistant hold the throttle wide open, and crank the engine on the starter motor. After one or two revolutions, the compression pressure should build-up to a maximum figure, and then stabilise. Record the highest reading obtained.
7 Repeat the test on the remaining cylinders, recording the pressure in each.
8 All cylinders should produce very similar pressures; a difference of more than 1 bar between any two cylinders may indicate a fault. Note that the compression should build-up quickly in a healthy engine; low compression on the first stroke, followed by gradually-increasing pressure on successive strokes, indicates worn piston rings. A low compression reading on the first stroke, which does not build-up during successive strokes, indicates leaking valves or a blown head gasket (a cracked head could also be the cause). Deposits on the undersides of the valve heads can also cause low compression.
9 Toyota minimum values for compression pressures are given in the Specifications.
10 If the pressure in any cylinder is low, carry out the following test to isolate the cause. Introduce a teaspoonful of clean oil into that cylinder through its spark plug hole, and repeat the test.
11 If the addition of oil temporarily improves the compression pressure, this indicates that bore or piston wear is responsible for the pressure loss. No improvement suggests that leaking or burnt valves, or a blown head gasket, may be to blame.
12 A low reading from two adjacent cylinders is almost certainly due to the head gasket having blown between them; the presence of coolant in the engine oil will confirm this.
13 If one cylinder is about 20 percent lower than the others and the engine has a slightly rough idle, a worn camshaft lobe could be the cause.
14 If the compression reading is unusually high, the combustion chambers are probably coated with carbon deposits. If this is the case, the cylinder head should be removed and decarbonised.
15 On completion of the test, refit the spark plugs (see Chapter 1) and refit the fuel pump fuse.

3 Top Dead Centre (TDC) for number one piston – locating

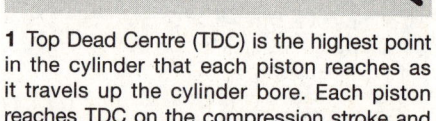

1 Top Dead Centre (TDC) is the highest point in the cylinder that each piston reaches as it travels up the cylinder bore. Each piston reaches TDC on the compression stroke and again on the exhaust stroke, but TDC generally refers to piston position on the compression stroke.
2 Positioning the piston(s) at TDC is an essential part of many procedures such as camshaft and timing belt/chain/pulley removal, and distributor (where applicable) removal.

2.5 Use a compression gauge with a threaded fitting for the spark plug hole

Engine in-car repair procedures 2A•5

3.6 Align the crankshaft drivebelt pulley notch (arrowed) with the 0 (zero) on the timing cover

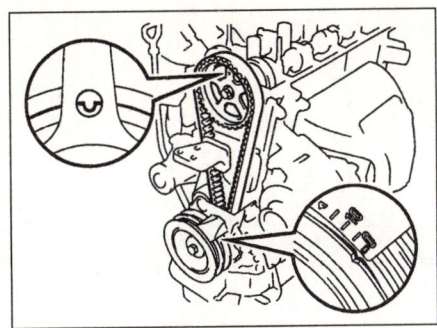

3.7a The camshaft sprocket is at TDC when the hole in the sprocket lines up with the notch in the bearing cap

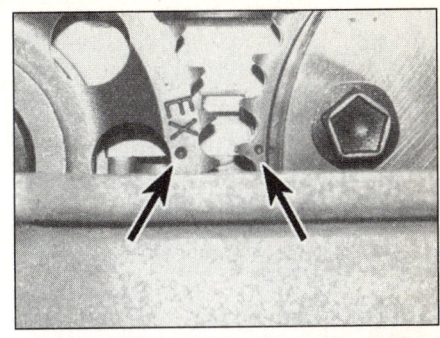

3.7b On VVT-i engines, the marks on the camshaft sprockets (arrowed) should align with the top edge of the cylinder head

3 Before beginning this procedure, be sure to place the transmission in Neutral and apply the handbrake or block the rear wheels. Remove the spark plugs (see Chapter 1).

4 In order to bring any piston to TDC, the crankshaft must be turned using the method outlined below. When looking at the timing belt/chain end of the engine, normal crankshaft rotation is clockwise. Turn the crankshaft with a socket and ratchet attached to the bolt threaded into the front of the crankshaft. Apply pressure on the bolt in a clockwise direction only. Never turn the bolt anti-clockwise.

5 Remove the cylinder head cover as described in Section 4.

6 Turn the crankshaft until the notch in the crankshaft pulley is aligned with the 0 on the timing cover **(see illustration)**.

7 Look at the camshaft lobes for No 1 cylinder. Both the intake and exhaust camshaft lobes should be pointing away from the camshaft followers. If they are not, use the socket/spanner to rotate the crankshaft one complete revolution (360°) – now the lobes should be pointing away from the followers. Additionally, on 1.3 litre 4E-FE and 1.6 litre 4A-FE engines, the mark on the No 1 camshaft bearing cap should be visible through the hole in the camshaft sprocket **(see illustration)**. On 1.4 litre 4ZZ-FE and 1.6 litre 3ZZ-FE VVT-i engines, the reference marks on the intake and exhaust camshaft sprockets should be aligned with the top of the cylinder head **(see illustration)**.

8 After the number one piston has been positioned at TDC on the compression stroke, TDC for any of the remaining pistons can be located by turning the crankshaft 180° and following the firing order.

4 Cylinder head cover – removal and refitting

Removal

1 Undo the two nuts, prise out the two plastic fasteners, and remove the plastic cover (where fitted) over the engine **(see illustrations)**.

2 Detach the PCV hoses from the cylinder head cover.

Non-VVT-i engines

3 Remove the HT leads from the spark plugs, handling them by the caps, not pulling on the leads, and release them from any clips on the cylinder head cover.

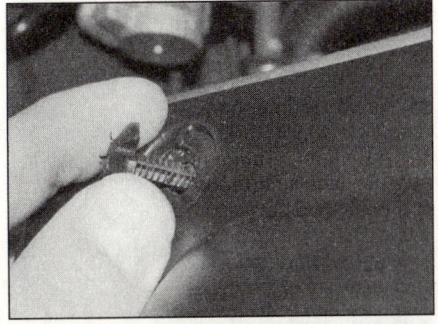

4.1a Prise out the plastic fasteners at the rear of the engine cover . . .

4.4 Remove the two harness cover mounting bolts at the timing belt end of the cover

4.6a On 1.6 litre engines, the cover is held by four nuts (arrowed). On 1.3 litre engines, there is an additional nut at the front

4 On 1.6 litre engines, remove two bolts at the timing belt end of the cylinder head cover, then pull up the wiring harness cover and wiring **(see illustration)**.

VVT-i engines

5 Remove the ignition coils as described in Chapter 5B.

All engines

6 Remove the cylinder head cover mounting nuts/bolts, then detach the cylinder head cover and gasket from the cylinder head **(see illustrations)**. If the cylinder head cover is stuck to the cylinder head, bump the end with a wood block and a hammer to jar it loose. If that doesn't work, try to slip a flexible putty knife between the cylinder head and cylinder head cover to break the seal.

Caution: Don't lever at the cylinder head cover-to-cylinder head joint or damage to

4.1b . . . then lift it from place

4.6b Cylinder head cover bolts/nuts/studs – VVT-i engines

2A•6 Engine in-car repair procedures

4.7a The cover gasket (left arrow) can be re-used if it hasn't hardened – ensure the spark plug tube seals (right arrow) are in place before refitting the cover

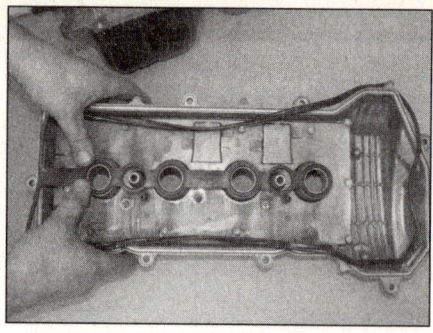

4.7b Ensure the one-piece cylinder head cover gasket is fitted to the spark plug tube grooves – VVT-i engines

the sealing surfaces may occur, leading to oil leaks after the valve cover is refitted.

Refitting

7 The mating surfaces of the housing or cylinder head and cylinder head cover must be clean when the cylinder head cover is refitted. The rubber sealing gasket can be re-used unless it has seen high mileage and the rubber has hardened or cracked, then pull out the rubber seal and clean the mating surfaces with brake cleaner. Install a new rubber gasket, pressing it evenly into the groove around the underside of the cylinder head cover. If there's residue or oil on the mating surfaces when the cylinder head cover is installed, oil leaks may develop. **Note:** *Make sure that the spark plug tube gaskets are in place on the underside of the valve cover before refitting it* **(see illustrations)**.

8 On VVT-i engines, apply sealant (Toyota No 08826-00080 or equivalent) to the area where the timing chain cover abuts the cylinder head.

9 On all engines, refit the cylinder head cover and tighten the nuts/bolts evenly to the specified torque.

10 Refit the remaining parts, run the engine and check for oil leaks.

5.8 After removing the centre bolt, remove the crankshaft pulley

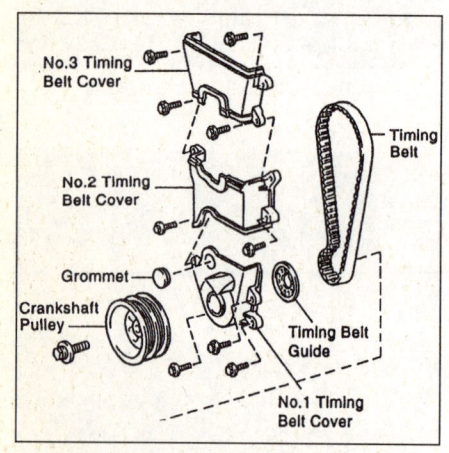

5.9 1.6 litre engine timing belt cover details. There are only two covers on the 1.3 litre engine

5 Timing belt and sprockets – removal, inspection and refitting

Note: *The following procedure applies only to the 4E-FE and 4A-FE non-VVT-i engines. The 4ZZ-FE and 3ZZ-FE VVT-i engines are fitted with a timing chain (see Section 6)*

Removal

1 Block the rear wheels and set the handbrake.
2 Loosen the nuts on the right front wheel and raise the vehicle. Support the front of the vehicle securely on axle stands (see *Jacking and vehicle support*). Remove the right-hand front roadwheel.
3 Remove the auxiliary drivebelt(s) as described in Chapter 1. To improve access, undo the screws and remove the right-hand engine undershield (where fitted).
4 Set the engine to TDC on No 1 cylinder as described in Section 3.

1.6 litre engines

5 Support the engine from underneath with a jack (use a wood block on the jack, but don't place the block under the oil sump drain plug). **Note:** *If you're planning on removing the oil sump in addition to the timing belt, support the engine with a hoist from above.*
6 Undo the four bolts and remove the coolant pump pulley.

All engines

7 To prevent the crankshaft from rotating whilst the crankshaft pulley central bolt is slackened, engage top gear and have an assistant press the brake pedal firmly. Slacken the pulley bolt. On automatic transmission models, it will be necessary to remove the starter motor (Chapter 5A) and have an assistant wedge a large flat-bladed screwdriver between the driveplate teeth and the transmission casing – ensure the screwdriver doesn't slip.
8 Check the timing marks are still aligned as described in Section 3, then slide the crankshaft pulley from the crankshaft **(see illustration)**.
9 Remove the two (1.3 litre engine) or three (1.6 litre engine) timing belt covers **(see illustration)**.
10 Remove the timing belt guide from the crankshaft, noting that the cupped side faces out and the smooth side is next to the belt.
11 If you plan to re-use the timing belt, apply match marks on the sprocket and belt and an arrow indicating direction of rotation on the belt. **Note:** *We recommend that the belt is renewed whenever it has been removed, regardless of mileage.*
12 Loosen the belt tensioner adjustment bolt, pry the tensioner to the rear and retighten the bolt in this position **(see illustration)**. Slip the timing belt off the sprocket. If you're removing the belt for camshaft seal renewal or cylinder head removal, it isn't necessary to detach the belt from the crankshaft sprocket or, on 1.6 litre engines, to unbolt the right engine mount. On 1.6 litre engines, if you are removing the belt completely, support the right engine mount with a jack, then remove the two nuts from the engine mount (from underneath) and the

5.12a Retighten the bolt to keep the tension off the belt for removal/installation

5.12b With the engine mounting supported by a jack, remove the two nuts (arrowed) from the right-hand engine mounting . . .

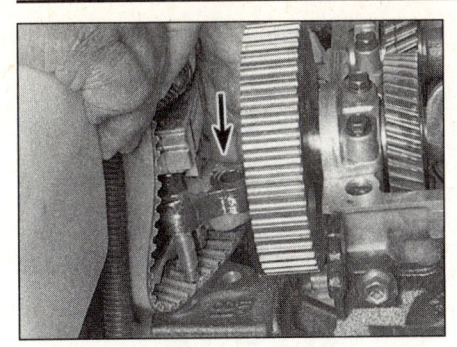

Engine in-car repair procedures 2A•7

5.12c ... and remove the upper engine mounting bolt (arrowed)

5.14 Paint marks (arrowed) on the crankshaft sprocket and the oil pump case so you can find TDC

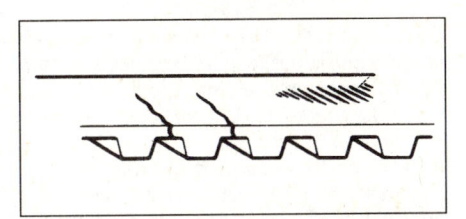

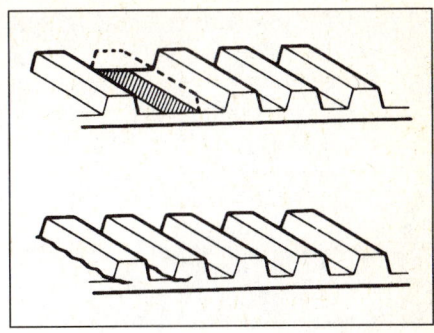

5.16 Check the timing belt for cracked and missing teeth

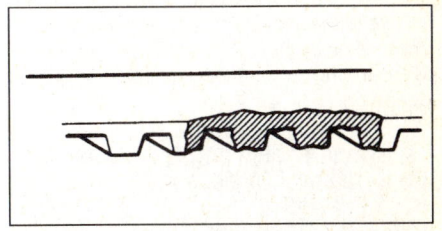

bolt from above **(see illustrations)**. Lower the engine, then pull the upper part of the mounting up (the rubber will allow movement) until the belt can be slipped out between the upper and lower sections of the mounting – this saves removing the mounting completely

13 If the camshaft sprocket is worn or damaged, hold the front (exhaust) camshaft with a large wrench and remove the bolt, then detach the sprocket (see Section 10).

14 Slip the timing belt off the crankshaft sprocket and remove it. If the sprocket is worn or damaged, or if you need to renew the crankshaft oil seal, remove the sprocket from the crankshaft. Before removing it, paint matching marks on the crankshaft sprocket and the oil pump case, so that you can find the TDC position without the crankshaft pulley in place **(see illustration)**.

Inspection

Caution: Do not bend, twist or turn the timing belt inside out. Do not allow it to come in contact with oil, coolant or fuel. Do not utilise timing belt tension to keep the camshaft or crankshaft from turning when installing the sprocket bolts. Do not turn the crankshaft or camshaft more than a few degrees (if necessary for tooth alignment) while the timing belt is removed.

15 If the timing belt broke during engine operation, the belt may have been contaminated or over-tightened.

Caution: If the timing belt broke during engine operation, the valves may have come in contact with the pistons, causing damage. Check the valve clearances (see Chapter 1) – bent valves usually will have excessive clearance, indicating damage that will require cylinder head removal to repair.

16 If the belt teeth are cracked or missing **(see illustration)**, the distributor (where applicable), oil pump or camshafts may have seized.

17 If there is noticeable wear or cracks on the face of the belt, check to see if there are nicks or burrs on the idler pulleys **(see illustration)**.

18 If there is wear or damage on only one side of the belt, check the belt guide and the alignment of the sprockets **(see illustration)**.

19 Renew the timing belt if obvious wear

5.17 If the face of the belt is cracked or worn, check the idler pulleys for nicks or burrs

or damage is noted or if it is the least bit questionable. Correct any problems which contributed to belt failure prior to belt refitting.

Note: Professionals recommend renewing the belt whenever it is removed, since belt failure can lead to expensive engine damage.

20 Release the bolt on the belt tensioner, then remove the tensioner and its spring. Check the idler for free rotation and measure the spring's free length **(see illustration)**. Renew the spring if it doesn't meet Specifications. Refit the tensioner and spring. On 1.3 litre engines, also check the condition of the upper idler pulley and renew it, by removing the centre securing bolt, if obvious wear or damage is noted. Fit the new idler and tighten the securing bolt to the torque listed in this Chapter's Specifications.

Refitting

21 Remove all dirt, oil and grease from the timing belt area at the front of the engine.

22 Recheck the camshaft and crankshaft timing marks to be sure they are properly aligned **(see illustration 3.7a)**. If the camshaft sprocket had been removed, reinstall it with the timing mark hole in the sprocket aligned with the notch in the bearing cap of the exhaust camshaft, and the locating pin in the end of the camshaft aligned with the 4E mark (1.3 litre engine) or A mark (1.6 litre engine) slot in the sprocket. Make sure the crankshaft sprocket is still aligned at the TDC marks you made in Step 14.

23 Fit the timing belt on the crankshaft, oil pump (1.3 litre engines) and camshaft sprockets. If the original belt is being reinstalled, align the marks made during removal.

24 Slip the belt guide onto the crankshaft with the cupped side facing out.

5.18 Wear on one side of the belt indicates sprocket misalignment problems

25 Reinstall the lower timing belt cover and crankshaft pulley and recheck the TDC marks.

26 Keeping tension on the side of the belt nearest the front of the vehicle, loosen the tensioner pulley bolt 1/2-turn, allowing the spring to apply pressure to the idler pulley.

27 Slowly turn the crankshaft clockwise two complete revolutions (720-degrees), then tighten the idler pulley mounting bolt to the torque listed in this Chapter's Specifications. Measure the deflection of the belt on the radiator side, halfway between the camshaft and crankshaft sprockets, and compare it to this Chapter's Specifications.

28 Recheck the timing marks. With the crankshaft at TDC for number one cylinder, the hole in the camshaft sprocket must align with the timing mark **(see illustration 3.7a)**. If the marks are not aligned exactly, repeat the belt refitting procedure.

Caution: DO NOT start the engine until you're absolutely certain that the timing belt is installed correctly. Serious and costly engine damage could occur if the belt is incorrectly fitted.

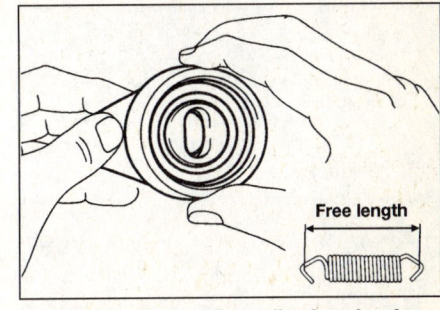

5.20 Check the idler pulley bearing for smooth operation and measure the free length of the tension spring

2A•8 Engine in-car repair procedures

6.7 If the crankshaft pulley is stuck, screw two 8 mm bolts into the threaded holes (arrowed) and push the pulley from place

29 Refit the remaining parts in the reverse order of removal.
30 Run the engine and check for proper operation.

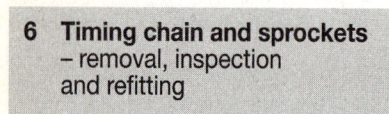

6 Timing chain and sprockets – removal, inspection and refitting

Note: *The following procedure applies only to the 4ZZ-FE and 3ZZ-FE VVT-i engines. Non-VVT-i engines are fitted with a timing belt (Section 5).*

Removal

1 Drain the coolant as described in Chapter 1.
2 Remove the auxiliary drivebelt as described in Chapter 1.
3 Remove the alternator (Chapter 5A).
4 Unbolt the power steering pump (Chapter 10).

6.11 Undo the two nuts and remove the chain tensioner assembly

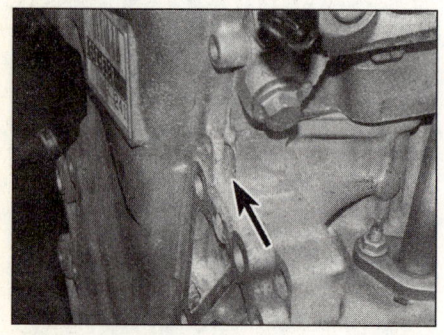

6.15 Insert a flat-bladed screwdriver into the leverage point provided (arrowed)

6.8 Undo the nut and bolt (arrowed) and remove the auxiliary belt tensioner assembly

There is no need to disconnect the fluid pipes from the pump, suspend it from the front panel/cowling using cable ties/wire.
5 Set the engine to TDC on No 1 cylinder as described in Section 3.
6 To prevent the crankshaft from rotating whilst the crankshaft pulley central bolt is slackened, engage top gear and have an assistant press the brake pedal firmly. Slacken the pulley bolt. On automatic transmission models, it will be necessary to remove the starter motor (Chapter 5A) and have an assistant wedge a large flat-bladed screwdriver between the driveplate teeth and the transmission casing – ensure the screwdriver doesn't slip.
7 Check the timing marks are still aligned as described in Section 3, then slide the crankshaft pulley from the crankshaft **(see illustration)**.
8 Undo the bolt/nut and remove the

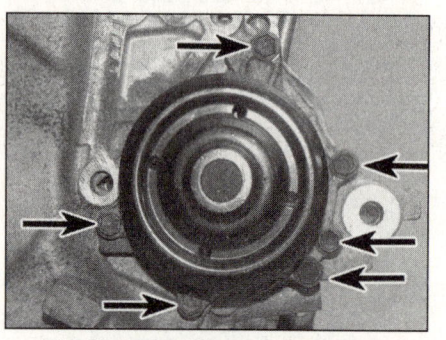

6.12 Undo the 6 bolts (arrowed) and remove the coolant pump

6.17 Undo the bolt (arrowed) and remove the tensioner slipper

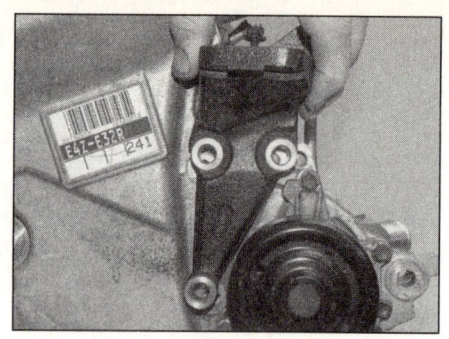

6.10 Undo the bolts/nuts and remove the right-hand engine mounting bracket from the engine block

auxiliary drivebelt tensioner assembly **(see illustration)**.
9 Support the engine from underneath with a jack (use a wood block on the jack, but don't place the block under the oil sump drain plug).
Note: *If you're planning on removing the oil sump in addition to the timing chain, support the engine with a hoist from above*.
10 Undo the bolts and remove the right-hand engine mounting bracket from the engine block **(see illustration)**. Where applicable, disconnect the earth lead from the mounting bracket.
11 Undo the two nuts and remove the chain tensioner assembly **(see illustration)**.
12 Undo the 6 bolts and remove the coolant pump **(see illustration)**. Discard the coolant pump O-ring seal, a new one must be fitted.
13 Undo the bolt and remove the crankshaft position sensor from the timing cover, then undo the bolt securing the wiring loom bracket clip and move the sensor to one side.
14 Undo the bolts/nuts securing the timing cover to the engine, then use a Torx socket to remove the stud in the upper left-hand corner.
15 Use a flat-bladed screwdriver to carefully prise the timing cover away **(see illustration)**. Take great care not to damage the sealing surfaces.
16 Note which way round it's fitted, then pull the crankshaft angle sensor plate from place.
17 Undo the bolt and remove the chain tensioner slipper **(see illustration)**.
18 Slide the sprocket (with the chain still fitted) from the crankshaft. If it's tight, use two flat-bladed screwdrivers to ease the sprocket from place, then lift the chain from the camshaft sprockets.
19 Undo the bolts and remove the chain guide **(see illustration)**.
20 Undo the centre bolt and remove the intake camshaft sprocket. Use a spanner on the hexagonal section of the camshaft to prevent it from rotating **(see illustration)**. Repeat this procedure on the exhaust camshaft sprocket. **Note:** *The intake sprocket with the VVT-i mechanism will be locked in the 'retarded' position*.

Inspection

21 Pull the timing chain taut by hand, and measure the length of 16 pins **(see**

Engine in-car repair procedures 2A•9

6.19 Undo the bolts (arrowed) and remove the chain guide

6.20 With a spanner on the hexagonal section, slacken the sprocket bolt

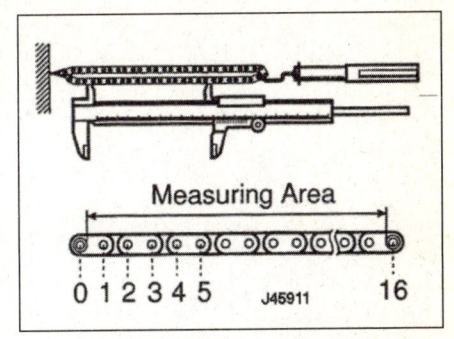

6.21 Pull the chain taut, and measure the length over 16 pins as shown

illustration). Repeat this procedure at 3 or more sections of the chain. If any of the measurements obtained exceed that given in the Specifications, the chain must be renewed.

22 Wrap the chain around the crankshaft sprocket and use a pair of vernier calipers to measure the diameter of the assembly **(see illustration)**. If the measurement obtained is less than that given in the Specifications, renew the chain and *all* the sprockets. Repeat this procedure on both camshaft sprockets.

23 Check the condition of the chain guide and tensioner slipper. There should be no sign of cracking or damage. As the chain runs along the guide/slipper it will create two grooves along the slipper/guide length. The maximum depth of these grooves is 1.0 mm. If their depth exceeds this, renew the slipper/guide.

24 Press the top of the locking pawl on the tensioner assembly to disengage the pawl from the plunger, and check that the plunger moves smoothly in and out of the housing **(see illustration)**. Release the pawl and check that the plunger cannot be pushed into the housing with your finger.

Refitting

25 Align the locating hole on the VVT-i unit/sprocket with the locating pin on the intake camshaft, then hold the camshaft in position with a spanner on the hexagonal section, and attempt to rotate the sprocket anti-clockwise whilst gently pushing it against the camshaft. This is to ensure it's locked in the 'retarded' position. If the VVT-i unit is already in the 'retarded' position (as it should be) the sprocket will not move. If it's not, the sprocket will rotate anti-clockwise slightly until the locating pin on the end of the camshaft aligns with a further locating slot inside the VVT-i assembly **(see illustration)**. Fit the sprocket retaining bolt and tighten it to the specified torque, using a spanner on the hexagonal section of the camshaft to prevent it from rotating.

26 Align the locating hole in the exhaust sprocket with the locating pin on the exhaust camshaft, then fit the bolt and tighten it to the specified torque, using a spanner on the camshaft hexagonal section to prevent it

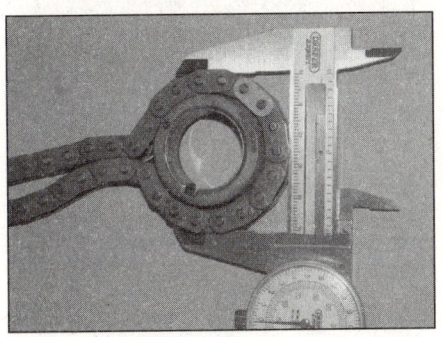

6.22 Wrap the chain around the sprocket and measure the diameter

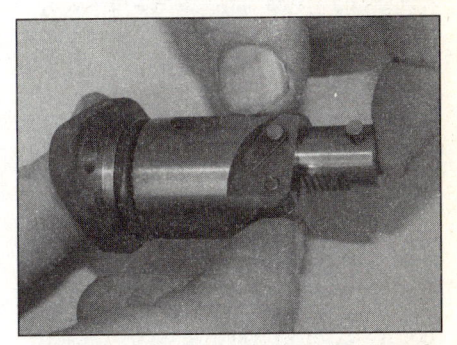

from rotating. Note that the sprocket must be fitted with timing mark facing outwards **(see illustrations)**.

27 Check that the camshaft sprockets are aligned **(see illustration)**. If necessary, using

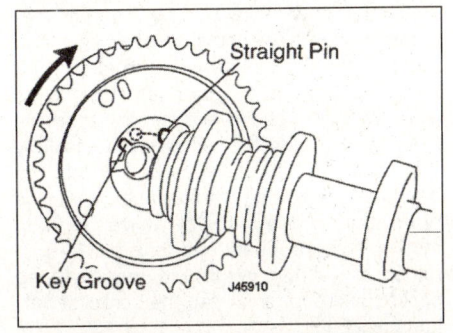

6.25 Align the pin on the camshaft with the locating hole in the VVT-i unit

6.26b . . . then tighten the bolt whilst holding the camshaft with a spanner at its hexagonal section

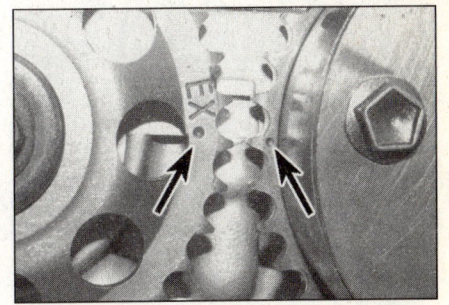

6.24 Press in the top of the locking pawl and check the plunger moves freely

a spanner on the hexagonal section, rotate the camshaft(s) slightly to bring them into alignment.

28 Check that the locating key in the end of the crankshaft is in the 12 o'clock position

6.26a Fit the exhaust camshaft sprocket with the timing marks facing outwards . . .

6.27 Align the camshaft sprocket marks (arrowed) with the top surface of the cylinder head

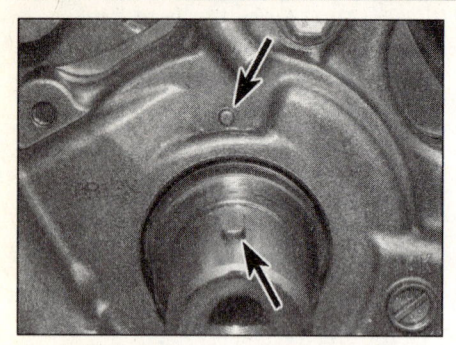

2A•10 Engine in-car repair procedures

6.28 Set the crankshaft key in the 12 o'clock position (the key aligns with the mark on the oil pump body – arrowed)

6.29 Align the yellow link of the timing chain with the mark on the crankshaft sprocket (arrowed)

6.30 Align the marks on the sprockets (arrowed) with the yellow links on the timing chain

6.33 Fit the crankshaft angle sensor plate with the B mark (4ZZ-FE) or F mark (3ZZ-FE) facing outwards (arrowed)

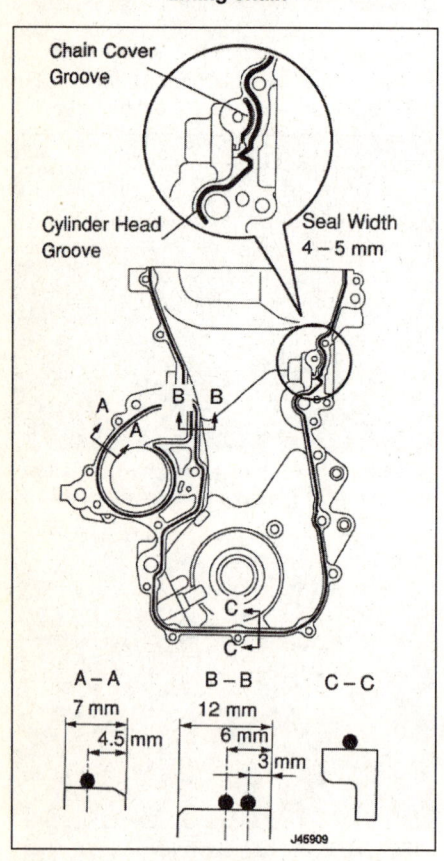

6.35 Apply a bead of sealant to the timing chain cover

6.36a Disengage the locking pawl and press in the plunger . . .

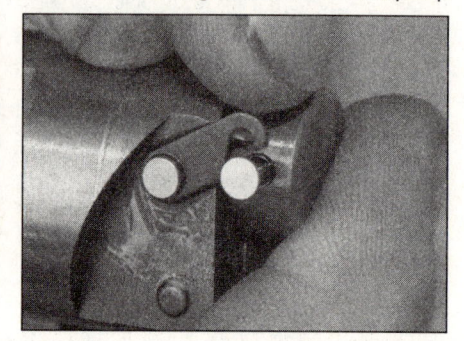

6.36b . . . then retain it with the hook

(upright). If necessary, temporarily insert the crankshaft pulley bolt and turn the crankshaft slightly to this position (see illustration).

29 There are three yellow-coloured links on the timing chain – two close together that correspond with the camshaft sprockets, and one which corresponds with the crankshaft sprocket. Engage the crankshaft sprocket with the timing chain, aligning the mark on the sprocket with the yellow-coloured link, then slide the sprocket over the end of the crankshaft, ensuring the locating key in the crankshaft aligns with the corresponding slot in the sprocket (see illustration). If necessary, using a tubular spacer (deep socket) and a hammer, tap the sprocket fully into position.

30 Engage the timing chain with the camshaft sprockets, ensuring the yellow-coloured links align with the marks on the sprockets (see illustration).

31 Refit the timing chain guide and tighten the bolts to the specified torque.

32 Refit the tensioner slipper and tighten the retaining bolt to the specified torque.

33 Refit the crankshaft angle sensor plate with the B mark (4ZZ-FE) or F mark (3ZZ-FE) facing outwards (see illustration).

34 Thoroughly clean the timing chain cover and engine block/cylinder gasket surfaces, removing all traces of the old sealant. Take the opportunity to renew the crankshaft oil seal in the timing chain cover as described in Section 8.

35 Apply a thin bead of sealant (Toyota part no 08826-00080 or equivalent) to the timing cover gasket surfaces as shown, then fit the timing chain cover, and tighten the bolts/nuts to the specified torques (see illustration).

36 Press in the top of the locking pawl to disengage it from the chain tensioner plunger, then use a finger to press the plunger fully into the tensioner housing, and retain it in place with the hook (see illustrations).

37 Check the condition of the tensioner housing O-ring seal and renew if necessary. Fit the housing to the timing chain cover, taking care not to disturb the plunger hook. If the hook is disturbed and the plunger released, remove the housing and reset the plunger as previously described. Tighten the housing retaining bolts to the specified torque.

38 Refit the crankshaft pulley and tighten the retaining bolt to the specified torque. Prevent the crankshaft from rotating using the same method employed during removal.

39 Rotate the crankshaft anti-clockwise a few degrees to release the hook retaining the tensioner plunger, then rotate it clockwise and check that the tensioner slipper is pushed against the chain by the plunger. If it isn't, use your finger or a screwdriver to push the slipper against the tensioner plunger and release the hook (see illustration).

40 Turn the crankshaft clockwise until the notch in the crankshaft pulley is aligned with the 0 on the timing plate located at the front of the engine, and check that the marks on the camshaft sprockets align with the top of the cylinder head (see illustrations 3.6 and 3.7b).

41 Fit a new O-ring seal to the coolant pump

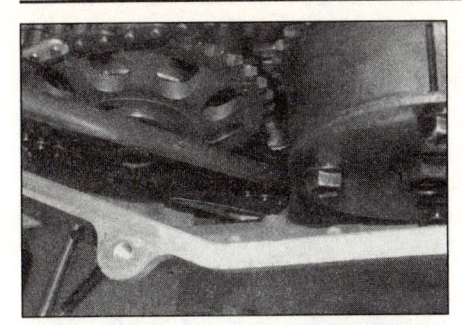

Engine in-car repair procedures 2A•11

6.39 If necessary, use a screwdriver to push the chain against the slipper to release the tensioner plunger

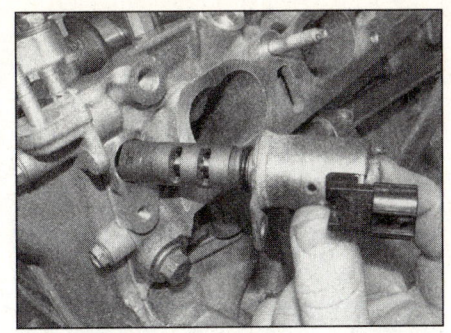

7.3 Undo the bolt and withdrawn the oil control valve from the cylinder head

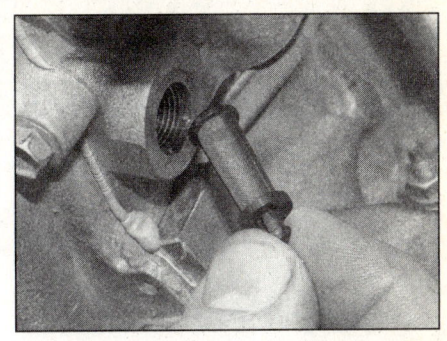

7.4 Pull the oil control valve filter from the cylinder head

and refit it, tightening the bolts to the specified torque.
42 The remainder of refitting is a reversal of removal.

7 VVT-i (Variable Valve Timing) components – removal, inspection and refitting

Removal

Camshaft VVT-i unit

1 The VVT-i unit is integral with the intake sprocket (see Section 6) – no dismantling is recommended.

Oil control valve

2 Unplug the wiring connector from the oil control valve at the timing chain end of the cylinder head.
3 Undo the bolt and withdraw the valve from the cylinder head (see illustration). Be prepared for oil spillage.

Oil control valve filter

4 The filter is located at the timing chain end of the cylinder head. Undo the plug and pull the filter from place (see illustration).

Inspection

Camshaft VVT-i unit

5 Testing the VVT-i unit is beyond the scope of the DIY mechanic. If the unit is faulty, the engine management ECM should store a relevant fault code. Have the system's self-diagnosis system interrogated by a Toyota dealer or suitably-equipped repairer.

Oil control valve

6 Disconnect the wiring plug from the control valve, and connect an ohmmeter to the valve terminals. The resistance should be 6.9 to 7.9Ω. If the resistance is not as specified the valve may be defective.

Oil control valve filter

7 Clean the filter and ensure it's free from debris and damage.

Refitting

Camshaft VVT-i unit

8 As the VVT-i unit is integral with the intake

camshaft sprocket, refitting is described in Section 6.

Oil control valve

9 Check the condition of the O-ring seal on the valve and renew if necessary.
10 Insert the valve into the cylinder head and tighten the retaining bolt to the specified torque. Reconnect the wiring plug.

Oil control valve filter

11 Insert the filter into the cylinder head.
12 Check the condition of the plug sealing washer and renew if necessary. Refit the plug and tighten it to the specified torque.

8 Crankshaft oil seal – renewal

Non-VVT-i engines

1 Remove the timing belt and crankshaft sprocket (see Section 5).
2 Note how far the seal is recessed in the bore, then carefully pry it out of the oil pump housing with a screwdriver or seal removal tool (see illustration). Don't scratch the housing bore or damage the crankshaft in the process (if the crankshaft is damaged, the new seal will end up leaking). Note: *The seal may be easier to remove if the old seal lip is cut with a sharp utility knife first* (see illustration).
3 Clean the bore in the housing and coat the outer edge of the new seal with engine oil or multi-purpose grease. Apply a little grease to the seal lip.

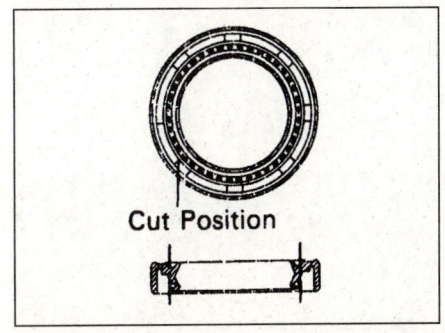

8.2b The seal may be removed more easily by carefully cutting the lip as indicated

4 Using a socket with an outside diameter slightly smaller than the outside diameter of the seal, carefully drive the new seal into place (see illustration). Make sure it's installed squarely and driven in to the same depth as the original. If a socket isn't available, a short section of large diameter pipe will also work.
5 Refit the crankshaft sprocket and timing belt (see Section 5).
6 Run the engine and check for oil leaks at the seal.

VVT-i engines

7 If the timing chain cover has been removed (part of the timing chain removal procedure), the seal can simply be driven from the cover using a hammer and punch. The new seal can then be fitted into place (spring towards the engine internals) using a block of wood and a hammer. The seal should be fitted with its outside edge flush with the timing cover (see illustrations).

8.2a Wrap tape around the screwdriver tip and pry the crankshaft oil seal out

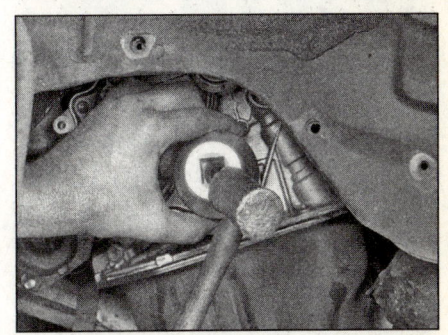

8.4 Gently drive the new seal into place with the spring side fitted towards the engine

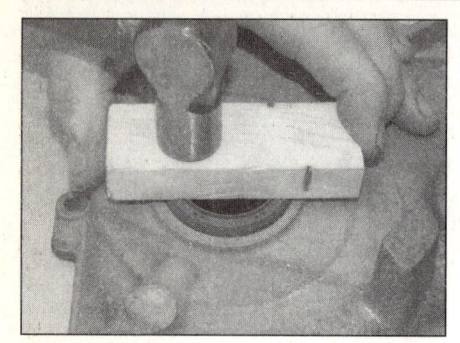

2A•12 Engine in-car repair procedures

8.7a Use a block of wood and a hammer to drive the new seal squarely into position

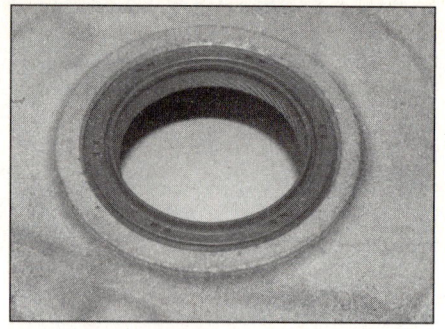

8.7b The new seal's outer edge should be flush with the timing cover

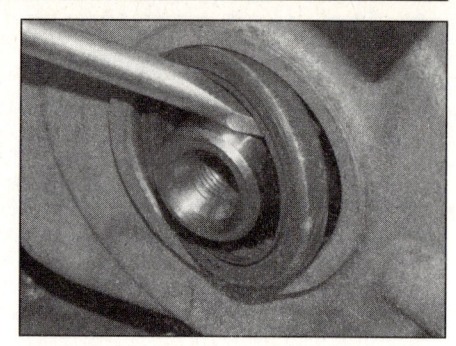

8.10 Carefully prise the oil seal out with a screwdriver

8 If the timing cover is still in place, remove the auxiliary drivebelt as described in Chapter 1.
9 Remove the crankshaft pulley. To prevent the crankshaft from rotating whilst the crankshaft pulley central bolt is slackened, engage top gear and have an assistant press the brake pedal firmly. Slacken the pulley bolt. On automatic transmission models, it will be necessary to remove the starter motor (Chapter 5A) and have an assistant wedge a large flat-bladed screwdriver between the driveplate teeth and the transmission casing – ensure the screwdriver doesn't slip.
10 Carefully prise the seal from the timing cover with a screwdriver or seal removal tool **(see illustration)**. Take great care not to scratch the cover bore or the surface of the crankshaft in the process. *Note: The seal may be easier to remove if the old seal lip is cut with a sharp utility knife first* **(see illustration 8.2b)**.
11 Clean the bore in the cover and coat the outer edge of the new seal with engine oil or multi-purpose grease. Apply a little grease to the seal lip.
12 Using a socket with an outside diameter slightly smaller than the outside diameter of the seal, carefully drive the new seal into place. Make sure it's installed squarely and driven in so the outer edge of the seal is flush with the timing cover. If a socket isn't available, a short section of large diameter pipe will also work.
13 Refit the crankshaft pulley and tighten the retaining bolt to the specified torque. Prevent the crankshaft from rotating using the same method employed during removal.

14 Refit the auxiliary drivebelt as described in Chapter 1.

9 Camshaft oil seal – renewal

Note: This procedure applies only to 4E-FE and 4A-FE non-VVT-i engines. No camshaft oil seals are fitted to the VVT-i engines.

1 Refer to Section 4 and remove the cylinder head cover, then remove the timing belt.
2 Use a large spanner to hold the exhaust camshaft at its hexagonal section, while removing the bolt from the camshaft sprocket **(see illustration)**, then pull off the sprocket.
3 Note how far the seal is seated in the bore, then carefully pry it out with a small screwdriver **(see illustration)**. Don't scratch the bore or damage the camshaft in the process (if the camshaft is damaged, the new seal will end up leaking).
4 Clean the bore and coat the outer edge of the new seal with engine oil or multi-purpose grease. Apply multi-purpose grease to the seal lip.
5 Using a socket with an outside diameter slightly smaller than the outside diameter of the seal, carefully drive the new seal into place with a seal installer or large socket. Make sure it's installed squarely and driven in to the same depth as the original. If a socket isn't available, a short section of pipe will also work. *Note: There isn't much room for a hammer, so you can also lever between the engine mounting and the socket to press the seal in* **(see illustration)**.
6 Refit the camshaft sprocket and timing belt (see Section 5). Refer to Section 4 and refit the cylinder head cover.
7 Run the engine and check for oil leaks at the camshaft seal.

10 Camshafts and followers – removal, inspection and refitting

1.3 litre 4E-FE engine

Note: Before beginning this procedure, obtain two 6 x 1.0 mm, bolts 16 to 20 mm long. They will be referred to as service bolts in the text.

Removal

1 Refer to Section 3 and place the engine on TDC for number 1 cylinder.
2 Remove the timing belt and camshaft sprocket (see Sections 5 and 9).
3 Measure the camshaft thrust clearance (end-float) with a dial indicator **(see illustration 10.41)**. If the clearance is greater than the service limit, renew the camshaft and/or the cylinder head.
4 Position the intake camshaft so that the service bolt hole in the camshaft gear is uppermost **(see illustration)**. This will position the intake camshaft lobes so the camshaft will be pushed up evenly by valve spring pressure.
Caution: This positioning is important to avoid damaging the cylinder head or camshaft as the camshaft is removed.

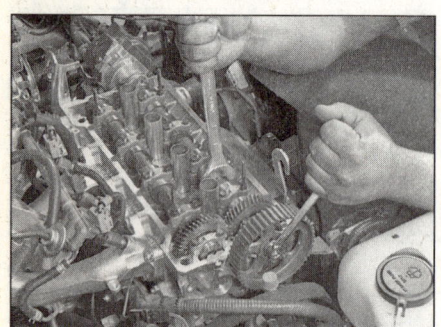

9.2 Use an open-ended spanner to hold the camshaft whilst removing the bolt

9.3 Carefully lever the camshaft seal out of the bore

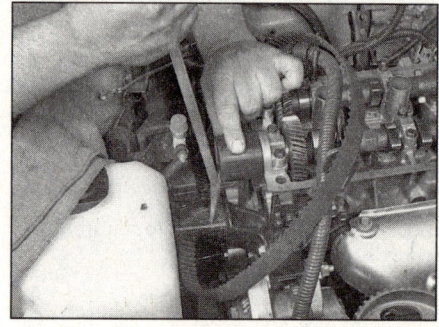

9.5 A new seal can be pressed into place with a lever against the engine mounting

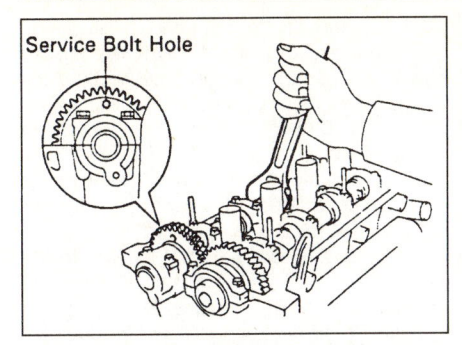

Engine in-car repair procedures 2A•13

10.4 Position the intake camshaft so that the bolt hole in the gear is uppermost

10.11a Mark the followers/shims and remove them with a magnetic tool

10.11b Mark up a cardboard box to store the followers/shims and bearing caps

5 Remove the four bolts and the right-hand bearing caps from the intake and exhaust camshafts. Remove the housing plug from its location in front of the intake camshaft, and remove the oil seal from the exhaust camshaft.
6 Secure the intake camshaft sub-gear to the main gear by fitting one of the service bolts into the threaded hole **(see illustration 10.44)**.
7 Following the reverse of the tightening sequence **(see illustration 10.36)**, loosen the remaining exhaust camshaft bearing cap bolts in 1/4-turn increments until the bolts can be removed by hand. Lift the bearing caps straight up and off.
Caution: As the centre bearing cap bolts are being loosened, make sure the camshaft is moving up evenly. If one end or the other stops moving and the camshaft gets jammed, start over by refitting the bearing caps. DO NOT try to lever or force the camshaft out.
8 Lift the exhaust camshaft straight up and out of the cylinder head.
9 Following the reverse of the tightening sequence **(see illustration 10.33)**, loosen the remaining intake camshaft bearing cap bolts in 1/4-turn increments until the bolts can be removed by hand. Lift the bearing caps straight up and off.
Caution: As the centre bearing cap bolts are being loosened, make sure the camshaft is moving up evenly. If one end or the other stops moving and the camshaft gets jammed, start over by refitting the bearing caps. DO NOT try to lever or force the camshaft out.
10 Lift the intake camshaft straight up and out of the cylinder head.
11 Clean the oil off the camshaft follower shims, marking them I for intake and E for exhaust (and number their location) with a felt-tip marker and remove the followers with a magnetic tool, keeping the shims with their followers. Store the camshaft bearing caps, followers and shims so they can be refitted without mixing them up **(see illustrations)**.
12 Position the intake camshaft in a vice, clamping it on the hexagonal section. Using a two-pin spanner, rotate the sub-gear clockwise and remove the service bolt from the threaded hole, then allow the sub-gear to rotate back until all tension is relieved **(see illustration)**.

13 Remove the sub-gear circlip. The wave washer, sub-gear and camshaft gear spring can now be removed from the camshaft **(see illustrations)**.

Inspection

14 Inspect each follower for scuffing and score marks **(see illustration)**.
15 Visually examine the cam lobes and bearing journals for score marks, pitting, galling and evidence of overheating (blue, discoloured areas). Look for flaking away of the hardened surface layer of each lobe.
16 If in any doubt as to the condition of the camshafts/gears, have them examined and measured by an automotive engineering workshop.

Refitting

17 Reassemble the intake camshaft sub-gear. Install the camshaft gear spring, sub-gear and wave washer. Secure them with the circlip **(see illustrations 10.13a and 10.13b)**.
18 Refer to paragraph 6 and install a service bolt.
19 Apply moly-base grease or engine assembly lube to the intake camshaft followers, then install them in their original locations. Make sure the valve adjustment shims are in place on the followers.
20 Apply moly-base grease or engine assembly lube to the intake camshaft lobes and bearing journals.
21 Position the intake camshaft so that the service bolt hole in the camshaft gear is uppermost then place the camshaft in position **(see illustration 10.4)**.
22 Install the intake camshaft bearing caps (except the right-hand cap) in numerical order with the arrows pointing toward the timing belt end of the engine.
23 Tighten the bearing cap bolts uniformly and alternately, in several stages, until the caps

10.12 Use a spanner to relieve the tension on the service bolt

10.13a Remove the circlip with a pair of circlip pliers

10.13b Remove the wave washer (1), then camshaft sub-gear (2) and the gear spring (3)

10.14 Wipe off the oil and inspect each follower for wear and scuffing

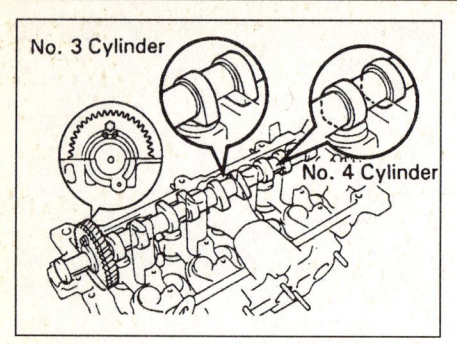

2A•14 Engine in-car repair procedures

10.26a Align the exhaust camshaft gear with the intake camshaft gear by matching up the timing marks on the gears

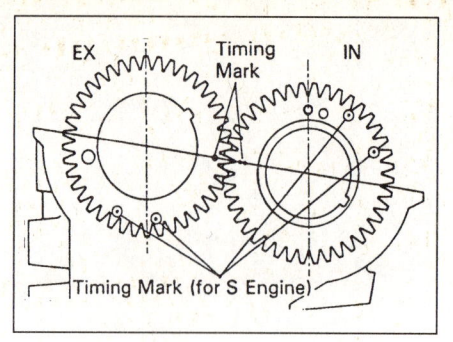

10.26b DO NOT use the timing marks for the S engines when installing the camshafts and gears

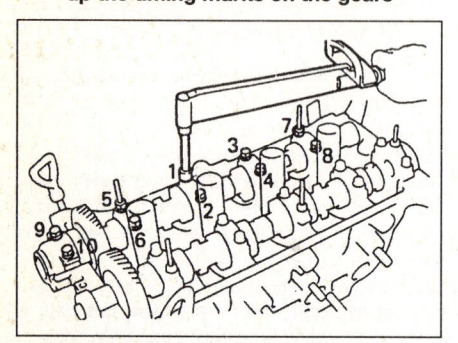

10.33 Intake camshaft bearing cap bolt tightening sequence – 1.3 litre

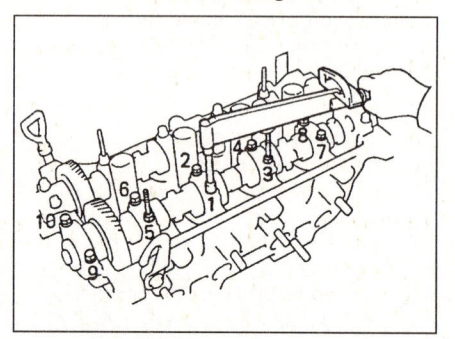

10.36 Exhaust camshaft bearing cap tightening sequence – 1.3 litre

are snug with the cylinder head. Do not tighten the bolts to the full torque setting at this stage.

24 Apply moly-base grease or engine assembly lube to the exhaust camshaft followers, then install them in their original locations. Make sure the valve adjustment shims are in place on the followers.

25 Apply moly-base grease or engine assembly lube to the exhaust camshaft lobes and bearing journals.

26 Align the exhaust camshaft gear with the intake camshaft gear by matching up the timing marks on the gears **(see illustration)**. On some 1.3 litre engines there are two sets of timing marks – DO NOT use the timing marks for the S engines when installing the camshafts and gears **(see illustration)**.

27 Roll the exhaust camshaft down into position. Turn the intake camshaft back-and-forth a little until the exhaust camshaft sits in the bearings evenly.

28 Install the exhaust camshaft bearing caps (except the right-hand cap) in numerical order with the arrows pointing toward the timing belt end of the engine.

29 Tighten the bearing cap bolts uniformly and alternately, in several stages, until the caps are snug with the cylinder head. Do not tighten the bolts to the full torque setting at this stage.

30 Remove the service bolt from the intake camshaft gear.

31 Apply a thin coat of RTV sealant to the intake camshaft right-hand bearing-cap-to-cylinder-head mating surface. **Note:** *The cap must be installed immediately or the sealer will dry prematurely.* Install the cap and tighten the two bearing cap bolts uniformly and alternately, in several stages, until the cap is snug with the cylinder head. Do not tighten the bolts to the full torque setting at this stage.

32 Install the housing plug to its location in front of the intake camshaft.

33 Following the recommended sequence **(see illustration)**, tighten all the intake camshaft bearing cap bolts uniformly to the torque listed in this Chapter's Specifications.

34 Lubricate the lips of a new exhaust camshaft oil seal with engine oil or multi-purpose grease and install the seal in the cylinder head. Push the seal fully into the recess in the head.

35 Apply a thin coat of RTV sealant to the exhaust camshaft right-hand bearing-cap-to-cylinder-head mating surface. **Note:** *The cap must be installed immediately or the sealer will dry prematurely.* Install the cap and tighten the two bearing cap bolts uniformly and alternately, in several stages, until the cap is snug with the cylinder head. Do not tighten the bolts to the full torque setting at this stage.

36 Following the recommended sequence **(see illustration)**, tighten all the exhaust camshaft bearing cap bolts uniformly to the torque listed in this Chapter's Specifications.

37 Install the timing belt sprocket on the exhaust camshaft and tighten the bolt to the torque listed in this Chapter's Specifications. Prevent the camshaft from turning by holding it with a spanner on the hexagonal section.

38 Install the timing belt (see Section 5).

39 The remainder of refitting is the reverse of the removal procedure.

1.6 litre 4A-FE engine

Note: *Before beginning this procedure, obtain two 6 x 1.0 mm, bolts 16 to 20 mm long. They will be referred to as service bolts in the text.*

Removal

40 Remove the distributor (see Chapter 5B). Remove the timing belt and camshaft sprocket (see Sections 5 and 9).

41 Measure the camshaft thrust clearance (endfloat) with a dial indicator **(see illustration)**. If the clearance is greater than the service limit, renew the camshaft and/or the cylinder head.

42 Position the knock pin in the *exhaust* camshaft just above the top of the cylinder head **(see illustration)**. This will position the intake camshaft lobes so the camshaft will be pushed up evenly by valve spring pressure. **Caution:** *This positioning is important to avoid damaging the cylinder head or camshaft as the camshaft is removed.*

10.41 With the dial zeroed, lever the camshaft forward and back, then read the endfloat on the dial

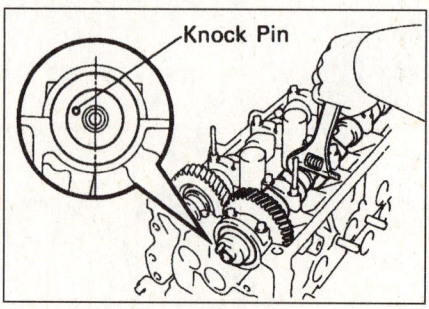

10.42 Place the exhaust camshaft knock pin between the 9 o'clock and 10 o'clock positions

10.43 Remove the two bolts and the right-hand camshaft bearing cap from the intake camshaft

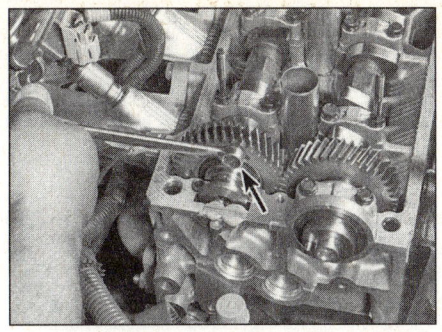

Engine in-car repair procedures 2A•15

43 Remove the two bolts and the right-hand bearing cap from the intake camshaft (see illustration).
44 Secure the intake camshaft sub-gear to the main gear by installing one of the service bolts into the threaded hole (see illustration).
45 Following the reverse of the tightening sequence (see illustration 10.70), loosen the remaining intake camshaft bearing cap bolts in 1/4-turn increments until the bolts can be removed by hand. Lift the bearing caps straight up and off.
Caution: As the centre bearing cap bolts are being loosened, make sure the camshaft is moving up evenly. If one end or the other stops moving and the camshaft gets jammed, start over by refitting the bearing caps. DO NOT try to lever or force the camshaft out.
46 Lift the camshaft straight up and out of the cylinder head.
47 Position the knock pin in the exhaust camshaft at approximately the 5 o'clock position (see illustration).
48 Remove the right-hand exhaust camshaft bearing cap bolts and detach the bearing cap and oil seal.
Caution: Do not lever the cap off. If it doesn't come loose easily, leave it in place without bolts.
49 Following the reverse of the tightening sequence (see illustration 10.60), loosen the remaining exhaust camshaft bearing cap bolts in 1/4-turn increments until the bolts can be removed by hand. Lift off the bearing caps.
Caution: As the centre bearing cap bolts are being loosened, make sure the camshaft is moving up evenly. If one end or the other stops moving and the camshaft gets jammed, start over by refitting the bearing caps and resetting the knock pin. DO NOT try to lever or force the camshaft out.
50 Lift the camshaft straight up and out of the cylinder head.
51 Clean the oil off the camshaft follower shims, mark them with a felt-tip marker and remove the followers, keeping the shims with their followers (see illustration 10.11a). Store the camshaft bearing caps, followers and shims so they can be reinstalled without mixing them up (see illustration 10.11b).
52 Position the intake camshaft in a vice,

10.44 Install a service bolt through the sub-gear and thread it into the main gear (arrowed)

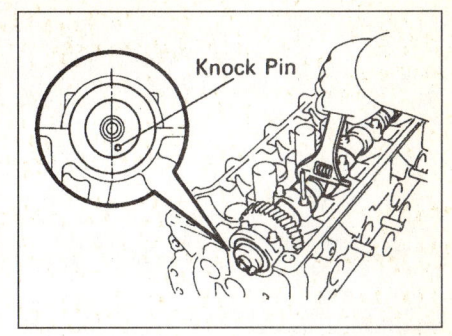

clamping it on the hexagon section. Using a two-pin spanner, rotate the sub-gear clockwise and remove the service bolt from the threaded hole, then allow the sub-gear to rotate back until all tension is relieved (see illustration 10.12).
53 Remove the sub-gear circlip (see illustration 10.13a). The wave washer, sub-gear and camshaft gear spring can now be removed from the camshaft (see illustration 10.13b).

Inspection

54 Follow the instructions given in paragraphs 14 to 16.

Refitting

55 Apply moly-base grease or engine assembly lube to the exhaust camshaft followers, then install them in their original locations. Make sure the valve adjustment shims are on place on the followers.
56 Apply moly-base grease or engine assembly lube to the exhaust camshaft lobes and bearing journals.
57 Position the exhaust camshaft in the cylinder head with the knock pin at approximately the 5 o'clock position (see illustration 10.47).
58 Apply a thin coat of RTV sealant to the outer edge of the right-hand bearing-cap-to-cylinder-head mating surface (see illustration). Note: *The cap must be installed immediately or the sealer will dry prematurely.*
59 Install the exhaust camshaft bearing caps in numerical order with the arrows pointing toward the timing belt end of the engine.
60 Following the recommended tightening

10.47 Turn the exhaust camshaft until the knock pin is pointed at about the 5 o'clock position

sequence (see illustration), tighten the bearing cap bolts in 1/4-turn increments to the torque listed in this Chapter's Specifications.
61 Refer to Section 9 and install a new camshaft oil seal.
62 Reassemble the intake camshaft sub-gear. Install the camshaft gear spring, sub-gear and wave washer. Secure them with the circlip (see illustrations 10.13a and 10.13b).
63 Refer to paragraph 44 and install a service bolt.
64 Apply moly-base grease or engine assembly lube to the intake camshaft followers, then install them in their original locations. Make sure the valve adjustment shims are in place on the followers.
65 Apply moly-base grease or engine assembly lube to the intake camshaft lobes and bearing journals.
66 Rotate the exhaust camshaft until the knock pin is positioned between the 9 o'clock and 10 o'clock position (see illustration 10.47).
67 Align the intake camshaft gear with the exhaust camshaft gear by matching up the *installation* marks on the gears (see illustration).
Caution: There are two sets of marks. Do not use the timing marks. The camshaft installation marks are the only marks that are duplicated on both sides of the two camshaft gears.
68 Roll the intake camshaft down into position. Turn the exhaust camshaft back-and-forth a little until the intake camshaft sits in the bearings evenly.
69 Install the intake camshaft bearing caps

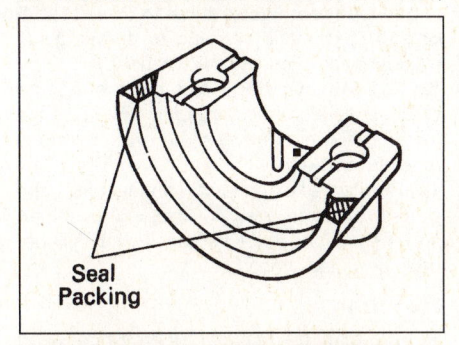

10.58 Apply sealant to the shaded areas of the exhaust camshaft bearing cap

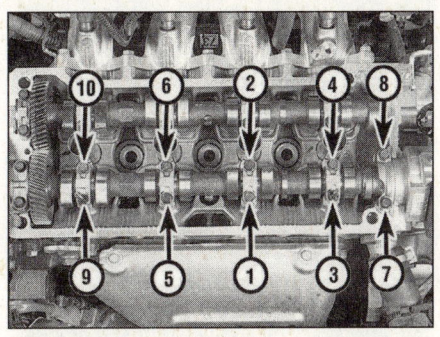

10.60 Exhaust camshaft bearing cap bolt tightening sequence – 1.6 litre

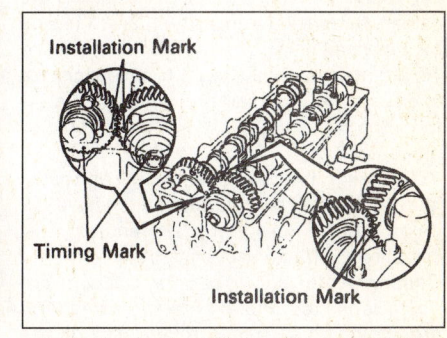

10.67 Use the installation marks, NOT the timing marks

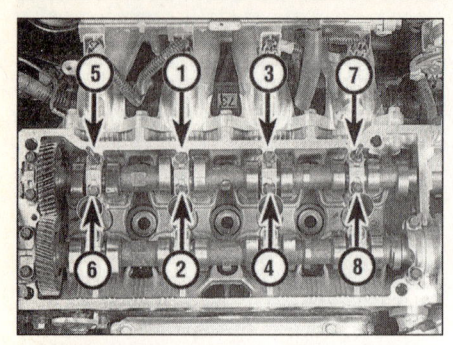

2A•16 Engine in-car repair procedures

10.70 Intake camshaft bearing cap bolt tightening sequence – 1.6 litre

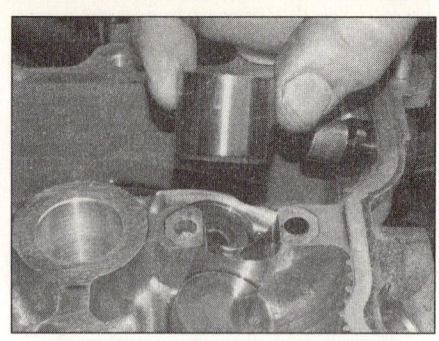

10.79 Lift the followers from position

10.83 Position the No 1 cylinder camshaft lobes away from the followers

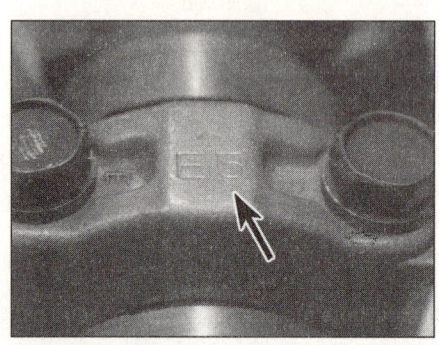

10.84 The camshaft bearing caps are marked (arrowed) E for exhaust, and I for intake

in numerical order with the arrows pointing toward the timing belt end of the engine.
70 Following the recommended sequence **(see illustration)**, tighten the bearing cap bolts in 1/4-turn increments to the torque listed in this Chapter's Specifications.
71 Remove the service bolt from the intake camshaft gear.
72 Install the timing belt sprocket on the exhaust camshaft and tighten the bolt to the torque listed in this Chapter's Specifications. Prevent the camshaft from turning by holding it with a spanner on the hexagonal section.
73 Install the timing belt (see Section 5).
74 The remainder of refitting is the reverse of the removal procedure.

VVT-i engines

Removal

75 Remove the timing chain as described in Section 6. There is no need to remove the camshaft sprockets unless you are renewing the camshafts.
76 Rotate the crankshaft 90° anti-clockwise to eliminate any possibility of accidental valve-to-piston contact during the camshaft removal procedure.
77 Working from the ends of the camshafts, gradually and evenly slacken and remove the bearing caps from the intake and exhaust camshafts. Lift off the bearing caps
Caution: As the centre bearing cap bolts are being loosened, make sure the camshafts are moving up evenly. If one end or the other stops moving and the camshaft gets jammed, start over by refitting the bearing caps. DO NOT try to lever or force the camshafts out.
78 Lift the camshaft straight up and out of the cylinder head.
79 Clean the oil off the camshaft followers, mark them with a felt-tip marker and remove them **(see illustration)**. Store the camshaft bearing caps and followers so they can be reinstalled without mixing them up **(see illustration 10.11b)**.

Inspection

80 Follow the instructions given in paragraphs 14 to 16.

Refitting

81 Apply a little clean engine oil to the exhaust camshaft followers, then install them in their original locations. Repeat this procedure for the intake camshaft.
82 Apply a little clean engine oil to the exhaust camshaft lobes and bearing journals. Repeat this procedure for the intake camshaft.
83 Position the exhaust and intake camshaft with the lobes for No 1 cylinder pointing upwards, away from the followers **(see illustration)**.
84 Refit the camshaft bearing caps to their original positions. Note that the exhaust bearing caps are marked E and the intake caps are marked I, as well as being numbered 2 to 5 from the timing chain end. No 1 bearing cap is the 'double' cap fitted adjacent to the timing chain. Apply a little clean engine oil to the threads and underside of the heads, then install the retaining bolts and tighten them gradually and evenly from the middle of the camshafts outwards **(see illustration)**.
85 Align the camshaft sprocket timing marks **(see illustration 3.7b)**, then rotate the crankshaft 90° clockwise, back to TDC position (with the crankshaft key upright in the 12 o'clock position).
86 Refit the timing chain as described in Section 6.

11 Cylinder head – removal and refitting

Note: *The engine must be completely cool before beginning this procedure.*

Removal

1 Drain the coolant from the engine block and radiator (see Chapter 1).
2 Drain the engine oil and remove the oil filter (see Chapter 1).
3 Remove the throttle body, fuel injectors, fuel rail, intake and exhaust manifolds (see Chapter 4A).

Non-VVT-i engines

4 Remove the timing belt and camshaft sprocket (see Sections 5 and 9).
5 Remove the alternator and distributor (1.6 litre engine only) – see Chapter 5A and 5B.
6 Unbolt the power steering pump and set the pump aside without disconnecting the hoses.
7 Remove the coolant junctions from each end of the cylinder head.

VVT-i engines

8 Remove the timing chain as described in Section 6.
9 Undo the bolt and withdraw the VVT-i oil control valve from the cylinder head **(see illustration 7.3)**.

All engines

10 Remove the camshafts and followers (see Section 10).
11 Label and remove any remaining items, such as coolant fittings, tubes, cables, hoses or wires.
12 Using an 8 mm Allen key bit (non-VVT-i engines) or an M12 bi-hexagon bit (VVT-i engines), loosen the cylinder head bolts in 1/4-turn increments until they can be removed by hand. Loosen the cylinder head bolts in the reverse of the recommended tightening sequence **(see illustrations 11.25a, 11.25b or 11.27)** to avoid warping or cracking the cylinder head. Recover the washers.
13 Lift the cylinder head off the engine block. If it's stuck, very carefully pry up at the transmission end, beyond the gasket surface **(see illustration)**.
14 Remove all external components from the cylinder head to allow for thorough cleaning and inspection. See Chapter 2B, for cylinder head servicing procedures.

Refitting

15 The mating surfaces of the cylinder head and block must be perfectly clean when the cylinder head is installed.

Engine in-car repair procedures 2A•17

11.13 Lever only at the overhang, not between the mating surfaces

11.16 Remove all traces of old gasket material

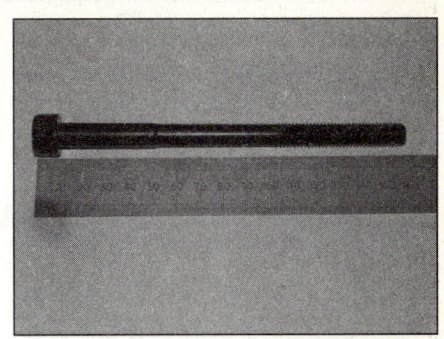

11.20 Measure the overall length of the cylinder head bolts – VVT-i engines

16 Use a gasket scraper to remove all traces of carbon and old gasket material (see illustration), then clean the mating surfaces with brake cleaner. If there's oil on the mating surfaces when the cylinder head is installed, the gasket may not seal correctly and leaks could develop. When working on the block, stuff the cylinders with clean rags to keep out debris. Use a vacuum cleaner to remove material that falls into the cylinders.

17 Check the block and cylinder head mating surfaces for nicks, deep scratches and other damage. If damage is slight, it can be removed with a file; if it's excessive, machining may be the only alternative.

18 Use a tap of the correct size to chase the threads in the cylinder head bolt holes, then clean the holes with compressed air – make sure that nothing remains in the holes.

⚠️ **Warning: Wear eye protection when using compressed air.**

19 Mount each bolt in a vice and run a die down the threads to remove corrosion and restore the threads. Dirt, corrosion, sealant and damaged threads will affect torque readings.

20 On VVT-i engines, measure the overall length of the cylinder head bolts. If any of the bolts lengths exceeds that given in the Specifications (indicating excessive stretching), renew all the cylinder head bolts (see illustration).

21 On all engines, install any components that were removed from the cylinder head.

22 Position the new gasket over the dowel pins in the block (see illustration). On VVT-i

11.22a Note the markings for UP on the gasket – non-VVT-i engines

engines, the 'Lot number' must be facing upwards (see illustration).

23 Carefully set the cylinder head on the block without disturbing the gasket.

24 Before installing the cylinder head bolts, apply a small amount of clean engine oil to the threads and under the bolt heads.

Non-VVT-i engines

25 Install the bolts and tighten them finger tight. Install the shorter bolts along the intake side of the cylinder head and the longer bolts along the exhaust side. Following the recommended sequence, tighten the bolts in three steps to the torque listed in this Chapter's Specifications (see illustrations). Some of the Stages of the tightening sequence require the bolts to be angle-tightened. If you don't have an angle-torque attachment for your torque wrench, simply apply a paint mark at one edge of each cylinder head bolt and tighten the bolt until that mark is 90 degrees from where you started.

11.22b On VVT-i engines, the 'Lot number' (arrowed) must face upwards

26 The remaining refitting steps are the reverse of removal. Note: *If the semi-circular rubber plug had been removed from the cylinder head, reinstall it with some RTV sealant.*

VVT-i engines

27 Install the cylinder head bolts and washers, then tighten them in sequence to the Stage 1 torque setting (see illustration).

28 Angle tighten the bolts. a further 90° in sequence.

All engines

29 Check and adjust the valve clearances as necessary (see Chapter 1).

30 The remainder of refitting is a reversal of removal, noting the following points:
a) *Refill the cooling system, install a new oil filter and add oil to the engine (see Chapter 1).*
b) *Run the engine and check for leaks.*
c) *Road test the vehicle.*

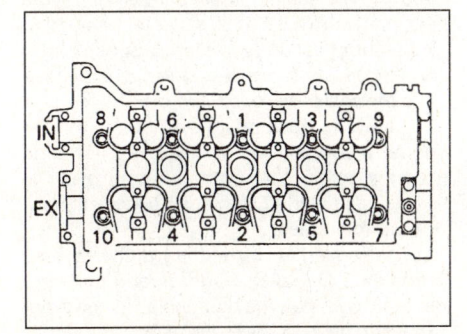

11.25a Cylinder head bolt tightening sequence – 1.3 litre

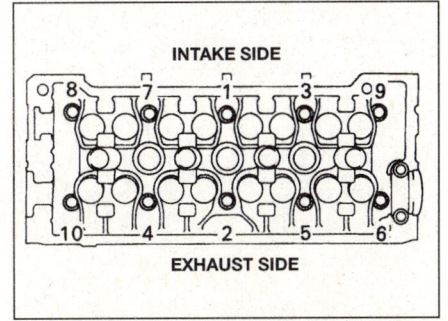

11.25b Cylinder head bolt tightening sequence – 1.6 litre non VVT-i engines

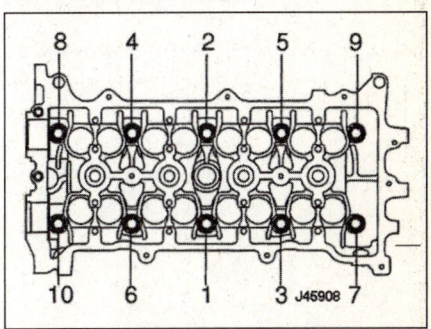

11.27 Cylinder head bolts tightening sequence – VVT-i engines

2A•18 Engine in-car repair procedures

12.7 Remove the front bolts of the chassis brace (arrowed)

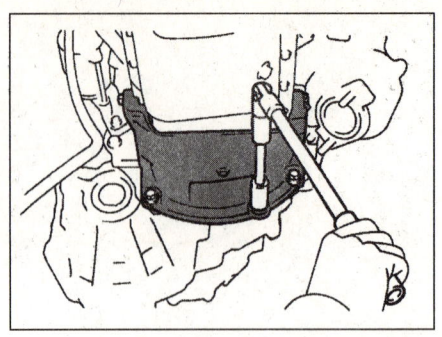

12.8 On 1.6 litre non-VVT-i engines, unbolt the block-to-transmission brace

12.9a Carefully lever the oil sump away from the block

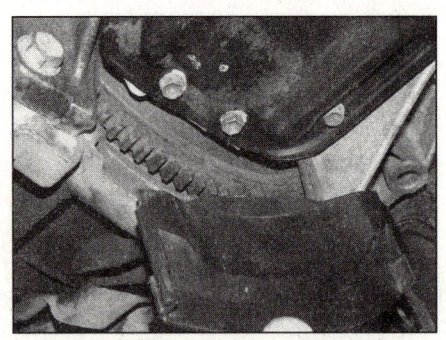

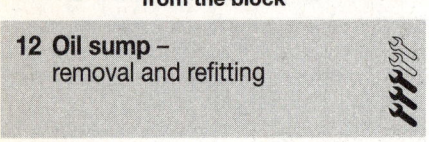

12.9b On VVT-i engines, pull down the plastic cover slotted into the engine block

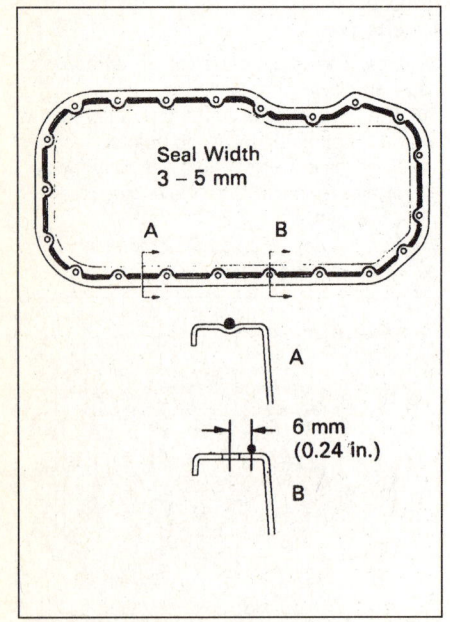

12.15a Sealant application details – non-VVT-i engines

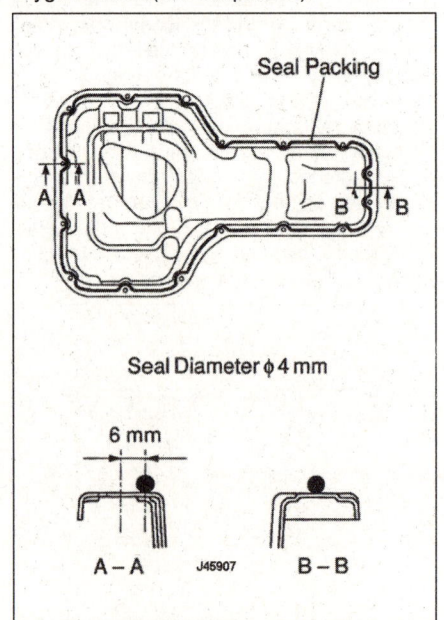

12.15b Sealant application details – VVT-i engines

12 Oil sump – removal and refitting

Removal

1 Set the parking brake and block the rear wheels.
2 Raise the front of the vehicle and support it securely on axle stands (see *Jacking and vehicle support*).
3 Remove the two splash shields under the engine.
4 Drain the engine oil and remove the oil filter (see Chapter 1). Remove the oil dipstick.

Non-VVT-i engines

5 Disconnect the electrical connector to the oxygen sensor (see Chapter 4B).
6 Remove the two nuts retaining the front exhaust pipe to the exhaust manifold, then the two bolts/nuts connecting the pipe to the rear of the exhaust system.
7 Remove the two front bolts of the longitudinal chassis brace and the two nuts securing the radiator side engine mounting (see illustration). For better access for sump removal, you'll have to insert a large lever bar between the brace and the chassis to lever the brace down.
8 On 1.6 litre engines, unbolt and remove the block-to-transmission brace (see illustration).

All engines

9 Remove the bolts and detach the oil sump. If it's stuck, pry it loose very carefully with a putty knife (see illustration). Don't damage the mating surfaces of the sump and block or oil leaks could develop. **Note:** *On VVT-i engines, pull down the plastic cover slotted into the left-hand end of the engine block to access the left-hand sump bolts (see illustration).*
10 Unbolt the pick-up tube/oil strainer assembly and remove it for cleaning. Discard the pick-up pipe gasket, a new one must be fitted.

Refitting

11 Use a scraper to remove all traces of old gasket material and sealant from the block and oil sump. Take great care not to gouge the mating surfaces. Clean the mating surfaces with brake cleaner.
12 Make sure the threaded bolt holes in the block are clean.
13 Check the oil sump flange for distortion, particularly around the bolt holes. On steel sumps, if necessary, place the oil sump on a wood block and use a hammer to flatten and restore the gasket surface.
14 Inspect the oil pump pick-up tube assembly for cracks and a blocked strainer. If the pick-up was removed, clean it thoroughly and install it now, using a new O-ring (non-VVT-i engines) or gasket (VVT-i engines). Tighten the nuts/bolts to the torque listed in this Chapter's Specifications.
15 Apply a 5 mm (approximately) wide bead of RTV sealant (steel sumps) or Toyota sealant No 08826-00080 (aluminium sumps) to the sump flange (see illustrations). **Note:** *Refitting must be completed within 5 minutes once the sealer has been applied.*
16 Carefully position the oil sump on the engine block and install the bolts. Working from the centre out. Tighten the bolts to the torque listed in this Chapter's Specifications in three or four steps.
17 The remainder of refitting is the reverse of removal. Be sure to add oil and fit a new oil filter. Use new gasket/seals on the front exhaust pipe (non-VVT-i engines).
18 Run the engine and check for oil pressure and leaks.

Engine in-car repair procedures 2A•19

13.3 Remove the bolt (arrowed) and withdraw the crankshaft position sensor from the oil pump body

13.4 Remove the oil pump body-to-block bolts (arrowed)

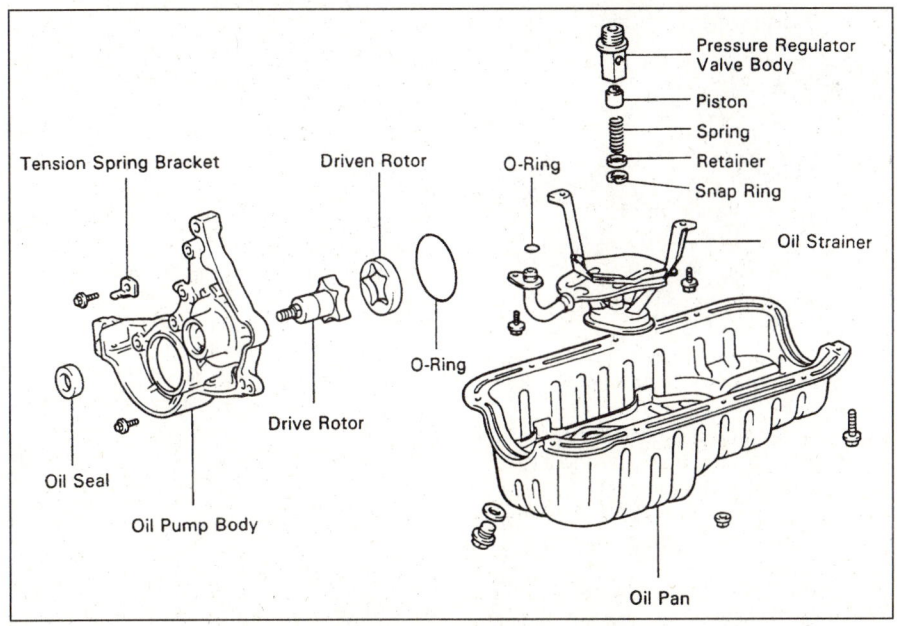

13.6a Oil pump components – 1.3 litre

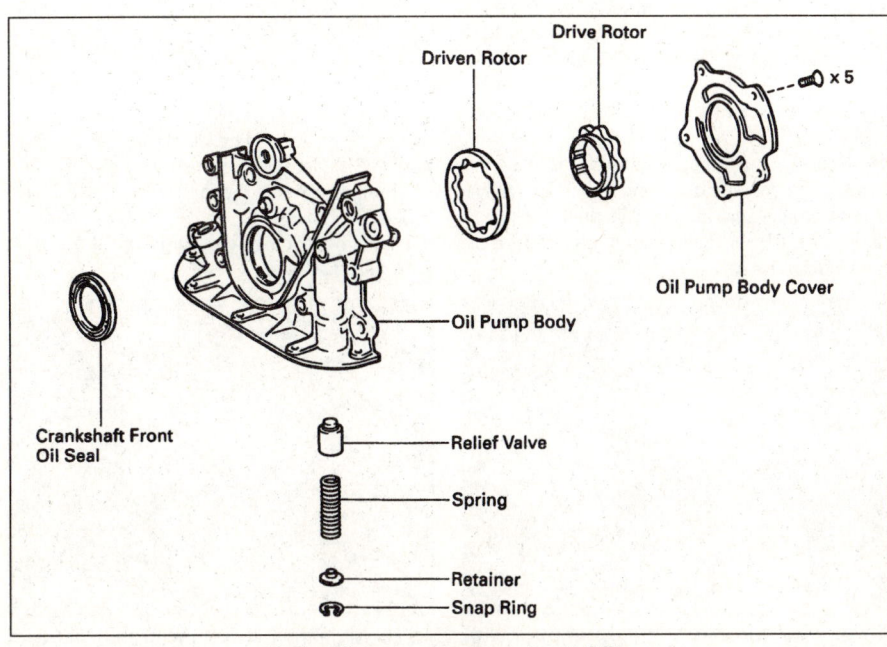

13.6b Oil pump components – 1.6 litre

13 Oil pump – removal, inspection and refitting

Removal

Non-VVT-i engines

1 Remove the oil dipstick, oil sump and the oil pick-up/strainer assembly (see Section 12).
2 Remove the timing belt, idler pulley and spring, crankshaft pulley, crankshaft sprocket (see Section 5) and, on 1.3 litre engines, undo the nut and remove the oil pump sprocket.
3 Where fitted, remove the crankshaft position sensor **(see illustration)**. Unbolt and remove the oil dipstick pipe. On 1.3 litre engines, remove the oil pressure relief valve from the engine block.
4 Remove the bolts and detach the oil pump body from the engine **(see illustration)**. You may have to pry carefully between the main bearing cap and the pump body with a screwdriver, or tap behind the oil pump with a soft-faced hammer. On 1.3 litre engines, remove the O-ring.
5 Use a scraper to remove all traces of sealant and old gasket material from the pump body and engine block, then clean the mating surfaces with lacquer thinner or acetone.
6 Remove the five Torx screws (1.6 litre engine) and separate the pump cover from the body. Lift out the drive and driven rotors **(see illustrations)**.
7 Remove the oil pressure relief valve circlip retainer, spring and piston.

⚠ **Warning: The spring is tightly compressed – be careful and wear eye protection.**

VVT-i engines

8 Remove the timing chain as described in Section 6.
9 Undo the five bolts and remove the oil pump from the engine block **(see illustration)**.
10 Undo the plug and remove the pressure relief spring and piston **(see illustration)**.
11 Undo the 3 screws remove the pump cover. Lift out the pump rotors **(see illustration)**.

Inspection

12 Clean all components with solvent, inspect

13.9 Oil pump bolts (arrowed) – VVT-i engines

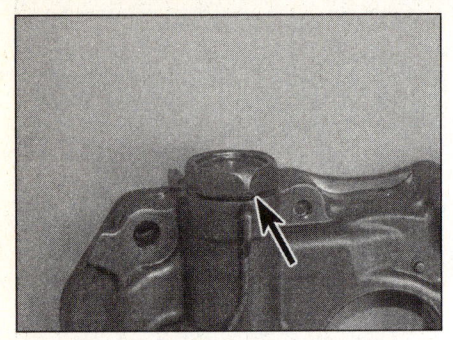

2A•20 Engine in-car repair procedures

13.10 Oil pressure relief valve plug (arrowed)

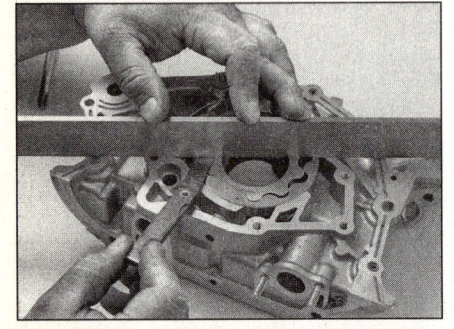

13.11 Undo the three screws (arrowed) and remove the pump cover

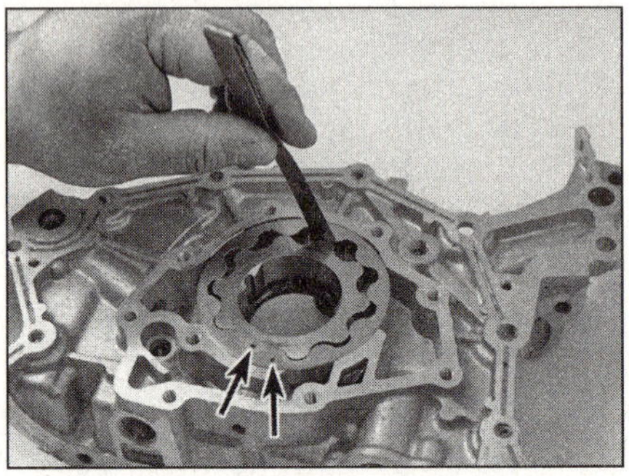

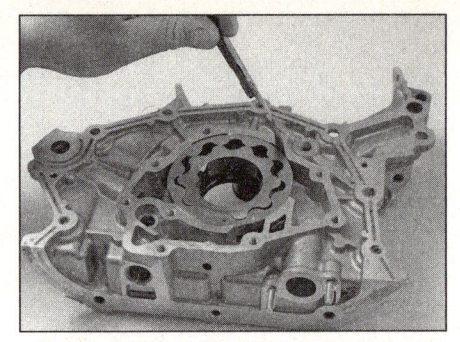

13.14a Measure the driven rotor-to-body clearance with a feeler gauge

13.14b Use a straight-edge and feeler gauges to measure the rotor-to-cover clearance

13.14c Measure the rotor tip clearance with a feeler gauge – rotor marks (arrowed)

them for wear and damage. Use compressed air to blow through the oilways in the pump body.
13 Check the oil pressure relief valve piston sliding surface and valve spring. If either the spring or the piston is damaged, they must be renewed as a set. The piston must free to slide up and down the bore in the pump body without binding at any point.
14 Check the driven rotor-to-body clearance, rotor-to-cover clearance and drive rotor tip clearance with a feeler gauge **(see illustrations)** and compare the results to this Chapter's Specifications. If any clearance is excessive, renew the rotors as a set. If necessary, renew the oil pump body.

Refitting

Non-VVT-i engines

15 Lubricate all rotors with clean engine oil and place them in the pump body with the marks facing in (1.3 litre engine) or out (1.6 litre engine) **(see illustration 13.14c)**.
16 Pack the pump cavity with petroleum jelly, attach the pump cover and tighten the screws (1.6 litre engine only).
17 Lubricate the oil pressure relief valve piston with clean engine oil and reinstall the valve components in the pump body or engine block.
18 On 1.3 litre engines, apply a bead of RTV sealant to the pump body **(see illustration)** and locate a new O-ring in the body groove. On 1.6 litre engines, place a new gasket on the engine block (the dowel pins should hold it in place).
19 Position the pump assembly against the block and install the mounting bolts. On 1.6 litre engines, make sure that the flats on the oil pump drive rotor align with the flats on the crankshaft **(see illustration)**.

20 Tighten the bolts to the torque listed in this Chapter's Specifications in three or four steps. Follow a criss-cross pattern to avoid warping the body.
21 The remainder of reassembly is a reversal of removal.

VVT-i engines

22 Lubricate the pump rotors with clean engine oil, and place them in the pump body with the marks facing the pump body cover side.
23 Refit the pump body cover and tighten the retaining screws to the specified torque.
24 Refit the oil pressure relief piston and spring, then tighten the plug to the specified torque.
25 Position a new gasket on the engine block, then refit the oil pump. Ensure the flats on the drive rotor align with the flats machined on the crankshaft, and tighten the bolts to the specified torque **(see illustration)**.
26 Refit the timing chain as described in Section 6.

14 Oil pressure switch – renewal

1 The oil pressure switch is located on the front face of the engine block, at the left-hand end (4E-FE engine), right-hand end (4A-FE engine), or above the oil filter (4ZZ-FE and 3ZZ-FE engines).
2 Disconnect the wiring plug from the switch **(see illustrations)**.

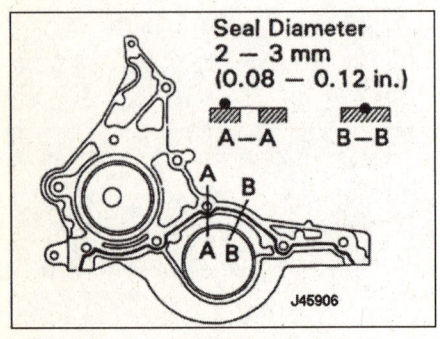

13.18 Apply a bead of sealant as shown – 1.3 litre

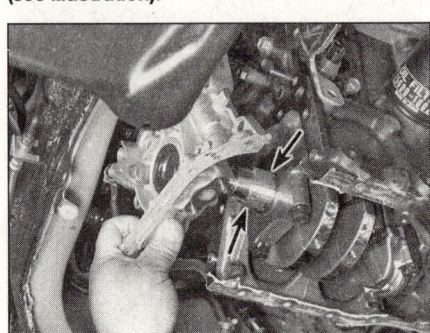

13.19 Align the flats in the pump rotor with the flats on the crankshaft

13.25 Align the flats on the crankshaft with the flats on the pump rotor

Engine in-car repair procedures 2A•21

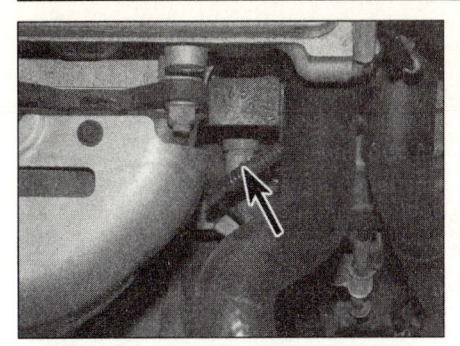

14.2a On 1.3 litre non-VVT-i engines, the oil pressure switch is located at the left-hand end of the cylinder block (arrowed)

14.2b On 1.6 litre non-VVT-i engines, the oil pressure switch is at the right-hand end of the cylinder block (arrowed)

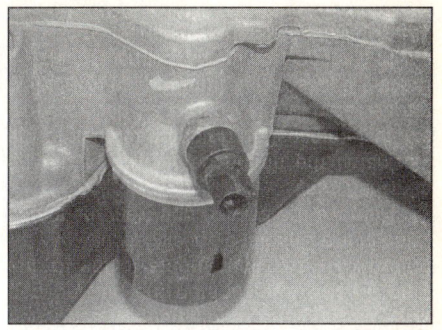

14.2c On VVT-i engines, the oil pressure switch is above the oil filter location

3 Unscrew the switch from the engine block. Be prepared for oil spillage.
4 Prior to refitting, apply a little Loctite Three Bond 1344 (or similar) to the threads of the switch.
5 Refit the switch and tighten it to the specified torque.
6 Reconnect the wiring plug.

15 Flywheel/driveplate – removal and refitting

Removal

1 Remove the transmission as described in Chapter 7A or 7B.
2 Remove the pressure plate and clutch disc (Chapter 6) (manual transmission vehicles).
3 Use a centre punch or paint to make alignment marks on the flywheel/driveplate and crankshaft to ensure correct alignment during refitting **(see illustration)**.
4 Remove the bolts that secure the flywheel/driveplate to the crankshaft. If the crankshaft turns, wedge a screwdriver in the ring gear teeth to jam the flywheel, or use a tool to lock the flywheel in position **(see illustration)**.
5 Remove the flywheel/driveplate from the crankshaft. Since the flywheel is fairly heavy, be sure to support it while removing the last bolt. Some automatic transmission equipped vehicles have spacers on both sides of the driveplate **(see illustration)**. Keep them with the driveplate.

⚠️ **Warning: The ring gear teeth may be sharp, wear gloves to protect your hands.**

Refitting

6 Clean the flywheel to remove grease and oil. Inspect the surface for cracks, rivet grooves, burned areas and score marks. Light scoring can be removed with emery cloth. Check for cracked and broken ring gear teeth. Lay the flywheel on a flat surface and use a straight-edge to check for warpage.
7 Clean and inspect the mating surfaces of the flywheel/driveplate and the crankshaft. If the crankshaft seal is leaking, renew it before reinstalling the flywheel/driveplate (see Section 16).
8 Position the flywheel/driveplate against the crankshaft. Be sure to align the marks made during removal. Note that some engines have an alignment dowel or staggered bolt holes to ensure correct refitting. Before installing the bolts, apply thread-locking compound to the threads.
9 Wedge a screwdriver in the ring gear teeth to keep the flywheel/driveplate from turning and tighten the bolts to the torque listed in this Chapter's Specifications. Follow a criss-cross pattern and work up to the final torque in three or four steps.
10 The remainder of refitting is the reverse of the removal procedure.

15.3 Mark the flywheel/driveplate and the crankshaft so they can be reassembled in the same relative positions

15.5 On vehicles equipped with a spacer plate, note the position of the locating pin (arrowed)

16 Main oil seal – renewal

1 Remove the flywheel/driveplate (Section 15).
2 The seal can be renewed without removing the oil sump or seal retainer. Carefully prise out the old seal with a screwdriver **(see illustration)**. Take great care not to damage the seal bore or the surface of the crankshaft.
3 Apply multi-purpose grease to the crankshaft seal journal and the lip of the new seal and carefully push the new seal into place. The lip is stiff so carefully work it onto the seal journal of the crankshaft with a smooth object like the

15.4 Lock the flywheel in place using a tool bolted to the engine block

16.2 Carefully prise out the old seal – take great care not to damage the crankshaft

2A•22 Engine in-car repair procedures

16.3a Tap the oil seal into place using a block of wood ...

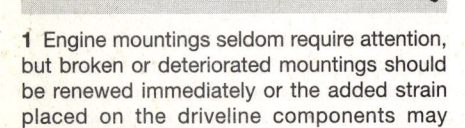

16.3b ... until the outer edge of the seal is flush with the engine block

end of an extension, then tap into place using a block of wood **(see illustrations)**. Don't rush it or you may damage the seal.
4 The remainder of refitting is the reverse of removal.

17 Engine mountings – check and renewal

1 Engine mountings seldom require attention, but broken or deteriorated mountings should be renewed immediately or the added strain placed on the driveline components may cause damage or wear.

Check

2 During the check, the engine must be raised slightly to remove the weight from the mountings.
3 Raise the vehicle and support it securely on axle stands (see *Jacking and vehicle support*), then position a jack under the engine oil sump. Place a large wood block between the jack head and the oil sump, then carefully raise the engine just enough to take the weight off the mountings. Do not position the wood block under the drain plug.

⚠️ *Warning: DO NOT place any part of your body under the engine when it's supported only by a jack.*

4 Check the mountings to see if the rubber is cracked, hardened or separated from the metal plates. Sometimes the rubber will split right down the centre.
5 Check for relative movement between the mounting plates and the engine or body (use a large screwdriver or pry bar to attempt to move the mountings). If movement is noted, lower the engine and tighten the mounting fasteners.
6 Rubber preservative should be applied to the mountings to slow deterioration.

Renewal

7 Raise the vehicle and support it securely on axle stands (if not already done). Support the engine as described in paragraph 3.
8 To remove the right engine mounting, remove the two nuts from underneath, one bolt from above, and the upper section will separate from the engine bracket.
9 Remove the mounting-to-chassis nuts and detach the mounting.
10 To remove the rear engine mounting, pull the rubber plugs from the longitudinal chassis brace to access the two nuts.
11 To remove the front engine mounting, remove the two nuts retaining the insulator to the longitudinal chassis brace, then the three nuts retaining the insulator to the chassis.
12 Refitting is the reverse of removal. Use thread-locking compound on the mounting bolts/nuts and be sure to tighten them securely.

Chapter 2 Part B:
Engine removal and overhaul procedures

Contents

	Section number		Section number
Crankshaft – inspection	16	Engine overhaul – reassembly sequence	18
Crankshaft – refitting	20	Engine rebuilding alternatives	5
Crankshaft – removal	12	Engine removal – methods and precautions	3
Cylinder head – cleaning and inspection	8	General information	1
Cylinder head – disassembly	7	Initial start-up after overhaul	22
Cylinder head – reassembly	10	Main and connecting rod bearings – inspection	17
Engine – removal and refitting	4	Piston rings – refitting	19
Engine block – cleaning	13	Pistons/connecting rods – inspection	15
Engine block – inspection	14	Pistons/connecting rods – refitting	21
Engine overhaul – disassembly sequence	6	Pistons/connecting rods – removal	11
Engine overhaul – general information	2	Valves – servicing	9

Degrees of difficulty

Easy, suitable for novice with little experience

Fairly easy, suitable for beginner with some experience

Fairly difficult, suitable for competent DIY mechanic

Difficult, suitable for experienced DIY mechanic

Very difficult, suitable for expert DIY or professional

Specifications

General
Engine codes:
- 1.3 litre (1332 cc) non-VVT-i engine ... 4E-FE
- 1.4 litre (1398 cc) VVT-i engine ... 4ZZ-FE
- 1.6 litre (1587 cc) non-VVT-i engine ... 4A-FE
- 1.6 litre (1598 cc) VVT-i engine ... 3ZZ-FE

Cylinder head
Warpage limits:
- Block surface ... 0.05 mm
- Manifold surfaces ... 0.10 mm

Engine block
Block warpage limit ... 0.05 mm
Cylinder bore diameter (nominal):
- 1.3 litre 4E-FE engine ... 74.00 to 74.03 mm
- 1.4 litre 4ZZ-FE engine ... 79.00 to 79.013 mm
- 1.6 litre 4A-FE engine ... 81.00 to 81.03 mm
- 1.6 litre 3ZZ-FE engine ... 79.00 to 79.013 mm

Valves and related components
Valve stem diameter:
- Non-VVT-i engines:
  - Intake ... 5.970 to 5.985 mm
  - Exhaust ... 5.965 to 5.980 mm
- VVT-i engines:
  - Intake ... 5.470 to 5.485 mm
  - Exhaust ... 5.465 to 5.480 mm
Valve spring:
- Free length:
  - 1.3 litre 4E-FE engine ... 39.80 mm
  - 1.4 litre 4ZZ-FE engine ... 43.40 mm
  - 1.6 litre 4A-FE engine ... 38.57 mm
  - 1.6 litre 3ZZ-FE engine ... 43.40 mm

Crankshaft

Crankshaft endfloat:
  Standard:
    1.3 litre 4E-FE engine .... 0.02 to 0.20 mm
    1.4 litre 4ZZ-FE engine .... 0.04 to 0.24 mm
    1.6 litre 4A-FE engine .... 0.02 to 0.22 mm
    1.6 litre 3ZZ-FE engine .... 0.04 to 0.24 mm
  Service limit .... 0.30 mm
Thrust washer thickness:
  1.3 litre 4E-FE engine .... 2.440 to 2.490 mm
  1.4 litre 4ZZ-FE engine .... 2.430 to 2.480 mm
  1.6 litre 4A-FE engine .... 2.440 to 2.490 mm
  1.6 litre 3ZZ-FE engine .... 2.430 to 2.480 mm

Pistons and rings

Piston diameter:
  1.3 litre 4E-FE engine .... 73.869 to 73.889 mm
  1.4 litre 4ZZ-FE engine (at 29.8 mm from the piston crown) .... 78.917 to 78.927 mm
  1.6 litre 4A-FE engine .... 80.905 to 80.935 mm
  1.6 litre 3ZZ-FE engine (at 29.8 mm from the piston crown) .... 78.955 to 78.965 mm
Piston ring end gap: **Standard**   **Service limit**
  1.3 litre 4E-FE engine:
    No 1 (top) compression ring .... 0.26 to 0.36 mm   0.95 mm
    No 2 (middle) compression ring .... 0.41 to 0.51 mm   1.10 mm
    Oil ring .... 0.13 to 0.38 mm   0.98 mm
  1.4 litre 4ZZ-FE engine:
    No 1 (top) compression ring: .... 0.02 to 0.07 mm   1.05 mm
    No 2 (middle) compression ring .... 0.03 to 0.07 mm   1.20 mm
    Oil ring: .... 0.04 to 0.12 mm   1.05 mm
  1.6 litre 4A-FE engine:
    No 1 (top) compression ring .... 0.25 to 0.45 mm   1.05 mm
    No 2 (middle) compression ring .... 0.35 to 0.60 mm   1.20 mm
    Oil ring .... 0.10 to 0.50 mm   1.10 mm
  1.6 litre 3ZZ-FE engine:
    No 1 (top) compression ring .... 0.02 to 0.07 mm   1.05 mm
    No 2 (middle) compression ring .... 0.03 to 0.07 mm   1.20 mm
    Oil ring .... 0.04 to 0.12 mm   1.05 mm

Torque wrench settings

Refer to Part A for torque specifications.

---

1 General information

Included in this portion of Chapter 2 are the general overhaul procedures for the cylinder head and internal engine components.

The information ranges from advice concerning preparation for an overhaul and the purchase of new parts to detailed, step-by-step procedures covering removal and installation of internal engine components and the inspection of parts.

The following Sections have been written based on the assumption that the engine has been removed from the vehicle. For information concerning in-vehicle engine repair, as well as removal and installation of the external components necessary for the overhaul, see Chapter 2A and Section 8 of this Chapter.

The Specifications included in this Part are only those necessary for the inspection and overhaul procedures which follow. Refer to Part A for additional Specifications.

2 Engine overhaul – general information

1 It is not always easy to determine when, or if, an engine should be completely overhauled, as a number of factors must be considered.
2 High mileage is not necessarily an indication that an overhaul is needed, while low mileage does not preclude the need for an overhaul. Frequency of servicing is probably the most important consideration. An engine which has had regular and frequent oil and filter changes, as well as other required maintenance, should give many thousands of miles of reliable service. Conversely, a neglected engine may require an overhaul very early in its life.
3 Excessive oil consumption is an indication that piston rings, valve seals and/or valve guides are in need of attention. Make sure that oil leaks are not responsible before deciding that the rings and/or guides are worn. Perform a compression test, as described in Part A of this Chapter, to determine the likely cause of the problem.

4 Check the oil pressure with a gauge fitted in place of the oil pressure switch, and compare it with that specified. If it is extremely low, the main and big-end bearings, and/or the oil pump, are probably worn out.
5 Loss of power, rough running, knocking or metallic engine noises, excessive valve gear noise, and high fuel consumption may also point to the need for an overhaul, especially if they are all present at the same time. If a complete service does not remedy the situation, major mechanical work is the only solution.
6 A full engine overhaul involves restoring all internal parts to the specification of a new engine. During a complete overhaul, the pistons and the piston rings are renewed, and the cylinder bores are reconditioned. New main and big-end bearings are generally fitted; if necessary, the crankshaft may be reground, to compensate for wear in the journals. The valves are also serviced as well, since they are usually in less-than-perfect condition at this point. Always pay careful attention to the condition of the oil pump when overhauling the engine, and renew it if there is any doubt as to

Engine removal and overhaul procedures 2B•3

its serviceability. The end result should be an as-new engine that will give many trouble-free miles.

7 Critical cooling system components such as the hoses, thermostat and water pump should be renewed when an engine is overhauled. The radiator should be checked carefully, to ensure that it is not clogged or leaking. Also, it is a good idea to renew the oil pump whenever the engine is overhauled.

8 Before beginning the engine overhaul, read through the entire procedure, to familiarise yourself with the scope and requirements of the job. Overhauling an engine is not difficult if you follow carefully all of the instructions, have the necessary tools and equipment, and pay close attention to all specifications. It can, however, be time-consuming. Plan on the car being off the road for a minimum of two weeks, especially if parts must be taken to an engineering works for repair or reconditioning. Check on the availability of parts and make sure that any necessary special tools and equipment are obtained in advance. Most work can be done with typical hand tools, although a number of precision measuring tools are required for inspecting parts to determine if they must be renewed. Often the engineering works will handle the inspection of parts and offer advice concerning reconditioning and renewal.

9 Always wait until the engine has been completely dismantled, and until all components (especially the cylinder block/crankcase and the crankshaft) have been inspected, before deciding what service and repair operations must be performed by an engineering works. The condition of these components will be the major factor to consider when determining whether to overhaul the original engine, or to buy a reconditioned unit. Do not, therefore, purchase parts or have overhaul work done on other components until they have been thoroughly inspected. As a general rule, time is the primary cost of an overhaul, so it does not pay to fit worn or sub-standard parts.

10 As a final note, to ensure maximum life and minimum trouble from a reconditioned engine, everything must be assembled with care, in a spotlessly-clean environment.

3 Engine removal – methods and precautions

1 If you have decided that the engine must be removed for overhaul or major repair work, several preliminary steps should be taken.

2 Locating a suitable place to work is extremely important. Adequate work space, along with storage space for the car, will be needed. If a workshop or garage is not available, at the very least, a flat, level, clean work surface is required.

3 Cleaning the engine compartment and engine/transmission before beginning the removal procedure will help keep tools clean and organised.

4 An engine hoist or A-frame will also be necessary. Make sure the equipment is rated in excess of the weight of the engine. Safety is of primary importance, considering the potential hazards involved in lifting the engine/transmission out of the car.

5 If this is the first time you have removed an engine, an assistant should ideally be available. Advice and aid from someone more experienced would also be helpful. There are many instances when one person cannot simultaneously perform all of the operations required when lifting the engine out of the vehicle.

6 Plan the operation ahead of time. Before starting work, arrange for the hire of or obtain all of the tools and equipment you will need. Some of the equipment necessary to perform engine/transmission removal and installation safely and with relative ease (in addition to an engine hoist) is as follows: a heavy duty trolley jack, complete sets of spanners and sockets (see *Tools and working facilities*), wooden blocks, and plenty of rags and cleaning solvent for mopping-up spilled oil, coolant and fuel. If the hoist must be hired, make sure that you arrange for it in advance, and perform all of the operations possible without it beforehand. This will save you money and time.

7 Plan for the car to be out of use for quite a while. An engineering works will be required to perform some of the work which the do-it-yourselfer cannot accomplish without special equipment. These places often have a busy schedule, so it would be a good idea to consult them before removing the engine, in order to accurately estimate the amount of time required to rebuild or repair components that may need work.

8 Always be extremely careful when removing and refitting the engine/transmission. Serious injury can result from careless actions. Plan ahead and take your time, and a job of this nature, although major, can be accomplished successfully.

Note: *Such is the complexity of the power unit arrangement on these vehicles, and the variations that may be encountered according to model and optional equipment fitted, that the following should be regarded as a guide to*

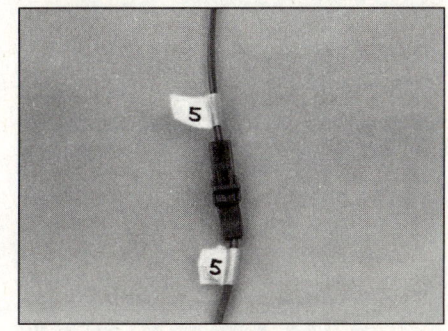

4.6 Label both ends of each wire and hose before disconnecting it

the work involved, rather than a step-by-step procedure. Where differences are encountered, or additional component disconnection or removal is necessary, make notes of the work involved as an aid to refitting.

4 Engine – removal and refitting

Note: *Read through the entire Section before beginning this procedure. The factory recommends removing the engine and transmission from the top as a unit, then separating the engine from the transmission on the workshop floor. If the transmission is not being serviced, it is possible to leave the transmission in the vehicle and remove the engine from the top by itself, by removing the crankshaft pulley and tilting up the timing belt/chain end of the engine for clearance.*

⚠ **Warning: These models are equipped with airbags. The airbag is armed and can deploy (inflate) anytime the battery is connected. To prevent accidental deployment (and possible injury), turn the ignition key to LOCK and disconnect the negative battery cable whenever working near airbag components. After the battery is disconnected, wait at least two minutes before beginning work (the system has a back-up capacitor that must fully discharge). For more information see Chapter 12.**

Removal

1 Relieve the fuel system pressure (see Chapter 4A).
2 Remove the battery as described in Chapter 5A, then lift out the plastic battery tray.
3 Remove the bonnet as described in Chapter 11.
4 Remove the air cleaner assembly (see Chapter 4A).
5 Raise the vehicle and support it securely on axle stands. Drain the cooling system and engine oil and remove the drivebelts (see Chapter 1).
6 Clearly label, then disconnect, all vacuum lines, coolant and emissions hoses, wiring harness connectors, earth straps and fuel lines. Masking tape and/or a touch up paint applicator work well for marking items **(see illustration)**. Take photos or sketch the locations of components and brackets.
7 Remove the windscreen washer tank and coolant reservoir tank.
8 Remove the cooling fan(s) and radiator (see Chapter 3).
9 Disconnect the heater hoses.
10 Release the residual fuel pressure in the tank by removing the fuel tank cap, then detach the fuel lines connecting the engine to the chassis. Plug or cap all open fittings.
11 Disconnect the accelerator cable, transmission Throttle Valve (TV) linkage and

speed control cable, if equipped, from the engine.
12 Refer Chapter 4A and remove the intake and exhaust manifolds.
13 On power steering-equipped vehicles, unbolt the power steering pump. If clearance allows, tie the pump aside without disconnecting the hoses. If necessary, remove the pump (see Chapter 10).
14 On air conditioned models, unbolt the compressor and set it aside. Do not disconnect the refrigerant hoses. **Note:** *Don't let the compressor hang on the hoses.*
15 Attach a lifting sling to the engine. Position a hoist and connect the sling to it. Take up the slack until there is slight tension on the hoist.
16 Refer to Chapter 8 and remove the driveshafts.
17 Remove the auxiliary drivebelt(s), coolant pump pulley and crankshaft pulley.
18 On automatic transmission-equipped models, pry out the plastic torque converter dust shield from the lower bellhousing. Remove the torque converter-to-driveplate fasteners (see Chapter 7B) and push the converter back slightly into the bellhousing.
19 Remove the engine-to-transmission bolts and separate the engine from the transmission (see Chapter 7A or 7B). The torque converter should remain in the transmission. **Note:** *If the transmission is to be removed at the same time, the left-side engine mounting should be removed, along with any wires, cables or hoses connected to the transmission. The engine-to-transmission bolts should remain in place at this time.*
20 Recheck to be sure nothing except the mountings are still connecting the engine to the vehicle or to the transmission. Disconnect and label anything still remaining.
21 Support the transmission with a trolley jack. Place a block of wood on the jack head to prevent damage to the transmission. Remove the bolts from the engine mountings, leaving those attached to the transmission in place.

⚠️ **Warning:** *Do not place any part of your body under the engine/transmission when its supported only by a hoist or other lifting device.*

22 Slowly lift the engine (or engine/transmission) out of the vehicle **(see illustration)**. It may be necessary to lever the mountings away from the frame brackets.
Note: *When removing the engine from a manual transmission-equipped vehicle and the transmission is to remain in the vehicle, you may have to use the jack supporting the transmission to tilt the transmission enough to allow the engine to be angled out of the vehicle.*
23 Move the engine away from the vehicle and carefully lower the hoist until the engine can be set on the floor; or remove the flywheel/driveplate and mount the engine on an engine stand. **Note:** *On automatic transmission-equipped models, mark the front and rear spacer plates (where fitted) and keep them with the driveplate.*

Refitting

24 Check the engine/transmission mountings. If they're worn or damaged, renew them.
25 On manual transmission-equipped models, inspect the clutch components (see Chapter 6) and on automatic models inspect the converter seal and bushing.
26 On automatic transmission-equipped models, apply a dab of grease to the nose of the converter.
27 Carefully guide the transmission into place, following the procedure outlined in Chapter 7A or 7B.
Caution: Do not use the bolts to force the engine and transmission into alignment. They may crack or damage major components.
28 Install the engine-to-transmission bolts and tighten them to the torque listed in the Chapter 7A or 7B Specifications.
29 Attach the hoist to the engine and carefully lower the engine/transmission assembly into the engine compartment. **Note:** *If the engine was removed with the transmission remaining in the car, lower the engine into the car until an assistant can help you line up the dowel pins on the block with the transmission. Some twisting and angling of the engine and/or the transmission will be necessary to secure proper alignment of the two.*
30 Install the mounting bolts and tighten them securely.
31 Reinstall the remaining components and fasteners in the reverse order of removal.
32 Add coolant, oil, power steering and transmission fluids as needed (see Chapter 1).
33 Run the engine and check for proper operation and leaks. Shut off the engine and recheck the fluid levels.

5 Engine rebuilding alternatives

The do-it-yourselfer is faced with a number of options when performing an engine overhaul. The decision to renew the engine block, piston/connecting rod assemblies and crankshaft depends on a number of factors, with the number one consideration being the condition of the block. Other considerations are cost, access to machine shop facilities, parts availability, time required to complete the project and the extent of prior mechanical experience on the part of the do-it-yourselfer.
Some of the rebuilding alternatives include:

Individual parts

If the inspection procedures reveal that the engine block and most engine components are in re-usable condition, purchasing individual parts may be the most economical alternative. The block, crankshaft and piston/connecting rod assemblies should all be inspected carefully. Even if the block shows little wear, the cylinder bores should be surface honed.

Short engine

A short engine consists of an engine block with a crankshaft and piston/connecting rod assemblies already installed. All new bearings are incorporated and all clearances will be correct. The existing camshafts, valve train components, cylinder head and external parts can be bolted to the short engine with little or no machine shop work necessary.

Reconditioned engine

A reconditioned engine usually consists of a short engine plus an oil pump, oil pan, cylinder head, valve cover, camshaft and valve train components, timing sprockets and timing belt covers. All components are installed with new bearings, seals and gaskets incorporated throughout. The installation of manifolds and external parts is all that's necessary.
Give careful thought to which alternative is best for you and discuss the situation with local automotive machine shops, auto parts dealers and experienced rebuilders before ordering or purchasing new parts.

6 Engine overhaul – disassembly sequence

1 It's much easier to disassemble and work on the engine if it's mounted on a portable engine stand. A stand can often be rented quite cheaply from an equipment rental yard. Before the engine is mounted on a stand, the flywheel/driveplate and oil seal retainer should be removed from the engine.
2 If a stand isn't available, it's possible to disassemble the engine with it blocked up on the floor. Be extra careful not to tip or drop the engine when working without a stand.
3 If you're going to obtain a reconditioned engine, all external components must come off first, to be transferred to the new engine, just as they will if you're doing a complete engine overhaul yourself. These include:
Alternator and brackets.
Emissions control components.
Thermostat and housing cover.
Water pump and remaining cooling system components.

4.22 Lift the engine out of the vehicle

Engine removal and overhaul procedures 2B•5

EFI components.
Intake/exhaust manifolds.
Oil filter.
Engine mountings.
Clutch and flywheel/driveplate.
Engine end plate.

Note: *When removing the external components from the engine, pay close attention to details that may be helpful or important during installation. Note the installed position of gaskets, seals, spacers, pins, brackets, washers, bolts and other small items.*

4 If you're obtaining a short engine, which consists of the engine block, crankshaft, pistons and connecting rods all assembled, then the cylinder head, oil sump and oil pump will have to be removed as well from your engine. See *Engine rebuilding alternatives* for additional information regarding the different possibilities to be considered.

5 If you're planning a complete overhaul, the engine must be disassembled and the internal components removed in the following order.

Intake and exhaust manifolds.
Cylinder head cover.
Timing belt/chain covers.
Timing belt/chain and sprockets.
Cylinder head.
Oil sump.
Oil pump.
Piston/connecting rod assemblies.
Crankshaft oil seal retainer.
Crankshaft and main bearings.

7 Cylinder head – disassembly

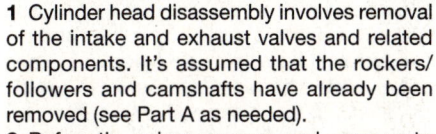

1 Cylinder head disassembly involves removal of the intake and exhaust valves and related components. It's assumed that the rockers/followers and camshafts have already been removed (see Part A as needed).
2 Before the valves are removed, arrange to label and store them, along with their related components, so they can be kept separate and reinstalled in the same valve guides they are removed from **(see illustration)**.
3 Compress the springs on the first valve with a spring compressor and remove the collets **(see illustration)**. Carefully release the valve spring compressor and remove the retainer, the spring and the spring seat (if used).

Caution: *Be very careful not to nick or otherwise damage the follower bores when compressing the valve springs.*

4 Pull the valve out of the head, then remove the oil seal from the guide. If the valve binds in the guide (won't pull through), push it back into the head and deburr the area around the keeper groove with a fine file or whetstone.
5 Repeat the procedure for the remaining valves. Remember to keep all the parts for each valve together so they can be reinstalled in the same locations.
6 Once the valves and related components have been removed and stored in an organised

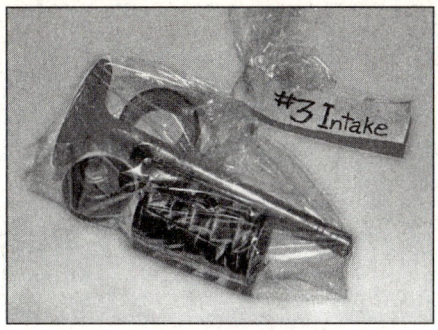

7.2 A small plastic bag, with an appropriate label, can be used to store the valve components

manner, the head should be thoroughly cleaned and inspected. If a complete engine overhaul is being done, finish the engine disassembly procedures before beginning the cylinder head cleaning and inspection process.

8 Cylinder head – cleaning and inspection

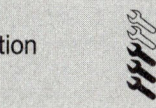

1 Thorough cleaning of the cylinder head and related valve train components, followed by a detailed inspection, will enable you to decide how much valve service work must be done during the engine overhaul. **Note:** *If the engine was severely overheated, the cylinder head is probably warped (see paragraph 12).*

Cleaning

2 Scrape all traces of old gasket material and sealing compound off the head gasket, intake manifold and exhaust manifold sealing surfaces. Be very careful not to gouge the cylinder head. Special gasket removal solvents that soften gaskets and make removal much easier are available at automotive accessory/parts retailers.
3 Remove all built-up scale from the coolant passages.
4 Run a stiff wire brush through the various holes to remove deposits that may have formed in them. If there are heavy rust deposits in the water passages, the bare head should be professionally cleaned.
5 Run an appropriate-size tap into each of the threaded holes to remove corrosion and thread sealant that may be present. If compressed air is available, use it to clear the holes of debris produced by this operation.

⚠ **Warning:** *Wear eye protection when using compressed air.*

6 Clean the exhaust and intake manifold stud threads with a wire brush.
7 Clean the cylinder head with solvent and dry it thoroughly. Compressed air will speed the drying process and ensure that all holes and recessed areas are clean. **Note:** *Decarbonising chemicals are available and may prove very useful when cleaning cylinder heads and valve*

7.3 Compress the spring until the collets can be removed with a small magnetic screwdriver or thin-nosed pliers

train components. They are very caustic and should be used with caution. Be sure to follow the instructions on the container.

8 Clean the followers with solvent and dry them thoroughly. Compressed air will speed the drying process and can be used to clean out the oil passages. Don't mix them up during the cleaning process; keep them in a box with numbered compartments.
9 Clean all the valve springs, spring seats, collets and retainers with solvent and dry them thoroughly. Work on the components from one valve at a time to avoid mixing up the parts.
10 Scrape off any heavy deposits that may have formed on the valves, then use a motorised wire brush to remove deposits from the valve heads and stems. Again, make sure the valves don't get mixed up.

Inspection

Note: *Be sure to perform all of the following inspection procedures before concluding that machine shop work is required. Make a list of the items that need attention. The inspection procedures for the followers and camshafts can be found in Part A.*

Cylinder head

11 Inspect the head very carefully for cracks, evidence of coolant leakage and other damage. If cracks are found, check with an automotive machine workshop concerning repair. If repair isn't possible, a new cylinder head should be obtained.
12 Using a straight-edge and feeler gauge, check the head gasket mating surface for warpage **(see illustration)**. If the warpage

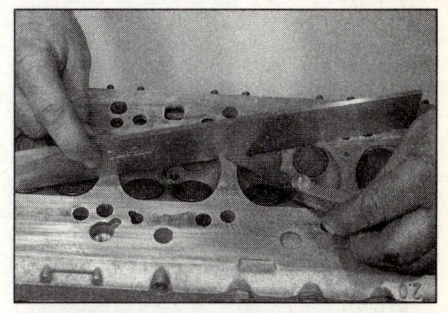

8.12 Check the cylinder head gasket surface for warpage by trying to slip a feeler gauge under the straight-edge

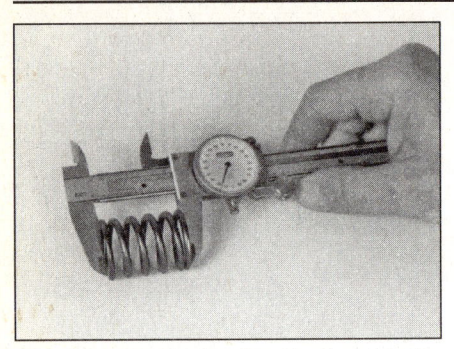

2B•6 Engine removal and overhaul procedures

8.17 Measure the free length of each valve spring

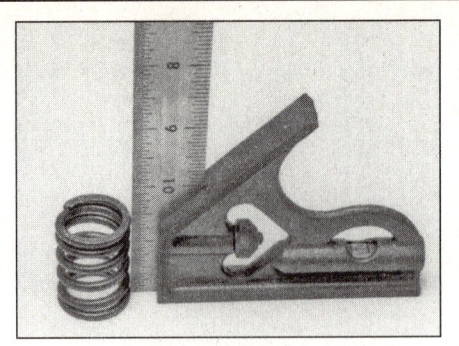

8.18 Check each valve spring for squareness

exceeds the limit found in this Chapter's Specifications, it can be resurfaced at an automotive machining workshop.

13 Examine the valve seats in each of the combustion chambers. If they're pitted, cracked or burned, the head will require valve service that's beyond the scope of the home mechanic.

14 If in any doubt as to the condition of the cylinder head, have it inspected by an automotive engine overhaul specialist.

Valves

15 Carefully inspect each valve face for uneven wear, deformation, cracks, pits and burned areas. Check the valve stem for scuffing and galling and the neck for cracks. Rotate the valve and check for any obvious indication that it's bent. Look for pits and excessive wear on the end of the stem. The presence of any of these conditions indicates the need for valve service by an automotive machine shop.

16 If in any doubt as to the condition of the valves, have them inspected by an automotive engine overhaul specialist.

Valve components

17 Check each valve spring for wear (on the ends) and pits. Measure the free length and compare it to this Chapter's Specifications **(see illustration)**. Any springs that are shorter than specified have sagged and should not be re-used.

18 Stand each spring on a flat surface and check it for squareness **(see illustration)**. If any of the springs are distorted or sagged, renew all of them.

19 Check the spring seats and collets for obvious wear and cracks. Any questionable parts should be renewed, as extensive damage will occur if they fail during engine operation.

20 Any damaged or excessively worn parts must be renewed.

21 If the inspection process indicates that the valve components are in generally poor condition and worn beyond the limits specified, which is usually the case in an engine that's being overhauled, reassemble the valves in the cylinder head and refer to Section 9 for valve servicing recommendations.

9 Valves – servicing

1 Because of the complex nature of the job and the special tools and equipment needed, servicing of the valves, the valve seats and the valve guides, commonly known as a valve job, should be done by a professional.

2 The home mechanic can remove and disassemble the head, do the initial cleaning and inspection, then reassemble and deliver them to an automotive engine overhaul specialist for the actual service work. Doing the inspection will enable you to see what condition the head and valve train components are in and will ensure that you know what work and new parts are required when dealing with the overhaul specialist.

3 The engine overhaul specialist will remove the valves and springs, recondition or renew the valves and valve seats, recondition the valve guides, check and renew the valve springs, spring retainers and collets (as necessary), renew the valve seals, reassemble the valve components and make sure the installed spring height is correct. The cylinder head gasket surface will also be resurfaced if it's warped.

4 After the valve job has been performed by a professional, the head will be in like new condition. When the head is returned, be sure to clean it again before installation on the engine to remove any metal particles and abrasive grit that may still be present from the valve service or head resurfacing operations. Use compressed air, if available, to blow out all the oil holes and passages.

10 Cylinder head – reassembly

1 Regardless of whether or not the head was sent for reconditioning, make sure it's clean before beginning reassembly. Note that there are several small core plugs in the head. These should be renewed whenever the engine is overhauled or the cylinder head is reconditioned (see Section 13 for renewal procedure).

2 If the head was sent out for valve servicing, the valves and related components will already be in place.

3 Install new seals on each of the valve guides. On non-VVT-i engines (4E-FE and 4A-FE) the intake seal lip is grey and the exhaust seal lip is black, whilst on VVT-i engines (4ZZ-FE and 3ZZ-FE) the intake seal *body* is grey and the exhaust seal *body* is black. **Note:** *Intake and exhaust valves require different seals – DO NOT mix them up.* Gently tap each intake valve seal into place until it's seated on the guide **(see illustration)**.

Caution: Don't hammer on the valve seals once they're seated or you may damage them. Don't twist or cock the seals during installation or they won't seat properly on the valve stems.

4 Beginning at one end of the head, lubricate and install the first valve. Apply clean engine oil to the valve stem.

5 Drop the spring seat or shim(s) over the valve guide and set the valve spring and retainer in place.

6 Compress the springs with a valve spring compressor and carefully install the collets in the upper groove, then slowly release the compressor and make sure the collets seat properly. Apply a small dab of grease to each collet to hold it in place if necessary **(see illustration)**.

7 Repeat the procedure for the remaining valves. Be sure to return the components to their original locations – don't mix them up.

10.3 Tap the valve stem seals (arrowed) into place with a deep socket and hammer

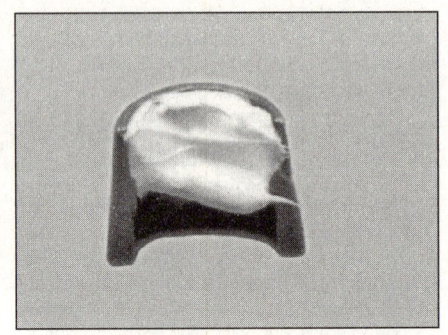

10.6 The small valve stem collets are easier to position when coated with grease

Engine removal and overhaul procedures 2B•7

11.1 A ridge reamer is required to remove the ridge from the top of each cylinder

11.3 Do not confuse these markings as rod numbers; they are bearing size identifications

11.5 Slip sections of hose over the rod bolts before removing the pistons

11 Pistons/connecting rods – removal

Note: *Prior to removing the piston/connecting rod assemblies, remove the cylinder head, the oil sump and the oil pump pick-up tube by referring to the appropriate Sections in Chapter 2A.*

1 Use your fingernail to feel if a ridge has formed at the upper limit of ring travel (about 8 mm down from the top of each cylinder). If carbon deposits or cylinder wear have produced ridges, they must be completely removed with a special tool **(see illustration)**. Follow the manufacturer's instructions provided with the tool. Failure to remove the ridges before attempting to remove the piston/connecting rod assemblies may result in piston damage.

2 After the cylinder ridges have been removed, turn the engine upside-down so the crankshaft is facing up.

3 Check the connecting rods and caps for identification marks. If they aren't plainly marked, use a small centre punch to make the appropriate number of indentations on each rod and cap (1, 2, 3, etc, depending on the engine type and cylinder they're associated with) **(see illustration)**.

4 Loosen each of the connecting rod cap nuts/bolts 1/2-turn at a time until they can be removed by hand. Remove the number one connecting rod cap and bearing shell. Don't drop the bearing shell out of the cap.

5 Slip a short length of plastic or rubber hose over each connecting rod cap bolt (where applicable) to protect the crankshaft journal and cylinder wall as the piston is removed **(see illustration)**.

6 Remove the bearing shell and push the connecting rod/piston assembly out through the top of the engine. Use a wooden hammer handle to push on the upper bearing surface in the connecting rod. If resistance is felt, double-check to make sure that all of the ridge was removed from the cylinder.

7 Repeat the procedure for the remaining cylinders. **Note:** *Turn the crankshaft as needed to put the rod to be removed close to parallel with the cylinder bore, ie, don't try to drive it out while at a large angle to the bore.*

8 After removal, reassemble the connecting rod caps and bearing shells in their respective connecting rods and install the cap nuts/bolts finger tight. Leaving the old bearing shells in place until reassembly will help prevent the connecting rod bearing surfaces from being accidentally nicked or gouged.

9 Don't separate the pistons from the connecting rods (see Section 15 for additional information).

12 Crankshaft – removal

Note: *The crankshaft can be removed only after the engine has been removed from the vehicle. It's assumed that the flywheel or driveplate, crankshaft sprocket, timing belt/chain, oil sump, oil pick-up tube, oil pump and piston/connecting rod assemblies have already been removed. The main oil seal and housing (where applicable) must be removed from the block before proceeding with crankshaft removal.*

1 Before the crankshaft is removed, check the endfloat. Mount a dial indicator with the stem in line with the crankshaft throws **(see illustration)**.

2 Push the crankshaft fully one way and zero the dial indicator. Next, lever the crankshaft the other way as far as possible and check the reading on the dial indicator. The distance that it moves is the endfloat. If it's greater than specified, check the crankshaft thrust surfaces for wear. If no wear is evident, new thrustwashers should correct the endfloat.

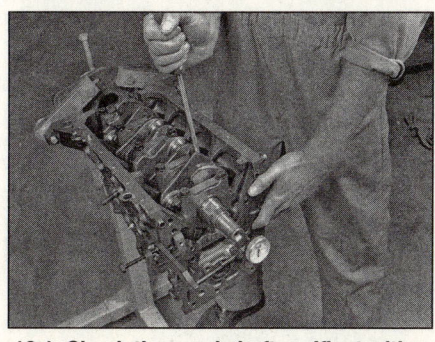

12.1 Check the crankshaft endfloat with a dial indicator . . .

3 If a dial indicator isn't available, feeler gauges can be used. Gently pry or push the crankshaft fully one way. Slip feeler gauges between the crankshaft and the face of the number 3 (thrust) main bearing to determine the clearance **(see illustration)**.

Non-VVT-i engines

4 Check the main bearing caps to see if they're marked to indicate their locations. They should be numbered consecutively from the right of the engine to the left. If they aren't, mark them with a centre punch. Main bearing caps generally have a cast-in arrow, which points to the right of the engine. Loosen the main bearing cap bolts 1/4-turn at a time each, in the reverse order of the recommended tightening sequence **(see illustration 20.9)**, until they can be removed by hand.

5 Gently tap the caps with a soft-face hammer, then separate them from the engine block. If necessary, use the bolts as levers to remove the caps. Try not to drop the bearing shells if they come out with the caps.

VVT-i engines

6 Working is the reverse of the tightening sequence **(see illustration 20.12)**, gradually and evenly slacken and remove the bolts securing the main bearing ladder to the engine block.

7 Use a flat-bladed screwdriver to gently prise the main bearing ladder from the engine block, at the cast-in leverage points. Ensure the lower bearing shells stay in their original positions in the bearing ladder.

12.3 . . . or a feeler gauge

2B•8 Engine removal and overhaul procedures

13.1a Use a hammer and punch to knock the core plugs sideways in their bores

13.1b Pull the core plugs from the block with pliers

All engines

8 Carefully lift the crankshaft out of the engine. It may be a good idea to have an assistant available, since the crankshaft is quite heavy. With the bearing shells in place in the engine block and main bearing caps or cap assembly, return the caps to their respective locations on the engine block and tighten the bolts finger tight.

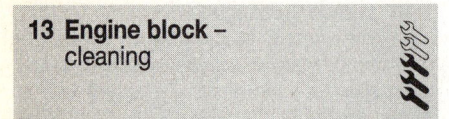

13 Engine block – cleaning

Caution: The core plugs may be difficult or impossible to retrieve if they're driven completely into the block coolant passages.

1 Using the blunt end of a punch, tap in on the outer edge of the core plug to turn the plug sideways in the bore. Then using pliers, pull the core plug from the engine block **(see illustrations)**.
2 Using a gasket scraper, remove all traces of gasket material from the engine block. Be very careful not to nick or gouge the gasket sealing surfaces.
3 Remove the main bearing caps or cap assembly and separate the bearing shells from the caps and the engine block. Tag the bearings, indicating which cylinder they were removed from and whether they were in the cap or the block, then set them aside.
4 Remove all of the threaded oil gallery plugs from the block. The plugs are usually very tight – they may have to be drilled out and the holes retapped. Use new plugs when the engine is reassembled.
5 If the engine is extremely dirty, it should be steam cleaned.
6 After the block is returned, clean all oil holes and oil galleries one more time. Brushes specifically designed for this purpose are available at most automotive accessory retailers. Flush the passages with warm water until the water runs clear, dry the block thoroughly and wipe all machined surfaces with a light, rust preventive oil. If you have access to compressed air, use it to speed the drying process and to blow out all the oil holes and galleries.

⚠ **Warning: Wear eye protection when using compressed air.**

7 If the block isn't extremely dirty or sludged up, you can do an adequate cleaning job with hot soapy water and a stiff brush. Take plenty of time and do a thorough job. Regardless of the cleaning method used, be sure to clean all oil holes and galleries very thoroughly, dry the block completely and coat all machined surfaces with light oil.
8 The threaded holes in the block must be clean to ensure accurate torque readings during reassembly. Run the proper size tap into each of the holes to remove rust, corrosion, thread sealant or sludge and restore damaged threads **(see illustration)**. If possible, use compressed air to clear the holes of debris produced by this operation. Now is a good time to clean the threads on the head bolts and the main bearing cap bolts as well.
9 Reinstall the main bearing caps and tighten the bolts finger tight.
10 After coating the sealing surfaces of the new core plugs with sealant, install them in the engine block **(see illustration)**. Make sure they're driven in straight and seated properly or leakage could result. Special tools are available for this purpose, but a large socket, with an outside diameter that will just slip into the core plug, a 1/2-inch drive extension and a hammer will work just as well.
11 Apply non-hardening sealant to the new oil gallery plugs and thread them into the holes in the block. Make sure they're tightened securely.
12 If the engine isn't going to be reassembled right away, cover it with a large plastic bag to keep it clean.

14 Engine block – inspection

1 Before the block is inspected, it should be cleaned as described in Section 13.
2 Visually check the block for cracks, rust and corrosion. Look for stripped threads in the threaded holes. It's also a good idea to have the block checked for hidden cracks by an engine overhaul specialist that has the equipment to do this type of work, especially if the vehicle had a history of overheating or using coolant. If defects are found, have the block repaired, if possible, or renewed.
3 If in any doubt as to the condition of the cylinder block, have it inspected and measured by an engine reconditioning specialist. If the bores are worn or damaged, they will be able to carry out any necessary reboring, and supply appropriate oversized pistons, etc.

15 Pistons/connecting rods – inspection

1 Before the inspection process can be carried out, the piston/connecting rod assemblies must be cleaned and the original piston rings removed from the pistons. **Note:** *Always use new piston rings when the engine is reassembled.*
2 Carefully expand the old rings over the top of the pistons. The use of two or three

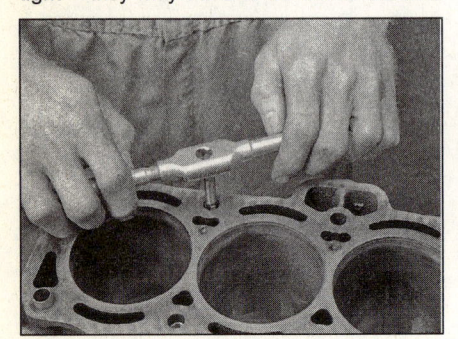

13.8 All bolt holes in the block should be cleaned and restored with a tap

13.10 A large socket can be used to drive the new core plugs into the bores

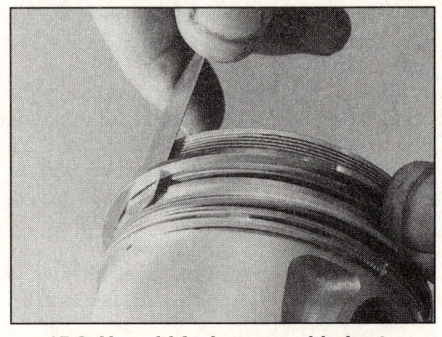

15.2 Use old feeler gauge blades to carefully expand the piston rings

Engine removal and overhaul procedures 2B•9

old feeler blades will be helpful in preventing the rings dropping into empty grooves **(see illustration)**. Be careful not to scratch the piston with the ends of the ring. The rings are brittle, and will snap if they are spread too far. They are also very sharp – protect your hands and fingers.

3 Scrape all traces of carbon from the top of the piston. A hand-held wire brush or a piece of fine emery cloth can be used once the majority of the deposits have been scraped away. Do not, under any circumstances, use a wire brush mounted in a drill motor to remove deposits from the pistons. The piston material is soft and may be eroded away by the wire brush.

4 Use a piston ring groove-cleaning tool to remove carbon deposits from the ring grooves. If a tool isn't available, a piece broken off the old ring will do the job. Be very careful to remove only the carbon deposits – don't remove any metal and do not nick or scratch the sides of the ring grooves **(see illustrations)**.

5 Once the deposits have been removed, clean the piston/rod assemblies with solvent and dry them with compressed air (if available). Make sure the oil return holes in the back sides of the ring grooves and the oil hole in the lower end of each rod are clear.

6 If the pistons and cylinder walls aren't damaged or worn excessively, and if the engine block is not rebored, new pistons won't be necessary. Normal piston wear appears as even vertical wear on the piston thrust surfaces and slight looseness of the top ring in its groove. New piston rings, however, should always be used when an engine is rebuilt.

7 Carefully inspect each piston for cracks around the skirt, at the pin bosses and at the ring lands.

8 Look for scoring and scuffing on the thrust faces of the skirt, holes in the piston crown and burned areas at the edge of the crown. If the skirt is scored or scuffed, the engine may have been suffering from overheating and/or abnormal combustion, which caused excessively high operating temperatures. The cooling and lubrication systems should be checked thoroughly. A hole in the piston crown is an indication that abnormal combustion (pre-ignition) was occurring. Burned areas at the edge of the piston crown are usually evidence of spark knock (detonation). If any of the above problems exist, the causes must be corrected or the damage will occur again. The causes may include intake air leaks, incorrect air/fuel mixture, incorrect ignition timing and EGR system malfunctions.

9 Corrosion of the piston, in the form of small pits, indicates that coolant is leaking into the combustion chamber and/or the crankcase. Again, the cause must be corrected or the problem may persist in the rebuilt engine.

10 If in any doubt as to the condition of the pistons and connecting rods, have them inspected and measured by an engine

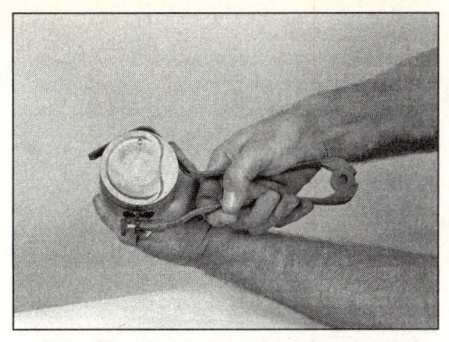

15.4a The ring grooves can be cleaned with a special tool, as shown here . . .

reconditioning specialist. If new parts are required, hw will be able to supply appropriate-sized pistons/rings, and rebore the cylinder block (where necessary).

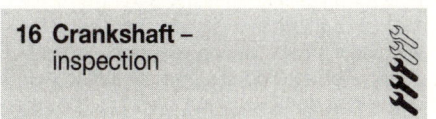

16 Crankshaft – inspection

1 Clean the crankshaft using paraffin or a suitable solvent, and dry it, preferably with compressed air if available. Be sure to clean the oil holes with a pipe cleaner or similar probe, to ensure that they are not obstructed.

> **Warning: Wear eye protection when using compressed air.**

2 Check the main and big-end bearing journals for uneven wear, scoring, pitting and cracking.

3 Big-end bearing wear is accompanied by distinct metallic knocking when the engine is running (particularly noticeable when the engine is pulling from low speed) and some loss of oil pressure.

4 Main bearing wear is accompanied by severe engine vibration and rumble – getting progressively worse as engine speed increases – and again by loss of oil pressure.

5 Check the bearing journal for roughness by running a finger lightly over the bearing surface. Any roughness (which will be accompanied by obvious bearing wear) indicates that the crankshaft requires regrinding (where possible) or renewal.

6 If the crankshaft has been reground, check for burrs around the crankshaft oil holes (the holes are usually chamfered, so burrs should not be a problem unless regrinding has been carried out carelessly). Remove any burrs with a fine file or scraper, and thoroughly clean the oil holes as described previously.

7 Have the crankshaft journals measured by an automotive engineering workshop. If the crankshaft is worn or damaged, they may be able to regrind the journals and supply suitable undersize bearing shells. If no undersize shells are available and the crankshaft has worn beyond the specified limits, it will have to be renewed. Consult your Toyota dealer or engine specialist for further information on parts availability.

15.4b . . . or a section of broken ring

17 Main and connecting rod bearings – inspection

Inspection

1 Even though the main and connecting rod bearings should be renewed during the engine overhaul, the old bearings should be retained for close examination, as they may reveal valuable information about the condition of the engine **(see illustration)**.

2 Bearing failure occurs because of lack of lubrication, the presence of dirt or other foreign particles, overloading the engine and corrosion. Regardless of the cause of bearing failure, it must be corrected before the engine is reassembled to prevent it from happening again.

3 When examining the bearings, remove them from the engine block, the main bearing caps, the connecting rods and the rod caps and lay them out on a clean surface in the same general position as their location in the engine. This will enable you to match any bearing problems with the corresponding crankshaft journal.

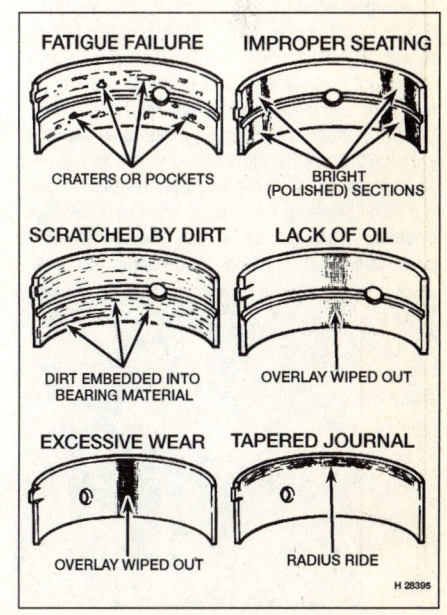

17.1 Typical bearing failures

2B•10 Engine removal and overhaul procedures

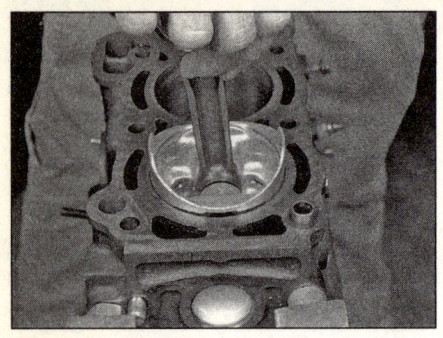

19.3 The ring must be square in the bore when checking the piston ring end gap

4 Dirt and other foreign particles get into the engine in a variety of ways. It may be left in the engine during assembly, or it may pass through filters or the PCV system. It may get into the oil, and from there into the bearings. Metal chips from machining operations and normal engine wear are often present. Abrasives are sometimes left in engine components after reconditioning, especially when parts are not thoroughly cleaned using the proper cleaning methods. Whatever the source, these foreign objects often end up embedded in the soft bearing material and are easily recognised. Large particles will not embed in the bearing and will score or gouge the bearing and journal. The best prevention for this cause of bearing failure is to clean all parts thoroughly and keep everything spotlessly clean during engine assembly. Frequent and regular engine oil and filter changes are also recommended.
5 Lack of lubrication (or lubrication breakdown) has a number of interrelated causes. Excessive heat (which thins the oil), overloading (which squeezes the oil from the bearing face) and oil leakage or throw off (from excessive bearing clearances, worn oil pump or high engine speeds) all contribute to lubrication breakdown. Blocked oil passages, which usually are the result of misaligned oil holes in a bearing shell, will also oil starve a bearing and destroy it. When lack of lubrication is the cause of bearing failure, the bearing material is wiped or extruded from the steel backing of the bearing. Temperatures may increase to the point where the steel backing turns blue from overheating.
6 Driving habits can have a definite effect on bearing life. Low speed operation in too high a gear (lugging the engine) puts very high loads on bearings, which tends to squeeze out the oil film. These loads cause the bearings to flex, which produces fine cracks in the bearing face (fatigue failure). Eventually the bearing material will loosen in pieces and tear away from the steel backing. Short trip driving leads to corrosion of bearings because insufficient engine heat is produced to drive off the condensed water and corrosive gases. These products collect in the engine oil, forming acid and sludge. As the oil is carried to the engine bearings, the acid attacks and corrodes the bearing material.
7 Incorrect bearing installation during engine assembly will lead to bearing failure as well. Tight-fitting bearings leave insufficient bearing oil clearance and will result in oil starvation. Dirt or foreign particles trapped behind a bearing insert results in high spots on the bearing which lead to failure.
8 *Do not* touch any shell's bearing surface with your fingers during reassembly; there is a risk of scratching the delicate surface, or of depositing particles of dirt on it.
9 As mentioned at the beginning of this Section, the bearing shells should be renewed as a matter of course during engine overhaul; to do otherwise is false economy.

18 Engine overhaul – reassembly sequence

1 Before beginning engine reassembly, make sure you have all the necessary new parts, gaskets and seals as well as the following items on hand:
   Common hand tools.
   A 1/2-inch drive torque wrench.
   Piston ring installation tool.
   Piston ring compressor.
   Short lengths of rubber or plastic hose to fit over connecting rod bolts.
   Feeler gauges.
   A fine-tooth file.
   New engine oil.
   Engine assembly lube or moly-base grease.
   Gasket sealant.
   Thread-locking compound.
2 In order to save time and avoid problems, engine reassembly must be done in the following general order:
   Piston rings (Part B).
   Crankshaft and main bearings (Part B).
   Piston/connecting rod assemblies (Part B).
   Main (crankshaft) oil seal (Part A).
   Cylinder head and followers (Part A).
   Camshafts (Part A).
   Oil pump (Part A).
   Timing belt/chain and sprockets (Part A).
   Timing covers (Part A).
   Oil pick-up (Part A).
   Oil sump (Part A).
   Intake and exhaust manifolds (Chapter 4A).
   Cylinder head cover (Part A).
   Flywheel/driveplate (Part A).

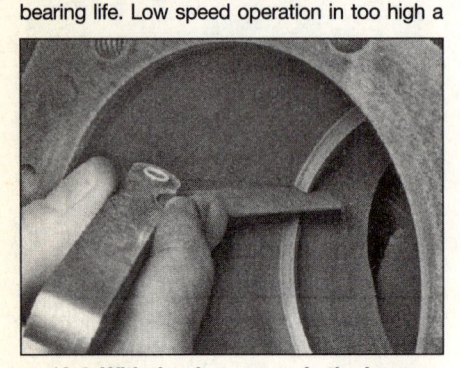

19.4 With the ring square in the bore, measure the end gap with a feeler gauge

19 Piston rings – refitting

1 Before installing the new piston rings, the ring end gaps must be checked.
2 Lay out the piston/connecting rod assemblies and the new ring sets so the ring sets will be matched with the same piston and cylinder during the end gap measurement and engine assembly.
3 Insert the top (number one) ring into the first cylinder and square it up with the cylinder walls by pushing it in with the top of the piston **(see illustration)**. The ring should be near the bottom of the cylinder, at the lower limit of ring travel.
4 To measure the end gap, slip feeler gauges between the ends of the ring until a gauge equal to the gap width is found **(see illustration)**. The feeler gauge should slide between the ring ends with a slight amount of drag. Compare the measurement to that found in this Chapter's Specifications. If the gap is larger or smaller than specified, double-check to make sure you have the correct rings before proceeding.
5 If the gap is too small (unlikely if genuine Toyota parts are used), it must be enlarged, or the ring ends may contact each other during engine operation, causing serious damage. Ideally, new piston rings providing the correct end gap should be fitted. As a last resort, the end gap can be increased by filing the ring ends very carefully with a fine file. Mount the file in a vice equipped with soft jaws, slip the ring over the file with the ends contacting the file face, and slowly move the ring to remove material from the ends. Take care, as piston rings are sharp, and are easily broken.
6 Excess end gap isn't critical unless it's greater than the service limit listed in this Chapter's Specifications. Again, double-check to make sure you have the correct rings for your engine.
7 Repeat the procedure for each ring that will be installed in the first cylinder and for each ring in the remaining cylinders. Remember to keep rings, pistons and cylinders matched up.
8 Once the ring end gaps have been checked/corrected, the rings can be installed on the pistons.
9 Fit the piston rings using the same technique as for removal. Fit the bottom (oil control) ring first, and work up. When fitting a three-piece oil control ring, first insert the expander, then fit the lower rail with its gap positioned 120° from the expander gap, then fit the upper rail with its gap positioned 120° from the lower rail. When fitting a two-piece oil control ring, first insert the expander, then fit the control ring with its gap positioned 180° from the expander gap. Ensure that the second compression ring is fitted the correct way up, with its identification mark (either a dot of paint or the word TOP stamped on the ring surface) at the top,

Engine removal and overhaul procedures 2B•11

19.9a Fit the spacer/expander in the oil control ring groove

19.9b Do not use a piston ring installation tool when installing the oil ring side rails

20.8a Rotate the thrustwasher into position with the oil grooves facing outwards

and the stepped surface at the bottom **(see illustrations)**. Arrange the gaps of the top and second compression rings 120° either side of the oil control ring gap, but make sure that none of the rings gaps are positioned over the gudgeon pin hole. **Note:** *Always follow any instructions supplied with the new piston ring sets – different manufacturers may specify different procedures. Do not mix up the top and second compression rings, as they have different cross-sections.*

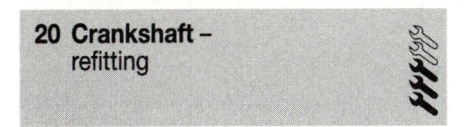

20 Crankshaft – refitting

1 Crankshaft installation is the first major step in engine reassembly. It's assumed at this point that the engine block and crankshaft have been cleaned, inspected and repaired or reconditioned.
2 Position the engine with the bottom facing up.
3 Remove the main bearing cap bolts and lift out the caps (where applicable). Lay the caps out in the proper order.
4 If they're still in place, remove the old bearing shells from the block and the main bearing caps/ladder. Wipe the main bearing surfaces of the block and caps/ladder with a clean, lint-free cloth. They must be kept spotlessly clean.
5 Clean the back sides of the new main bearing inserts and lay the bearing half with the oil groove in each main bearing saddle in the block. Lay the other bearing half from each bearing set in the corresponding main bearing cap/ladder. Make sure the tab on each bearing insert fits into the recess in the block or cap/ladder. Also, the oil holes in the block must line up with the oil holes in the bearing insert.
6 Clean the bearing faces in the block, then apply a thin, uniform layer of clean moly-based grease or engine assembly lube to each of the bearing surfaces. Coat the thrustwashers as well and position them either side of the No 3 bearing position with the oil grooves facing outwards.
7 Lubricate the crankshaft surfaces that contact the oil seals with moly-based grease, engine assembly lube or clean engine oil.

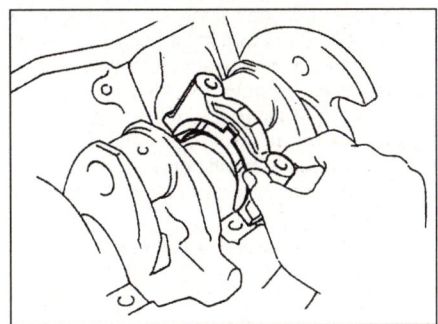

20.8b Fit the thrustwasher in the number three cap with the oil grooves facing out

Non-VVT-i engines

8 Make sure the crankshaft journals are clean, then lay the crankshaft back in place in the block. Clean the faces of the bearings in the caps, then apply lubricant to them. Install the caps in their respective positions with the arrows pointing toward the front of the engine. The tanged lower thrustwashers should be placed on the caps with their grooves OUT and the tangs fitting into the cap slots **(see illustrations)**.
9 Apply a light coat of oil to the bolt threads and the undersides of the bolt heads, then install them. Tighten all main bearing cap bolts to the correct torque, following the recommended sequence **(see illustration)**.

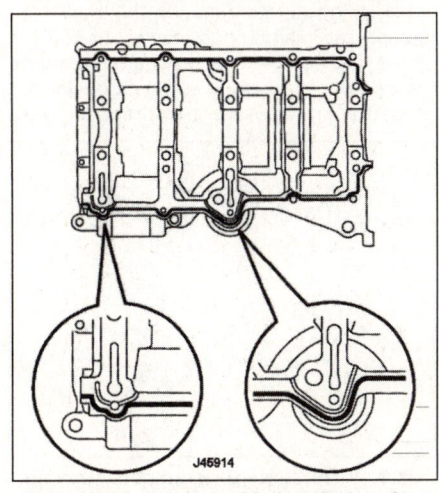

20.11 Apply a 2 mm wide bead of sealant to the main bearing ladder

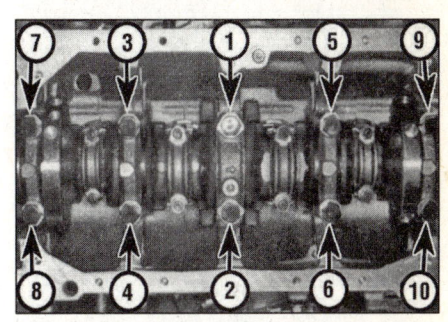

20.9 Main bearing cap bolt tightening sequence – 4E-FE and 4A-FE non-VVT-i engines

VVT-i engines

10 Make sure the crankshaft journals are clean, then lay the crankshaft back in place in the block. Clean the faces of the bearings in the main bearing ladder, the apply lubricant to them.
11 Apply a 2 mm wide bead of sealant (Toyota No 08826-00080) to the main bearing ladder **(see illustration)**. Install the main bearing ladder within 3 minutes or the sealant will harden.
12 Refit the main bearing ladder bolts, and tighten the inner row of 10 bolts in sequence to the Stage 1 torque setting, followed by the Stage 2 angle-tightening setting **(see illustration)**. Tighten the remaining main bearing ladder bolts to the specified torque.

All engines

13 Rotate the crankshaft a number of times by hand to check for any obvious binding.

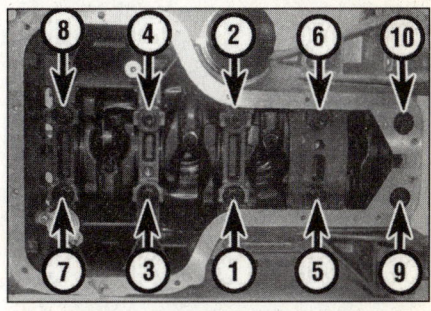

20.12 Main bearing ladder bolt tightening sequence – 4ZZ-FE and 3ZZ-FE VVT-i engines

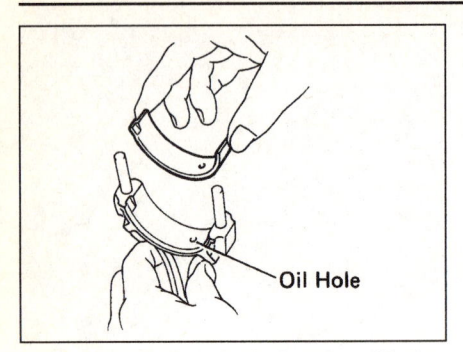

2B•12 Engine removal and overhaul procedures

21.3 Align the hole in the bearing with the oil hole in the rod

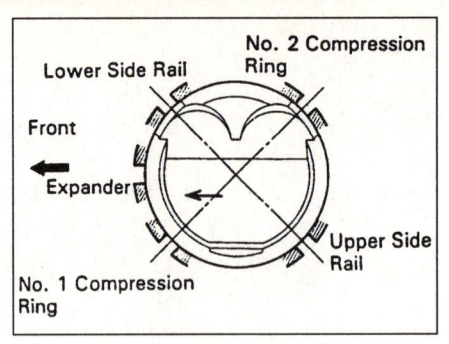

21.5a Piston ring end gap positions for the 1.3 litre engine

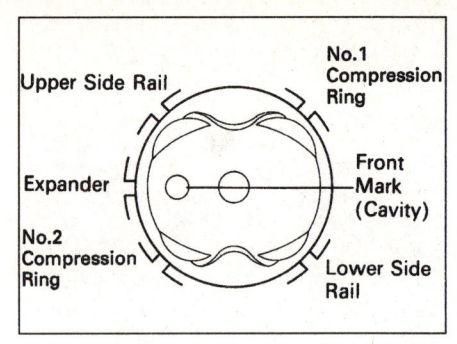

21.5b Piston ring end gap positions for the 1.6 litre non-VVT-i engine

14 Check the crankshaft endfloat with a feeler gauge or a dial indicator as described in Section 12. The endfloat should be correct if the crankshaft thrust faces aren't worn or damaged and new thrustwashers have been installed.

15 Install a new main oil seal, then bolt the retainer to the block (where applicable) – see Part A of this Chapter.

21 Pistons/connecting rods – refitting

1 Before installing the piston/connecting rod assemblies, the cylinder walls must be perfectly clean, the top edge of each cylinder must be chamfered, and the crankshaft must be in place.

2 Remove the cap from the end of the number one connecting rod (refer to the marks made during removal). Remove the original bearing shells and wipe the bearing surfaces of the connecting rod and cap with a clean, lint-free cloth. They must be kept spotlessly clean.

3 Clean the back side of the new upper bearing shell, then lay it in place in the connecting rod. Make sure the tab on the bearing fits into the recess in the rod so the oil holes line up (see illustration). Don't hammer the bearing insert into place and be very careful not to nick or gouge the bearing face.

4 Clean the back side of the other bearing shell and install it in the rod cap. Again, make sure the tab on the bearing fits into the recess in the cap, and don't apply any lubricant. It's critically important that the mating surfaces of the bearing and connecting rod are perfectly clean and oil-free when they're assembled.

5 Position the piston ring gaps at staggered intervals around the piston (see illustrations).

6 Slip a section of plastic or rubber hose over each connecting rod cap bolt to protect the cylinder bore.

7 Lubricate the piston and rings with clean engine oil and attach a piston ring compressor to the piston. Leave the skirt protruding about 8.0 mm to guide the piston into the cylinder. The rings must be compressed until they're flush with the piston.

8 Rotate the crankshaft until the number one connecting rod journal is at BDC (bottom dead centre) and apply a coat of engine oil to the cylinder wall.

9 With the dimple or arrow on top of the piston (see illustration) facing the front of the engine, gently insert the piston/connecting rod assembly into the number one cylinder bore and rest the bottom edge of the ring compressor on the engine block.

10 Tap the top edge of the ring compressor to make sure it's contacting the block around its entire circumference.

11 Gently tap on the top of the piston with the end of a wooden hammer handle (see illustration) while guiding the end of the connecting rod into place on the crankshaft journal. The piston rings may try to pop out of the ring compressor just before entering the cylinder bore, so keep some downward pressure on the ring compressor. Work slowly, and if any resistance is felt as the piston enters the cylinder, stop immediately. Find out what's binding and fix it before proceeding.

Caution: Do not, for any reason, force the piston into the cylinder – you might break a ring and/or the piston.

12 Make sure the bearing faces are perfectly clean, then apply a uniform layer of clean moly-based grease or engine assembly lube to both of them. You'll have to push the piston higher into the cylinder to expose the face of the bearing shell in the connecting rod, be sure to slip the protective hoses over the rod bolts first.

13 Slide the connecting rod back into place on the journal, remove the protective hoses from the rod cap bolts, install the rod cap and tighten the nuts to the correct torque.

14 Repeat the entire procedure for the remaining pistons/connecting rods.

15 The important points to remember are:
a) Keep the back sides of the bearing shells and the insides of the connecting rods and caps perfectly clean when assembling them.
b) Make sure you have the correct piston/rod assembly for each cylinder.
c) The dimple or arrow on the piston must face the front of the engine.
d) Lubricate the cylinder walls with clean oil.
e) Lubricate the bearing faces.

16 After all the piston/connecting rod assemblies have been properly installed, rotate the crankshaft a number of times by hand to check for any obvious binding.

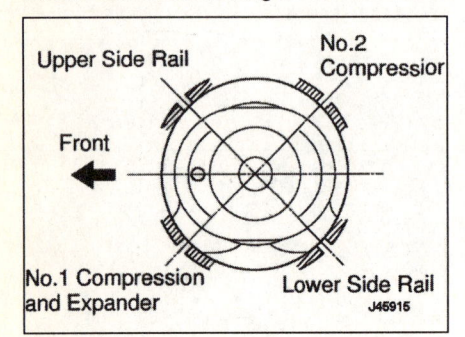

21.5c Piston ring end gap positions for 1.4 litre 4ZZ-FE and 1.6 litre 3ZZ-FE VVT-i engines

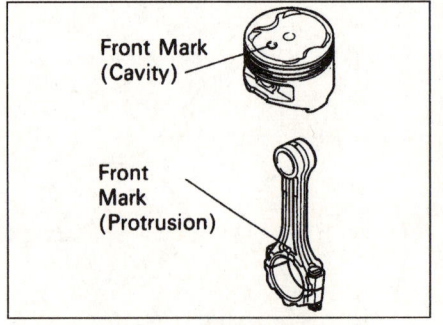

21.9 Check to be sure both the mark on the piston and the mark on the connection rod are aligned

21.11 The piston can be (gently) driven into the cylinder bore with the end of a hammer handle

22 Initial start-up after overhaul

⚠️ **Warning: Have a fire extinguisher handy when starting the engine for the first time.**

1 Once the engine has been installed in the vehicle, double-check the engine oil and coolant levels.

2 With the spark plugs out of the engine and the ignition system and fuel pump disabled (see Section 2 of Chapter 4A), crank the engine until oil pressure registers on the gauge or the light goes out.

3 Install the spark plugs, connect the HT leads/coils (where applicable) and restore the ignition system and fuel pump functions.

4 Start the engine. It may take a few moments for the fuel system to build-up pressure, but the engine should start without a great deal of effort.

5 After the engine starts, it should be allowed to warm-up to normal operating temperature. While the engine is warming-up, make a thorough check for fuel, oil and coolant leaks.

6 Shut the engine off and recheck the engine oil and coolant levels.

7 Drive the vehicle to an area with minimum traffic, accelerate from 30 to 50 mph, then allow the vehicle to slow to 30 mph with the throttle closed. Repeat the procedure 10 or 12 times. This will load the piston rings and cause them to seat properly against the cylinder walls. Check again for oil and coolant leaks.

8 Drive the vehicle gently for the first 500 miles (no sustained high speeds) and keep a constant check on the oil level. It is not unusual for an engine to use oil during the run-in period.

9 At approximately 500 to 600 miles, change the oil and filter.

10 For the next few hundred miles, drive the vehicle normally. Do not pamper it or abuse it.

11 After 2000 miles, change the oil and filter again and consider the engine run-in.

Notes

Chapter 3
Cooling, heating and air conditioning systems

Contents

	Section number
Air conditioning and heating system – testing and maintenance	12
Air conditioning compressor – removal and refitting	14
Air conditioning condenser – removal and refitting	15
Air conditioning evaporator and expansion valve – removal and refitting	16
Air conditioning receiver/drier – removal and refitting	13
Air conditioning system sensors – renewal	17
Antifreeze/coolant – general information	2
Blower motor and resistor – removal and refitting	9
Coolant level check	See *Weekly checks*
Coolant pump – removal and refitting	7
Coolant pump – testing	6
Coolant temperature gauge sender unit – testing and renewal	8

	Section number
Cooling system servicing (draining, flushing and refilling)	See Chapter 1
Cooling system testing	See Chapter 1
Drivebelt check, adjustment and renewal	See Chapter 1
Engine cooling fan and relay – testing and renewal	4
General information	1
Heater and air conditioning control assembly – removal and refitting	11
Heater matrix – removal and refitting	10
Radiator and coolant reservoir – removal and refitting	5
Thermostat – testing and renewal	3
Underbonnet hose check and renewal	See Chapter 1

Degrees of difficulty

Easy, suitable for novice with little experience | **Fairly easy**, suitable for beginner with some experience | **Fairly difficult**, suitable for competent DIY mechanic | **Difficult**, suitable for experienced DIY mechanic | **Very difficult**, suitable for expert DIY or professional

Specifications

General
Engine codes:
- 1.3 litre (1332 cc) non-VVT-i engine ... 4E-FE
- 1.4 litre (1398 cc) VVT-i engine ... 4ZZ-FE
- 1.6 litre (1587 cc) non-VVT-i engine ... 4A-FE
- 1.6 litre (1598 cc) VVT-i engine ... 3ZZ-FE

Radiator cap pressure rating ... 0.74 to 1.03 bar
Thermostat rating ... 82°C

Air conditioning system refrigerant:
- Type ... R-134a
- Quantity ... 650 ± 50g

Thermostatic switch:
- Open at ... 93°C
- Closed at ... 83°C

Air conditioning oil type ... ND-Oil 9

Torque wrench settings

	Nm	lbf ft
Compressor mounting bolts	25	18
Coolant pump-to-block bolts:		
4E-FE engine	19	14
4A-FE engine	14	10
4ZZ-FE engine	10	7
3ZZ-FE engine	10	7
Thermostat cover bolts:		
4E-FE engine	6	4
4A-FE engine	10	7
4ZZ-FE engine	9	7
3ZZ-FE engine	9	7

3•2 Cooling, heating and air conditioning systems

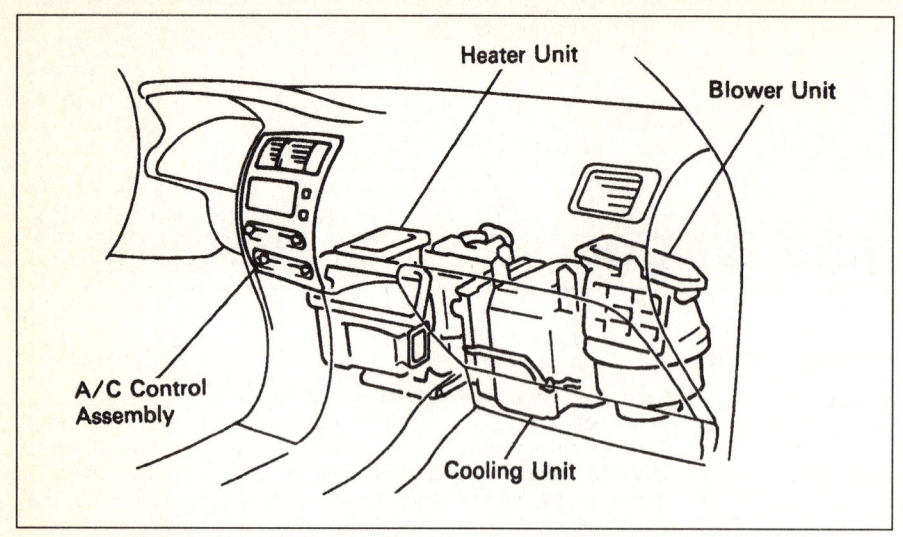

1.1 Underfacia arrangement of the blower unit, evaporator, and heater unit (LHD model shown, RHD is a mirror image)

1 General information

Engine cooling system

All vehicles covered by this manual employ a pressurised engine cooling system with thermostatically-controlled coolant circulation. An impeller type coolant pump mounted on the front of the block pumps coolant through the engine. The coolant flows around each cylinder and toward the rear of the engine. Cast-in coolant passages direct coolant around the intake and exhaust ports, near the spark plug areas and in proximity to the exhaust valve guides.

A wax-pellet type thermostat is located in the thermostat housing at the transmission end of the engine (non-VVT-i engines) or on the front face of the engine block (VVT-i engines). During warm-up, the closed thermostat prevents coolant from circulating through the radiator. When the engine reaches normal operating temperature, the thermostat opens and allows hot coolant to travel through the radiator, where it is cooled before returning to the engine.

The cooling system is sealed by a pressure-type radiator cap. This raises the boiling point of the coolant, and the higher boiling point of the coolant increases the cooling efficiency of the radiator. If the system pressure exceeds the cap pressure-relief value, the excess pressure in the system forces the spring-loaded valve inside the cap off its seat and allows the coolant to escape through the overflow tube into a coolant reservoir. When the system cools, the excess coolant is automatically drawn from the reservoir back into the radiator.

The coolant reservoir does double duty as both the point at which fresh coolant is added to the cooling system to maintain the proper fluid level and as a holding tank for overheated coolant.

This type of cooling system is known as a closed design because coolant that escapes past the pressure cap is saved and re-used.

Heating system

The heating system consists of a blower fan and heater matrix located within the heater box under the facia, the inlet and outlet hoses connecting the heater matrix to the engine cooling system and the heater/air conditioning control panel on the facia (see illustration). Engine coolant is circulated through the heater matrix. When the heater mode is activated, a flap door opens to expose the heater box to the passenger compartment. A fan switch on the control head activates the blower motor, which forces air through the matrix, heating the air.

Air conditioning system

The air conditioning system consists of a condenser mounted in front of the radiator, an evaporator mounted adjacent to the heater matrix, a compressor mounted on the engine, a receiver/drier which contains a high pressure relief valve and the plumbing connecting all of the above.

2.1 Use a hydrometer to test the strength of the antifreeze mixture

A blower fan forces the warmer air of the passenger compartment through the evaporator matrix (sort of a radiator-in-reverse), transferring the heat from the air to the refrigerant. The liquid refrigerant boils off into low pressure vapour, taking the heat with it when it leaves the evaporator. The compressor keeps refrigerant circulating through the system, pumping the warmed refrigerant through the condenser where it is cooled and then circulated back to the evaporator.

2 Antifreeze/coolant – general information

⚠ **Warning: Do not allow antifreeze to come in contact with your skin or painted surfaces of the vehicle. Rinse off spills immediately with plenty of water. Antifreeze is highly toxic if ingested. Never leave antifreeze lying around in an open container or in puddles on the floor; children and pets are attracted by its sweet smell and may drink it. Check with local authorities about disposing of used antifreeze. Many communities have collection centres which will see that antifreeze is disposed of safely. Never dump used antifreeze on the ground or into drains.**

The cooling system should be filled with a water/ethylene-glycol based antifreeze solution, which will prevent freezing down to at least -30° C, or lower if local climate requires it. It also provides protection against corrosion and increases the coolant boiling point.

The cooling system should be drained, flushed and refilled regularly (see Chapter 1). The use of antifreeze solutions for extended periods is likely to cause damage and encourage the formation of rust and scale in the system. If your tap water is 'hard', ie, contains a lot of dissolved minerals, use distilled water with the antifreeze.

Before adding antifreeze to the system, check all hose connections, because antifreeze tends to search out and leak through very minute openings. Engines do not normally consume coolant. Therefore, if the level goes down, find the cause and correct it.

The exact mixture of antifreeze-to-water you should use depends on the relative weather conditions. The mixture should contain at least 50 percent antifreeze, but should never contain more than 70 percent antifreeze. Consult the mixture ratio chart on the antifreeze container before adding coolant. Hydrometers are available at most motor parts/accessory stores to test the ratio of antifreeze to water (see illustration). Use antifreeze which meets the vehicle manufacturer's specifications.
Note: *The antifreeze available from a Toyota dealer is ready-mixed and doesn't require further dilution.*

Cooling, heating and air conditioning systems 3•3

3.6 Disconnect the switch connector (arrowed) and remove the two nuts (arrow indicates upper nut)

3.8 The thermostat is fitted with the spring towards the cylinder head

3.9 The thermostat gasket fits around the edge of the thermostat

3 Thermostat – testing and renewal

Warning: Do not attempt to remove the radiator cap, coolant or thermostat until the engine has cooled completely.

Testing

1 Before assuming the thermostat is responsible for a cooling system problem, check the coolant level (Chapter 1), drivebelt tension (Chapter 1) and temperature gauge (or light) operation.
2 If the engine takes a long time to warm-up (as indicated by the temperature gauge or heater operation), the thermostat is probably stuck open. Renew the thermostat.
3 If the engine runs hot, use your hand to check the temperature of the radiator top hose. If the hose is not hot, but the engine is, the thermostat is probably stuck in the closed position, preventing the coolant inside the engine from travelling through the radiator. Renew the thermostat.
Caution: Do not drive the vehicle without a thermostat. The engine management ECM may stay in open loop and emissions and fuel economy will suffer.
4 If the radiator top hose is hot, it means that the coolant is flowing and the thermostat is open. Consult the *Fault finding* Section at the rear of this manual for further diagnosis.

Renewal

5 Drain the coolant from the radiator (see Chapter 1).

Non-VVT-i engines

6 Disconnect the cooling fan temperature switch connector from the thermostat cover located at the left end of the cylinder head **(see illustration)**.
7 Detach the thermostat cover from the housing. Be prepared for some coolant to spill as the gasket seal is broken. The radiator hose can be left attached to the cover, unless the cover itself is to be renewed.
8 Remove the thermostat, noting the direction in which it was fitted in the cover or housing, and thoroughly clean the sealing surfaces **(see illustration)**.
9 Fit a new gasket onto the thermostat **(see illustration)**. Make sure it is evenly fitted all the way around.
10 On 4A-FE engines, install the thermostat and the cover, positioning the jiggle pin at the highest point. On 4E-FE engines, position the thermostat in the cover with the jiggle pin aligned with the raised projection on the cover, then install the cover and thermostat.
11 Tighten the cover fasteners to the torque listed in this Chapter's Specifications and reinstall the remaining components in the reverse order of removal.

VVT-i engines

12 Remove the alternator as described in Chapter 5A.
13 Undo the two nuts and remove the thermostat cover **(see illustration)**.
14 Remove the thermostat. Discard the seal, a new one must be fitted **(see illustration)**.
15 Fit a new seal to the thermostat, and fit it into position on the engine block, with the jiggle pin at the 12 o'clock position **(see illustration)**.
16 Refit the thermostat cover and tighten the nuts to the specified torque.
17 Refit the alternator as described in Chapter 5A.

All engines

18 Refill the cooling system (see Chapter 1), run the engine and check for leaks and proper operation.

4 Engine cooling fan and relay – testing and renewal

Warning: To avoid possible injury, keep clear of the fan blades, as they may start turning at any time.

Testing

Non-VVT-i engines

Note: No cooling fan temperature switch is fitted to VVT-i engines. The coolant temperature is monitored by the engine management ECM via the coolant temperature sensor, and the fans are operated by energising the cooling fan relay(s).

1 If the radiator fan won't turn off when the engine is cool, disconnect the wiring

3.13 Undo the thermostat cover nuts

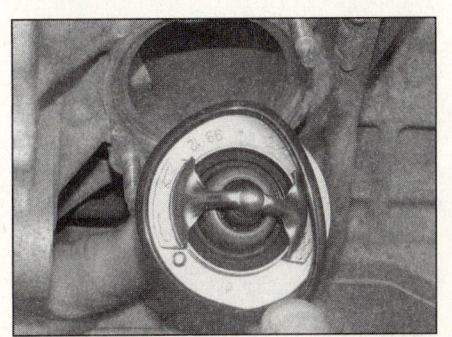

3.14 Discard the thermostat seal, and fit a new one

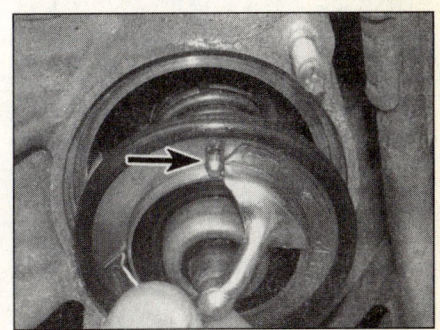

3.15 Fit the thermostat with the jiggle pin at the 12 o'clock position

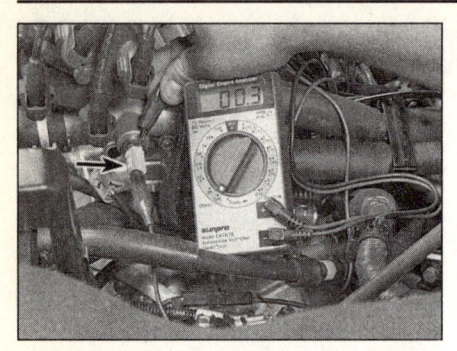

3•4 Cooling, heating and air conditioning systems

4.2 The switch (arrowed) for the cooling fan control on the thermostat cover

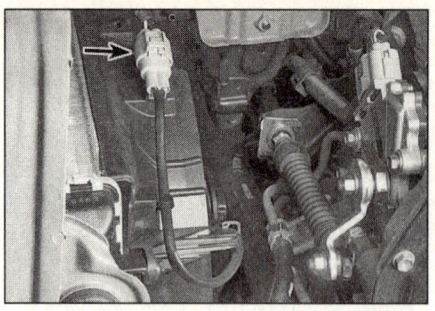

4.3 Disconnect the connector (arrowed) and connect jumper wires to the positive and negative terminals of the battery

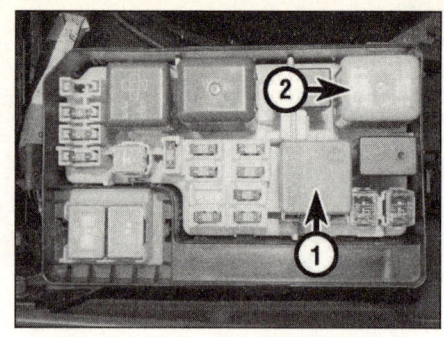

4.5 No 1 cooling fan relay (1) and main engine relay (2)

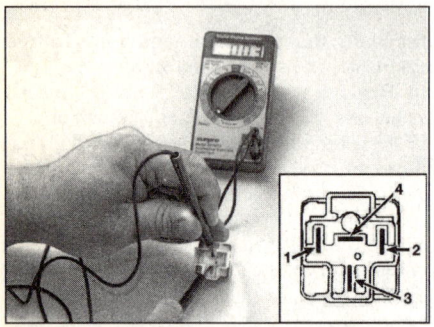

4.6 Test the fan relay (Nippondenso). With no voltage applied, there should be continuity between 1 and 2, and 3 and 4 – with voltage applied across 1 and 2, there should be NO continuity between 3 and 4

On Bosch relays, disregard the terminal numbers, test it just like this Nippondenso relay

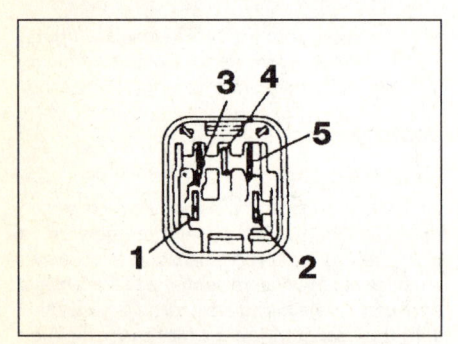

4.7 Main engine relay terminal guide

connector from the cooling fan temperature switch **(see illustration 3.6)**. With the key ON, the fan should now operate. If not, check the fan relay, wiring between the temperature switch and the relay, and the fan motor itself.

2 The cooling fan temperature switch can be tested for continuity with an ohmmeter. Disconnect the wiring connector and attach one lead of the ohmmeter to the terminal on the switch, and the other lead to the body of the switch **(see illustration)**. When the engine is cold (below 83°C) there should be continuity. When the engine is warm (above 93°C), there should be NO continuity.

All engines

3 To test an inoperative fan motor (one that doesn't come on when the engine gets hot or when the air conditioner is on), first check the fuses and/or fusible links (see Chapter 12). Then disconnect the electrical connector at the motor and use fused jumper wires to connect the fan directly to the battery **(see illustration)**. If the fan still does not work, renew the fan motor.

⚠️ **Warning: Do not allow the test clips to contact each other or any metallic part of the vehicle.**

4 If the motor tested OK in the previous test but is still inoperative, then the fault lies in the relays, fuse, or wiring. The fan relay and main engine relay can be tested as described below.

Relay testing

5 Locate the main relay box, located in the engine compartment, on the left-side.

Air conditioned models have extra relays in a separate box next to the battery **(see illustration)**.

6 Remove the No 1 cooling fan relay and, using an ohmmeter, test for continuity **(see illustration)**. Both Nippondenso and Bosch-made relays are used, and the terminals are numbered differently. Be sure to test either relay as shown in the illustration.

7 If the fan relay tests OK, remove the main engine relay and test it **(see illustration)**. There should be continuity between terminals 3 and 5, and between 2 and 4. There should be NO continuity between terminals 1 and 2. With battery voltage applied across terminals 3 and 5, there should be continuity between 1 and 2, and NO continuity between 2 and 4. If both relays test OK, take the vehicle to a suitably-equipped repairer who will be able to interrogate the vehicles self-diagnosis system.

Renewal

Radiator cooling fan

8 Disconnect the negative battery cable (see Chapter 5A).
9 Disconnect the wiring connector at the fan motor.
10 Drain enough coolant to disconnect the upper radiator hose at the radiator (see Chapter 1).
11 Unbolt the fan shroud from the radiator and lift the fan/shroud assembly from the vehicle **(see illustrations)**.
12 Hold the fan blades and remove the fan retaining nut (and spacer, if equipped) **(see illustration)**.

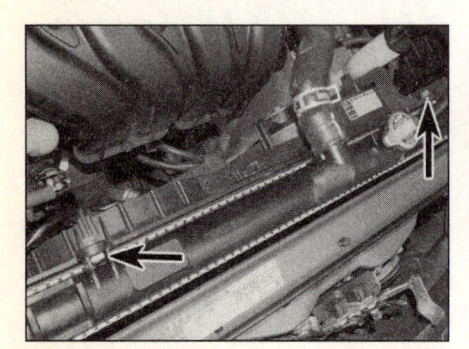

4.11a Undo the fan shroud retaining bolts (arrowed)

4.11b On single headlight models the fan shroud is also bolted at the lower edge (left-hand lower bolt arrowed)

4.12 Undo the fan blade retaining nut

Cooling, heating and air conditioning systems 3•5

13 Unbolt the fan motor from the shroud (see illustration).
14 Refitting is the reverse of removal.

Condenser cooling fan

15 On single headlight models (pre-October '99), a separate cooling fan for air conditioned models is located in front of the condenser. Undo the three screws and remove the radiator grille – see Chapter 11 if necessary.
16 Disconnect the wiring plug from the cooling fan motor.
17 Undo the bolt securing the fan to the slam panel brace (see illustration).
18 Prise out the upper and lower retaining pins at the right-hand edge of the fan (see illustration).
19 Undo the bolts securing the bonnet catch and bonnet slam panel centre brace, then manoeuvre the fan assembly from place (see illustration).
20 If required, undo the three fan retaining screws, then undo the screws and remove the motor.
21 Refitting is a reversal of removal.

5 Radiator and coolant reservoir – removal and refitting

Warning: Do not start this procedure until the engine is completely cool.

Radiator

1 Drain the coolant into a container (see Chapter 1).
2 Remove both the upper and lower radiator hoses.
3 Disconnect the reservoir hose from the radiator filler neck.
4 Remove the cooling fan (see Section 4).
5 If equipped with an automatic transmission, disconnect the fluid cooler pipes from the radiator (see illustration). Place a drip pan to catch the fluid and cap the fittings.
6 Remove the two upper radiator mounting brackets (see illustration). Note: *The bottom of the radiator is retained by grommeted projections that fit into holes in the body.*
7 Lift out the radiator. Be aware of dripping fluids and the sharp fins.
8 With the radiator removed, it can be inspected for leaks, damage and internal blockage. If in need of repairs, have a professional radiator workshop or dealer service department perform the work as special techniques are required.
9 Insects and dirt can be cleaned from the radiator with compressed air and a soft brush. Don't bend the cooling fins as this is done.

Warning: Wear eye protection when using compressed air.

10 Refitting is the reverse of the removal procedure. Be sure the rubber mounts are in place on the bottom of the radiator.

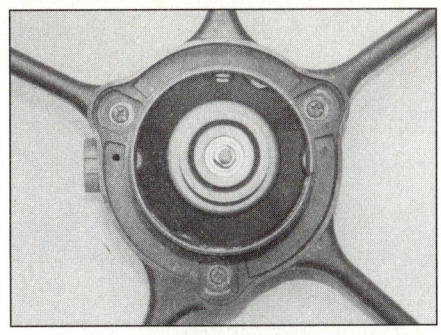

4.13 Unbolt the fan motor from the shroud

4.18 Prise out the upper and lower retaining pins (upper pin arrowed)

11 After refitting, fill the cooling system with the proper mixture of antifreeze and water. Refer to Chapter 1 if necessary.
12 Start the engine and check for leaks. Allow the engine to reach normal operating temperature, indicated by both radiator hoses becoming hot. Recheck the coolant level and add more if required.
13 On automatic transmission-equipped models, check and add fluid as needed.

Coolant reservoir

14 Remove the battery and battery tray (Chapter 5A), then undo the reservoir retaining bolt.
15 Pour the coolant into a container. Wash out and inspect the reservoir for cracks and chafing. Renew it if damaged.
16 Refitting is the reverse of removal.

4.17 Undo the fan shroud-to-panel brace bolt (arrowed)

4.19 Remove the bonnet slam panel brace

6 Coolant pump – testing

1 A failure in the coolant pump can cause serious engine damage due to overheating.
2 With the engine running and warmed to normal operating temperature, squeeze the upper radiator hose. If the coolant pump is working properly, a pressure surge should be felt as the hose is released.

Warning: Keep hands away from fan blades.

3 Coolant pumps are normally equipped with weep or vent holes (see illustration 7.12). If a failure occurs in the pump seal, coolant will leak from this hole. In most cases it will be necessary to use a flashlight to find the hole

5.5 Release the clips and disconnect the automatic transmission fluid cooler pipes (arrowed)

5.6 Undo the radiator upper retaining bracket bolts (arrowed)

3•6 Cooling, heating and air conditioning systems

7.9 Use a screwdriver to lever the wiring clip from the dipstick tube bracket

7.10 Disconnect the coolant temperature gauge sender wiring plug (arrowed)

7.11a Remove the two nuts (smaller arrows) retaining the coolant neck to the cylinder head, then remove the top bolt (larger arrow) from the coolant pump

7.11b Remove the remaining coolant pump bolts – do not remove the bolts retaining the pump halves together until the assembly is removed

on the coolant pump by looking through the space behind the pulley just below the coolant pump shaft.

4 If the coolant pump shaft bearings fail there may be a howling sound at the front of the engine while it is running. Bearing wear can be felt if the coolant pump pulley is rocked up-and-down. Do not mistake drivebelt slippage, which causes a squealing sound, for coolant pump failure.

7 Coolant pump – removal and refitting

Warning: Do not start this procedure until the engine is completely cool.

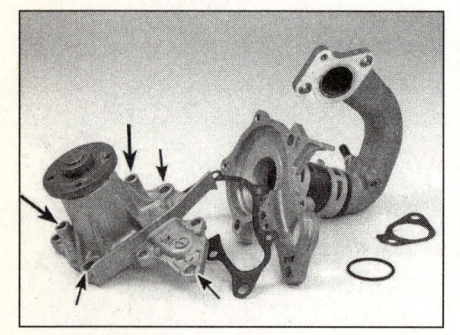

7.12 Small arrows indicate the pump-to-block bolts. Larger arrows show weep holes

Removal

4E-FE engine

1 Refer to Chapter 5A and remove the alternator.
2 Remove the nut and two bolts retaining the intake manifold stay at the rear of the engine and remove the stay.
3 Remove the coolant inlet hose and bypass hose from the coolant inlet at the rear of the coolant pump. Remove the retaining bolt and pull the coolant inlet pipe from the coolant pump. Collect the sealing O-ring from the end of the pipe.
4 Remove the oil dipstick. Remove the bolt retaining the dipstick tube and alternator adjustment arm to the engine and pull the dipstick tube from the oil pump housing.
5 Remove the bolt and two nuts retaining the

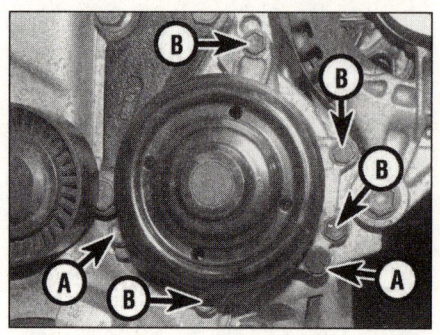

7.15 The bolts marked (A) are 30 mm long whilst the ones marked (B) are 35 mm long

coolant pump to the engine block and remove the coolant pump assembly. The pulley can remain on the coolant pump during removal.
6 Disassemble the coolant pump and renew the gaskets. Thoroughly clean all sealing surfaces, removing all traces of old sealant from the housing-to-engine mating faces. Reassemble the coolant pump using new gaskets.

4A-FE engine

7 Refer to Chapter 1 and remove the power steering belt, alternator/coolant pump belt and air conditioning belt. Then remove the upper power steering mounting bracket.
8 Refer to Chapter 2A and remove the cylinder head cover and the upper timing belt covers.
9 Remove the oil dipstick. Remove the bolt retaining the dipstick tube to the engine and pull the dipstick tube from the oil pump housing (see illustration).
10 Behind the coolant pump, remove the two nuts retaining the right-side coolant neck to the cylinder head, and unplug the connector from the coolant temperature sender (see illustration).
11 Remove the three bolts retaining the coolant pump to the engine block and remove the coolant pump and coolant neck assembly. The pulley can remain on the coolant pump during removal (see illustrations).
12 Disassemble the coolant pump and renew the gaskets. Thoroughly clean all sealing surfaces, removing the O-ring and cleaning the groove (see illustration). Reassemble the coolant pump using new gaskets.

4ZZ-FE and 3ZZ-FE engines

13 Drain the engine coolant as described in Chapter 1.
14 Remove the auxiliary drivebelt as described in Chapter 1.
15 Undo the 6 bolts, and remove the coolant pump (see illustration). Discard the O-ring seal, a new one must be fitted.

Refitting

4E-FE engine

16 Obtain a tube of sealant (Part No 08826-00100 or 3Bond 1282B available from Toyota dealers) and apply a 2.0 mm band of the sealant to the sealing groove on the housing, following the instructions supplied with the sealant.
17 Install the pump assembly to the block and secure with the bolt and two nuts.
18 Refit the remaining parts in the reverse order of removal. When reinstalling the dipstick tube, use a new O-ring where it pushes into the oil pump. Also use a new O-ring on the coolant inlet pipe.
19 With refitting complete, wait at least two hours for the sealant to set then refill the cooling system (see Chapter 1), run the engine and check for leaks and proper operation.

4A-FE engine

20 Using a new O-ring, fit the pump assembly to the block. Use a new gasket on the coolant

Cooling, heating and air conditioning systems 3•7

7.23 Renew the coolant pump O-ring

8.7a Engine coolant temperature sender (arrowed) – 4E-FE non-VVT-i engine

8.7b Engine coolant temperature sender (arrowed) – VVT-i engine

neck. **Note:** *If the pump has been renewed after many miles of usage, it's a good idea to also renew the hose connecting the coolant pump to the coolant neck.*

21 Refit the remaining parts in the reverse order of removal. When refitting the dipstick tube, use a new O-ring where it pushes into the oil pump.
22 Refill the cooling system (see Chapter 1), run the engine and check for leaks and proper operation.

4ZZ-FE and 3ZZ-FE engines

23 Ensure the mating faces of the coolant pump and timing chain cover are clean, then refit the pump using a new O-ring seal **(see illustration)**.
24 Refit the retaining bolts and tighten them to the specified torque.
25 Refill the coolant system (Chapter 1), then run the engine and check for leaks.

8 Coolant temperature gauge sender unit – testing and renewal

⚠ **Warning:** *Do not start this procedure until the engine is completely cool.*

Testing

Note: *The following procedures only apply to the 1.3 and 1.6 litre non-VVT-i engines. On VVT-i engines have the engine management ECM self-diagnosis system interrogated by a suitably-equipped repair workshop. The vehicle's diagnostic connector is located under the right-hand side of the facia.*

1 If the coolant temperature gauge is inoperative, check the fuses first (see Chapter 12).
2 If the temperature gauge indicates excessive temperature after running a while, see the *Fault finding* Section in the rear of the manual.
3 If the temperature gauge indicates Hot as soon as the engine is started from cold, disconnect the wire at the coolant temperature sender. The sender is located on the side of the thermostat housing on 4E-FE engines, and on the coolant pump coolant neck on 4A-FE engines. If the gauge reading drops, renew the sender unit. If the reading remains high, the wire to the gauge may be shorted to earth or the gauge may be faulty.
4 If the coolant temperature gauge fails to show any indication after the engine has been warmed-up (approximately 10 minutes) and the fuses checked out OK, shut off the engine. Disconnect the wire at the sender unit and, using a jumper wire, connect the wire to a clean earth on the engine. Briefly turn on the ignition without starting the engine. If the gauge now indicates Hot, renew the sender unit.
5 If the gauge fails to respond, the circuit may be open or the gauge may be faulty – see Chapter 12 for additional information.

Renewal

6 Drain the coolant (see Chapter 1).
7 Disconnect the wiring connector from the sender unit **(see illustrations)**. On 4A-FE engines, the sender is located on the rear of the engine **(see illustration 7.10)**
8 Using a deep socket or a spanner, remove the sender unit.

9 Fit the new unit and tighten it securely. Do not use thread sealer as it may electrically insulate the sender unit.
10 Reconnect the wiring connector, refill the cooling system and check for coolant leakage and proper gauge function.

9 Blower motor and resistor – removal and refitting

Testing

1 The blower unit is located in the passenger compartment above the left-hand front footwell. If the blower doesn't work, check the fuse and all connections in the circuit for looseness and corrosion. Make sure the battery is fully-charged.
2 Remove the glovebox (see Chapter 11, Section 27).

Removal

3 Disconnect the electrical connector from the blower motor resistor. Remove the screws and withdraw the resistor from the housing **(see illustration)**.
4 Using a continuity tester on the blower motor resistor, there should be continuity between all terminals. If not, renew the resistor.
5 If the blower motor must be renewed, Disconnect the wiring plug, then remove the three mounting screws and lower the blower assembly from the housing **(see illustrations)**. The fan can be removed and re-used on the new blower motor.

9.3 Undo the blower motor resistor retaining screws (arrowed)

9.5a Undo the three retaining screws (arrowed) ...

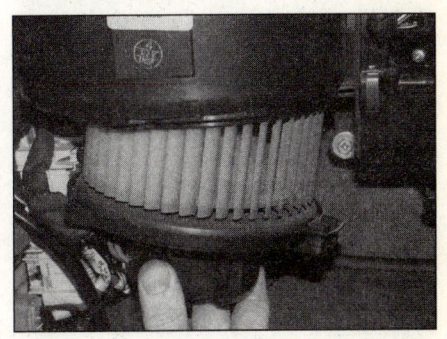

9.5b ... and lower the blower motor from position

3•8 Cooling, heating and air conditioning systems

10.4a If available, use clamps on the heater hoses . . .

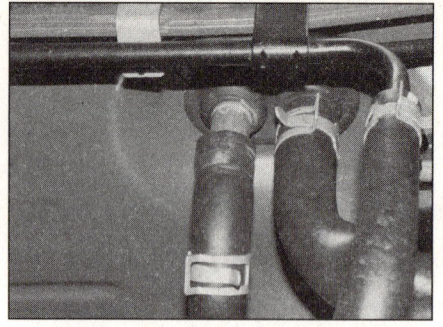

10.4b . . . then release the clips and disconnect the heater hoses from the bulkhead stubs

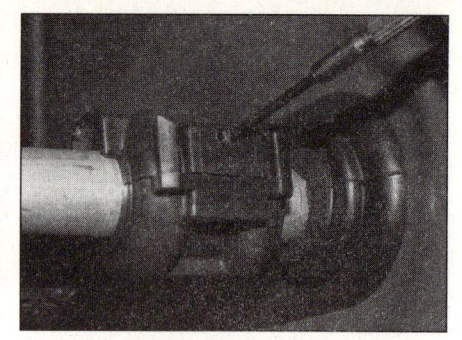

10.5 Depress the silver clip and release the air conditioning pipe clamps

Refitting

6 Refitting is the reverse of removal. Check for proper operation.

10 Heater matrix – removal and refitting

⚠ **Warning:** *These models are equipped with airbags. The airbag is armed and can deploy (inflate) anytime the battery is connected. To prevent accidental deployment (and possible injury), turn the ignition key to LOCK and disconnect the negative battery cable whenever working near airbag components. After the battery is disconnected, wait at least two minutes before beginning work (the system has a back-up capacitor that must fully discharge). For more information see Chapter 12.*

Removal

1 Have the air conditioning refrigerant discharged (where applicable) by an automotive air conditioning specialist.
2 Disconnect the negative cable from the battery (see Chapter 5A).
3 Drain the cooling system (see Chapter 1), unless you have access to hose clamps (see next paragraph).
4 Working in the engine compartment, release the clips and disconnect the heater hoses at the bulkhead. If you have access to hose clamps, use them on the heater hoses – then there's no need to drain the coolant **(see illustrations)**. Recover the rubber grommet from the bulkhead.

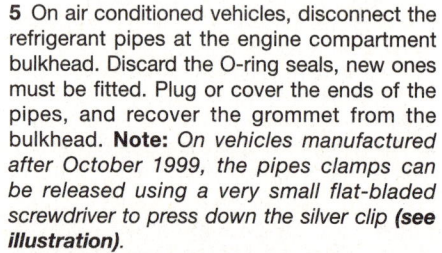

5 On air conditioned vehicles, disconnect the refrigerant pipes at the engine compartment bulkhead. Discard the O-ring seals, new ones must be fitted. Plug or cover the ends of the pipes, and recover the grommet from the bulkhead. **Note:** *On vehicles manufactured after October 1999, the pipes clamps can be released using a very small flat-bladed screwdriver to press down the silver clip* **(see illustration)**.
6 Remove the entire facia and support crossbrace as described in Chapter 11.
7 Note their fitted positions, then disconnect any wiring plugs from the heater unit.
8 Undo the nuts, and remove the blower motor/evaporator housing from the left-hand side of the heater housing **(see illustrations)**.
9 Undo the nuts securing the heater unit to the bulkhead, and remove the unit from the vehicle **(see illustrations)**.
10 Undo the screw and remove the matrix pipe clamp.
11 Lift the matrix from the housing **(see illustration)**.

Refitting

12 Refitting is the reverse order of removal, noting that new air conditioning pipe O-rings must be fitted.
13 Refill the cooling system, reconnect the battery and run the engine. Check for leaks and proper system operation.

10.8a Undo the blower motor/evaporator housing upper nuts (arrowed) . . .

10.8b . . . and the three lower ones (arrowed)

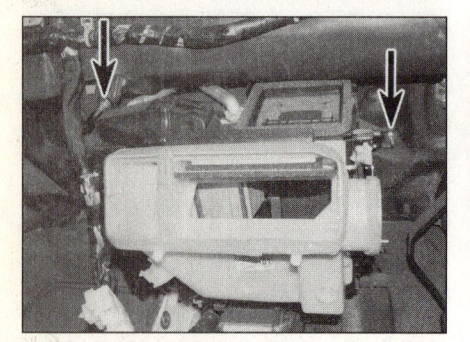

10.9a Undo the nuts (arrowed) securing the heater housing to the bulkhead . . .

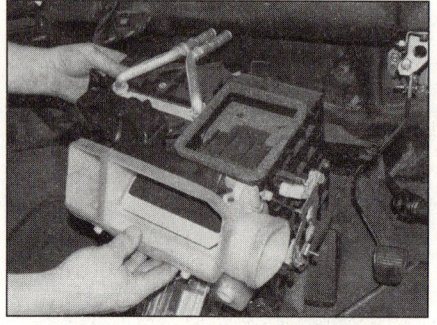

10.9b . . . and remove the housing

10.11 Lift the heater matrix from the housing

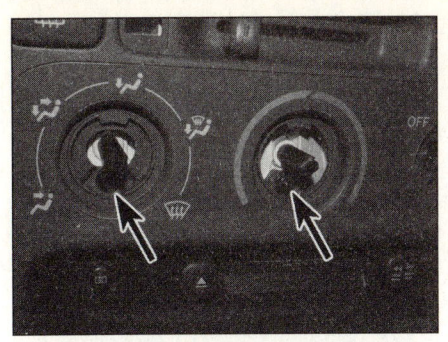

Cooling, heating and air conditioning systems 3•9

11.3a Remove the two screws in the heater knob recesses (arrowed) . . .

11.3b . . . and carefully pull the centre cluster finish panel from place

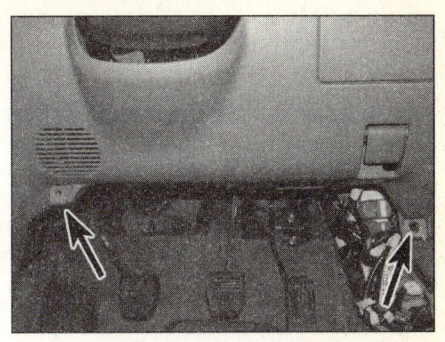

11.4 Undo the two bolts (arrowed) securing the lower facia panel

11 Heater and air conditioning control assembly – removal and refitting

Removal

1 Remove the rear section of the centre console (see Chapter 11).
2 Pull off the control knobs, and the air recirculation knob.
3 Undo the two screws in the knob recesses, the carefully pull away the centre cluster finish panel. Disconnect the wiring plugs as the panel is removed **(see illustrations)**.
4 Pull up the driver's door sill trim panel, remove the footwell kick panel, then undo the two bolts and remove the lower facia panel under the steering column **(see illustration)**. Disconnect the bonnet release cable if required.
5 Undo the two screws and remove the metal shield (where fitted) from underneath the steering column **(see illustration)**.
6 Prise out the clip and remove the right-hand side heater ducting from under the steering column.
7 Release the clip either side and pull the control out slightly.
8 Disconnect the control cable (black) from the heater control valve in the engine compartment, adjacent to the bulkhead **(see illustration)**.
9 Working through the ashtray aperture, disconnect the temperature control cable (blue) from the rear of the heater housing.
10 Remove the glovebox as described in Chapter 11, Section 27.
11 Disconnect the heat distribution cable (grey) from the linkage at the right-hand side of the heater housing **(see illustration)**.
12 Disconnect the recirculation control cable (yellow) from the left-hand side of the heater housing.
13 Pull the control unit outwards then disconnect the wiring plugs and remove the control unit **(see illustration)**.

Refitting

14 Refitting is the reverse of the removal procedure.
15 Run the engine and check for proper functioning of the heater (and air conditioning, if equipped).

Cable adjustment

16 With the cables attached at the control end and the control assembly installed in the dash, adjust the cables at their ends. The controls should be set to: RECIRC, COOL, and DEF.
17 To adjust the recirculation control cable set the damper lever to RECIRC, install the cable and clamp it in place.
18 To adjust the temperature control cable, set the air mix damper to COOL, install the cable and lock the clamp while applying slight pressure on the outer cable.
19 To adjust the heat distribution control cable, set the mode damper to the DEF mode, hook the cable end on and tighten the clamp.

11.5 Undo the metal shield retaining screws (arrowed)

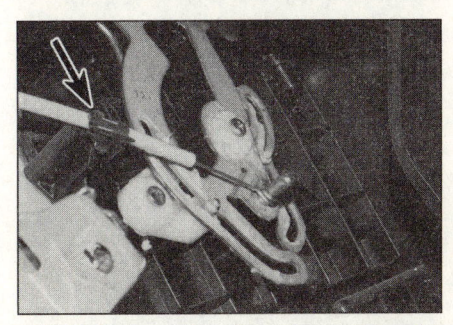

11.11 Release the clamp (arrowed) and disconnect the heat distribution cable from the right-hand side of the heater housing

12 Air conditioning and heating system – testing and maintenance

Air conditioning system

⚠ **Warning: The air conditioning system is under high pressure. Do not loosen any hose fittings or remove any components until the system has been discharged. Air conditioning refrigerant may only be discharged by a dealer service department or an automotive air conditioning specialist. Always wear eye protection when disconnecting air conditioning system fittings even after the system has been discharged.**

1 The following maintenance checks should be performed on a regular basis to ensure

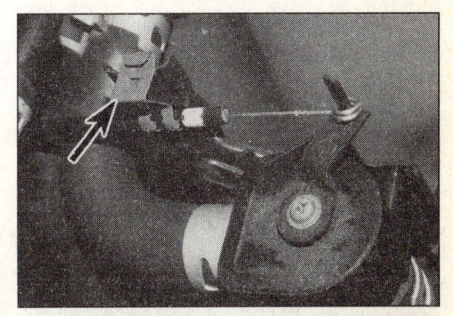

11.8 Release the clamp (arrowed) and disconnect the heater control valve cable in the engine compartment

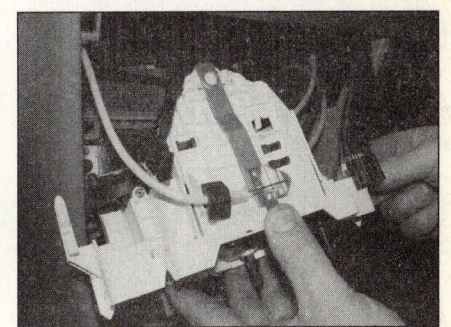

11.13 Disconnect the control panel wiring plugs

12.10 Air conditioning refrigerant sight glass (arrowed)

that the air conditioner continues to operate at peak efficiency:
a) Inspect the condition of the compressor drivebelt. If it is worn or deteriorated, renew it (see Chapter 1).
b) Check the drivebelt tension and, if necessary, adjust it (see Chapter 1).
c) Inspect the system hoses. Look for cracks, bubbles, hardening and deterioration. Inspect the hoses and all fittings for oil bubbles or seepage. If there is any evidence of wear, damage or leakage, renew the hose(s).
d) Inspect the condenser fins for leaves, insects and any other foreign material that may have embedded itself in the fins. Use a 'fin comb' or compressed air to remove debris from the condenser.

2 It's a good idea to operate the system for about ten minutes at least once a month. This is particularly important during the winter months because long term non-use can cause hardening, and subsequent failure, of the seals.

3 Leaks in the air conditioning system are best spotted when the system is brought up to operating temperature and pressure, by running the engine with the air conditioning ON for five minutes. Shut the engine off and inspect the air conditioning hoses and connections. Traces of oil usually indicate refrigerant leaks.

4 If the air conditioning system doesn't operate at all, check the fuse panel and the air conditioning relay, located in the fuse/relay box in the engine compartment.

5 The most common cause of poor cooling

TOOL TIP

Many car accessory shops sell one-shot air conditioning recharge aerosols. These generally contain refrigerant, compressor oil, leak sealer and system conditioner. Some also have a dye to help pinpoint leaks.

⚠️ **Warning: These products must only be used as directed by the manufacturer, and do not remove the need for regular maintenance.**

is simply a low system refrigerant charge. If a noticeable drop in cool air output occurs, the following quick check will help you determine if the refrigerant level is low.

Checking refrigerant charge

6 Warm the engine up to normal operating temperature.

7 Place the air conditioning temperature selector at the coldest setting and put the blower at the highest setting. Open the doors (to make sure the air conditioning system doesn't cycle off as soon as it cools the passenger compartment).

8 With the compressor engaged – the clutch will make an audible click and the centre of the clutch will rotate. After the system reaches operating temperature, feel the two pipes connected to the evaporator at the bulkhead (see illustration 12.13).

9 The pipe leading from the condenser outlet to the evaporator (small tubing) should be cold, and the evaporator outlet line (the larger tubing that leads back to the compressor) should be slightly colder. If the evaporator outlet is considerably warmer than the inlet, the system needs a charge. If the air isn't as cold as it used to be, the system probably needs a charge. Further inspection or testing of the system is beyond the scope of the home mechanic and should be left to a professional.

10 Inspect the sight glass. If the refrigerant looks foamy when running, it's low (see illustration). When ambient temperatures are very hot, bubbles may show in the sight glass even with the proper amount of refrigerant. With the proper amount of refrigerant, when the air conditioning is turned off, the sight glass should show refrigerant that foams, then clears.

11 If the previous checks indicate that the refrigerant charge is low, take the vehicle to a Toyota dealer or automotive air conditioning repair facility to have the system recharged (see Tool tip).

Air conditioning service ports

12 The high-pressure service port is located in front of the condenser (see illustrations).
13 The low-pressure service port is located where the air conditioning pipes enter the engine compartment bulkhead at the left-hand side (see illustration).

Heating systems

14 If the air coming out of the heater vents isn't hot, the problem could stem from any of the following causes:
a) The thermostat is stuck open, preventing the engine coolant from warming-up enough to carry heat to the heater matrix. Renew the thermostat (see Section 3).
b) A heater hose is blocked, preventing the flow of coolant through the heater matrix. Feel both heater hoses at the bulkhead. They should be hot. If one of them is cold, there is an obstruction in one of the hoses or in the heater matrix, or the heater control valve is shut. Detach the hoses and back flush the heater matrix with a garden hose. If the heater matrix is clear but circulation is impeded, remove the two hoses and flush them out with a garden hose.
c) If flushing fails to remove the blockage from the heater matrix, the matrix must be renewed (see Section 10).

15 If the blower motor speed does not

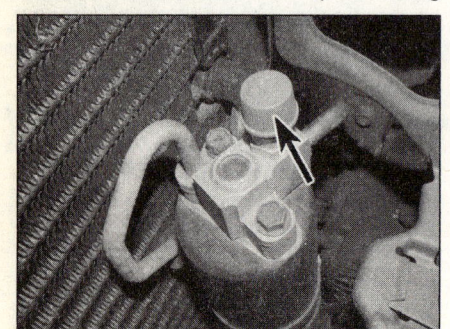

12.12a High-pressure service port (arrowed) – single headlight models

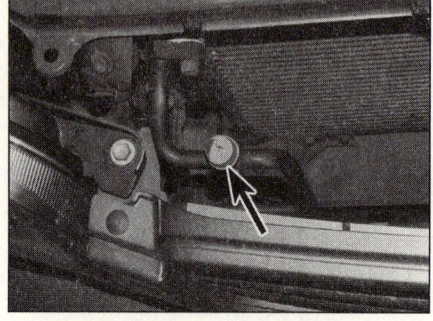

12.12b High-pressure service port (arrowed) – twin headlight models

12.13 Low-pressure service port – all models

Cooling, heating and air conditioning systems 3•11

correspond to the setting selected on the blower switch, the problem could be a bad fuse, circuit, switch, blower motor resistor or motor (see Sections 9 and 11).
16 If there isn't any air coming out of the vents:
a) Turn the ignition ON and activate the fan control. Place your ear at the heating/air conditioning register (vent) and listen. Most motors are audible. Can you hear the motor running?
b) If you can't (and have already verified that the blower switch and the blower motor resistor are good), the blower motor itself is probably defective (see Section 9).
17 If the carpet under the heater matrix is damp, or if antifreeze vapour or steam is coming through the vents, the heater matrix is leaking. Remove it (see Section 10) and install a new unit (most radiator workshops will not repair a leaking heater matrix).
18 Inspect the drain hose from the heater/air conditioning assembly at the left-hand side of the bulkhead, make sure it is not clogged.

13 Air conditioning receiver/drier – removal and refitting

Warning: *The air conditioning system is under high pressure. Do not loosen any hose fittings or remove any components until the system has been discharged. Air conditioning refrigerant may only be discharged by a dealer service department or an automotive air conditioning specialist. Always wear eye protection when disconnecting air conditioning system fittings even after the system has been discharged.*
Note: *On models manufactured after October 1999, the receiver/drier is integral with the condenser. If faulty, the condenser must be renewed – consult a Toyota dealer.*

Removal
1 Have the refrigerant discharged and recovered by a Toyota dealer or automotive air conditioning specialist.
2 Refer to Chapter 11 and remove the radiator grille.
3 Undo the two bolts and disconnect the refrigerant pipes **(see illustration)** from the top of the receiver/drier and cap the open fittings to prevent entry of moisture. Discard the pipes O-ring seals, new ones must be fitted.
4 Loosen the pinch-bolt and slip the receiver/drier out of the bracket.

Refitting
5 Refitting is the reverse of removal.
6 Have the system evacuated, charged and leak-tested by the workshop that discharged it. Note that if a new receiver/drier is fitted, 20 cc of air conditioning oil must be added during the recharge.

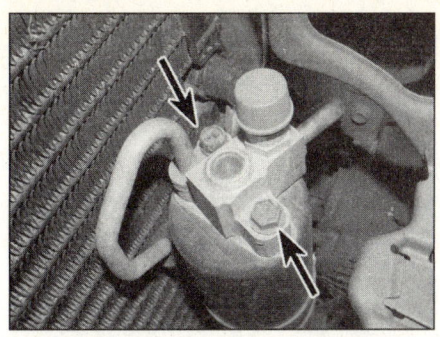

13.3 Disconnect the refrigerant pipes from the receiver/drier (arrowed)

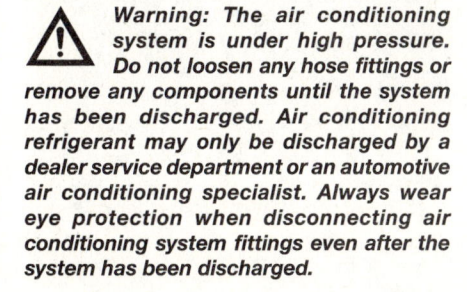

14 Air conditioning compressor – removal and refitting

Warning: *The air conditioning system is under high pressure. Do not loosen any hose fittings or remove any components until the system has been discharged. Air conditioning refrigerant may only be discharged by a dealer service department or an automotive air conditioning specialist. Always wear eye protection when disconnecting air conditioning system fittings even after the system has been discharged.*

Removal
1 Have the refrigerant discharged and recovered by a Toyota dealer or automotive air conditioning specialist.
2 Remove the drivebelt from the compressor (see Chapter 1).
3 Detach the wiring connector and disconnect the refrigerant pipes, then cap the open fittings to prevent entry of moisture **(see illustration)**. Discard the pipe O-ring seals, new ones must be fitted.
4 Unbolt the compressor and lift it from the vehicle.
5 If a new or rebuilt compressor is being installed, follow the directions supplied with the compressor regarding the proper level of oil prior to refitting.

15.3 Undo the bolts (arrowed) and disconnect the refrigerant pipe connections

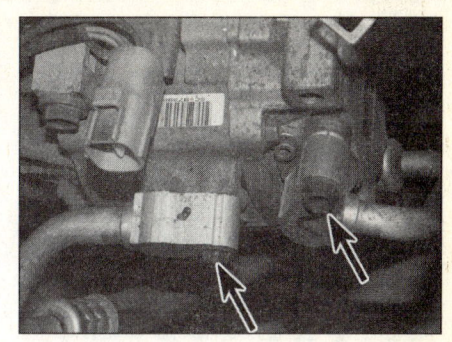

14.3 Undo the compressor refrigerant pipe bolts (arrowed)

Refitting
6 Refitting is the reverse of removal. Renew any O-rings with new ones specifically made for the type of refrigerant in your system and lubricate them with refrigerant oil, also designed specifically for your system.
7 Have the system evacuated, recharged and leak-tested by the workshop that discharged it.

15 Air conditioning condenser – removal and refitting

Warning: *The air conditioning system is under high pressure. Do not loosen any hose fittings or remove any components until the system has been discharged. Air conditioning refrigerant may only be discharged by a dealer service department or an automotive air conditioning specialist. Always wear eye protection when disconnecting air conditioning system fittings even after the system has been discharged.*

Removal
1 Have the refrigerant discharged and recovered by a Toyota dealer or automotive air conditioning repair facility.
2 Undo the three screws and remove the radiator grille.
3 Disconnect the condenser inlet and outlet fittings **(see illustration)**. Cap the open fittings immediately to keep moisture and contamination out of the system. Discard the O-ring seals, new ones must be fitted. **Note:** *On pre-October '99 models, the left-side fitting is connected to the receiver/drier (see Section 13), on models after this date, the receiver/drier is integral with the condenser.*
4 Undo the bolts securing the pipe support brackets to the condenser **(see illustrations)**.
5 Undo the bolts for the upper and lower condenser supports on both sides **(see illustrations)**.
6 Undo the radiator upper support bolts, and push the top of the radiator backwards – there is no need to disconnect the hoses.
7 Push the radiator back towards the engine,

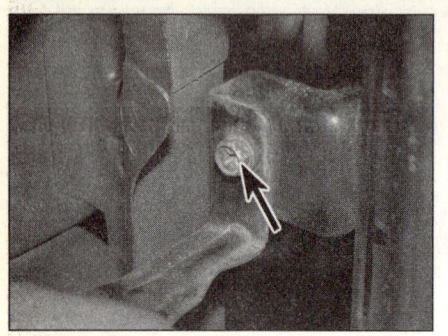

3•12 Cooling, heating and air conditioning systems

15.4a Condenser pipe support bracket bolt (arrowed) – right-hand side . . .

15.4b . . . and left-hand side (arrowed)

15.5a Condenser upper support bolt (arrowed) . . .

the lift the condenser upwards from place **(see illustration)**.

Refitting

8 Fit the condenser, brackets and bolts, making sure the rubber cushions fit on the mounting points properly.
9 Reconnect the refrigerant pipes, using new O-rings.
10 Refit the remaining parts in the reverse order of removal.
11 Have the system evacuated, charged and leak-tested by the workshop that discharged it. If a new condenser has been installed, add approximately 40 cc of new refrigerant oil of the correct type.

16 Air conditioning evaporator and expansion valve
– removal and refitting

⚠ **Warning: The air conditioning system is under high pressure. Do not loosen any hose fittings or remove any components until the system has been discharged. Air conditioning refrigerant may only be discharged by a dealer service department or an automotive air conditioning specialist. Always wear eye protection when disconnecting air conditioning system fittings even after the system has been discharged.**

Removal

1 Have the refrigerant discharged and

15.5b . . . and lower support (arrowed)

recovered by a Toyota dealer or automotive air conditioning specialist.
2 Remove the complete facia assembly and crossbrace as described in Chapter 11.
3 Disconnect the air conditioning pipes at the bulkhead, use a second spanner so as not to damage the fittings. Cap the open fittings after disassembly to prevent the entry of air or dirt. **Note:** *On vehicles manufactured after October 1999, the pipes clamps can be released using a small flat-bladed screwdriver to press down the silver clip (see illustration 10.5).*
4 On models with manual air conditioning, disconnect the wiring plug, release the clips and remove the air conditioning amplifier from above the cooling unit **(see illustration)**.
5 Remove nuts/screw retaining the evaporator unit and pull the unit out of the vehicle **(see illustrations 10.8a and 10.8b)**. Disconnect the wiring plug(s) as the unit is withdrawn.
6 With the evaporator unit on the bench,

15.7 Push the radiator rearwards, and slide the condenser from position

remove the two bolts and separate the blower motor housing from the evaporator housing **(see illustration)**.
7 Remove the screws and clips and separate the top and bottom halves of the case and pull out the evaporator **(see illustration)**.
8 Pull the thermistor sensor probe from the evaporator matrix, and unbolt the expansion valve and the two short refrigerant pipes **(see illustrations)**. Discard the O-ring seals, new ones must be fitted.
9 The evaporator matrix can be cleaned with a 'fin comb' and blown off with compressed air.

⚠ **Warning: Be sure to wear eye protection when using compressed air.**

Refitting

10 Refitting is the reverse of the removal process. Be sure to use new O-rings, and new gaskets on the expansion valve.

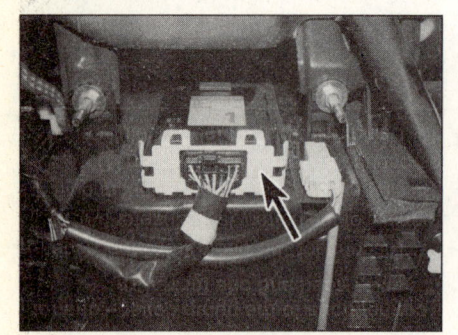

16.4 Unclip the amplifier from above the cooling unit (arrowed)

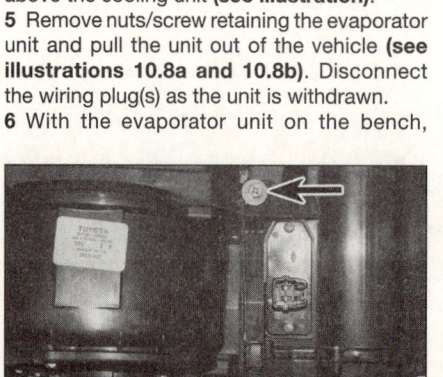

16.6 Undo the two bolts (arrowed) to separate the blower motor housing

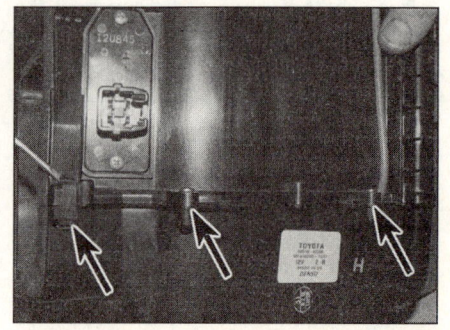

16.7 Undo the screws and clips (arrowed) and separate the two halves of the housing

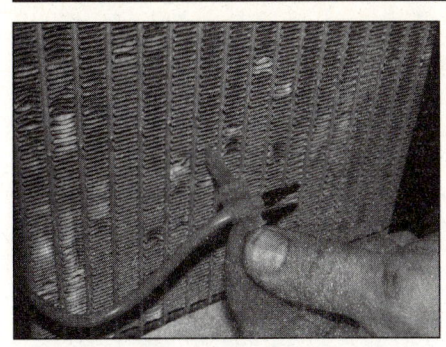

Cooling, heating and air conditioning systems 3•13

16.8a Pull the temperature sensor probe from the matrix fins

16.8b Undo the two bolts and remove the expansion valve

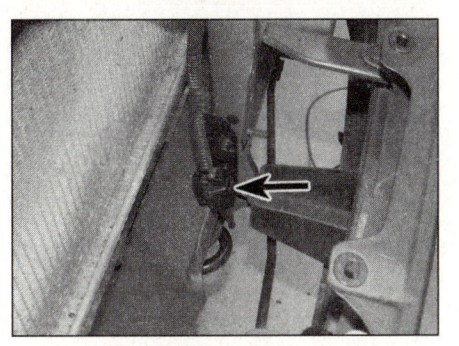

16.11 Feed the drain tube through the hole in the bulkhead

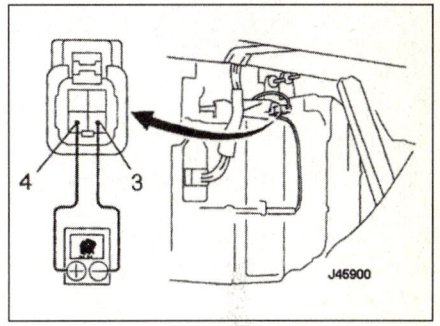

11 When refitting the evaporator housing, ensure the drain hose is correctly located at the bulkhead **(see illustration)**.
12 Have the system evacuated, charged and leak-tested by the workshop that discharged it. If the evaporator matrix is renewed, add 40 cc of new refrigerant oil of the correct type to the system during the recharge.

17 Air conditioning system sensors – renewal

Sunlight sensor

1 Use a flat-bladed screwdriver to carefully prise the sensor from the facia.
2 Disconnect the wiring plug as the sensor is withdrawn.
3 To test the sensor, cover it with a cloth and connect the leads from an ohmmeter to the sensor terminals. No continuity should exist. Conversely, next to a strong light source, continuity should exist.
4 Refitting is a reversal of removal.

Cabin temperature sensor

5 Undo the two screws and remove the lower facia panel from under the steering column (see Chapter 11).
6 Release the two clips, then disconnect the wiring plug and remove the sensor.

17.10 Ambient temperature sensor (arrowed)

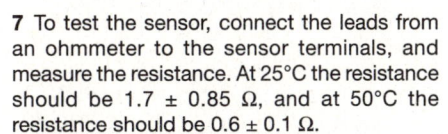

17.13 Connect the leads of an ohmmeter to evaporator temperature sensor terminals 3 and 4

7 To test the sensor, connect the leads from an ohmmeter to the sensor terminals, and measure the resistance. At 25°C the resistance should be 1.7 ± 0.85 Ω, and at 50°C the resistance should be 0.6 ± 0.1 Ω.
8 Refitting is a reversal of removal.

Ambient temperature sensor

9 Remove the radiator grille as described in Chapter 11.
10 Disconnect the wiring plug, release the connector clamp, then carefully prise the sensor from position **(see illustration)**.
11 To test the sensor, connect the leads from an ohmmeter to the sensor terminals, and measure the resistance. At 25°C the resistance should be 1.6 to 1.8 kΩ, and at 40°C the resistance should be 0.5 to 0.7 kΩ.
12 Refitting is a reversal of removal.

Evaporator temperature sensor

13 To test the sensor in place, remove the glovebox (Chapter 11, Section 27), connect the leads from an ohmmeter to the sensor terminals 3 and 4, and measure the resistance. At 25°C the resistance should be 1.5 kΩ (see illustration).
14 To renew the sensor, remove the evaporator as described in Section 16.
15 Carefully pull the sensor from position **(see illustration 16.8a)**.
16 Refitting is a reversal of removal.

Chapter 4 Part A:
Fuel and exhaust systems

Contents

	Section number
Accelerator cable – removal, refitting and adjustment	9
Air cleaner assembly – removal and refitting	8
Catalytic converter	See Chapter 4B
Exhaust manifold – removal and refitting	14
Exhaust system – removal and refitting	15
Exhaust system check	See Chapter 1
Fuel filter renewal	See Chapter 1
Fuel injection system – component testing and renewal	12
Fuel injection system – depressurisation	2
Fuel injection system – general information	10

	Section number
Fuel injection system – testing and adjustment	11
Fuel level sender unit – testing and renewal	4
Fuel pipes and fittings – inspection and renewal	5
Fuel pump – removal and refitting	3
Fuel tank – removal and refitting	6
Fuel tank cleaning and repair – general information	7
General information	1
Intake manifold – removal and refitting	13
Underbonnet hose check and renewal	See Chapter 1

Degrees of difficulty

Easy, suitable for novice with little experience | **Fairly easy,** suitable for beginner with some experience | **Fairly difficult,** suitable for competent DIY mechanic | **Difficult,** suitable for experienced DIY mechanic | **Very difficult,** suitable for expert DIY or professional

Specifications

General
Engine codes:
1.3 litre (1332 cc) non-VVT-i engine	4E-FE
1.4 litre (1398 cc) VVT-i engine	4ZZ-FE
1.6 litre (1587 cc) non-VVT-i engine	4A-FE
1.6 litre (1598 cc) VVT-i engine	3ZZ-FE

Fuel system
Fuel pressure:
  Engine idling:
    Vacuum sensing hose detached:
1.3 litre 4E-FE engine	2.81 to 2.87 bar
1.6 litre 4A-FE engine	2.62 to 3.03 bar

    Vacuum sensing hose attached:
1.3 litre 4E-FE engine	2.27 to 2.55 bar
1.6 litre 4A-FE engine	2.13 to 2.55 bar

  Fuel system hold pressure:
Non-VVT-i engines	1.44 bar
VVT-i engines	3.01 to 3.47 bar
Fuel injector resistance	13.4 to 14.2 Ω
Air control valve resistance – cold (1.3 litre 4E-FE engine)	17.0 to 24.5 Ω
Air conditioning idle-up valve solenoid resistance	30 to 34 Ω

Crankshaft position sensor resistance:
  1.3 litre 4E-FE engine:
Hot	1265 to 1890 Ω
Cold	985 to 1600 Ω

  1.4 litre 4ZZ-FE and 1.6 litre 3ZZ-FE engines:
Hot	2065 to 3225 Ω
Cold	1630 to 2740 Ω

Camshaft timing oil control valve:
1.4 litre 4ZZ-FE and 1.6 litre 3ZZ-FE engines at 20°C	6.9 to 7.9 Ω

Idle speed
Automatic transmission	700 rpm
Manual transmission	650 rpm

4A•2 Fuel and exhaust systems

Torque wrench settings

	Nm	lbf ft
Non VVT-i engines		
Crankshaft position sensor (1.3 litre)	8	6
Exhaust manifold bolts/nuts:		
1.3 litre engines	48	35
1.6 litre engines	34	25
Fuel pipe fittings	30	22
Fuel pressure regulator bolts	8	6
Fuel rail mounting bolts	15	11
Intake manifold bolt/nuts	19	14
Throttle body mounting bolts/nuts:		
1.3 litre engine	19	14
1.6 litre engine	22	16
VVT-i engines		
Camshaft oil control valve	7	5
Camshaft position sensor	9	7
Crankshaft position sensor	9	7
Exhaust manifold	37	27
Fuel rail mounting bolts	18	13
Intake manifold	30	23
Throttle body	30	22

1 General information

The fuel system consists of a fuel tank, an electric fuel pump (located in the fuel tank), an EFI/fuel pump relay, fuel injectors, a fuel pressure regulator, an air cleaner assembly and a throttle body unit. All models covered by this manual are equipped with the Multi Point Fuel Injection (MPFI) system.

Multi Point Fuel Injection

Multi Point Fuel Injection (MPFI) uses timed impulses to sequentially inject the fuel directly into the intake port of each cylinder. The injectors are controlled by the Electronic Control Module (ECM). The ECM monitors various engine parameters and delivers the exact amount of fuel, in the correct sequence, into the intake ports. The throttle body serves only to control the amount of air passing into the system. Because each cylinder is equipped with an injector mounted immediately adjacent to the intake valve, much better control of the fuel/air mixture ratio is possible.

On VVT-i engines, the engine management ECM also varies the timing of the intake camshaft. The camshaft timing is varied according to engine speed and load. Retarding the timing (opening the valves later) at low and high engine speeds, improves low speed driveability and maximum power respectively, whilst advancing the timing at medium engine speeds increases mid-range torque and reduces exhaust emissions.

Fuel pump and pipes

Non-VVT-i engines

Fuel is circulated from the fuel tank to the fuel injection system, and back to the fuel tank, through a pair of metal pipes running along the underside of the vehicle. An electric fuel pump is attached to the fuel level sender unit inside the fuel tank. A return system routes hot fuel back to the fuel tank through a separate return line, whilst fuel vapour is routed into a carbon canister where it is stored, until it's then fed back into the intake manifold and burnt during the normal combustion process.

VVT-i engines

On these engines, the fuel sender/pump unit incorporates a pressure regulator. Fuel is pumped along a single pipe to the front of the vehicle – any excess pressure created by the pump is released directly back into the tank via the regulator.

Fuel vapour is routed into a carbon canister where it is stored, until it's then fed back into the intake manifold and burnt during the normal combustion process.

All engines

The fuel pump will operate as long as the engine is cranking or running and the ECM is receiving ignition reference pulses from the electronic ignition system (see Chapter 5B). If there are no reference pulses, the fuel pump will shut off after 2 or 3 seconds.

Exhaust system

The exhaust system includes a manifold fitted with an exhaust oxygen sensor, a catalytic converter, an exhaust pipe, and a silencer. On models with VVT-i engines, an additional oxygen sensor is fitted after the catalytic converter to further fine tune the engine and monitor the performance of the converter.

The catalytic converter is an emission control device added to the exhaust system to reduce pollutants. A single-bed converter is used in combination with a three-way (reduction) catalyst. Refer to Chapter 4B for more information regarding the catalytic converter.

Warning: *Petrol is extremely flammable, so take extra precautions when you work on any part of the fuel system. Don't smoke or allow open flames or bare light bulbs near the work area, and don't work in a garage where a natural gas-type appliance (such as a water heater or a clothes dryer) with a pilot light is present. Since petrol is carcinogenic, wear latex gloves when there's a possibility of being exposed to fuel, and, if you spill any fuel on your skin, rinse it off immediately with soap and water. Mop-up any spills immediately and do not store fuel-soaked rags where they could ignite. The fuel system is under constant pressure, so, if any fuel pipes are to be disconnected, the fuel pressure in the system must be relieved first. When you perform any kind of work on the fuel system, wear safety glasses and have a Class B type fire extinguisher on hand.*

2 Fuel injection system – depressurisation

1 Before servicing any fuel system component, you must relieve the fuel pressure to minimise the risk of fire or personal injury.
2 Remove the fuel filler cap – this will relieve any pressure built-up in the tank.
3 Remove the rear seat from the passenger cabin, then prise up the fuel pump/sender unit access cover **(see illustration 3.4)**.
4 Remove the fuel pump connector **(see illustration 3.5a)**.
5 Start the engine and wait for the engine to stall, then turn the ignition off.
6 The fuel system is now depressurised. **Note:** *Place a rag around the fuel line before removing any hose clamp or fitting to prevent any residual fuel from spilling onto the engine.*

Fuel and exhaust systems 4A•3

7 Before working on the fuel system, disconnect the cable from the negative terminal of the battery (see Chapter 5A).
8 Refit the connector when the job is completed.

3 Fuel pump – removal and refitting

⚠️ **Warning:** *Petrol is extremely flammable, so take extra precautions when you work on any part of the fuel system. Don't smoke or allow open flames or bare light bulbs near the work area, and don't work in a garage where a natural gas-type appliance (such as a water heater or a clothes dryer) with a pilot light is present. Since petrol is carcinogenic, wear latex gloves when there's a possibility of being exposed to fuel, and, if you spill any fuel on your skin, rinse it off immediately with soap and water. Mop-up any spills immediately and do not store fuel-soaked rags where they could ignite. The fuel system is under constant pressure, so, if any fuel pipes are to be disconnected, the fuel pressure in the system must be relieved first. When you perform any kind of work on the fuel system, wear safety glasses and have a Class B type fire extinguisher on hand.*

Non-VVT-i engines

1 Remove the fuel tank cap.
2 Disconnect the cable from the negative terminal of the battery (see Chapter 5A).
3 Remove the rear seat cushion, and lift the carpet underneath it (see Chapter 11).
4 Using a flat-bladed tool, carefully prise up the fuel pump/sender unit access cover **(see illustration)**.
5 Disconnect the electrical connector, and disconnect the fuel pipe(s) **(see illustrations)**.
6 Remove the fuel pump/sender unit cover retaining bolts **(see illustration)**.
7 Carefully withdraw the fuel pump/fuel level sender unit assembly from the fuel tank **(see illustration)**.
8 Pry the lower end of the fuel pump loose from the bracket **(see illustration)**.
9 Remove the rubber cushion from the lower end of the fuel pump.
10 Remove the clip securing the inlet screen to the pump.
11 Remove the screen and inspect it for contamination. If it is dirty, renew it.
12 If you are only renewing the fuel pump inlet screen, install the new screen, the clip and the rubber cushion, push the lower end of the pump back into the bracket and install the pump/sender unit assembly in the fuel tank.
13 If you are renewing the fuel pump, remove the hose clamp at the upper end of the pump and disconnect the pump from the hose **(see illustration)**.
14 Disconnect the wires from the pump terminals and remove the pump.

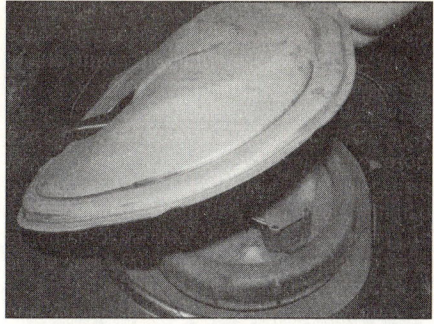

3.4 Prise up the access cover over the fuel pump

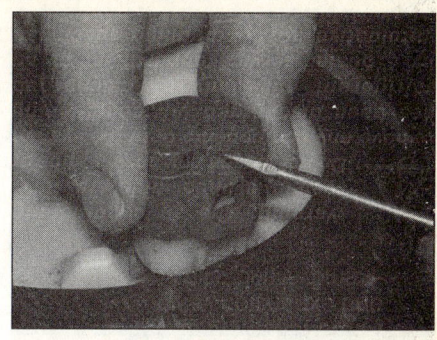

3.5a Depress the clips and disconnect the pump/sender wiring plug

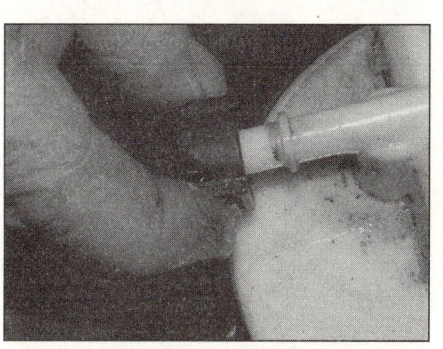

3.5b Squeeze in the release buttons and pull the fuel pipe from the pump cover

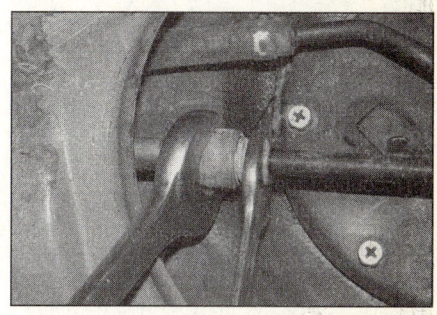

3.5c On some models, there are two fuel connections to the pump cover – one for feed and one for return

15 Refitting is the reverse of removal.

VVT-i engines

TMC (Toyota Motor Co) manufactured

16 Remove the fuel tank cap.

3.6 Undo the pump/sender unit cover retaining bolts

3.7 Carefully lift the pump/sender unit from the tank

3.8 Pull the lower end of the pump from the bracket

3.13 Disconnect the fuel hose and wiring plug from the pump (arrowed)

17 Disconnect the cable from the negative terminal of the battery (see Chapter 5A).
18 Remove the rear seat cushion, and lift the carpet underneath it (see Chapter 11).
19 Using a flat-bladed tool, carefully prise up

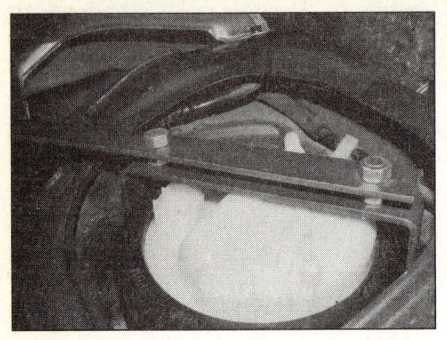

4A•4 Fuel and exhaust systems

3.46 Improvise a tool to unscrew the plastic collar

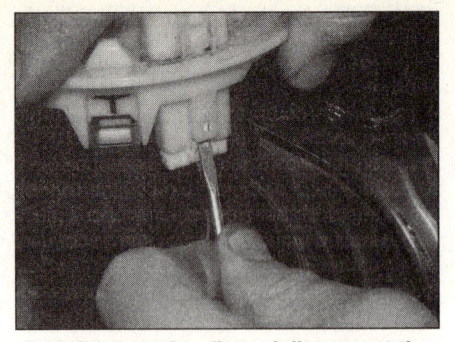

3.47 Depress the clip and disconnect the sender unit wiring plug

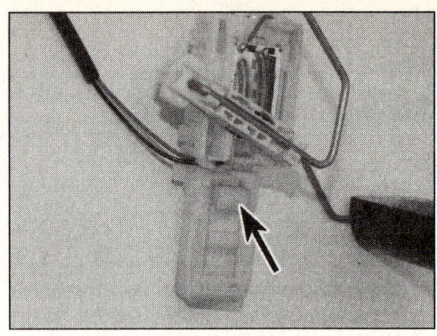

3.48 Press-in the clip (arrowed) and slide the sender unit upwards from the tank

the fuel pump/sender unit access cover **(see illustration 3.4)**.
20 Disconnect the electrical connector, and disconnect the fuel pipe(s) **(see illustrations 3.5a, 3.5b and 3.5c)**.
21 Remove the fuel pump/sender unit retaining bolts **(see illustration 3.6)**.
22 Carefully withdraw the fuel pump/fuel level sender unit assembly from the fuel tank.
23 Undo the screw and disconnect the earth wire from the pump earth clamp.
24 Disconnect the pump wiring connector, then ease the lower end of the pump from the bracket, and remove the rubber cushion from the bracket.
25 Disconnect the fuel hose, and remove the pump.
26 Prise out the clip and remove the filter from the base of the pump.
27 Refitting is the reverse of removal.

Denso manufactured

28 Remove the fuel tank cap.
29 Disconnect the cable from the negative terminal of the battery (see Chapter 5A).
30 Remove the rear seat cushion, and lift the carpet underneath it (see Chapter 11).
31 Using a flat-bladed tool, carefully prise up the fuel pump/sender unit access cover **(see illustration 3.4)**.
32 Disconnect the electrical connector, and disconnect the fuel pipe(s) **(see illustrations 3.5a, 3.5b and 3.5c)**.
33 Unscrew the sender unit plastic retaining collar using a pair of large, crossed-screwdrivers, or improvise a tool **(see illustration 3.46)**. Make alignment marks

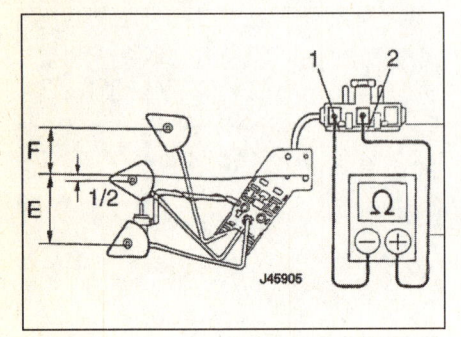

4.8 Connect an ohmmeter to the sender unit terminals

between the collar and the tank to aid refitting.
34 Carefully lift the sender/pump assembly from position.
35 Carefully prise off the plastic bracket at the base of the assembly, and remove the rubber cushion.
36 Pull the fuel pressure regulator from place, and recover the O-ring.
37 Remove the clip and withdraw the filter from the base of the pump.
38 Release the clips securing the top 'suction plate' of the assembly, then disconnect the fuel pump connector. Recover the O-ring seal.
39 Pull the fuel pump from position.
40 Refitting is the reverse of removal. On vehicles where the pump/sender assembly is retained by a locking collar, the collar must be tightened up to the same point as before disassembly.

Bosch manufactured

41 Remove the fuel tank cap.
42 Disconnect the cable from the negative terminal of the battery (see Chapter 5A).
43 Remove the rear seat cushion, and lift the carpet underneath it (see Chapter 11).
44 Using a flat-bladed tool, carefully prise up the fuel pump/sender unit access cover **(see illustration 3.4)**.
45 Disconnect the electrical connector, and disconnect the fuel pipe(s) **(see illustrations 3.5a, 3.5b and 3.5c)**.
46 Unscrew the sender unit plastic retaining collar using a pair of large, crossed-screwdrivers, or improvise a tool **(see illustration)**. Make alignment marks between the collar and the tank to aid reassembly.
47 Carefully lift the pump assembly from position, disconnecting the sender unit wiring plug as the assembly is withdrawn **(see illustration)**.
48 Depress the clip and slide the sender unit upwards from the tank **(see illustration)**.
49 No further dismantling is recommended.
50 Refitting is the reverse of removal. On vehicles where the pump/sender assembly is retained by a locking collar, the collar must be tightened upto the same point as before disassembly.

4 Fuel level sender unit – testing and renewal

> **Warning:** *Petrol is extremely flammable, so take extra precautions when you work on any part of the fuel system. Don't smoke or allow open flames or bare light bulbs near the work area, and don't work in a garage where a natural gas-type appliance (such as a water heater or a clothes dryer) with a pilot light is present. Since petrol is carcinogenic, wear latex gloves when there's a possibility of being exposed to fuel, and, if you spill any fuel on your skin, rinse it off immediately with soap and water. Mop-up any spills immediately and do not store fuel-soaked rags where they could ignite. The fuel system is under constant pressure, so, if any fuel pipes are to be disconnected, the fuel pressure in the system must be relieved first. When you perform any kind of work on the fuel system, wear safety glasses and have a Class B type fire extinguisher on hand.*

Testing

1 Before performing any tests on the fuel level sender unit, completely fill the tank with fuel.
2 Remove the rear seat and the fuel pump/sending unit access cover **(see illustration 3.4)**.
3 Disconnect the fuel level sender unit electrical connector located on top of the fuel tank.
4 Position the ohmmeter probes on the electrical connector terminals (terminals 1 and 2) check for resistance **(see illustration 4.8)**. Use the 200 ohm scale on the ohmmeter.
5 With the fuel tank completely full, the resistance should be about 4.0 ohms.
6 Reconnect the electrical connector and drive the vehicle until the tank is nearly empty (or syphon the fuel into an approved fuel container using a syphoning kit – not your mouth).
7 Check the resistance. The resistance of the sending unit should now be about 110 ohms.
8 If the readings are incorrect, renew the sender unit. **Note:** *The test can also be performed with the fuel level sending*

Fuel and exhaust systems 4A•5

unit removed from the fuel tank. Using an ohmmeter, check the resistance of the sending unit with the float arm completely down (tank empty) and with the arm up (tank full) **(see illustration)**. The resistance should change steadily from 62 ohms to approximately 2.0 ohms.

Renewal

9 Remove the fuel pump/fuel level sending unit assembly from the fuel tank (see Section 3).
10 Carefully angle the sending unit out of the opening without damaging the fuel level float located at the bottom of the assembly **(see illustration 3.7)**. **Note:** *On Bosch units, the sender unclips from the container inside the tank – see Section 3.*
11 Disconnect the electrical connectors from the sending unit.
12 Remove the screw from the side of the sending unit bracket and separate the sending unit from the assembly.
13 Refitting is the reverse of removal.

5 Fuel pipes and fittings – inspection and renewal

⚠️ **Warning:** *Petrol is extremely flammable, so take extra precautions when you work on any part of the fuel system. Don't smoke or allow open flames or bare light bulbs near the work area, and don't work in a garage where a natural gas-type appliance (such as a water heater or a clothes dryer) with a pilot light is present. Since petrol is carcinogenic, wear latex gloves when there's a possibility of being exposed to fuel, and, if you spill any fuel on your skin, rinse it off immediately with soap and water. Mop-up any spills immediately and do not store fuel-soaked rags where they could ignite. The fuel system is under constant pressure, so, if any fuel pipes are to be disconnected, the fuel pressure in the system must be relieved first. When you perform any kind of work on the fuel system, wear safety glasses and have a Class B type fire extinguisher on hand.*

Inspection

1 Once in a while, you will have to raise the vehicle to service or renew some component (an exhaust pipe mounting, for example). Whenever you work under the vehicle, always inspect fuel pipes and all fittings and connections for damage or deterioration.
2 Check all hoses and pipes for cracks, kinks, deformation or obstructions.
3 Make sure all hoses and pipe clips attach their associated hoses or pipes securely to the underside of the vehicle.
4 Verify all hose clamps attaching rubber hoses to metal fuel pipes or pipes are snug enough to assure a tight fit between the hoses and pipes.

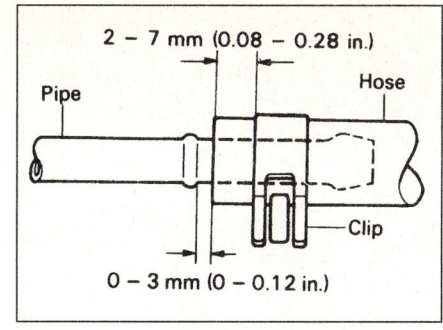

5.6 When attaching a section of rubber hose to a metal fuel line, be sure to overlap the hose as shown

Renewal

5 If you must renew any damaged sections, use original equipment hoses or pipes constructed from exactly the same material as the section you are renewing. Do not install substitutes constructed from inferior or inappropriate material or you could cause a fuel leak or a fire.
6 Always, before detaching or disassembling any part of the fuel line system, note the routing of all hoses and pipes and the orientation of all clamps and clips to ensure that new sections are installed in exactly the same manner. When attaching hoses to metal pipes, overlap them as shown **(see illustration)**.
7 Before detaching any part of the fuel system, be sure to relieve the fuel line and tank pressure by removing the fuel tank cap and disconnecting the battery (see Chapter 5A). Cover the fitting being disconnected with a rag to absorb any fuel that may spray out.

6 Fuel tank – removal and refitting

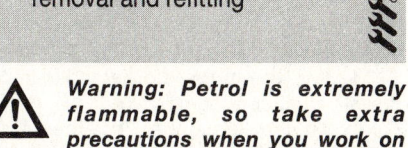

⚠️ **Warning:** *Petrol is extremely flammable, so take extra precautions when you work on any part of the fuel system. Don't smoke or allow open flames or bare light bulbs near the work area, and don't work in a garage where a natural gas-type appliance (such as a water heater or a clothes dryer) with a pilot light is present. Since petrol is carcinogenic, wear latex gloves when there's a possibility of being exposed to fuel, and, if you spill any fuel on your skin, rinse it off immediately with soap and water. Mop-up any spills immediately and do not store fuel-soaked rags where they could ignite. The fuel system is under constant pressure, so, if any fuel pipes are to be disconnected, the fuel pressure in the system must be relieved first. When you perform any kind of work on the fuel system, wear safety glasses and have a Class B type fire extinguisher on hand.*

Removal

1 This procedure is much easier to perform if the fuel tank is empty. Some models may have a drain plug for this purpose. If for some reason the drain plug can't be removed, postpone the job until the tank is empty or syphon the fuel into an approved container using a siphoning kit (available at most automotive parts/accessory stores).

⚠️ **Warning:** *Do not start the syphoning action by mouth.*

2 Remove the fuel filler cap to relieve fuel tank pressure. Relieve the fuel system pressure (see Section 2).
3 Raise the vehicle and place it securely on axle stands (see *Jacking and vehicle support*).
4 Remove the centre exhaust pipe and the heat insulator from the vehicle (see Section 15).
5 Support the fuel tank with a trolley jack. Place a sturdy plank between the jack head and the fuel tank to protect the tank.
6 Disconnect the fuel pipe(s), and the fuel filler hose **(see illustration)**. **Note:** *Be sure to plug the hoses to prevent leakage and contamination of the fuel system.*
7 Remove the bolts from the fuel tank retaining straps **(see illustration)**.
8 Lower the tank enough to disconnect the electrical connector and earth strap from the fuel pump/fuel gauge sender unit, if you have not already done so.
9 Remove the tank from the vehicle.

Refitting

10 Refitting is the reverse of removal.

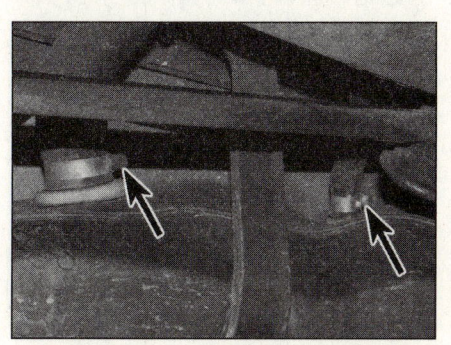

6.6 Slacken the clamps (arrowed) and disconnect the fuel filler and breather hoses

6.7 Remove the fuel retaining strap bolts (left-hand bolt arrowed)

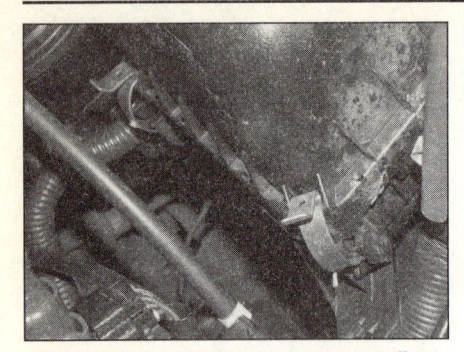

4A•6 Fuel and exhaust systems

8.1a Release the air cleaner cover clips – single headlight models . . .

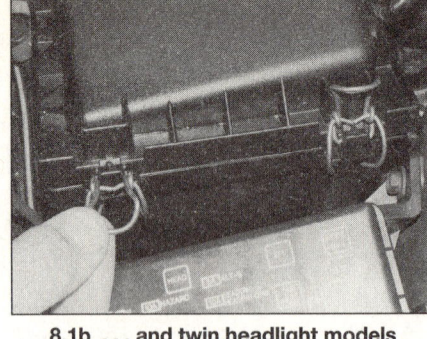

8.1b . . . and twin headlight models

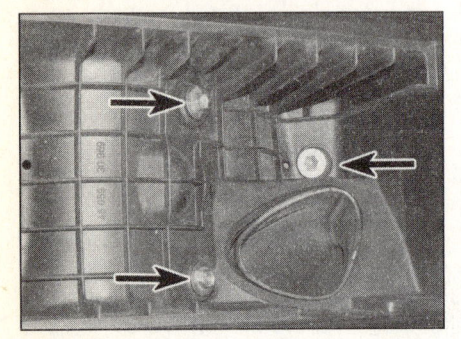

8.2a Undo the three air cleaner housing bolts (arrowed) . . .

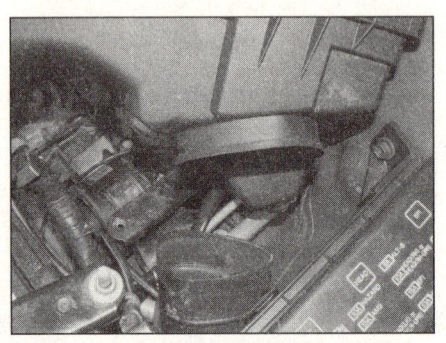

8.2b . . . and disconnect the intake hose

7 Fuel tank cleaning and repair – general information

1 Any repairs to the fuel tank or filler neck should be carried out by a professional who has experience in this critical and potentially dangerous work. Even after cleaning and flushing of the fuel system, explosive fumes can remain and ignite during repair of the tank.
2 If the fuel tank is removed from the vehicle, it should not be placed in an area where sparks or open flames could ignite the fumes coming out of the tank. Be especially careful inside garages where a natural gas-type appliance is located, because the pilot light could cause an explosion.

8 Air cleaner assembly – removal and refitting

Removal

1 Detach the clips, and remove the air filter cover and the filter element (see illustrations).
2 Remove the three bolts and remove the air cleaner assembly from the engine compartment, disconnecting the intake hose as the assembly is withdrawn (see illustrations).

Refitting

3 Refitting is the reverse of removal.

9 Accelerator cable – removal, refitting and adjustment

Removal

1 Loosen the locknut on the threaded portion of the throttle cable at the throttle body (see illustration).
2 Rotate the throttle lever and slip the cable end out of the slot in the lever (see illustration). Release the cable from the retaining clips/brackets in the engine compartment.
3 Remove the driver's side lower facia panel as described in Chapter 11.
4 Squeeze together the ends of the retaining clips, and pull the plastic grommet/fitting from the accelerator pedal, then detach the cable (see illustration). Remove the two bolts securing the cable retainer to the bulkhead.
5 From inside the vehicle, pull the cable through the bulkhead.

Refitting and adjustment

6 Refitting is the reverse of removal. Make sure the cable casing grommet seats properly in the bulkhead.
7 To adjust the cable, fully depress the accelerator pedal and check that the throttle is fully opened.
8 If not fully opened, loosen the locknuts, depress accelerator pedal and adjust the cable until the throttle is fully open.
9 Tighten the locknuts and recheck the adjustment. Make sure the throttle closes fully when the pedal is released.

10 Fuel Injection system – general information

These models are equipped with a Sequential Electronic Fuel Injection (SEFI) system. The SEFI system is composed of three basic subsystems: fuel system, air induction system and electronic control system.

Fuel system

An electric fuel pump located inside the fuel tank supplies fuel under constant pressure to

9.1 Slacken the locknut on the accelerator cable

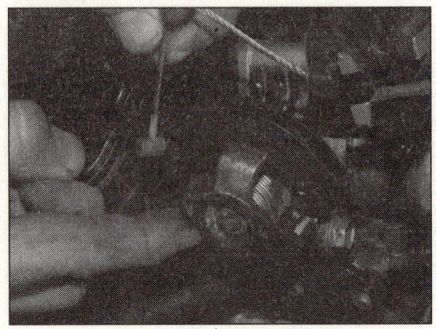

9.2 Remove the cable end fitting from the slot in the lever

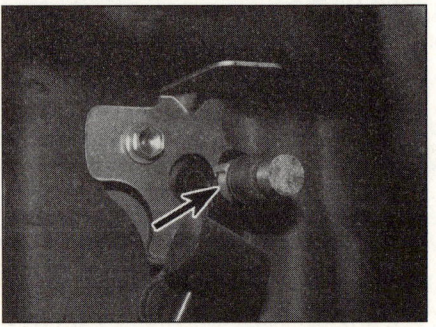

9.4 Squeeze the ends of the retaining clip (arrowed) and pull the plastic grommet/fitting from the pedal

Fuel and exhaust systems 4A•7

11.6 Use carburettor cleaner, a brush and a rag to clean the throttle body – open the throttle plate to clean behind it

11.7 The injectors should make a clicking sound that rises and falls with the engine speed

11.8 Using and ohmmeter, measure the resistance across the terminals of the injector

the fuel rail, which distributes fuel evenly to all injectors. From the fuel rail, fuel is injected into the intake ports, just above the intake valves, by fuel injectors. The amount of fuel supplied by the injectors is precisely controlled by an Electronic Control Module (ECM). A pressure regulator controls system pressure in relation to intake manifold vacuum (non-VVT-i engines). A fuel filter between the fuel pump and the fuel rail filters fuel to protect the components of the system is only fitted to non-VVT-i engines.

Air induction system

The air induction system consists of an air filter housing, the throttle body and the duct connecting the two. On non-VVT-i engines, an Intake Air Temperature (IAT) sensor monitors the temperature of the incoming air, and a Vacuum Sensor (VS) monitors the level of vacuum in the intake manifold, and therefore the engine load. On VVT-i engines, an airflow meter is located in the air filter outlet ducting, which also measures the air temperature. This information helps the ECM determine the amount of fuel to be injected by the injectors.

The throttle plate inside the throttle body is controlled by the driver. As the throttle plate opens, the speed of the incoming air increases, which lowers the temperature of the air, and the manifold vacuum decreases. The sensors send this information to the ECM, which then signals the injectors to increase the amount of fuel delivered to the intake ports.

Electronic control system

The Computer Control System controls the SEFI and other systems by means of an Electronic Control Module (ECM), which employs a microcomputer. The ECM receives signals from a number of information sensors which monitor such variables as intake air temperature, throttle angle, coolant temperature, engine rpm, vehicle speed and exhaust oxygen content. These signals help the ECM determine the injection duration necessary for the optimum air/fuel ratio. Some of these sensors and their corresponding ECM-controlled relays are not contained within SEFI components, but are located throughout the engine compartment.

11 Fuel Injection system – testing and adjustment

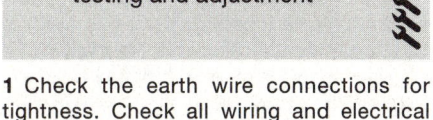

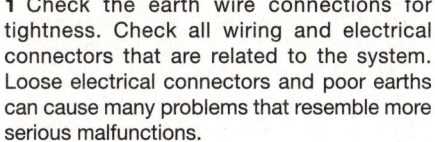

1 Check the earth wire connections for tightness. Check all wiring and electrical connectors that are related to the system. Loose electrical connectors and poor earths can cause many problems that resemble more serious malfunctions.

2 Check to see that the battery is fully-charged, as the control unit and sensors depend on an accurate supply voltage in order to properly meter the fuel.

3 Check the air filter element – a dirty or partially-blocked filter will severely impede performance and economy (see Chapter 1).

4 If a blown fuse is found, renew it and see if it blows again. If it does, search for a earthed wire in the harness related to the system.

5 Check the air intake duct from the air cleaner housing to the intake manifold for leaks, which will result in an excessively lean mixture. Also check the condition of the vacuum hoses connected to the intake manifold.

6 Remove the air intake duct from the throttle body and check for carbon and residue build-up. If it's dirty, clean it with aerosol carburettor cleaner (make sure the can says it's safe for use with oxygen sensors and catalytic converters) and a toothbrush (see illustration).

7 With the engine running, place a stethoscope against each injector, one at a time, and listen for a clicking sound, indicating operation (see illustration). If you don't have an automotive stethoscope you can use a long screwdriver; just place the tip of the screwdriver against the injector body and press your ear against the handle.

8 With the engine OFF and the fuel injector electrical connectors disconnected, measure the resistance of each injector (see illustration). Each injector should measure about 13.4 to 14.2 ohms. If not, the injector is probably faulty.

9 The remainder of the system checks should be left to a dealer service department or other suitably-equipped repairer, as there is a chance that the control unit may be damaged if not performed properly.

10 All models are equipped with a sophisticated self-diagnosis system, whereby any faults are stored as codes within the engine management ECM. By connecting suitable hand-held diagnostic equipment to the relevant connector (see illustrations), the stored code can be retrieved, and the fault identified. See your dealer or repair specialist.

12 Fuel Injection system – component testing and renewal

⚠ *Warning: Petrol is extremely flammable, so take extra precautions when you work on any part of the fuel system. Don't smoke or allow open flames or bare light bulbs near the work area, and don't work in a*

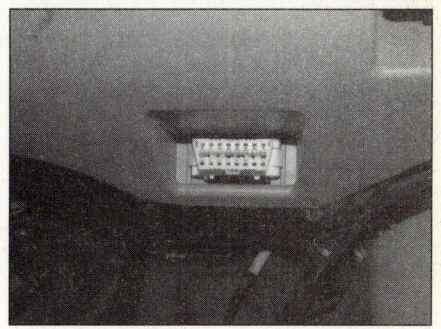

11.10a On non-VVT-i engines, the diagnostic plug is located adjacent to the left-hand front suspension turret

11.10b On VVT-i engines, the 16-pin diagnostic plug is located under the driver's side of the facia

4A•8 Fuel and exhaust systems

12.10a Throttle body mounting bolts (arrowed) – non-VVT-i engines

12.10b Throttle body mounting bolts (arrowed) – VVT-i engines

12.11 Fit a new throttle body gasket/seal

garage where a natural gas-type appliance (such as a water heater or a clothes dryer) with a pilot light is present. Since petrol is carcinogenic, wear latex gloves when there's a possibility of being exposed to fuel, and, if you spill any fuel on your skin, rinse it off immediately with soap and water. Mop up any spills immediately and do not store fuel-soaked rags where they could ignite. The fuel system is under constant pressure, so, if any fuel pipes are to be disconnected, the fuel pressure in the system must be relieved first. When you perform any kind of work on the fuel system, wear safety glasses and have a Class B type fire extinguisher on hand.

Throttle body

Testing

1 Verify that the throttle linkage operates smoothly.
2 Start the engine, detach each vacuum hose and, using a vacuum gauge, check there is no vacuum at idle, but that there is vacuum at all other times.

Renewal

⚠ **Warning: Wait until the engine is completely cool before beginning this procedure.**

3 Drain the cooling system (see Chapter 1).
4 Loosen the hose clamps and remove the air intake duct, then undo the nuts, prise out the two rear fasteners, and remove the plastic cover from the top of the engine (where fitted).

5 Detach the accelerator cable from the throttle lever (see Section 9).
6 Where applicable, detach the throttle cable bracket and set it aside (it's not necessary to detach the throttle cable from the bracket).
7 If your vehicle is equipped with an automatic transmission, detach the throttle valve (TV) cable from the throttle linkage (see Chapter 7B), detach the TV cable brackets from the engine and set the cable and brackets aside.
8 Clearly label, then detach, all vacuum, coolant hoses and breather hose from the throttle body.
9 Disconnect the electrical connector from the throttle position sensor (TPS), and idle speed control valve on the underside of the throttle body (where applicable)
10 Remove the throttle body mounting bolts/nuts **(see illustrations)**.
11 Detach the throttle body and gasket **(see illustration)** from the intake manifold. Discard the gasket, a new one must be fitted.
12 Using a soft brush and carburettor cleaner, thoroughly clean the throttle body casting, then blow out all passages with compressed air.

Caution: Do not clean the throttle position sensor with anything. Just wipe it off carefully with a clean, soft cloth.

13 Refitting of the throttle body is the reverse of removal, remembering to use a new gasket.
14 Be sure to tighten the throttle body mounting bolts to the torque listed in this Chapter's Specifications. Refill the cooling system (see Chapter 1).

Throttle position sensor (TPS)

Testing

15 Disconnect the electrical connector from the throttle position sensor (TPS).
16 Using an ohmmeter, measure the resistance between the indicated terminal pairs. The resistances should be as follows **(see illustration)**:

Throttle valve position	Between terminals	Resistance value
Fully closed	VTA and E2	0.2 to 5.7 kΩ
Fully open	VTS and E2	2.0 to 10.2 kΩ
Any position	VC and E2	2.5 to 5.9 kΩ

17 If the resistance values are not as specified, renew the sensor.

Renewal

18 Undo the screws and remove the sensor **(see illustrations)**.
19 Refitting is a reversal of removal.

Fuel pressure regulator

Renewal – non-VVT-i engines

20 Relieve the fuel pressure (see Section 2).
21 Detach the vacuum sensing hose from the regulator.
22 On 1.3 litre engines, remove the fuel return hose banjo bolt and washers, then disconnect the return hose from the regulator. On 1.6 litre engines, slide the clamp down the hose and remove the fuel return hose from the regulator.
23 Remove the pressure regulator mounting bolts **(see illustration)** and detach the pressure regulator from the fuel rail.

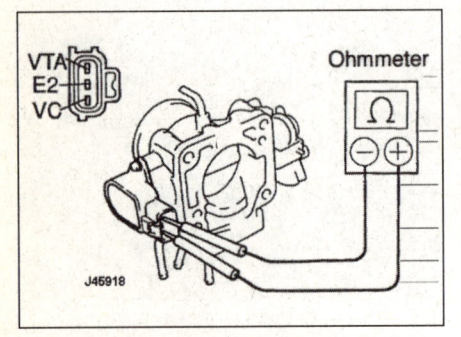

12.16 Throttle body connector terminal identification (see text)

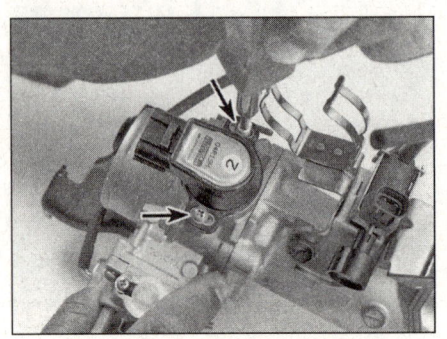

12.18a Throttle position sensor screws (arrowed) – non-VVT-i engines

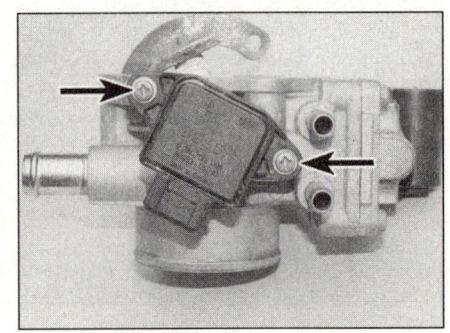

12.18b Throttle position sensor screws (arrowed) – VVT-i engines

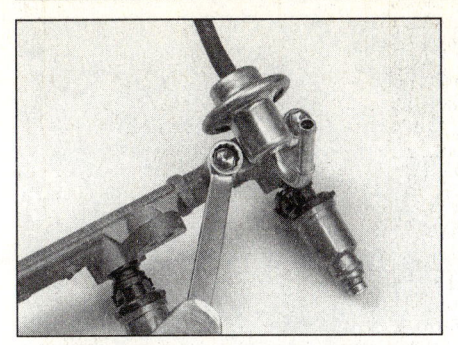

Fuel and exhaust systems 4A•9

12.23 Detach the fuel return hose and remove the two mounting bolts (arrowed)

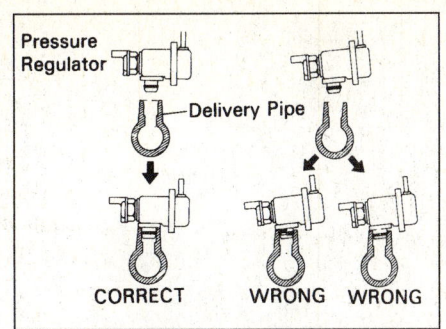

12.24 If the fuel pressure regulator is cocked during refitting, it will not seal properly

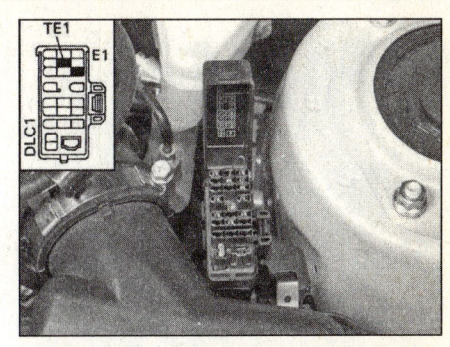

12.27 Using a jumper wire or paper clip, bridge terminals TE1 and E1

12.32a Idle speed control (ISC) valve mounting screws – non-VVT-i engines

12.32b Idle speed control (ISC) valve mounting screws (arrowed) – VVT-i engines

12.38 Number each injector electrical connector before disconnecting them from the fuel rail

24 Use a new O-ring and make sure that the pressure regulator is installed properly on the fuel rail **(see illustration)**.
25 The remainder of refitting is the reverse of removal. On 1.3 litre engines, use new copper washers each side of the banjo fitting.

Renewal – VVT-i engines

26 On these engines, the fuel pressure regulator is incorporated into the fuel pump/ level sender unit fitted into the fuel tank. Refer to Section 3 for details.

Idle speed control (ISC) valve

Testing – non-VVT-i engines

27 Using a jumper wire, bridge terminals TE1 and E1 of the test connector **(see illustration)**.
28 Start the engine. The engine speed should increase to approximately 1000 to 1200 rpm for five seconds then return to normal idle speed.
 a) If the engine speed changes as described, the ISC valve is okay.
 b) If the engine speed does not change as described, remove the valve as described below.
29 With the valve removed, reconnect the wiring plug.
30 Turn the ignition on. The valve should move from fully open, to fully closed, then to halfway closed in that order, with a gap of 0.5 seconds between each position. If it does not perform as specified, renew the valve.

Renewal – non-VVT-i engines

31 Remove the throttle body (see paragraphs 3 to 11). **Note:** *The ISC valve and assembly are difficult to reach, therefore it is recommended to remove the throttle body so that the new ISC valve assembly can be installed properly.*
32 Remove the mounting screws and detach the ISC valve and gasket **(see illustrations)**.
33 If the ISC assembly was renewed, be sure to install the temperature vacuum valve (TVV) from the original assembly into the new unit (if equipped).
34 Refitting of the ISC valve is the reverse of removal. Be sure to use a new gasket when installing the ISC valve.

Fuel rail and fuel injectors

Testing

35 Refer to the fuel injection system checking procedure (see Section 11).

Renewal – non-VVT-i engines

36 Relieve the fuel pressure (see Section 2).

12.41 Remove the bolts (arrowed) that retain the fuel rail to the intake manifold

37 Remove the PCV hose(s) from the cylinder head and intake manifold.
38 Carefully mark each injector connector with a felt pen or paint **(see illustration)**. Disconnect the fuel injector electrical connectors and set the injector wire harness aside. On 1.3 litre engines remove the bolt and detach the harness from the air intake plenum stay bar. Remove the nut and bolt, then remove the stay bar.
39 Detach the vacuum sensing hose from the fuel pressure regulator.
40 Disconnect the fuel pipes from the fuel pressure regulator and the fuel rail.
41 Remove the fuel rail mounting bolts **(see illustration)**.
42 Remove the fuel rail with the fuel injectors attached **(see illustration)**.
43 Remove the fuel injector(s) from the fuel rail and set them aside in a clearly labelled storage container.

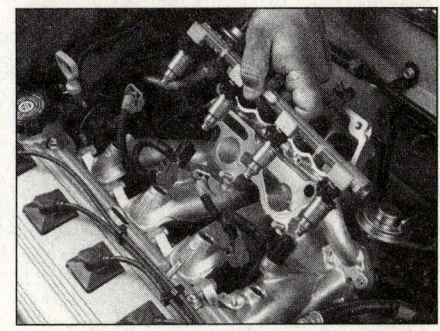

12.42 Lift the fuel rail assembly from the engine. Be prepared for fuel spillage

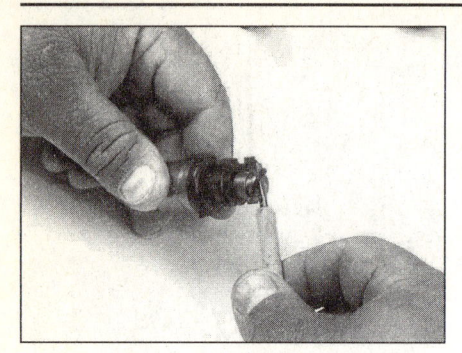

4A•10 Fuel and exhaust systems

12.44a Remove the O-ring from the injector

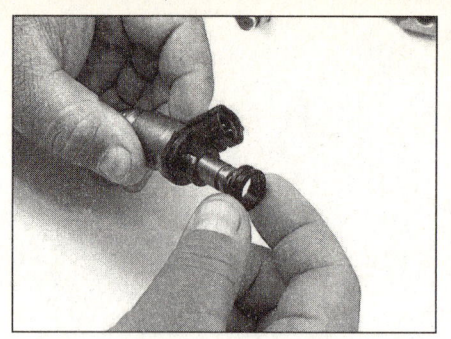

12.44b Remove the grommet from the top of the injector

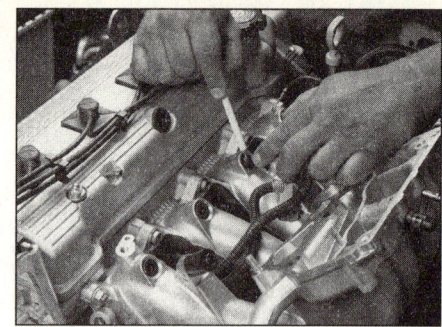

12.44c Remove the O-rings from the bores in the intake manifold

12.49 Depress the clip (arrowed) and disconnect the injector wiring plugs

12.51a Slide the clamp from the fuel hose connection . . .

12.51b . . . then using a stiff piece of plastic . . .

44 If you intend to re-use the same injectors, renew the grommets and O-rings **(see illustrations)**.

45 Refitting of the fuel injectors is the reverse of removal.

46 Tighten the fuel rail mounting bolts to the torque listed in this Chapter's Specifications.

Renewal – VVT-i engines

47 Relieve the fuel pressure (Section 2).

48 Remove the PCV hose from the cylinder head cover.

49 Disconnect the wiring plugs from the top of the injectors **(see illustration)**.

50 Undo the bolt securing the fuel pipe to the cylinder head.

51 Disconnect the fuel supply pipe from the fuel rail by sliding the clamp from the pipe then using a piece of stiff plastic to release the internal clips inside the connection **(see illustrations)**.

52 Undo the two mounting bolts and remove the fuel rail complete with injectors **(see illustration)**.

53 Remove the two spacers and 4 grommets, then pull the injectors from the fuel rail **(see illustrations)**.

54 If you intend to re-use the same injectors, renew the grommets and O-rings **(see illustration)**.

12.51c . . . release the internal catches and disconnect the fuel hose

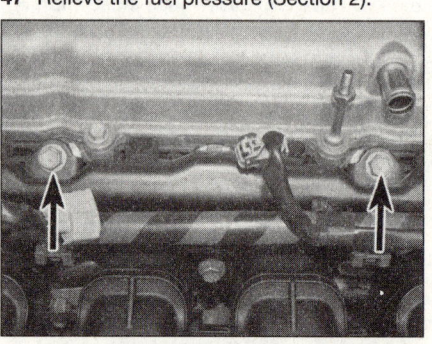

12.52 Undo the two fuel rail mounting bolts (arrowed)

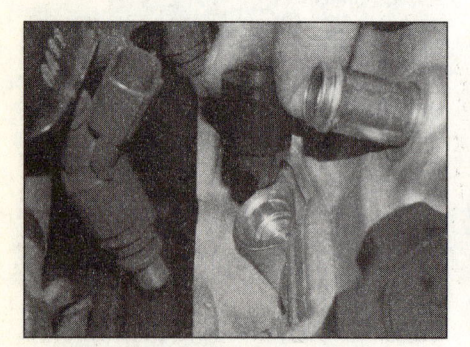

12.53a Recover the spacers from the cylinder head . . .

12.53b . . . and pull the grommets from the injector bores

12.54 Renew the injector O-rings and grommets (arrowed)

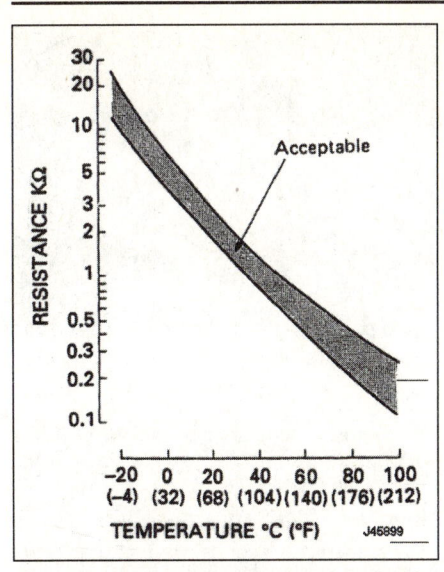

Fuel and exhaust systems 4A•11

12.59 Temperature/resistance chart for the intake air temperature sensor

12.62a Intake air temperature sensor – 1.3 litre 4E-FE engine (arrowed)

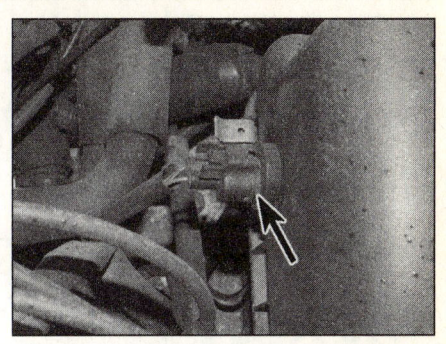

12.62b Intake air temperature sensor – 1.6 litre 4A-FE engine (arrowed)

12.65 The vacuum sensor is located on the engine compartment bulkhead

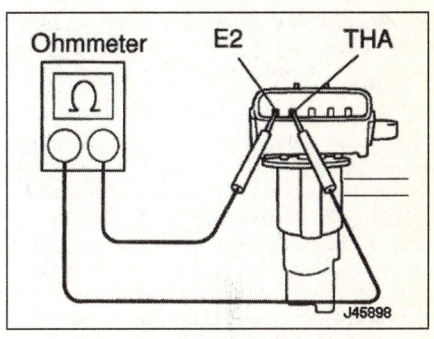

12.68 Connector an ohmmeter to the airflow meter terminals as shown

55 Refitting of the fuel injectors is the reverse of removal.
56 Tighten the fuel rail mounting bolts to the torque listed in this Chapter's Specifications.

Intake air temperature sensor

Testing – non-VVT-i engines

57 Remove the sensor as described below.
58 Connect the leads of an ohmmeter to the terminals of the sensor, and suspend the sensor in a saucepan of water.
59 Insert a thermometer into the water, then measure the temperature and resistance, and compare the readings with those shown **(see illustration)**.
60 If the resistance is not as specified, the sensor may be faulty.

Renewal – non-VVT-i engines

61 Disconnect the wiring plug from the sensor, located in the air cleaner cover.
62 Pull the sensor from the cover **(see illustrations)**.
63 Refitting is a reversal of removal.

Vacuum (MAP) sensor

Testing – non-VVT-i engines

64 No testing procedure is available for the sensor. Have the engine management ECM self-diagnosis system interrogated for any stored fault codes relating to the sensor (see Section 11).

Renewal – non-VVT-i engines

65 The sensor is located on the bulkhead at the rear of the engine compartment. Disconnect the sensor wiring plug, and the vacuum hose **(see illustration)**.
66 Release the wiring clip, undo the retaining bolt and remove the sensor along with the bracket.
67 Refitting is a reversal of removal.

Airflow meter

Testing – VVT-i engines

68 Connect the leads of an ohmmeter to the terminals E2 and THA of the sensor **(see illustration)**.
69 At -20°C the resistance across the terminals should be 13.6 to 18.4 kΩ, at 20° it should be 2.21 to 2.69 kΩ, and at 60°C 0.49 to 0.67 kΩ.

Renewal – VVT-i engines

70 The airflow meter is located in the air filter outlet ducting. Disconnect the sensor wiring plug **(see illustration)**.
71 Undo the two screws, and pull the sensor from the ducting. Discard the O-ring, a new one must be fitted.
72 Fit the sensor to the ducting, using a new O-ring seal, and tighten the screws securely.

12.70 The airflow meter is located in the air filter outlet ducting

Engine management ECM

Testing

73 Have the engine management ECM self-diagnosis system interrogated for any stored fault codes relating to the ECM (see Section 11).

Removal

74 Disconnect the battery negative lead (see Chapter 5A). **Note:** *Disconnecting the battery will erase any fault codes stored in the ECM. It is recommended that the fault code memory of the module is interrogated using special test equipment prior to battery disconnection. Entrust this task to a Toyota dealer or suitably-equipped specialist.*
75 Remove the complete centre console as described in Chapter 11.
76 Undo the three bolts and remove the ECM **(see illustration)**.

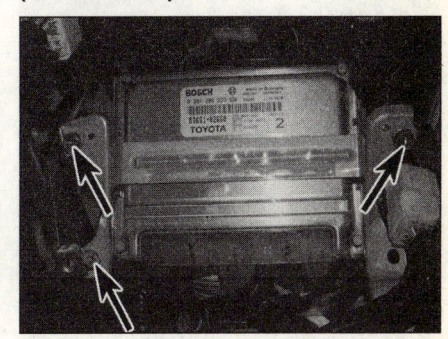

12.76 ECM retaining bolts (arrowed)

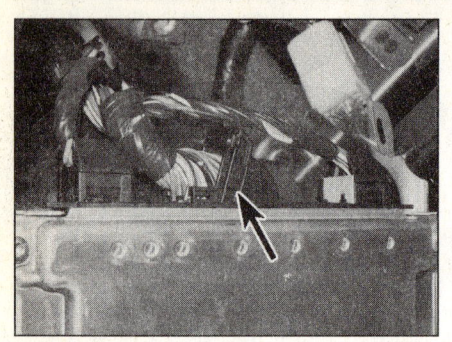

4A•12 Fuel and exhaust systems

12.77 Release the locking catch (arrowed) and disconnect the ECM wiring plugs

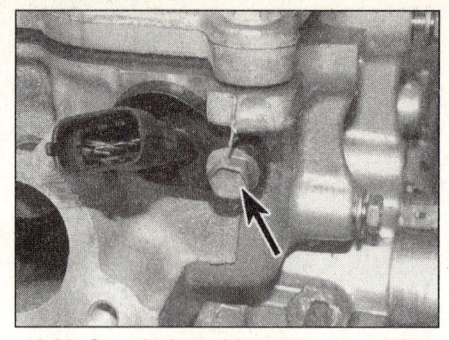

12.82 Camshaft position sensor retaining bolt (arrowed)

12.87 Crankshaft position sensor wiring plug (arrowed)

77 Release the catch and disconnect the ECM wiring plugs **(see illustration)**.

Refitting

78 Refitting is a reversal of removal. **Note:** *If a new module has been fitted, it may be necessary to be recode it using special test equipment. Entrust this task to a Toyota dealer or suitably-equipped specialist. After reconnecting the battery, the vehicle must be driven for several miles so that the ECM can learn its basic settings. If the engine still runs erratically, the basic settings may be reinstated by a Toyota dealer or specialist using special diagnostic equipment.*

Camshaft position sensor

Testing – VVT-i engines

Note: *The following procedure only applies to those sensors manufactured by Denso. No information concerning Bosch sensors was available.*

79 The sensor is located at the front, left-hand end of the cylinder head. Disconnect the sensor wiring plug, and connect the leads of an ohmmeter to the sensor terminals.
80 On a cold engine, then resistance should be 835 to 1400 Ω. On a hot engine, the resistance should be 1060 to 1645 Ω.

Renewal – VVT-i engines

81 Disconnect the sensor wiring plug.
82 Undo the retaining bolt, and pull the sensor from position **(see illustration)**. Discard the O-ring seal, a new one must be fitted.
83 Insert the sensor into the cylinder head, with a new O-ring seal.

84 Tighten the retaining bolt to the specified torque, and reconnect the wiring plug.

Crankshaft position/speed sensor

Testing – 1.3 litre 4E-FE engines

85 Disconnect the wiring plug from the sensor, and connect the leads of an ohmmeter to the sensor terminals.
86 Measure the resistance of the sensor and compare the readings obtained with those given in the Specifications at the start of this Chapter.

Renewal – 1.3 litre 4E-FE engines

87 Disconnect the sensor wiring plug, and unclip it from the bracket adjacent to the oil level dipstick **(see illustration)**.
88 Remove the auxiliary drivebelt(s) as described in Chapter 1.
89 Remove the crankshaft pulley and timing belt covers as described in Chapter 2A.
90 Undo the bolt and remove the sensor from the mounting bracket **(see illustration)**.
91 Refitting is a reversal of removal. Tighten the sensor bolt to the specified torque.

Testing – VVT-i engines

92 Remove the alternator as described in Chapter 5A.
93 The sensor is located adjacent to the crankshaft pulley at the front of the engine. Trace the wiring back from the sensor and disconnect the wiring plug **(see illustration)**.
94 Connect the leads of an ohmmeter to the sensor terminals, and measure the resistance of the sensor. Compare the readings obtained with those given in the Specifications at the start of this Chapter.

Renewal – VVT-i engines

95 Proceed as described in paragraphs 92 and 93
96 Undo the bolt securing the sensor wiring loom retaining bracket to the engine block.
97 Undo the retaining bolt and withdraw the sensor from position **(see illustration)**. Discard the sensor O-ring seal, a new one must be fitted.
98 Insert the sensor into position, with a new O-ring seal.
99 Tighten the retaining bolt to the specified torque, and reconnect the wiring plug.

13 Intake manifold – removal and refitting

Removal

Non-VVT-i engines

Note: *If the intake manifold is to be unbolted only for removal of the cylinder head, then the intake manifold can simply be unbolted from the cylinder head and pushed toward the bulkhead, without disconnecting any hoses, wires or linkage. The following procedure is for complete removal of the manifold from the vehicle.*

1 Remove the throttle body as described in Section 12.

12.90 Undo the bolt (arrowed) and remove the crankshaft position sensor

12.93 The crankshaft position sensor is located adjacent to the crankshaft pulley (arrowed)

12.97 Undo the bolt and pull the sensor from the timing chain cover. Renew the O-ring (arrowed)

Fuel and exhaust systems 4A•13

13.2 The various hoses should be marked to ensure correct refitting

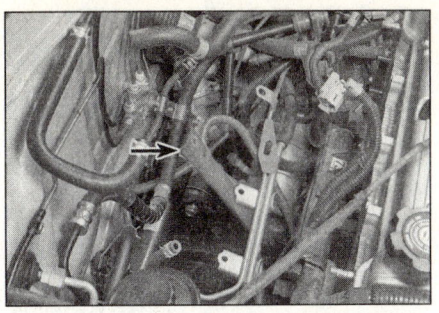

13.5 From underneath the vehicle, remove the bolt retaining this brace (arrowed) to the intake manifold

13.6a Unbolt the wiring harness (right arrow), then remove the lower manifold bolts (left arrow indicates one of the four bolts)

2 Label and detach the PCV and vacuum hoses connected to the intake manifold, including those from the vacuum sensor, vacuum servo unit and the air conditioning idle-up actuator – where fitted **(see illustration)**.
3 The intake manifold can be removed with the injectors and fuel rail in place. If the injectors are to be removed from the intake manifold, refer to Section 12.
4 Disconnect the idle speed control valve electrical connector and the hoses from the air pipe at the rear of the manifold.
5 Unbolt the upper end of the intake manifold-to-block brace (accessible from under the vehicle), and the upper manifold brace, where fitted **(see illustration)**.
6 Remove the earth strap and mounting nuts/bolts, then detach the manifold from the engine **(see illustrations)**. **Note:** *From under the vehicle, it will be necessary to unbolt the wiring harness, the lower intake manifold bolts, and the two nuts securing the pair of steel pipes to the underside of the intake manifold.*

VVT-i engines

7 Remove the throttle body as described in Section 12.
8 Release the clips securing the engine wiring loom to the 2 brackets on the top of the manifold, then disconnect the camshaft position sensor plug and move the loom to one side.
9 Undo the two bolts and release the hose bracket from the manifold **(see illustration)**.
10 Disconnect the brake servo vacuum pipe and the PCV (positive crankcase ventilation) hose from the manifold **(see illustration)**.
11 Undo the three bolts, two nuts, remove the 2 brackets, then remove the intake manifold **(see illustration)**. Recover the intake manifold O-ring seals. Release the wiring loom clip as the manifold is removed.

Refitting

12 Clean the mating surfaces of the intake manifold and the cylinder head mounting surface with brake cleaner or a suitable solvent. If the gasket shows signs of leaking, have the manifold checked for warpage at an automotive machine workshop and resurfaced if necessary.
13 On 1.6 litre 4A-FE engines, the manifold is a two-piece design, and a new gasket set

13.6b Remove the intake manifold bolts/nuts and remove the intake manifold

may include the gasket for the air chamber cover. Unless the engine has covered a high mileage or you suspect a vacuum leak at the mating surfaces, don't unbolt the air chamber cover. If it's necessary to renew the gasket, unbolt the cover, clean the surfaces, position the new gasket and reinstall the cover.
14 Fit a new gasket/O-ring seals, then position the manifold on the cylinder head and refit the nuts/bolts.
15 Tighten the nuts/bolts in three or four equal steps to the torque listed in this Chapter's Specifications. Work from the centre out towards the ends to avoid warping the manifold.
16 Refit the remaining parts in the reverse order of removal.
17 Before starting the engine, check the throttle linkage for smooth operation.
18 Run the engine and check for coolant and vacuum leaks.

13.10 Release the clamps and disconnect the servo vacuum hose (right arrow) and the PCV hose (left arrow)

13.9 Undo the two bolts (arrowed) and remove the hose bracket

19 Road test the vehicle and check for proper operation of all accessories.

14 Exhaust manifold – removal and refitting

⚠️ **Warning:** *The engine must be completely cool before beginning this procedure.*

Removal

1 Remove the upper heat shield from the manifold **(see illustration)**. **Note:** *There may also be a lower heat shield, but this is attached to the manifold from underneath and does not need to be removed.*
2 Apply penetrating oil to the exhaust manifold mounting nuts/bolts, and the nuts/bolts retaining the exhaust pipe to the manifold. After the nuts/bolts have soaked, remove the

13.11 Undo the nuts and bolts (arrowed) and remove the intake manifold

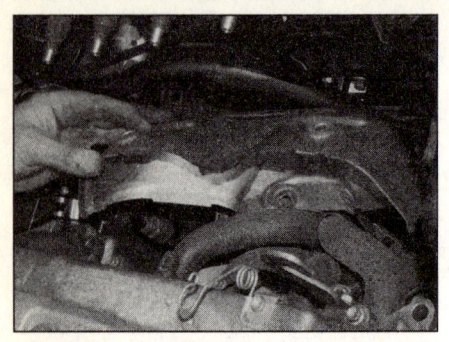

4A•14 Fuel and exhaust systems

14.1 Remove the upper heat shield from the manifold

14.2a Remove the upper bolt retaining the brace (top arrow) and slacken the brace to block bolts (lower arrows)

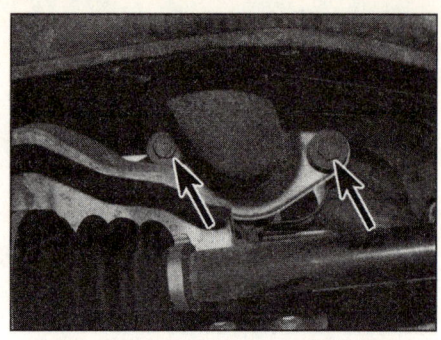

14.2b Exhaust pipe-to-manifold bolts (arrowed) – VVT-i engines

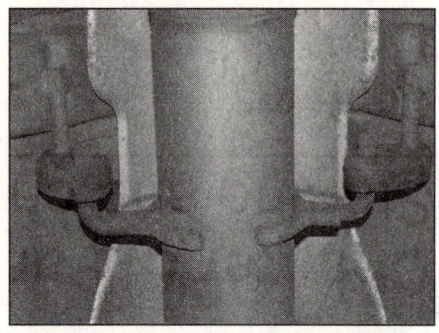

nuts/bolts retaining the exhaust pipe to the manifold **(see illustrations)**
3 Where fitted, unbolt the exhaust manifold brace.
4 Where the manifold has an oxygen sensor fitted, trace the wiring from the sensor back to the connector and unplug it.
5 Remove the nuts/bolts and detach the manifold and gasket.

Refitting

6 Use a scraper to remove all traces of old gasket material and carbon deposits from the manifold and cylinder head mating surfaces. If the gasket was leaking, have the manifold checked for warpage at an automotive machine workshop and resurfaced if necessary.
7 Position a new gasket over the cylinder head studs. **Note:** *The marks on the gasket should face out (away from the cylinder head) and the arrow should point toward the transmission end of the engine.*
8 Refit the manifold and thread the mounting nuts/bolts into place.
9 Working from the centre out, tighten the nuts/bolts to the torque listed in this Chapter's Specifications in three or four equal steps.
10 Refit the remaining parts in the reverse order of removal.
11 Run the engine and check for exhaust leaks.

15 Exhaust system – removal and refitting

⚠️ *Warning: Inspection and repair of exhaust system components should be done only after the system components have cooled completely.*

1 The exhaust system consists of the exhaust manifold, catalytic converter, the silencer, the tailpipe and all connecting pipes, brackets, rubber-mountings and clamps. The exhaust system is attached to the body with mounting brackets and rubber hangers **(see illustration)**. If any of these parts are damaged or deteriorated, excessive noise and vibration will be transmitted to the body.
2 Conducting regular inspections of the exhaust system will keep it safe and quiet. Look for any damaged or bent parts, open seams, holes, loose connections, excessive corrosion or other defects, which could allow exhaust fumes to enter the vehicle. Deteriorated exhaust system components should not be repaired – they should be renewed.
3 If the exhaust system components are extremely corroded or rusted together, they will probably have to be cut from the exhaust system. The convenient way to accomplish this is to have a exhaust specialist remove the corroded sections with a cutting torch. If, however, you want to save money by doing it yourself and you don't have an oxy/acetylene welding outfit with a cutting torch, simply cut off the old components with a hacksaw. If you have compressed air, special pneumatic cutting chisels can also be used. If you do decide to tackle the job at home, be sure to wear eye protection to protect your eyes from metal chips and work gloves to protect your hands.
4 Here are some simple guidelines to apply when repairing the exhaust system:
 a) Work from the back to the front when removing exhaust system components.

15.1 The exhaust system is attached to the vehicle body with rubber hangers

 b) Apply penetrating oil to the exhaust system component fasteners to make them easier to remove.
 c) Use new gaskets, rubber-mountings and clamps when installing exhaust system components.
 d) Apply anti-seize compound to the threads of all exhaust system fasteners during reassembly.
 e) Be sure to allow sufficient clearance between newly fitted parts and all points on the underbody to avoid overheating the floorpan and possibly damaging the interior carpet and insulation. Pay particularly close attention to the catalytic converter and its heat shield.

⚠️ *Warning: The catalytic converter operates at very high temperatures and takes a long time to cool. Wait until it's completely cool before attempting to remove the converter. Failure to do so could result in serious burns.*

Chapter 4 Part B:
Emission control systems

Contents

	Section number		Section number
Catalytic converter	4	General information	1
Evaporative Emission Control (EVAP) system	2	Positive Crankcase Ventilation (PCV) system	3

Degrees of difficulty

Easy, suitable for novice with little experience	**Fairly easy,** suitable for beginner with some experience	**Fairly difficult,** suitable for competent DIY mechanic	**Difficult,** suitable for experienced DIY mechanic	**Very difficult,** suitable for expert DIY or professional

Specifications

General
Engine codes:
1.3 litre (1332 cc) non-VVT-i engine	4E-FE
1.4 litre (1398 cc) VVT-i engine	4ZZ-FE
1.6 litre (1587 cc) non-VVT-i engine	4A-FE
1.6 litre (1598 cc) VVT-i engine	3ZZ-FE

Torque wrench settings
	Nm	lbf ft
Oxygen sensor:		
Non-VVT-i engines	20	15
VVT-i engines	44	32

1 General information

To minimise pollution of the atmosphere from incompletely burned and evaporating gases, and to maintain good driveability and fuel economy, a number of emission control systems are used on these vehicles, according to market territory. They include the:
Positive Crankcase Ventilation (PCV) system.
Evaporative Emission Control (EVAP) system.
Three-way catalytic converter (TWC) system.
The Sections in this Chapter include general descriptions, checking procedures within the scope of the home mechanic and component renewal procedures (when possible) for each of the systems listed above.

Before assuming an emissions control system is malfunctioning, check the fuel and ignition systems carefully (see Chapters 4A and 5A). The diagnosis of some emission control devices requires specialised tools, equipment and training. If checking and servicing become too difficult or if a procedure is beyond the scope of your skills, consult your dealer service department or other repair workshop.

This doesn't mean, however, that emission control systems are particularly difficult to maintain and repair. You can quickly and easily perform many checks and do most of the regular maintenance at home with common tune-up and hand tools. **Note:** *The most frequent cause of emissions problems is simply a loose or broken electrical connector or vacuum hose, so always check the electrical connectors and vacuum hoses first.*

Pay close attention to any special precautions outlined in this Chapter. It should be noted that the illustrations of the various systems may not exactly match the system installed on your vehicle because of changes made by the manufacturer during production or from year-to-year.

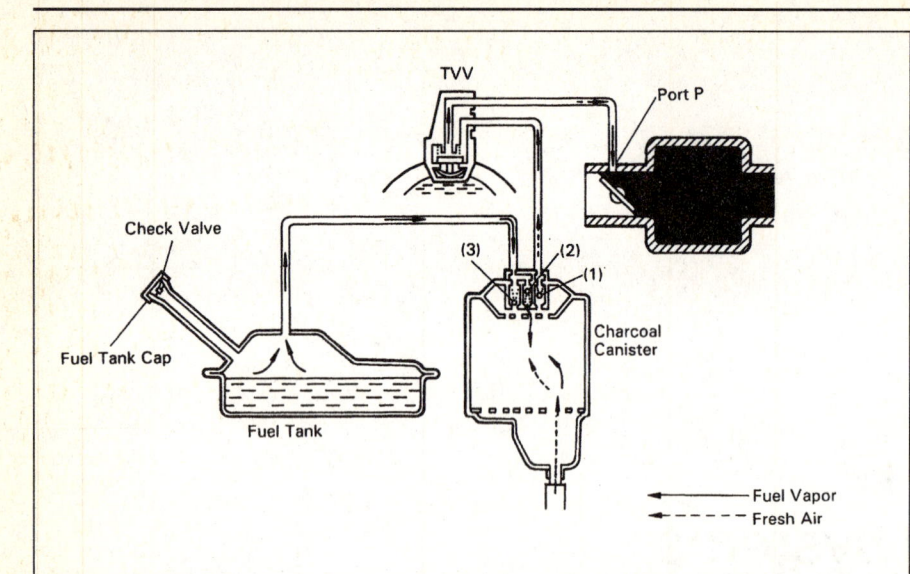

4B•2 Emission control systems

ECT	TVV	Throttle Position	Canister Check Valve (1)	Canister Check Valve (2)	Canister Check Valve (3)	Check Valve in Cap	Evaporated Fuel (HC)
Below 35°C (95°F)	CLOSED	—	—	—	—	—	HC from tank is absorbed into the canister.
Above 54°C (129°F)	OPEN	Below port P	CLOSED	—	—	—	HC from tank is absorbed into the canister.
		Above port P	OPEN	—	—	—	HC from canister is led into air intake chamber.
High pressure in tank	—	—	—	OPEN	CLOSED	CLOSED	HC from tank is absorbed into the canister.
High vacuum in tank	—	—	—	CLOSED	OPEN	OPEN	Air is led into the fuel tank.

2.2a Typical EVAP system and operation chart – non-VVT-i models

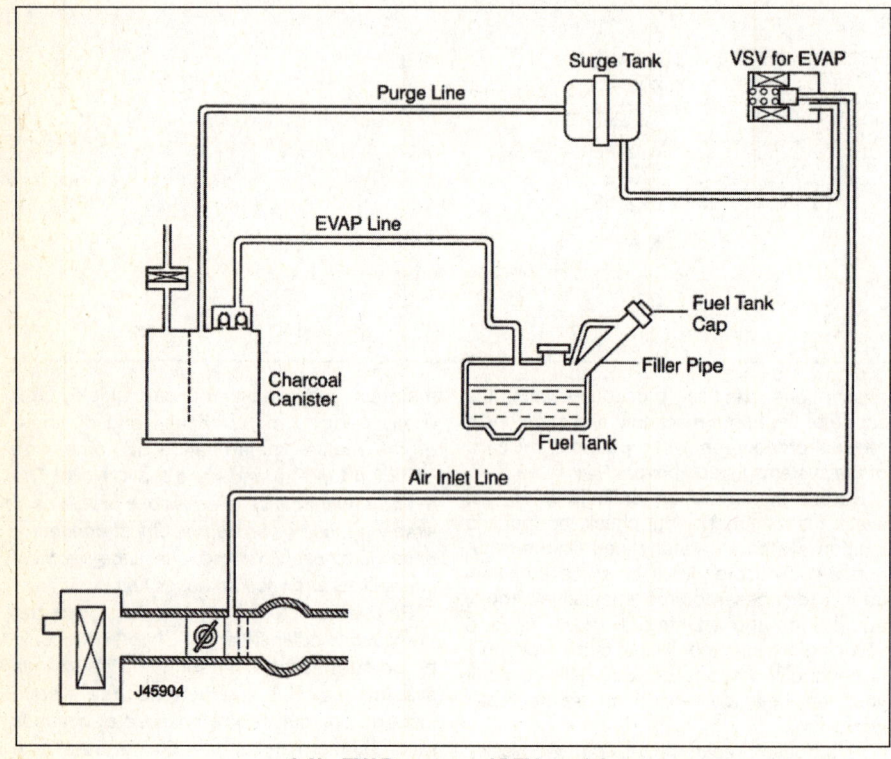

2.2b EVAP system – VVT-i models

2 Evaporative Emission Control (EVAP) system

General description

1 This system is designed to trap and store fuel that evaporates from the fuel tank, throttle body and intake manifold that would normally enter the atmosphere in the form of hydrocarbon (HC) emissions.

2 The Evaporative Emission Control (EVAP) system for non-VVT-i engines consists of a charcoal-filled canister, the lines connecting the canister to the fuel tank, the Temperature Vacuum Valve (TVV) and a check valve (see illustration). On VVT-i engines, the system consists of a charcoal-filled canister, the pipes connecting the canister to the fuel tank, the Vacuum Switching Valve (VSV) and a surge tank (see illustration).

3 Fuel vapours are transferred from the fuel tank and throttle body to a canister where they're stored when the engine isn't running. When the engine is running, the fuel vapours are purged from the canister by intake airflow and consumed in the normal combustion process.

4 The charcoal canister is equipped with a check valve that incorporates three check balls. Depending upon the running conditions and the pressure in the fuel tank, the check balls open and close the passageways to the TVV/VSV (consequently the throttle body) and fuel tank.

Check

5 Poor idle, stalling and poor driveability can be caused by an inoperative check valve, a damaged canister, split or cracked hoses, or hoses connected to the wrong fittings. Check the fuel filler cap for a damaged or deformed gasket.

6 Evidence of fuel loss or fuel odour can be caused by liquid fuel leaking from fuel lines, a cracked or damaged canister, an inoperative check valve, or disconnected, misrouted, kinked, deteriorated or damaged vapour or control hoses.

7 Inspect each hose attached to the canister for kinks, leaks and cracks along its entire length. Repair or renew as necessary.

8 Look for fuel leaking from the bottom of the canister. If fuel is leaking, renew the canister and check the hoses and hose routing.

9 Inspect the canister. If it's cracked or damaged, renew it.

10 Check for a clogged filter or a stuck check valve. Using low pressure compressed air, blow into the canister tank pipe (see illustration). Air should flow freely from the other pipes. If a problem is found, renew the canister.

11 On non-VVT-i engines, check the operation of the TVV. With the engine completely cold, use a hand-held pump and direct air into port A (see illustration). Air should not pass

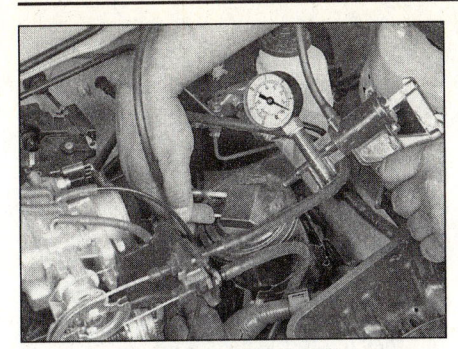

Emission control systems 4B•3

2.10 Apply air pressure into the purge control valve A (inlet) and confirm that the valve allows air to pass into the charcoal canister

2.11 Apply air pressure to the port A on the TVV (top port) and confirm that air does not pass when the temperature is below 53°C

2.15 Lift the cap (arrowed) then label the hoses before disconnecting them

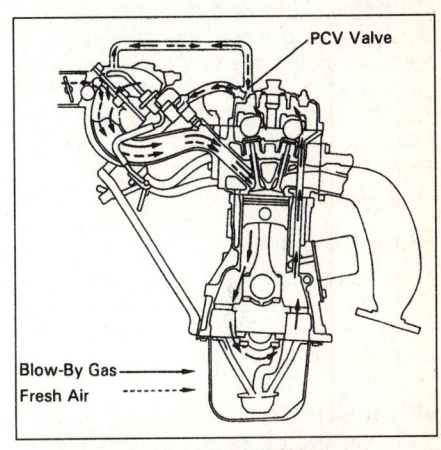

through the TVV. Now warm the engine to operating temperature (above 53°C) and check that air passes through the TVV. Renew the valve if the test results are incorrect.

12 On VVT-i engines, disconnect the VSV (purge) valve wiring plug (located on the rear of the air filter housing) and connect the leads of an ohmmeter to the valve terminals. The correct resistance should be 27 to 33 Ω at 20°C.

Charcoal canister renewal

13 Clearly label, then detach the vacuum hoses from the canister (located behind the air filter housing).
14 On non-VVT-i engines, remove the mounting clamp bolts, lower the canister with the bracket, disconnect the hoses from the check valve and remove it from the vehicle.
15 On VVT-i engines, lift the cap from the top of the canister (located behind the air filter housing), label and disconnect the hoses from the canister **(see illustration)**. Release the clips and lift the canister from position.
16 Installation is the reverse of removal.

3 Positive Crankcase Ventilation (PCV) system

General description

1 The Positive Crankcase Ventilation (PCV) system reduces hydrocarbon emissions by scavenging crankcase vapours. It does this by circulating fresh air from the air cleaner through the crankcase, where it mixes with blow-by gases and is then rerouted through a PCV valve to the intake manifold **(see illustrations)**.
2 The main components of the PCV system are the PCV valve, a fresh air intake and the vacuum hoses connecting these components to the engine.
3 To maintain idle quality, the PCV valve restricts the flow when the intake manifold vacuum is high. If abnormal operating conditions (such as piston ring problems) arise, the system is designed to allow excessive amounts of blow-by gases to flow back through the crankcase vent tube into the air cleaner to be consumed by normal combustion.
4 This system directs the blow-by into the throttle body which, over time, can cause an oily residue build-up in the area near the throttle plate. Consequently, it's a good idea to periodically clean this residue from the throttle body. Refer to Chapter 4A for this cleaning procedure.

Check

5 To check the valve, first pull it out of the grommet in the valve cover (non-VVT-i engines), or unscrew it from the cover (VVT-i engines) and shake the valve. It should rattle, indicating that it's not clogged with deposits. If the valve does not rattle, renew it.

3.1a Diagram of the PCV system – non-VVT-i engines

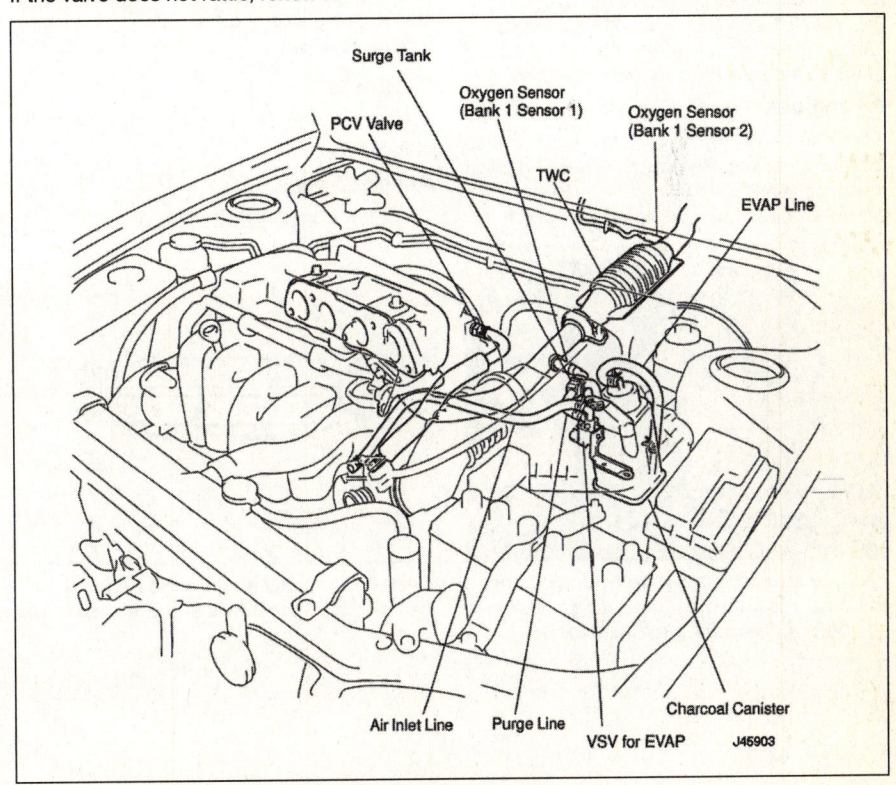

3.1b Emission systems pipework – VVT-i engines

4B•4 Emission control systems

3.9 Disconnect the hose and unscrew the PCV valve

6 Start the engine and allow it to idle, then place your finger over the valve opening. If vacuum is felt, the PCV valve is working properly. If no vacuum is felt, the PCV valve may be defective or the hose may be blocked. Also check for vacuum leaks at the valve, filler cap and all the hoses.

Renewal

Non-VVT-i engines

7 Pull straight up on the valve (located in the breather hose attached to the cylinder head cover) to remove it. Check the rubber grommet for cracks and distortion. If it's damaged, renew it.

VVT-i engines

8 Undo the two nuts, prise out the plastic fasteners at the rear and remove the cover from the top of the engine.
9 Release the clamp, disconnect the hose, and unscrew the valve from the left-hand end of the cylinder head cover **(see illustration)**.

All engines

10 If the valve is clogged, the hose is also probably blocked. Remove the hose and clean it with solvent.
11 After cleaning the hose, inspect it for damage, wear and deterioration. Make sure it fits snugly on the fittings.
12 If necessary, install a new PCV valve.
13 Install the clean PCV hose. Make sure that the PCV valve and hose are secure.

4 Catalytic converter

General description

1 To reduce hydrocarbon, carbon monoxide and oxides of nitrogen emissions, all vehicles are equipped with a three-way catalyst system which oxidises and reduces these chemicals, converting them into harmless nitrogen, carbon dioxide and water.
2 The catalytic converter is mounted in the exhaust system much like a silencer **(see illustration)**.

Check

3 Periodically inspect the catalytic converter-to-exhaust pipe mating flanges and bolts. Make sure that there are no loose bolts and no leaks between the flanges.
4 Look for dents in or damage to the catalytic converter protector **(see illustration)**. If any part of the protector is damaged or dented enough to touch the converter, repair or renew it.
5 Inspect the heat insulator for damage. Make sure that there is adequate clearance between the heat insulator and the catalytic converter **(see illustration)**.

Renewal

6 To renew the catalytic converter, refer to Chapter 4A.

Precautions

a) DO NOT use leaded petrol or LRP – the lead will coat the precious metals, reducing their converting efficiency, and will eventually destroy the converter.
b) Always keep the ignition and fuel systems well-maintained in accordance with the manufacturer's schedule (see Chapter 1).
c) If the engine develops a misfire, do not drive the vehicle at all (or at least as little as possible) until the fault is cured.
d) DO NOT push – or tow-start the vehicle – this will soak the catalytic converter in unburned fuel, causing it to overheat when the engine does start.
e) DO NOT switch off the ignition at high engine speeds, ie, do not blip the throttle immediately before switching off.
f) DO NOT use fuel or engine oil additives – these may contain substances harmful to the catalytic converter.
g) DO NOT continue to use the vehicle if the engine burns oil to the extent of leaving a visible trail of blue smoke.
h) Remember that the catalytic converter operates at very high temperatures. DO NOT, therefore, park the vehicle in dry undergrowth, over long grass or piles of dead leaves, after a long run.
i) Remember that the catalytic converter is FRAGILE. Do not strike it with tools during servicing work.
j) In some cases, a sulphurous smell (like that of rotten eggs) may be noticed from the exhaust. This is common to many catalytic converter-equipped vehicles. Once the vehicle has covered a few thousand miles, the problem should disappear – in the meantime, try changing the brand of petrol used.
k) The catalytic converter used on a well-maintained and well-driven vehicle should last for between 50 000 and 100 000 miles. If the converter is no longer effective, it must be renewed.

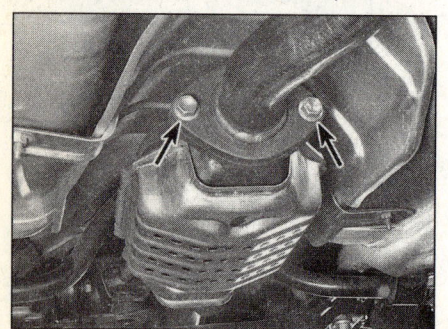

4.2 Be sure to spray penetrating oil onto the catalytic converter mounting bolts/nuts before attempting to unscrew them

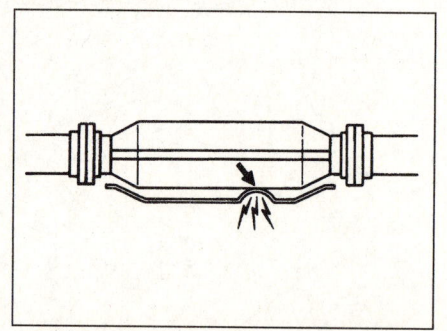

4.4 Periodically inspect the heat shield (where fitted) for dents and other damage

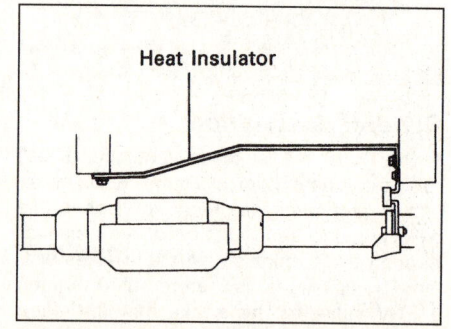

4.5 Periodically inspect the heat insulation panels to make sure there's adequate clearance

Chapter 5 Part A:
Starting and charging systems

Contents

	Section number		Section number
Alternator – removal and refitting	6	Charging system – general information and precautions	4
Alternator – testing and overhaul	8	Charging system – testing	5
Alternator drivebelt inspection, adjustment and renewal	See Chapter 1	General information	1
		Starter motor – removal and refitting	11
Alternator regulator/brush pack – renewal	7	Starter motor – testing in vehicle	10
Battery – removal and refitting	3	Starting system – general information and precautions	9
Battery – testing and charging	2		

Degrees of difficulty

Easy, suitable for novice with little experience	Fairly easy, suitable for beginner with some experience	Fairly difficult, suitable for competent DIY mechanic	Difficult, suitable for experienced DIY mechanic	Very difficult, suitable for expert DIY or professional

Specifications

General

Engine codes:
- 1.3 litre (1332 cc) non-VVT-i engine 4E-FE
- 1.4 litre (1398 cc) VVT-i engine 4ZZ-FE
- 1.6 litre (1587 cc) non-VVT-i engine 4A-FE
- 1.6 litre (1598 cc) VVT-i engine 3ZZ-FE

Charging system

Charging voltage ..... 13.9 to 15.1 volts
Standard amperage:
- All lights and accessories turned off ..... Less than 10 amps
- Headlights (hi-beam) and heater blower motor turned on ..... 30 amps or more

Alternator brush exposed length:
- Denso alternator:
  - Standard ..... 9.5 to 11.5 mm
  - Minimum ..... 1.5 mm
- Bosch alternator:
  - Standard ..... 11.0 to 13.6 mm
  - Minimum ..... 1.5 mm

5A•2 Starting and charging systems

1 General information

General information

The engine electrical system consists mainly of the charging and starting systems. Because of their engine-related functions, these components are covered separately from the body electrical devices such as the lights, instruments, etc (which are covered in Chapter 12). Refer to Part B for information on the ignition system.

The electrical system is of the 12 volt negative earth type.

The battery is of the low maintenance or 'maintenance-free' (sealed for life) type and is charged by the alternator, which is belt-driven from the crankshaft pulley.

The starter motor is of the pre-engaged type incorporating an integral solenoid. On starting, the solenoid moves the drive pinion into engagement with the flywheel ring gear before the starter motor is energised. Once the engine has started, a one-way clutch prevents the motor armature being driven by the engine until the pinion disengages from the flywheel.

Precautions

Further details of the various systems are given in the relevant Sections of this Chapter. While some repair procedures are given, the usual course of action is to renew the component concerned. The owner whose interest extends beyond mere component renewal should obtain a copy of the *Automotive Electrical & Electronic Systems Manual*, available from the publishers of this manual.

It is necessary to take extra care when working on the electrical system to avoid damage to semi-conductor devices (diodes and transistors), and to avoid the risk of personal injury. In addition to the precautions given in *Safety first!* at the beginning of this manual, observe the following when working on the system:

- Always remove rings, watches, etc, before working on the electrical system. Even with the battery disconnected, capacitive discharge could occur if a component's live terminal is earthed through a metal object. This could cause a shock or nasty burn.
- Do not reverse the battery connections. Components such as the alternator, electronic control units, or any other components having semi-conductor circuitry could be irreparably damaged.
- If the engine is being started using jump leads and a slave battery, connect the batteries positive-to-positive and negative-to-negative (see *Jump starting*). This also applies when connecting a battery charger.
- Never disconnect the battery terminals, the alternator, any electrical wiring or any test instruments when the engine is running.
- Do not allow the engine to turn the alternator when the alternator is not connected.
- Never 'test' for alternator output by 'flashing' the output lead to earth.
- Never use an ohmmeter of the type incorporating a hand-cranked generator for circuit or continuity testing.
- Always ensure that the battery negative lead is disconnected when working on the electrical system.
- Before using electric-arc welding equipment on the car, disconnect the battery, alternator and components such as the fuel injection/ignition electronic control unit to protect them from the risk of damage.
- When the battery is disconnected, any fault codes stored in the engine management ECM memory will be erased. If any faults are suspected, do not disconnect the battery until the fault codes have been read by a Toyota dealer or specialist.
- Several systems fitted to the vehicle require battery power to be available at all times, either to ensure their continued operation (such as the clock) or to maintain control unit memories of security codes which would be wiped if the battery were to be disconnected. To ensure that there are no unforeseen consequences of this action, refer to *Disconnecting the battery* in the Reference Section of this manual for further information.

2 Battery – testing and charging

Testing

Standard and low maintenance battery

1 If the vehicle covers a small annual mileage, it is worthwhile checking the specific gravity of the electrolyte every three months to determine the state of charge of the battery. Use a hydrometer to make the check and compare the results with the following table. Note that the specific gravity readings assume an electrolyte temperature of 15°C (60°F); for every 10°C (18°F) below 15°C (60°F) subtract 0.007. For every 10°C (18°F) above 15°C (60°F) add 0.007.

	Above 25°C	Below 25°C
Fully-charged	1.210 to 1.230	1.270 to 1.290
70% charged	1.170 to 1.190	1.230 to 1.250
Discharged	1.050 to 1.070	1.110 to 1.130

2 If the battery condition is suspect, first check the specific gravity of electrolyte in each cell. A variation of 0.040 or more between any cells indicates loss of electrolyte or deterioration of the internal plates.

3 If the specific gravity variation is 0.040 or more, the battery should be renewed. If the cell variation is satisfactory but the battery is discharged, it should be charged as described later in this Section.

Maintenance-free battery

4 In cases where a 'sealed for life' maintenance-free battery is fitted, topping-up and testing of the electrolyte in each cell is not possible. The condition of the battery can therefore only be tested using a battery condition indicator or a voltmeter.

5 Certain models may be fitted with a particular type of maintenance-free battery, with a built-in charge condition indicator. The indicator is located in the top of the battery casing, and indicates the condition of the battery from its colour. If the indicator shows green, then the battery is in a good state of charge. If the indicator shows black, then the battery requires charging, as described later in this Section. If the indicator shows blue, then the electrolyte level in the battery is too low to allow further use, and the battery should be renewed.

Caution: Do not attempt to charge, load or jump start a battery when the indicator shows clear/yellow.

6 If testing the battery using a voltmeter, connect the voltmeter across the battery and compare the result with those given in paragraph 7. The test is only accurate if the battery has not been subjected to any kind of charge for the previous six hours. If this is not the case, switch on the headlights for 30 seconds, then wait four to five minutes before testing the battery after switching off the headlights. All other electrical circuits must be switched off, so check that the doors, boot and/or tailgate are fully shut when making the test.

7 If the voltage reading is less than 12.2 volts, then the battery is discharged, whilst a reading of 12.2 to 12.4 volts indicates a partially-discharged condition.

8 If the battery is to be charged, remove it from the vehicle (Section 3) and charge it as described later in this Section.

Charging

Note: *The following is intended as a guide only. Always refer to the manufacturer's recommendations (often printed on a label attached to the battery) before charging a battery.*

Standard and low maintenance battery

9 Charge the battery at a rate of 3.5 to 4 amps and continue to charge the battery at this rate until no further rise in specific gravity is noted over a four hour period.

10 Alternatively, a trickle charger charging at the rate of 1.5 amps can safely be used overnight.

11 Specially rapid 'boost' charges which are claimed to restore the power of the battery in 1 to 2 hours are not recommended, as they can cause serious damage to the battery plates through overheating.

12 While charging the battery, note that the temperature of the electrolyte should never exceed 37.8°C (100°F).

Maintenance-free battery

13 This battery type takes considerably longer to fully recharge than the standard type, the time taken being dependent on the

Starting and charging systems 5A•3

extent of discharge, but it can take anything up to three days.

14 A constant voltage type charger is required to be set, when connected, to 13.9 to 14.9 volts with a charger current below 25 amps. Using this method, the battery should be usable within three hours, giving a voltage reading of 12.5 volts, but this is for a partially-discharged battery and, as mentioned, full charging can take considerably longer.

15 If the battery is to be charged from a fully-discharged state (reading less than 12.2 volts), have it recharged by your Toyota dealer or local automotive electrician, as the charge rate is higher and constant supervision during charging is necessary.

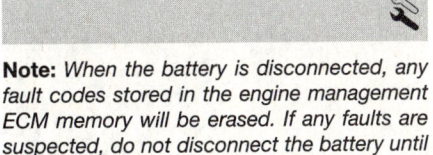

3 Battery – removal and refitting

Note: *When the battery is disconnected, any fault codes stored in the engine management ECM memory will be erased. If any faults are suspected, do not disconnect the battery until the fault codes have been read by a Toyota dealer or specialist.*

Removal

1 Starting with the negative battery cable **(see illustration)**, disconnect both cables from the battery terminals.
Caution: *If the stereo in your vehicle is equipped with an anti-theft system, make sure you have the correct activation code before disconnecting the battery.*
2 Remove the battery hold-down clamp **(see illustration)**.
3 Lift out the battery. Be careful, it's heavy.
4 While the battery is out, lift out the plastic tray and inspect the bracket for corrosion.
5 If you are renewing the battery, make sure that you get one that's identical, with the same dimensions, amperage rating, cold cranking rating, etc, as the original.

Refitting

6 Refitting is the reverse of removal, but smear petroleum jelly on the terminals after reconnecting the leads, to combat corrosion, and always reconnect the positive lead first, and the negative lead last.

4 Charging system – general information and precautions

General information

The charging system includes the alternator, an internal voltage regulator, a charge indicator, the battery, a fusible link and the wiring between all the components. The charging system supplies electrical power for the ignition system, the lights, the radio, etc. The alternator is driven by a drivebelt at the right-hand side of the engine.

3.1 Slacken the nut and disconnect the lead from the battery negative terminal

The purpose of the voltage regulator is to limit the alternator's voltage to a preset value. This prevents power surges, circuit overloads, etc, during peak voltage output.

The fusible link is located in the engine compartment fusebox **(see illustration)**.

The instrument cluster warning light should come on when the ignition key is turned to Start, then should go off immediately. If it remains on, there is a malfunction in the charging system. Some vehicles are also equipped with a voltage gauge. If the voltage gauge indicates abnormally high or low voltage, check the charging system (see Section 5).

Precautions

Be very careful when making electrical circuit connections to a vehicle equipped with an alternator and note the following:

a) *When reconnecting wires to the alternator from the battery, be sure to note the polarity.*
b) *Before using arc welding equipment to repair any part of the vehicle, disconnect the wires from the alternator and the battery terminals.*
c) *Never start the engine with a battery charger connected.*
d) *Always disconnect both battery leads before using a battery charger.*
e) *The alternator is driven by an engine drivebelt which could cause serious injury if your hand, hair or clothes become entangled in it with the engine running.*
f) *Because the alternator is connected directly to the battery, it could arc or cause a fire if overloaded or shorted out.*

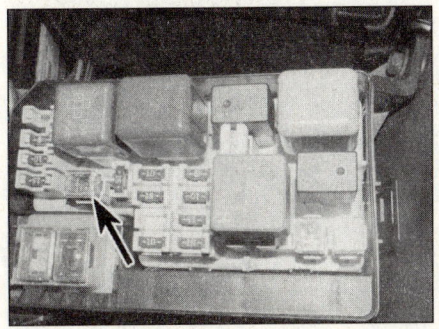

4.1 Main fusible link (arrowed)

3.2 Undo the nut and bolt (arrowed), then remove the battery hold-down clamp

g) *Wrap a plastic bag over the alternator and secure it with rubber bands before steam cleaning the engine.*

5 Charging system – testing

Note: *Refer to the warnings given in 'Safety first!' and in Section 1 of this Chapter before starting work.*

1 If the ignition warning light fails to illuminate when the ignition is switched on, first check the alternator wiring connections for security. If satisfactory, check that the warning light bulb has not blown, and that the bulbholder is secure in its location in the instrument panel. If the light still fails to illuminate, check the continuity of the warning light feed wire from the alternator to the bulbholder. If all is satisfactory, the alternator is at fault and should be renewed or taken to an auto-electrician for testing and repair.

2 If the ignition warning light illuminates when the engine is running, stop the engine and check that the drivebelt is correctly tensioned (see Chapter 1) and that the alternator connections are secure. If all is so far satisfactory, have the alternator checked by an auto-electrician for testing and repair.

3 If the alternator output is suspect even though the warning light functions correctly, the regulated voltage may be checked as follows.

4 Connect a voltmeter across the battery terminals and start the engine.

5 Increase the engine speed until the voltmeter reading remains steady; the reading should be approximately 12 to 13 volts, and no more than 14.2 volts.

6 Switch on as many electrical accessories as possible (eg, the headlights, heated rear window and heater blower), and check that the alternator maintains the regulated voltage at around 13 to 14 volts.

7 If the regulated voltage is not as stated, the fault may be due to worn alternator brushes, weak brush springs, a faulty voltage regulator, a faulty diode, a severed phase winding or worn or damaged slip-rings. The alternator should be renewed or taken to an auto-electrician for testing and repair.

5A•4 Starting and charging systems

6 Alternator – removal and refitting

Removal

1 Detach the cable from the negative terminal of the battery (see Section 3).
2 Detach the electrical connectors from the alternator **(see illustrations)**.

Non-VVT-i engines

3 Loosen the alternator adjustment, pivot and lock bolts and detach the drivebelt.
4 Remove the adjustment and lockbolts from the alternator adjustment bracket.
5 Separate the alternator and bracket from the engine.

VVT-i engines

6 Remove the drivebelt as described in Chapter 1.
7 Undo the two mounting bolts and remove the alternator **(see illustration)**.

All engines

8 If you are renewing the alternator, take the old alternator with you when purchasing a new unit. Make sure that the new/rebuilt unit is identical to the old alternator. Look at the terminals – they should be the same in number, size and locations as the terminals on the old alternator. Finally, look at the identification markings – they will be stamped in the housing or printed on a tag or plaque affixed to the housing. Make sure that these numbers are the same on both alternators.

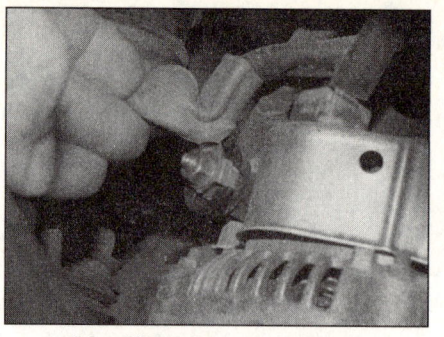

6.2a Alternator connections – 1.3 litre non-VVT-i models

6.2b Alternator connections – 1.6 litre non-VVT-i models

6.2c Alternator connections – VVT-i models

6.7 Alternator mounting bolts (arrowed) – VVT-i models

9 Many new/rebuilt alternators do not have a pulley installed, so you may have to switch the pulley from the old unit to the new/rebuilt one. When buying an alternator, find out the workshop's policy regarding refitting of pulleys – some workshops will perform this service free of charge.

Refitting

10 Refitting is the reverse of removal, tightening the mounting bolts securely.
11 After the alternator is installed, adjust the drivebelt tension (see Chapter 1).
12 Check the charging voltage to verify proper operation of the alternator (see Section 5).

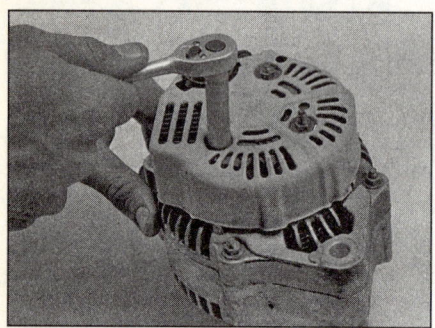

7 Alternator regulator/brush pack – renewal

1 Remove the alternator (see Section 6) and place it on a clean workbench.
2 Remove the rear cover nuts, the screw and terminal insulator, and the rear cover **(see illustrations)**.
3 Undo the 5 screws (Denso alternator) or 3 screws (Bosch alternator) and remove the brush holder and the regulator from the rear end frame **(see illustrations)**.
4 Measure the exposed length of each brush **(see illustration)** and compare it to the minimum length listed in this Chapter's Specifications. If the length of either brush is less than the specified minimum, renew the brushes and brush holder assembly. **Note:** *On some models, it may be necessary to solder the new brushes in place.*
5 Make sure that each brush moves smoothly in the brush holder.

7.2a Remove the three nuts from the rear cover (Denso alternator)

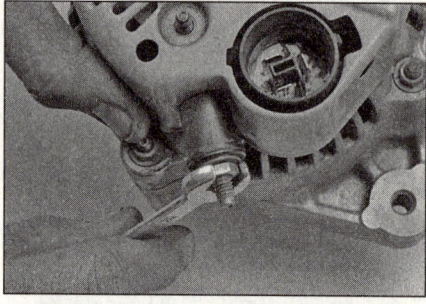

7.2b Take the nut, washer and insulator off terminal B and remove the rear cover (Denso alternator)

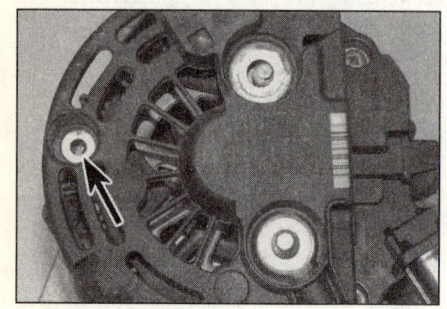

7.2c Undo the two nuts and undo the screw (arrowed), then lift off the rear cover (Bosch alternator)

7.3a Undo the 5 screws (arrowed) . . .

Starting and charging systems 5A•5

7.3b ... remove the brush holder ...

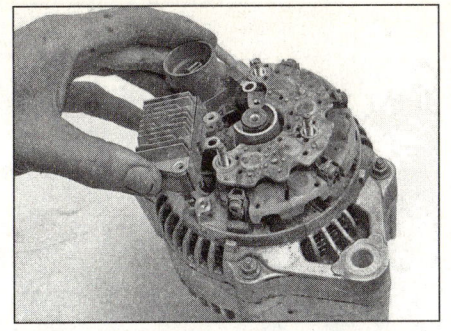

7.3c ... and regulator (Denso alternator)

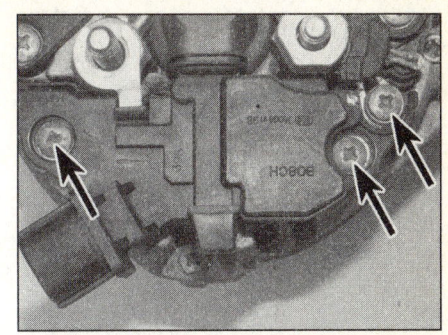

7.3d Undo the 3 screws (arrowed) and remove the brush holder (Bosch alternator)

6 Install the components in the reverse order of removal, noting the following:
7 On Denso alternators, install the brush holder by depressing each brush with a small screwdriver to clear the shaft **(see illustration)**.
8 Install the voltage regulator and brush holder screws into the rear frame.
9 Install the rear cover and tighten the nuts/screw securely.
10 Install the terminal insulator and tighten it with the nut (where applicable).
11 Refit the alternator.

8 Alternator – testing and overhaul

If the alternator is thought to be suspect, it should be removed from the vehicle and taken to an auto-electrician for testing. Most auto-electricians will be able to supply and fit brushes at a reasonable cost. However, check on the cost of repairs before proceeding as it may prove more economical to obtain a new or exchange alternator.

9 Starting system – general information and precautions

General information

The function of the starting system is to turn over the engine quickly enough to allow it to start.
The system consists of the battery, the starter motor, the starter solenoid and the electrical circuit connecting the components. The solenoid is mounted directly on the starter motor **(see illustration)**.
The solenoid/starter motor assembly is installed on the upper part of the engine, next to the transmission bellhousing.
When the ignition key is turned to the Start position, the starter solenoid is actuated through the starter control circuit. The starter solenoid then connects the battery to the starter. The battery supplies the electrical energy to the starter motor, which does the actual work of cranking the engine.

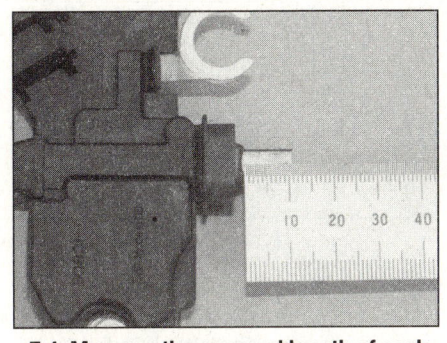

7.4 Measure the exposed length of each brush

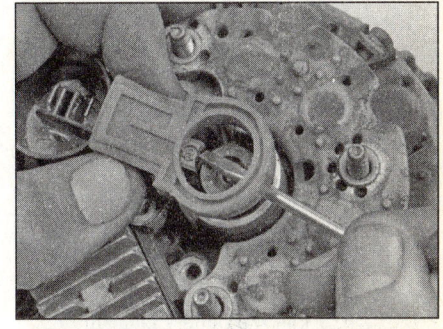

The starter motor on a vehicle equipped with a manual transmission can be operated only when the clutch pedal is depressed; the starter on a vehicle equipped with an automatic transmission can be operated only when the transmission selector lever is in Park or Neutral.

Precautions

Always observe the following precautions when working on the starting system:
a) *Excessive cranking of the starter motor can overheat it and cause serious damage. Never operate the starter motor for more than 15 seconds at a time without pausing to allow it to cool for at least two minutes.*
b) *The starter is connected directly to the battery and could arc or cause a fire if mishandled, overloaded or short-circuited.*
c) *Always detach the cable from the negative terminal of the battery before working on the starting system (see Section 3).*

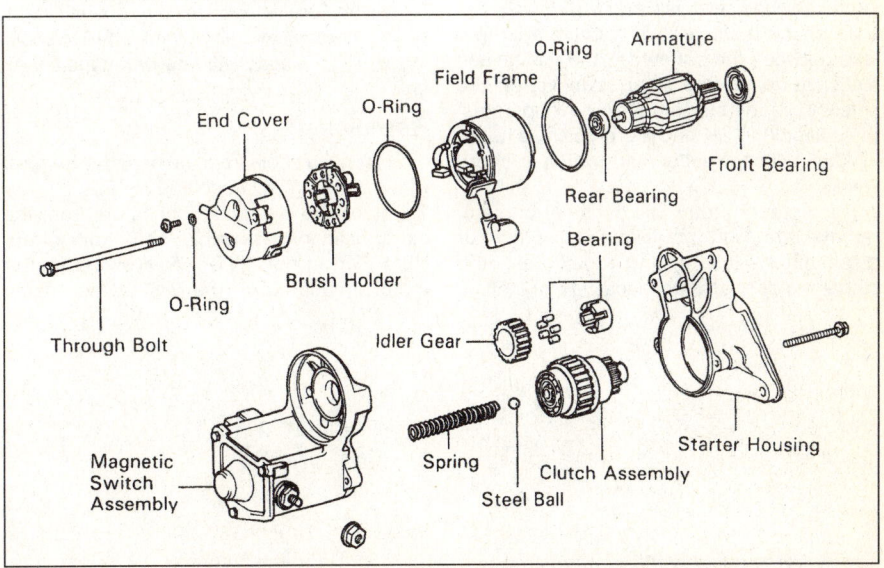

7.7 On Denso alternators, depress each brush with a small screwdriver to ease refitting

9.1 Exploded view of a typical starter/solenoid assembly

5A•6 Starting and charging systems

11.2 Disconnect the wiring from the starter motor/solenoid

10 Starter motor – testing in vehicle

Note: *Before diagnosing starter problems, make sure the battery is fully-charged.*

1 If the starter motor does not turn at all when the switch is operated, make sure that the selector lever is in Neutral or Park (automatic transmission) or that the clutch pedal is depressed (manual transmission).
2 Make sure that the battery is charged and that all cables, both at the battery and starter solenoid terminals, are clean and secure.
3 If the starter motor spins but the engine is not cranking, the overrunning clutch in the starter motor is slipping and the starter motor must be renewed.
4 If, when the switch is actuated, the starter motor does not operate at all but the solenoid clicks, then the problem lies with either the battery, the main solenoid contacts or the starter motor itself (or the engine is seized).
5 If the solenoid plunger cannot be heard when the switch is actuated, the battery is faulty, the fusible link is burned (the circuit is open), the starter relay is defective or the starter solenoid itself is defective.
6 To check the solenoid, connect a jumper lead between the battery (+) and the ignition switch terminal (the small terminal) on the solenoid. If the starter motor now operates, the solenoid is OK and the problem is in the ignition switch, Neutral start switch or in the wiring.
7 If the starter motor still does not operate, remove the starter/solenoid assembly for disassembly, testing and repair. Take the starter motor to an auto-electrician for testing.

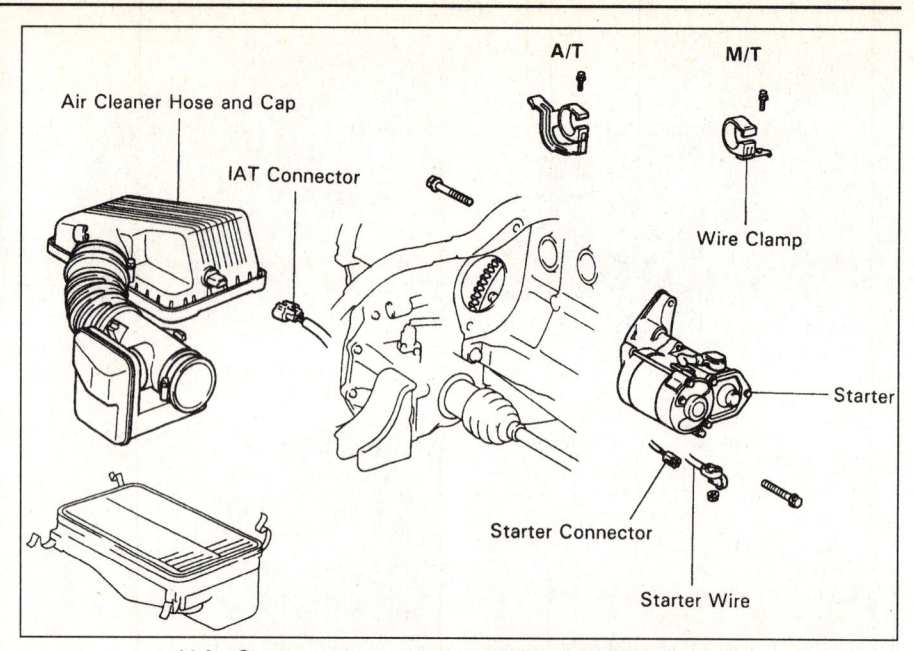

11.3a Starter motor mounting details – non-VVT-i engines

Most auto-electricians will be able to supply and fit brushes at a reasonable cost. However, check on the cost of repairs before proceeding as it may prove more economical to obtain a new or exchange motor.
8 If the starter motor cranks the engine at an abnormally slow speed, first make sure that the battery is charged and that all terminal connections are tight. If the engine is partially seized, or has the wrong viscosity oil in it, it will crank slowly.

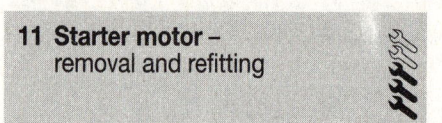

11 Starter motor – removal and refitting

Note: *The starter/solenoid assembly cannot be repaired using separate components. In the event of failure, exchange the starter/solenoid assembly for a complete new or reconditioned unit.*

Removal

1 Detach the cable from the negative terminal of the battery (see Section 3).
2 Detach the electrical connectors from the starter/solenoid assembly **(see illustration)**. Note that on non-VVT-i engines, the starter motor is located on the rear of the engine

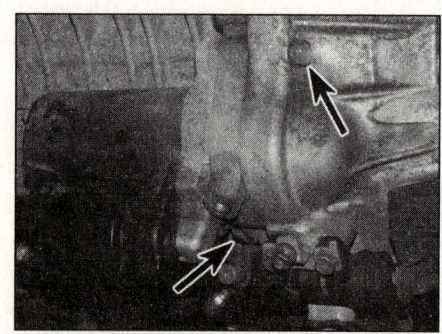

11.3b Starter motor mounting bolts (arrowed) – VVT-i engines

block, whilst on VVT-i engines, the motor is located at the front of the engine block.
3 Remove the starter motor mounting bolts **(see illustrations)**.
4 On non-VVT-i engines, remove the bracket from the upper section of the starter/solenoid assembly. **Note:** *It is necessary to loosen one or two of the bracket bolts to allow the starter/solenoid assembly to partially drop down to gain access to the remaining bracket assembly bolts and hardware.*

Refitting

5 Refitting is the reverse of removal.

Chapter 5 Part B:
Ignition systems

Contents

	Section number
Crankshaft position sensor	See Chapter 4A
Distributor – removal and refitting	3
Distributor pick-up coil – testing and renewal	5
General information	1
Igniter – renewal	6

	Section number
Ignition coil – testing and renewal	2
Ignition timing – check and adjustment	4
Knock sensor – removal, testing and refitting	7
Spark plug renewal	See Chapter 1

Degrees of difficulty

Easy, suitable for novice with little experience | **Fairly easy,** suitable for beginner with some experience | **Fairly difficult,** suitable for competent DIY mechanic | **Difficult,** suitable for experienced DIY mechanic | **Very difficult,** suitable for expert DIY or professional

Specifications

General
Engine codes:
1.3 litre (1332 cc) non-VVT-i engine	4E-FE
1.4 litre (1398 cc) VVT-i engine	4ZZ-FE
1.6 litre (1587 cc) non-VVT-i engine	4A-FE
1.6 litre (1598 cc) VVT-i engine	3ZZ-FE

Ignition timing (4A-FE engines only)
With test terminals TE1 and E1 earthed.................. 10 ± 2° BTDC

Firing order
All models.................. 1 – 3 – 4 – 2

Ignition coil resistance (cold)
4E-FE engine:
  Primary resistance.................. Not available
  Secondary resistance.................. 9.7 to 16.7 kΩ
4A-FE engine:
  Primary resistance.................. 1.11 to 1.75 Ω
  Secondary resistance.................. 9.0 to 15.7 kΩ
4ZZ-FE and 3ZZ-FE engines.................. Not available

HT leads
Resistance.................. 25 kΩ max

Distributor (4A-FE only)
Air gap.................. 0.2 to 0.4 mm
Pick-up coil resistance:
  Cold:
    G+ to G-.................. 185 to 275 Ω
    NE+ to NE-.................. 370 to 550 Ω

Torque wrench settings
	Nm	lbf ft
Ignition coil to cylinder head:		
4E-FE engine	20	15
4ZZ-FE and 3ZZ-FE engines	7	5
Knock sensor:		
4E-FE engine	45	33
4ZZ-FE engine:		
Stud	10	7
Nut	20	15
3ZZ-FE engine	39	29

5B•2 Ignition systems

2.3 Carefully prise the plastic shield at the locking tab to release it from the ignition coil

1 General information

There are three types of ignition system fitted to models covered by this manual.

The first type, fitted to the 1.6 litre 4A-FE engine, has a distributor fitted to the left-hand end of the cylinder head, which incorporates the ignition pick-up sensors to monitor the position and speed of the camshaft, and therefore the firing cycle. The engine management ECM uses the information from the sensors to calculate the precise moment to interrupt the current to the primary ignition coil, which causes the secondary ignition coil to generate high voltage which passes down the HT lead to the distributor cap. This is then passed to the correct HT lead by the spinning rotor, and then jumps across the spark plug electrodes, causing a spark which ignites the air/fuel mixture. This type of system, where the ignition coil and igniter is integrated into the distributor, Toyota call their Integrated Ignition Assembly (IIA).

The second type, fitted to the 1.3 litre 4E-FE engines, is a distributorless ignition system. Here the crankshaft speed and position is monitored by a sensor fitted adjacent to the crankshaft pulley at the right-hand end of the engine. The engine management ECM calculates the optimum moment to trigger the spark, then interrupts the primary signal to one of the two ignition coils bolted to the left-hand end of the cylinder head. The positive and negative ends of secondary coils are connected to the spark plugs on cylinders 1 and 4, and 2 and 3. When the primary current is interrupted, the secondary coil generates a spark at the two cylinders it's connected to. However, only one of these sparks occurs at the correct combustion phase and causes ignition, the other spark occurs harmlessly during the exhaust stroke, and is known as a 'wasted' spark. A knock sensor is also fitted, to monitor for any signs of pre-ignition. Should any be detected, the ECM will gradually retard the ignition timing until the symptoms disappear.

The third type, fitted to the 1.4 litre 4ZZ-FE and 1.6 litre 3ZZ-FE engines, has one ignition coil per cylinder, fitted directly above each spark plug. The engine management ECM information from the crankshaft and camshaft position sensors to calculate the optimum to generate a spark at each cylinder sequentially. A knock sensor is also fitted, to monitor for any signs of pre-ignition. Should any be detected, the ECM will gradually retard the ignition timing until the symptoms disappear.

Precautions

When working on the ignition system, take the following precautions:
a) *Do not keep the ignition switch on for more than 10 seconds if the engine will not start.*
b) *Always connect a tachometer in accordance with the manufacturer's instructions. Some tachometers may be incompatible with this ignition system. Consult a dealer service department before buying a tachometer for use with this vehicle.*
c) *Never allow the ignition coil terminals to touch earth. Earthing the coil could result in damage to the igniter and/or the ignition coil.*
d) *Do not disconnect the battery when the engine is running.*

2 Ignition coil – testing and renewal

Testing

1 Ensure the ignition is turned off.

4A-FE engine

2 Undo the screws, and remove the distributor cap **(see illustration 3.4)**.
3 Remove the plastic shield from the coil **(see illustration)**.
4 Remove the mounting bolts from the coil electrical connectors, and connect the ohmmeter leads.
5 Using an ohmmeter:
a) *Measure the resistance between the positive and negative terminals of the coil **(see illustration)**. Compare your reading with the specified coil primary resistance listed in this Chapter's Specifications.*
b) *Measure the resistance between the positive terminal and the high tension terminal **(see illustration)**. Compare your reading with the specified coil secondary resistance listed in this Chapter's Specifications.*

6 If either of the above tests yield resistance values outside the specified amount, the coil may be defective.

4E-FE engine

7 Note their fitted positions, then disconnect the HT leads from the ignition coils **(see illustration)**.
8 Using an ohmmeter, measure the resistance between the positive and negative HT terminals of each coil **(see illustration)**.

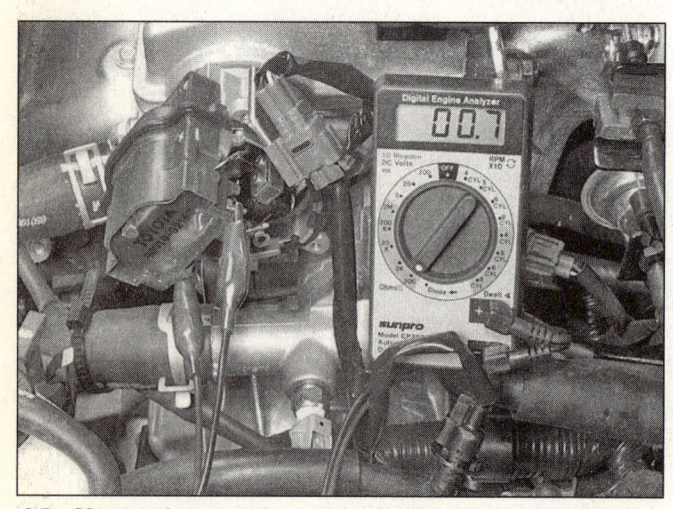

2.5a Measure between the positive and negative terminals of the coil to the check the primary resistance

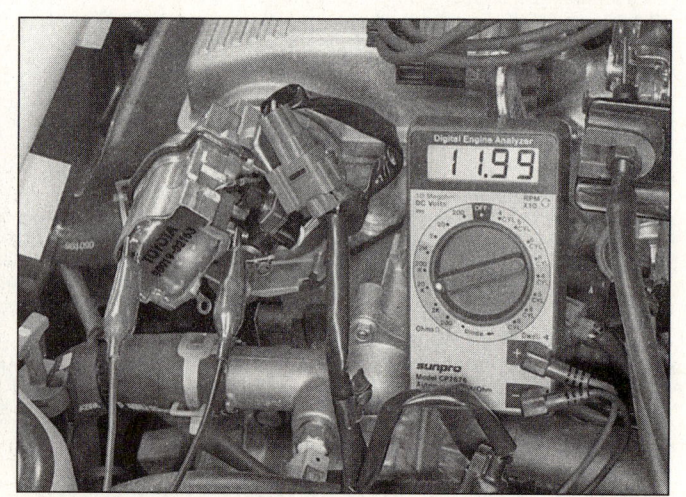

2.5b Measure between the positive terminal and the high tension terminal to check the coil secondary resistance

Ignition systems 5B•3

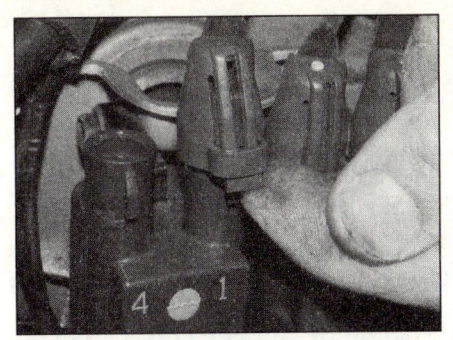

2.7 Lift the clip the pull the HT caps from the ignition coils

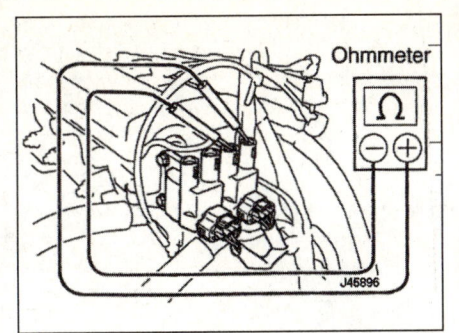

2.8 Measure the resistance between the positive and negative HT terminals of each coil

2.14 Remove the retaining screws (arrowed) and lift the coil from the distributor housing

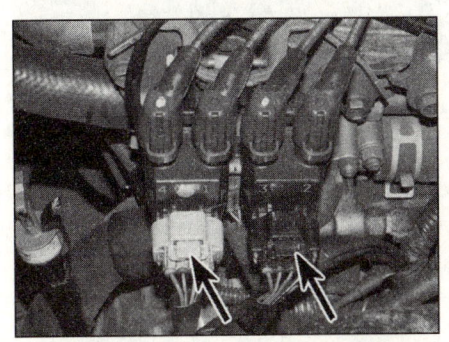

2.16 Press the clips and disconnect the ignition coil wiring plugs (arrowed)

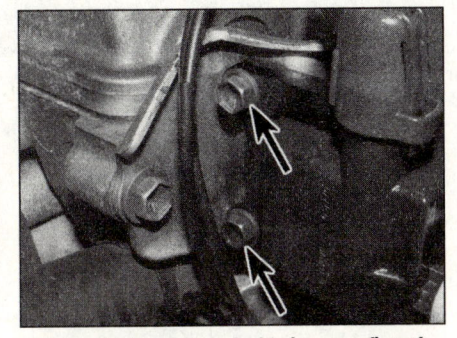

2.17 Undo the two bolts (arrowed) and detach the ignition coil from the bracket

2.21 Depress the clip (arrowed) and disconnect the ignition coil's wiring plugs

9 If the resistances measured for either coil is outside those given in the Specifications, the coil(s) may be defective.

4ZZ-FE and 3ZZ-FE engines

10 At the time of writing, no testing specifications were available for these engines.

Renewal

11 Ensure the ignition is turned off.

4A-FE engine

12 Remove the distributor cap, then remove the heat shield from the coil (see illustration 2.3)
13 Label and disconnect the wires from the coil terminals.
14 Undo the coil mounting screws (see illustration).
15 Refitting is a reversal of removal.

4E-FE engine

16 Note their fitted positions, then disconnect the HT leads (see illustration 2.7) and wiring plugs (see illustration) from the ignition coils.
17 Undo the bolts and separate the coil(s) from the mounting bracket (see illustration).
18 If required, undo the two bolts and one nut securing the coil mounting bracket to the cylinder head.
19 Refitting is the reverse of removal.

4ZZ-FE and 3ZZ-FE engines

20 Undo the two nuts, prise out the plastic fasteners at the rear, and remove the plastic cover from the top of the engine.

21 Disconnect the wiring plugs from the ignition coils (see illustration).
22 Undo the bolts and pull the ignition coils from the top of the spark plugs (see illustration). Recover the dust seal (where fitted).
23 Refitting is a reversal of removal.

3 Distributor – removal and refitting

Note: This procedure applies only to the 1.6 litre 4A-FE engine.

Removal

1 Ensure the ignition is turned off.
2 Disconnect the wiring plug from the distributor.

2.22 Undo the bolt and pull the coil from the cylinder head cover

3 Look for the raised 1 on the distributor cap. This marks the location for the number one cylinder spark plug HT lead terminal. If the cap doesn't have a mark for the number one terminal, locate the number one spark plug and trace the HT lead back to the terminal on the cap.
4 Undo the two screws and remove the distributor cap (see illustration).
5 Turn the engine over until the timing mark on the crankshaft pulley aligns with the 0 mark on the scale adjacent to the pulley, and the distributor rotor is pointing to the number one spark plug terminal. Make a mark on the edge of the distributor base directly below the rotor tip and in line with it. Also mark the distributor base and the cylinder head cover to ensure the distributor is correctly refitted (see illustration).

3.4 Undo the two screws (arrowed) and remove the distributor cap

5B•4 Ignition systems

3.5 Make marks (arrowed) on the distributor housing below the rotor, and across the cylinder head cover and the distributor body

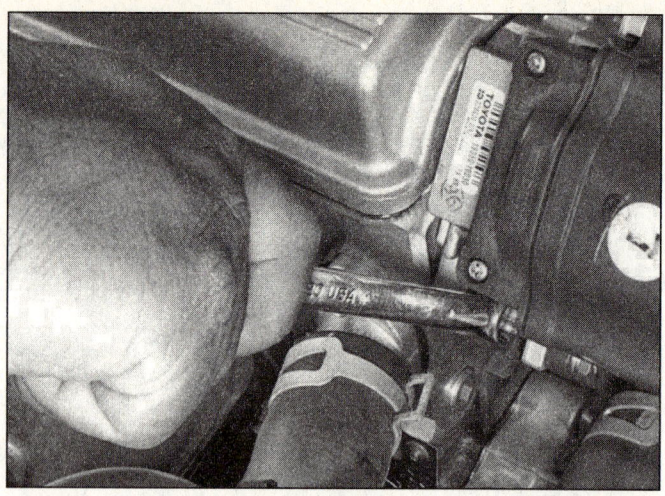

3.6 Undo the distributor retaining bolts and pull the distributor straight out

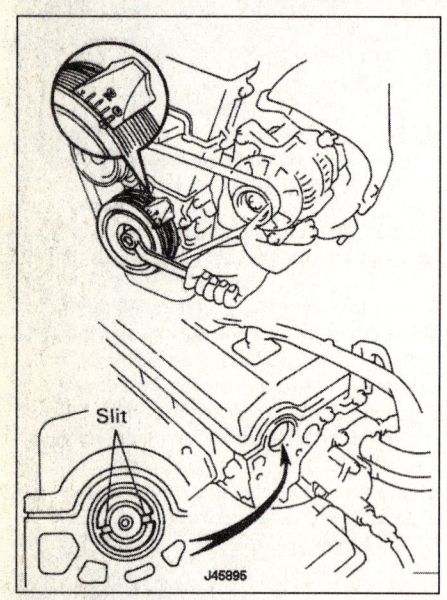

3.7 Align the timing mark on the pulley with the 0 mark on the scale; the slot in the end of the camshaft should be almost horizontal

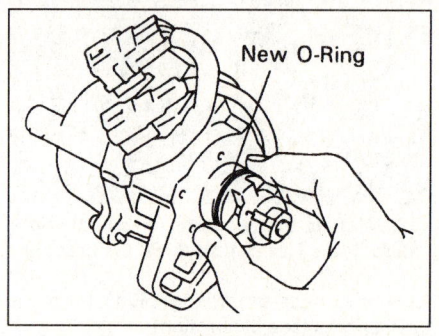

3.8 Fit a new O-ring to the distributor housing

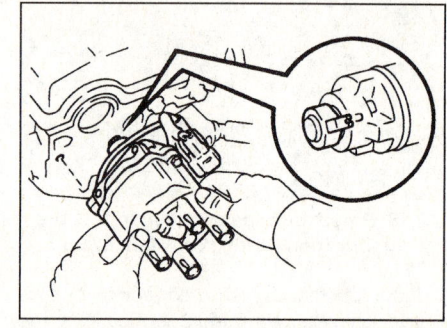

3.9 Align the cut-out portion of the coupling with the groove in the distributor housing

6 Undo the two mounting bolts and remove the distributor **(see illustration)**.

Refitting

Note: *If the crankshaft has been moved while the distributor is out, locate Top Dead Centre (TDC) for the number one cylinder (see Chapter 2A) and position the distributor and rotor accordingly.*

7 Rotate the crankshaft so the drive slot in the end of the camshaft is almost horizontal, and the timing mark on the crankshaft pulley aligns with the 0 mark on the scale adjacent to the pulley **(see illustration)**. In this position, then engine should be at TDC for No 1 cylinder (right-hand end of the engine).

8 Install a new O-ring onto the distributor housing **(see illustration)**.

9 Align the cut-out portion of the drive coupling with the protrusion on the distributor housing **(see illustration)**.

10 Align the distributor drive with the slot in the end of the camshaft and fit the distributor to the cylinder head without twisting it.

11 Lightly tighten the distributor mounting bolts, and reconnect the HT leads. Make sure the leads are fitted to their original positions.

12 Refit the distributor cap and reconnect the distributor wiring plug.

13 Check the ignition timing (see Section 4) and tighten the distributor mounting bolts securely.

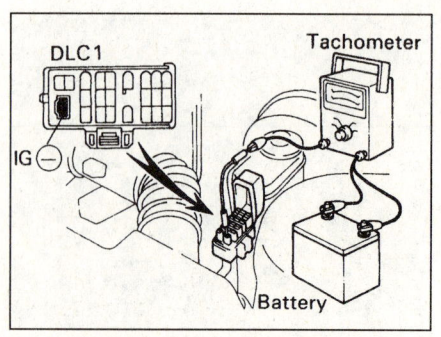

4 Ignition timing – check and adjustment

Note: *This procedure only applies to the 1.6 litre 4A-FE engines. On all other engines, the timing is not adjustable.*

1 Connect a tachometer according to the manufacturer's specifications **(see illustration)**.

2 Locate the diagnostic connector and insert a jumper wire between terminals E1 and TE1 **(see illustration)**.

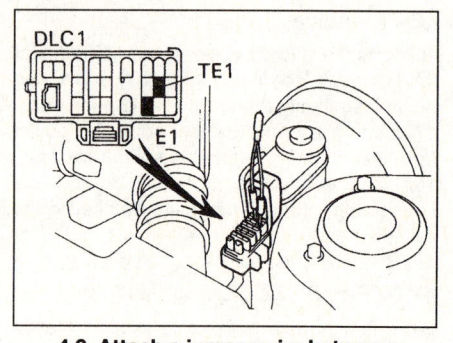

4.1 Connect the tachometer lead to the IG terminal of the test connector

4.2 Attach a jumper wire between terminals E1 and TE1 of the test connector

Ignition systems 5B•5

4.3 Tools needed to check and adjust the ignition timing

1 **Vacuum plugs** – Vacuum hoses will, in most cases, have to be disconnected and plugged. Moulded plugs in various shapes and sizes are available for this
2 **Inductive pick-up timing light** – Flashes a bright, concentrated beam of light when the number one spark plug fires. Connect the leads according to the instructions supplied with the light
3 **Distributor spanner** – Sometimes the distributor retaining bolts can be difficult to reach with conventional spanners

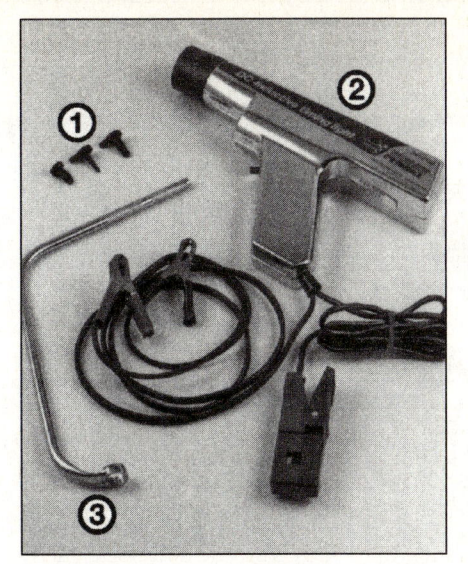

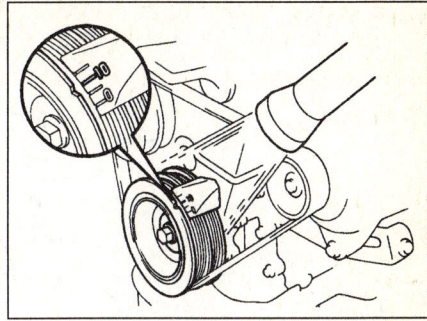

4.5 Point the timing light at the timing marks with the engine at idle

3 With the ignition switched off, connect a timing light according to the manufacturer's specifications **(see illustration)**. Most timing lights are powered by the battery. Also, an inductive style pick-up is installed onto the number one cylinder spark plug wire.
4 Locate the timing marks on the front cover and the crankshaft pulley.
5 Start the engine and allow it to warm-up to normal operating temperature (upper radiator hose hot). Verify that the engine idle is correct (see Chapter 4A Specifications). Aim the timing light at the timing scale on the engine cover **(see illustration)**. The mark on the crankshaft pulley should line up with the 10-degree mark on the scale. If necessary, loosen the distributor mounting bolts and slowly rotate the distributor until the timing marks align. Tighten the mounting bolts and recheck the timing.
6 Remove the jumper wire from the diagnostic connector and confirm that the ignition timing advances in accordance with the figures listed in this Chapter's Specifications.
7 Turn the engine off, and remove the tachometer and the timing light.

5 Distributor pick-up coil – testing and renewal

Note: *This procedure applies only to the 1.6 litre 4A-FE engine.*

1 Ensure the ignition is switched off.

Pick-up coil check

2 Disconnect the electrical connector at the distributor and, using an ohmmeter, measure the resistance between the pick-up coil terminals **(see illustration)**.
3 Compare the measurements to those listed in this Chapter's Specifications. If the resistance is not as specified, it may be necessary to renew the complete distributor housing as, at the time of writing, it appears that parts are not available separately.

Air gap check

4 Undo the bolts and remove the distributor cap.
5 Using a brass feeler gauge, measure the gap between the signal rotor and the pick-up coil projections **(see illustration)**. Compare your measurement to the air gap listed in this Chapter's Specifications. If the air gap is not as specified, renew the distributor, as the air gap is not adjustable. Excessive air gap is usually a sign of wear in the distributor shaft bushing.

Renewal

6 It would appear that, at the time of writing, no parts are available for the distributor. Check with a Toyota dealer or specialist.

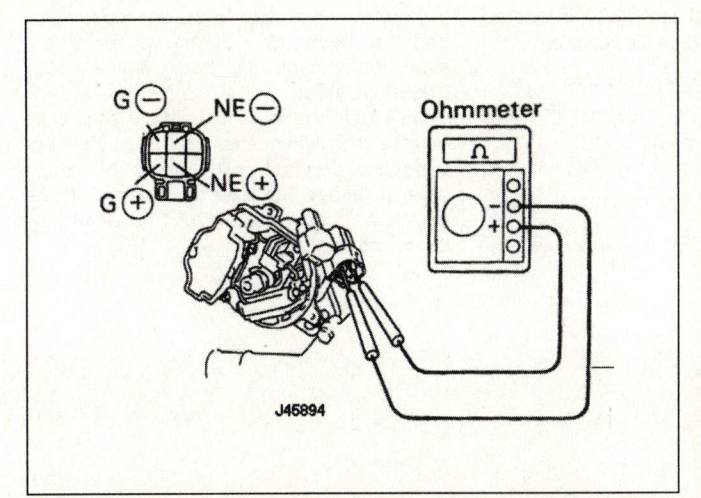

5.2 Connect an ohmmeter to the pick-up coil connections and compare the resistances with those given in the Specifications

5.5 Measure the air gap between the signal rotor and the pick-up coil projection

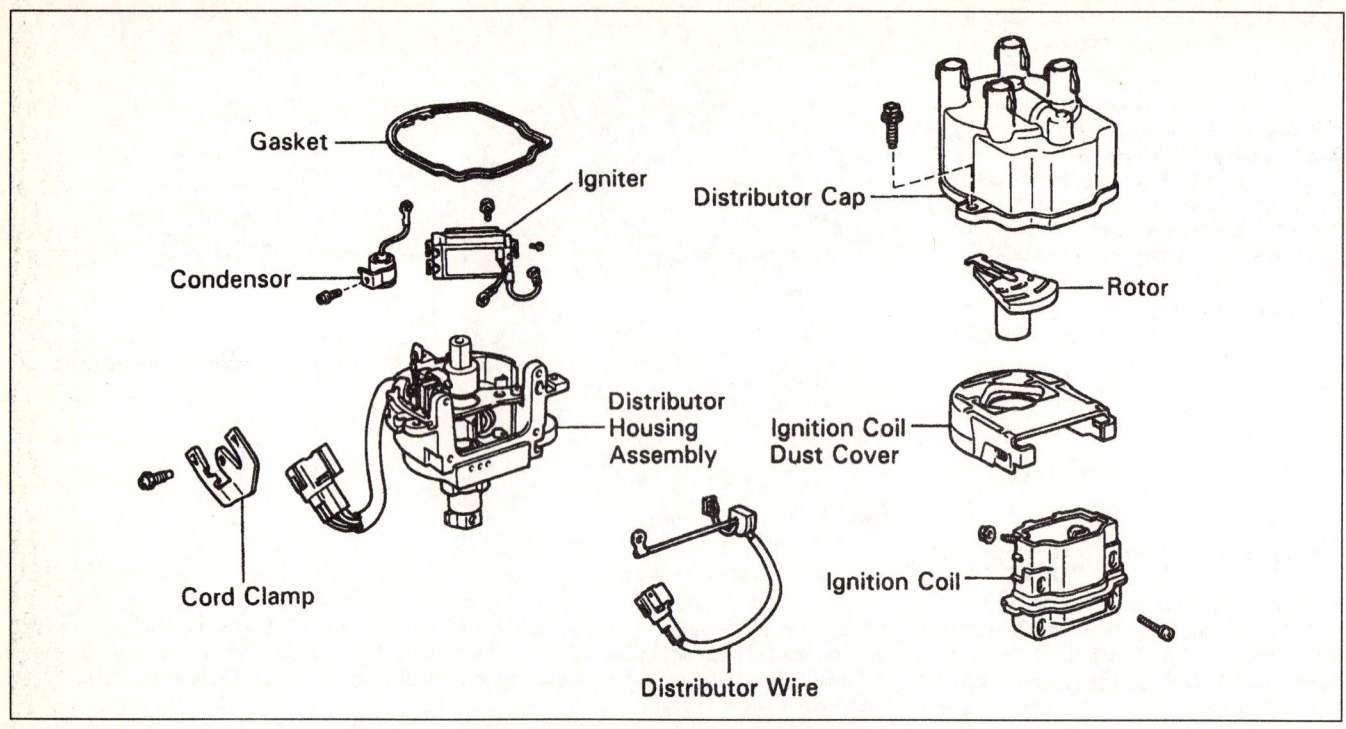

5B•6 Ignition systems

6.3 Exploded view of the distributor – 1.6 litre 4A-FE engines only

6 Igniter – renewal

1 Remove the ignition coil from the distributor as described in Section 2.
2 Disconnect the wiring plug from the igniter.
3 Remove the screws from the igniter assembly, and pull the igniter/bracket from place **(see illustration)**.
4 Refitting is a reversal of removal.

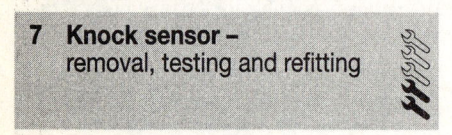

7 Knock sensor – removal, testing and refitting

Removal

4ZZ-FE and 3ZZ-FE engines

1 Remove the intake manifold as described in Chapter 4A.
2 Disconnect the sensor wiring plug, then unscrew the sensor (3ZZ-FE engine) or undo the nut and pull the sensor (4ZZ-FE engine) from the engine block **(see illustration)**.

4E-FE engine

3 Reach underneath the intake manifold and disconnect the sensor wiring plug.
4 Unscrew the sensor from the engine block.

Testing

5 On 3ZZ-FE and 4E-FE engines, connect the

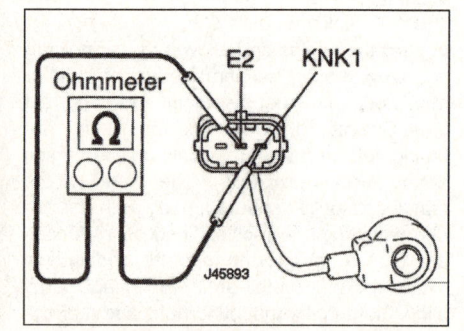

7.2 Undo the nut and remove the knock sensor from the cylinder block (4ZZ-FE engine shown)

leads of an ohmmeter to the sensor terminal and the metal body of the sensor. There should be no continuity. If there is, the sensor may be defective.
6 On 4ZZ-FE engines, connect the leads of an ohmmeter between terminals E2 and KNK1 of the sensor connector. The resistance should be less than 1 MΩ **(see illustration)**. If the resistance is not as specified, the sensor may be defective.

7.6 On 4ZZ-FE engines, connect the ohmmeter to terminals E2 and KNK1 of the knock sensor connector

Chapter 6
Clutch

Contents

	Section number
Clutch components – removal, inspection and refitting	3
Clutch fluid level check	See *Weekly checks*
Clutch hydraulic system – bleeding	2
Clutch master cylinder – removal, overhaul and refitting	5
Clutch pedal height and freeplay check and adjustment	See Chapter 1
Clutch release bearing and lever – removal, inspection and refitting	4
Clutch release cylinder – removal, overhaul and refitting	6
Clutch start switch – check and renewal	7
Flywheel – removal and refitting	See Chapter 2A
General information	1

Degrees of difficulty

Easy, suitable for novice with little experience	Fairly easy, suitable for beginner with some experience	Fairly difficult, suitable for competent DIY mechanic	Difficult, suitable for experienced DIY mechanic	Very difficult, suitable for expert DIY or professional

Specifications

Clutch
Fluid type .... See *Lubricants and fluids* on page 0•17
Pedal height:
   RHD .... 141.1 to 151.1 mm
   LHD .... 138.4 to 148.4 mm
Pedal freeplay .... 1.0 to 5.0 mm

Torque wrench settings

	Nm	lbf ft
Clutch cover-to-flywheel bolts	19	14
Clutch master cylinder mounting nuts	12	9
Clutch release cylinder mounting bolts	12	9

1 General information

The clutch consists of a friction disc, a clutch cover assembly, a release bearing and release fork; all of these components are contained in the large cast-aluminium alloy bellhousing, sandwiched between the engine and the transmission. The release mechanism is hydraulic on all models **(see illustration)**.

The friction disc is fitted between the engine flywheel and the clutch cover, and is allowed to slide on the transmission input shaft splines.

The clutch cover assembly is bolted to the engine flywheel. When the engine is running, drive is transmitted from the crankshaft, via the flywheel, to the friction disc (these components being clamped securely together by the clutch cover assembly) and from the friction disc to the transmission input shaft.

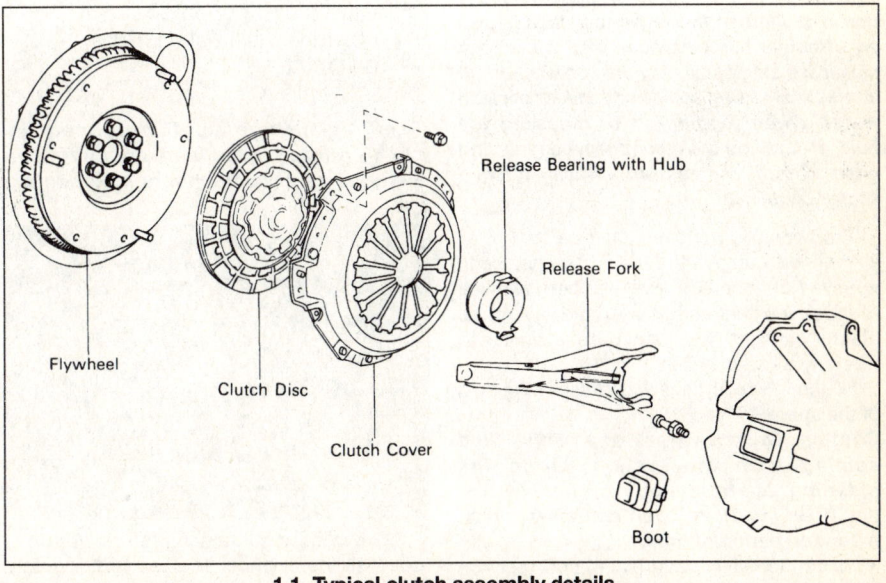

1.1 Typical clutch assembly details

6•2 Clutch

To interrupt the drive, the spring pressure must be relaxed. This is done by means of the clutch release bearing, fitted concentrically around the transmission input shaft. The bearing is pushed onto the clutch cover assembly by means of the release fork actuated by clutch slave cylinder pushrod.

The clutch pedal is connected to the clutch master cylinder by a short pushrod. The master cylinder is mounted on the engine side of the bulkhead in front of the driver and receives its hydraulic fluid supply from the brake master cylinder reservoir. Depressing the clutch pedal moves the piston in the master cylinder forwards, so forcing hydraulic fluid through the clutch hydraulic pipe to the slave cylinder. The piston in the slave cylinder moves forward on the entry of the fluid and actuates the clutch release fork by means of a short pushrod. The release fork pivots on its mounting stud, and the other end of the fork then presses the release bearing against the clutch cover spring fingers. This causes the springs to deform and releases the clamping force on the clutch cover.

On all models the clutch operating mechanism is self-adjusting, and no manual adjustment is required.

2 Clutch hydraulic system – bleeding

Warning: Hydraulic fluid is poisonous; wash off immediately and thoroughly in the case of skin contact, and seek immediate medical advice if any fluid is swallowed or gets into the eyes. Certain types of hydraulic fluid are inflammable, and may ignite when allowed into contact with hot components; when servicing any hydraulic system, it is safest to assume that the fluid IS inflammable, and to take precautions against the risk of fire as though it is petrol that is being handled. Hydraulic fluid is also an effective paint stripper, and will attack plastics; if any is spilt, it should be washed off immediately, using copious quantities of clean water. When topping-up or renewing the fluid, always use the recommended type, and ensure that it comes from a freshly-opened sealed container.

1 The hydraulic system should be bled of all air whenever any part of the system has been removed or if the fluid level has been allowed to fall so low that air has been drawn into the master cylinder. The procedure is similar to bleeding a brake system.

2 Fill the master cylinder with fresh brake fluid of the specified type.

Caution: Do not re-use any of the fluid coming from the system during the bleeding operation or use fluid which has been inside an open container for an extended period of time.

3 Raise the vehicle and place it securely on axle stands to gain access to the release

2.4 The clutch release cylinder bleed screw (arrowed) is adjacent to the hydraulic pipe

cylinder, which is located on the front side of the clutch housing.

4 Locate the bleed screw on the clutch release cylinder (adjacent to the fitting for the hydraulic fluid pipe) **(see illustration)**. Remove the dust cap which fits over the bleed screw and push a length of plastic hose over the valve. Place the other end of the hose into a clear container with sufficient fluid to submerge the end of the hose.

5 Have an assistant depress the clutch pedal and hold it. Open the bleed screw on the release cylinder, allowing fluid to flow through the hose. Close the bleed screw when fluid stops flowing from the hose. Once closed, have your assistant release the pedal.

6 Continue this process until all air is evacuated from the system, indicated by a full, solid stream of fluid being ejected from the bleed screw each time and no air bubbles in the hose or container. Keep a close watch on the fluid level inside the master cylinder reservoir; if the level drops too low, air will be sucked back into the system and the process will have to be started all over again.

7 Install the dust cap and lower the vehicle. Check carefully for proper operation before placing the vehicle in normal service.

3 Clutch components – removal, inspection and refitting

Warning: Dust produced by clutch wear and deposited on clutch components may contain

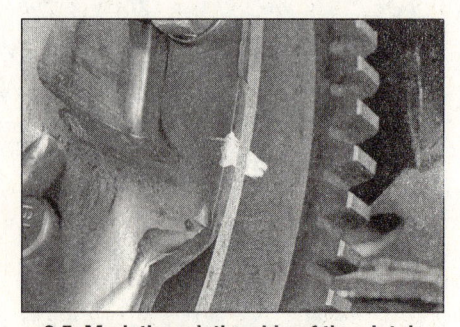

3.5 Mark the relationship of the clutch cover to the flywheel (in case you're going to re-use the same clutch cover)

asbestos, which is hazardous to your health. DO NOT blow it out with compressed air and DO NOT inhale it. DO NOT use petrol or petroleum-based solvents to remove the dust. Brake system cleaner should be used to flush the dust into a drain pan. After the clutch components are wiped clean with a rag, dispose of the contaminated rags and cleaner in a labelled, covered container.

Removal

1 Access to the clutch components is normally by removing the transmission, leaving the engine in the vehicle. If the engine is being removed for major overhaul, then the opportunity should be taken to check the clutch for wear and renew worn components as necessary. However, the relatively low cost of the clutch components compared to the time and labour involved in gaining access to them warrants their renewal any time the engine or transmission is removed, unless they are new or in near-perfect condition. The following procedures assume that the engine will stay in place.

2 Remove the release cylinder (see Section 6). Position it to one side out of the way – it isn't necessary to disconnect the hose.

3 Remove the transmission from the vehicle (see Chapter 7A). Support the engine while the transmission is out. Preferably, an engine hoist should be used to support it from above. **Note:** *If a jack is used underneath the engine, make sure a piece of wood is used between the jack and oil sump to spread the load.*

Caution: The pick-up for the oil pump is very close to the bottom of the oil sump. If the sump is bent or distorted in any way, engine oil starvation could occur.

4 The release fork and release bearing can remain attached to the transmission for the time being.

5 Carefully inspect the flywheel and clutch cover for alignment marks. The marks are usually an X an O or a white letter. If they cannot be found, scribe marks yourself so the clutch cover and the flywheel will be in the same alignment during refitting **(see illustration)**.

6 Slowly loosen the clutch cover-to-flywheel bolts. Work in a diagonal pattern and loosen each bolt a little at a time until all spring pressure is relieved. Then hold the clutch cover securely and completely remove the bolts, followed by the clutch cover and clutch disc.

Inspection

7 Ordinarily, when a problem occurs in the clutch, it can be attributed to wear of the clutch driven plate assembly (clutch disc). However, all components should be inspected at this time.

8 Inspect the flywheel for cracks, score marks and other damage. If the imperfections are slight, a machine workshop can resurface it to make it flat and smooth. Refer to Chapter 2A for the flywheel removal procedure.

Clutch 6•3

3.9 Examine the clutch disc

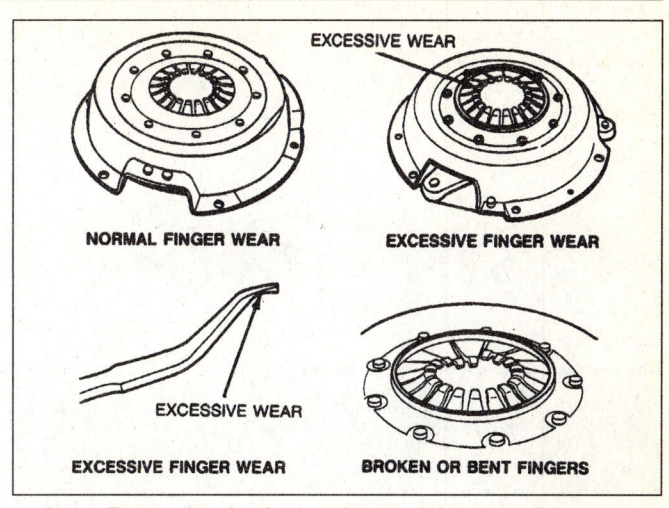

3.11a Renew the clutch cover is any of these conditions are noted

9 Inspect the lining on the clutch disc. There should be at least 0.3 mm of lining above the rivet heads. Check for loose rivets, distortion, cracks, broken springs and other obvious damage **(see illustration)**. As mentioned above, ordinarily the clutch disc is renewed as a matter of course, so if in doubt about the condition, renew it.

10 The release bearing should be renewed along with the clutch disc (see Section 4).

11 Check the machined surface and the diaphragm spring fingers of the clutch cover **(see illustrations)**. If the surface is grooved or otherwise damaged, renew the clutch cover assembly. Also check for obvious damage, distortion, cracking, etc. Light glazing can be removed with emery cloth or sandpaper. If a new clutch cover is indicated, new or factory rebuilt units are available.

Refitting

12 Before refitting, carefully wipe the flywheel and clutch cover machined surfaces clean. It's important that no oil or grease is on these surfaces or the lining of the clutch disc. Handle these parts with clean hands.

13 Position the clutch disc and clutch cover, with the clutch held in place with an alignment tool **(see illustration)**. Make sure it's installed properly (most new clutch discs will be marked 'flywheel side' or something similar – if not marked, install the clutch disc with the damper springs or cushion toward the transmission).

14 Tighten the clutch cover-to-flywheel bolts only finger tight, working around the clutch cover.

15 Centralise the clutch disc by ensuring the alignment tool is through the splined hub and into the recess in the crankshaft. Wiggle the tool up, down or side-to-side as needed to bottom the tool. Tighten the clutch cover-to-flywheel bolts a little at a time, working in a crisscross pattern to prevent distortion of the cover. After all of the bolts are snug, tighten them to the torque listed in this Chapter's Specifications. Remove the alignment tool.

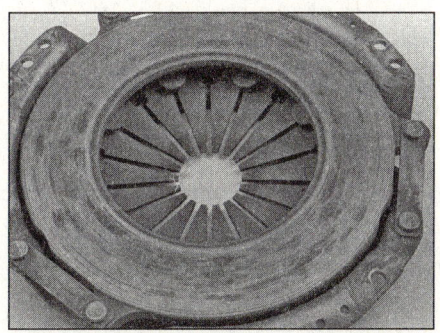

3.11b Examine the clutch cover friction surface for score marks, cracks and evidence of overheating (blue spots)

16 Using clutch assembly grease, lubricate the inner groove of the release bearing (see Section 4). Also place grease on the release lever contact areas and the transmission input shaft bearing retainer.

17 Fit the clutch release bearing (see Section 4).

18 Refit the transmission, release cylinder and all components removed previously, tightening all fasteners to the proper torque specifications.

4 Clutch release bearing and lever – removal, inspection and refitting

> **Warning:** Dust produced by clutch wear and deposited on clutch components may contain asbestos, which is hazardous to your health. DO NOT blow it out with compressed air and DO NOT inhale it. DO NOT use petrol or petroleum-based solvents to remove the dust. Brake system cleaner should be used to flush it into a drain pan. After the clutch components are wiped clean with a rag, dispose of the contaminated rags and cleaner in a labelled, covered container.

3.13 Centre the clutch disc in the clutch cover with a clutch alignment tool

Removal

1 Remove the transmission (see Chapter 7A).
2 Remove the clutch release lever from the ball-stud, then remove the bearing from the lever **(see illustration)**.

Inspection

3 Hold the bearing by the outer race and rotate the inner race while applying pressure **(see illustration)**. If the bearing doesn't turn smoothly or if it's noisy, renew the bearing/hub assembly. Wipe the bearing with a clean rag

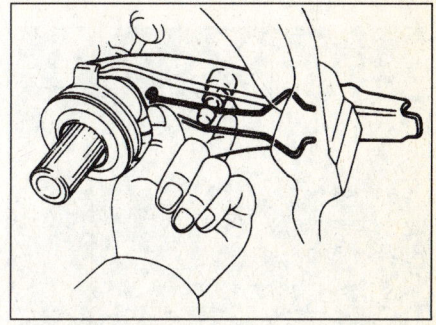

4.2 Disengage the lever from the ball-stud by pulling on the retention spring, then remove the lever and bearing

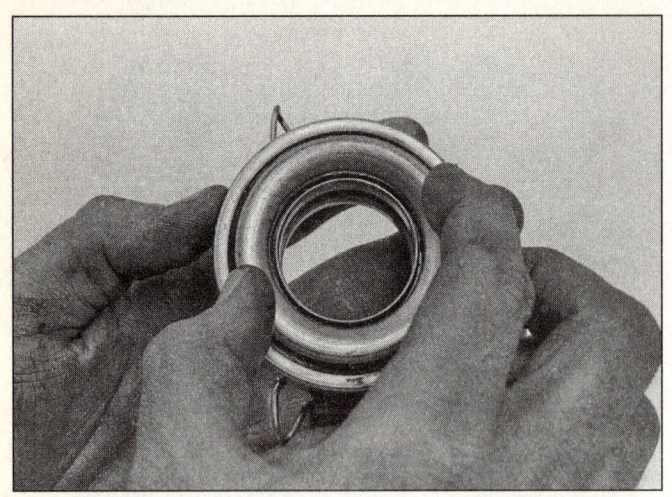

6•4 Clutch

4.3 Hold the bearing by the outer race and rotate the inner race while applying pressure – the bearing should turn smoothly

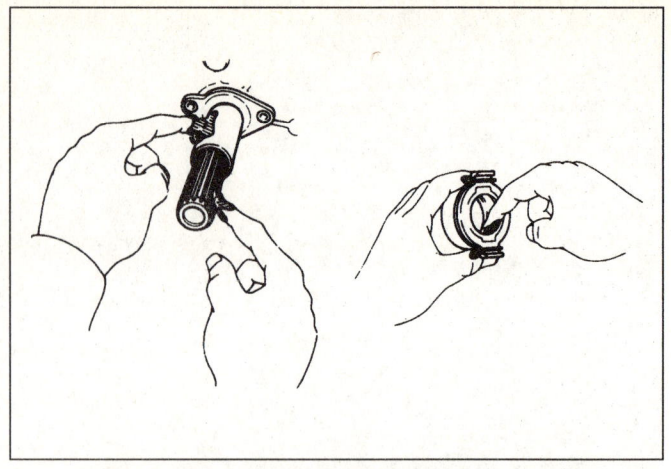

4.4 Apply a light coat of clutch assembly grease to the transmission bearing guide tube and also fill the release bearing groove

and inspect it for damage, wear and cracks. Don't immerse the bearing in solvent – it's sealed for life and to do so would ruin it. Also check the release lever for cracks and bends.

Refitting

4 Fill the inner groove of the release bearing with clutch assembly grease. Also apply a light coat of the same grease to the transmission input shaft splines and the bearing guide tube **(see illustration)**.

5 Lubricate the release lever ball socket, lever ends and release cylinder pushrod socket with clutch assembly grease **(see illustration)**.

6 Attach the release bearing to the release lever.

7 Slide the release bearing onto the transmission input shaft front bearing retainer while passing the end of the release lever through the opening in the clutch housing. Push the clutch release lever onto the ball-stud until it's firmly seated.

8 Apply a light coat of clutch assembly grease to the face of the release bearing where it contacts the clutch cover diaphragm fingers.

9 The remainder of refitting is the reverse of the removal procedure.

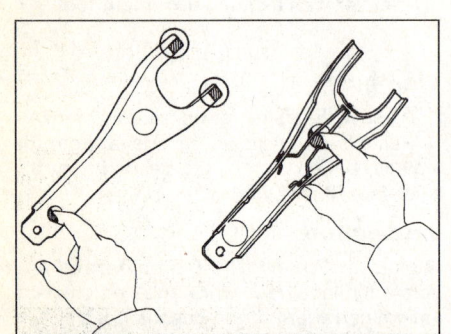

5 Clutch master cylinder – removal, overhaul and refitting

Note: *Before beginning this procedure, contact local motor factors and dealer service departments concerning the purchase of a rebuild kit or a new master cylinder. Availability and cost of the necessary parts may dictate whether the cylinder is rebuilt or renewed. If you decide to rebuild the cylinder, inspect the bore as described in paragraph 11 before purchasing parts.*

Removal

1 Remove the driver's side lower facia panel as described in Chapter 11.

2 Working under the driver's side of the facia, Undo the four nuts securing the brake servo unit to the bulkhead, then pull the servo away from the bulkhead a little, to allow sufficient clearance between the servo and the clutch master cylinder.

3 Under the dashboard, unclip the return spring, and disconnect the pushrod from the top of the clutch pedal. It's held in place with a clevis pin. To remove the clevis pin, remove the clip **(see illustrations)**.

4 Disconnect the hydraulic pipe at the clutch master cylinder. If available, use a flare-nut spanner on the fitting, to protect the fitting from being rounded off. Have rags handy as some fluid will be lost as the pipe is removed.

Caution: Don't allow clutch fluid to come into contact with paint, as it will damage it.

5 From under the facia, remove the nuts which attach the master cylinder to the bulkhead **(see illustration)**. Remove the master cylinder, again being careful not to spill any of the fluid.

Overhaul

6 Remove the reservoir cap and drain all fluid from the master cylinder. Drive out the spring pin **(see illustration)** with a hammer and punch, then carefully lever off the reservoir.

4.5 Apply clutch assembly grease to the release lever in the areas indicated

5.3a Unhook the clutch pedal return spring (arrowed)

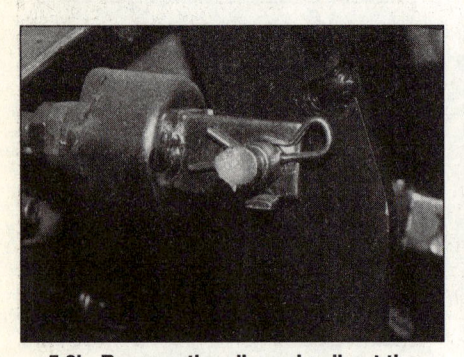

5.3b Remove the clip and pull out the clevis pin

5.5 Master cylinder retaining nuts (arrowed)

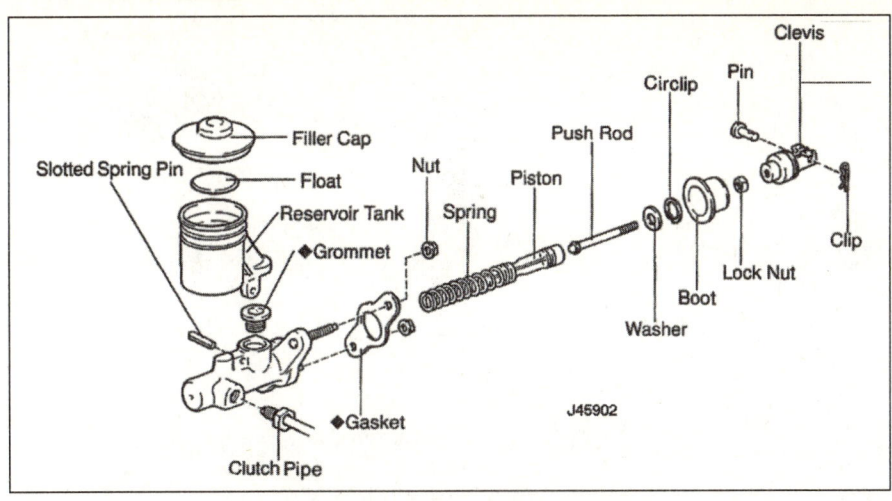

Clutch 6•5

5.6 Typical master cylinder details

5.8 Invert the cylinder and tap it against a block of wood to eject the piston

7 Remove the dust boot, depress the pushrod and remove the circlip with a pair of circlip pliers. Pull out the pushrod and washer.
8 Tap the master cylinder on a block of wood to eject the piston assembly from inside the bore (see illustration). Note: *If the rebuild kit supplies a complete piston assembly, ignore the paragraphs which don't apply.*
9 Separate the spring from the piston.
10 Carefully remove the seal from the piston.
11 Inspect the bore of the master cylinder for deep scratches, score marks and ridges. The surface must be smooth to the touch. If the bore isn't perfectly smooth, the master cylinder must be renewed or factory rebuilt unit used.
12 If the cylinder will be rebuilt, use the new parts contained in the rebuild kit and follow any specific instructions which may have accompanied the rebuild kit. Wash all parts to be re-used with brake cleaner or clean brake fluid. DO NOT use petroleum-based solvents.
13 Attach the seal to the piston. The seal lips must face away from the pushrod end of the piston.
14 Assemble the spring on the other end of the piston.

15 Lubricate the bore of the cylinder and the seals with plenty of fresh brake fluid.
16 Carefully guide the piston assembly into the bore, being careful not to damage the seals. Make sure the spring end is installed first, with the pushrod end of the piston closest to the opening.
17 Refit the pushrod and washer, depress the pushrod and install a new circlip, making sure it seats completely in its groove. Fit a new dust boot.
18 Install the fluid reservoir with a new grommet. Drive in the spring pin with a small hammer and punch. Make sure the pin protrudes about 2.0 mm on each side of the reservoir bracket.

Refitting

19 Position the master cylinder on the bulkhead, refitting the mounting nuts finger-tight.
20 Connect the hydraulic pipe to the master cylinder, moving the cylinder slightly as necessary to thread the fitting properly into the bore. Don't cross-thread the fitting as it's installed.
21 Tighten the mounting nuts and the hydraulic pipe fitting securely.

22 Connect the pushrod to the clutch pedal.
23 Fill the clutch master cylinder reservoir with fresh brake fluid of the specified type and then bleed the clutch system (see Section 2).
24 Check the clutch pedal height and freeplay (see Chapter 1).

6 Clutch release cylinder – removal, overhaul and refitting

Note: *Before beginning this procedure, contact local motor factors and dealer service departments concerning the purchase of a rebuild kit or a new release cylinder. Availability and cost of the necessary parts may dictate whether the cylinder is rebuilt or renewed. If it's decided to rebuild the cylinder, inspect the bore as described in paragraph 7 before purchasing parts.*

Removal

1 Raise the vehicle and support it securely on axle stands (see *Jacking and vehicle support*). Undo the screws and remove the engine undershield (where fitted).
2 Disconnect the hydraulic pipe at the release cylinder. If available, use a flare-nut spanner on the fitting, which will prevent the fitting from being rounded off (see illustrations). Have a small can and rags handy, as some fluid will be spilled as the pipe is removed.

6.2a Use a flare-nut spanner on the hydraulic pipe fitting (left arrow), then remove the mounting bolts (right arrows) – non-VVT-i models

6.2b Pipe fitting and release cylinder mounting bolts (arrowed) – VVT-i models. The right-hand bolt is behind the pipe bracket

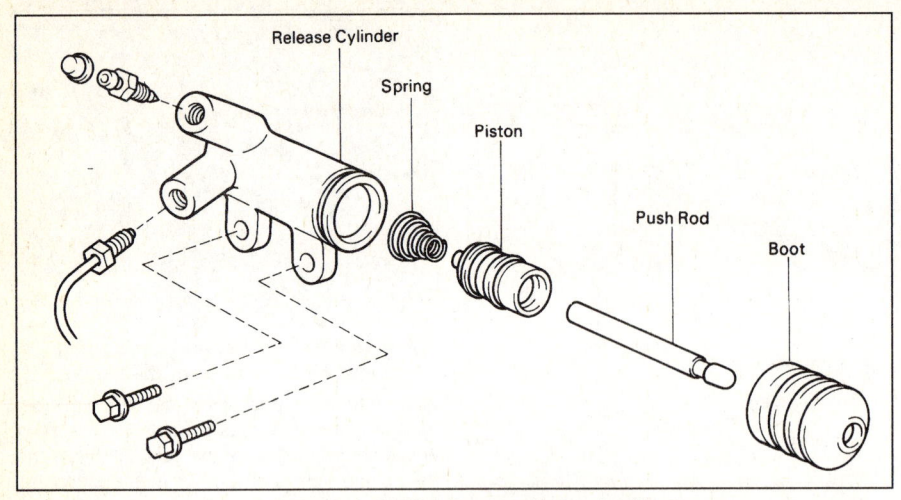

6.5 Typical clutch release cylinder details

3 Remove the release cylinder mounting bolts.
4 Remove the release cylinder.

Overhaul

5 Remove the pushrod and the boot **(see illustration)**.
6 Tap the cylinder on a block of wood to eject the piston and seal. Remove the spring from inside the cylinder.
7 Carefully inspect the bore of the cylinder. Check for deep scratches, score marks and ridges. The bore must be smooth to the touch. If any imperfections are found, the release cylinder must be renewed.
8 Using the new parts in the rebuild kit, assemble the components using plenty of fresh brake fluid for lubrication. Note the installed direction of the spring and the seal.

Refitting

9 Refit the release cylinder on the clutch housing. Make sure the pushrod is seated in the release fork pocket.
10 Connect the hydraulic pipe to the release cylinder. Tighten the connection.
11 Fill the clutch master cylinder with fresh brake fluid of the specified type.
12 Bleed the system (see Section 2).
13 Lower the vehicle.

7 Clutch start switch – check and renewal

Note: *A clutch pedal start switch is not fitted to all models.*

Check

1 Check the clutch pedal height and freeplay, and the pushrod freeplay (see Chapter 1).
2 Verify that the engine will not start when the clutch pedal is released. Verify that the engine will start when the clutch pedal is depressed all the way.
3 If the clutch start switch doesn't perform as described, adjust and, if necessary, renew it.
4 Locate the switch **(see illustration)** and unplug the electrical connector.
5 Verify that there is continuity between the clutch start switch terminals when the switch is on (pedal depressed) **(see illustration)**.
6 Verify that no continuity exists between the switch terminals when the switch is off (pedal released).
7 If the switch fails either of the tests, renew it.

Renewal

8 Remove the nut nearest the plunger end of

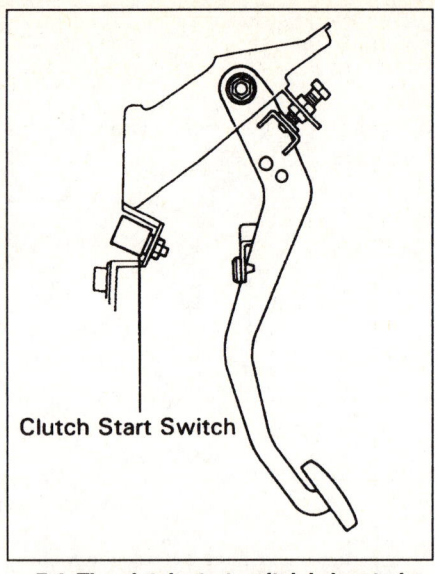

7.4 The clutch start switch is located under the facia on a bracket in front of the clutch pedal

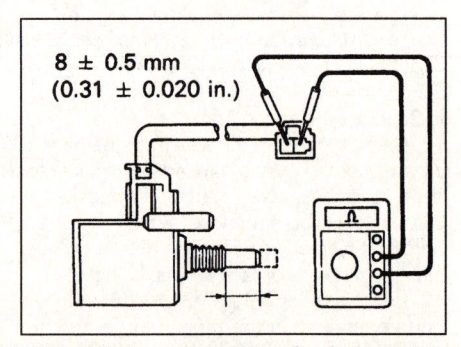

7.5 Using an ohmmeter, check the start switch

the switch and unscrew the switch. Unplug the electrical connector.
9 Refitting is the reverse of removal. The switch is self-adjusting, so there's no need for adjustment.
10 Verify again that the engine doesn't start when the clutch pedal is released, and does start when the pedal is depressed.

Chapter 7 Part A:
Manual transmission

Contents

	Section number		Section number
Gearchange cables – removal and refitting	2	Manual transmission – removal and refitting	5
Gearchange lever – removal and refitting	3	Manual transmission overhaul – general information	6
General information	1	Oil seals – renewal	7
Lubricant change	See Chapter 1	Reversing light switch – testing and renewal	4
Lubricant level check	See Chapter 1		

Degrees of difficulty

| **Easy,** suitable for novice with little experience | **Fairly easy,** suitable for beginner with some experience | **Fairly difficult,** suitable for competent DIY mechanic | **Difficult,** suitable for experienced DIY mechanic | **Very difficult,** suitable for expert DIY or professional |

Specifications

Torque wrench settings — Nm — lbf ft
Lower transmission-to-engine bolts — 23 — 17
Reversing light switch — 40 — 30
Stiffener plate bolts — 23 — 17
Upper transmission-to-engine bolts **(see illustration 5.28):**
  Bolts A — 64 — 47
  Bolt B — 46 — 34

1 General information

The vehicles covered by this manual are equipped with a 5- or 6-speed manual transmission or a 3- or 4-speed automatic transmission. Information on the manual transmission is included in this Part of Chapter 7. Service procedures for the automatic transmission are contained in Chapter 7B.

The transmission is contained in a cast-aluminium alloy casing bolted to the engine's left-hand end, and consists of the gearbox and final drive differential – often called a transaxle.

Drive is transmitted from the crankshaft via the clutch to the input shaft, which has a splined extension to accept the clutch friction disc, and rotates in sealed ball-bearings. From the input shaft, drive is transmitted to the output shaft, which rotates in a roller bearing at its right-hand end and a sealed ball-bearing at its left-hand end. From the output shaft, the drive is transmitted to the differential crownwheel, which rotates with the differential case and planetary gears, thus driving the sun gears and driveshafts. The rotation of the planetary gears on their shaft allows the inner roadwheel to rotate at a slower speed than the outer roadwheel when the car is cornering.

The input and output shafts are arranged side by side, parallel to the crankshaft and driveshafts, so that their gear pinion teeth are in constant mesh. In the neutral position, the output shaft gear pinions rotate freely, so that drive cannot be transmitted to the crownwheel.

Gear selection is via a floor-mounted lever and cable mechanism. The selector/gearchange cables causes the appropriate selector fork to move its respective synchro-sleeve along the shaft, to lock the gear pinion to the synchro-hub. Since the synchro-hubs are splined to the output shaft, this locks the pinion to the shaft, so that drive can be transmitted. To ensure that gearchanging can be made quickly and quietly, a synchromesh system is fitted to all forward gears, consisting of baulk rings and spring-loaded fingers, as well as the gear pinions and synchro-hubs. The synchromesh cones are formed on the mating faces of the baulk rings and gear pinions.

2 Gearchange cables – removal and refitting

Removal

1 In the engine compartment, remove the retaining clips and washers and disconnect the gearchange cables from the selecting bellcrank **(see illustration).**

2.1 Prise out the clips and disconnect the gearchange cables from the levers

7A•2 Manual transmission

2.2 Slide up the cable retaining clips (arrowed)

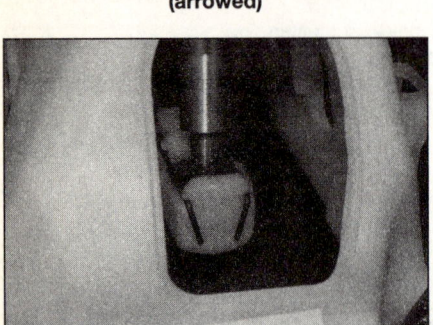

2.4 Slide up the cable retainers

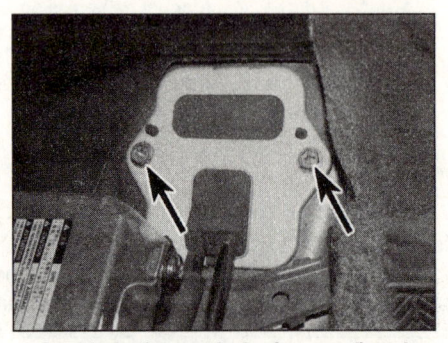

2.5a Remove the cable clip and recover the washer

2.5b Prise the gearchange cable downwards to disconnect it

2.7 Undo the two bolts (arrowed) and remove the cable grommet/retaining plate assembly

2 Remove the cable retaining clips from the cable bracket **(see illustration)**.
3 Inside the vehicle, remove the centre console (see Chapter 11).
4 Remove the cable retainers from the gearchange lever base **(see illustration)**.
5 Remove the retaining clips and washers from the cable ends **(see illustrations)** and disconnect the cables from the gearchange lever assembly.
6 Pull the outer cables upwards from the lever housing.
7 Trace the cable assembly to the bulkhead, undo the bolts and remove the weatherproofing grommet and retaining plate **(see illustration)**. Pull the cable assembly through the bulkhead.

Refitting

8 Refitting is the reverse of removal.

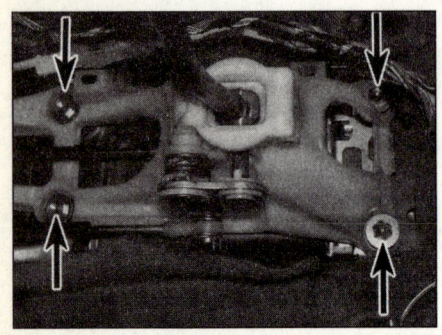

3.3 Undo the 4 bolts (arrowed) and remove the gearchange lever base

3 Gearchange lever – removal and refitting

Removal

1 Remove the centre console (see Chapter 11).
2 Remove the gearchange cable retainers and disconnect both cables from the gearchange lever (see Section 2).
3 Remove the retaining bolts from the gearchange lever base **(see illustration)** and detach the gearchange lever from the vehicle.

Refitting

4 Refitting is the reverse of removal.

4 Reversing light switch – testing and renewal

Check

1 The reversing light switch is located on top of the transmission.
2 Turn the ignition key to the on position and move the gearchange lever to the Reverse position. The switch should close the reversing light circuit and turn on the reversing lights.
3 If it doesn't, check the reversing light fuse (see Chapter 12).
4 If the fuse is okay, verify that there's voltage available on the battery side of the switch (with the ignition turned on).
5 If there's no voltage on the battery side of the switch, check the wire between the fuse and the switch; if there is voltage, put the gearchange lever in reverse and see if there's voltage on the earth side of the switch.
6 If there's no voltage on the earth side of the switch, renew the switch (see below); if there is voltage, note whether one or both reversing lights are out.
7 If only one bulb is out, renew it; if they're both out, the bulbs could be the problem, but it's more likely that the wire between the switch and the bulbs has an open circuit somewhere.

Renewal

8 Disconnect the electrical connector from the reversing light switch **(see illustration)**.
9 Unscrew and remove the old switch. Recover the sealing washer (where applicable)
10 To test the new switch before refitting, simply check continuity across the switch terminals: with the plunger depressed, there should be continuity; with the plunger free, there should be no continuity.
11 Check the condition of the sealing washer (where fitted) and renew where necessary. Screw in the new switch and tighten it to the specified torque.
12 Connect the electrical connector.
13 Check the switch to ensure that the circuit is working properly.

4.8 The reversing light switch (arrowed) is located on the top of the transmission housing

Manual transmission 7A•3

5 Manual transmission
– removal and refitting

Removal

1 Disconnect the negative cable from the battery (see Chapter 5A).
2 Remove the air cleaner assembly (see Chapter 4A).
3 Slacken the front roadwheel bolts, then jack up the front of the vehicle, and support it securely on axle stands (see *Jacking and vehicle support*). Remove the front roadwheels.
4 Undo the screws and remove the engine undershields.
5 Remove the clutch release cylinder and the clutch hydraulic pipe (see Chapter 6).
6 Note their fitted locations, then unplug the electrical connectors from the transmission.
7 Locate the earth cable on top of the transmission. Remove the cable retaining bolt and detach the earth cable from the transmission.
8 Disconnect the gearchange cables from the transmission (see Section 2).
9 Remove the starter motor as described in Chapter 5A.
10 Remove the two upper and the single front transmission-to-engine mounting bolts. Note the location of any earth connectors or brackets, so that they may be refitted in their original location.
11 Remove the left-hand engine mounting stay and the left-hand engine mounting retaining bolt **(see illustrations)**.
12 Support the engine. This can be done from above by using an engine hoist, or by placing a jack (with a wood block as an insulator) under the engine oil sump pan. The engine must be supported at all times while the transmission is out of the vehicle.
13 Drain the transmission fluid (see Chapter 1).
14 Remove the driveshafts (see Chapter 8), and unbolt the shield over the right-hand driveshaft inner joint (where fitted).
15 Remove the front exhaust pipe (see Chapter 4A).
16 Disconnect the front engine mounting **(see illustration)**.

5.11a Remove the mounting stay (arrowed) ...

5.11b ... and the engine mounting through-bolt (arrowed)

17 Remove the rear engine mounting **(see illustration)**.
18 Remove the centre support member **(see illustration)**.
19 Remove the bolts securing the rear engine plate or sump reinforcement section (stiffener plate) to the transmission (where fitted) **(see illustration)**.
20 Remove the left-hand engine mounting **(see illustration)**.
21 Support the transmission with a jack (preferably a special jack made for this purpose). If you're using a floor jack, be sure to place a wood block between the lifting pad and the transmission to protect the cast aluminium housing. Safety chains will help steady the transmission on the jack.
22 Remove the rest of the bolts securing the transmission to the engine.
23 Make a final check that all wires and hoses have been disconnected from the transmission.
24 Lower the left-hand end of the engine, then roll the transmission and jack toward the side of the vehicle. Once the input shaft is clear of the splines in the clutch hub, lower the transmission and remove it from under the vehicle. Try to keep the transmission as level as possible.

Caution: Do not depress the clutch pedal while the transmission is removed from the vehicle.

25 The clutch components can now be inspected (see Chapter 6). In most cases, new clutch components should be routinely fitted whenever the transmission is removed.

Refitting

26 If removed, fit the clutch components (see Chapter 6).

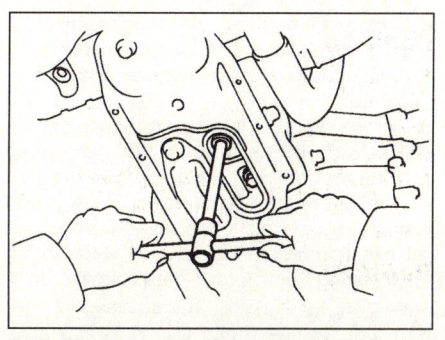

5.16 Disconnect the front engine mounting

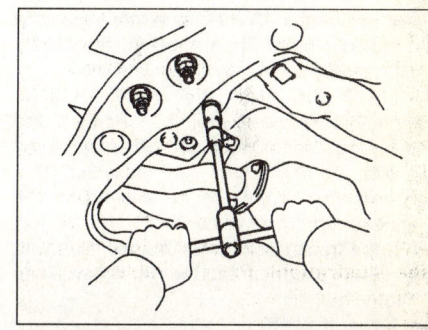

5.17 Remove the rear engine mounting

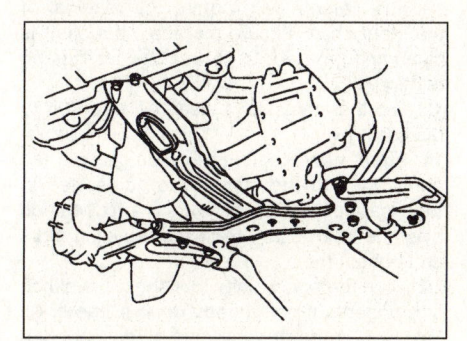

5.18 Remove the centre support member

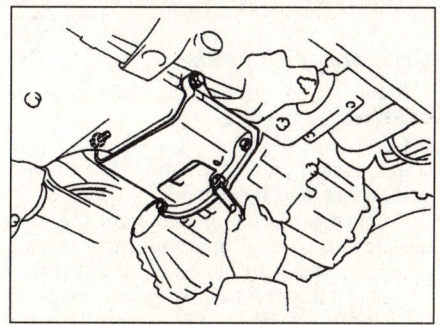

5.19 On 1.6 litre non-VVT-i engines, remove the stiffener plate

5.20 Remove the left-hand engine mounting (arrowed)

7A•4 Manual transmission

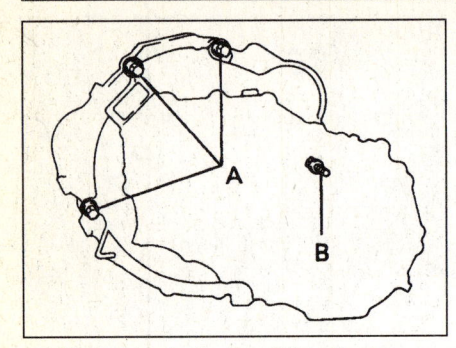

5.28 Tighten bolts A and B to the torque listed in the Specifications

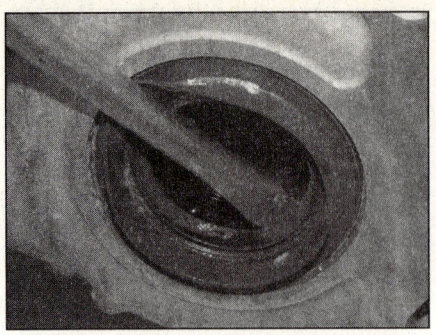

7.2 Prise out the driveshaft oil seal from the transmission casing using a large flat-bladed screwdriver

7.3 Use a suitable tubular drift or socket which bears only on the hard, outer edge of the new seal

27 With the transmission secured to the jack as on removal, raise it into position and then carefully slide it forward, engaging the input shaft with the splines in the clutch hub. Do not use excessive force to install the transmission – if the input shaft does not slide into place, readjust the angle of the transmission so it is level and/or turn the input shaft so the splines engage properly with the clutch.
28 Refit the transmission-to-engine bolts **(see illustration)**. Tighten the bolts to the torque listed in this Chapter's Specifications.
29 Refit the transmission mounting nuts and bolts. Tighten all nuts and bolts securely.
30 Refit any suspension components which were detached or removed. Tighten all nuts and bolts to the torque listed in the Chapter 10 Specifications.
31 Remove the jacks supporting the transmission and the engine.
32 Refit the various items removed previously. Refer to Chapter 4A for information regarding the exhaust pipe, Chapter 5A for the starter motor and Chapter 8 for the driveshafts.
33 Make sure that the wiring harness connectors for the reversing light switch and the speed sensor, and any other electrical devices, are plugged in. And make sure that all harness clamps are reattached to the engine and/or transmission.
34 If the transmission was drained, fill it with the specified lubricant to the proper level (see Chapter 1).
35 Lower the vehicle.
36 Connect the gearchange cables (see Section 2).
37 Connect the negative battery cable (see Chapter 5A). Road test the vehicle to check for proper transmission operation, and check for leakage.

6 Manual transmission overhaul – general information

1 Overhauling a manual transmission is a difficult and involved job for the DIY home mechanic. In addition to dismantling and reassembling many small parts, clearances must be precisely measured and, if necessary, changed by selecting shims and spacers. Internal transmission components are also often difficult to obtain, and in many instances, extremely expensive. Because of this, if the transmission develops a fault or becomes noisy, the best course of action is to have the unit overhauled by a specialist repairer, or to obtain an exchange reconditioned unit.
2 Nevertheless, it is not impossible for the more experienced mechanic to overhaul the transmission, provided the special tools are available, and the job is done in a deliberate step-by-step manner, so that nothing is overlooked.
3 The tools necessary for an overhaul include internal and external circlip pliers, bearing pullers, a slide hammer, a set of pin punches, a dial test indicator, and possibly a hydraulic press. In addition, a large, sturdy workbench and a vice will be required.
4 During dismantling of the transmission, make careful notes of how each component is fitted, to make reassembly easier and more accurate.
5 Before dismantling the transmission, it will help if you have some idea what area is malfunctioning. Certain problems can be closely related to specific areas in the transmission, which can make component examination and renewal easier. Refer to the *Fault finding* Section for more information.

7 Oil seals – renewal

Driveshaft oil seals

1 Remove the appropriate driveshaft as described in Chapter 8.
2 Carefully prise the oil seal out of the transmission, using a large flat-bladed screwdriver **(see illustration)**.
3 Remove all traces of dirt from the area around the oil seal aperture, then apply a smear of grease to the outer lip of the new oil seal. Fit the new seal into its aperture, and drive it squarely into position using a suitable tubular drift (such as a socket) which bears only on the hard outer edge of the seal, until it abuts its locating shoulder. If the seal was supplied with a plastic protector sleeve, leave this in position until the driveshaft has been refitted **(see illustration)**.
4 Apply a thin film of grease to the oil seal lip.
5 Refit the driveshaft as described in Chapter 8.

Input shaft oil seal

Note: *The C60 5-speed transmission fitted to many 1.4 litre post-October '99 models has an integral release bearing guide sleeve, and an oil seal fitted to the inside of the transmission casing. As the transmission must be disassembled to change the seal, entrust this task to a Toyota dealer or suitably-equipped specialist.*

6 Remove the transmission as described in Section 5, and the clutch release mechanism as described in Chapter 6.
7 Undo the three bolts securing the clutch release bearing guide sleeve in position, and slide the guide off the input shaft. Recover any shims or thrustwashers which have stuck to the rear of the guide sleeve, and refit them to the input shaft.
8 Carefully lever the oil seal out of the transmission casing using a suitable flat-bladed screwdriver.
9 Before fitting a new seal, check the input shaft's seal rubbing surface for signs of burrs, scratches or other damage, which may have caused the seal to fail in the first place. It may be possible to polish away minor faults of this sort using fine abrasive paper; however, more serious defects will require the renewal of the input shaft. Ensure that the input shaft is clean and greased, to protect the seal lips on refitting.
10 Dip the new seal in clean oil, and fit it to the casing.
11 Fit a new sealing ring or gasket (as applicable) to the rear of the guide sleeve, then carefully slide the sleeve into position over the input shaft. Refit the retaining bolts and tighten them securely.
12 Take the opportunity to inspect the clutch components if not already done (Chapter 6). Finally, refit the transmission as described in Section 5.

Chapter 7 Part B:
Automatic transmission

Contents

	Section number
Automatic transmission – removal and refitting	8
Automatic transmission/differential fluid change	See Chapter 1
Automatic transmission/differential lubricant level check	See Chapter 1
Diagnosis – general	2
General information	1
Neutral start switch – testing, adjustment and renewal	6
Oil seal renewal	3
Selector cable – removal, refitting and adjustment	5
Throttle valve (TV) cable – check, adjustment and renewal	4
Transmission mounting – check and renewal	7

Degrees of difficulty

Easy, suitable for novice with little experience	Fairly easy, suitable for beginner with some experience	Fairly difficult, suitable for competent DIY mechanic	Difficult, suitable for experienced DIY mechanic	Very difficult, suitable for expert DIY or professional

Specifications

Torque wrench settings

	Nm	Ft-lbs
Manual valve	10	7
Neutral start switch:		
4-speed transmissions	6	4
3-speed transmissions	13	10
Speed sensor (A245E – 4-speed transmission)	11	8
Torque converter-to-driveplate bolts	26	19
Transmission-to-engine bolts:		
Upper bolts	64	47
Lower bolts	46	34
Valve body	10	7

1 General information

All vehicles covered in this manual are equipped with either a 5- or 6-speed manual transmission or a 3- or 4-speed automatic transmission. All information on the automatic transmission is included in this Part of Chapter 7. Information for the manual transmission can be found in Part A of this Chapter.

The A132L is a three-speed automatic transmission, and the A240L is a 4-speed transmission. Their shift points are controlled by the governor and the throttle valve. The A245E is a 4-speed automatic transmission with the shift points controlled electronically, determined by throttle position and roadspeed. All transmissions utilise a lock-up torque converter.

Because of the complexity of the automatic transmissions and the specialised equipment necessary to perform most service operations, this Chapter contains only those procedures related to general diagnosis, routine maintenance, adjustment, and removal and refitting.

If the transmission requires major repair work, it should be left to a dealer service department or an automotive or transmission repair workshop. You can, however, remove and install the transmission yourself and save the expense, even if the repair work is done by a transmission workshop.

2 Diagnosis – general

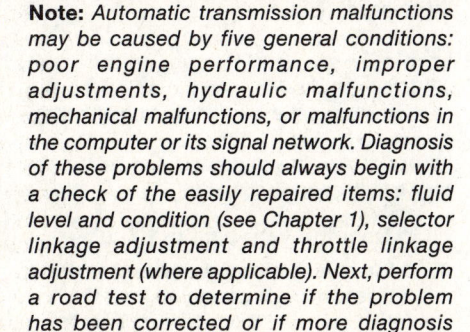

Note: *Automatic transmission malfunctions may be caused by five general conditions: poor engine performance, improper adjustments, hydraulic malfunctions, mechanical malfunctions, or malfunctions in the computer or its signal network. Diagnosis of these problems should always begin with a check of the easily repaired items: fluid level and condition (see Chapter 1), selector linkage adjustment and throttle linkage adjustment (where applicable). Next, perform a road test to determine if the problem has been corrected or if more diagnosis is necessary. If the problem persists after the preliminary tests and corrections are completed, additional diagnosis should be done by a dealer service department or transmission repair workshop. Refer to the 'Fault finding' section at the rear of this manual for information on symptoms of transmission problems.*

Preliminary checks

1 Drive the vehicle to warm the transmission to normal operating temperature.
2 Check the fluid level as described in Chapter 1:
  a) *If the fluid level is unusually low, add enough fluid to bring the level within the designated area of the dipstick, then check for external leaks (see below).*
  b) *If the fluid level is abnormally high, drain off the excess, then check the drained fluid for contamination by coolant. The presence of engine coolant in the automatic transmission fluid indicates that a failure has occurred in the internal radiator walls that separate the coolant from the transmission fluid (see Chapter 3).*
  c) *If the fluid is foaming, drain it and refill the transmission, then check for coolant in the fluid, or a high fluid level.*
3 Check the engine idle speed. **Note:** *If the*

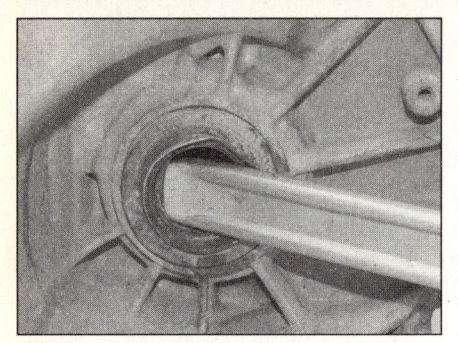

7B•2 Automatic transmission

3.4 Lever the driveshaft oil seal from the transmission casing

3.6 Drive the seal into place using a tubular drift or socket that bears only on the hard, outer edge of the seal

3.9 Unplug the speed sensor electrical connector (arrowed), remove the bolt (arrowed) and pull the speed sensor out

engine is malfunctioning, do not proceed with the preliminary checks until it has been repaired and runs normally.

4 Check the throttle valve cable for freedom of movement. Adjust it if necessary (see Section 4). **Note:** *The throttle cable may function properly when the engine is shut off and cold, but malfunction once the engine is hot. Check it when cold and at normal engine operating temperature.*

5 Inspect the selector cable (see Section 5). Make sure that it's properly adjusted and that the cable operates smoothly.

Fluid leak diagnosis

6 Most fluid leaks are easy to locate visually. Repair usually consists of renewing a seal or gasket. If a leak is difficult to find, the following procedure may help.

7 Identify the fluid. Make sure it's transmission fluid and not engine oil or brake fluid (automatic transmission fluid is a deep red colour).

8 Try to pinpoint the source of the leak. Drive the vehicle several miles, then park it over a large sheet of cardboard. After a minute or two, you should be able to locate the leak by determining the source of the fluid dripping onto the cardboard.

9 Make a careful visual inspection of the suspected component and the area immediately around it. Pay particular attention to gasket mating surfaces. A mirror is often helpful for finding leaks in areas that are hard to see.

10 If the leak still cannot be found, clean the suspected area thoroughly with a degreaser or solvent, then dry it.

11 Drive the vehicle for several miles at normal operating temperature and varying speeds. After driving the vehicle, visually inspect the suspected component again.

12 Once the leak has been located, the cause must be determined before it can be properly repaired. If a gasket is renewed but the sealing flange is bent, the new gasket will not stop the leak. The bent flange must be straightened.

13 Before attempting to repair a leak, check to make sure that the following conditions are corrected or they may cause another leak. **Note:** *Some of the following conditions cannot be fixed without highly-specialised tools and expertise. Such problems must be referred to a transmission workshop or a dealer service department.*

Gasket leaks

14 Check the pan periodically. Make sure the bolts are tight, no bolts are missing, the gasket is in good condition and the pan is flat (dents in the pan may indicate damage to the valve body inside).

15 If the pan gasket is leaking, the fluid level or the fluid pressure may be too high, the vent may be plugged, the pan bolts may be too tight, the pan sealing flange may be warped, the sealing surface of the transmission housing may be damaged, the gasket may be damaged or the transmission casting may be cracked or porous. If sealant instead of gasket material has been used to form a seal between the pan and the transmission housing, it may be the wrong sealant.

Seal leaks

16 If a transmission seal is leaking, the fluid level or pressure may be too high, the vent may be plugged, the seal bore may be damaged, the seal itself may be damaged or improperly installed, the surface of the shaft protruding through the seal may be damaged or a loose bearing may be causing excessive shaft movement.

17 Make sure the dipstick tube seal is in good condition and the tube is properly seated. Periodically check the area around the speedometer gear or sensor for leakage. If transmission fluid is evident, check the O-ring for damage.

Case leaks

18 If the case itself appears to be leaking, the casting is porous and will have to be repaired or renewed.

19 Make sure the oil cooler hose fittings are tight and in good condition.

Fluid from the vent pipe or fill tube

20 If this condition occurs, the transmission is overfilled, there is coolant in the fluid, the case is porous, the dipstick is incorrect, the vent is plugged or the drain-back holes are plugged.

3 Oil seal renewal

1 Oil leaks frequently occur due to wear of the driveshaft oil seals and/or the speedometer drive gear oil seal and O-rings. Renewal of these seals is relatively easy, since the repairs can usually be performed without removing the transmission from the vehicle.

Driveshaft oil seals

2 The driveshaft oil seals are located on the sides of the transmission, where the inner ends of the driveshafts are splined into the differential side gears. If you suspect that a driveshaft oil seal is leaking, raise the vehicle and support it securely on axle stands (see *Jacking and vehicle support*). If the seal is leaking, you'll see lubricant on the side of the transmission, below the seal.

3 Remove the driveshaft (see Chapter 8).

4 Using a screwdriver or pry bar, carefully lever the oil seal out of the transmission bore **(see illustration)**.

5 If the oil seal cannot be removed with a screwdriver or pry bar, a special oil seal removal tool (available at motor factors) will be required.

6 Using a seal installer, a large section of pipe or a large deep socket as a drift, install the new oil seal. Drive it into the bore squarely and make sure it's completely seated **(see illustration)**. On 3-speed transmissions, a fully-seated seal should be flush with the surface of the transmission housing; on 4-speed units, a fully-seated left seal should be recessed about 5.3 mm, a right seal about 3.1 mm.

7 Lubricate the lip of the new seal with multi-purpose grease, then refit the driveshaft (see Chapter 8). Be careful not to damage the lip of the new seal.

Speed sensor O-ring

8 The speed sensor is located on the transmission housing. Look for lubricant around the sensor housing to determine if the O-ring is leaking.

9 Unplug the electrical connector and unbolt the vehicle speed sensor from the transmission **(see illustration)**.

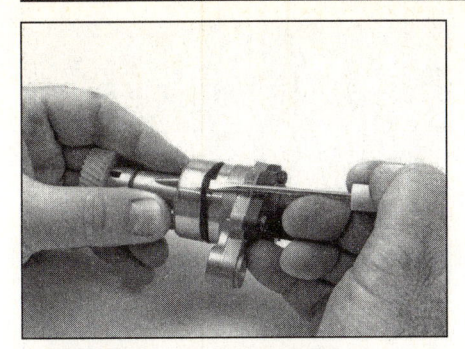

Automatic transmission 7B•3

3.10 Remove the O-ring; make sure you don't scratch the surface of the sensor or gouge the O-ring groove

10 Using a scribe or a small screwdriver, remove the O-ring from the sensor (see illustration) and install a new O-ring. Lubricate the new O-ring with automatic transmission fluid to protect it during refitting of the sensor.
11 Refitting is the reverse of removal.

4 Throttle valve (TV) cable – check, adjustment and renewal

Check

1 Remove the duct between the air cleaner and the throttle body (see Chapter 4A).
2 Have an assistant press the accelerator pedal all the way to the floor and hold it while you measure the distance between the end of the boot and the stopper on the cable.
3 If the measurement taken is as shown (see illustration), the cable is properly adjusted. If it's out-of-range, adjust it as follows.

Adjustment

4 Have your assistant continue to hold the pedal down while you loosen the adjusting nuts and adjust the cable housing so that the distance between the end of the boot and the stopper on the cable is within the range shown.
5 Tighten the adjusting nuts securely, recheck the clearance and make sure the throttle valve opens all the way when the throttle is depressed.

Renewal

6 Loosen the cable locknut and detach the cable from the bracket at the throttle body.
7 Disconnect the cable from the throttle linkage.
8 Detach the cable from the bracket on the transmission.
9 Follow the cable down to the front of the transmission, where it enters the transmission housing right behind the neutral start switch. Remove the cable hold-down bolt.
10 Drain the transmission fluid (see Chapter 1). Working underneath the vehicle, undo the bolts and remove the transmission oil sump pan, then remove the filter.

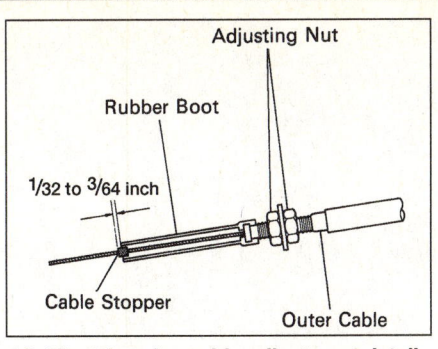

4.3 Throttle valve cable adjustment details
1/32 to 3/64 inches = 0.78 to 1.19 mm

11 Remove the two oil tube bracket bolts and remove the oil tubes (see illustrations).
12 On A240L models, unplug the electrical connectors for the solenoids.
13 Remove the manual detent spring (see illustration).
14 Remove the manual valve on A132L models then, on all models, remove the valve body (see illustrations). On A132L models, the valve body is retained by 14 bolts, and on A240L models by 12 bolts. Note the different bolt lengths and their locations.
15 Disconnect the throttle valve cable from the cam on top of the valve body (see illustration).
16 Refitting is the reverse of removal. Be sure to tighten the valve body, manual valve and detent spring bolts to the torque listed in this Chapter's Specifications, where given. Refer to Chapter 1 for the torque specifications

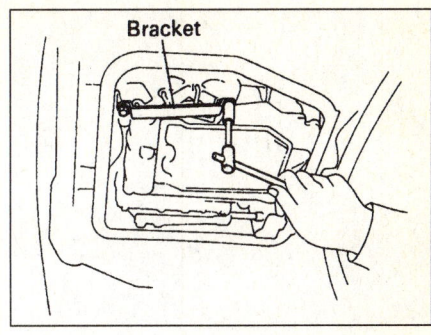

4.11a Remove the two bolts that attach the tube bracket, remove the bracket . . .

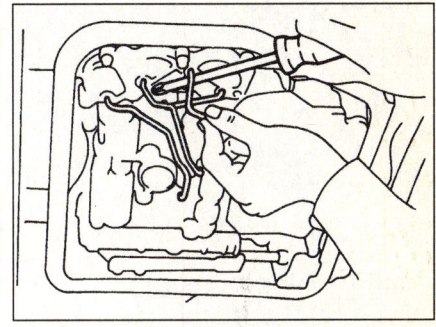

4.11b . . . and carefully lever out both ends of all four oil tubes – make sure you don't bend or kink the tubes (A132L transmission)

for the pan bolts and the type and quantity of transmission fluid required to refill the transmission.

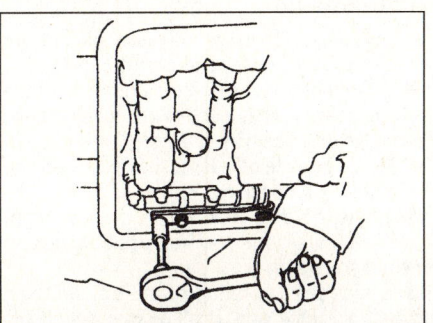

4.13 Remove the manual detent spring (A132L transmission)

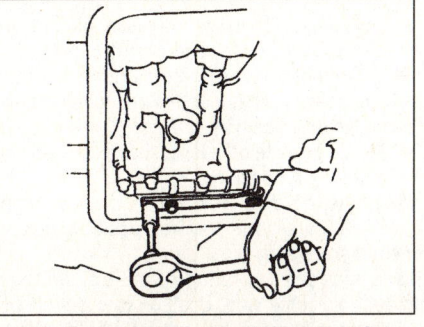

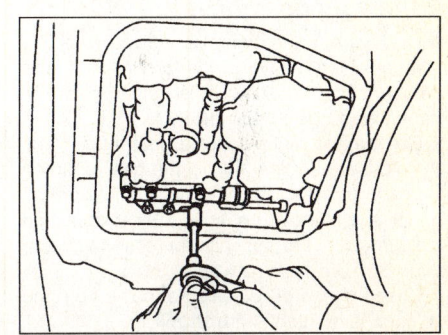

4.14a On A132L models, remove the manual valve . . .

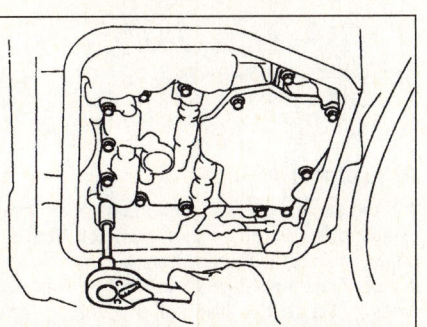

4.14b . . . remove the valve body retaining bolts and remove the valve body

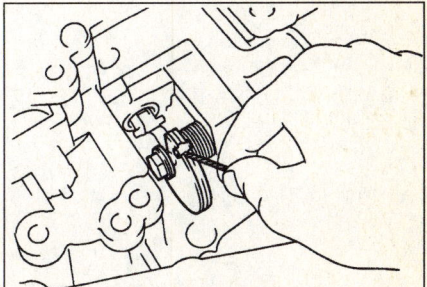

4.15 Disengage the fitting on the lower end of the throttle valve cable from the cam on top of the valve body

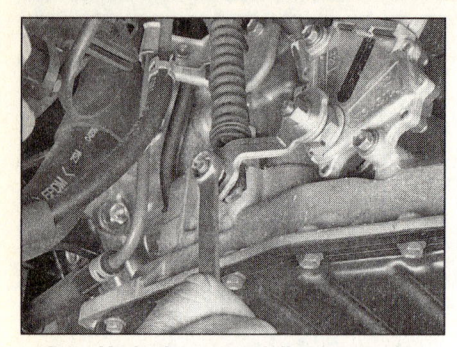

7B•4 Automatic transmission

5.1a Undo the nut and disconnect the selector cable from the lever

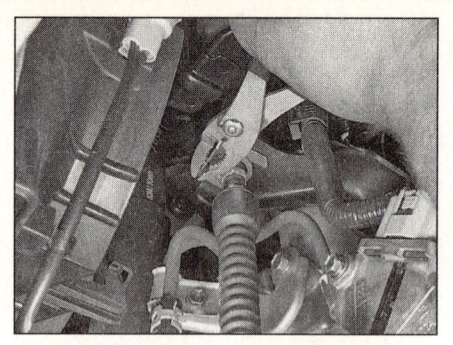

5.1b Pull out the cable retaining clip

5.3a Release the indicator panel clips (arrowed)

5.3b Pull the light bulb and holder from the panel

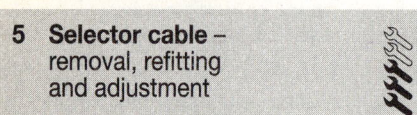

5.4 Prise the end of the selector cable from the lever

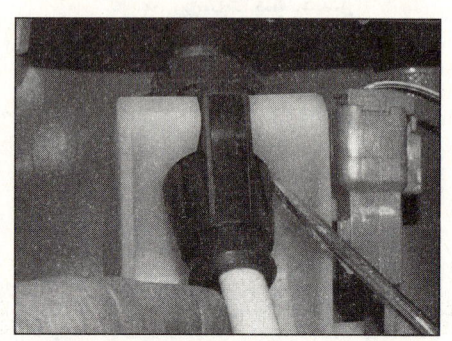

5.5 Depress the clip either side and pull the outer cable from the selector lever base

5 Selector cable – removal, refitting and adjustment

Removal and refitting

1 Disconnect the selector cable from the manual selector lever at the transmission and detach it from the bracket on the front of the transmission (see illustrations).
2 Remove the centre console (see Chapter 11).
3 Release the clips, lift up the gear-position indicator panel and pull the light bulb from the panel (see illustrations). Tie the gear-position indicator panel to the selector lever handle so that you have room to work.
4 Prise the end of the selector cable from the selector lever (see illustration).
5 Depress the two retaining clips, and pull the selector lever outer cable from the front edge of the selector lever base (see illustration).

6 Pull the cable through the grommet in the firewall.
7 Refitting is the reverse of removal.
8 When you're done, adjust the selector cable.

Adjustment

9 Loosen the nut on the manual selector lever at the transmission (see illustration 5.1a).
10 Push the lever toward the right side of the vehicle until it stops, then return it two notches to the Neutral position.
11 Move the selector lever inside the vehicle to the Neutral position.
12 While holding the lever with a slight pressure toward the Reverse position, tighten the nut securely.
13 Check the operation of the transmission in each selector lever position (try to start the engine in each gear – the starter should operate in the Park and Neutral positions only).

6 Neutral start switch – check, adjustment and renewal

Adjustment

1 If the engine will start with the selector lever in any position other than Park or Neutral, adjust the neutral start switch.
2 Apply the handbrake and block the rear wheels. Raise the front of the vehicle and place it securely on axle stands (see *Jacking and vehicle support*). Shift the transmission into Neutral.

3-speed and A240L 4-speed transmissions

3 Unplug the electrical connector from the switch and loosen the switch retaining bolts.
4 Touch the ohmmeter leads to the switch terminals inside the electrical connector and rotate the switch until there is continuity between the terminals, indicating that it's now in the Neutral position (see illustration). Tighten the bolts securely.

A245E 4-speed transmission

5 Disconnect the switch connector.
6 Check for continuity between the terminals of the switch when the selector lever is moved to the various positions (see illustration).

Selector position	Terminal number continuity
P	1 and 3, 6 and 9
R	2 and 3
N	3 and 5, 6 and 9
D	3 and 7
2	3 and 4
L	3 and 8

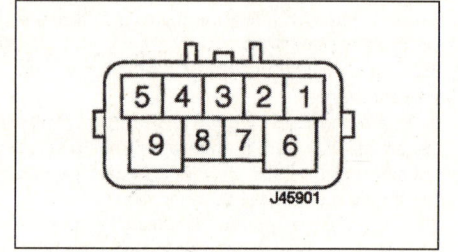

6.4 With the transmission in neutral, check continuity with an ohmmeter as shown

6.6 A245E transmission neutral start switch connector details

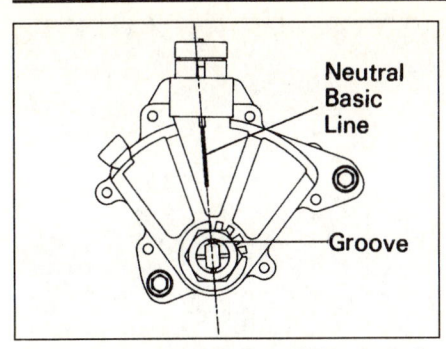

6.15 Rotate the switch until the neutral basic line aligns with the groove and tighten the bolts

7 If the switch continuity is not as described, renew it.

Renewal

8 Shift the transmission into Neutral.
9 Remove the nut and lift off the selector lever.
10 Unplug the electrical connector.
11 Using a screwdriver, prise back the tab on the lockwasher under the nut securing the switch to the valve shaft.
12 Unscrew the nut, and recover the lockwasher and shim(s).
13 Remove the retaining bolts and lift the switch off the shaft.
14 To install, line up the flats on the valve shaft with the flats in the switch and push the switch onto the shaft. Refit the shim(s), the lockwasher and securing nut. Tighten the securing nut, and bend over the lockwasher tab.
15 Rotate the switch until the neutral basic line aligns with the groove **(see illustration)**. Tighten the bolts securely and connect the electrical connector.
16 Install the selector lever, connect the negative battery cable and verify the engine will not start with the selector lever in any position other than Park or Neutral, if necessary follow the adjustment procedure above.

7 Transmission mounting – check and renewal

Check

1 Insert a large screwdriver or pry bar between the transmission mounting and the body and try to lever it away from the body.
2 The transmission mounting should not move excessively. If it does, renew the mounting.

Renewal

3 To renew a mounting, support the transmission with a jack, remove the nuts and bolts and remove the mounting. It may be necessary to raise the transmission slightly to provide enough clearance to remove the mounting.
4 Refitting is the reverse of removal.

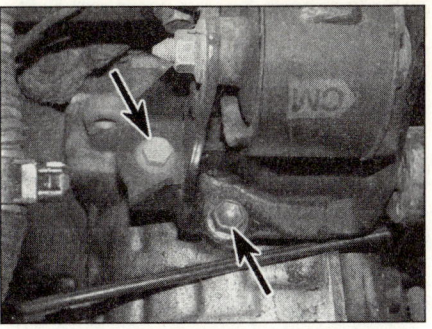

8.4 Undo the mounting-to-transmission casing bolts (rear ones arrowed)

8 Automatic transmission – removal and refitting

Removal

1 Detach the cable from the negative battery terminal (see Chapter 5A).
2 If you're planning to re-use the same transmission, simply remove the cable retaining clip from the bracket and disconnect the throttle valve cable from the linkage on the throttle body; if you're planning to renew the transmission, disconnect the throttle valve cable from the valve body (in either case, see Section 4). **Note:** *A throttle valve is not fitted to A245E transmissions.*
3 Remove the air cleaner housing (see Chapter 4A).
4 Remove the bolts from the left-hand transmission mounting **(see illustration)**.
5 Note their fitted positions, then disconnect any all electrical connectors from the transmission, and detach any wiring harness clamps from the transmission and set the wiring harnesses aside.
6 Remove the upper transmission-to-engine bolts **(see illustration)**. Remove the upper transmission-to-starter motor bolt (see Chapter 5A).
7 Raise the vehicle and support it securely on axle stands (see *Jacking and vehicle support*).
8 Release the screws and remove the engine undershields.
9 Disconnect the selector cable from the transmission (see Section 5).

8.14b ... the three rear support brace bolts (arrowed) ...

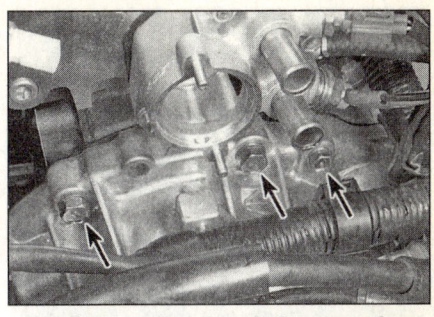

8.6 Remove the transmission-to-engine bolts (arrowed). Right-hand side bolt secures the starter motor on non-VVT-i models

8.14a Remove the four front support brace bolts (arrowed) ...

10 Remove the exhaust pipe section between the exhaust manifold and the catalytic converter (see Chapter 4A).
11 Drain the transmission fluid and, on three-speed models, the differential fluid (see Chapter 1).
12 Remove the driveshafts (see Chapter 8). **Note:** *It's not absolutely necessary to completely remove the driveshafts; you can detach the inner CV joints and suspend them out of the way. However, you'll have more room to work if you remove the driveshafts. And this is a good time to inspect the CV joint boots for tears and deterioration and, if necessary, repack them with new CV joint grease (see Chapter 8).*
13 Support the engine using a hoist from above, or a jack and a wood block under the oil sump to spread the load.
14 Remove the bolts and nuts that attach the centre support brace and suspension member to the vehicle **(see illustrations)**.

8.14c ... and the five bolts (arrowed) from the each suspension member

7B•6 Automatic transmission

8.16 Unbolt the oil cooler pipe clamps (arrowed) from the transmission and unscrew the pipe fittings (arrowed)

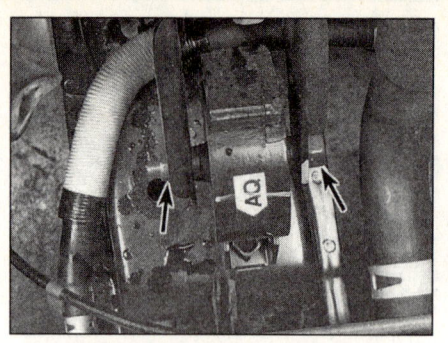

8.19 Remove the nut and through-bolt (arrowed) from the front and rear mountings (front mounting shown, rear mounting similar)

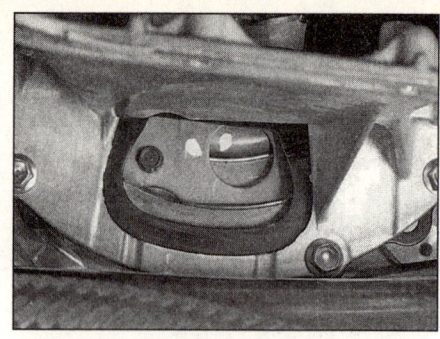

8.20 Mark the relationship of the torque converter to the driveplate to ensure proper dynamic balance when it's reattached

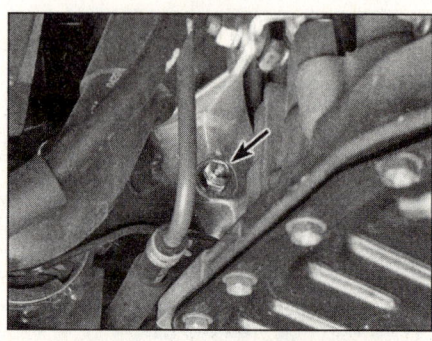

8.21 Remove this front lower transmission-to-engine bolt (arrowed)

15 Detach the starter motor leads, remove the lower starter-to-transmission bolt and remove the starter (see Chapter 5A).

16 Detach the oil cooler pipe retaining clamps from the transmission, then disconnect the two pipe fittings from the transmission **(see illustration)**.

17 To detach the dipstick tube from the transmission, remove the single bracket bolt from the front of the bellhousing, then pull straight up on the tube.

18 Support the transmission with a jack – preferably a special jack made for this purpose. Safety chains will help steady the transmission on the jack.

19 Remove the remaining bolts from the left-hand transmission mounting. Remove the bolts from the front and rear mountings **(see illustration)** so that the engine can be tilted slightly to the left to allow easier removal and refitting of the transmission.

20 Remove the torque converter inspection cover. Mark the relationship of the torque converter to the driveplate so they can be installed in the same position **(see illustration)**. Remove the six torque converter mounting bolts. Turn the crankshaft for access to each one in turn.

21 Remove the lower engine-to-transmission bolts: the three lowest bolts are shown in **illustration 8.20**, and there's another bolt on the rear of the engine, right below the lower starter bolt. Remove the lower transmission-to-engine bolt, on the front side of the transmission **(see illustration)**.

22 Move the transmission to the side to disengage it from the engine block dowel pins and make sure the torque converter is detached from the driveplate. Secure the torque converter to the transmission so that it will not fall out during removal. Lower the transmission from the vehicle.

Refitting

23 Make sure that the torque converter is securely engaged in the transmission prior to refitting.

24 With the transmission secured to the jack, raise it into position. Be sure to keep it level so the torque converter does not slide forward. Connect the cooler lines.

25 Move the transmission carefully into place until the dowel pins are engaged and the torque converter is engaged.

26 Rotate the torque converter to align the bolt holes with the holes in the driveplate. The match marks on the torque converter and driveplate, made during paragraph 20, must align.

27 Install the lower transmission-to-engine bolts and tighten them to the torque listed in this Chapter's Specifications.

28 Install the torque converter-to-driveplate bolts. Tighten them to the torque listed in this Chapter's Specifications. Install the torque converter cover.

29 Install the support brace and suspension member. Tighten the bolts and nuts securely.

30 Remove the jacks supporting the transmission and the engine.

31 Install the starter motor (see Chapter 5A). (It's easier to install the upper bolt after the vehicle has been lowered.)

32 Install the dipstick tube into the transmission and attach the dipstick bracket to the transmission.

33 Connect the oil cooler pipe fittings and the line retaining clamps to the transmission.

34 Install and/or connect the driveshafts to the transmission (see Chapter 8).

35 Install and adjust the neutral start switch (see Section 6).

36 Connect and adjust the selector cable (see Section 5) and the throttle valve cable (see Section 4).

37 Reconnect all electrical connectors. Make sure that the wiring harnesses are routed properly and clamped to the transmission housing.

38 Refit the exhaust pipe between the exhaust manifold and the catalytic converter (see Chapter 4A).

39 Remove the axle stands and lower the vehicle.

40 Refit the upper transmission bolts and tighten them to the torque listed in this Chapter's Specifications. Install the upper starter motor bolt, if you haven't already done so.

41 Fill the transmission with the proper type and amount of fluid (see Chapter 1). Run the vehicle and check for fluid leaks.

Chapter 8
Driveshafts

Contents

	Section number		Section number
Driveshaft gaiter check	See Chapter 1	Driveshafts – removal and installation	2
Driveshaft gaiter renewal and CV joint inspection	3	Driveshafts – general information and inspection	1

Degrees of difficulty

Easy, suitable for novice with little experience

Fairly easy, suitable for beginner with some experience

Fairly difficult, suitable for competent DIY mechanic

Difficult, suitable for experienced DIY mechanic

Very difficult, suitable for expert DIY or professional

Specifications

Driveshaft CV joints
Grease capacity:
 Up to October 1999 (single headlight models):
  Inboard joint... 180 to 190g
  Outboard joint... 120 to 130g
 From October 1999 (twin headlight models):
  Inboard joint... 80g
  Outboard joint... 108.5g

Driveshaft length
Left-hand driveshaft....................................... 541.3 ± 5.0 mm
Right-hand driveshaft...................................... 855.8 ± 5.0 mm

Torque wrench settings | Nm | lbf ft
Driveshaft/hub nut.. 216 | 159
Wheel nuts... 103 | 76

1 General information

1 Power is transmitted from the transmission to the wheels through a pair of driveshafts. The inner end of each driveshaft is splined into the differential side gears. The outer ends of the driveshafts are splined to the axle hubs and locked in place by a large nut.

2 The inner ends of the driveshafts are equipped with sliding constant velocity joints, which are capable of both angular and axial motion. Each inner joint assembly consists of a tripod bearing and a joint housing (outer race) in which the joint is free to slide in and out as the driveshaft moves up and down with the wheel. The joints can be disassembled and cleaned in the event of a gaiter failure (see Section 3), but if any parts are damaged, the joints must be renewed as a unit.

3 The outer CV joints are the Rzeppa type, which consists of ball-bearings running between an inner race and an outer cage, is capable of angular but not axial movement. The outer joints should be cleaned, inspected and repacked, but they cannot be disassembled. If an outer joint is damaged, it must be renewed along with the driveshaft (the outer joint and driveshaft are sold as a single component).

4 The gaiters should be inspected periodically for damage and leaking lubricant. Torn CV joint gaiters must be renewed immediately or the joints can be damaged. Gaiter renewal involves removal of the driveshaft (see Section 2). **Note:** *Some motor accessory/parts stores carry 'split' type renewal gaiters, which can be fitted without removing the driveshaft from the vehicle. This is a convenient alternative; however, the driveshaft should be removed and the CV joint disassembled and cleaned to ensure the joint is free from contaminants such as moisture and dirt which will accelerate CV joint wear.* The most common symptom of worn or damaged CV joints, besides lubricant leaks, is a clicking noise in turns, a clunk when accelerating after coasting, and vibration at highway speeds. To check for wear in the CV joints and driveshaft shafts, grasp each driveshaft (one at a time) and rotate it in both directions while holding the CV joint housings, feeling for play indicating worn splines or sloppy CV joints. Also check the driveshaft shafts for cracks, dents and distortion.

8•2 Driveshafts

2.2a Remove the split pin...

2.2b ...and the locking cap

2.3 Use a large lever to immobilise the hub while slackening the driveshaft nut

2.4 Use a brass punch to loosen the driveshaft splines from the hub

2 Driveshafts – removal and refitting

Removal

1 Loosen the front wheel nuts, raise the vehicle and support it securely on axle stands (see *Jacking and vehicle support*). Remove the wheel.
2 Remove the split pin and locking cap from the driveshaft hub nut **(see illustrations)**.
3 Remove the driveshaft hub nut and washer. To prevent the hub from turning, wedge a lever between two of the wheel studs and allow the lever to rest against the ground or the floor of the vehicle **(see illustration)**.
4 To loosen the driveshaft from the hub splines, tap the end of the driveshaft with a soft-faced hammer or a hammer and a brass punch **(see illustration)**. **Note:** *Don't attempt to push the end of the driveshaft through the hub yet. Applying force to the end of the driveshaft, beyond just breaking it loose from the hub, can damage the driveshaft or transmission.* If the driveshaft is stuck in the hub splines and won't move, it may be necessary to remove the brake disc (see Chapter 9) and push it from the hub with a two-jaw puller after the procedure in paragraph 6 is performed.
5 Release the screws and remove the engine undershields. Place a drain pan underneath the transmission to catch the lubricant that will spill out when the driveshafts are removed.
6 Remove the nuts and bolt securing the balljoint to the control arm, then lever the control arm down to separate the components (see Chapter 10)
7 Pull out on the hub carrier and detach the driveshaft from the hub **(see illustration)**. Don't let the driveshaft hang by the inner CV joint after the outer end has been detached from the hub carrier, as the inner joint could become damaged. Support the outer end of the driveshaft with a piece of wire, if necessary.
8 Carefully lever the inner CV joint out of the transmission – you may need to give the lever bar a sharp rap with a soft hammer **(see illustration)**.
9 Refer to Chapter 7A or 7B for the driveshaft oil seal renewal procedure.

Refitting

10 Refitting is the reverse of the removal procedure, but with the following additional points:
 a) Push the driveshaft sharply in to seat the retaining ring on the inner CV joint in the groove in the differential side gear.
 b) Tighten the driveshaft hub nut to the torque listed in this Chapter's Specifications, then install the locking cap and a new split pin.
 c) Refit the wheel and nuts, lower the vehicle and tighten the nuts to the torque listed in the Specifications.
 d) Check the transmission or differential lubricant and add, if necessary, to bring it to the proper level (see Chapter 1).

2.7 Pull the hub carrier out and slide the end of the driveshaft out of the hub

2.8 To separate the end of the driveshaft from the transmission, lever on the CV joint housing

Driveshafts 8•3

3.3 Lift the tabs on all the gaiter clamps with a screwdriver, then open the clamps

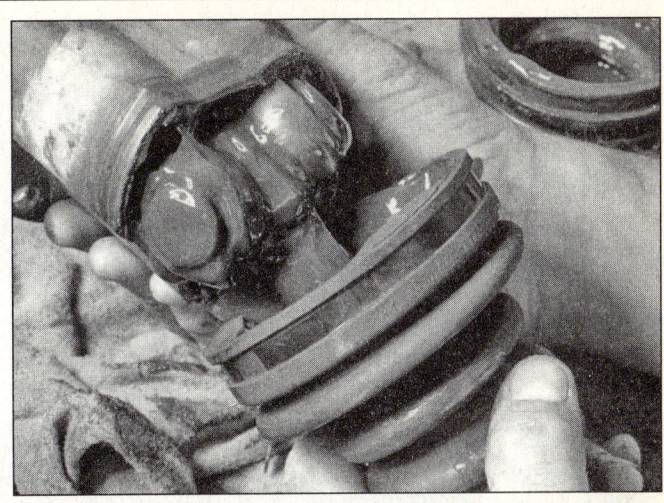

3.4 Remove the gaiter from the inner CV joint and slide the joint housing from the tripod

3 Driveshaft gaiter renewal and CV joint inspection

Note: *If the CV joints must be overhauled (usually due to torn gaiters), explore all options before beginning the job. Complete rebuilt driveshafts are available on an exchange basis, which eliminates much time and work. Whichever route you choose to take, check on the cost and availability of parts before disassembling the vehicle.*

1 Remove the driveshaft (see Section 2).

Disassembly

2 Mount the driveshaft in a vice with wood lined jaws (to prevent damage to the driveshaft). Check the CV joint for excessive play in the radial direction, which indicates worn parts. Check for smooth operation throughout the full range of motion for each CV joint. If a gaiter is torn, disassemble the joint, clean the components and inspect for damage due to loss of lubrication and possible contamination by foreign matter.

3 Working on the inboard joint, using a small screwdriver, lever the retaining tabs on the clamps up to loosen them and slide them off **(see illustration)**.

4 Using a screwdriver, carefully lever up on the edge of the outer gaiter and push it away from the CV joint. Old and worn gaiters can be cut off. Pull the inner CV joint gaiter back from the housing and slide the housing from the tripod **(see illustration)**.

5 Mark the tripod and driveshaft to ensure that they are reassembled properly.

6 Remove the tripod joint circlip with a pair of circlip pliers **(see illustration)**.

7 Use a hammer and a brass punch to drive the tripod joint from the driveshaft; be careful not to damage the bearing surfaces or the splines on the shaft **(see illustration)**.

8 If you haven't already cut them off, remove both gaiters. If you're working on a right-hand driveshaft, you'll also have to cut off the clamp for the dynamic damper and slide the damper off, after first marking its position for reassembly.

9 Do not disassemble the outer joint.

Check

10 Thoroughly clean all components, including the outer CV joint assembly, with solvent until the old CV joint grease is completely removed. Inspect the bearing surfaces of the inner tripods and housings for cracks, pitting, scoring and other signs of wear. It's very difficult to inspect the bearing surfaces of the inner and outer races of the outer CV joint, but you can at least check the surfaces of the ball-bearings themselves. If they're in good shape, the races probably are too; if they're not, neither are the races. If the inner CV joint is worn, you can buy a new inner CV joint and install it on the old driveshaft; if the outer CV joint is worn, you'll have to purchase a new outer CV joint *and* driveshaft (they're sold preassembled).

Reassembly

11 Wrap the splines on the end of the driveshaft with electrical tape to protect the gaiters from the sharp edges of the splines **(see illustration)**. Slide the clamps and gaiter(s) onto the driveshaft, then place the tripod on the shaft. **Note:** *If you're working on a right-hand driveshaft, be sure to install the dynamic damper and a new clamp before installing the inner gaiter.* Apply grease to the tripod assembly and inside the housing. Insert the tripod into the housing and pack the remainder of the grease around the tripod **(see illustrations)**.

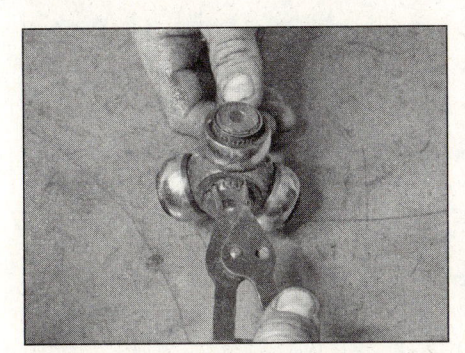

3.6 Remove the circlip with a pair of circlip pliers

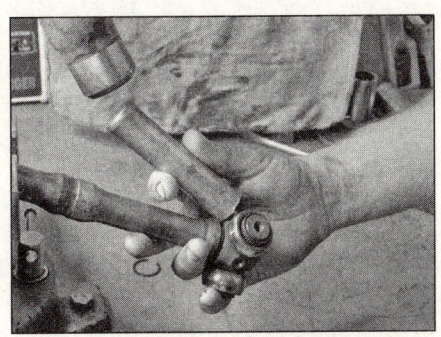

3.7 Drive the tripod joint from the driveshaft with a brass punch and hammer

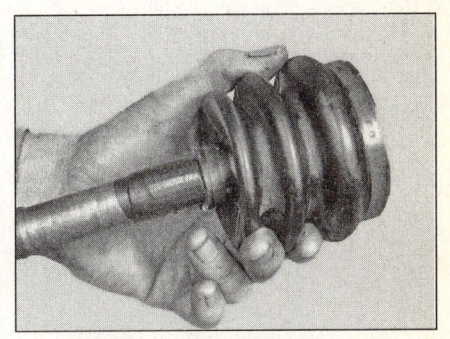

3.11a Wrap the splined areas of the driveshaft with tape to prevent damage to the gaiters

8•4 Driveshafts

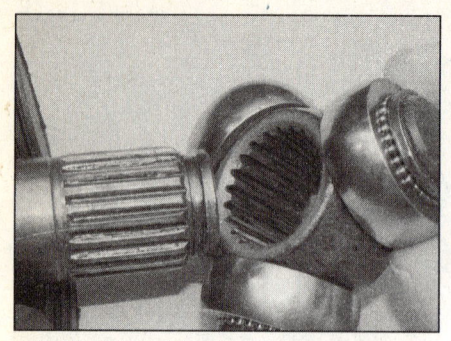

3.11b Fit the tripod with the chamfered section facing the driveshaft

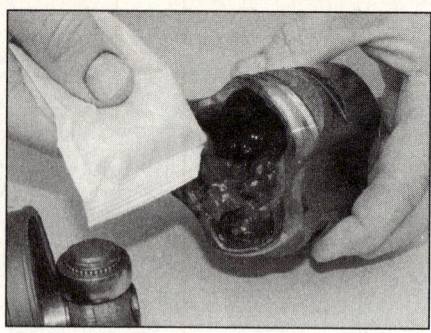

3.11c Apply the supplied grease to the joint housing

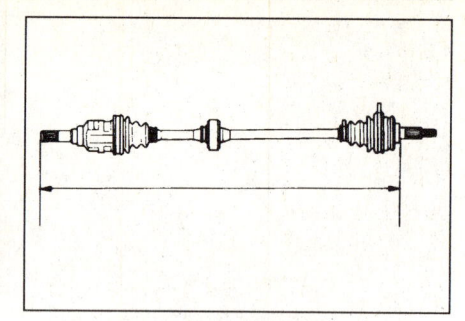

3.12 The driveshaft standard length should be set before the gaiter clamps are tightened

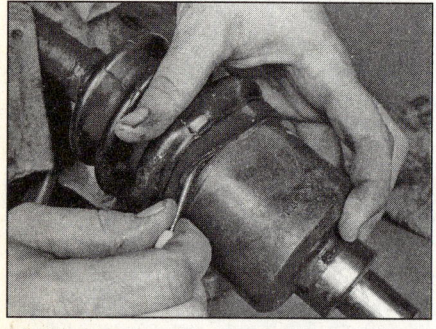

3.13a Equalise the pressure in the gaiter with a screwdriver between the gaiter and the housing

3.13b Use pinchers . . .

3.13c . . . to tighten the gaiter clamps

12 Slide the gaiter into place, making sure both ends seat in their grooves. Adjust the length of the driveshaft to the dimension listed in this Chapter's Specifications **(see illustration)**.

13 Equalise the pressure in the gaiter, then tighten and secure the gaiter clamps **(see illustrations)**.

Chapter 9
Braking system

Contents

	Section number		Section number
Anti-lock Braking System (ABS) – general information	22	Hydraulic pipes and hoses – renewal	3
Anti-lock Braking System (ABS) components – removal and refitting	23	Hydraulic system – bleeding	2
		Load-sensing proportioning valve – removal and refitting	21
Brake pedal – removal and refitting	14	Master cylinder – removal, overhaul and refitting	13
Front brake caliper – removal, overhaul and refitting	8	Rear brake caliper – removal, overhaul and refitting	9
Front brake disc – inspection, removal and refitting	6	Rear brake disc – inspection, removal and refitting	7
Front brake pad wear check	See Chapter 1	Rear brake drum – removal, inspection and refitting	10
Front brake pads – renewal	4	Rear brake pad wear check	See Chapter 1
General information	1	Rear brake pads – renewal	5
Handbrake – adjustment	17	Rear brake shoes – renewal	11
Handbrake cables – renewal	19	Rear wheel cylinder – removal, overhaul and refitting	12
Handbrake lever – removal and refitting	18	Stop-light switch – removal, refitting and adjustment	20
Hydraulic fluid level check	See *Weekly checks*	Vacuum servo unit – testing, removal and refitting	15
Hydraulic fluid renewal	See Chapter 1	Vacuum servo unit check valve – removal, testing and refitting	16

Degrees of difficulty

| Easy, suitable for novice with little experience | Fairly easy, suitable for beginner with some experience | Fairly difficult, suitable for competent DIY mechanic | Difficult, suitable for experienced DIY mechanic | Very difficult, suitable for expert DIY or professional |

Specifications

Front disc brakes
Type.. Disc, with single-piston sliding caliper
Disc thickness:
  1.6 litre models:
    New... 22.0 mm
    Minimum... 20.0 mm
  All other models:
    New... 18.0 mm
    Minimum... 16.0 mm
Maximum disc run-out.. 0.05 mm
Brake pad friction material thickness:
  New... 13.0 mm
  Minimum... 1.0 mm

Rear disc brakes
Type.. Disc, with single-piston sliding caliper and integral handbrake mechanism

Disc thickness:
  New... 9.0 mm
  Minimum... 8.0 mm
Maximum disc run-out.. 0.15 mm
Brake pad friction material thickness:
  New... 10.0 mm
  Minimum... 1.0 mm

Rear drum brakes
Drum diameter:
  New... 200.0 mm
  Maximum... 201.0 mm
Brake shoe friction material thickness:
  New... 4.0 mm
  Minimum... 1.0 mm

Brake pedal

Height from floor to centre of pedal pad:
- LHD .... 148.6 to 158.6 mm
- RHD .... 138.7 to 148.7 mm

Torque wrench settings

	Nm	lbf ft
Front brake caliper:		
Guide pin bolts	34	25
Mounting bracket bolts	88	65
Handbrake lever nuts	15	11
Hydraulic hose/pipe union nuts	15	11
Master cylinder retaining nuts	13	10
Rear brake caliper:		
Guide pin bolts:		
Up to October 1999 (single headlight models)	20	15
From October 1999 (twin headlight models)	27	20
Mounting bracket	47	35
Rear wheel cylinder bolts	10	7
Roadwheel bolts	103	76
Vacuum servo unit mounting nuts	13	10
Vacuum servo unit pushrod nut	25	18
Wheel speed sensor	8	6

1 General information

The braking system is of the servo-assisted, dual-circuit hydraulic type. The arrangement of the hydraulic system is such that each circuit operates one front and one rear brake from a tandem master cylinder. Under normal circumstances, both circuits operate in unison. However, in the event of hydraulic failure in one circuit, full braking force will still be available at two wheels.

All models are equipped with front disc brakes, and may be fitted with drum or disc brakes at the rear wheels. ABS is fitted as standard (refer to Section 22 for further information on ABS operation).

The disc brakes are actuated by single-piston sliding type calipers, which ensure that equal pressure is applied to each disc pad. The rear drum brakes are actuated by a twin piston wheel cylinder at each wheel which acts upon the brake shoes.

On all models, the handbrake provides an independent mechanical means of rear brake application. Models with rear discs are fitted with rear brake calipers with an integral handbrake function. The handbrake cable operates a lever on the caliper which forces the piston to press the pad against the disc surface. A self-adjust mechanism is incorporated, to automatically compensate for brake pad wear. On models with rear drum brakes, the handbrake cable operates an expanding link positioned between the two brake shoes, forcing them against the inside of the brake drum.

Note: *When servicing any of the system, work carefully and methodically; also observe scrupulous cleanliness when overhauling any of the hydraulic system. Always renew components (in axle sets, where applicable) if in doubt about their condition, and use only genuine Toyota parts, or at least those of known good quality. Note the warnings given in 'Safety first!' and at relevant points in this Chapter concerning the dangers of asbestos dust and hydraulic fluid.*

2 Hydraulic system – bleeding

Warning: *Hydraulic fluid is poisonous; wash off immediately and thoroughly in the case of skin contact, and seek immediate medical advice if any fluid is swallowed or gets into the eyes. Certain types of hydraulic fluid are inflammable, and may ignite when allowed into contact with hot components; when servicing any hydraulic system, it is safest to assume that the fluid is inflammable, and to take precautions against the risk of fire as though it is petrol that is being handled. Hydraulic fluid is also an effective paint stripper, and will attack plastics; if any is spilt, it should be washed off immediately, using copious quantities of fresh water. Finally, it is hygroscopic (it absorbs moisture from the air) – old fluid may be contaminated and unfit for further use. When topping-up or renewing the fluid, always use the recommended type, and ensure that it comes from a freshly-opened sealed container.*

Caution: *Ensure the ignition is switched off before starting the bleeding procedure, to avoid any possibility of voltage being applied to the hydraulic modulator before the bleeding procedure is complete. Ideally, the battery should be disconnected. If voltage is applied to the modulator before the bleeding procedure is complete, this will effectively drain the hydraulic fluid in the modulator, rendering the unit unserviceable. Do not, therefore, attempt to 'run' the modulator in order to bleed the brakes.*

General

1 The correct operation of any hydraulic system is only possible after removing all air from the components and circuit; this is achieved by bleeding the system.

2 During the bleeding procedure, add only clean, unused hydraulic fluid of the recommended type; never re-use fluid that has already been bled from the system. Ensure that sufficient fluid is available before starting work.

3 If there is any possibility of incorrect fluid being already in the system, the brake components and circuit must be flushed completely with uncontaminated, correct fluid, and new seals should be fitted to the various components.

4 If hydraulic fluid has been lost from the system, or air has entered because of a leak, ensure that the fault is cured before proceeding further.

5 Park the vehicle on level ground, switch off the engine and select first or reverse gear, then chock the wheels and release the handbrake.

6 Check that all pipes and hoses are secure, unions tight and bleed screws closed. Clean any dirt from around the bleed screws.

7 Unscrew the master cylinder reservoir cap, and top the master cylinder reservoir up to the MAX level line; refit the cap loosely, and remember to maintain the fluid level at least above the MIN level line throughout the procedure, or there is a risk of further air entering the system.

Braking system 9•3

8 There is a number of one-man, do-it-yourself brake bleeding kits currently available from motor accessory shops. It is recommended that one of these kits is used whenever possible, as they greatly simplify the bleeding operation, and also reduce the risk of expelled air and fluid being drawn back into the system. If such a kit is not available, the basic (two-man) method must be used, which is described in detail below.

9 If a kit is to be used, prepare the vehicle as described previously, and follow the kit manufacturer's instructions, as the procedure may vary slightly according to the type being used; generally, they are as outlined below in the relevant sub-section.

10 Whichever method is used, the same sequence must be followed (paragraphs 11 and 12) to ensure that the removal of all air from the system.

Bleeding

Sequence

11 If the system has been only partially disconnected, and suitable precautions were taken to minimise fluid loss, it should be necessary only to bleed that of the system (ie, the primary or secondary circuit).

12 If the complete system is to be bled, then it should be done working in the following sequence:
a) Left-hand front brake.
b) Right-hand front brake.
c) Left-hand rear brake.
d) Right-hand rear brake.

Basic (two-man) method

13 Collect a clean glass jar, a suitable length of plastic or rubber tubing which is a tight fit over the bleed screw, and a ring spanner to fit the screw **(see illustration)**. The help of an assistant will also be required.

14 Remove the dust cap from the first screw in the sequence. Fit the spanner and tube to the screw, place the other end of the tube in the jar, and pour in sufficient fluid to cover the end of the tube.

15 Ensure that the master cylinder reservoir fluid level is maintained at least above the MIN level line throughout the procedure.

16 Have the assistant fully depress the brake pedal several times to build-up pressure, then maintain it on the final down stroke.

17 While pedal pressure is maintained, unscrew the bleed screw (approximately one turn) and allow the compressed fluid and air to flow into the jar. The assistant should maintain pedal pressure, following it down to the floor if necessary, and should not release it until instructed to do so. When the flow stops, tighten the bleed screw again, have the assistant release the pedal slowly, and recheck the reservoir fluid level.

18 Repeat the steps given in paragraphs 16 and 17 until the fluid emerging from the bleed screw is free from air bubbles. If the master cylinder has been drained and refilled, and air is being bled from the first screw in the sequence, allow approximately five seconds between cycles for the master cylinder passages to refill.

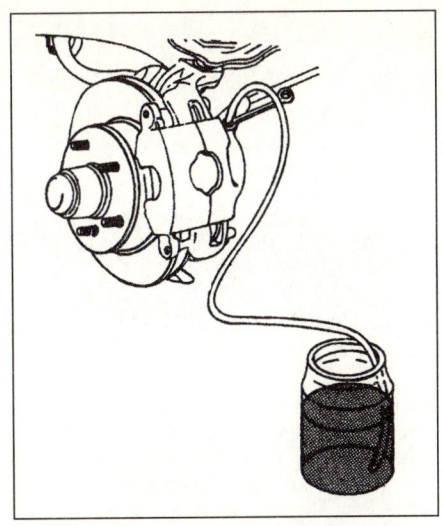

2.13 When bleeding the brakes, a hose is connected to the bleed screw at the caliper or wheel cylinder

19 When no more air bubbles appear, tighten the bleed screw securely, remove the tube and spanner, and refit the dust cap. Do not overtighten the bleed screw.

20 Repeat the procedure on the remaining screws in the sequence, until all air is removed from the system and the brake pedal feels firm again.

Using a one-way valve kit

21 As their name implies, these kits consist of a length of tubing with a one-way valve fitted, to prevent expelled air and fluid being drawn back into the system; some kits include a translucent container, which can be positioned so that the air bubbles can be more easily seen flowing from the end of the tube.

22 The kit is connected to the bleed screw, which is then opened. The user returns to the driver's seat, depresses the brake pedal with a smooth, steady stroke, and slowly releases it; this is repeated until the expelled fluid is clear of air bubbles.

23 Note that these kits simplify work so much that it is easy to forget the master

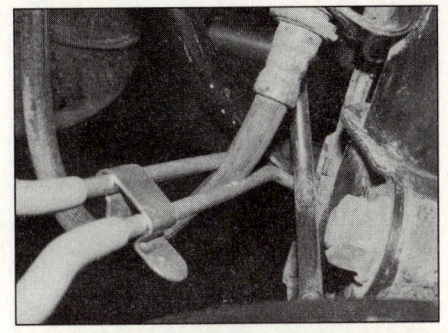

3.1 Use a propriety hose clamp to seal the rubber flexible hoses

cylinder reservoir fluid level; ensure that this is maintained at least above the MIN level line at all times.

Using a pressure-bleeding kit

24 These kits are usually operated by the reservoir of pressurised air contained in the spare tyre. However, note that it will probably be necessary to reduce the pressure to a lower level than normal; refer to the instructions supplied with the kit.

25 By connecting a pressurised, fluid-filled container to the master cylinder reservoir, bleeding can be carried out simply by opening each screw in turn (in the specified sequence), and allowing the fluid to flow out until no more air bubbles can be seen in the expelled fluid.

26 This method has the advantage that the large reservoir of fluid provides an additional safeguard against air being drawn into the system during bleeding.

27 Pressure-bleeding is particularly effective when bleeding 'difficult' systems, or when bleeding the complete system at the time of routine fluid renewal.

All methods

28 When bleeding is complete, and firm pedal feel is restored, wash off any spilt fluid, tighten the bleed screws securely, and refit their dust caps.

29 Check the hydraulic fluid level in the master cylinder reservoir, and top-up if necessary (see Weekly checks).

30 Discard any hydraulic fluid that has been bled from the system; it will not be fit for re-use.

31 Check the feel of the brake pedal. If it feels at all spongy, air must still be present in the system, and further bleeding is required. Failure to bleed satisfactorily after a reasonable repetition of the bleeding procedure may be due to worn master cylinder seals.

3 Hydraulic pipes and hoses – renewal

Note: Before starting work, refer to the note at the beginning of Section 2 concerning the dangers of hydraulic fluid.

1 If any pipe or hose is to be renewed, minimise fluid loss by first removing the master cylinder reservoir cap, then tightening it down onto a piece of polythene to obtain an airtight seal. Alternatively, flexible hoses can be sealed, if required, using a proprietary brake hose clamp **(see illustration)**; metal brake pipe unions can be plugged (if care is taken not to allow dirt into the system) or capped immediately they are disconnected. Place a wad of rag under any union that is to be disconnected to catch any spilt fluid.

2 If a flexible hose is to be disconnected, unscrew the brake pipe union nut before removing the spring clip which secures the hose to its mounting bracket **(see illustrations)**.

9•4 Braking system

3.2a Unscrew the brake pipe threaded fitting with a flare-nut spanner to protect the union corners from being rounded off

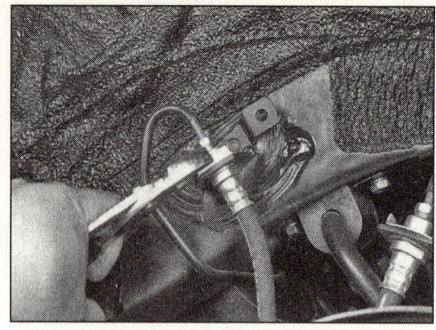

3.2b Pull of the union clip with a pair of pliers

3 To unscrew the union nuts, it is preferable to obtain a brake pipe (flare-nut) spanner of the correct size; these are available from most large motor accessory shops. Failing this, a close-fitting open-ended spanner will be required, though if the nuts are tight or corroded, their flats may be rounded-off if the spanner slips. In such a case, a self-locking wrench is often the only way to unscrew a stubborn union, but it follows that the pipe and the damaged nuts must be renewed on reassembly. Always clean a union and surrounding area before disconnecting it. If disconnecting a component with more than one union, make a careful note of the connections before disturbing any of them.

4 If a brake pipe is to be renewed, it can be obtained, cut to length and with the union nuts and end flares in place, from Toyota dealers. All that is then necessary is to bend it to shape, following the line of the original, before fitting it to the car. Alternatively, most motor accessory shops can make up brake pipes from kits, but this requires very careful measurement of the original, to ensure that the new one is of the correct length. The safest answer is usually to take the original to the shop as a pattern.

5 On refitting, do not overtighten the union nuts. It is not necessary to exercise brute force to obtain a sound joint.

6 Ensure that the pipes and hoses are correctly routed, with no kinks, and that they are secured in the clips or brackets provided. After fitting, remove the polythene from the reservoir, and bleed the hydraulic system as described in Section 2. Wash off any spilt fluid, and check carefully for fluid leaks.

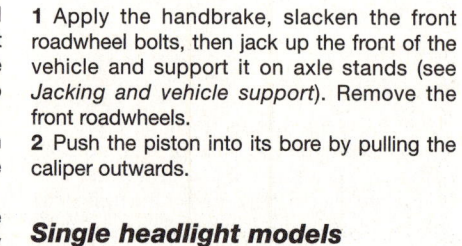

4 Front brake pads – renewal

⚠ **Warning: Renew both sets of front brake pads at the same time – never renew the pads on only one wheel, as uneven braking may result. Note that the dust created by wear of the pads may contain asbestos, which is a health hazard. Never blow it out with compressed air, and don't inhale any of it. An approved filtering mask should be worn when working on the brakes. DO NOT use petrol or petroleum-based solvents to clean brake parts; use brake cleaner or methylated spirit only.**

1 Apply the handbrake, slacken the front roadwheel bolts, then jack up the front of the vehicle and support it on axle stands (see *Jacking and vehicle support*). Remove the front roadwheels.

2 Push the piston into its bore by pulling the caliper outwards.

Single headlight models

3 Follow the accompanying photos **(illustrations 4.3a to 4.3s)** for the actual pad renewal procedure. Be sure to stay in order and read the caption under each illustration.

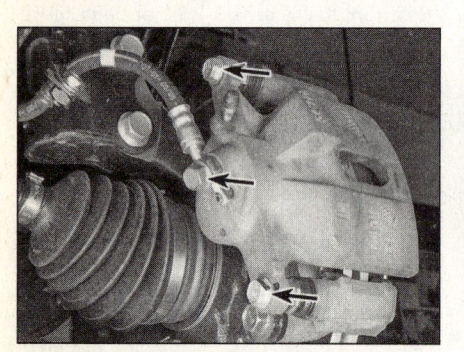

4.3a Remove the bolts (upper and lower arrows). The hose union (middle arrow) shouldn't be unscrewed unless the caliper is being removed

4.3b Remove the caliper . . .

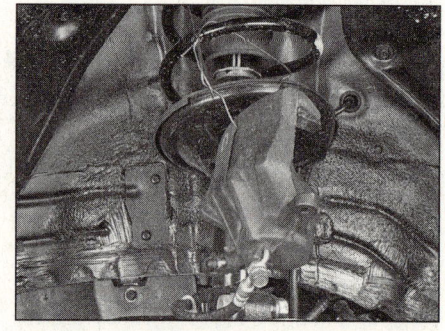

4.3c . . . and suspend it from the coil spring with a piece of wire; don't allow it to hang by the brake hose

4.3d Remove the upper anti-squeal spring . . .

4.3e . . . and the lower anti-squeal spring

4.3f Remove the outer shim . . .

Braking system 9•5

4.3g ... and, where fitted, the inner shim from the outer brake pad

4.3h Remove the outer brake pad

4.3i Remove the outer shim ...

4.3j ... and, where fitted, the inner shim from the inner brake pad

4.3k Remove the inner brake pad

4.3l Remove the four pad support plates; inspect the plates for damage and renew as necessary (good plates should 'snap' into place in the mounting plate; if they're weak or distorted, renew them)

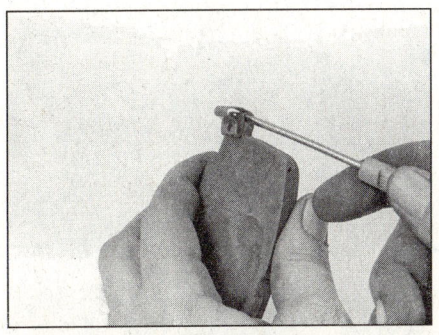

4.3m Lever the wear indicator off the old inner brake pad and transfer it to the new inner pad (if the wear indicator is worn or bent, renew it)

4.3n Install the pad support plates, then new inner brake pads and the shims; make sure the ears on the pad are properly engaged with the pad support plates

4.3o Fit the pad support plates, the outer pad and shims

4.3p Fit the upper and lower anti-squeal springs; make sure both are properly engaged with the pads as shown

4.3q Pull out the upper and lower sliding pins and clean them off (if either boot is damaged, remove it by levering the flange of the metal bushing that retains the boot) ...

4.3r ... apply a coat of high-temperature grease to the caliper sliding pins before installing them

9•6 Braking system

4.3s Refit the caliper and tighten the caliper bolts to the specified torque

Twin headlight models

4 Follow the accompanying photos (illustrations 4.4a to 4.4k) for the actual pad renewal procedure. Be sure to stay in order and read the caption under each illustration.

All models

5 If new brake pads are to be fitted, the caliper piston must be pushed back into the cylinder to make room for them. Either use a G-clamp or similar tool, or use suitable pieces of wood as levers. Clamp off the flexible brake hose leading to the caliper then connect a brake bleeding kit to the caliper bleed nipple. Open the bleed nipple as the piston is retracted, the surplus brake fluid will then be collected in the bleed kit vessel **(see illustration 4.4j)**. Close the bleed nipple just before the caliper piston is pushed fully into the caliper. This should ensure no air enters the hydraulic system.

Note: *The ABS unit contains hydraulic components that are very sensitive to impurities in the brake fluid. Even the smallest particles can cause the system to fail through blockage. The pad retraction method described here prevents any debris in the brake fluid expelled from the caliper from being passed back to the ABS hydraulic unit, as well as preventing any chance of damage to the master cylinder seals.*

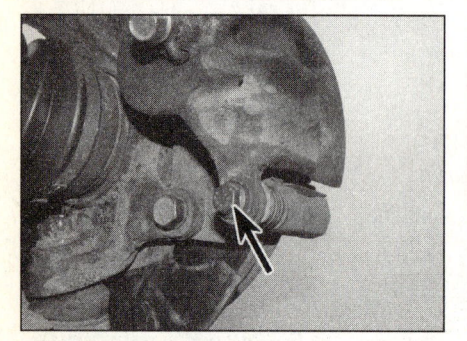

4.4a Remove the caliper lower guide pin bolt (arrowed)

4.4b Pivot the caliper away and suspend it from the coil spring using a length of wire or string

4.4c Remove the inner and outer pad from the caliper mounting bracket

4.4d Check the pad support plates (arrowed) in the caliper mounting bracket; if they are worn or distorted, renew them

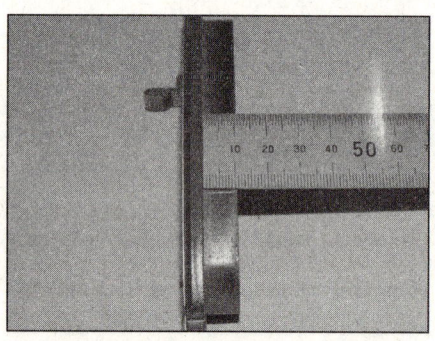

4.4e Measure the thickness of the pad's friction material; if it's less than 2.0 mm, renew all four pads

4.4f Check the caliper guide pins slide easily and the rubber gaiters are not damaged

4.4g Peel the protective covering from the back of the new pads

4.4h Fit the pads in the caliper mounting bracket, ensuring the ears of the pads engage correctly with the pad support plates

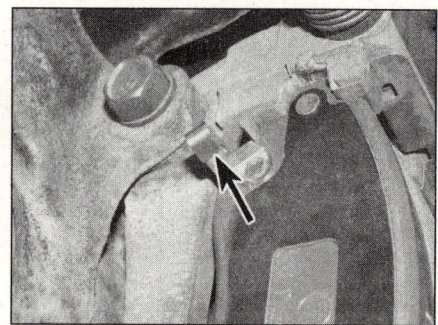

4.4i The pad with the audible wear indicator (arrowed) should be fitted to the inboard side of the mounting bracket

Braking system 9•7

6 Depress the brake pedal repeatedly, until the pads are pressed into firm contact with the brake disc, and normal (non-assisted) pedal pressure is restored.
7 Repeat the above procedure on the remaining front brake caliper.
8 Refit the roadwheels, then lower the vehicle to the ground and tighten the roadwheel bolts to the specified torque.
9 Check the hydraulic fluid level as described in *Weekly checks*.
Caution: New pads will not give full braking efficiency until they have bedded-in. Be prepared for this, and avoid hard braking as far as possible for the first hundred miles or so after pad renewal.

5 Rear brake pads – renewal

Warning: Renew both sets of rear brake pads at the same time – never renew the pads on only one wheel, as uneven braking may result. Note that the dust created by wear of the pads may contain asbestos, which is a health hazard. Never blow it out with compressed air, and don't inhale any of it. An approved filtering mask should be worn when working on the brakes. DO NOT use petrol or petroleum-based solvents to clean brake parts; use brake cleaner or methylated spirit only.

1 Chock the front wheels, slacken the rear roadwheel bolts, then jack up the rear of the vehicle and support it on axle stands (see *Jacking and vehicle support*). Remove the rear roadwheels.
2 Slacken and remove the caliper lower guide pin bolt, and swing the caliper up, pivoting around the top guide pin bolt, and tie it in place.
3 Withdraw the inner and outer pads from the caliper bracket, along with the anti-rattle shims **(see illustration)**.
4 Recover the upper and lower pad support plates from the caliper mounting bracket.
5 First measure the thickness of the friction material of each brake pad. If either pad is worn at any point to the specified minimum thickness or less, all four pads must be renewed. Also, the pads should be renewed if any are fouled with oil or grease; there is no satisfactory way of degreasing friction material, once contaminated. If any of the brake pads are worn unevenly, or fouled with oil or grease, trace and rectify the cause before reassembly.
6 If the brake pads are still serviceable, carefully clean them using a clean, fine wire brush or similar, paying particular attention to the sides and back of the metal backing. Clean out the grooves in the friction material, and pick out any large embedded particles of dirt or debris. Carefully clean the pad locations in the caliper body/mounting bracket.

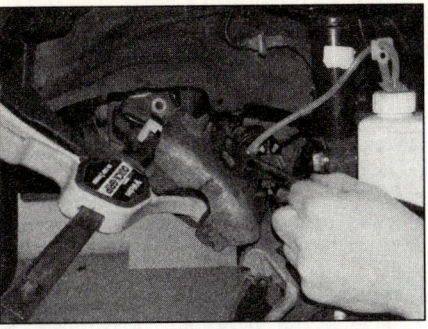

4.4j If new pads have been fitted, before refitting the caliper, push back the caliper piston whilst opening the bleed screw. This is to prevent any dirt/debris being forced back up the hydraulic circuit in the ABS modulator

7 Prior to fitting the pads, check that the guide pins are free to slide easily in the caliper body, and check that the rubber guide pin gaiters are undamaged. Brush the dust and dirt from the caliper and piston, but **do not** inhale it, as it is a health hazard. Inspect the dust seal around the piston for damage, and the piston for evidence of fluid leaks, corrosion or damage. If attention to any of these components is necessary, refer to Section 9.
8 If new brake pads are to be fitted, the caliper piston must be pushed back into the cylinder to make room for them. In order to retract the piston, the piston must be turned clockwise

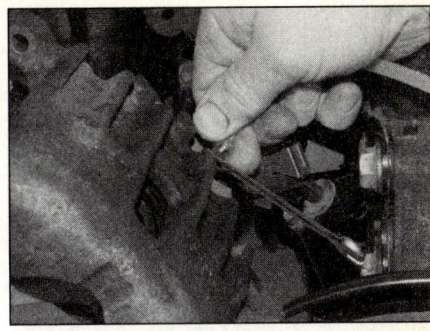

4.4k Close the bleed screw as soon as the piston is retracted, then refit the caliper and tighten the bolts to the specified torque

as it is pushed into the caliper. Toyota tool No SST 09719-14020 is available to retract the pistons, as are several available from good accessory/parts retailers. Clamp off the flexible brake hose leading to the caliper then connect a brake bleeding kit to the caliper bleed nipple. Open the bleed nipple as the piston is retracted, the surplus brake fluid will then be collected in the bleed kit vessel. Apply pressure to the piston and rotate it clockwise at the same time, until the piston rotates freely, then align the piston 'stopper' groove with the caliper protrusion. Close the bleed nipple just before the caliper piston is pushed fully

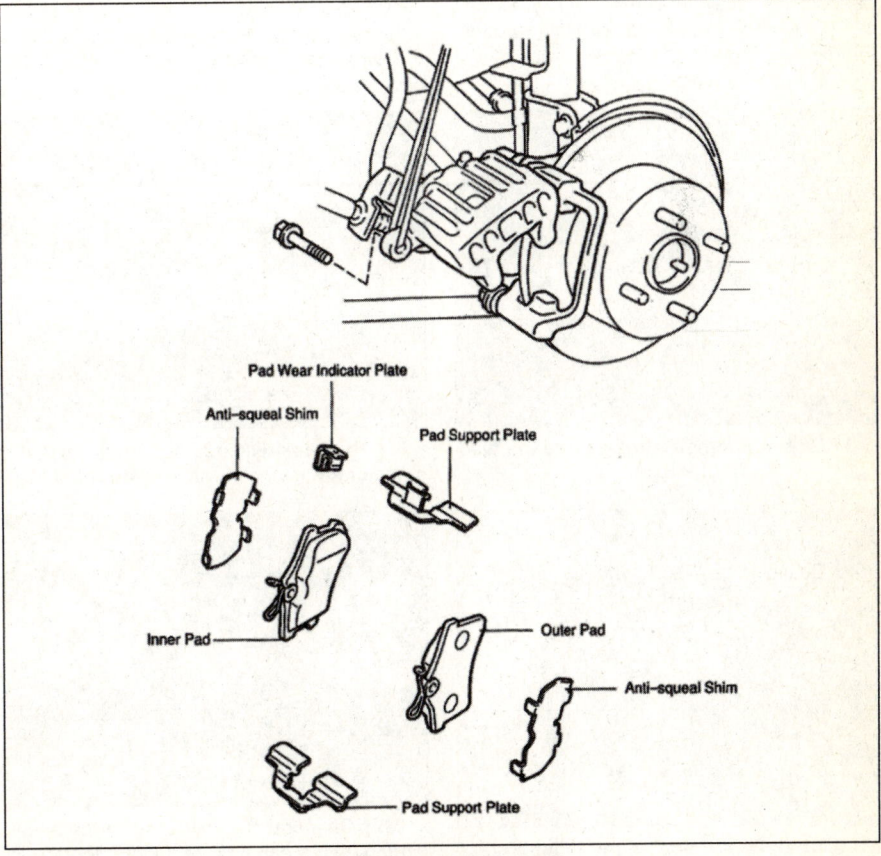

5.3 Rear brake pad details

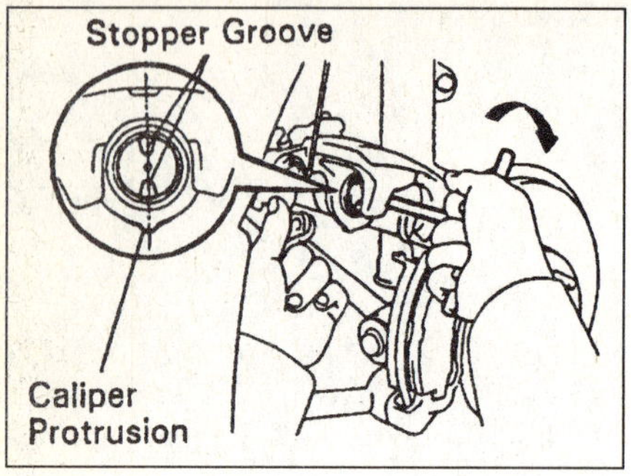

5.8 Retract the caliper piston by turning it clockwise until it turns freely, then align the stopper grooves and caliper protrusion into the caliper **(see illustration)**. This should ensure no air enters the hydraulic system

Note: *The ABS unit contains hydraulic components that are very sensitive to impurities in the brake fluid. Even the smallest particles can cause the system to fail through blockage. The pad retraction method described here prevents any debris in the brake fluid expelled from the caliper from being passed back to the ABS hydraulic unit, as well as preventing any chance of damage to the master cylinder seals.*

9 Refit the pad support plates to the caliper mounting bracket, then slide the brake pads into position in the caliper, ensuring each pad's friction material is facing the brake disc. Fit the anti-rattle shims to the back of each pad, ensuring they are correctly located.

10 Untie the caliper and lower it into position. Insert the caliper lower guide pin bolt, and tighten it to the specified torque.

11 Depress the brake pedal repeatedly until the pads are pressed into firm contact with the brake disc, and normal (non-assisted) pedal pressure is restored.

12 Repeat the above procedure on the remaining rear brake caliper.

13 Check the operation of the handbrake and, if necessary, carry out the adjustment procedure as described in Section 17.

14 Refit the roadwheels, then lower the vehicle to the ground and tighten the roadwheel bolts to the specified torque setting.

15 Check the hydraulic fluid level as described in *Weekly checks*.

Caution: *New pads will not give full braking efficiency until they have bedded-in. Be prepared for this, and avoid hard braking as far as possible for the first hundred miles or so after pad renewal.*

6 Front brake disc – inspection, removal and refitting

Note: *Before starting work, refer to the note at the beginning of Section 4 concerning the dangers of asbestos dust.*

Inspection

Note: *If either disc requires renewal, BOTH should be renewed at the same time, to ensure even and consistent braking. New brake pads should also be fitted.*

1 Apply the handbrake, slacken the front roadwheel bolts, then jack up the front of the car and support it on axle stands (see *Jacking and vehicle support*). Remove the appropriate front roadwheel.

2 Slowly rotate the brake disc so that the full area of both sides can be checked; remove the brake pads if better access is required to the inboard surface. Light scoring is normal in the area swept by the brake pads, but if heavy scoring or cracks are found, the disc must be renewed.

3 It is normal to find a lip of rust and brake dust around the disc's perimeter; this can be scraped off if required. If, however, a lip has formed due to excessive wear of the brake pad swept area, then the disc's thickness must be measured using a micrometer. Take measurements at several places around the disc, at the inside and outside of the pad swept area; if the disc has worn at any point to the specified minimum thickness or less, the disc must be renewed **(see illustration)**.

4 If the disc is thought to be warped, it can be checked for run-out. Either use a dial gauge mounted on any convenient fixed point, while the disc is slowly rotated, or use feeler blades to measure (at several points all around the disc) the clearance between the disc and a fixed point, such as the caliper mounting bracket **(see illustration)**. If the measurements obtained are at the specified maximum or beyond, the disc is excessively warped and must be renewed; however, it is worth checking first that the hub bearing is in good condition (Chapter 1). Also try the effect of removing the disc and turning it through 180°, to reposition it on the hub; if the run-out is still excessive, the disc must be renewed.

5 Check the disc for cracks, especially around the wheel bolt holes, and any other wear or damage, and renew if necessary.

Removal

6 Slacken and remove the two bolts securing the brake caliper mounting bracket to the hub carrier. Undo the bolt securing the brake hose to the bracket on the strut. Slide the assembly off the disc and tie it to the coil spring, using a piece of wire or string, to avoid placing any strain on the hydraulic brake hose **(see illustrations)**.

7 Use chalk or paint to mark the relationship of the disc to the hub, then remove the disc. If it is tight, lightly tap its rear face with a hide or plastic mallet.

Refitting

8 Refitting is the reverse of the removal procedure, noting the following points:
a) Ensure that the mating surfaces of the disc and hub are clean and flat.
b) Align (if applicable) the marks made on removal.
c) If a new disc has been fitted, use a suitable solvent to wipe any preservative coating from the disc before refitting the caliper.
d) Refit the roadwheel then lower the vehicle to the ground and tighten the wheel bolts to the specified torque. Apply the

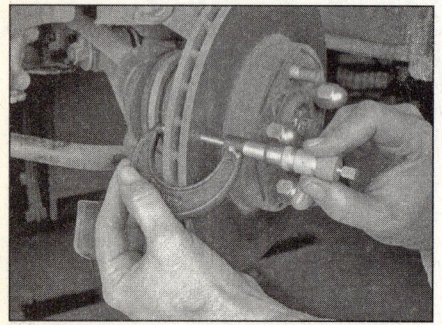

6.3 Use a micrometer to measure the disc thickness

6.4 To check disc run-out, mount a dial indicator as shown and rotate the disc

6.6a Undo the two caliper mounting bracket bolts (arrowed)

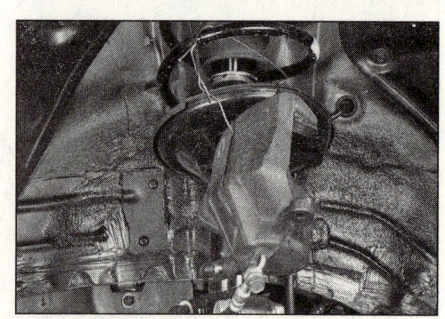

6.6b Suspend the caliper from the coil spring with a cable tie or string; don't let it hang by the brake hose alone

footbrake several times to force the pads back into contact with the disc before driving the vehicle.

7 Rear brake disc – inspection, removal and refitting

Note: *Before starting work, refer to the note at the beginning of Section 5 concerning the dangers of asbestos dust.*

Inspection

Note: *If either disc requires renewal, BOTH should be renewed at the same time, to ensure even and consistent braking. New brake pads should also be fitted.*

1 Firmly chock the front wheels, slacken the appropriate rear roadwheel bolts, then jack up the rear of the car and support it on axle stands (see *Jacking and vehicle support*). Remove the relevant rear roadwheel.
2 Inspect the disc as described in Section 6.

Removal

3 Slacken and remove the two bolts securing the brake caliper mounting bracket to the hub carrier. Slide the assembly off the disc and tie it to the coil spring, using a piece of wire or string, to avoid placing any strain on the hydraulic brake hose.
4 Use chalk or paint to mark the relationship of the disc to the hub, then pull the disc from the hub. If necessary, gently tap the disc from behind and release it from the hub.

Refitting

5 Refitting is the reverse of the removal procedure, noting the following points:
 a) Ensure that the mating surfaces of the disc and hub are clean and flat.
 b) Align (if applicable) the marks made on removal.
 c) If a new disc has been fitted, use a suitable solvent to wipe any preservative coating from the disc before refitting the caliper.
 d) Refit the roadwheel, then lower the vehicle to the ground and tighten the roadwheel bolts to the specified torque. Depress the brake pedal several times to force the pads back into contact with the disc.

8 Front brake caliper – removal, overhaul and refitting

Caution: *Ensure the ignition is switched off before disconnecting any braking system hydraulic union and do not switch it on until after the hydraulic system has been bled. Failure to do this could lead to air entering the regulator unit.*
Note: *Before starting work, refer to the note at the beginning of Section 2 concerning the dangers of hydraulic fluid, and to the warning at the beginning of Section 4 concerning the dangers of asbestos dust.*

Removal

1 Apply the handbrake, slacken the relevant front roadwheel bolts, then jack up the front of the vehicle and support it on axle stands (see *Jacking and vehicle support*). Remove the appropriate roadwheel.
2 Minimise fluid loss by first removing the master cylinder reservoir cap, and then tightening it down onto a piece of polythene, to obtain an airtight seal. Alternatively, use a brake hose clamp, a G-clamp or a similar tool to clamp the flexible hose **(see illustration 3.1)**.
3 Clean the area around the caliper hose union, then loosen the union.
4 Slacken and remove the upper and lower caliper guide pin bolts **(see illustrations 4.3a or 4.4a)**. Lift the caliper away from the brake disc, then unscrew the caliper from the end of the brake hose. Note that the brake pads need not be disturbed, and can be left in position in the caliper mounting bracket.
5 If required, the caliper mounting bracket can be unbolted from the hub carrier.

Overhaul

Note: *Check the availability of repair kits for the caliper before dismantling.*
6 With the caliper on the bench, wipe away all traces of dust and dirt, but *avoid inhaling the dust, as it is a health hazard.*
7 Withdraw the partially ejected piston from the caliper body, and remove the dust seal. The dust seal is retained by a circlip **(see illustration)**.

HAYNES HINT *If the piston cannot be withdrawn by hand, it can be pushed out by applying compressed air to the brake hose union hole. Only low pressure should be required, such as is generated by a foot pump. As the piston is expelled, take great care not to trap your fingers between the piston and caliper.*

8 Using a small screwdriver, extract the piston hydraulic seal, taking great care not to damage the caliper bore.
9 Thoroughly clean all components, using only methylated spirit, isopropyl alcohol or clean

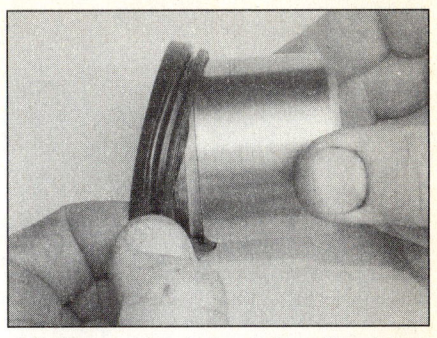

8.7 Remove the dust seal from the piston

hydraulic fluid as a cleaning medium. Never use mineral-based solvents such as petrol or paraffin, as they will attack the hydraulic system's rubber components. Dry the components immediately, using compressed air or a clean, lint-free cloth. Use compressed air to blow clear the fluid passages.
10 Check all components, and renew any that are worn or damaged. Check particularly the cylinder bore and piston; these should be renewed (note that this means the renewal of the complete body assembly) if they are scratched, worn or corroded in any way. Similarly check the condition of the guide pins and their gaiters; both pins should be undamaged and (when cleaned) a reasonably tight sliding fit in the caliper bracket. If there is any doubt about the condition of any component, renew it.
11 If the assembly is fit for further use, obtain the appropriate repair kit; the components should be available from Toyota dealers in various combinations. All rubber seals should be renewed as a matter of course; these should never be re-used.
12 On reassembly, ensure that all components are clean and dry.
13 Soak the piston and the new piston (fluid) seal in clean brake fluid. Smear clean fluid on the cylinder bore surface.
14 Fit the new piston (fluid) seal, using only your fingers (no tools) to manipulate it into the cylinder bore groove **(see illustration)**.
15 Fit the new dust seal to the rear of the piston and seat the outer lip of the seal in the caliper body groove. Carefully ease the piston squarely into the cylinder bore using a twisting motion **(see illustrations)**. Press the piston

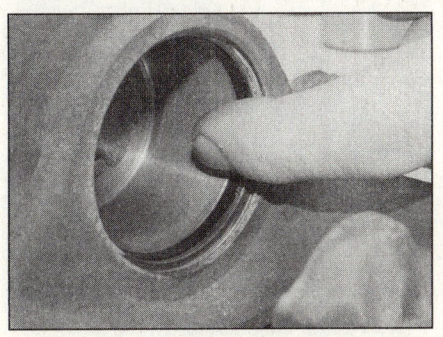

8.14 Fit the seal into the groove in the caliper bore

8.15a Fit the seal to the rear of the piston, and the outer lip to the caliper body groove . . .

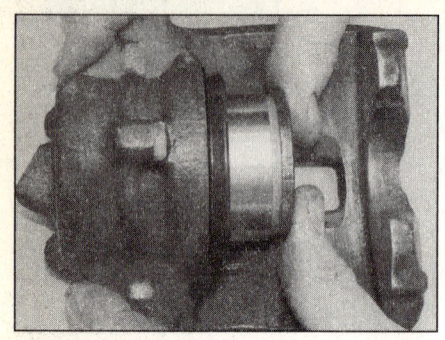

8.15b ... then push and twist the piston into the bore

fully into position, and seat the inner lip of the dust seal in the piston groove. Fit the circlip which retains the dust seal.
16 If the guide pins are being renewed, lubricate the pin shafts with the special grease supplied in the repair kit, and fit the gaiters to the pin grooves. Insert the pins into the caliper bracket and seat the gaiters correctly in the bracket grooves.

Refitting

17 If previously removed, refit the caliper mounting bracket to the hub carrier, and tighten the new bolts to the specified torque.
18 Screw the caliper body fully onto the flexible hose union.
19 Ensure that the brake pads are correctly fitted in the caliper mounting bracket and refit the caliper (see Section 4).
20 Fit the lower guide pin bolt, then press the caliper into position and fit the upper guide pin bolt. Tighten both guide pin bolts to the specified torque.
21 Tighten the brake hose union nut to the specified torque, then remove the brake hose clamp or polythene (where fitted).
22 Bleed the hydraulic system as described in Section 2. Note that, providing the precautions described were taken to minimise brake fluid loss, it should only be necessary to bleed the relevant front brake.
23 Refit the roadwheel, then lower the vehicle to the ground and tighten the roadwheel bolts to the specified torque.

9 Rear brake caliper – removal, overhaul and refitting

Caution: Ensure the ignition is switched off before disconnecting any braking system hydraulic union and do not switch it back on until after the hydraulic system has been bled. Failure to do this could lead to air entering the regulator unit requiring the unit to be bled (see Section 2).
Note: *Before starting work, refer to the note at the beginning of Section 2 concerning the dangers of hydraulic fluid, and to the warning at the beginning of Section 5 concerning the dangers of asbestos dust.*

Removal

1 Chock the front wheels, slacken the relevant rear roadwheel bolts, then jack up the rear of the vehicle and support on axle stands (see *Jacking and vehicle support*). Remove the relevant rear wheel.
2 Prise off the clip and remove the pin securing the handbrake inner cable to the caliper lever, then remove the clip and pull the cable from the support bracket.
3 Minimise fluid loss by first removing the master cylinder reservoir cap, and then tightening it down onto a piece of polythene, to obtain an airtight seal. Alternatively, use a brake hose clamp, a G-clamp or a similar tool to clamp the flexible hose at the nearest convenient point to the brake caliper.
4 Wipe away all traces of dirt around the brake hose union on the caliper. Unscrew the union nut and disconnect the brake pipe from the caliper. Plug the pipe and caliper unions to minimise fluid loss and prevent dirt entry.
5 Slacken and remove the guide pin bolts. Remove the caliper from the vehicle.

Overhaul

6 At the time of writing, no parts were available to recondition the rear caliper assembly, with the excepting of the guide pin bolts, guide pins and guide pin gaiters. Check the condition of the guide pins and their gaiters; both pins should be undamaged and (when cleaned) a reasonably tight sliding fit in the caliper bracket. If there is any doubt about the condition of any component, renew it.

Refitting

7 Refit the caliper and tighten the guide pin bolts to the specified torque settings.
8 Reconnect the brake pipe to the caliper, and tighten the brake hose union nut to the specified torque. Remove the brake hose clamp or polythene (where fitted).
9 Refit the handbrake cable to the support bracket and secure it with the retaining clip.
10 Align the end of the handbrake inner cable with the lever on the caliper, then refit the pin and the retaining clip.
11 Bleed the hydraulic system as described in Section 2. Note that, providing the precautions described were taken to minimise brake fluid loss, it should only be necessary to bleed the relevant rear brake.
12 Refit the roadwheel, then lower the vehicle to the ground and tighten the roadwheel bolts to the specified torque.

10 Rear brake drum – removal, inspection and refitting

Removal

1 Chock the front wheels, slacken the relevant rear roadwheel bolts, then jack up the rear of the vehicle and support on axle stands (see *Jacking and vehicle support*). Remove the relevant rear wheel.
2 Ensure the handbrake is released, then pull the brake drum from place. If the shoes are sticking gently tap the drum with a soft-faced hammer, whilst pulling the drum at the same time. If necessary, use two 8 mm bolts to pull the drum from place **(see illustration)**.

Inspection

3 Brush the dirt and dust from the drum, taking care not to inhale it.
4 Examine the internal friction surface of the drum. If deeply scored, or so worn that the drum had become ridged to the width of the shoes, then both drums must be renewed.
5 Regrinding of the friction surface may be possible, provided the maximum diameter given in the Specifications is not exceeded, but note that both rear drums must be reground to an identical diameter.

Refitting

6 Refit the brake drum over the shoes. If necessary, back off the adjuster wheel on the strut until the drum will pass over the shoes **(see illustration)**.
7 Adjust the brakes by operating the footbrake a number of times. A clicking noise will be heard as the automatic adjuster operates. When the clicking stops, the adjustment is complete.
8 Refit the roadwheel, and lower the vehicle to the ground.

10.2 Use two 8 mm bolts to pull the drum from place

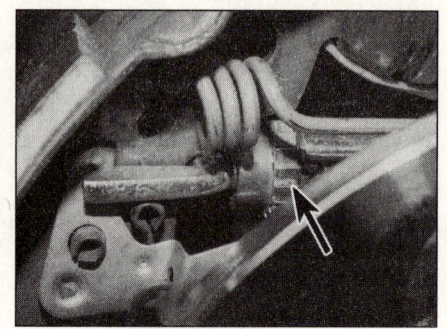

10.6 Rotate the adjuster wheel (arrowed) to shorten the adjuster strut and retract the brake shoes

Braking system 9•11

11 Rear brake shoes – renewal

Warning: *Renew both sets of brake shoes at the same time – never renew the shoes on only one wheel, as uneven braking may result. Note that the dust created by wear of the shoes may contain asbestos, which is a health hazard. Never blow it out with compressed air, and don't inhale any of it. An approved filtering mask should be worn when working on the brakes. DO NOT use petrol or petroleum-based solvents to clean brake parts; use brake cleaner or methylated spirit only.*

1 Remove the brake drum as described in Section 10.
2 Taking precautions to avoid inhalation of dust, remove the brake dust from the brake drum, shoes and backplate. We recommend the use of aerosol brake cleaners, available from most automotive part/accessory retailers.
3 Measure the thickness of the friction material at several points; if either shoe is worn at any point to the specified minimum thickness or less, all four shoes must be renewed as a set **(see illustration)**. The shoes should also be renewed if any are contaminated with oil or grease, since there is no satisfactory way of degreasing the friction material.
4 Note the location and orientation of all components before disassembly as an aid to reassembly.

Single headlight models

5 Follow the accompanying illustrations for the brake shoe renewal procedure **(see illustrations 11.5a to 11.5cc)**. Be sure to stay in order and read the caption under each illustration.

11.3 Measure the thickness of the brake shoe friction material

11.5a Before removing anything, place a drain tray under the brake assembly and clean the brakes with aerosol brake cleaner

11.5b Unhook the return spring from its hole in the front shoe . . .

11.5c . . . then pull the other end out of the hole in the rear shoe and remove the adjuster and spring

11.5d Using a hold-down spring tool (or pliers), remove the hold-down spring by pushing in and rotating in 1/4 turn . . .

11.5e . . . remove the outer cup, the spring and the inner cup . . .

11.5f and pull the pin through the backing plate

11.5g Remove the front shoe and unhook the anchor spring from the rear shoe

11.5h Remove the rear shoe hold-down spring, cups and pin

9•12 Braking system

11.5i Flip the rear shoe over, force the spring back from the handbrake lever as shown . . .

11.5j . . . and disengage the cable from the handbrake lever

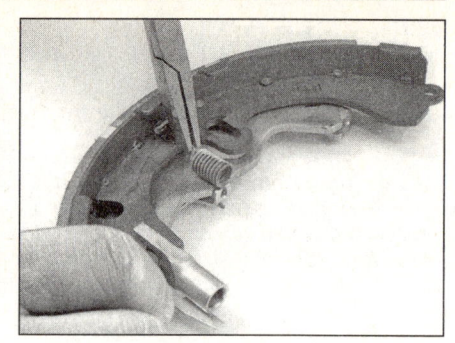

11.5k Unhook the adjusting lever spring from the rear shoe

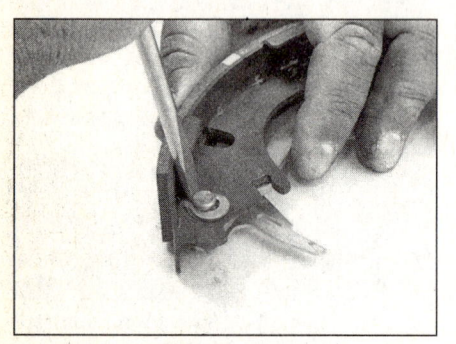

11.5l Lever off the C-washer (don't lose the shim underneath) . . .

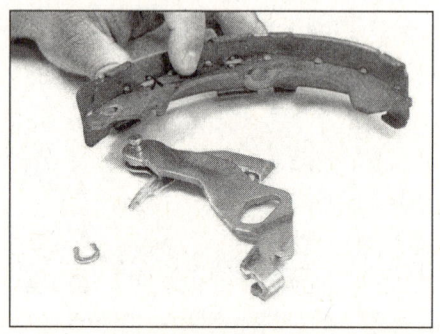

11.5m . . . and remove the handbrake lever and the adjusting lever from the old rear brake shoe

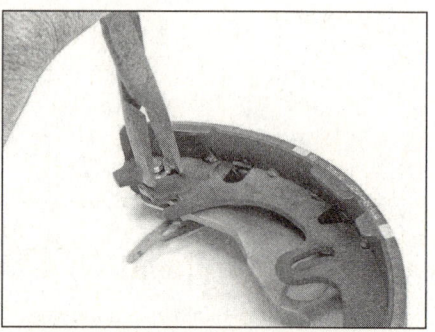

11.5n Attach the handbrake lever and adjusting lever to the new rear shoe and secure them with a new C-washer (don't forget the shim)

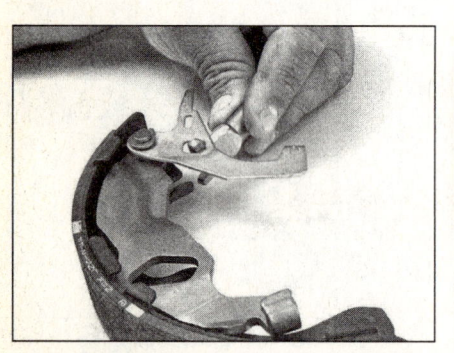

11.5o Engage the rear part of the adjuster with the shoe lever as shown . . .

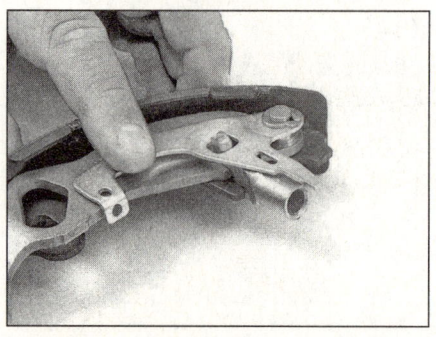

11.5p . . . rotate the shoe lever back against the rear shoe . . .

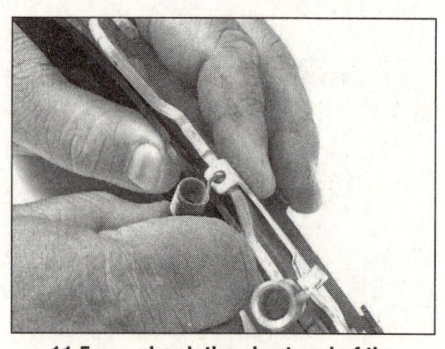

11.5q . . . hook the short end of the adjusting lever spring into the shoe lever . . .

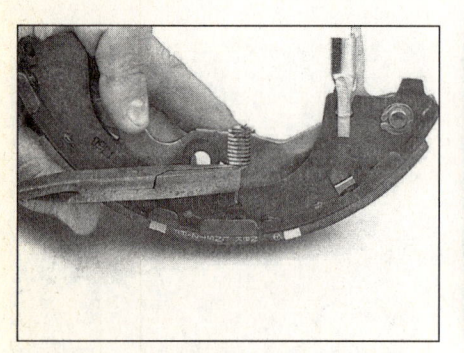

11.5r . . . and hook the long end of the spring into the hole in the rear shoe

11.5s Apply high-temperature grease to the friction points of the backing plate

11.5t Insert the pin for the rear shoe hold-down spring through the hole in the backplate

11.5u Attach the cable to the handbrake lever

11.5v Bring the rear shoe into position, insert the hold-down pin through the shoe, refit the inner cup on the pin . . .

11.5w . . . refit the hold-down spring and outer cup . . .

11.5x . . . compress the spring, give the outer cup a 1/4 turn and lock it down

11.5y Place the adjusting assembly in position and insert it into the rear part of the adjuster that you installed on the rear shoe

11.5z Attach the anchor spring to the rear shoe . . .

11.5aa . . . attach it to the front shoe . . .

11.5bb . . . place the front shoe in position and hook both ends of the return spring into their respective holes in the front and rear shoes

11.5cc Refit the front shoe hold-down pin, spring and inner and outer cups and lock the hold-down assembly into place

6 Using a screwdriver inserted through the adjusting hole in the backing plate **(see illustration)**, turn the adjuster star wheel until the brake shoes drag on the brake drum as the drum is rotated, then back off the start wheel until the shoes don't drag.

11.6 Rotate the adjuster star wheel using a screwdriver

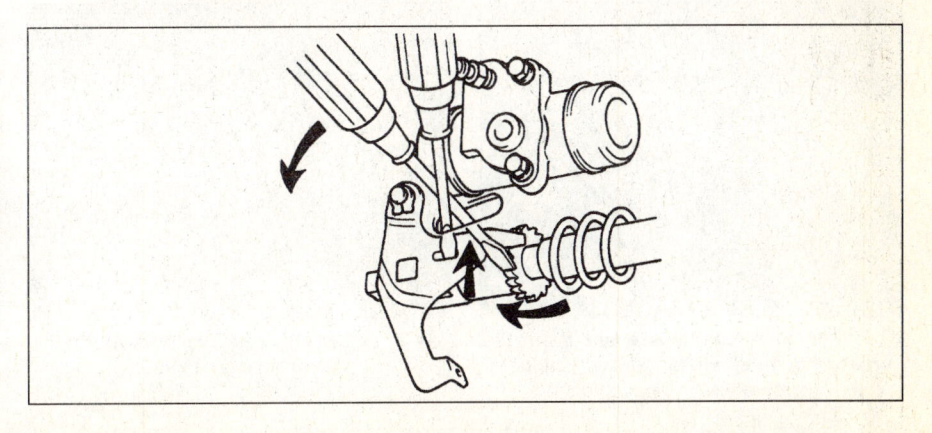

9•14 Braking system

Twin headlight models

7 Follow the accompanying illustrations for the brake shoe renewal procedure **(see illustrations 11.7a to 11.7o)**. Be sure to stay in order and read the caption under each illustration.

8 Install the shoe retaining pin, then position the clip. Compress the clip and slide it under the head of the pin, then slowly release it **(see illustration 11.7a)**.

9 Remove the elastic band or cable tie from the wheel cylinder. Make sure that both shoes are correctly positioned on the wheel cylinder pistons.

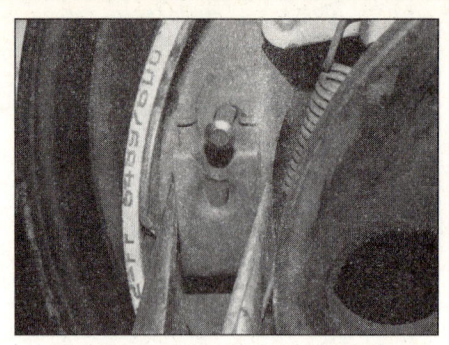

11.7a Depress the clip and slide it from the pin

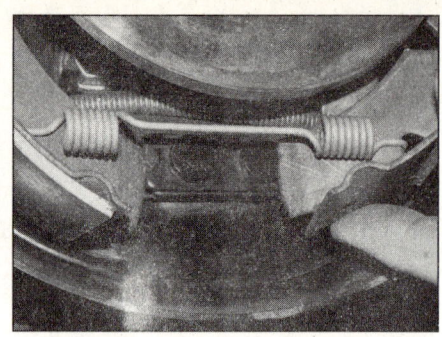

11.7b Pull the ends of the shoes from the lower anchor . . .

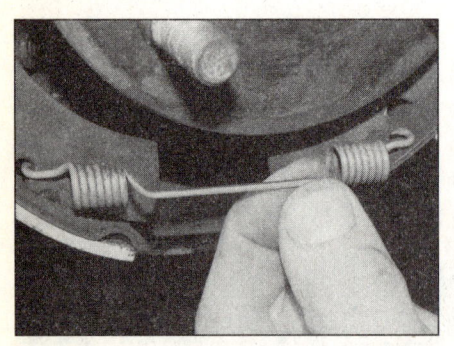

11.7c . . . and remove the lower return spring

11.7d Manoeuvre the shoe assembly over the hub

11.7e Turn the shoe over, force back the spring, and disengage the handbrake cable from the brake lever

11.7f Fit a strong elastic band around the wheel cylinder pistons to retain them

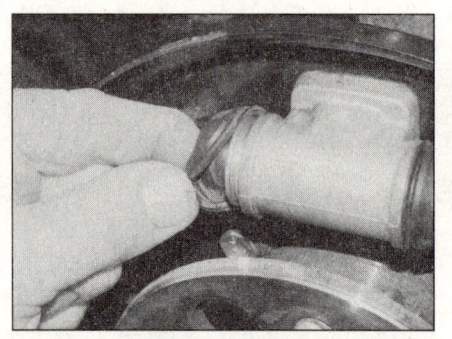

11.7g Peel back the wheel cylinder rubber boots to check for leaks

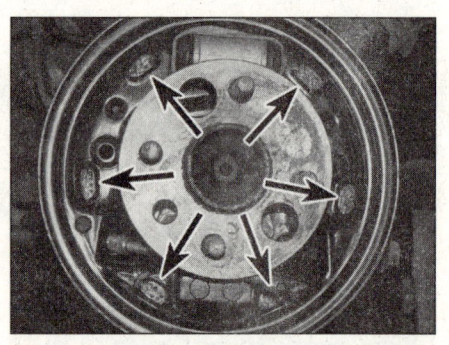

11.7h Apply anti-seize grease to the wheel cylinder piston faces and the backplate as shown (arrowed)

11.7i Position the rear shoe, and insert the brake shoe retaining pin through the hole (arrowed) in the backplate

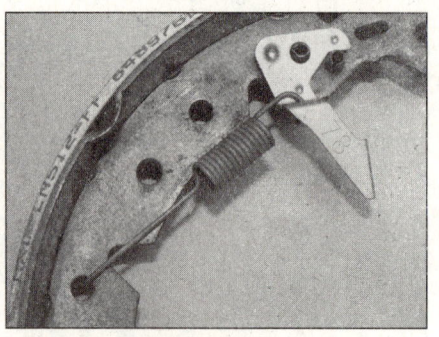

11.7j Fit the adjuster lever and spring to the front brake shoe

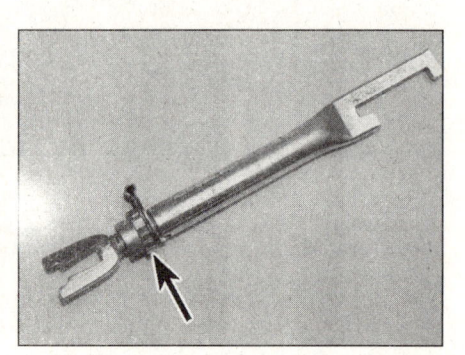

11.7k Rotate the adjuster wheel (arrowed) to set the strut at its shortest possible length

All models

10 Refit the brake drum as described in Section 10.
11 Repeat the operation on the remaining brake.
12 Once both sets of rear shoes have been renewed, with the handbrake fully released, adjust the lining-to-drum clearance by repeatedly depressing the brake pedal at least 20 to 25 times. Whilst depressing the pedal, have an assistant listen to the rear drums, to check that the adjuster strut is functioning correctly; if so, a clicking sound will be heard as the pedal is depressed.
13 Check, and if necessary, adjust the handbrake as described in Section 17.

Caution: New shoes will not give full braking efficiency until they have bedded-in. Be prepared for this, and avoid hard braking as far as possible for the first hundred miles or so after shoe renewal.

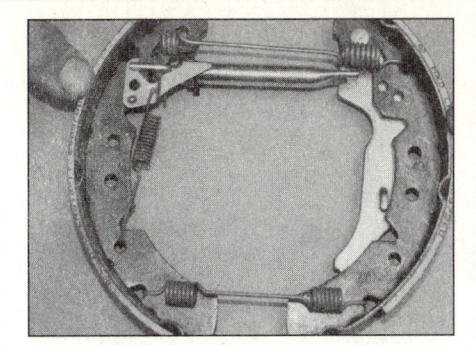

12 Rear wheel cylinder – removal, overhaul and refitting

Caution: Ensure the ignition is switched off before disconnecting any braking system hydraulic union and do not switch it back on until after the hydraulic system has been bled. Failure to do this could lead to air entering the regulator unit requiring the unit to be bled (see Section 2).

Removal

1 Remove the brake drum as described in Section 10.
2 Minimise fluid loss by first removing the master cylinder reservoir cap, and then tightening it down onto a piece of polythene to obtain an air tight seal. Alternatively, use a brake hose clamp, a G-clamp or similar tool to clamp the flexible hose at the nearest convenient point to the wheel cylinder **(see illustration 3.1)**.
3 Wipe away any traces of dirt around the brake pipe union nut at the rear of the wheel cylinder, and unscrew the nut. Carefully ease the pipe out of the cylinder, and plug or tape over its end to prevent dirt ingress **(see illustration)**. Wipe up any spilt fluid immediately.
4 Unscrew the retaining bolts from the rear of the backplate, and remove the wheel cylinder, taking care not to allow surplus hydraulic fluid to contaminate the brake shoe friction linings **(see illustration)**.

Overhaul

Note: Check the availability of a wheel cylinder overhaul kit prior to dismantling.
5 Brush the dirt and dust from the wheel cylinder. We recommend the use of aerosol brake cleaners, available from most automotive parts/accessory retailers.
6 Pull the rubber dust seals from the ends of the cylinder body **(see illustration)**.
7 The pistons will normally be ejected by the pressure of the coil spring, but if they are not, simply pull them from place. If they are stuck, apply low air pressure (eg. from a foot pump) to the hydraulic fluid union hole to eject the pistons from their bores, followed by the spring.
8 Inspect the surfaces of the pistons and their bores in the cylinder body for scoring, or evidence of metal-to-metal contact. If evident, renew the complete wheel cylinder.
9 If the pistons and bores are in good condition, discard the seals and obtain a repair/overhaul kit, which will contain all the necessary renewable items.
10 Lubricate the piston seals with clean brake fluid, then fit them to the pistons as shown **(see illustrations)**.

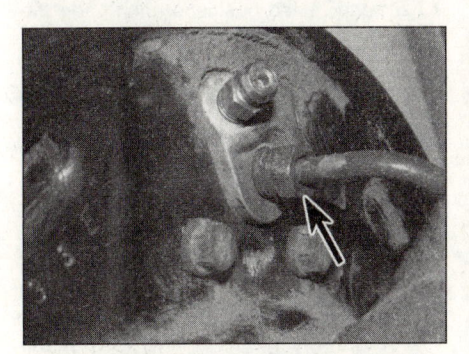

11.7l Brake shoe assembly

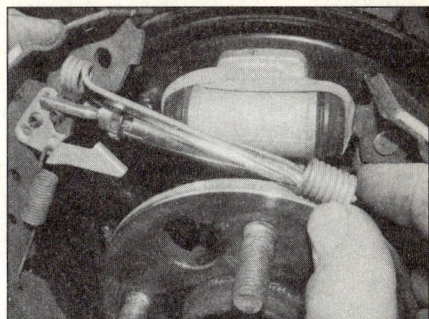

11.7m Fit the adjuster strut and spring to the front brake shoe . . .

11.7n . . . ensure the rear end of the strut locates in the slot on the handbrake lever

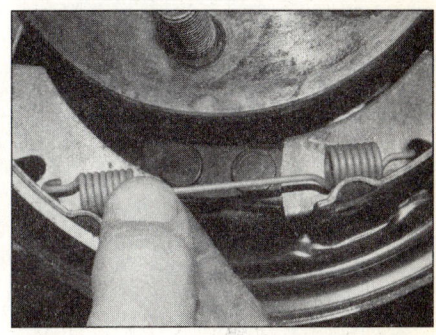

11.7o Hook the return springs into place, then use a large screwdriver to manoeuvre the front shoe over the end of the wheel cylinder and lower anchor

12.3 Unscrew the pipe union (arrowed) from the wheel cylinder

12.4 Undo the two bolts and remove the wheel cylinder

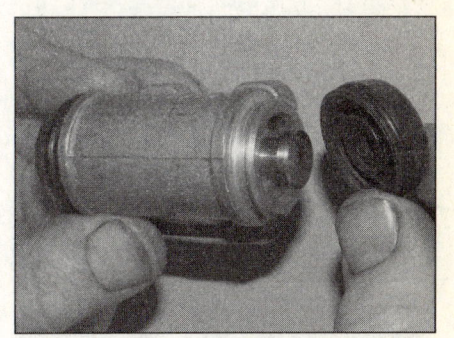

12.6 Pull the rubber dust seals from the cylinder

9•16 Braking system

12.10a Manoeuvre the seal . . .

12.10b . . . onto the piston

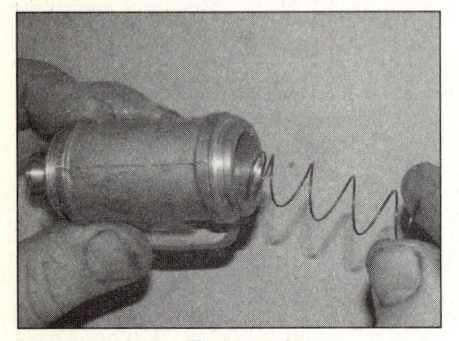

12.11a Fit the spring . . .

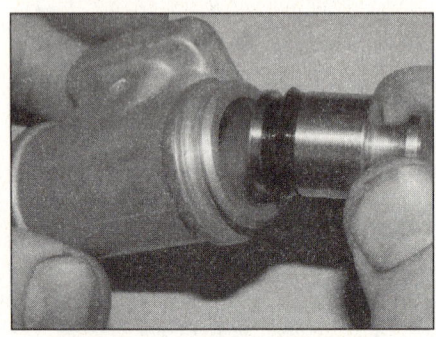

12.11b . . . followed by the piston

11 Smear a little clean brake fluid onto the cylinder bore, pistons and seals, then insert the spring, followed by the pistons, into the cylinder bore **(see illustrations)**. Ease the piston seals into the bore using a thumbnail, or blunt plastic tool.

12 Fit the rubber dust seals, and check the pistons can move freely in their bores.

Refitting

13 Ensure the backplate and wheel cylinder mating surfaces are clean, then spread the brake shoes and manoeuvre the wheel cylinder into position.

14 Insert the brake pipe, and screw in the union nut two or three turns to ensure that the thread has started.

15 Insert the wheel cylinder retaining bolts, and tighten them to the specified torque, then tighten the pipe union securely.

16 Ensure the wheel cylinder bleed screw is closed, then remove the clamp from the flexible brake pipe, or the polythene from the master cylinder.

17 Ensure the brake shoes are correctly located against the cylinder pistons.

18 Refit the brake drum as described in Section 10.

19 Bleed the brake hydraulic system as described in Section 2. Providing suitable precautions were taken to minimise fluid loss, it should only be necessary to bleed the relevant rear wheel.

13 Master cylinder – removal, overhaul and refitting

Caution: Ensure the ignition is switched off before disconnecting any braking system hydraulic union and do not switch it back on until after the hydraulic system has been bled. Failure to do this could lead to air entering the regulator unit requiring the unit to be bled (see Section 2).

Note: *Before starting work, refer to the warning at the beginning of Section 2 concerning the dangers of hydraulic fluid.*

Removal

1 Disconnect the fluid level sensor wiring plug **(see illustration)**.

2 Remove the master cylinder reservoir cap and filter, and syphon the hydraulic fluid from the reservoir. **Note:** *Do not syphon the fluid by mouth, as it is poisonous; use a syringe or an old antifreeze tester.* Alternatively, open any convenient bleed screw in the system, and gently pump the brake pedal to expel the fluid through a plastic tube connected to the screw until the reservoir is emptied (see Section 2).

3 Note their fitted positions, then undo the brake pipe unions from the master cylinder **(see illustration)**. Be prepared for fluid spillage. Plug or tape over the pipe ends and master cylinder orifices, to minimise the loss of brake fluid, and to prevent the entry of dirt into the system. Wash off any spilt fluid immediately with cold water.

4 Undo the nuts and pull the master cylinder from the brake servo unit **(see illustration)**. Recover the gasket fitted between the cylinder and brake servo.

5 Undo the screw, and pull the reservoir upwards from the master cylinder. Recover the two rubber grommets from the master cylinder ports **(see illustration)**. Note that on models produced after December 1999 with Toyota

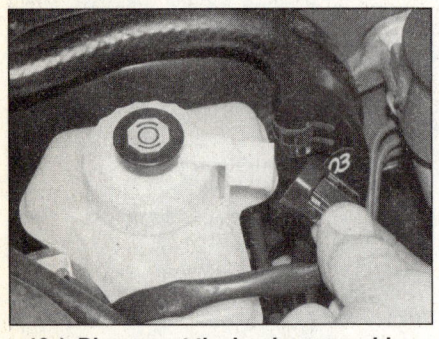

13.1 Disconnect the level sensor wiring plug

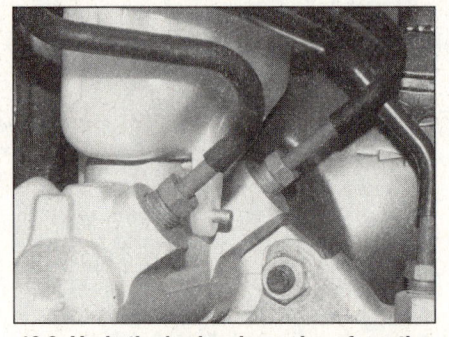

13.3 Undo the brake pipe unions from the master cylinder

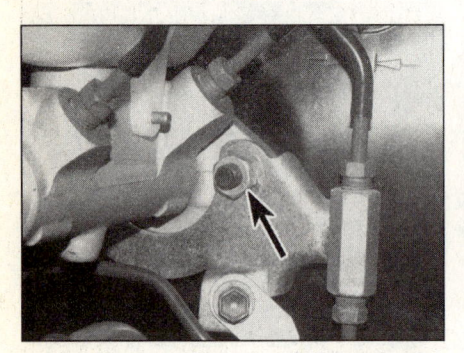

13.4 Master cylinder nut (left-hand nut arrowed)

13.5a Pull the grommets from the master cylinder; if they're hard, cracked or damaged, or have been leaking, renew them

Motor Co manufactured master cylinders, the reservoir is retained by fitting the reservoir bracket over a pin **(see illustration)**.

Overhaul

6 The master cylinder may be overhauled after obtaining the relevant repair kit from a Toyota dealer. Ensure that the correct repair kit is obtained for the master cylinder being worked on. Note the locations of all components to ensure correct refitting, and lubricate the new seals using clean brake fluid. Follow the assembly instructions supplied with the repair kit.

Refitting

7 Remove all traces of dirt from the master cylinder and servo unit mating surfaces and check the condition of the gasket – renew if necessary.
8 Fit the master cylinder to the servo unit. Refit the master cylinder mounting nuts, and tighten them to the specified torque.
9 Wipe clean the brake pipe unions and refit them to the master cylinder ports, tightening them to the specified torque.
10 Press the mounting seals fully into the master cylinder ports then carefully ease the fluid reservoir into position. Refit and tighten the retaining screw, or refit the retaining clip as applicable.
11 Reconnect the level sensor wiring plug.
12 Refill the master cylinder reservoir with new fluid. Bleed the complete hydraulic system as described in Section 2.

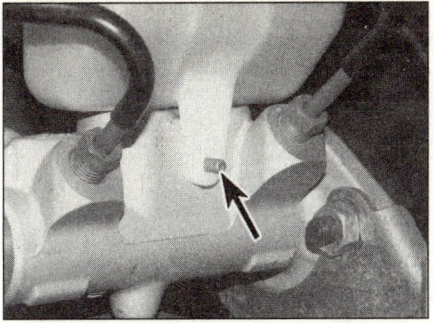

13.5b On post-99 models, the reservoir may be secured by fitting the bracket over a pin (arrowed)

14 Brake pedal – removal and refitting

Removal

1 Remove the driver's side lower facia panel as described in Chapter 11.
2 Release the return spring, slide off the retaining clip and withdraw the clevis pin securing the servo pushrod to the pedal **(see illustrations)**.
3 Slacken and remove the pivot bolt and nut **(see illustration)**, and remove the brake pedal from the vehicle. Slide the spacer and washer (where fitted) out from the pedal pivot. Examine all components for signs of wear or damage, renewing them as necessary.

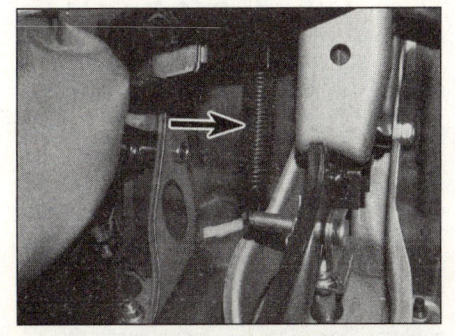

Refitting

4 Apply a smear of multi-purpose grease to the spacer and washer, and insert it into the pedal pivot bore.
5 Manoeuvre the pedal into position, making sure it is correctly engaged with the pushrod, and insert the pivot bolt. Refit the nut to the pivot bolt and tighten it securely.
6 Align the pedal with the pushrod and insert the clevis pin, securing it in position with the retaining clip.
7 Pull back the carpet and measure the distance from the centre of the pedal pad to the metal floor. Compare the measurement obtained and compare it with that given in the Specifications. Slacken the servo pushrod locknut and adjust the length of the pushrod if necessary **(see illustration)**.
8 Refit the lower panel to the facia.

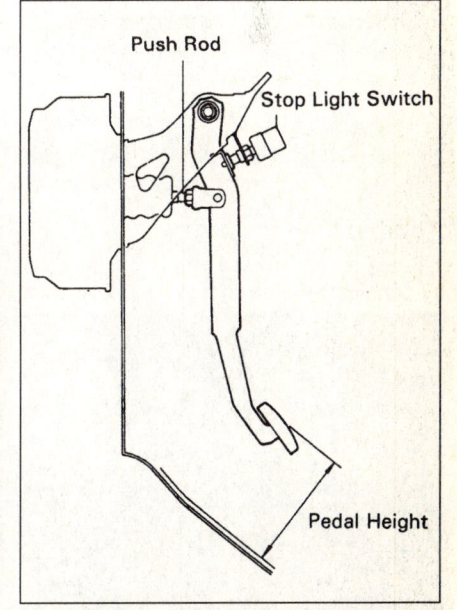

15 Vacuum servo unit – testing, removal and refitting

Testing

1 To test the operation of the servo unit, depress the footbrake several times to exhaust the vacuum, then start the engine whilst keeping the pedal firmly depressed. As the engine starts, there should be a noticeable 'give' in the brake pedal as the vacuum builds-up. Allow the engine to run for at least two minutes, then switch it off. If the brake pedal is now depressed it should feel normal, but further applications should result in the pedal feeling firmer, with the pedal stroke decreasing with each application.
2 If the servo does not operate as described, first inspect the servo unit check valve as described in Section 16.
3 If the servo unit still fails to operate satisfactorily, the fault lies within the unit itself. Repairs to the unit are not possible – if faulty, the servo unit must be renewed.

Removal

4 Remove the master cylinder as described in Section 13.
5 Slacken or release the retaining clip (depending on type of securing clip), then disconnect the vacuum pipe from the servo unit check valve.
6 Working in the passenger's footwell, prise up the centre pins, lever out the complete

14.2a Unhook the brake pedal return spring (arrowed) . . .

14.2b . . . then pull out the servo pushrod clevis pin (arrowed)

14.3 Undo the nut (arrowed) and withdraw the brake pedal pivot bolt (shown with the facia removed for clarity)

14.7 Brake pedal height is the distance between the pedal and the metal floor when the pedal is released

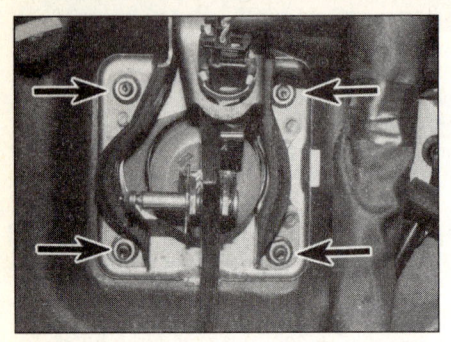

9•18 Braking system

15.10 Remove the four nuts (arrowed) securing the servo to the bulkhead

plastic expanding rivets, and remove the trim beneath the passenger's glovebox.

7 Disconnect the pedal return spring **(see illustration 14.2a)**.

8 Remove the clip and extract the servo pushrod clevis pin from the linkage **(see illustration 14.2b)**.

9 On RHD manual transmission models, remove the clutch master cylinder as described in Chapter 6.

10 Slacken and remove the four nuts securing the servo to the bulkhead **(see illustration)**.

11 Manoeuvre the servo unit out of position, along with its gasket which is fitted between the servo and bulkhead. Renew the gasket if it shows signs of damage.

Refitting

12 Refitting is the reverse of removal, noting the following points.
a) Lubricate all linkage pivot points with multi-purpose grease.
b) Tighten the servo unit and mounting bracket nuts and bolts to their specified torque settings.
c) Refit the master cylinder as described in Section 13 and bleed the complete hydraulic system as described in Section 2.

16 Vacuum servo unit check valve – removal, testing and refitting

Removal

1 Slacken or release the retaining clip (depending on type of securing clip), then disconnect the vacuum hose from the servo unit check valve.

2 Withdraw the valve from its rubber sealing grommet, using a pulling and twisting motion **(see illustration)**. Remove the grommet from the servo.

Testing

3 Examine the check valve for signs of damage, and renew if necessary. The valve may be tested by blowing through it in both directions. Air should flow through the valve in one direction only – when blown through from the servo unit end of the valve. Renew the valve if this is not the case.

4 Examine the rubber sealing grommet and flexible vacuum hose for signs of damage or deterioration, and renew as necessary.

Refitting

5 Fit the sealing grommet into position in the servo unit.

6 Carefully ease the check valve into position, taking great care not to displace or damage the grommet. Reconnect the vacuum hose to the valve and, where necessary, securely tighten its retaining clip.

7 On completion, start the engine and check for air leaks from the check valve-to-servo unit connection.

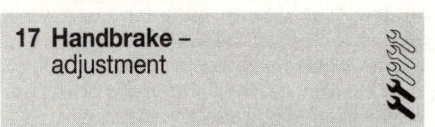

17 Handbrake – adjustment

1 To check the handbrake adjustment, applying normal moderate pressure, pull the handbrake lever to the fully-applied position, counting the number of clicks emitted from the handbrake ratchet mechanism. If adjustment is correct, the handbrake should be fully applied after 4 to 7 (rear drum brake models) or 5 to 8 (rear disc models) clicks have been emitted. If this is not the case, adjust as follows.

2 Remove the rear section of the centre console as described in Chapter 11.

3 Slacken the locknut, then rotate the adjusting nut until the correct setting is achieved. Tighten the locknut **(see illustration)**.

4 Refit the centre console.

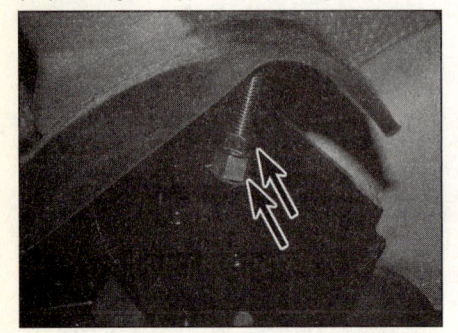

18 Handbrake lever – removal and refitting

Removal

1 Chock the front wheels then jack up the rear of the vehicle and support it on axle stands (see *Jacking and vehicle support*).

2 Referring to Section 17, release the handbrake lever and back off the adjuster nut to obtain maximum freeplay in the cable.

3 Remove the centre console as described in Chapter 11.

4 Disconnect the wiring connector from the handbrake warning light switch.

16.2 Servo check valve (arrowed)

5 Slacken and remove the locknut and adjuster nut, then detach the handbrake cable from the lever.

6 Slacken and remove the lever retaining nuts, and remove the lever from the vehicle **(see illustration)**.

Refitting

7 Refitting is a reversal of removal. Tighten the lever retaining nuts to the specified torque, and adjust the handbrake (see Section 17).

19 Handbrake cables – renewal

Equaliser-to-handbrake cable

1 Firmly chock the front wheels, slacken the relevant rear roadwheel bolts, then jack up the rear of the vehicle and support it on axle stands (see *Jacking and vehicle support*). Remove the rear wheel.

2 Ensure the handbrake is completely released then, on drum brake models, remove the relevant brake drum (see Section 10).

3 On drum brake models, remove the brake shoes and disconnect the cable from the lever on the shoe (see Section 11). Squeeze together the tangs of the retaining clip and pull the cable through the backing plate **(see illustration)**.

4 On rear disc brake models, disconnect the cable at the caliper end by removing the pin clip then pulling out the hole pin while pushing the handbrake crank. Remove the outer cable retaining clip and remove the cable.

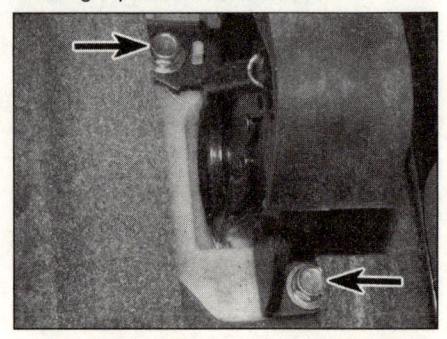

17.3 Slacken the locknut (top arrow) and rotate the adjusting nut (lower arrow)

18.6 Undo the two bolts (arrowed) and remove the handbrake lever

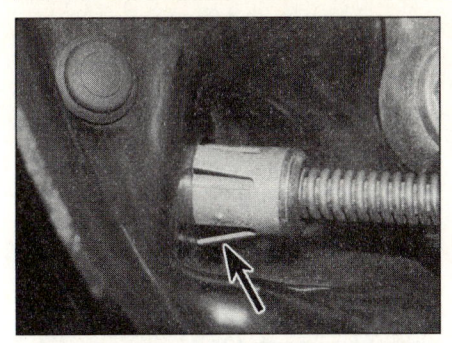

Braking system 9•19

19.3 Squeeze together the tangs of the retaining clip (arrowed) and pull the cable from the backplate

19.6 Remove the bolt (arrowed) and detach the cable bracket from the floor

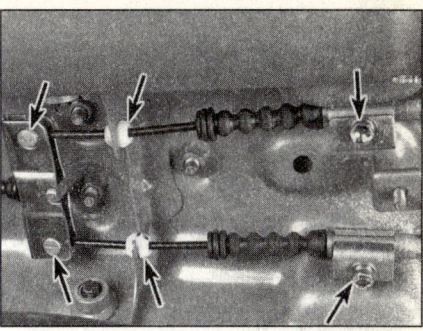

19.8 Remove the clamp retaining bolt (right arrows), lever the bushing out of the bracket (centre arrows) and disengage the cable from the equaliser (left arrows)

5 Unbolt the cable clamp near the forward end of the suspension rod.
6 Unbolt the cable clamp from the floorpan, just to the left of the centre tunnel **(see illustration)**.
7 Remove the exhaust pipe and catalytic converter heat shields (see Chapter 4A).
8 Unclamp the cable from the rear retaining bracket, pull the nylon bushing out of the front bracket and disconnect the cable from the equaliser **(see illustration)**.
9 Refitting is a reversal of the removal procedure, adjusting the handbrake as described in Section 17.

Equaliser-to-handbrake lever

10 Remove the centre console as described in Chapter 11.
11 Ensure the handbrake lever is fully released, then remove the locknut and adjusting nut (see Section 17), and detach the cable from the lever.
12 Firmly chock the front wheels, slacken the relevant rear roadwheel bolts, then jack up the rear of the vehicle and support it on axle stands (see *Jacking and vehicle support*). Remove the rear wheel.
13 Remove the exhaust pipe and catalytic converter heat shields (see Chapter 4A).
14 Rotate the cable end 90° and disconnect it from the equaliser **(see illustration 19.8)**.
15 Prise out the rubber grommet, and pull the cable through the hole.
16 Refitting is a reversal of removal. Apply a light coat of grease to the portion of the cable end the engages with the equaliser, and coat the sealing edge of the rubber grommet with silicone sealant to ensure that it remains watertight.
17 Adjust the handbrake as described in Section 17.

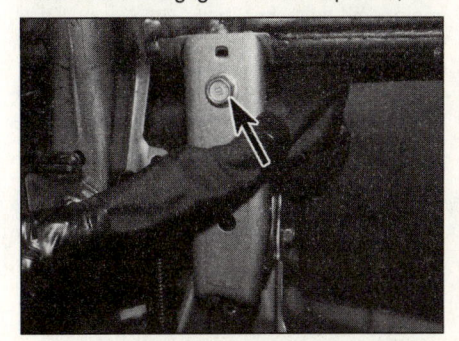

20 Stop-light switch – removal, refitting and adjustment

1 The stop-light switch is located on a bracket at the top of the brake pedal. The switch activates the brake lights at the rear of the vehicle when the brake pedal is depressed.

Removal

2 Remove the driver's side lower facia panel as described in Chapter 11.
3 Undo the bolt and remove metal plate under the switch **(see illustration)**.
4 Disconnect the wiring, then undo the locknut and unscrew the switch from the bracket **(see illustration)**.

Refitting and adjustment

5 Screw the switch into the pedal bracket and loosely refit the locknut.
6 Continue to screw in the switch until the plunger makes light contact with the pedal, then rotate the switch anti-clockwise one complete turn. Tighten the locknut.
7 Check the clearance between the switch and the pedal **(see illustration)**.
8 Reconnect the wiring connector, and check the operation of the stop-lights. Refit the metal plate and facia panel.

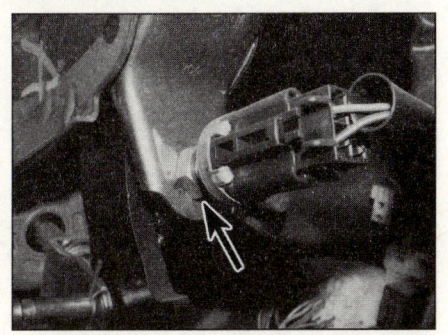

21 Load-sensing proportioning valve – removal and refitting

Note: Due to the specialised equipment required to check and accurately adjust the brake fluid pressure after refitting (or reconnecting) the valve, you are advised to entrust this task to a Toyota dealer or suitably-equipped specialist. The following procedure is given for circumstances where the task must be undertaken, but it is vitally important that the brake fluid pressure is checked and adjusted as necessary upon completion.

⚠ **Warning:** *If the fluid pressure is not checked and accurately adjusted, brake system performance may be severely impaired.*

Removal

1 Position the car over an inspection pit or raise it in such a manner is level with its weight on the wheels.
2 To minimise fluid loss, remove the master cylinder reservoir filler cap an place a piece of polythene over the filler neck. Secure the polythene with an elastic band ensuring that an airtight seal is obtained.
3 Undo the unions at the ends of the brake pipes where they enter the proportioning valve.
4 Pull the brake pipes from the valve, and plug the ends to prevent contamination.
5 Remove the locknut and adjusting nut, then

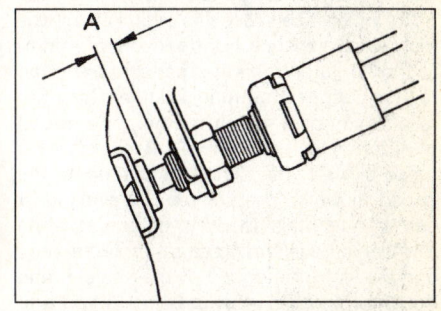

20.3 Undo the bolt (arrowed) and remove the plate to access the stop-light switch

20.4 Undo the locknut (arrowed) and unscrew the stop-light switch

20.7 Clearance A between the end of the light switch body and the pedal should be 0.5 to 2.4 mm

9•20 Braking system

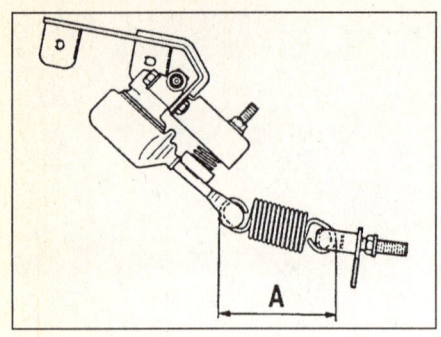

21.8 Set the load-sensing proportioning valve spring length A to an initial set-up dimension of 105 mm

remove the spring retaining bracket from the suspension member.
6 Remove the three bolts and remove the valve and mounting bracket assembly.

Refitting

7 Refit the valve and tighten the three bolts securely.
8 Refit the spring retaining bracket and temporarily tighten the locknut below the adjusting nut. Turn the adjusting nut and locknut to set the spring length to the initial set-up dimension of approximately 105 mm **(see illustration)**.
9 Reconnect the brake pipes and bleed the system (see Section 2).
10 Lower the vehicle to the ground and have the brake fluid pressure checked by a Toyota dealer.

22 Anti-lock Braking System (ABS) – general information

ABS is fitted to all models as standard, the system comprises a hydraulic regulator unit and the four roadwheel sensors. The regulator unit contains the electronic control unit (ECU), the hydraulic solenoid valves and the electrically-driven return pump. The purpose of the system is to prevent the wheel(s) locking during heavy braking. This is achieved by automatic release of the brake on the relevant wheel, followed by re-application of the brake.

The solenoid valves are controlled by the ECU, which itself receives signals from the four wheel sensors (front sensors are fitted to the hubs, and the rear sensors are fitted to the caliper mounting brackets or stub axle assembly), which monitor the speed of rotation of each wheel. By comparing these signals, the ECU can determine the speed at which the vehicle is travelling. It can then use this speed to determine when a wheel is decelerating at an abnormal rate, compared to the speed of the vehicle, and therefore predicts when a wheel is about to lock. During normal operation, the system functions in the same way as a non-ABS braking system.

If the ECU senses that a wheel is about to lock, it closes the relevant outlet solenoid valves in the hydraulic unit, which then isolates the relevant brake(s) on the wheel(s) which is/are about to lock from the master cylinder, effectively sealing-in the hydraulic pressure.

If the speed of rotation of the wheel continues to decrease at an abnormal rate, the ECU opens the inlet solenoid valves on the relevant brake(s), and operates the electrically-driven return pump which pumps the hydraulic fluid back into the master cylinder, releasing the brake. Once the speed of rotation of the wheel returns to an acceptable rate, the pump stops; the solenoid valves switch again, allowing the hydraulic master cylinder pressure to return to the brake.

The action of the solenoid valves and return pump creates pulses in the hydraulic circuit. When the ABS system is functioning, these pulses can be felt through the brake pedal.

The operation of the ABS system is entirely dependent on electrical signals. To prevent the system responding to any inaccurate signals, a built-in safety circuit monitors all signals received by the ECU. If an inaccurate signal or low battery voltage is detected, the ABS system is automatically shut-down, and the warning light on the instrument panel is illuminated, to inform the driver that the ABS system is not operational. Normal braking should still be available, however.

If a fault does develop in the any of these systems, the vehicle must be taken to a Toyota dealer or suitably-equipped specialist for fault diagnosis and repair.

23 Anti-lock Braking System (ABS) components – removal and refitting

Regulator assembly

Caution: Disconnect the battery (see Chapter 5A) before disconnecting the regulator hydraulic unions, and do not reconnect the battery until after the hydraulic system has been bled. Also ensure that the unit is stored upright (in the same position as it is fitted to the vehicle) and is not tipped onto its side or upside down.

23.6 Note the location of the pipes before disconnecting them from the regulator

Note: *Before starting work, refer to the warning at the beginning of Section 2 concerning the dangers of hydraulic fluid.*

Removal

1 Disconnect the battery (see Chapter 5A).
2 Slacken the right-hand front roadwheel bolts, jack up the front of the vehicle and support it securely on axle stands (see *Jacking and vehicle support*). Remove the roadwheel.
3 Undo the five screws/clips and remove the right-hand front wheel arch liner.
4 Remove the washer fluid reservoir as described in Chapter 12.
5 Disconnect the regulator wiring plug.
6 Mark the locations of the hydraulic fluid pipes to ensure correct refitting, then unscrew the union nuts, and disconnect the pipes from the regulator assembly **(see illustration)**. Be prepared for fluid spillage, and plug the open ends of the pipes and the regulator, to prevent dirt ingress and further fluid loss.
7 Slacken and remove the regulator mounting nuts and remove the assembly from the engine compartment. If necessary, the mounting bracket can then be unbolted and removed from the vehicle. Renew the regulator mountings if they show signs of wear or damage.

Refitting

8 Manoeuvre the regulator into position and locate it in the mounting bracket. Refit the mounting nuts and tighten them securely.
9 Reconnect the hydraulic pipes to the correct unions on the regulator and tighten the union nuts to the specified torque.
10 Reconnect the wiring connector to the regulator and connect the earth lead (where fitted), tightening its retaining nut securely.
11 Bleed the complete hydraulic system as described in Section 2. Once the system is correctly bled, refit the wheels arch liner, roadwheel and reconnect the battery.

Electronic control unit (ECU)

12 The ECU is integral with the regulator assembly, and is not available separately.

Wheel speed sensors

Removal

13 Ensure the ignition is turned off.
14 Apply the handbrake, slacken the appropriate roadwheel bolts, then jack up the front/rear (as applicable) of the vehicle and support securely on axle stands (see *Jacking and vehicle support*). Remove the relevant roadwheel.
15 Trace the wiring back from the sensor, releasing it from all the relevant clips and ties whilst noting its correct routing, and disconnect the wiring connector.
16 Slacken and remove the retaining bolt and withdraw the sensor from the hub carrier, caliper bracket or stub axle assembly, as appropriate **(see illustration)**.

Refitting

17 Ensure that the mating faces of the sensor

and the swivel hub are clean, and apply a little anti-seize grease to the hub carrier bore before refitting.
18 Make sure the sensor tip is clean and ease it into position in the hub carrier.
19 Refit the retaining bolt and tighten it to the specified torque.

20 Work along the sensor wiring, making sure it is correctly routed, and securing it in position with all the relevant clips and ties. Reconnect the wiring connector.
21 Refit the roadwheel, then lower the vehicle and tighten the wheel bolts to the specified torque.

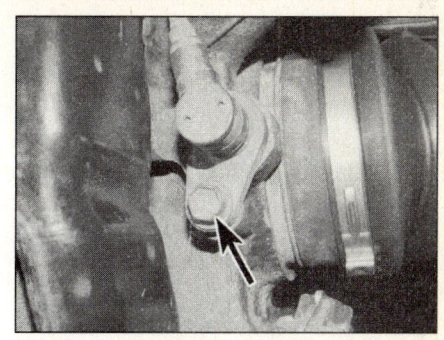

23.16 Undo the bolt (arrowed) and pull the sensor from the hub carrier

Notes

Chapter 10
Suspension and steering systems

Contents

	Section number		Section number
Anti-roll bar and bushings (front) – removal and installation	4	Steering rack gaiters – renewal	18
Anti-roll bar and bushings (rear) – removal and installation	9	Steering system – general information	15
Balljoints – renewal	6	Steering wheel – removal and refitting	16
Control arm – removal, inspection and installation	5	Strut rod – removal and refitting	11
General information	1	Strut/spring assembly – renewal	3
Hub and bearing assembly (front) – removal and refitting	8	Suspension arms – removal and refitting	12
Hub and bearing assembly (rear) – removal and refitting	13	Suspension strut assembly (front) – removal, inspection and refitting	2
Hub carrier and hub (front) – removal and refitting	7		
Power steering fluid level check	See Weekly checks	Suspension strut assembly (rear) – removal, inspection and refitting	10
Power steering pump – removal and refitting	20		
Power steering system – bleeding	21	Track rod ends – removal and refitting	17
Rear hub carrier – removal and refitting	14	Tyre pressures	See Weekly checks
Steering and suspension check	See Chapter 1	Wheel alignment – general information	23
Steering rack – removal and refitting	19	Wheels and tyres – general information	22

Degrees of difficulty

| Easy, suitable for novice with little experience | Fairly easy, suitable for beginner with some experience | Fairly difficult, suitable for competent DIY mechanic | Difficult, suitable for experienced DIY mechanic | Very difficult, suitable for expert DIY or professional |

Specifications

General
Engine codes:
1.3 litre (1332 cc) non-VVT-i engine	4E-FE
1.4 litre (1398 cc) VVT-i engine	4ZZ-FE
1.6 litre (1587 cc) non-VVT-i engine	4A-FE
1.6 litre (1598 cc) VVT-i engine	3ZZ-FE

Front wheel alignment
Toe setting	0°06' ± 12' toe-in
Camber	-0°13' ± 45'
Caster	1°24' ± 45'

Rear wheel alignment
| Toe setting | 0°24' ± 12' toe-in |
| Camber | -1°00' ± 45' |

10•2 Suspension and steering systems

Torque wrench settings	Nm	lbf ft
Front suspension		
Balljoints:		
Balljoint-to-control arm bolt/nuts	142	105
Balljoint-to-hub carrier nut	124	92
Control arm:		
Front pivot bolt	215	159
Rear pivot bolt	175	129
Rear pivot mounting bracket bolts	147	108
Front anti-roll bar:		
Clamp:		
Kinked type anti-roll bar:		
Rear bolt	225	166
Front bolt	147	108
Straight type anti-roll bar:		
Rear bolt	50	37
Front bolt	147	108
Front suspension struts:		
Strut-to-hub carrier bolts/nuts	274	202
Strut upper mounting nuts	39	29
Strut piston rod nut	47	35
Roadwheel nuts	103	76
Rear suspension		
No 1 (front) suspension arm nuts/bolts	125	92
No 2 (rear) suspension arm nuts/bolts	125	92
Rear hub and bearing assembly-to-hub carrier	80	59
Rear anti-roll bar:		
Link nuts	44	32
Clamp bolts	19	14
Rear suspension struts:		
Strut-to-hub carrier nuts/bolts	150	111
Strut upper mounting nuts	39	29
Strut piston rod nut	49	36
Roadwheel nuts	103	76
Strut rod nuts/bolts	91	67
Steering		
Steering column mounting bolts/nuts	26	19
Steering rack bracket bolts/nuts	71	52
Steering wheel nut	34	25
Track rod ends		
Track rod end-to-hub carrier nut	49	36
Track rod end locknut	56	41
Universal joint-to-pinion shaft pinch-bolt	35	26
Power steering pressure line banjo bolts	54	40
Power steering pump mounting bolts	39	29

1 General information

The front suspension **(see illustration)** is a MacPherson strut design. The upper end of each strut/coil spring assembly is attached to the vehicle's body. The lower end of the strut assembly is connected to the upper end of the hub carrier. The hub carrier is attached to a balljoint mounted on the outer end of the suspension control arm. An anti-roll bar reduces body roll.

The rear suspension **(see illustration)** also utilises strut/coil spring assemblies. The upper end of each strut is attached to the vehicle body. The lower end of each strut is attached to a hub carrier. The carrier is located by a pair of suspension arms on each side, and a longitudinally mounted strut rod between the body and each carrier.

The rack-and-pinion steering rack is located behind the engine/transmission assembly on the bulkhead and actuates the track rods, which are attached to the hub carriers. The inner ends of the track rods are protected by rubber gaiters which should be inspected periodically for secure attachment, tears and leaking lubricant.

The steering power assist system consists of a belt-driven pump and associated lines and hoses. The fluid level in the power steering pump reservoir should be checked periodically (see *Weekly checks*).

The steering wheel operates the steering column, which actuates the steering rack through universal joints. Looseness in the steering can be caused by wear in the steering shaft universal joints, the steering rack, the track rod ends and loose retaining bolts.

Precautions

Frequently, when working on the suspension or steering system components, you may come across fasteners which seem impossible to loosen. These fasteners on the underside of the vehicle are continually subjected to water, road grime, mud, etc, and can become rusted or 'frozen', making them extremely difficult to remove. In order to unscrew these stubborn fasteners without damaging them (or other components), be sure to use lots of penetrating fluid and allow it to soak in for a while. Using a wire brush to clean exposed threads will also ease removal of the nut or bolt and prevent damage to the threads.

Suspension and steering systems 10•3

1.1 Front suspension components

1. Front anti-roll bar (VVT-i models have a straight bar)
2. Anti-roll bar bush clamp
3. Control arm
4. Balljoint
5. Strut/coil spring assembly (McPherson strut)
6. Right-hand driveshaft
7. Left-hand driveshaft
8. Steering rack
9. Support brace
10. Suspension crossmember

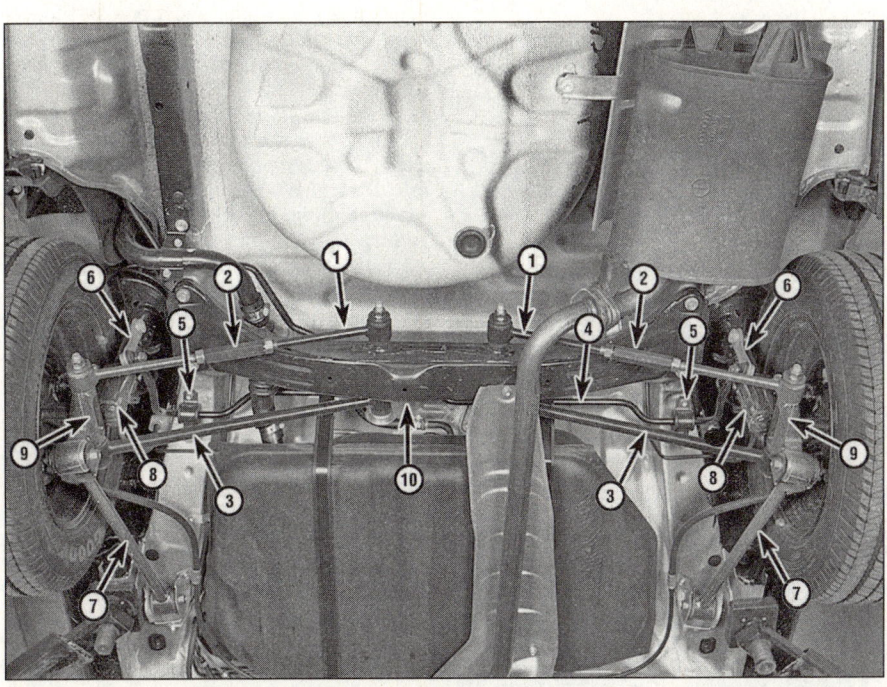

1.2 Rear suspension components

1. No 2 lower suspension arm. Note that some models are fitted with a brace between the inboard ends of the arms
2. No 2 arm toe adjuster
3. No 1 lower suspension arm
4. Rear anti-roll bar
5. Anti-roll bar bush clamp
6. Anti-roll bar link
7. Strut rod
8. Strut/coil spring assembly (McPherson strut)
9. Hub carrier
10. Rear suspension crossmember

Sometimes a sharp blow with a hammer and punch will break the bond between a nut and bolt threads, but care must be taken to prevent the punch from slipping off the fastener and ruining the threads. Heating the stuck fastener and surrounding area with a torch sometimes helps too, but isn't recommended because of the obvious dangers associated with fire. Sometimes tightening the nut or bolt first will help to break it loose. Fasteners that require drastic measures to remove should always be renewed.

Since most of the procedures dealt with in this Chapter involve jacking up the vehicle and working underneath it, a good pair of axle stands will be needed. A hydraulic trolley jack is the preferred type of jack to lift the vehicle, and it can also be used to support certain components during various operations.

⚠ **Warning:** *Never, under any circumstances, rely on a jack to support the vehicle while working on it. Whenever any of the suspension or steering fasteners are loosened or removed they must be inspected and, if necessary, renewed with ones of the same part number or of original equipment quality and design. Torque specifications must be followed for proper reassembly and component retention. Never attempt to heat or straighten any suspension or steering components. Instead, renew any bent or damaged part.*

2 Suspension strut assembly (front) – removal, inspection and refitting

Removal

1 Loosen the wheel nuts, raise the vehicle and support it securely on axle stands (see *Jacking and vehicle support*). Remove the wheel.

2 Unbolt the brake hose bracket from the strut. Release the clip and detach the speed sensor wiring harness from the strut **(see illustrations)**.

3 Remove the strut-to-hub carrier nuts **(see illustration)** and knock the bolts out with a hammer and punch.

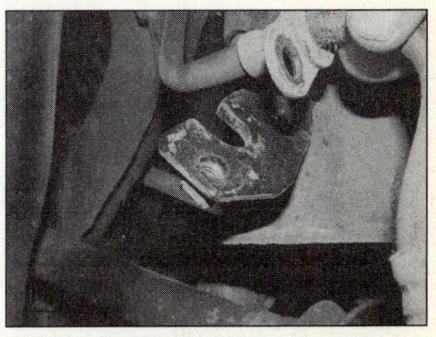

2.2a Unbolt the brake hose bracket from the strut . . .

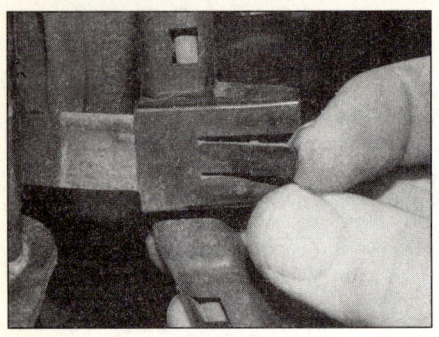

10•4 Suspension and steering systems

2.2b . . . and unclip the ABS sensor wiring harness

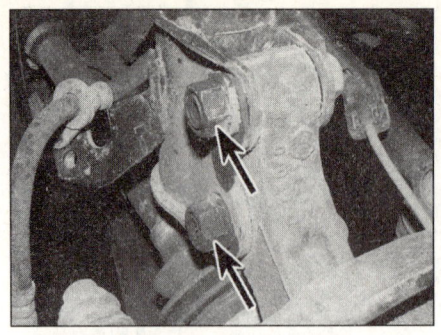

2.3 Undo the nuts (arrowed) and remove the strut-to-hub carrier bolts

2.5 Undo the three strut-to-body nuts

4 Separate the strut from the hub carrier. Be careful not to overextend the inner CV joint. Also, don't let the hub carrier fall outward and strain the brake hose.

5 Support the strut and spring assembly with one hand and remove the three strut-to-body nuts **(see illustration)**. Remove the assembly out from the wheel arch.

Inspection

6 Check the strut body for leaking fluid, dents, cracks and other obvious damage which would warrant repair or renewal.

7 Check the coil spring for chips or cracks in the spring coating (this will cause premature spring failure due to corrosion). Inspect the spring seat for cuts, hardness and general deterioration.

8 If any undesirable conditions exist, proceed to the strut disassembly procedure (see Section 3).

Refitting

9 Guide the strut assembly up into the wheel arch and insert the upper mounting studs through the holes in the body. Once the studs protrude, install the nuts so the strut won't fall back through. This is most easily accomplished with the help of an assistant, as the strut is quite heavy and awkward.

10 Slide the hub carrier into the strut flange and insert the two bolts from the rear. Install the nuts and tighten them to the torque listed in this Chapter's Specifications.

11 Connect the brake hose bracket to the strut and tighten the bolt securely. Install the speed sensor wiring harness bracket.

12 Install the wheel and nuts, then lower the vehicle and tighten the nuts to the torque listed in the Specifications.

13 Tighten the upper mounting nuts to the torque listed in this Chapter's Specifications.

3.3 Compress the spring until all pressure is relieved from the upper spring seat

3.4 Slacken the piston rod nut

3.5a Lift off the upper mounting/bearing . . .

3.5b . . . and the foam washer

14 We recommend that the front wheel alignment be checked after fitting the suspension struts (see Section 23).

3 Strut/spring assembly – renewal

1 If the struts or coil springs exhibit the telltale signs of wear (leaking fluid, loss of damping capability, chipped, sagging or cracked coil springs) explore all options before beginning any work. The strut/shock absorber assemblies are not serviceable and must be renewed if a problem develops. However, strut assemblies complete with springs may be available on an exchange basis, which eliminates much time and work. Whichever route you choose to take, check on the cost and availability of parts before disassembling your vehicle.

⚠ **Warning:** *Disassembling a strut is potentially dangerous and utmost attention must be directed to the job, or serious injury may result. Use only a high-quality spring compressor and carefully follow the manufacturer's instructions furnished with the tool. After removing the coil spring from the strut assembly, set it aside in a safe, isolated area.*

Disassembly

2 Remove the strut assembly following the procedure described in the relevant Section. Mount the strut assembly in a vice. Line the vice jaws with wood or rags to prevent damage to the unit and don't tighten the vice excessively.

3 Following the tool manufacturer's instructions, install the spring compressor (which can be obtained at most automotive parts/accessory retailers or tool hire shops) on the spring and compress it sufficiently to relieve all pressure from the upper spring seat **(see illustration)**. This can be verified by wiggling the spring.

Front strut

4 Loosen the piston rod nut with a socket **(see illustration)**.

5 Lift off the upper mounting, bearing and foam washer **(see illustrations)**. Inspect

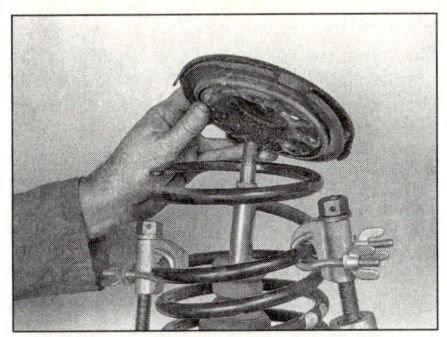

Suspension and steering systems 10•5

3.6 Remove the upper spring seat

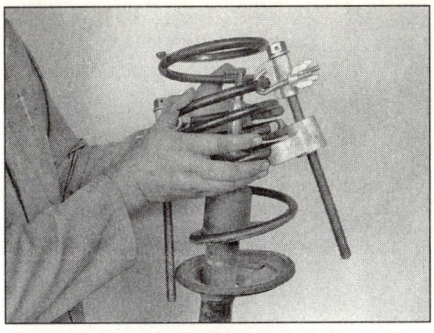

3.7 Lift the compressed spring from the strut

3.8 Slide the bump stop from the piston rod

3.10 Undo the rear strut piston rod nut and recover the spacer

3.11 Lift off the upper spring seat, complete with gaiter

3.13 Slide the bump stop from the piston rod

the bearing in the mounting for smooth operation. If it doesn't turn smoothly, renew the mounting.

6 Remove the upper spring seat **(see illustration)**. Check the rubber portion of the suspension seat for cracking and general deterioration. If there is any separation of the rubber, renew it.

7 Carefully lift the compressed spring from the assembly **(see illustration)** and set it in a safe place.

8 Slide the bump stop off the piston rod **(see illustration)**.

9 Check the lower rubber insulator/seat for wear, cracking and hardness and renew it if necessary.

Rear strut

10 Remove the piston rod nut with a socket. Recover the spacer **(see illustration)**.

11 Remove upper spring seat, complete with gaiter **(see illustration)**. Check the rubber portion of the suspension seat for cracking and general deterioration. If there is any separation of the rubber, renew it.

12 Carefully lift the compressed spring from the assembly and set it in a safe place.

13 Slide the bump stop off the piston rod **(see illustration)**.

14 Check the lower insulator for wear, cracking and hardness and renew it if necessary **(see illustration)**.

Reassembly

15 If the lower insulator is being renewed, set it into position with the dropped portion seated in the lowest part of the seat. Extend the piston rod to its full length and install the rubber bump stop **(see illustration)**.

16 Carefully place the coil spring onto the lower insulator, with the end of the spring resting in the lowest part of the insulator **(see illustration)**.

3.14 Check the rubber insulator for deterioration

3.16 The end of the spring must rest in the lowest part of the insulator (arrowed)

Front strut

17 Fit the rubber element of the spring seat to the top of the spring, aligning the end of the spring coil with the step in the rubber **(see illustration)**.

3.15 The dropped portion of the insulator must fit in the lowest part of the seat (arrowed)

3.17 The step in the rubber (arrowed) must align with the end of the spring

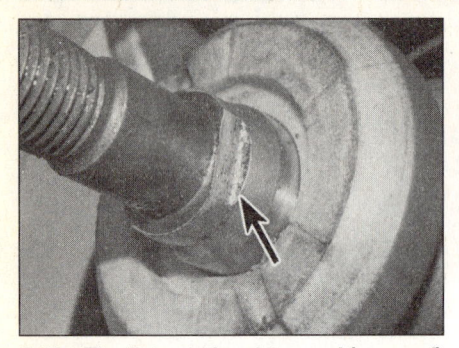

10•6 Suspension and steering systems

3.18a The flats on the piston rod (arrowed) must align with the flats on the spring seat underside

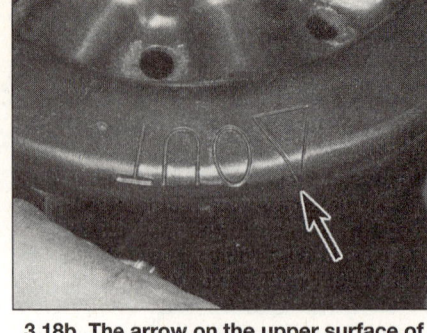

3.18b The arrow on the upper surface of the upper spring seat must point towards the outside of the vehicle (arrowed)

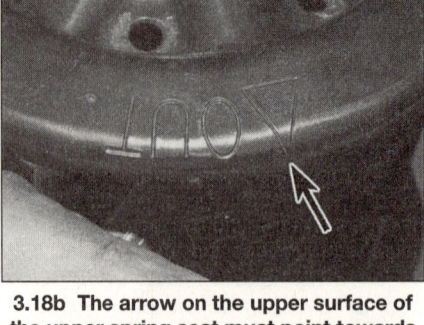

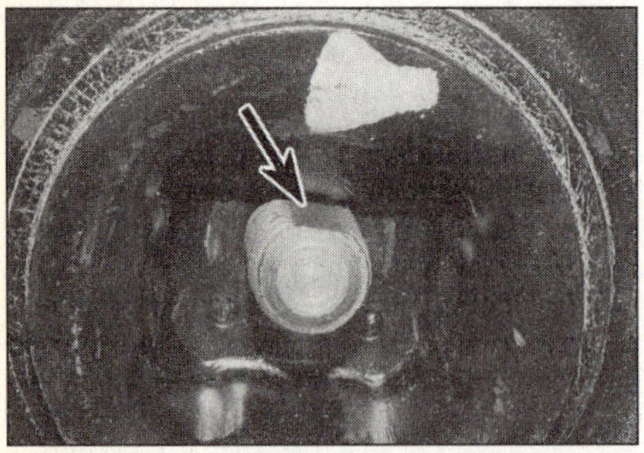

3.21 Ensure the flat on the piston rod aligns with the flat on the upper spring seat (arrowed)

3.22 Refit the spacer

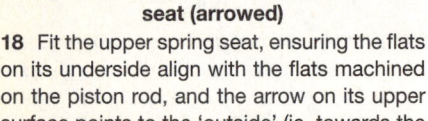

18 Fit the upper spring seat, ensuring the flats on its underside align with the flats machined on the piston rod, and the arrow on its upper surface points to the 'outside' (ie, towards the hub side of the strut) **(see illustrations)**.

19 Fit the foam washer and upper mounting, then tighten the piston rod nut to the specified torque.

20 Install the strut assembly following the procedure as described in the relevant Section.

4.2 Use an Allen key to hold the anti-roll bar link shank whilst slackening the nut

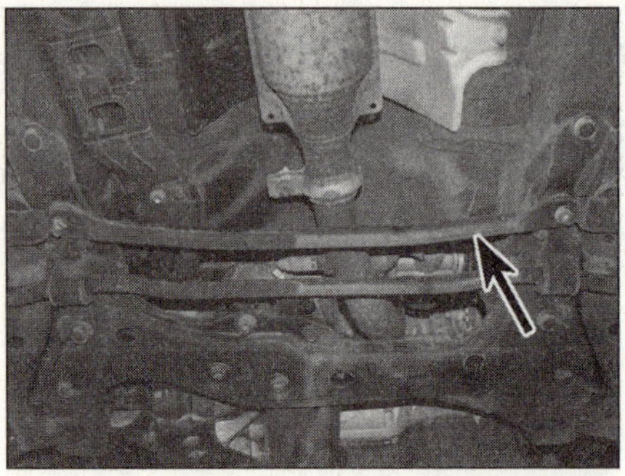

4.3 Remove the brace (arrowed) between the anti-roll bar bushing clamps

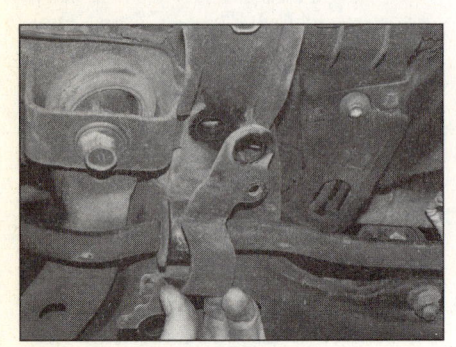

4.4 Unbolt the anti-roll bar bush clamps

4.6a Pull the rubber bushes from the anti-roll bar and inspect them

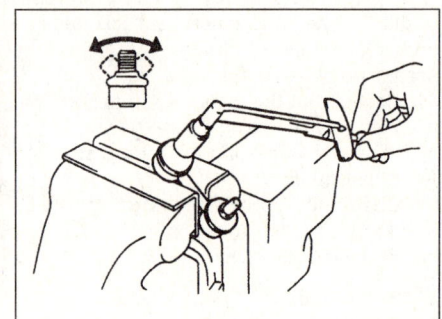

Rear strut

21 Install the upper spring seat and gaiter, making sure that the flat in the hole in the seat matches up with the flat on the piston rod **(see illustration)**.

22 Install the spacer and nut and tighten it securely **(see illustration)**.

23 Install the strut assembly following the procedure as described in the relevant Section.

4 Anti-roll bar and bushings (front) – removal and refitting

Removal

1 Loosen the front wheel nuts. Raise the front of the vehicle and support it securely on axle stands (see *Jacking and vehicle support*). Apply the handbrake and block the rear wheels to keep the vehicle from rolling off the stands. Remove the front wheels.

2 Remove the anti-roll bar link **(see illustration)**. If the balljoint shank turns with the nut, use an Allen key to hold the shank.

3 Undo the nuts and remove the brace between the left- and right-hand anti-roll bar bushing clamps **(see illustration)**.

4 Unbolt the anti-roll bar bushing clamps **(see illustration)**.

5 Two different types of anti-roll bar may be fitted. A 'kinked' type which fits over the exhaust pipe, and a 'straight' type which runs under the exhaust pipe. On 'kinked' type anti-roll bars, unbolt the front exhaust pipe from the flange in front of the catalytic converter (see Chapter 4A) and pull it down far enough to remove the anti-roll bar.

6 While the anti-roll bar is off the vehicle, slide off the rubber bushings and inspect them **(see illustration)**. If they're cracked, worn or deteriorated, renew them. It's also a good idea to inspect the anti-roll bar link. To check it, flip the balljoint shank side to side five or six times **(see illustration)**, then install the nut. Using a torque wrench, turn the nut continuously one turn every two to four seconds and note the torque reading on the fifth turn. It should be about 0.05 to 1.0 Nm. If it isn't, renew the link assembly.

4.6b Check the balljoint in the anti-roll bar link as described in the text

Suspension and steering systems 10•7

7 Clean the bushing area of the anti-roll bar with a stiff wire brush to remove any rust or dirt.

Installation

8 Lubricate the inside and outside of the new bushing with vegetable oil (as used in cooking) to simplify reassembly.
Caution: Don't use petroleum or mineral-based lubricants or brake fluid – they will lead to deterioration of the bushings.
9 Refitting is the reverse of removal.

5 Control arm – removal, inspection and refitting

Removal

1 Loosen the wheel nuts on the side to be dismantled, raise the front of the vehicle, support it securely on axle stands (see *Jacking and vehicle support*) and remove the wheel.
2 Disconnect the anti-roll bar link from the control arm as described in Section 4.
3 Remove the bolt and two nuts holding the control arm to the balljoint. Use a lever to disconnect the control arm from the balljoint **(see illustrations)**.
4 Remove the control arm front pivot bolt **(see illustration)**.
5 Remove the rear pivot bolt **(see illustration)**.
6 Remove the control arm.

Inspection

7 Check the control arm for distortion and the bushings for wear, renewing parts as necessary. Do not attempt to straighten a bent control arm.

Refitting

8 Refitting is the reverse of removal. Tighten all of the fasteners to the torque values listed in this Chapter's Specifications. **Note:** *Before tightening the pivot bolts, raise the outer end of the control arm with a floor jack to simulate normal ride height, or only tighten the bolts once the vehicle is lowered to the ground.*
9 Refit the wheel and nuts, lower the vehicle and tighten the nuts to the torque listed in the Specifications.
10 It's a good idea to have the front wheel alignment checked, and if necessary, adjusted after this job has been performed.

6 Balljoints – renewal

1 Loosen the wheel nuts, raise the vehicle and support it securely on axle stands (see *Jacking and vehicle support*). Remove the wheel.
2 Remove the split pin (if equipped) from the balljoint shank and loosen the nut (but don't remove it yet).
3 Separate the balljoint from the hub carrier

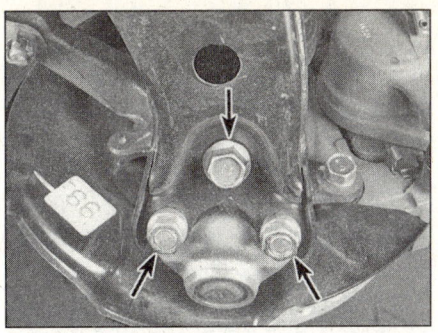

5.3a Undo the bolt and two nuts (arrowed) . . .

5.3b . . . then lever the balljoint from the control arm

5.4 Remove the control arm front pivot bolt (arrowed)

5.5 Undo the control arm rear pivot bolt (arrowed)

with a balljoint separator **(see illustration)**. Lubricate the rubber boot with grease and work carefully, so as not to tear the boot. Remove the balljoint shank nut. The clearance between the balljoint shank and the CV joint is very tight. To remove the stud nut, you'll have to alternately back off the nut a turn or two, pull down the balljoint, turn the nut another turn or two, etc, until the nut is off.
4 Remove the bolt and nuts securing the balljoint to the control arm. Separate the balljoint from the control arm with a lever **(see illustration 5.3a and 5.3b)**.
5 To install the balljoint, insert the balljoint shank through the hole in the hub carrier and install the nut, but don't tighten it yet. Don't push the balljoint stud all the way up into and through the hole; instead, thread the nut onto the stud as soon as the stud protrudes through the hole, then turn the nut to draw the shank up through the hole.

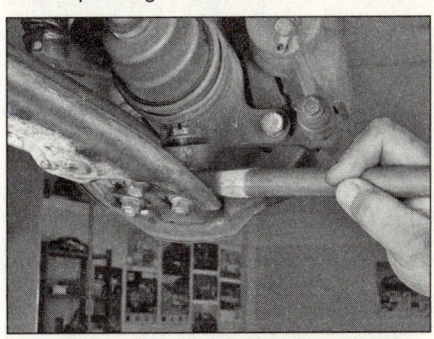

6.3 Detach the balljoint shank from the hub carrier using a separator tool

6 Attach the balljoint to the control arm and install the bolt and nuts, tightening them to the torque listed in this Chapter's Specifications.
7 Tighten the balljoint shank nut to the torque listed in this Chapter's Specifications and install a new split pin. If the split pin hole doesn't line up with the slots on the nut, tighten the nut additionally until it does line up – don't loosen the nut to insert the split pin.
8 Refit the wheel and nuts. Lower the vehicle and tighten the nuts to the torque listed in the Specifications.

7 Hub carrier and hub (front) – removal and refitting

⚠️ **Warning:** *Dust created by the brake system may contain asbestos, which is harmful to your health. Never blow it out with compressed air and don't inhale any of it. Do not, under any circumstances, use petroleum-based solvents to clean brake parts. Use an aerosol brake cleaner.*

Removal

1 Loosen the wheel nuts, raise the vehicle and support it securely on axle stands (see *Jacking and vehicle support*). Remove the wheel.
2 Remove the split pin and the locking cap from the driveshaft hub nut.
3 Remove the driveshaft hub nut and washer. To prevent the hub from turning, wedge a lever between two of the wheel studs and allow the

10•8 Suspension and steering systems

lever to rest against the ground or the floorpan of the vehicle.

4 To loosen the driveshaft from the hub splines, tap the end of the driveshaft with a soft-faced hammer or a hammer and a brass punch. **Note:** *Don't attempt to push the end of the driveshaft through the hub yet. Applying force to the end of the driveshaft, beyond just breaking it loose from the hub, can damage the driveshaft or transmission*

5 Remove the brake caliper and the brake disc (see Chapter 9), and disconnect the brake hose from the strut.

6 Disconnect and remove the wheel speed sensor.

7 Loosen, but don't remove the strut-to-hub carrier nuts and bolts (see Section 2).

8 Separate the track rod end from the hub carrier arm (see Section 17).

9 Remove the balljoint-to-lower arm bolt and nuts **(see illustrations 5.3a and 5.3b)**.

10 Push the driveshaft from the hub and support the end of the driveshaft with a piece of wire.

11 Using a balljoint separator tool **(see illustration 6.3)** or a small puller, remove the balljoint from the hub carrier.

12 The strut-to-hub carrier bolts can now be removed.

13 Carefully separate the hub carrier from the strut.

Refitting

14 Guide the hub carrier and hub assembly into position, inserting the driveshaft into the hub.

15 Push the hub carrier into the strut flange and install the bolts and nuts, but don't tighten them yet.

16 If you removed the balljoint from the old hub carrier, and are planning to use it with the new hub carrier, connect the balljoint to the hub carrier and tighten the balljoint shank nut to the torque listed in this Chapter's Specifications.

17 Attach the balljoint to the control arm (see Section 5), but don't tighten the bolt and nuts yet.

18 Attach the track rod to the hub carrier arm (see Section 17). Tighten the strut bolt nuts, the balljoint-to-control arm bolt and nuts and the track rod nut to the torque listed in this Chapter's Specifications.

19 Place the brake disc on the hub and install the caliper as outlined in Chapter 9.

20 Install the driveshaft/hub washer and nut, then tighten it to the torque listed in the Chapter 8 Specifications. Fit the locking cap and a new split pin.

21 Install the wheel and nuts.

22 Lower the vehicle and tighten the nuts to the torque listed in the Specifications.

23 Drive the vehicle to an alignment workshop to have the front alignment checked and, if necessary, adjusted

8 Hub and bearing assembly (front) – removal and refitting

Removal

1 Remove the hub carrier and hub assembly as described in Section 7.

2 The hub must now be removed from the bearing inner races. It is preferable to use a press to do this, but it is possible to drive out the hub using a length of metal tube/socket of suitable diameter **(see illustration)**.

3 Part of the inner race may remain on the hub, and this should be removed using a puller or chisel **(see illustration)**.

4 Note that when renewing the hub, the wheel bearing will have to be renewed also, as it will be damaged on removal.

5 Using circlip pliers, extract the circlip securing the bearing in the hub carrier **(see illustration)**.

6 Press or drive out the bearing, using a length of metal tubing of diameter slightly less than the bearing outer race. Alternatively, refit the bearing inner race and press or drive against this – after all, as the bearing assembly is to be renewed, any damage to the bearing balls/races is of no importance **(see illustrations)**.

7 Clean the bearing seating faces in the hub carrier.

Refitting

8 Using a length of metal tube of diameter slightly less than the outer race, press or drive the new bearing into the hub carrier until it is fully located. Do not apply any pressure to the inner race.

9 Locate the circlip into the groove in the hub carrier.

10 Support the inner race on a length of metal tube, then press or drive the hub fully into the bearing.

11 Refit the hub carrier and hub assembly as described in Section 7.

9 Anti-roll bar and bushings (rear) – removal and refitting

Note: *As the fuel filler and breather hoses need to be disconnected during this procedure, ensure minimal fuel is present in the tank.*

Removal

1 Loosen the rear wheel nuts. Raise the rear of the vehicle and place it securely on axle stands (see *Jacking and vehicle support*). Remove the rear wheels.

2 Remove the anti-roll bar-to-link nuts (see

8.2 Drive the hub from the bearing using a suitable tube or drift

8.3 If the bearing inner race remains on the hub, remove it using a puller or chisel

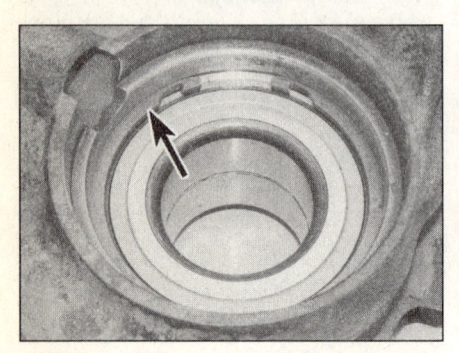

8.5 Extract the bearing circlip (arrowed) from the hub carrier

8.6a Refit the bearing inner race . . .

8.6b . . . and drive the bearing from the hub carrier

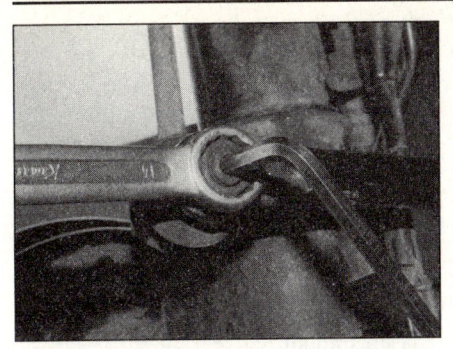

Suspension and steering systems 10•9

9.2 Use an Allen key to hold the shank whilst undoing the anti-roll bar link nut

9.3 Unbolt the anti-roll bar clamps from the vehicle body (arrowed)

9.4 Undo the fuel tank strap bolts at the rear, and the left-hand front bolt (arrowed)

illustration). If the balljoint shank turns with the nut, use an Allen key to hold the shank.
3 Unbolt the anti-roll bar bushing clamps from the body **(see illustration)**.
4 Support the fuel tank with a trolley jack, then undo the fuel tank retaining strap bolts at the rear. Undo the left-hand strap front bolt, and remove the strap **(see illustration)**.
5 Undo the clips and disconnect the fuel filler and breather hoses from the tank **(see illustration)**.
6 The anti-roll bar can now be lowered from the vehicle. Pull the clamps off the anti-roll bar (if they haven't fallen off already) using a rocking motion.
7 Check the bushings for wear, hardness, distortion, cracking and other signs of deterioration, renewing them if necessary **(see illustration)**. Also check the link bushings for these signs.
8 Using a wire brush, clean the areas of the bar where the bushings ride. Refitting is the reverse of the removal procedure. If necessary, use a light coat of vegetable oil to ease bushing and U-bracket installation (don't use petroleum-based products or brake fluid, as these will damage the rubber).
9 To inspect the links, refer to paragraph 6 in Section 4.

Refitting
10 Refitting is the reverse of removal.

10 Suspension strut assembly (rear) – removal, inspection and refitting

Removal
1 On models with a one-piece rear seat, remove the rear seat back; on models with separate rear seat backs, fold the rear seats forward; on all Hatchback, Liftback and Estate models, prise up and remove the rear strut cover (the plastic trim piece on top of the side trim panel) (see Chapter 11) **(see illustration)**.
2 Loosen the rear wheel nuts, raise the rear of the vehicle and support it securely on axle stands (see *Jacking and vehicle support*). Remove the wheel.
3 Fit a hose clamp to the brake flexible rubber

9.5 Slacken the hose clamps and disconnect the filler and breather hoses (arrowed) from the fuel tank

hose, and undo the hose-to-pipe union. Remove the clip and detach the brake hose from the bracket on the strut. Release the clips and detach the ABS sensor wire from the strut **(see illustrations)**.

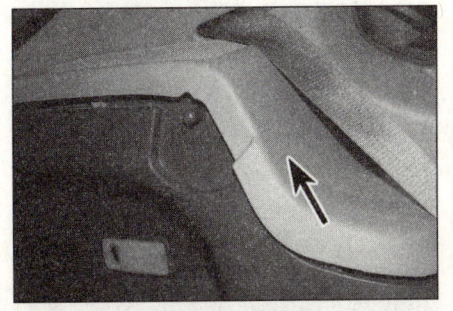

9.7 Check the condition of the anti-roll bar bushes (arrowed)

4 Disconnect the anti-roll bar link from the strut **(see illustration 9.2)**.
5 Support the hub carrier with a trolley jack.
6 Loosen the strut-to-hub carrier bolt nuts **(see illustration)**.

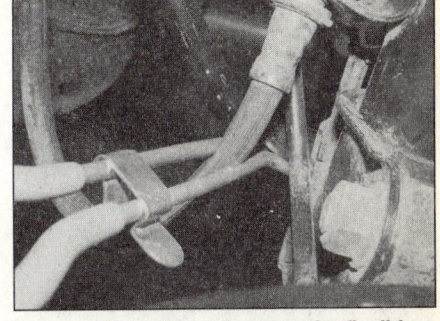

10.1 On Hatchback, Liftback and Estate models, prise up the trim piece (arrowed) over the top of the rear strut mounting

10.3a Use a hose clamp on the flexible rubber brake hose . . .

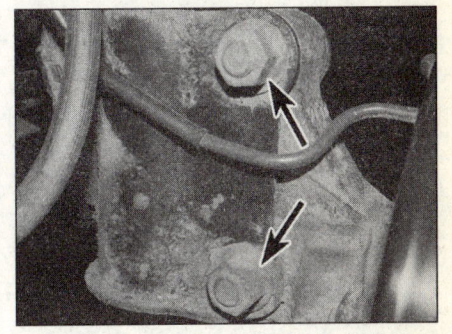

10.3b . . . then undo the hose union, and pull out the hose retaining clip (arrowed)

10.6 Slacken the strut-to-carrier bolt nuts (arrowed)

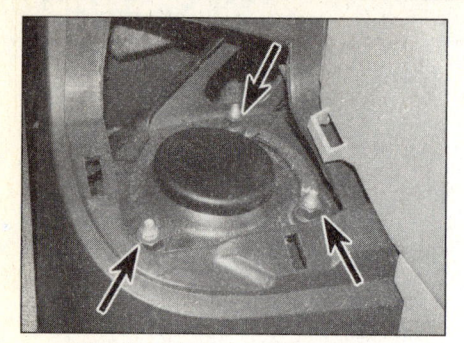

10•10 Suspension and steering systems

10.7 Undo the upper strut-to-body mounting nuts (arrowed)

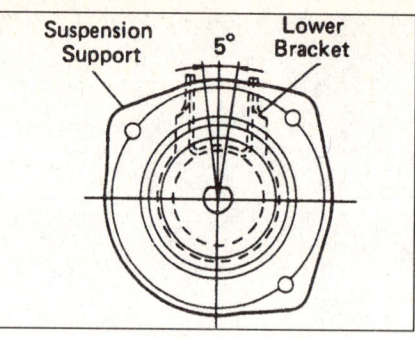

10.11 Fit the strut upper support so that it's in line (within 5°) with the hub carrier mounting brackets on the strut lower bracket

7 Remove the three upper strut-to-body mounting nuts **(see illustration)**.
8 Lower the hub carrier with the jack and remove the two strut-to-hub carrier bolts.
9 Remove the strut assembly.

Inspection

10 Follow the inspection procedures described in Section 3. If you determine that the strut assembly must be disassembled for renewal of the strut or the coil spring, refer to Section 3.
11 When reassembling the strut, make sure the suspension upper support is aligned as shown **(see illustration)**.

Refitting

12 Manoeuvre the assembly up into the wheel arch and insert the mounting studs through the holes in the body. Install the nuts, but don't tighten them yet.

11.2 Remove the strut rod-to-hub carrier bolt (arrowed)

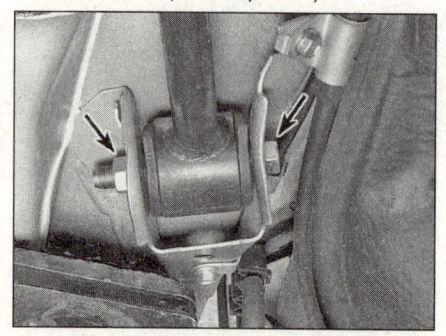

11.3 Remove the strut rod-to-body bracket bolt (arrowed)

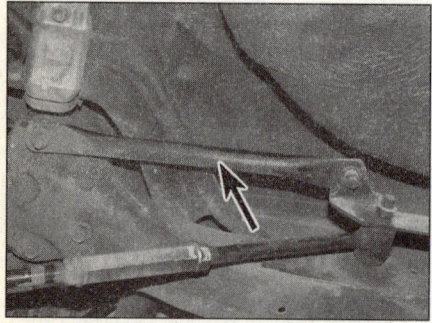

13 Push the hub carrier into the strut lower bracket and install the bolts and nuts, tightening them to the torque listed in this Chapter's Specifications.
14 Connect the anti-roll bar link to the strut bracket.
15 Attach the brake hose to the strut bracket and install the clip, then reconnect the brake hose. Attach the ABS wire to the strut.
16 Bleed the brakes as described in Chapter 9.
17 Install the wheel and nuts, lower the vehicle and tighten the nuts to the torque listed in the Specifications.
18 Tighten the three strut upper mounting nuts to the torque listed in this Chapter's Specifications.
19 Repeat paragraphs 1 to 18 for the other strut.
20 Refit the seat, rear side seat backs and rear strut covers (see Chapter 11).

12.3 Remove the brace (arrowed) between the bracket and the crossmember

12.6 Undo the nut and remove the through-bolt (arrowed)

11 Strut rod – removal and refitting

Removal

1 Loosen the wheel nuts, raise the vehicle and support it securely on axle stands (see *Jacking and vehicle support*). Remove the wheel.
2 Remove the strut rod-to-hub carrier bolt **(see illustration)**.
3 Remove the strut rod-to-body bracket bolt **(see illustration)** and detach the rod from the vehicle.

Refitting

4 Refitting is the reverse of the removal procedure, but don't tighten the bolts until the suspension is raised by a jack to simulate normal ride height, or the weight of the vehicle is back on its wheels. Be sure to tighten the bolts to the torque listed in this Chapter's Specifications. Tighten the wheel nuts to the torque listed in the Specifications.

12 Suspension arms – removal and refitting

Removal

1 Loosen the rear wheel nuts, raise the rear of the vehicle and support it securely on axle stands (see *Jacking and vehicle support*).
2 Block the front wheels and remove the rear wheel.

No 2 (rear) suspension arms

3 On vehicles manufactured after October 1999, undo the two nuts and remove the brace from the bracket at the inboard end of the suspension arms to the outer edge of the crossmember **(see illustration)**. If removing the right-hand No 2 suspension arm, remove the exhaust tailpipe as described in Chapter 4A.
4 Where a load-sensing proportioning valve is fitted, unscrew the locknut securing the valve lower spring anchor to the right-hand No 2 suspension arm.
5 Take care not to alter the position of the adjusting nut fitted just above. It is advisable to mark the adjusting nut and the spring anchor threads with quick drying paint so that the relative positions can be maintained.
6 Remove the nut, washer and through-bolt from the outer end of the suspension arm at the hub carrier **(see illustration)**.
7 Remove the nuts, washers, and plate (where fitted) from the inner end of the suspension arms at the suspension crossmember **(see illustration)**.
8 Remove the No 2 suspension arm.
Caution: Do NOT loosen the locknuts and turn the adjusting tube; moving this tube will affect the rear wheel toe adjustment.

Suspension and steering systems 10•11

No 1 (front) suspension arms

9 Loosen the nut and bolt securing the inner end of the arms **(see illustration 12.7)**. Also loosen the nut and bolt attaching the outer ends of the arms to the hub carrier **(see illustration 12.6)**. Remove the exhaust system centre pipe and the exhaust pipe insulator (see Chapter 4A). Where a load-sensing proportioning valve is fitted, disconnect the lower spring anchor (see paragraph 5).

10 Support the suspension crossmember with a trolley jack. Remove the two bolts and one stud each side retaining the crossmember **(see illustration)**. Lower the crossmember far enough to allow the long through-bolt at the inner end of the suspension arm to be pulled forward, out of the crossmember.

11 Remove the front suspension arm-to-rear hub carrier nut and washer.

12 Remove the front suspension arm-to-suspension crossmember nut and bolt.

13 Remove the No 1 suspension arm.

Refitting

14 Refitting is the reverse of removal. Be sure to tighten all suspension fasteners to the torque listed in this Chapter's Specifications.

15 Refit the wheel and nuts, then lower the vehicle to the ground. Tighten the wheel nuts to the torque listed in the Specifications.

16 Have the rear wheel alignment checked by a suitably-equipped workshop.

13 Hub and bearing assembly (rear) – removal and refitting

Warning: *Dust created by the brake system may contain asbestos, which is harmful to your health. Never blow it out with compressed air and don't inhale any of it. Do not use petroleum-based solvents. Use brake system cleaner only.*

Note: *Due to the special tools required to renew the bearing, the hub and bearing assembly should not be disassembled by the home mechanic. The assembly can be removed, however, and taken to a dealer service department or other repair workshop to have the bearing renewed.*

Removal

1 Loosen the wheel nuts, raise the vehicle and support it securely on axle stands (see *Jacking and vehicle support*). Remove the wheel.

2 Pull the brake drum from the hub (drum brake models) or remove the rear disc and caliper (disc brake models) (see Chapter 9).

3 Undo the bolt and pull the ABS sensor from place.

4 Remove the four hub-to-hub carrier bolts, accessible by turning the hub flange so that the large circular cut-out exposes each bolt **(see illustration)**.

5 Remove the hub and bearing assembly

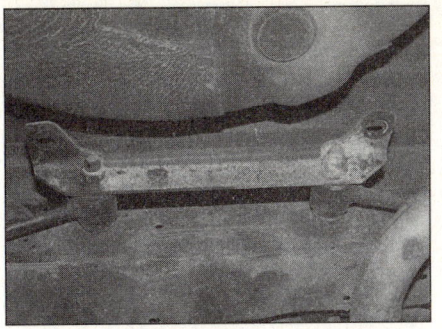

12.7 Remove the plate from the inner end of the suspension arms

from its seat, manoeuvring it out through the brake assembly.

6 Remove the old O-ring from the hub seat.

7 Due to the special tools required to do this, you'll have to take the hub and bearing assembly to an automotive machine workshop and have the old bearing pulled off the hub and a new bearing pressed on (you can re-use the hub itself, as long as it's in good condition).

Refitting

8 Apply a light coat of oil to the new O-ring and install it on the outer circumference of the raised hub in the backing plate.

9 Position the hub and bearing assembly on the axle carrier and align the holes in the backing plate. Install the bolts. A magnet is useful in guiding the bolts through the hub flange and into position. After all four bolts have been installed, tighten them to the torque listed in this Chapter's Specifications.

10 Refit the brake drum, or disc and caliper, and the wheel. Lower the vehicle and tighten the nuts to the torque listed in the Specifications.

14 Rear hub carrier – removal and refitting

Warning: *Dust created by the brake system may contain asbestos, which is harmful to your health. Never blow it out with compressed air and don't inhale any of it. Do not, under*

13.4 Remove the hub-to-carrier bolts

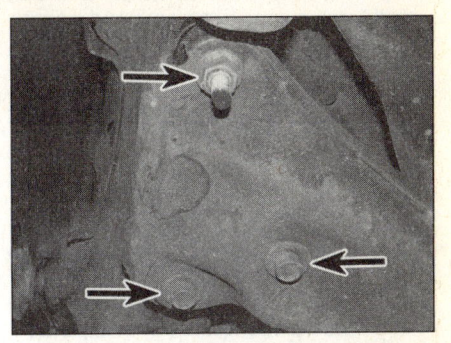

12.10 Remove the two bolts and one nut each side (arrowed) securing the crossmember

any circumstances, use petroleum-based solvents to clean brake parts. Use brake system cleaner only.

Removal

1 Loosen the wheel nuts, raise the vehicle and support it on axle stands (see *Jacking and vehicle support*). Block the front wheels and remove the rear wheel.

2 Remove the rear brake drum (drum brake models) or remove the rear disc and caliper (disc brake models). Detach the brake pipe from the bracket on the strut **(see illustration 10.3)**.

3 Remove the rear hub and bearing assembly (see Section 13).

4 Detach the backing plate and rear brake assembly (drum brake models) from the hub carrier. It isn't necessary to disassemble the brake shoe assembly or disconnect the handbrake cable from the backing plate. Suspend the backing plate and brake assembly from the coil spring with a piece of wire. Be careful not to kink the brake line.

5 Remove the wheel speed sensor from the hub carrier.

6 Loosen, but don't remove the strut-to-hub carrier bolts **(see illustration 10.6)**.

7 Remove the suspension arm-to-hub carrier bolt, nut and washers and remove the rear strut rod-to-hub carrier bolt **(see illustrations 11.2 and 12.6)**.

8 Remove the loosened strut-to-hub carrier bolts while supporting the carrier so it doesn't fall and detach the hub carrier from the strut bracket.

Refitting

9 Inspect the carrier bushing for cracks, deformation and signs of wear. If it is worn out, take the carrier to a dealer service department or other repair workshop to have the old one pressed out and a new one pressed in.

10 Push the hub carrier into the strut bracket, aligning the two bolt holes. Insert the two strut-to-carrier bolts and tighten them to the torque listed in this Chapter's Specifications.

11 Refit the suspension arm-to-hub carrier bolt (from the front), washers and nut. Tighten the nut by hand.

12 Connect the strut rod to the hub carrier and tighten the nut and bolt finger tight.

10•12 Suspension and steering systems

16.2 Insert a T30 Torx bit through holes each side of the steering wheel boss, and slacken the retaining screws

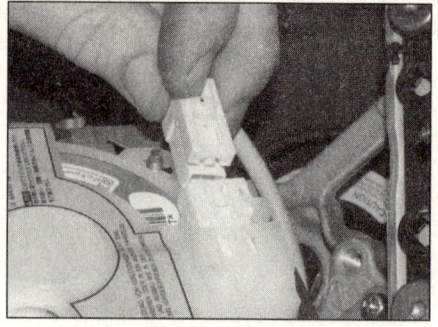

16.3a Airbag connector – single headlight models (pre-October '99)

16.3b On twin headlight models (post-October '99), pull out the locking clip . . .

16.3c . . . and disconnect the airbag wiring plug

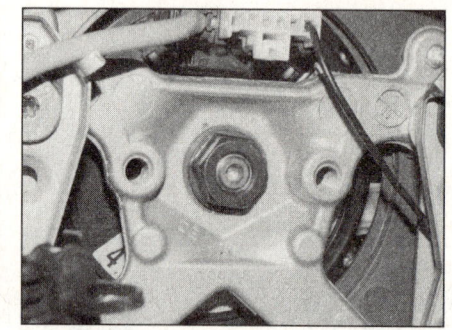

16.5 Remove the steering wheel nut

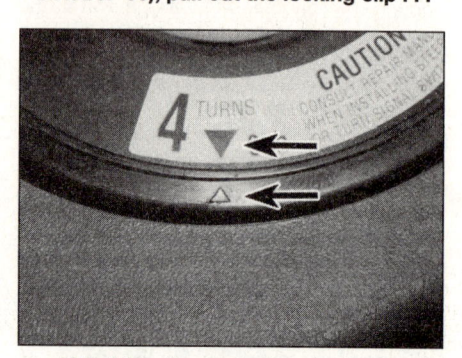

16.7 Align the contact reel pointers (arrowed)

13 Place a jack under the carrier and raise it to simulate normal ride height.
14 Tighten the suspension arm bolt/nut and the strut rod bolt/nut to the torque values listed in this Chapter's Specifications. Remove the floor jack from under the rear hub carrier.
15 On models with ABS, reattach the wheel speed sensor to the hub carrier.
16 Attach the brake backing plate to the hub carrier, install the hub and tighten the four bolts to the torque listed in this Chapter's Specifications.
17 Connect the brake line to the strut bracket and install the clip. Make sure the hose isn't twisted.
18 Refit the rear brake drum or disc and caliper (see Chapter 9).
19 Refit the wheel and nuts.
20 Lower the vehicle and tighten the nuts to the torque listed in the Specifications.

15 Steering system – general information

All models are equipped with rack-and-pinion steering. The steering gear is bolted to the engine compartment bulkhead and operates the hub carriers via track rods. The inner ends of the track rods are protected by rubber gaiters which should be inspected periodically for secure attachment, tears and leaking lubricant.

All models are equipped with power-assisted steering. The power assist system consists of a belt-driven pump and associated lines and hoses. The fluid level in the power steering pump reservoir should be checked periodically (see *Weekly checks*).

The steering wheel operates the steering column, which actuates the steering rack through universal joints. Looseness in the steering can be caused by wear in the steering column universal joints, the steering rack, the track rod ends and loose retaining bolts.

16 Steering wheel – removal and refitting

Warning: *These models are equipped with airbags. The airbag is armed and can deploy (inflate) whenever the battery is connected. To prevent accidental deployment (and possible injury), turn the ignition key to LOCK and disconnect the negative battery cable whenever working near airbag components (see Chapter 5A). After the battery is disconnected, wait at least five minutes before beginning work (the system has a back-up capacitor that must fully discharge). For more information see Chapter 12.*

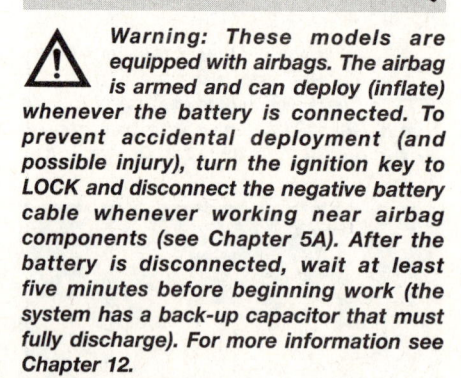

Removal

1 Turn the ignition key to off, then disconnect the cable from the negative terminal of the battery (see Chapter 5A), then wait at least 5 minutes before proceeding.
2 Turn the steering wheel so the wheels are pointing straight-ahead, prise out the blanking grommets (where fitted), and undo the T30 Torx screw each side of the steering wheel boss, securing the airbag. There is no need to remove the screws, simply undo them to the 'released' position **(see illustration)**.
3 Pull the airbag module off the steering wheel and disconnect the module electrical connector **(see illustrations)**.

Warning: *Set the airbag module down with the trim side facing up.*

4 Unplug the electrical connector for the cruise control (if equipped) and horn contact.
5 Remove the steering wheel retaining nut, then mark the relationship of the steering column to the hub (if marks don't already exist or don't line up) to simplify installation and ensure steering wheel alignment **(see illustration)**.
6 Pull the wheel from the steering column using a rocking motion. If necessary, use a puller to disconnect the steering wheel from the column.

Refitting

7 Make sure that the front wheels are facing straight-ahead. Turn the spiral contact reel anti-clockwise by hand until it becomes harder to turn the reel. Rotate the reel clockwise about two turns and align the two pointers **(see illustration)**.
8 To install the wheel, align the mark on the steering wheel hub with the mark on the shaft and slip the wheel onto the shaft. Install the nut and tighten it to the torque listed in this Chapter's Specifications.
9 Plug in the cruise control/horn contact connector.

Suspension and steering systems 10•13

10 Plug in the electrical connector for the airbag module and flip down the locking tab.
11 Make sure the airbag module electrical connector is positioned correctly and that the wires don't interfere with anything, then install the airbag module and tighten the Torx retaining screws.
12 Connect the negative battery cable (see Chapter 5A).

17 Track rod ends – removal and refitting

Removal

1 Loosen the wheel nuts. Raise the front of the vehicle, support it securely on axle stands (see *Jacking and vehicle support*), block the rear wheels and set the handbrake. Remove the front wheel.
2 Remove the split pin (see illustration) and loosen the nut on the track rod end balljoint shank.
3 Hold the track rod with a pair of locking pliers or spanner and loosen the locknut enough to mark the position of the track rod end in relation to the threads (see illustrations).
4 Disconnect the track rod from the hub carrier arm using a universal balljoint separator (see illustration). Remove the nut and detach the track rod.
5 Unscrew the track rod end from the track rod.

Refitting

6 Thread the track rod end on to the marked position and insert the track rod end balljoint shank into the hub carrier arm. Tighten the lock nut securely.
7 Refit the castellated nut on the balljoint shank and tighten it to the torque listed in this Chapter's Specifications. Install a new split pin. If the hole for the split pin doesn't line up with one of the slots in the nut, turn the nut an additional amount until it does.
8 Refit the wheel and nuts. Lower the vehicle and tighten the nuts to the torque listed in the Specifications.
9 It's advisable to have the wheel alignment checked by a dealer service department or an alignment workshop.

18 Steering rack gaiters – renewal

1 Loosen the nuts, raise the vehicle and support it securely on axle stands (see *Jacking and vehicle support*). Remove the wheel.
2 Remove the track rod end and lock nut (see Section 17).
3 Remove the outer steering rack gaiter clamp with a pair of pliers. Release the inner gaiter clamp and slide off the gaiter (see illustrations).
4 Before fitting the new gaiter, wrap the

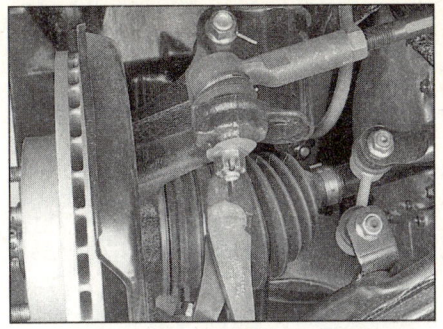

17.2 Remove the split pin from the track rod end retaining nut

17.3b ... then mark the position of the track rod end in relation to the threads

threads and serrations on the end of the steering rod with a layer of tape so the small end of the new gaiter isn't damaged.
5 Slide the new gaiter into position on the steering rack until it seats in the groove in the steering rod and install new clamps (where necessary).
6 Remove the tape and install the track rod end (see Section 17).
7 Refit the wheel and nuts. Lower the vehicle and tighten the nuts to the torque listed in the Specifications.

19 Steering rack – removal and refitting

Warning: *These models are equipped with airbags. Make sure the steering column is not*

18.3a The outer ends of the gaiters are secured by band type clamps; they're easily released with a pair of pliers

17.3a Slacken the locknut ...

17.4 Disconnect the track rod end from the hub carrier arm with a puller

turned while the steering rack is removed or you could damage the airbag system. To prevent the column from turning, turn the ignition key to the LOCK position before beginning work or run the seat belt through the steering wheel and clip the seat belt into place.

Removal

1 Loosen the front wheel nuts, raise the front of the vehicle and support it securely on axle stands (see *Jacking and vehicle support*). Apply the handbrake and remove the wheels. Remove the engine undershields.
2 Undo the nuts/bolts and remove the heat shields (where fitted) from the front of the steering rack (see illustration).
3 Place a drain pan under the steering rack. Detach the power steering pressure and return pipes (see illustration) and cap the

18.3b The inner ends of the gaiters are retained by clamps that must be cut off and discarded

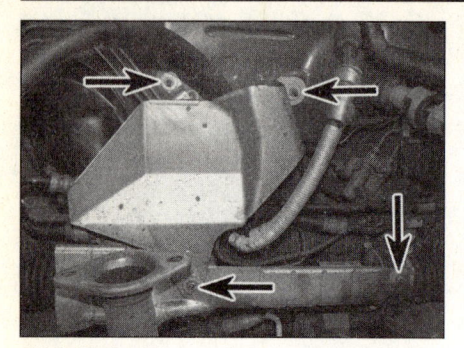

10•14 Suspension and steering systems

19.2 Undo the nuts (arrowed) and remove the steering rack heat shields

19.3 Disconnect the fluid pressure and return pipes (arrowed)

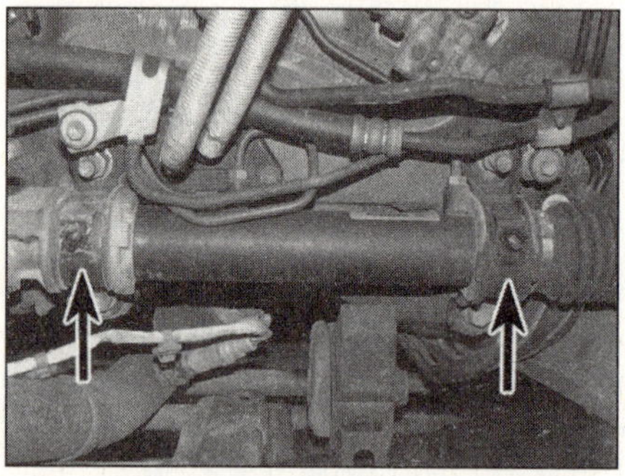

19.4a Remove the cover over the steering column universal joint . . .

19.4b . . . then undo the intermediate shaft pinch-bolt (arrowed)

19.6 Undo the nuts and remove the rack mounting brackets (arrowed)

ends to prevent excessive fluid loss and contamination.
4 Remove the universal joint cover. Mark the relationship of the lower universal joint to the steering rack pinion and remove the lower intermediate shaft pinch-bolt **(see illustrations)**.
5 Separate the track rod ends from the hub carrier arms (see Section 17).
6 Support the steering rack and remove the steering rack bracket-to-bulkhead mounting bolts/nuts **(see illustration)**. Separate the intermediate shaft from the steering rack input shaft and remove the steering rack assembly through the right-hand wheel arch.

⚠ **Warning: Do NOT turn the steering wheel while the steering rack is removed. If the steering wheel is inadvertently turned, remove the steering wheel and centre the spiral cable (see Section 16).**

7 Check the steering rack mounting grommets for excessive wear or deterioration, renewing them if necessary.

Refitting

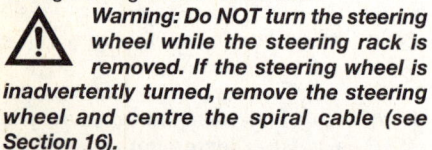

8 Position the steering rack and connect the universal joint, aligning the marks.
9 Refit the mounting brackets and bolts/nuts and tighten them to the torque listed in this Chapter's Specifications.
10 Connect the track rod ends to the hub carrier arms (see Section 17).
11 Refit the universal joint pinch-bolt and tighten it to the torque listed in this Chapter's Specifications.
12 Connect the power steering pressure and return hoses to the steering rack and fill the power steering pump reservoir with the recommended fluid (see *Lubricants and fluids*).

13 Refit the roadwheels, lower the vehicle and bleed the steering system (see Section 21). Tighten the roadwheel nuts to the torque listed in the Specifications.

20 Power steering pump – removal and refitting

Removal

1 Using a large syringe, suck as much fluid out of the power steering fluid reservoir as possible. Place a drain pan under the vehicle to catch any fluid that spills out when the hoses are disconnected.

4E-FE engines

2 Loosen the clamp and disconnect the fluid return hose from the pump **(see illustration)**.
3 Unscrew the pressure line to pump union nut, and detach the line from the pump.
4 Detach the two vacuum lines from the pump air control valve.
5 Loosen the pivot bolt (above) and adjuster bolt (below) and remove the drivebelt (see Chapter 1). Remove the pivot and adjuster bolts, then remove the pump from the vehicle.

4A-FE engines

6 Loosen the clamp and disconnect the fluid return hose from the pump **(see illustration)**.
7 Remove the pressure line-to-pump banjo bolt **(see illustration 20.6)**, then detach the line from the pump. Remove and discard

20.2 Power steering pump fluid return hose (left arrow), pressure pipe (centre arrow) and vacuum pipes (right arrow)

20.6 Power steering pump return hose (left arrow) and pressure pipe union bolt (right arrow)

20.9 Working from underneath, disconnect the two vacuum hoses (arrowed) from the pump

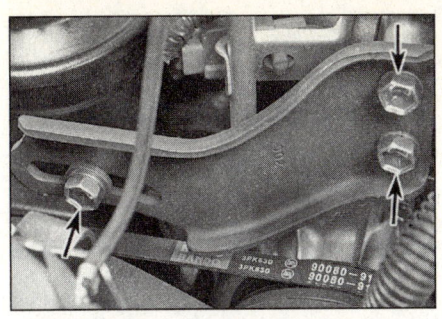

Suspension and steering systems 10•15

20.10a Undo the adjuster bolt (left arrow); if you need to remove the bracket, undo the two bolts (right arrows)

the copper sealing washers. They must be renewed when refitting the pump.
8 Raise the front of the vehicle and place it securely on axle stands (see *Jacking and vehicle support*).
9 Working from underneath the vehicle, detach the two vacuum lines from the pump **(see illustration)**.
10 Loosen the pivot bolt (underneath) and adjuster bolt (above) and remove the drivebelt (see Chapter 1). Remove the pivot, adjuster and mounting bolts **(see illustrations)**, then remove the pump from the vehicle.

4ZZ-FE and 3ZZ-FE engines

11 Remove the auxiliary drivebelt as described in Chapter 1.
12 Disconnect the power steering pressure switch wiring plug, then undo the union and disconnect the pressure hose from the pump **(see illustration)**.
13 Release the clamp and disconnect the fluid return hose from the pump **(see illustration)**.
14 The pump is secured to the engine block by two bolts. Working through the gap in the drive pulley, undo the nuts and pull the bolts from the pump and bracket. Remove the pump.

Refitting

15 Refitting is the reverse of removal. Be sure to tighten the pressure line banjo bolt to the torque listed in this Chapter's Specifications. Adjust the drivebelt tension following the procedure described in Chapter 1.
16 Top-up the fluid level in the reservoir (see *Weekly checks*) and bleed the system (Section 21).

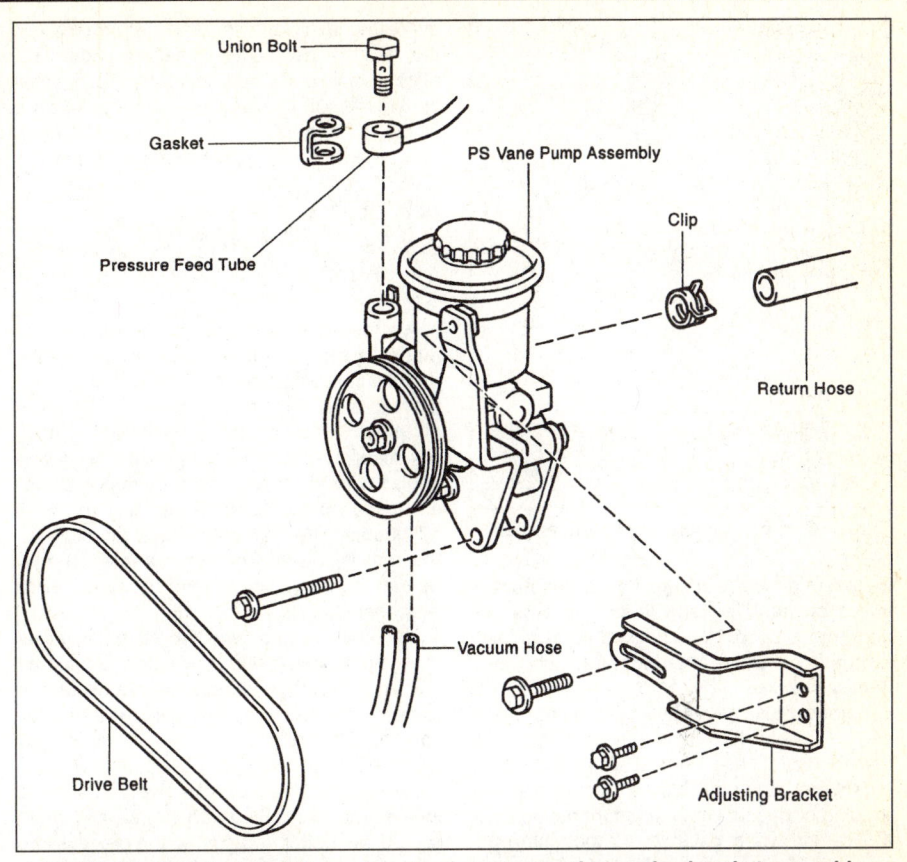

21 Power steering system – bleeding

1 Following any operation in which the power steering fluid lines have been disconnected, the power steering system must be bled to remove all air and obtain proper steering performance.
2 With the front wheels in the straight-ahead position, check the power steering fluid level and, if low, add fluid of the specified type (see *Lubricants and fluids*) until it reaches the Cold mark on the dipstick.
3 Start the engine and allow it to run at fast idle. Recheck the fluid level and add more if necessary to reach the Cold mark on the dipstick.
4 Bleed the system by turning the wheels from side-to-side, without hitting the stops. This will work the air out of the system. Keep the reservoir full of fluid as this is done.
5 When the air is worked out of the system, return the wheels to the straight-ahead position and leave the vehicle running for several more minutes before shutting it off.
6 Road test the vehicle to be sure the steering system is functioning normally and noise-free.
7 Recheck the fluid level to be sure it is up to the Hot mark on the dipstick while the engine is at normal operating temperature. Add fluid if necessary (see *Weekly checks*).

20.10b Exploded view of the power steering pump and mounting bracket assembly

22 Wheels and tyres – general information

1 All vehicles covered by this manual are equipped with metric-sized fibreglass or steel belted radial tyres. Use of other size or type of tyres may affect the ride and handling of the vehicle. Don't mix different types of tyres, such as radials and bias belted, on the same vehicle as handling may be seriously affected. It's recommended that tyres be renewed in pairs on the same axle, but if only one tyre is being renewed, be sure it's the same size, structure and tread design as the other.

20.12 Working at the back of the engine, disconnect the power steering pressure switch wiring plug

20.13 Release the clamp and disconnect the fluid return hose from the pump

10•16 Suspension and steering systems

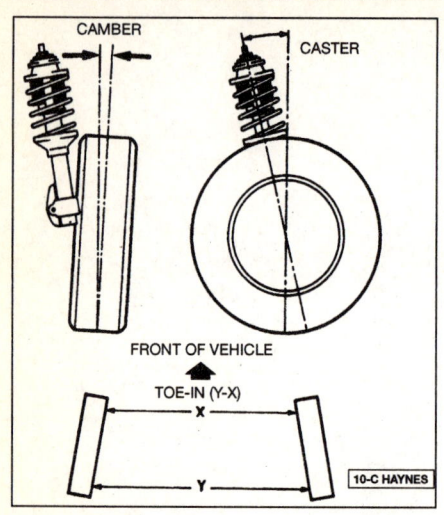

23.1 Camber, castor and toe-in angles

2 Because tyre pressure has a substantial effect on handling and wear, the pressure on all tyres should be checked at least once a month or before any extended trips (see *Weekly checks*).

3 Wheels must be renewed if they are bent, dented, leak air, have elongated bolt holes, are heavily rusted, out of vertical symmetry or if the nuts won't stay tight. Wheel repairs that use welding or peening are not recommended.

4 Tyre and wheel balance is important in the overall handling, braking and performance of the vehicle. Unbalanced wheels can adversely affect handling and ride characteristics as well as tyre life. Whenever a tyre is installed on a wheel, the tyre and wheel should be balanced by a workshop with the proper equipment.

23 Wheel alignment – general information

A wheel alignment refers to the adjustments made to the wheels so they are in proper angular relationship to the suspension and the ground. Wheels that are out of proper alignment not only affect vehicle control, but also increase tyre wear. The front end angles normally measured are camber, caster and toe-in **(see illustration)**; only toe-in is adjustable. The only adjustment possible on the rear is toe-in. The other angles should be measured to check for bent or worn suspension parts.

Getting the proper wheel alignment is a very exacting process, one in which complicated and expensive machines are necessary to perform the job properly. Because of this, you should have a technician with the proper equipment perform these tasks. We will, however, use this space to give you a basic idea of what is involved with a wheel alignment so you can better understand the process and deal intelligently with the workshop that does the work.

Toe-in is the turning in of the wheels. The purpose of a toe specification is to ensure parallel rolling of the wheels. In a vehicle with zero toe-in, the distance between the front edges of the wheels will be the same as the distance between the rear edges of the wheels. The actual amount of toe-in is normally only millimetre or so. On the front end, toe-in is controlled by the track rod end position on the track rod. On the rear end, it's controlled by altering the length of the rear (No 2) suspension arm. Incorrect toe-in will cause the tyres to wear improperly by making them scrub against the road surface.

Camber is the tilting of the wheels from vertical when viewed from one end of the vehicle. When the wheels tilt out at the top, the camber is said to be positive (+). When the wheels tilt in at the top the camber is negative (-). The amount of tilt is measured in degrees from vertical and this measurement is called the camber angle. This angle affects the amount of tyre tread which contacts the road and compensates for changes in the suspension geometry when the vehicle is cornering or travelling over an undulating surface.

Caster is the tilting of the front steering axis from the vertical. A tilt toward the rear is positive caster and a tilt toward the front is negative caster.

Chapter 11
Bodywork and fittings

Contents

	Section number		Section number
Body exterior fittings – removal and refitting	23	Interior trim – removal and refitting	27
Bonnet – removal, refitting and adjustment	8	Maintenance – bodywork and underframe	2
Bonnet lock – removal and refitting	10	Maintenance – upholstery and carpets	3
Bonnet release cable – removal and refitting	9	Major body damage – repair	5
Boot lid and lock components – removal and refitting	16	Minor body damage – repair	4
Central locking components – removal and refitting	18	Mirrors and associated components – removal and refitting	20
Centre console – removal and refitting	28	Radiator grille – removal and refitting	11
Door – removal, refitting and adjustment	12	Rear bumper – removal and refitting	7
Door glass and regulator – removal and refitting	15	Seat belt components – removal and refitting	26
Door handle and lock components – removal and refitting	14	Seats – removal and refitting	24
Door inner trim panel – removal and refitting	13	Sunroof – general information and motor renewal	22
Electric window components – removal and refitting	19	Tailgate, lock components and support struts – removal and refitting	17
Facia panel assembly – removal and refitting	29	Windscreen, fixed windows and rear screen/tailgate glass – general information	21
Front bumper – removal and refitting	6		
Front seat belt tensioning mechanism – general information	25		
General information	1		

Degrees of difficulty

Easy, suitable for novice with little experience	**Fairly easy**, suitable for beginner with some experience	**Fairly difficult**, suitable for competent DIY mechanic	**Difficult**, suitable for experienced DIY mechanic	**Very difficult**, suitable for expert DIY or professional

Specifications

Torque wrench settings	Nm	lbf ft
Seat belt mounting bolts	41	30
Seat belt tensioner stalk on seat	41	30
Seat mounting bolts	42	31

1 General information

The bodyshell is made of pressed-steel sections. Most components are welded together, but some use is made of structural adhesives.

The bonnet, door and some other vulnerable panels are made of zinc-coated metal, and are further protected by being coated with an anti-chip primer before being sprayed.

Extensive use is made of plastic materials, mainly in the interior, but also in exterior components. The front and rear bumpers and front grille are injection-moulded from a synthetic material that is very strong and yet light. Plastic components such as wheel arch liners are fitted to the underside of the vehicle, to improve the body's resistance to corrosion.

2 Maintenance – bodywork and underframe

1 The condition of a vehicle's bodywork is the one thing that significantly affects its value. Maintenance is easy, but needs to be regular. Neglect, particularly after minor damage, can lead quickly to further deterioration and costly repair bills. It is important also to keep watch on those parts of the vehicle not immediately visible, for instance the underside, inside all the wheel arches, and the lower part of the engine compartment.

2 The basic maintenance routine for the bodywork is washing – preferably with a lot of water, from a hose. This will remove all the loose solids which may have stuck to the vehicle. It is important to flush these off in such a way as to prevent grit from scratching the finish. The wheel arches and underframe need washing in the same way, to remove any accumulated mud which will retain moisture and tend to encourage rust. Oddly enough, the best time to clean the underframe and wheel arches is in wet weather, when the mud is thoroughly wet and soft. In very wet weather, the underframe is usually cleaned of large accumulations automatically, and this is a good time for inspection.

3 Periodically, except on vehicles with a wax-based underbody protective coating, it is a good idea to have the whole of the underframe

of the vehicle steam-cleaned, engine compartment included, so that a thorough inspection can be carried out to see what minor repairs and renovations are necessary. Steam cleaning is available at many garages, and is necessary for the removal of the accumulation of oily grime, which sometimes is allowed to become thick in certain areas. If steam-cleaning facilities are not available, there are some excellent grease solvents available which can be brush-applied; the dirt can then be simply hosed off. Note that these methods should not be used on vehicles with wax-based underbody protective coating, or the coating will be removed. Such vehicles should be inspected annually, preferably just before Winter, when the underbody should be washed down, and repair any damage to the wax coating. Ideally, a completely fresh coat should be applied. It would also be worth considering the use of such wax-based protection for injection into door panels, sills, box sections, etc, as an additional safeguard against rust damage, where such protection is not provided by the vehicle manufacturer.

4 After washing paintwork, wipe off with a chamois leather to give an unspotted clear finish. A coat of clear protective wax polish will give added protection against chemical pollutants in the air. If the paintwork sheen has dulled or oxidised, use a cleaner/polisher combination to restore the brilliance of the shine. This requires a little effort, but such dulling is usually caused because regular washing has been neglected. Care needs to be taken with metallic paintwork, as special non-abrasive cleaner/polisher is required to avoid damage to the finish. Always check that the door and ventilator opening drain holes and pipes are completely clear, so that water can be drained out. Brightwork should be treated in the same way as paintwork. Windscreens and windows can be kept clear of the smeary film which often appears, by proprietary glass cleaner. Never use any form of wax or other body or chromium polish on glass.

3 Maintenance – upholstery and carpets

Mats and carpets should be brushed or vacuum-cleaned regularly, to keep them free of grit. If they are badly stained, remove them from the vehicle for scrubbing or sponging, and make quite sure they are dry before refitting. Seats and interior trim panels can be kept clean by wiping with a damp cloth and a proprietary brand of cleaner. If they do become stained (which can be more apparent on light-coloured upholstery), use a little liquid detergent and a soft nail brush to scour the grime out of the grain of the material. Do not forget to keep the headlining clean in the same way as the upholstery. When using liquid cleaners inside the vehicle, do not over-wet the surfaces being cleaned. Excessive damp could get into the seams and padded interior, causing stains, offensive odours or even rot. If the inside of the vehicle gets wet accidentally, it is worthwhile taking some trouble to dry it out properly, particularly where carpets are involved. Do not leave oil or electric heaters inside the vehicle for this purpose.

4 Minor body damage – repair

Minor scratches

1 If the scratch is very superficial, and does not penetrate to the metal of the bodywork, repair is very simple. Lightly rub the area of the scratch with a paintwork renovator or a very fine cutting paste to remove loose paint from the scratch, and to clear the surrounding bodywork of wax polish. Rinse the area with clean water.
2 Apply touch-up paint to the scratch using a fine paint brush; continue to apply fine layers of paint until the surface of the paint in the scratch is level with the surrounding paintwork. Allow the new paint at least two weeks to harden, then blend it into the surrounding paintwork by rubbing the scratch area with a paintwork renovator or a very fine cutting paste. Finally, apply wax polish.
3 Where the scratch has penetrated right through to the metal of the bodywork, causing the metal to rust, a different repair technique is required. Remove any loose rust from the bottom of the scratch with a penknife, then apply rust-inhibiting paint to prevent the formation of rust in the future. Using a rubber or nylon applicator, fill the scratch with bodystopper paste. If required, this paste can be mixed with cellulose thinners to provide a very thin paste which is ideal for filling narrow scratches. Before the stopper-paste in the scratch hardens, wrap a piece of smooth cotton rag around the top of a finger. Dip the finger in cellulose thinners, and quickly sweep it across the surface of the stopper-paste in the scratch; this will ensure that the surface of the stopper-paste is slightly hollowed. The scratch can now be painted over as described earlier in this Section.

Dents

4 When deep denting of the vehicle's bodywork has taken place, the first task is to pull the dent out, until the affected bodywork almost attains its original shape. There is little point in trying to restore the original shape completely, as the metal in the damaged area will have stretched on impact, and cannot be reshaped fully to its original contour. It is better to bring the level of the dent up to a point which is about 3 mm below the level of the surrounding bodywork. In cases where the dent is very shallow anyway, it is not worth trying to pull it out at all. If the underside of the dent is accessible, it can be hammered out gently from behind, using a mallet with a wooden or plastic head. Whilst doing this, hold a suitable block of wood firmly against the outside of the panel, to absorb the impact from the hammer blows and thus prevent a large area of the bodywork from being 'belled-out'.
5 Should the dent be in a section of the bodywork which has a double skin, or some other factor making it inaccessible from behind, a different technique is called for. Drill several small holes through the metal inside the area – particularly in the deeper section. Then screw long self-tapping screws into the holes, just sufficiently for them to gain a good purchase in the metal. Now the dent can be pulled out by pulling on the protruding heads of the screws with a pair of pliers.
6 The next stage of the repair is the removal of the paint from the damaged area, and from an inch or so of the surrounding 'sound' bodywork. This is accomplished most easily by using a wire brush or abrasive pad on a power drill, although it can be done just as effectively by hand, using sheets of abrasive paper. To complete the preparation for filling, score the surface of the bare metal with a screwdriver or the tang of a file, or alternatively, drill small holes in the affected area. This will provide a good 'key' for the filler paste.
7 To complete the repair, see the Section on filling and respraying.

Rust holes or gashes

8 Remove all paint from the affected area, and from an inch or so of the surrounding 'sound' bodywork, using an abrasive pad or a wire brush on a power drill. If these are not available, a few sheets of abrasive paper will do the job most effectively. With the paint removed, you will be able to judge the severity of the corrosion, and therefore decide whether to renew the whole panel (if this is possible) or to repair the affected area. New body panels are not as expensive as most people think, and it is often quicker and more satisfactory to fit a new panel than to attempt to repair large areas of corrosion.
9 Remove all fittings from the affected area, except those which will act as a guide to the original shape of the damaged bodywork (eg headlamp shells etc). Then, using tin snips or a hacksaw blade, remove all loose metal and any other metal badly affected by corrosion. Hammer the edges of the hole inwards, to create a slight depression for the filler paste.
10 Wire-brush the affected area to remove the powdery rust from the surface of the remaining metal. Paint the affected area with rust-inhibiting paint; if the back of the rusted area is accessible, treat this also.
11 Before filling can take place, it will be necessary to block the hole in some way. This can be achieved with aluminium or plastic mesh, or aluminium tape.
12 Aluminium or plastic mesh, or glass-fibre matting, is probably the best material to use for a large hole. Cut a piece to the approximate

size and shape of the hole to be filled, then position it in the hole so that its edges are below the level of the surrounding bodywork. It can be retained in position by several blobs of filler paste around its periphery.

13 Aluminium tape should be used for small or very narrow holes. Pull a piece off the roll, trim it to the approximate size and shape required, then pull off the backing paper (if used) and stick the tape over the hole; it can be overlapped if the thickness of one piece is insufficient. Burnish down the edges of the tape with the handle of a screwdriver or similar, to ensure that the tape is securely attached to the metal underneath.

Filling and respraying

14 Before using this Section, see the Sections on dent, deep scratch, rust holes and gash repairs.

15 Many types of bodyfiller are available, but generally speaking, those proprietary kits which contain a tin of filler paste and a tube of resin hardener are best for this type of repair which can be used directly from the tube. A wide, flexible plastic or nylon applicator will be found invaluable for imparting a smooth and well-contoured finish to the surface of the filler.

16 Mix up a little filler on a clean piece of card or board – measure the hardener carefully (follow the maker's instructions on the pack), otherwise the filler will set too rapidly or too slowly. Using the applicator, apply the filler paste to the prepared area; draw the applicator across the surface of the filler to achieve the correct contour and to level the surface. When a contour that approximates to the correct one is achieved, stop working the paste – if you carry on too long, the paste will become sticky and begin to 'pick-up' on the applicator. Continue to add thin layers of filler paste at 20-minute intervals, until the level of the filler is just proud of the surrounding bodywork.

17 Once the filler has hardened, the excess can be removed using a metal plane or file. From then on, progressively-finer grades of abrasive paper should be used, starting with a 40-grade production paper, and finishing with a 400-grade wet-and-dry paper. Always wrap the abrasive paper around a flat rubber, cork, or wooden block – otherwise the surface of the filler will not be completely flat. During the smoothing of the filler surface, the wet-and-dry paper should be periodically rinsed in water. This will ensure that a very smooth finish is imparted to the filler at the final stage.

18 At this stage, the 'dent' should be surrounded by a ring of bare metal, which in turn should be encircled by the finely 'feathered' edge of the good paintwork. Rinse the repair area with clean water, until all the dust produced by the rubbing-down operation has gone.

19 Spray the whole area with a light coat of primer – this will show up any imperfections in the surface of the filler. Repair these imperfections with fresh filler paste or bodystopper, and again smooth the surface with abrasive paper. If bodystopper is used, it can be mixed with cellulose thinners, to form a thin paste which is ideal for filling small holes. Repeat this spray-and-repair procedure until you are satisfied that the surface of the filler, and the feathered edge of the paintwork, are perfect. Clean the repair area with clean water, and allow to dry fully.

20 The repair area is now ready for final spraying. Paint spraying must be carried out in a warm, dry, windless and dust-free atmosphere. This condition can be created artificially if you have access to a large indoor working area, but if you are forced to work in the open, you will have to pick your day very carefully. If you are working indoors, dousing the floor in the work area with water will help to settle the dust which would otherwise be in the atmosphere. If the repair area is confined to one body panel, mask off the surrounding panels; this will help to minimise the effects of a slight mis-match in paint colours. Bodywork fittings (eg chrome strips, door handles etc) will also need to be masked off. Use genuine masking tape, and several thickness of newspaper, for the masking operations.

21 Before starting to spray, agitate the aerosol can thoroughly, then spray a test area (an old tin, or similar) until the technique is mastered. Cover the repair area with a thick coat of primer; the thickness should be built up using several thin layers of paint, rather than one thick one. Using 400 grade wet-and-dry paper, rub down the surface of the primer until it is smooth. While doing this, the work area should be thoroughly doused with water, and the wet-and-dry paper periodically rinsed in water. Allow to dry before spraying on more paint.

22 Spray on the top coat, again building up the thickness by using several thin layers of paint. Start spraying at the top of the repair area, and then, using a side-to-side motion, work downwards until the whole repair area and about 2 inches of the surrounding original paintwork is covered. Remove all masking material 10 to 15 minutes after spraying on the final coat of paint.

23 Allow the new paint at least two weeks to harden, then, using a paintwork renovator or a very fine cutting paste, blend the edges of the paint into the existing paintwork. Finally, apply wax polish.

Plastic components

24 With the use of more and more plastic body components by the vehicle manufacturers (eg bumpers. spoilers, and in some cases major body panels), rectification of more serious damage to such items has become a matter of either entrusting repair work to a specialist in this field, or renewing complete components. Repair of such damage by the DIY owner is not feasible, owing to the cost of the equipment and materials required for effecting such repairs. The basic technique involves making a groove along the line of the crack in the plastic, using a rotary burr in a power drill. The damaged part is then welded back together, using a hot air gun to heat up and fuse a plastic filler rod into the groove. Any excess plastic is then removed, and the area rubbed down to a smooth finish. It is important that a filler rod of the correct plastic is used, as body components can be made of different types (eg polycarbonate, ABS, polypropylene).

25 Damage of a less serious nature (abrasions, minor cracks etc) can be repaired by the DIY owner using a two-part epoxy filler repair material which can be used directly from the tube. Once mixed in equal proportions, this is used in similar fashion to the bodywork filler used on metal panels. The filler is usually cured in twenty to thirty minutes, ready for sanding and painting.

26 If the owner is renewing a complete component himself, or if he has repaired it with epoxy filler, he will be left with the problem of finding a suitable paint for finishing which is compatible with the type of plastic used. At one time, the use of a universal paint was not possible, owing to the complex range of plastics met with in body component applications. Standard paints, generally speaking, will not bond to plastic or rubber satisfactorily, but professional matched paints, to match any plastic or rubber finish, can be obtained from some dealers. However, it is now possible to obtain a plastic body parts finishing kit which consists of a pre-primer treatment, a primer and coloured top coat. Full instructions are normally supplied with a kit, but basically the method of use is to first apply the pre-primer to the component concerned, and allow it to dry for up to 30 minutes. Then the primer is applied, and left to dry for about an hour before finally applying the special-coloured top coat. The result is a correctly coloured component, where the paint will flex with the plastic or rubber, a property that standard paint does not normally possess.

5 Major body damage – repair

Where serious damage has occurred, or large areas need renewal due to neglect, it means that complete new panels will need welding-in, and this is best left to professionals. If the damage is due to impact, it will also be necessary to check completely the alignment of the bodyshell, and this can only be carried out accurately by a Toyota dealer using special jigs. If the body is left misaligned, it is primarily dangerous, as the car will not handle properly, and secondly, uneven stresses will be imposed on the steering, suspension and possibly transmission, causing abnormal wear, or complete failure, particularly to such items as the tyres.

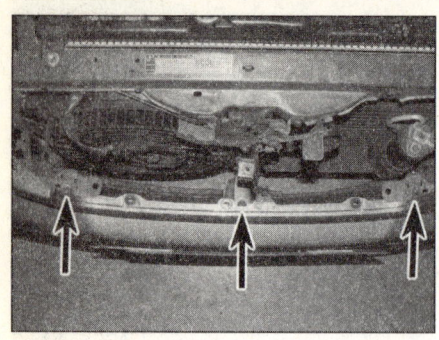

11•4 Bodywork and fittings

6.2a Front bumper centre clips (arrowed)

6.2b Undo the bolt each side securing the bumper to the wing

6.5 Bumper fasteners (three right-hand bolts arrowed)

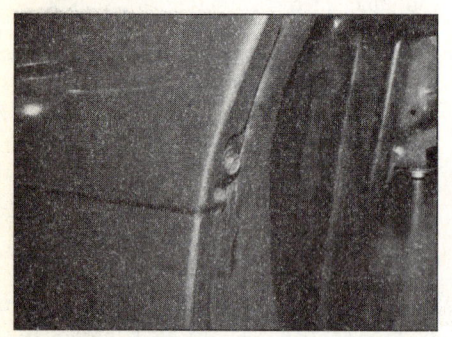

6.6 Undo the two screw each side securing the bumper to the wheel arch liner

6.7 Prise out the plastic grille each side and undo the bolt (arrowed) in the recesses

6.8 Undo the bolt in the centre grille (arrowed)

6 Front bumper – removal and refitting

Removal

Single headlamp models

1 Remove the radiator grille as described in Section 11.
2 The bumper is held by three clips at the centre top, one screw each side securing the bumper to the wing, one each side securing the bumper to the side support, and one bolt in the centre below the number plate. Unscrew the centre pins and prise out the clips, then undo the bolts (see illustrations).
3 Undo the bolts under the bumper securing it to the engine undershields.
4 With the help of an assistant, pull the bumper forwards, disconnecting any wiring plugs as the bumper is withdrawn.

Twin headlamp models

5 Undo the 6 bolts on the underside of the bumper (see illustration). The two outer bolts are screwed into plastic expansion rivets. Prise out the rivets, once the screws are removed.
6 Undo the screw each side securing the rear edge of the bumper to the wheel arch liner (see illustration).
7 Prise out the plastic grille each side or remove the front foglights (as applicable – see Chapter 12), and undo the bolt in each recess (see illustration).
8 Undo the bolt in the centre grille (see illustration).
9 Pull the wheel arch liner away from the rear edge of the bumper a little, then undo the bolt securing the bumper to the wing (see illustration).
10 Open the bonnet, undo the three screws and remove the radiator grille.
11 Undo the three screws and prise out the clips in the radiator grille aperture securing the front panel to the bumper (see illustration 6.2a).
12 Pull the rear edges of the bumper outwards a little, and with the help of an assistant, pull the bumper forwards away from the vehicle. Disconnect any wiring plugs as the bumper is withdrawn.

Refitting

13 Refitting is a reverse of the removal procedure, ensuring that the bumper mounting screws are securely tightened.

7 Rear bumper – removal and refitting

Removal

Saloon models

1 No information was available at the time of writing.

Hatchback and Liftback models

2 Open the tailgate, and undo the two plastic nuts securing the sill trim panel. Remove the trim panel.
3 Pull the trim panels behind the rear lights forward, then undo the four nuts securing the bumper to the rear panel (see illustration).
4 Undo the two screws and remove the mudflaps from both sides, then undo the screw

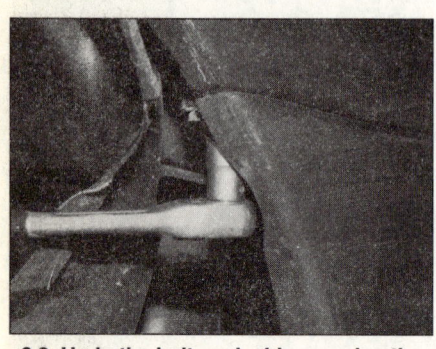

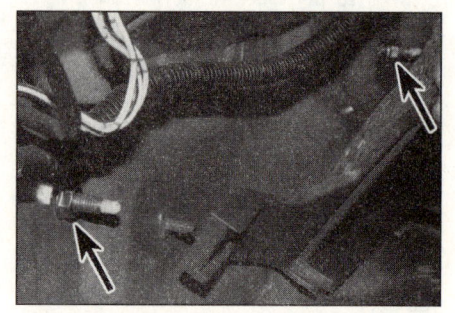

6.9 Undo the bolt each side securing the bumper to the wing

7.3 Pull the panel behind the rear lights forwards and undo the bumper mounting nuts (two right-hand side nuts arrowed)

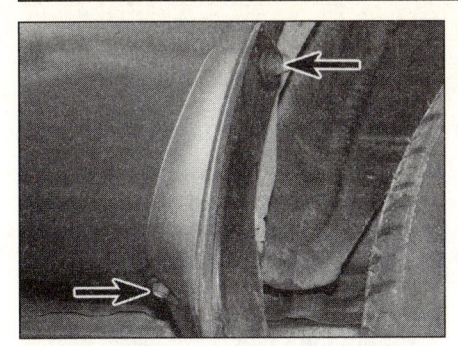

Bodywork and fittings 11•5

7.4a Undo the two screws (arrowed) and remove the mudflap each side . . .

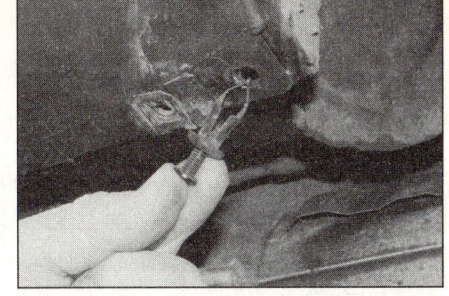

7.4b . . . then undo the screw, and prise out the clip at the lower edge of the bumper

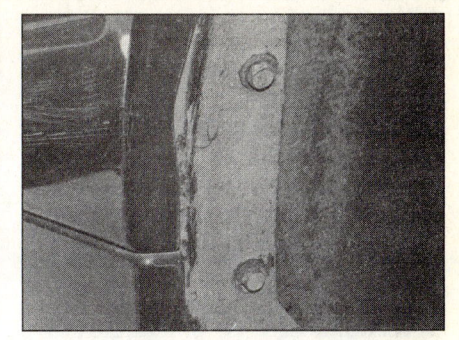

7.5 Undo the screws and pull the insert away from the bumper

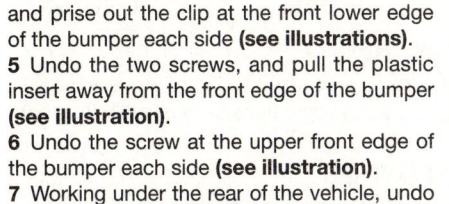

and prise out the clip at the front lower edge of the bumper each side **(see illustrations)**.

5 Undo the two screws, and pull the plastic insert away from the front edge of the bumper **(see illustration)**.

6 Undo the screw at the upper front edge of the bumper each side **(see illustration)**.

7 Working under the rear of the vehicle, undo the screws and prise out the two clips on the bumper cover underside **(see illustration)**.

8 With the help of an assistant, slide the bumper to the rear. On models with parking distance sensors, disconnect the wiring plugs as the bumper is withdrawn.

Estate models

9 No information was available at the time or writing.

Refitting

10 Refitting is a reverse of the removal procedure, ensuring that the mounting bolts/nuts are tightened securely.

8 Bonnet – removal, refitting and adjustment

Bonnet

Note: *The bonnet is heavy and somewhat awkward to remove and refit – at least two people should perform this procedure.*

Removal and refitting

1 Make marks around the bolt heads to

7.6 Undo the screw each side (arrowed) at the front, upper edge of the bumper

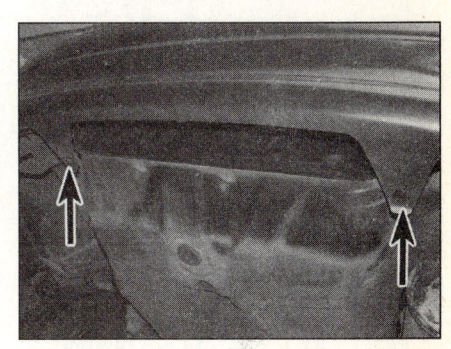

ensure proper alignment during refitting **(see illustration)**.

2 Use blankets or pads to cover the scuttle area of the body and wings. This will protect the body and paint as the bonnet is lifted off.

3 Disconnect any cables or wires that will interfere with removal.

4 Have an assistant support the bonnet. Remove the hinge-to-bonnet bolts.

5 Lift off the bonnet.

6 Refitting is the reverse of removal.

Adjustment

7 Fore-and-aft and side-to-side adjustment of the bonnet is done by moving the hinge plate slot after loosening the bolts.

8 Scribe a line around the entire hinge plate so you can judge the amount of movement **(see illustration 8.1)**

9 Loosen the bolts or nuts and move the bonnet into correct alignment. Move it only

7.7 Undo the screws and prise out the clips (arrowed)

a little at a time. Tighten the hinge bolts and carefully lower the bonnet to check the position.

10 If necessary after refitting, the entire bonnet latch assembly can be adjusted up-and-down as well as from side-to-side on the radiator support so the bonnet closes securely, flush with the wings. To make the adjustment, scribe a line around the bonnet latch mounting bolts to provide a reference point, then loosen them and reposition the latch assembly, as necessary **(see illustration)**. Following adjustment, retighten the mounting bolts.

11 Finally, adjust the bonnet bumpers on the radiator support so the bonnet, when closed, is flush with the wings **(see illustration)**.

12 The bonnet latch assembly, as well as the hinges, should be periodically lubricated with white, lithium-base grease to prevent binding and wear.

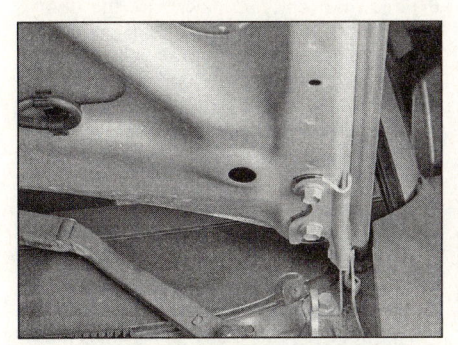

8.1 Before removing the bonnet, make marks around the hinge plate

8.10 Slacken the bolts, move the catch and retighten the bolts, then close the bonnet to check the fit

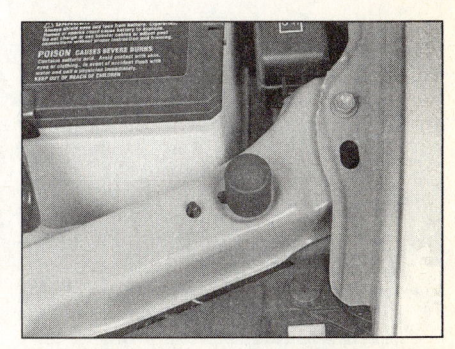

8.11 Adjust the bonnet height by screwing the bonnet bumpers in-or-out

11•6 Bodywork and fittings

9.6 Disconnect the bonnet release cable from the catch

9 Bonnet release cable – removal and refitting

Removal

1 The one-piece bonnet release cable connects the release handle under the driver's side of the facia, to the release mechanism in the centre of the bonnet slam panel.
2 Pull the release handle to open the bonnet, then disengage the outer cable and cable end fitting from the handle **(see illustration 27.51)**.
3 Remove the driver's side lower facia panel as described in Section 27.
4 Undo the three screws and remove the radiator grille **(see illustration 11.1)**.
5 Make alignment marks around the bonnet lock to aid refitting, then undo the two retaining screws **(see illustration 8.10)**.

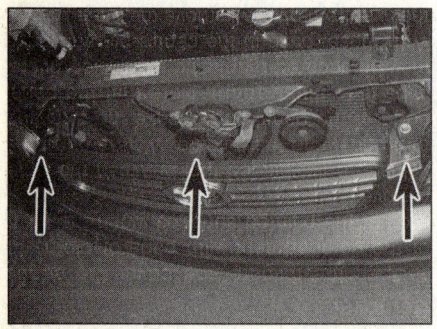

11.1 Undo the three screws (arrowed)

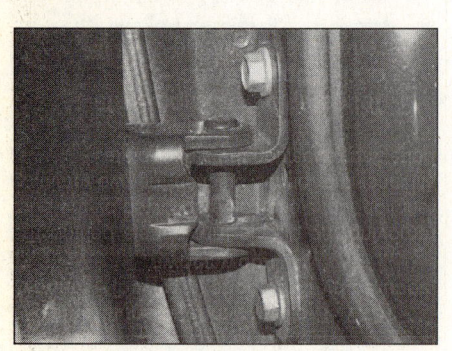

12.5 Draw around the hinge plate before slackening the retaining bolts

6 Disconnect the outer cable and end fitting from the bonnet lock **(see illustration)**.
7 Release the cable from any retaining clips along its length.
8 Tie a length of string to the end of the cable in the engine compartment, then carefully pull the cable through into the passenger compartment. Untie the string from the end of the cable, and leave it in position to aid refitting.

Refitting

9 Locate the cable in position in the passenger compartment.
10 Tie the end of the new cable to the string, and pull it through into the engine compartment. You may have to guide the cable through the grommet at the bulkhead.
11 Check that the cable is correctly routed, then secure it in place with the retaining clips. Untie the string.
12 Reconnect the cable to the bonnet lock, then refit the lock using the previously-made alignment marks.
13 Refit the radiator grille.
14 Refit the facia lower panel, and reconnect the cable to the release lever. Check that the bonnet lock operates correctly before closing the bonnet.

10 Bonnet lock – removal and refitting

Removal

1 Remove the radiator grille (see Section 11).

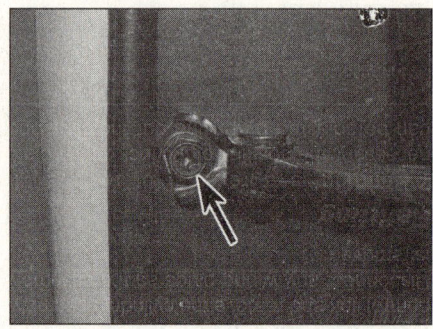

12.3 Undo the check strap bolt (arrowed)

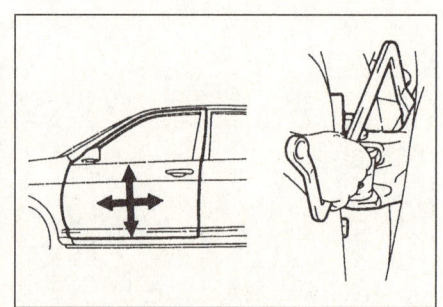

12.6a When adjusting the door up-and-down, or forward-and-backward, a special spanner such as this one will make the job easier

2 Make alignment marks around the bonnet lock to aid refitting, then undo the two retaining screws **(see illustration 8.10)**.
3 Disengage the outer cable and end fitting from the lock **(see illustration 9.6)**.

Refitting

4 Refitting is a reversal of removal, using the alignment marks. Check that the mechanism functions correctly before closing the bonnet.

11 Radiator grille – removal and refitting

Removal

1 Open the bonnet, and undo the three screws at the top edge of the grille **(see illustration)**.
2 Lift the grille from position.

Refitting

3 Refitting is a reversal of removal.

12 Door – removal, refitting and adjustment

Removal and installation

1 Remove the door trim panel (see Section 13). Disconnect any electrical connectors and push them through the door opening so they won't interfere with removal.
2 Position a jack or axle stand under the door or have an assistant on hand to support the door when the hinge bolts are removed. **Note:** *If a jack or stand is used, place a rag between it and the door to protect the door's paint.*
3 Remove the door check strap bolt **(see illustration)**.
4 Scribe around the door bolts to aid refitting.
5 Remove the hinge-to-door bolts and carefully detach the door **(see illustration)**. Refitting is the reverse of removal.

Adjustment

6 Following refitting, make sure the door is aligned properly. Adjust it if necessary as follows:
a) Up-and-down and forward-and-backward adjustments are made by loosening the hinge-to-body bolts and moving the door as necessary. A special offset tool may be required to reach some of the bolts **(see illustration)**.
b) In-and-out and up-and-down adjustments are made by loosening the door side hinge bolts and moving the door as necessary. A special offset tool may be required to reach some of the bolts **(see illustration)**.
c) The door lock striker can also be adjusted

Bodywork and fittings 11•7

both up-and-down and sideways to provide a positive engagement with the locking mechanism. This is done by loosening the screws and moving the striker as necessary (see illustration).

13 Door inner trim panel – removal and refitting

Removal – front door

Hatchback models

1 On manual window regulator-equipped models, remove the window crank by working a cloth back-and-forth behind the handle to dislodge the retaining clip (see illustration). A special tool is available for this purpose but it's not essential. With the retaining clip released, pull off the handle, and recover the plastic washer behind the handle. On power window models, pry out the switch assembly, unplug the electrical connector and remove it (see illustration).

2 Prise open the plastic cap, undo the screw securing the interior release handle surround trim, then use a flat-bladed screwdriver to lever the trim rearwards and carefully prise the trim from place (see illustrations).

3 Carefully prise the outside mirror inner trim from place (see illustration).

4 Undo the two screws securing the door pull handle. The rearmost screw is accessed after prising open the flap – open the flap and undo the screws (see illustrations).

5 The panel is now secured by three expanding plastic clips and 6 panel clips. Push in the centre pins and prise out the expanding clips, then insert a flat-bladed tool between the trim panel and the door to disengage the panel clips. Work around the outer edge of the door until the panel is free.

6 Once all of the clips are disengaged, detach the trim panel, unplug any electrical connectors and remove the trim panel from the vehicle by gently pulling it up and out.

7 For access to the inner door remove the plastic weathershield. Peel back the plastic cover, taking care not to tear it (see illustration 13.14).

All models except Hatchback

8 Remove the window regulator handle or power window switch as described in paragraph 1.

9 Undo the screw securing the interior release handle surround trim, then slide the trim

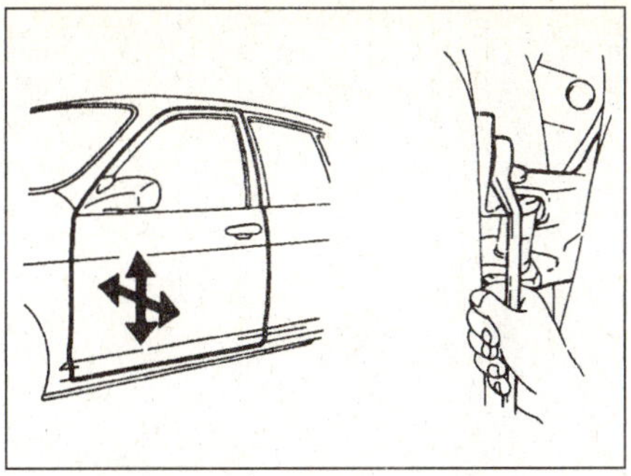

12.6b Adjust the door up-and-down or in-and-out after slackening the hinge-to-door bolts

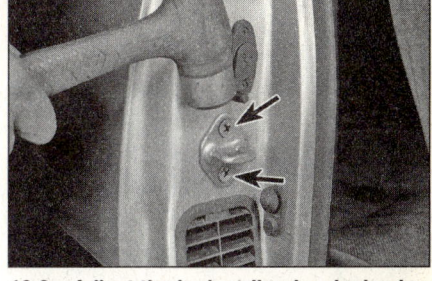

12.6c Adjust the lock striker by slackening the mounting screws (arrowed) and tapping the striker

forwards to remove it (see illustration). Release the link rod and remove the handle assembly.

10 Carefully prise the outside mirror inner trim from place (see illustration 13.3).

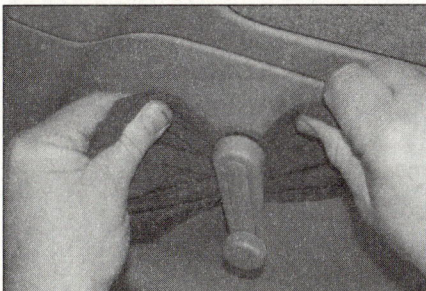

13.1a Work a cloth backwards-and-forwards behind the handle to dislodge the retaining clip

13.1b Prise the power window switch from the door trim

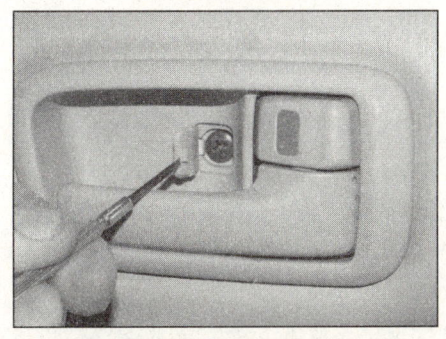

13.2a Open the cap and undo the screw . . .

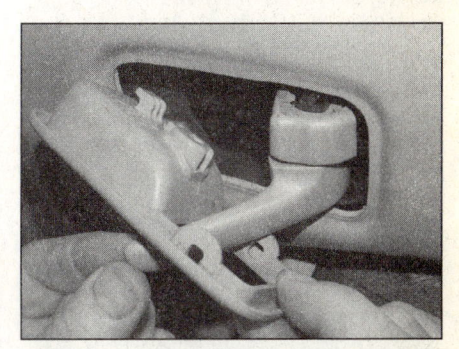

13.2b . . . then slide the handle surround rearwards to remove it

13.3 Prise off the mirror trim

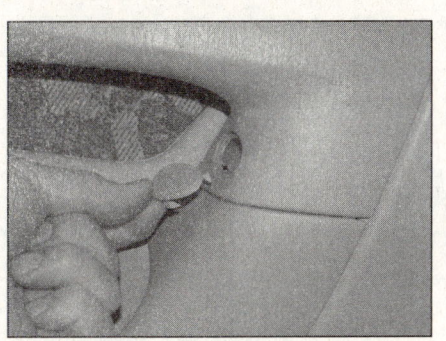

13.4a Prise open the flap . . .

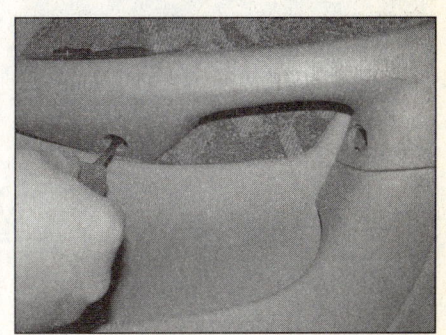

13.4b . . . and remove the door trim screws

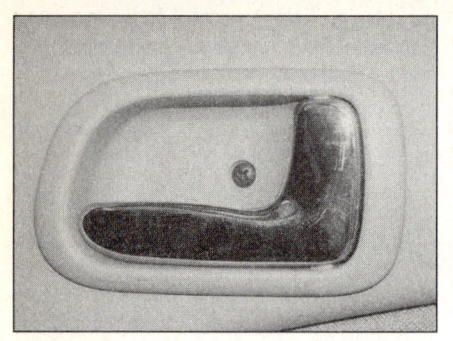

11•8 Bodywork and fittings

13.9 Undo the screw in the interior hand recess

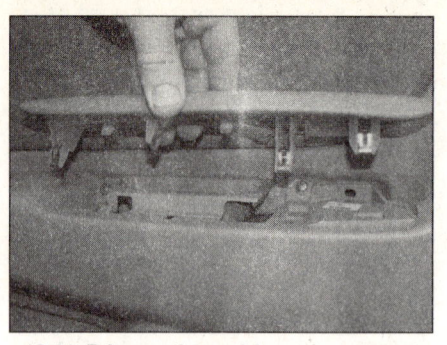

13.11 Prise up the pad from the armrest

11 Carefully prise up the armrest with a screwdriver (see illustration).
12 The inner trim panel is now secured by two screws in the armrest recess, one or two expanding plastic clips (depending on trim level), and 6 panel clips. Undo the screws, push in the centre pins and prise out the expanding clips, then insert a flat-bladed tool between the trim panel and the door to disengage the panel clips. Work around the outer edge of the door until the panel is free (see illustrations).
13 Once all of the clips are disengaged, detach the trim panel, unplug any electrical connectors and remove the trim panel from the vehicle by gently pulling it up and over the lock button (see illustration).
14 For access to the inner door remove the plastic weathershield. Peel back the plastic cover, taking care not to tear it (see illustration).

Removal – rear door

15 Remove the window winder handle or power window switch as described in paragraph 1.
16 Undo the screw and remove the door inner release handle surround trim (see illustration 13.9). Disconnect the link rod as the handle is removed.
17 Carefully prise up the armrest with a screwdriver (see illustration).
18 Undo the two screws in the armrest recess.
19 The inner trim panel is secured by panel clips around the edge of the door. Insert a flat-bladed tool between the door and the panel to disengage the clips. Work around the edge of the door until the panel is free. Note that on some models, a plastic expanding clip may be fitted at the rear edge of the trim. Unscrew the centre pin, and prise out the clip (see illustration).

20 Once all of the clips are disengaged, detach the trim panel, unplug any electrical connectors and remove the trim panel from the vehicle by gently pulling it up and over the lock button.
21 For access to the inner door remove the plastic weathershield. Peel back the plastic cover, taking care not to tear it (see illustration 13.14).

Refitting

22 To refit the trim panel, first press the weathershield back into place. If necessary, add more sealant to hold it in place.
23 Prior to refitment of the door panel, be sure to refit any clips in the panel which may have come out during the removal procedure and stayed in the door.
24 Plug in any electrical connectors and place the panel in position. Press it into place until the clips are seated and install any retaining screws and armrest/door pulls. Refit the manual regulator window handle or power switch assembly.

14 Door handle and lock components – removal and refitting

1 Remove the door trim panel and the plastic weathershield (Section 13).

Door latch

Removal

2 Undo the bolt and remove the window guide from rear of the door (see illustrations).

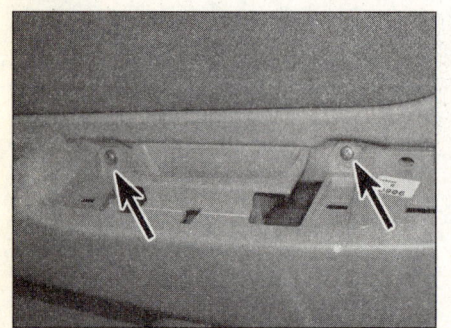

13.12a Undo the two screws in the armrest (arrowed)

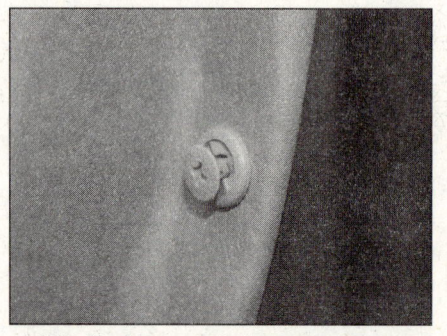

13.12b On this type of clip, undo the screw and prise the rest of the clip from place

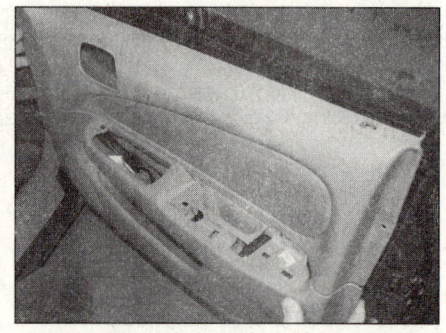

13.13 With all the clips released, lift the trim panel upwards to remove it

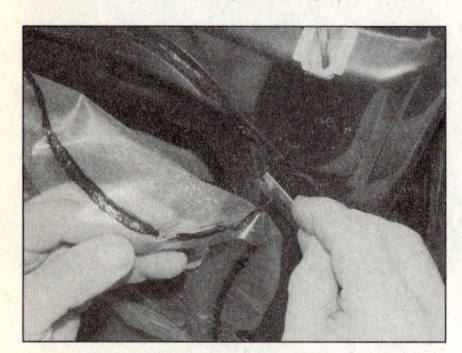

13.14 Carefully cut through the sealant securing the plastic weathershield

13.17 Prise up the armrest pad and undo the two screws (arrowed)

13.19 Unscrew the centre pin and prise the clip out (arrowed)

Bodywork and fittings 11•9

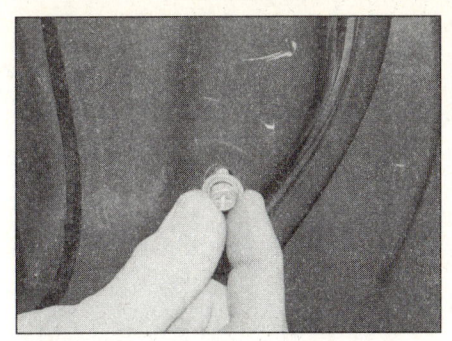

14.2a Undo the window guide screw . . .

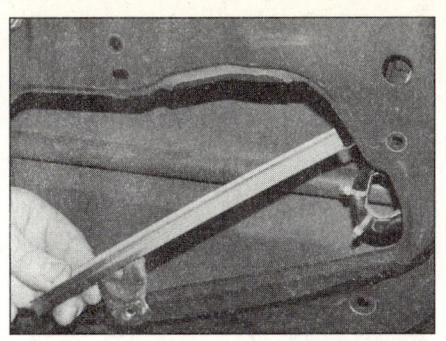

14.2b . . . and lift out the window guide

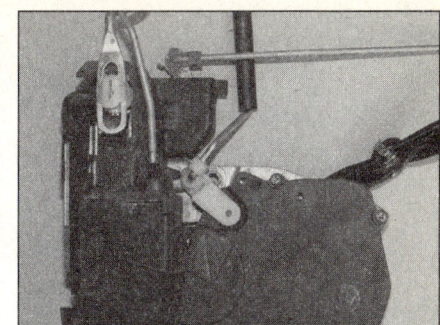

14.3 Front door latch control rods

14.4a Undo the three latch screws

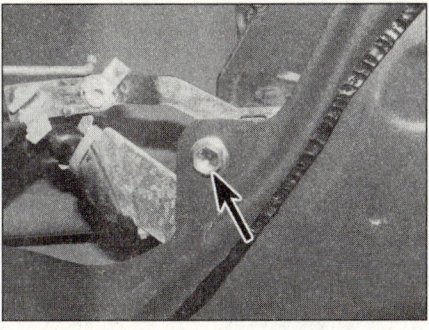

14.4b On rear doors, the latch is secured by an additional bolt (arrowed)

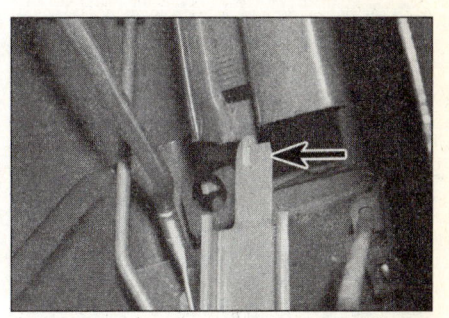

14.6 Note how the lug (arrowed) at the top rear window guide engages with the fixed guide

On rear doors, remove the guide as described in Section 15, paragraphs 10 and 11.

3 Reach behind the inside the door panel and disconnect the control links from the latch, outside handle and lock cylinder **(see illustration)**. To disconnect the lock cylinder rod on some models, it will be necessary to undo the nut and remove the metal cover from the rear of the lock cylinder **(see illustration 14.7)**.

4 Remove the latch retaining Torx screws from the end of the door **(see illustration)**. On rear doors, the latch is also secured by an additional bolt **(see illustration)**.

5 Detach the door latch and (if equipped) the door lock solenoid – disconnect the wiring plugs as the assembly is withdrawn.

Refitting

6 Refitting is the reverse of removal. Note the lug on the top of the front door rear window guide engages with the fixed window guide **(see illustration)**.

Lock cylinder and outside handle

Removal

7 Disconnect the control rods from the lock cylinder (front doors only) and outside handle. To disconnect the lock cylinder rod on some models, it will be necessary to undo the nut and remove the metal cover from the rear of the lock cylinder **(see illustration)**.

8 Remove the two outside handle retention bolts, then pull the handle from the door **(see illustrations)**. Note that on rear doors, it's necessary to remove the door latch to gain access to the outside handle rear mounting bolt.

9 Undo the stud, then remove the lock cylinder assembly from the handle assembly – front doors only.

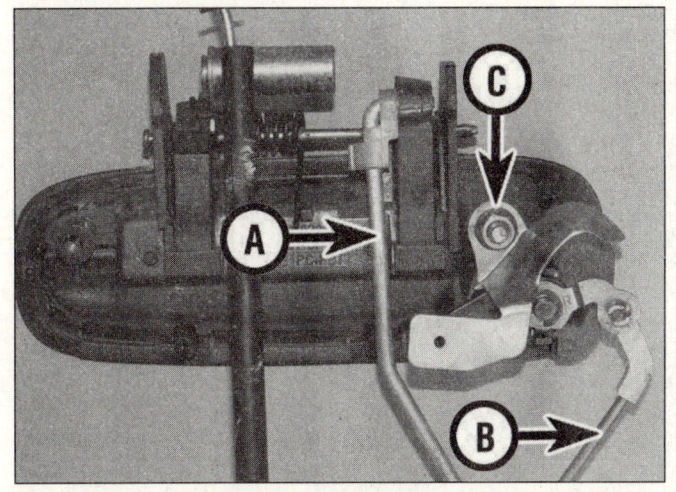

14.7 Exterior handle control rod (A), lock cylinder control rod (B) and metal cover retaining nut (C)

14.8a Exterior handle retaining bolts and lock cylinder stud (arrowed)

11•10 Bodywork and fittings

14.8b Remove the handle from the door

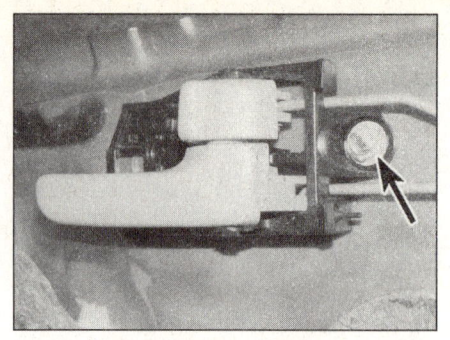

14.11 Undo the interior handle retaining bolt (arrowed)

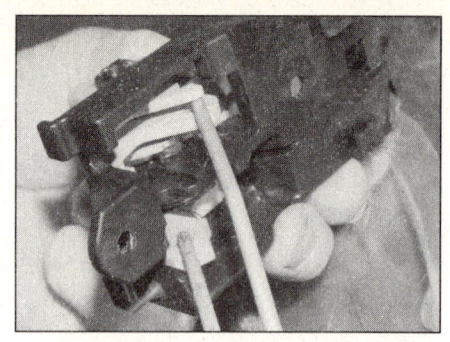

14.12 Disengage the link rods from the handle

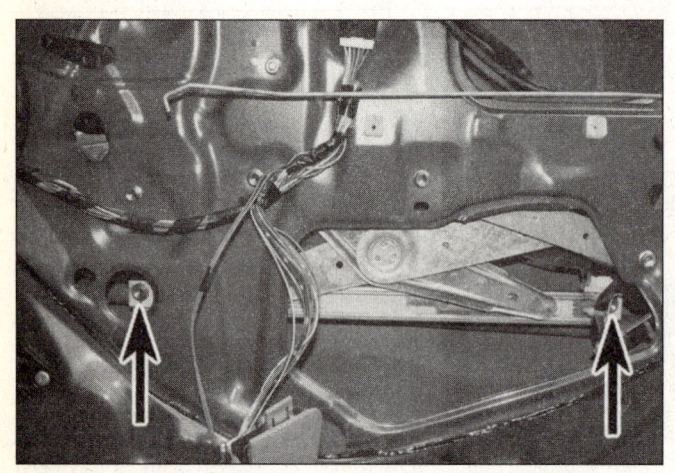

15.3 Undo the glass mounting bolts (arrowed)

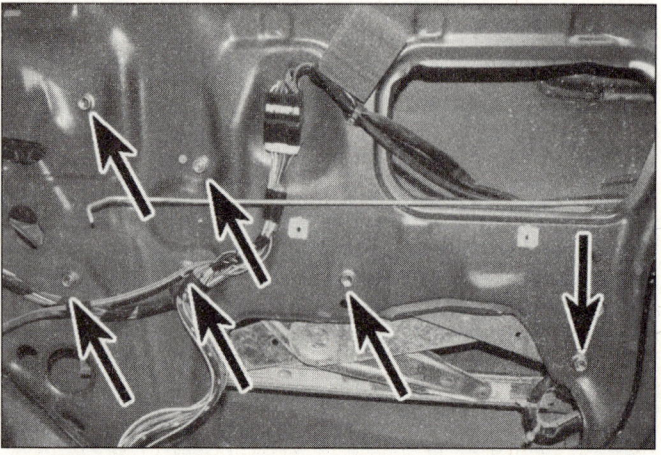

15.8 Window regulator bolts (arrowed – models with electric windows)

Refitting
10 Refitting is the reverse of removal.

Inside handle

Removal
Note: *On post-facelift models (after Oct '99), the handle is removed as part of the door inner trim panel removal procedure.*
11 Remove the retaining screw **(see illustration)**.
12 Pull the handle free, disconnect the link from the inside handle control and remove the handle from the door **(see illustration)**.

Refitting
13 Refitting is the reverse of removal.

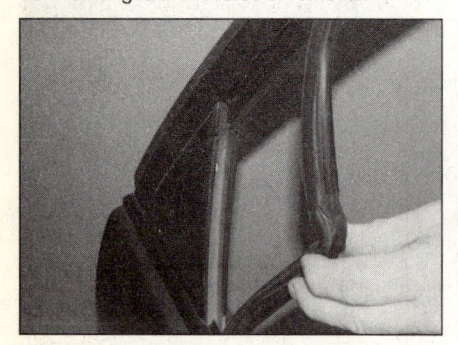

15.10 Prise out the window rubber guide from the door frame

15 Door glass and regulator
– removal and refitting

Removal

Front door window
1 Lower the window glass approximately 1/2 of full travel.
2 Remove the door trim panel and the plastic weathershield (Section 13).
3 Place a rag inside the door panel to help prevent scratching the glass and remove the two glass mounting bolts **(see illustration)**.

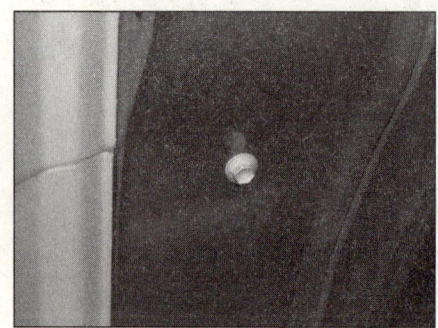

15.11a Undo the window guide lower screw . . .

4 Remove the glass by pulling it up.

Front door window regulator
5 Remove the door inner trim panel and the plastic weathershield (Section 13).
6 Undo the two bolts securing the window to the regulator, then lift the window upwards and secure it at the top of the door using tape **(see illustration 15.3)**.
7 Disconnect the window regulator wiring plug (where applicable).
8 The regulator is retained by 4 bolts and one nut (manual windows) or 5 bolts and one nut (power windows). Undo the bolts/nut and manoeuvre the regulator from the door **(see illustration)**.
9 Manoeuvre the regulator from the door. At the time of writing, it would appear that the electric motor is integral with the regulator, and must be renewed as an assembly. Check with your Toyota dealer or specialist.

Rear door window glass
10 Lower the window completely, then carefully prise out and remove the window rubber guide from the door frame **(see illustration)**.
11 Undo the screw securing the lower edge and the screw securing the upper edge of the rear window guide, and remove the guide **(see illustrations)**.
12 Undo the 2 or 3 screws (depending on model) and remove the rear triangular

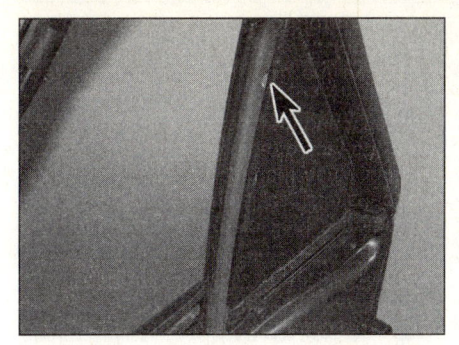

Bodywork and fittings 11•11

15.11b . . . and upper screw (arrowed)

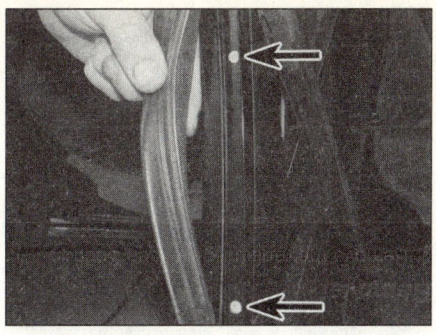

15.12a Pull away the door weatherstrip and undo the two trim retaining screws (arrowed)

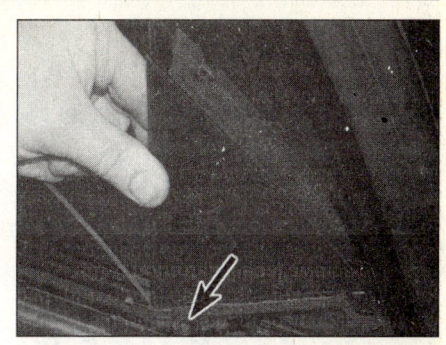

15.12b Lift away the triangular shaped trim. Note the trim retaining screw position on some models (arrowed)

guide trim and/or window guide **(see illustrations)**.

13 Manoeuvre the window sideways to disengage the lift channel at the base of the window from the regulator arm roller and remove it from the window **(see illustration)**.

Rear door fixed window glass

14 Remove the rear door window as previously described.
15 Pull the glass and weatherstrip from place.

Rear door window regulator

16 Remove the rear window as described in this Section.
17 Undo the bolts and remove the regulator assembly. On models with power windows, the regulator is secured by 4 bolts, and on models with manual windows, by three bolts **(see illustration)**. Disconnect the motor wiring plug as the assembly is withdrawn (where applicable).
18 At the time of writing, it would appear that the electric motor is integral with the regulator, and must be renewed as an assembly. Check with your Toyota dealer or specialist.

Refitting

19 Refitting is the reverse of removal, but prior to refitting the plastic weatherstrip, check the window operates smoothly.
20 After refitting the window, it may be necessary to manually operate the power window switch to fully close the window. This allows the system to 'learn' the fully-closed position.

16 Boot lid and lock components – removal and refitting

Removal

Boot lid

1 Open the boot, and paint alignment marks around the hinges on the underside of the boot lid.
2 Undo the four bolts and remove the boot lid.

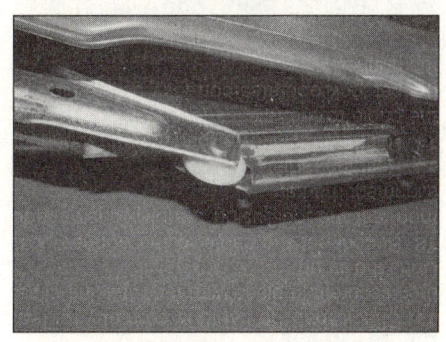

15.13 Disengage the window lift channel from the regulator arm roller

Boot lock

3 Release the clips and remove the boot lid trim panel.
4 Undo the two retaining bolts, disconnect the control link and remove the lock assembly. Disconnect any wiring plugs as the assembly is removed (where applicable).

Boot lock cylinder

5 Release the clips and remove the boot lid trim panel.
6 Undo the two retaining bolts, disconnect the control link and remove the cylinder assembly. Disconnect any wiring plugs as the assembly is removed.

Refitting

7 Refitting is a reversal of removal. If necessary, the position of the lock striker plate can be adjusted by prising out the clips and

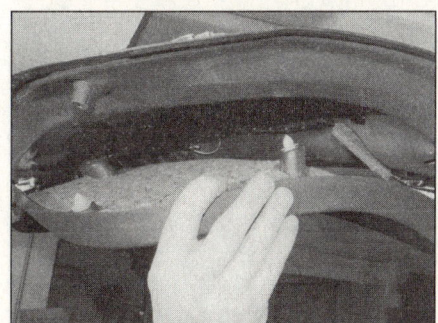

17.2 Work around the edge of the tailgate trim panel and release the clips

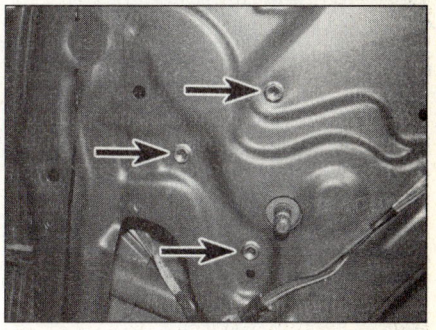

15.17 The rear window regulator is secured by three bolts (arrowed) – manual window shown

removing the plastic trim panels behind the rear light units each side, followed by the boot sill inner trim panel. Slacken the two retaining bolts and reposition the striker plate.

17 Tailgate, lock components and support struts – removal and refitting

Tailgate

Removal

1 Open the tailgate and cover the edges of the compartment with pads or cloths to protect the painted surfaces when the lid is removed.
2 Insert a flat-bladed tool between the inner trim panel and the tailgate. Work around the edge of the panel and release the retaining clips **(see illustration)**. Note that the panel may be secured by plastic expansion rivets. With these, push in the centre pin and prise the rivet from place. Remove the panel.
3 Disconnect any cables or wire harness connectors attached to the tailgate that would interfere with removal.
4 Use a marking pen to make alignment marks around the hinge mounting flanges.
5 Have an assistant support the tailgate and detach the support struts as described in this Section.
6 While an assistant supports the tailgate, remove the tailgate-to-hinge bolts on both sides and lift it off **(see illustration)**.

11•12 Bodywork and fittings

17.6 Tailgate hinge bolts

17.12 Tailgate lock screws

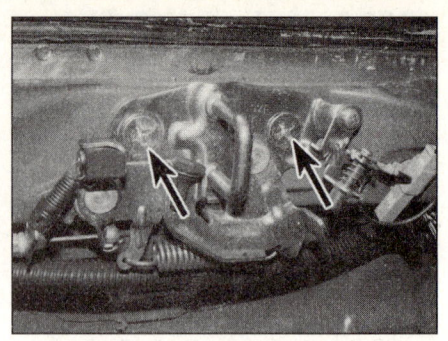

17.14 Undo the tailgate lock striker screws (arrowed)

Refitting and adjustment

7 Refitting is the reverse of removal. **Note:** When refitting the tailgate, align the hinges with the marks made during removal.
8 After refitting, close the tailgate and make sure it's in proper alignment with the surrounding panels.
9 Adjustments to the tailgate position are made by loosening the hinge to tailgate bolts or nuts and gently moving the tailgate into correct alignment.
10 The tailgate latch position can be adjusted by loosening the adjusting bolts and moving the latch. The latch striker can be adjusted by loosening the mounting screws and gently tapping it into position with a plastic hammer.

Tailgate lock

Hatchback and Liftback models

11 Remove the tailgate inner trim panel as described in paragraph 2.

17.18 Undo the three screws and remove the lock cylinder bracket

12 Undo the three retaining screws, disconnect the control link and remove the lock (see illustration). Disconnect any wiring plugs as the lock is withdrawn (where applicable).
13 To remove the tailgate lock striker, open the tailgate, undo the two plastic nuts and remove the sill trim panel.
14 Make alignment marks around the striker plate, then undo the two screws and remove the striker. Disconnect the release cable as the striker is withdrawn (see illustration).
15 Refitting is a reversal of removal.

Estate models

16 No information was available at the time of writing.

Tailgate lock cylinder

Hatchback andLiftback models

17 Remove the tailgate inner trim panel as described in paragraph 2.

17.19 Slide up the clip (arrowed) and remove the lock cylinder

18 Disconnect the control link from the cylinder operating arm, then undo the three screws and remove the lock cylinder bracket (see illustration).
19 Slide up the retaining clip, and remove the lock cylinder from the tailgate (see illustration).
20 Refitting is a reversal of removal.

Estate models

21 No information was available at the time of writing.

Tailgate lock control

Estate models

22 No information was available at the time of writing.

Tailgate support struts

⚠️ **Warning:** The support strut is filled with pressurised gas – do not disassemble this component. If it is faulty renew it with a new one.

Note: The rear tailgate is heavy and somewhat awkward to hold securely while renewing the struts – at least two people should perform this procedure.
23 Open the tailgate and support it in the open position. On single headlight models, undo the bolts holding the bracket at the lower end of the strut, and undo the stud at the top. On twin headlight models, prise out the retaining clips and pull the struts from the mounting studs (see illustrations).
24 Installation is the reverse of the removal procedure.

18 Central locking components – removal and refitting

Note: The central locking system is equipped with a sophisticated self-diagnosis capability. Before removing any of the central locking components, have the system interrogated by a Toyota dealer or suitably-equipped specialist, to pinpoint the fault.

Removal

Electronic control unit (ECU)

1 The central locking system is controlled by an ECU, which is located behind the driver's

17.23a Undo the bolts and remove the tailgate strut – single headlight models

17.23b Prise and the clip and remove the tailgate strut – twin headlight models

Bodywork and fittings 11•13

side lower facia panel. To access the control unit, remove the facia panel as described in Section 27.
2 Release the retaining clips and lower the ECU out of position.
3 Disconnect the wiring connector(s) and remove the ECU from the vehicle (see illustration). Note: *If the control unit is renewed, it may need to be programmed before use. Entrust this task to a Toyota dealer or specialist.*

Door lock actuator
4 Remove the door lock as described in Section 14. The central locking actuator is integral with the door lock assembly.

Boot lock actuator
5 Remove the boot lock as described in Section 16. The actuator is integral with the boot lock assembly.

Tailgate lock actuator
6 Refer to Section 17.

Refitting
7 Refitting is the reverse of removal. Prior to refitting any trim panels removed for access thoroughly check the operation of the central locking system.

19 Electric window components – removal and refitting

Window switches
1 Refer to Chapter 12, Section 4.

Window motors
2 At the time of writing, it would appear that the electric motor is integral with the regulator (see Section 15), and must be renewed as an assembly. Check with your Toyota dealer or specialist.

20 Mirrors and associated components – removal and refitting

Exterior mirror assembly
1 On models with manually adjustable mirrors, carefully prise off the triangular plastic trim panel over the mirror mounting.
2 On models with electrically adjustable mirrors, remove the door inner trim panel as described in Section 13, then disconnect the mirror wiring plug.
3 On all models, undo the three mounting nuts and remove the mirror assembly (see illustration).
4 Refitting is the reverse of removal, tightening the mirror nuts securely.

Exterior mirror glass
5 Slide the mirror glass a little to the outside, then pull the outer edge rearwards, and remove it (see illustration).
6 Disconnect the mirror heater wiring plugs (where applicable) as the mirror is withdrawn.
7 Refitting is a reversal of removal.

Exterior mirror switch
8 Refer to Chapter 12, Section 4.

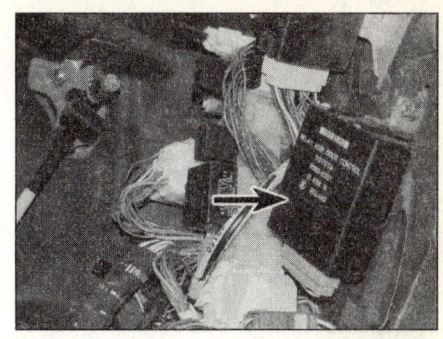

18.3 Door lock control relay/unit (arrowed)

Exterior mirror motor
9 Remove the mirror glass as previously described.
10 Undo the three screws, and remove the motor (see illustration). Note that it is necessary to cut the wires to the mirror motor as the plug is too large to pass through the cable guide. When refitting the motor, splice the new wires to the plug.
11 Refitting is a reversal of removal.

Interior mirror

Single headlight models
12 Prise away the plastic cap, and undo the two mounting screws (see illustration).
13 If required, rotate the mirror 180° and undo the clamp screw to separate the mirror from the mounting (see illustration).
14 Refitting is a reversal of removal.

Twin headlight models
15 Carefully slide the mirror upwards from its mounting.
16 Refitting is a reversal of removal.

21 Windscreen, fixed windows and rear screen/tailgate glass – general information

1 These areas of glass are secured by the tight fit of the weatherstrip in the body aperture, and are bonded in position with a special adhesive. Renewal of such fixed glass is a difficult, messy and time-consuming task, which is beyond the scope of the home mechanic. It is difficult, unless one has plenty

20.3 Undo the three mounting nuts and remove the mirror assembly

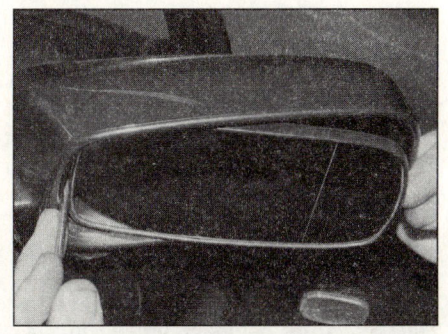

20.5 Slide the mirror glass to the outside, then pull it rearwards

20.10 Undo the three screws (arrowed) and remove the mirror motor

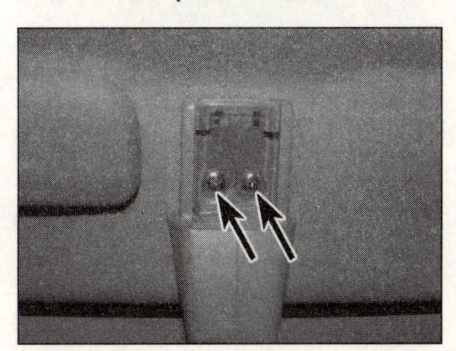

20.12 Prise off the plastic cap and undo the mirror mounting screws (arrowed)

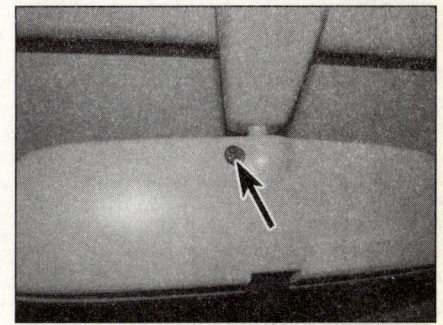

20.13 Undo the screw (arrowed) and pull the mirror from the mounting

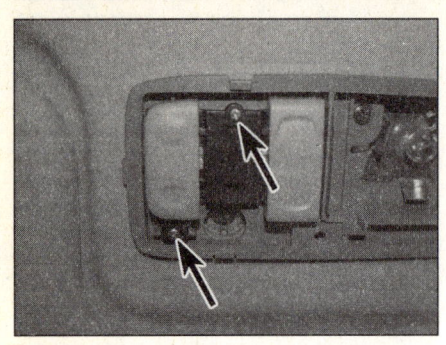

11•14 Bodywork and fittings

22.4 Sunroof switch retaining screws (arrowed)

of practice, to obtain a secure, waterproof fit. Furthermore, the task carries a high risk of breakage; this applies especially to the laminated glass windscreen. In view of this, owners are strongly advised to have this sort of work carried out by one of the many specialist windscreen fitters.

22 Sunroof – general information and motor renewal

General information

1 Due to the complexity of the sunroof mechanism, considerable expertise is needed to repair, renew or adjust the sunroof components successfully. Removal of the roof first requires the headlining to be removed, which is a complex and tedious operation, and not a task to be undertaken lightly. Therefore, any problems with the sunroof (except sunroof motor renewal) should be referred to a Toyota dealer or specialist.

Renewal

Motor

2 Motor renewal required the front section of the headlining to be lowered (See paragraph 1). Once the headlining has been lowered, disconnect the wiring plug, undo the three retaining bolts, and remove the motor complete with relay. Once removed, do not attempt to rotate the motor spindle.
3 Refitting is a reversal of removal.

Switch

4 Remove the interior light lens as described in Chapter 12, Section 8, then undo the two switch retaining screws, disconnect the wiring plug and remove the switch **(see illustration)**.
5 Refitting is a reversal of removal.

23 Body exterior fittings – removal and refitting

Wheel arch liners and body under-panels

1 The various plastic covers fitted to the underside of the vehicle are secured in position by a mixture of screws, nuts and retaining clips, and removal will be fairly obvious on inspection. Work methodically around, removing its retaining screws and releasing its retaining clips until the panel is free and can be removed from the underside of the vehicle. Most clips used on the vehicle are simply prised out of position. Other clips can be released by unscrewing/prising out the centre pins and then removing the clip.

Body trim strips and badges

2 The various body trim strips and badges are held in position with a special adhesive tape. Removal requires the trim/badge to be heated, to soften the adhesive, and then cut away from the surface. Due to the high risk of damage to the vehicle's paintwork during this operation, it is recommended that this task should be entrusted to a Toyota dealer or suitably-equipped specialist.

24 Seats – removal and refitting

Front seat removal

⚠️ **Warning: The front seats may be fitted with side airbags. If they are, disconnect the battery negative lead (Chapter 5A), then wait at least 5 minutes before commencing work on any aspect of the seat.**

1 Slide the seat fully forwards and prise up the plastic covers over the seat rails rear mounting bolts. Undo the bolts **(see illustration)**.
2 Slide the seat fully rearwards, and prise up the plastic covers (where fitted) over the seat rails front mounting bolts. Undo the bolts.
3 Tip the seat rearwards a little, then disconnect any wiring plug(s) and remove the seat from the passenger cabin.

Folding rear seat removal

Saloon

4 Pull up on the front of the seat cushion to release the left- and right-hand retaining clips, and remove it forwards and out from the vehicle.
5 Fold the seat backrests forwards, and undo the two bolts securing the outer seat hinges to the vehicle body.
6 Undo the two bolts at the seat's centre hinge and remove the seat assembly from the passenger cabin.

Hatchback, Liftback and Estate

7 Fold the seat cushion forwards, then undo the bolt each side at the front securing the seat cushion to the vehicle body. Lift the front of the cushion and remove it from the cabin **(see illustration)**.
8 Undo the centre seat belt anchorage point on the vehicle floor.
9 Fold the seat backrests forwards, and undo the bolt each side securing the seat to the hinges, and remove the seat backrest **(see illustration)**.

Fixed rear seat removal

10 Pull up on the seat base cushion to release the left- and right-hand retaining clips and remove it from the vehicle. Pull the centre headrest from place.
11 Undo the screw each side at the lower, outer edge of the seat back, and the one at the lower centre edge of the seat back, then unclip the top of the seat back then slide it upwards to release its lower retaining pins. Remove it from the vehicle.

Front seat refitting

12 Refitting is the reverse of removal, noting the following points.
a) Fit the seat retaining bolts and tighten them by hand only. Slide the seat fully

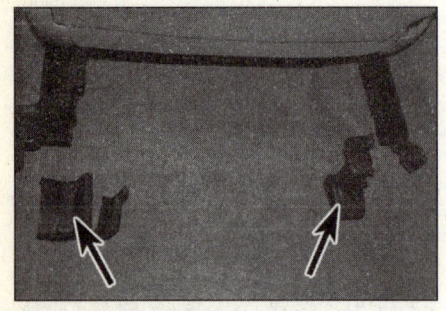

24.1 Prise off the plastic covers (arrowed) and undo the front seat rail rear mounting bolts

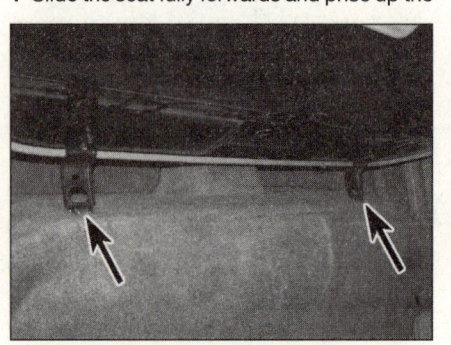

24.7 Fold the seat cushion forwards, and undo the retaining bolts (arrowed)

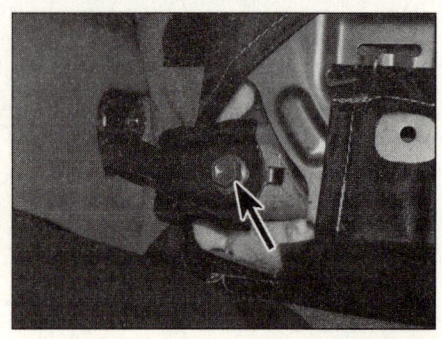

24.9 Seat backrest outer hinge retaining bolt (arrowed)

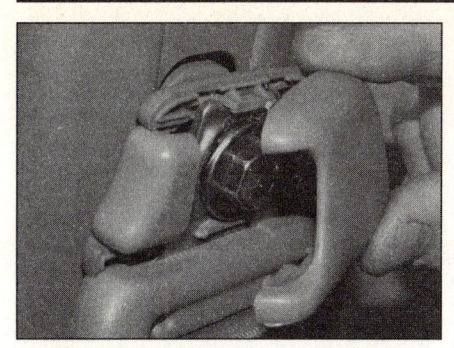

Bodywork and fittings 11•15

26.3 Prise off the cap and undo the seat belt upper anchorage bolt

26.4 Undo the four nuts and remove the metal shield over the B-pillar

26.5 Prise out the locking clip and disconnect the inertia reel wiring plug

forwards and then slide it back by two stops of the seat locking mechanism. Rock the seat to ensure that the seat locking mechanism is correctly engaged then tighten the mounting bolts to the specified torque.
b) Ensure that the wiring is connected and correctly routed.

Folding rear seats refitting

13 Refitting is a reversal of removal.

Fixed rear seat refitting

14 Refitting is the reverse of removal, making sure the seat back lower locating pegs are correctly engaged with the body, and the seat belt buckles and lap belt are fed through the intended openings.

25 Front seat belt tensioning mechanism – general information

1 Most models are fitted with a front seat belt tensioner system. The system is designed to instantaneously take up any slack in the seat belt in the case of a sudden frontal impact, therefore reducing the possibility of injury to the front seat occupants. The tensioner is incorporated into the design of the inertia reels, located behind the B-pillar lower trim panels.
2 The seat belt tensioner is triggered by a frontal impact above a predetermined force. Lesser impacts, including impacts from behind, will not trigger the system.
3 When the system is triggered, a pyrotechnic device causes the inertia reel to retract. This prevents the seat belt moving and keeps the occupant in position in the seat. Once the tensioner has been triggered, the seat belt will be permanently locked and the assembly must be renewed.
4 There is a risk of injury if the system is triggered inadvertently when working on the vehicle. If any work is to be carried out on the seat belt disable, the tensioner by disconnecting the battery negative lead (see Chapter 5A), and waiting at least 5 minutes before proceeding.
5 Also note the following warnings before contemplating any work on the front seat belt inertia reel.

26 Seat belt components – removal and refitting

Warning: Read Section 25 before proceeding.

Removal – front seat belts

1 Remove the front seat as described in Section 24.
2 Remove the front door sill trim panel and the lower B-pillar trim panel (5-door Hatchback, Liftback, Saloon and Estate models) or B/C pillar trim (3-door Hatchback models) as described in Section 27.
3 Prise off the cap, and undo the bolt securing the front seat belt upper anchorage to the vehicle body (see illustration).
4 Undo the four nuts and remove the metal shield from the B-pillar (see illustration).
5 Release the catch and disconnect the wiring plug from the inertia reel (where fitted) (see illustration).
6 Unscrew the inertia reel retaining bolt(s) and

Warning: If the tensioner mechanism is dropped, it must be renewed, even it has suffered no apparent damage.
• Do not allow any solvents to come into contact with the tensioner mechanism.
• Do not subject the inertia reel to any form of shock as this could accidentally trigger the seat belt tensioner.

remove the seat belt from the door pillar (see illustrations).
7 On single headlight models undo the screws and remove the lower seat belt mounting rail.
8 On twin headlight models prise off the plastic cap, then undo the bolt securing the lower seat belt anchorage.

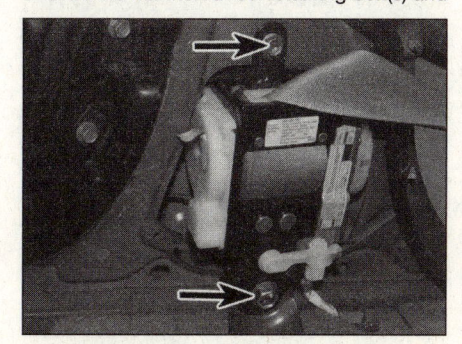

Removal – rear seat belts

Fixed rear seat

9 Remove the rear seat as described in Section 24.
10 Remove the parcel shelf and C-pillar trims as described in Section 27.
11 Slacken and remove the bolts and washers securing the rear seat belts to the vehicle body and remove the centre belt and buckle.
12 Unscrew the inertia reel retaining bolt and remove the seat belt(s).

Folding rear seat side belts

13 Fold the rear seats forward.
14 Remove the rear parcel shelf.
15 Remove the C-pillar trim as described in Section 27.
16 Slacken and remove the bolt securing the lower end of the belt to the body (if not already done) (see illustration).
17 Undo the upper seat belt anchorage bolt (see illustrations)
18 The inertia reel is secured by one bolt. Slacken and remove the bolt and washer (see illustration).
19 Manoeuvre the assembly from the vehicle, feeding the belt through the slot in the trim panel.

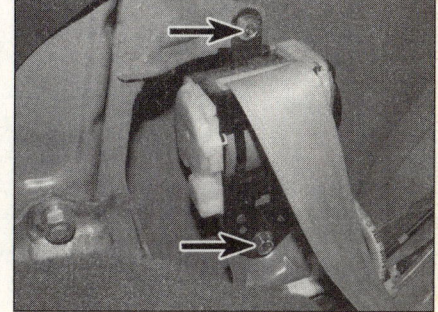

26.6a Inertia reel retaining bolts – 4/5-door models (arrowed)

26.6b Inertia reel retaining bolts – 3-door models (arrowed)

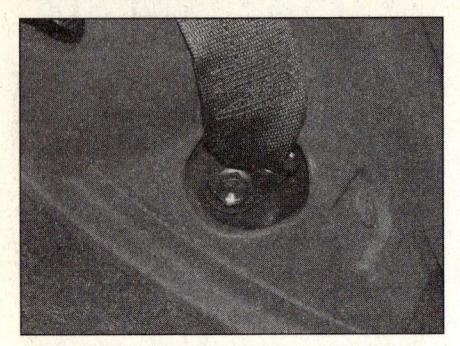

11•16 Bodywork and fittings

26.16 Rear side seat belt lower anchorage point

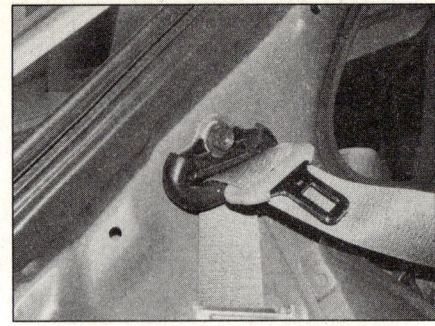

26.17a Rear side seat belt upper anchorage point – 4/5-door models

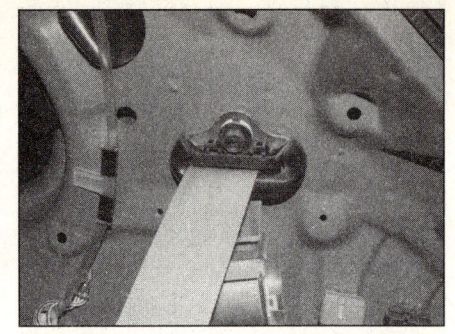

26.17b Rear side seat belt upper anchorage point – 3-door models

26.18 Rear side seat belt inertia reel bolt (arrowed)

26.21 Centre seat belt lower anchorage point

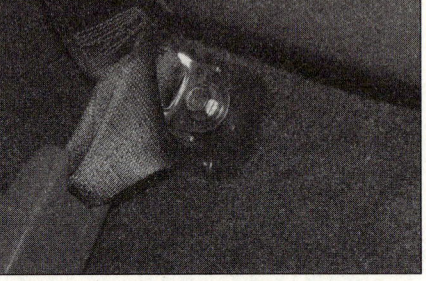

26.22 Undo the four screws and remove the cover over the centre inertia reel

Rear centre belt

20 Remove the rear seat cushion as described in Section 24.
21 Undo the bolts securing the seat belt anchorage to the floor. Note the positions of any washers/spacers fitted **(see illustration)**.
22 Fold the seat backrest forward, unclip the fabric cover, and undo the four screws securing the cover over the inertia reel **(see illustration)**.
23 Undo the nut and pull the inertia reel from position **(see illustration)**.
24 Prise up the plastic trim at the top of the seat backrest, and feed the seat belt through the slot **(see illustration)**.

Refitting

25 Refitting is a reversal of the removal procedure, ensuring that all the seat belt mounting bolts are tightened to the specified torque, and all disturbed trim panels are securely retained by all the relevant retaining clips.

27 Interior trim – removal and refitting

Interior trim panels

1 The interior trim panels are secured using either screws or various types of trim fasteners, usually studs or clips.
2 Check that there are no other panels overlapping the one to be removed; usually there is a sequence that has to be followed that will become obvious on close inspection.
3 Remove all obvious fasteners, such as screws. If the panel will not come free, it is held by hidden clips or fasteners. These are usually situated around the edge of the panel and can be prised up to release them; note, however, that they can break quite easily so new ones should be available. The best way of releasing such clips, without the correct type of tool, is to use a large flat-bladed screwdriver. Note that some panels are secured by plastic expanding rivets, where the centre pin must be prised up before the rivet can be removed. Note in many cases that the adjacent sealing strip must be prised back to release a panel.
4 When removing a panel, never use excessive force or the panel may be damaged; always check carefully that all fasteners have been removed or released before attempting to withdraw a panel.
5 Refitting is the reverse of the removal procedure; secure the fasteners by pressing them firmly into place and ensure that all disturbed components are correctly secured to prevent rattles.

A-pillar trim

6 Using a wooden or plastic flat-bladed lever, starting at the top, carefully prise the trim away from the pillar **(see illustration)**.

26.23 Undo the nut (arrowed) and remove the centre inertia reel

26.24 Prise up the plastic trim and feed the seat belt through the slot

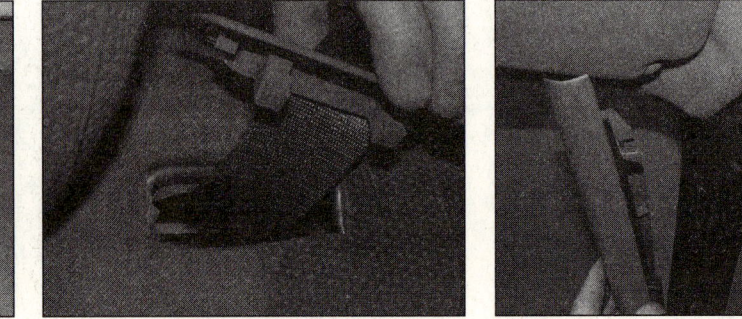

27.6 Pull away the top of the A-pillar trim

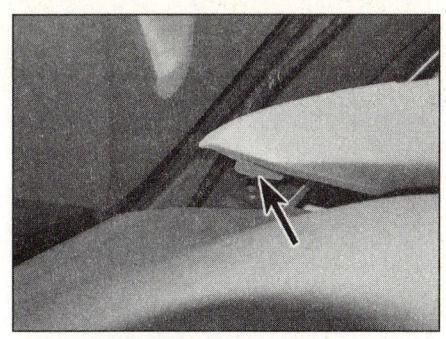

Bodywork and fittings 11•17

27.7 Note the lug at the base of the A-pillar trim (arrowed)

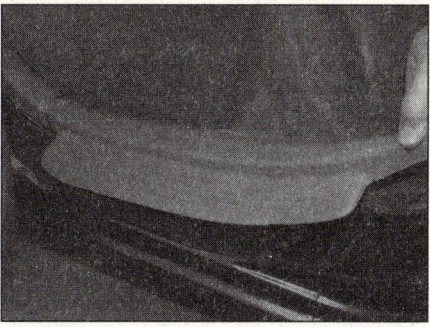

27.9 Pull up the door sill trim panel

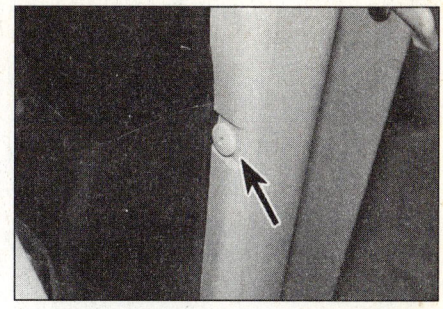

27.10 Slacken the screw, then prise out the expanding clip at the top of the B-pillar trim (arrowed)

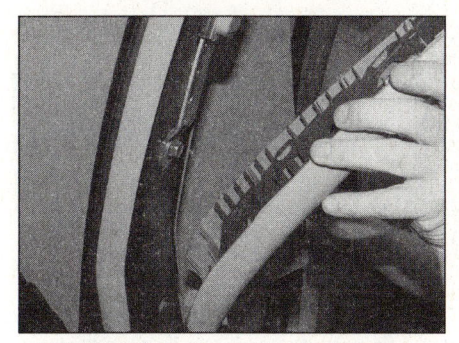

27.12 Pull the top of the B-pillar trim towards the centre of the vehicle

27.17a Slacken the screw (arrowed) and prise out the expanding clip . . .

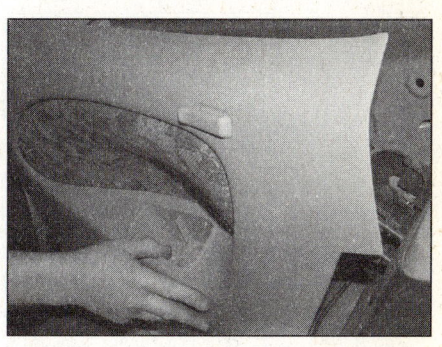

27.17b . . . then pull the side panel from place

7 Lift the trim to disengage it from the facia. Note the lug at the base of the trim **(see illustration)**.

8 Refitting is the reverse of the removal procedure; secure the fasteners by pressing them firmly into place.

B-pillar trim

Saloon, 5-door Hatchback, Liftback and Estate models

9 Begin by carefully prising up the front door sill trim panel with its retaining clips **(see illustration)**.

10 Pull the bottom edge of the lower trim in towards the centre of the vehicle to release it from the retaining clips, then undo the screw and prise out the clip at the top of the lower panel **(see illustration)**.

11 Prise apart the plastic cover, then undo the bolt securing the upper seat belt anchorage to the pillar **(see illustration 26.3)**.

12 Pull the top of the pillar upper trim in towards the centre of the vehicle and release it from the retaining clips **(see illustration)**.

13 Refitting is the reverse of the removal procedure; secure the fasteners by pressing them firmly into place and ensure that all disturbed components are correctly secured to prevent rattles.

B/C-pillar trim

3-door Hatchback models

14 Begin by carefully prising up the front door sill trim panel with its retaining clips.

15 Remove the rear seat backrest as described in Section 24.

16 Undo the rear side seatbelt lower anchorage bolt, then prise off the cap and undo the upper seat belt anchorage bolt from the B-pillar.

17 Undo the screw, prise out the clip, and pull the lower B-pillar/side panel from place **(see illustrations)**.

18 Remove the luggage compartment carpet, then unscrew the two plastic nuts and remove the tailgate sill trim panel **(see illustration)**.

19 Prise up and remove the plastic trim at the top of the luggage compartment side trim panel **(see illustration)**.

20 Undo the screws/prise out the clips and remove the luggage compartment side trim panel **(see illustrations)**. Disconnect the speaker wiring plug as the panel is removed.

21 Undo the screws and pull the B/C pillar trim from place **(see illustration)**. Feed the seat belt through the slot in the panel.

22 Refitting is the reverse of the removal procedure; secure the fasteners by pressing them firmly into place and ensure that all disturbed components are correctly secured to prevent rattles.

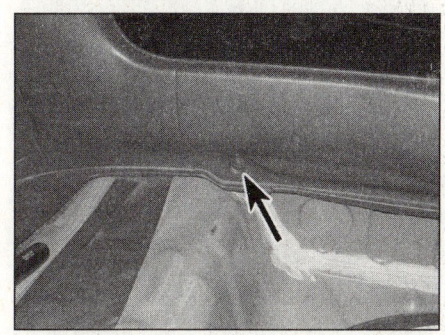

27.18 Unscrew the tailgate sill trim panel plastic nuts (right-hand nut arrowed)

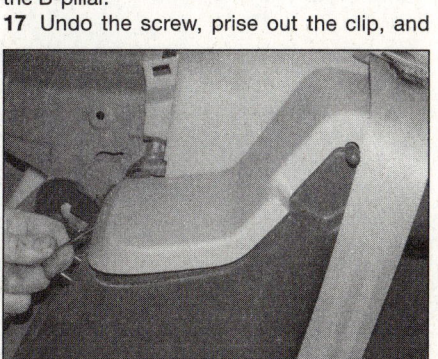

27.19 Prise up the trim panel over the rear speaker

27.20a Undo the three screw adjacent to the rear speaker (arrowed) . . .

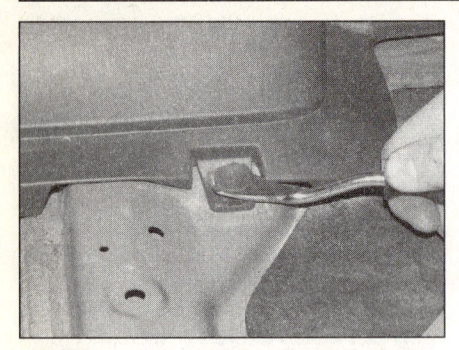

11•18 Bodywork and fittings

27.20b ... prise out the clip on the lower edge ...

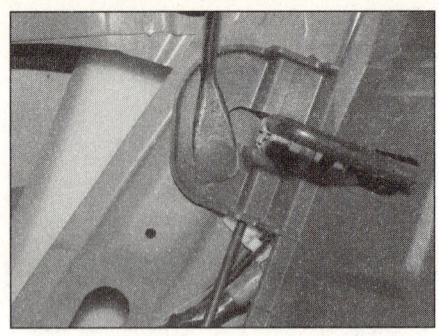

27.20c ... and the clip at the front edge

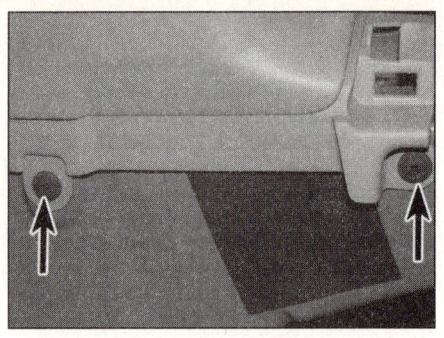

27.21 B/C-pillar trim retaining screws (arrowed)

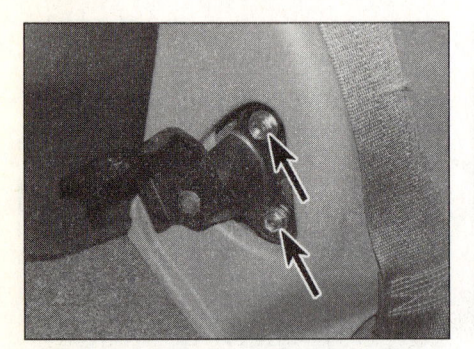

27.28 Undo the two bolts securing the seat outer hinge (arrowed)

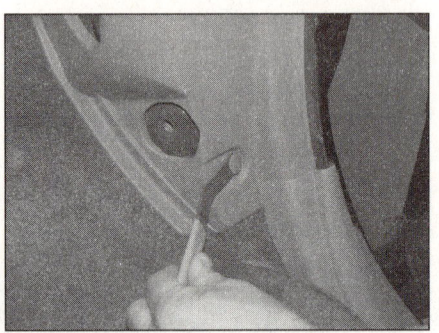

27.29 Prise out the clip at the lower edge of the side panel

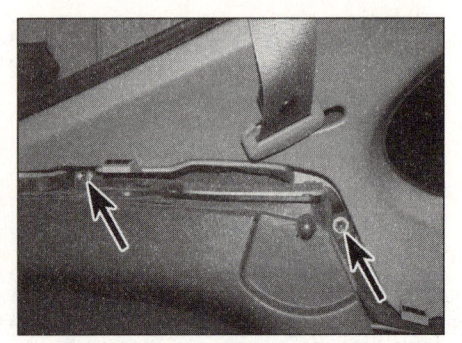

27.31 Undo the two bolts (arrowed) above the rear speaker

C-pillar trim

Saloon

23 No information was available at the time of writing.

5-door Hatchback and Liftback

24 Remove the rear seat cushion as described in Section 24.
25 Remove the rear parcel shelf.
26 Prise up and remove the plastic trim at the top of the luggage compartment side trim panel **(see illustration 27.19)**.
27 Pull the weatherstrip from the door aperture adjacent to the C-pillar trim and seat lower side panel.
28 Undo the outer seat belt lower anchorage point, and undo the two bolts securing the seat backrest hinge to the vehicle body **(see illustration)**.
29 Prise out the retaining clip at the lower edge of the seat lower side panel, and pull the panel from the pillar **(see illustration)**.
30 Undo the two plastic nuts and remove the tailgate sill trim panel **(see illustration 27.18)**.
31 Undo the two bolts **(see illustration)**, prise out the two clips **(see illustrations 27.20b and 27.20c)** and remove the luggage compartment side trim panel. Where applicable, undo the bolt and remove the baggage anchorage point. Disconnect any wiring plugs as the panel is withdrawn.
32 Prise out the clip at the lower edge, then pull the trim panel from the pillar **(see illustrations)**.
33 Refitting is a reversal of removal.

C/D-pillar trim

Estate models

34 At the time of writing, no information was available.

Luggage area side trim panel

Saloon

35 No information was available at the time of writing.

5-door Hatchback and Liftback

36 This operation is described as part of the C-pillar trim removal procedure – see paragraph 24.

3-door Hatchback

37 This operation is described as part of the B/C-pillar trim removal procedure – see paragraph 14.

Tailgate trim panel

38 Open the tailgate and insert a flat-bladed tool between the inner trim panel and the tailgate. Work around the edge of the panel and release the retaining clips **(see illustration 17.2)**. Remove the panel.
39 Refitting is a reversal of removal, ensuring any damaged clips are renewed.

Glovebox

40 Pull the passenger's side sill trim panel up to release the clips, then undo the bolt and remove the footwell kick panel **(see illustration)**.
41 Open the glovebox and undo the 5 screws securing the glovebox to the facia **(see illustrations)**.
42 Pull the glovebox from position, disconnecting any wiring plugs as it's withdrawn.
43 Disconnect the yellow air recirculation control cable from the left-hand side of the heater housing.
44 Refitting is a reversal of removal.

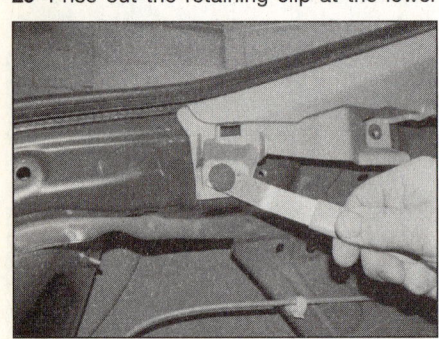

27.32a Prise out the clip ...

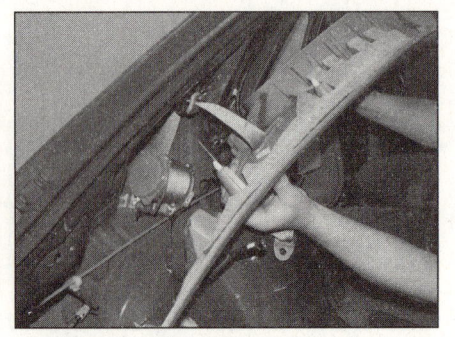

27.32b ... and pull the C-pillar trim from place

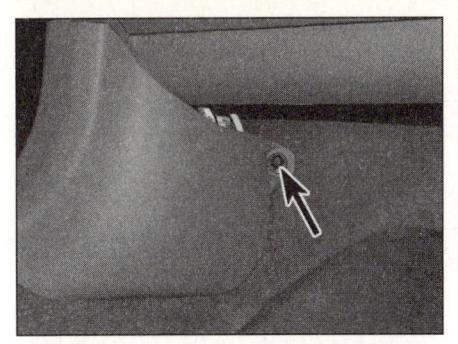

27.40 Undo the nut and remove the passenger's side kick panel (arrowed)

27.41a Undo the three screws at the top (arrowed) . . .

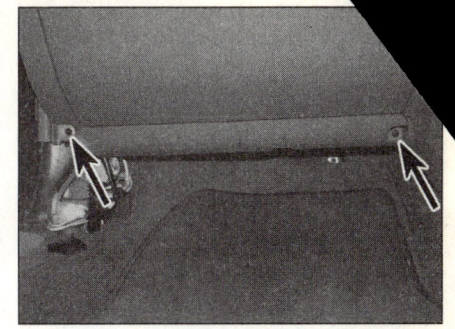

27.41b . . . and the two at the bottom (arrowed)

Carpets

45 The passenger compartment floor carpet is in one piece, secured at its edges by screws or clips, usually the same fasteners used to secure the various adjoining trim panels.

46 Carpet removal and refitting is reasonably straightforward but very time-consuming because all adjoining trim panels must be removed first, as must components such as the seats, the centre console and seat belt lower anchorages.

Headlining

47 The headlining is clipped to the roof and can be withdrawn only once all fittings such as the grab handles, sunvisors, sunroof (if fitted), windscreen, rear quarter windows and related trim panels have been removed, and the door, tailgate and sunroof aperture sealing strips have been prised clear.

48 Note that headlining removal and refitting requires considerable skill and experience if it is to be carried out without damage and is therefore best entrusted to an expert.

Driver's side facia lower panel

49 Pull the driver's side door sill trim panel upwards to release the retaining clips.

50 Undo the screw and remove the driver's side footwell kick panel.

51 Pull the bonnet release handle, and disengage the outer cable and end fitting from the handle **(see illustration)**.

52 Undo the two lower fixing screws and pull the out the lower edge of the panel **(see illustration)**.

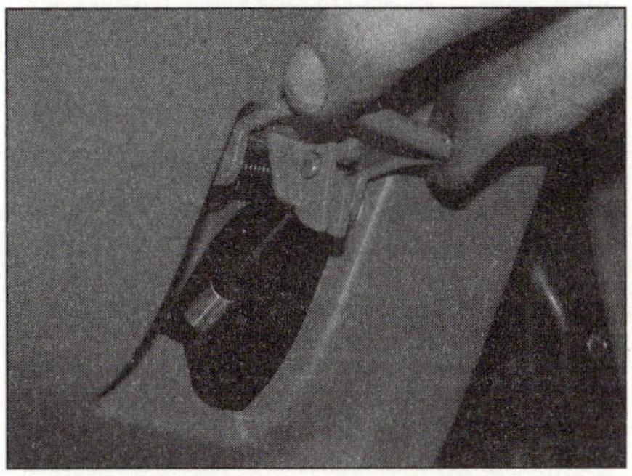

27.51 Disengage the bonnet release cable from the handle

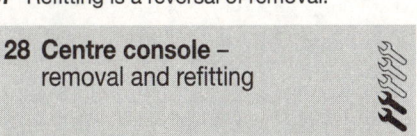

53 Unhook the top edge, and remove the panel.

54 If required, release the clips/screws and detach the diagnostic plug from the panel.

55 Refitting is a reversal of removal.

Sunvisors

56 Unclip the sunvisor from the inner mounting, then undo the screw(s) and remove the mounting.

57 Refitting is a reversal of removal.

28 Centre console – removal and refitting

Removal

1 Two different types of rear centre consoles are fitted. On the type with a lid over the rear storage compartment, lift the lid and undo the

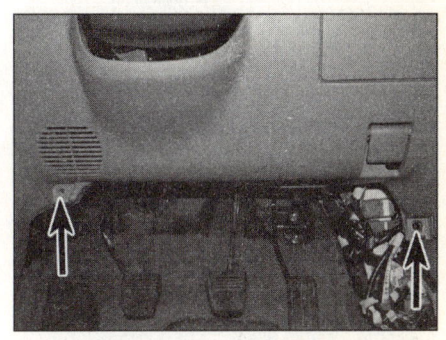

27.52 Undo the two fasteners (arrowed) and remove the lower facia panel

two screws in the base of the compartment. On the second type (no lid), undo the screw each side at the rear outer edge of the console **(see illustration)**.

2 On manual transmission models, unscrew the knob from the top of the gear lever. Starting at the front, prise up the gaiter surround trim and pull the gaiter and trim over the gear lever.

3 On automatic transmission models, carefully prise up the selector lever surround trim.

4 Undo the screw each side where the rear section of the console meets the front **(see illustration)**. Staring at the front, lift the console over the handbrake lever and remove it from the cabin. Disconnect the wiring plugs as the console is removed.

5 Pull the heater control knobs from place, then undo the two screws in the knob recesses **(see illustration)**. Carefully pull the recirculation knob from the lever.

28.1 Lift the lid on the storage box, and undo the two screws at the rear of the centre console

28.4 The front edge of the centre console rear section is secured by a screw (arrowed) each side

28.5 Pull the heater control knobs from place, and undo the two screws (arrowed) in the knob recesses

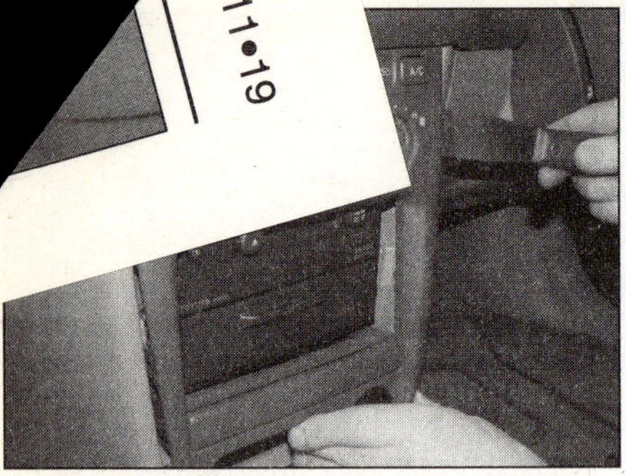

28.6 Prise the centre cluster trim panel from place

28.7 Undo the four screws and remove the audio unit/storage box (arrowed)

28.9 Undo the screw each side and remove the centre console (arrowed)

6 Carefully prise the centre cluster trim panel from position **(see illustration)**. Disconnect any wiring plugs as the panel is withdrawn.

7 Open the front console storage box lid, then undo the two screws and pull the box from the centre cluster. On some models, an audio unit/storage box is fitted, and retained by 4 screws **(see illustration)**. Disconnect any wiring plugs as the audio unit/box is withdrawn.

8 Remove the glovebox and driver's side lower facia panel as described in Section 27.

9 Undo the two screws each side and remove the centre cluster (console front section) **(see illustration)**.

Refitting

10 Refitting is the reverse of removal, making sure all fasteners are securely tightened.

29 Facia panel assembly
– removal and refitting

Note: *The driver's side facia lower panel is covered in Section 27.*

Removal

1 Disconnect the battery negative lead as described in Chapter 5A.

2 Remove the centre console as described in Section 28.

3 Remove the steering wheel as described in Chapter 10.

4 Remove the instrument cluster and central information/audio unit as described in Chapter 12.

5 Remove the A-pillar trims as described in Section 27.

6 Undo the three screws and remove the steering column lower shroud, then undo the single screw and remove the upper shroud **(see illustrations)**.

7 Remove the steering column combination switches as described in Chapter 12, Section 4.

> **HAYNES HiNT** Label each wiring connector as it is disconnected from its relevant component. The labels will prove useful on refitting, when routing the wiring and feeding the wiring through the facia apertures.

8 Reach through the central aperture in the facia and disconnect the passenger airbag wiring connector **(see illustration)**.

9 Carefully prise the mirror switch and rear foglight switch assembly from the right-hand end of the facia. Disconnect the wiring plugs as the assembly is removed.

10 Undo the two screws securing the passenger's airbag to the crossmember **(see illustration)**.

11 The facia is secured by two screws in the instrument cluster aperture, and one under the passenger's side of the facia **(see illustrations)**. Undo the screws and pull the facia away a little.

12 Note the routing of the wiring loom, then release it from all the retaining clips on the facia. Note the location of the clips. The loom connectors will slide out of the connection box in the instrument cluster aperture, then unclip the connection box from the facia.

29.6a Undo the three screws (arrowed) and remove the lower steering column shroud . . .

29.6b . . . and the one (arrowed) securing the upper steering column shroud

29.8 Reach through the aperture in the centre of the facia and disconnect the passenger's airbag connector (arrowed)

29.10 Undo the passenger's airbag bolts (arrowed)

29.11a Undo the two screws in the instrument panel aperture (arrowed) . . .

Bodywork and fittings 11•21

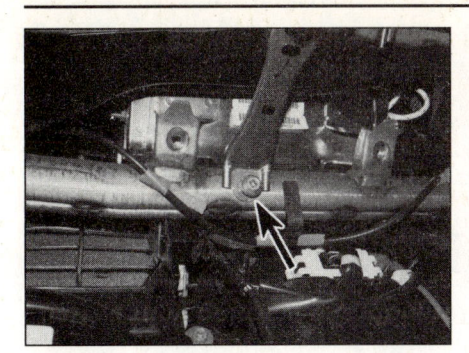

29.11b . . . and the one (arrowed) under the passenger's side of the facia

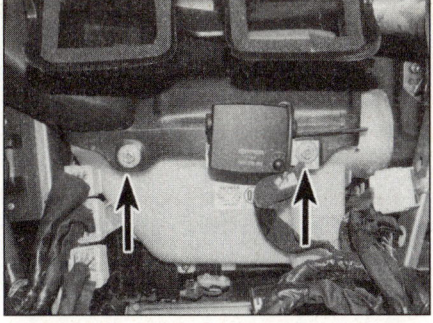

29.14 The centre air vent is secured by two screws (arrowed)

29.17 Lower the steering column, and support it to prevent damage to the column joints

13 Reach around the back of the facia, undo the two screws and remove the ducting from the right-hand facia air vent. This should allow the facia wiring loom to remain in place, whilst the facia is removed. With the help of and assistant, manoeuvre the facia from the vehicle.

14 If the facia is being removed in order to remove the heater housing, undo the bolts and remove the centre air vents **(see illustration)**.

15 Undo the bolts and remove the side upright braces (either side of the centre tunnel).

16 Unclip the fusebox from the right-hand side of the facia crossbrace.

17 Undo the two bolts, and two nuts securing the steering column to the crossbrace, and lower the steering column. Support the column to prevent undue stress being placed on the column joints **(see illustration)**.

18 Undo the bolts/nuts securing the crossbrace to the vehicle, make a note of the fitted positions and routing of any wiring looms before releasing the cable ties attached to the brace, then manoeuvre the brace from the vehicle.

Refitting

19 Refitting is a reversal of the removal procedure, noting the following points:

a) Manoeuvre the facia into position and ensure that the wiring is correctly routed and securely retained by its facia clips.
b) Clip the facia back into position, ensure the locating lugs at the front edge of the facia engage correctly, making sure all the wiring connectors are fed through their respective apertures, then refit all the facia fasteners and tighten them securely.
c) On completion, reconnect the battery and check that all the electrical components and switches function correctly.

Notes

Chapter 12
Body electrical system

Contents

	Section number
Audio units – removal and refitting	17
Battery check	See *Weekly checks*
Bulbs (exterior lights) – renewal	7
Bulbs (interior lights) – renewal	8
Electric windows	See Chapter 11
Electrical fault finding – general information	2
Exterior light units – removal and refitting	9
Fuses and relays – general information	3
General information and precautions	1
Headlight beam alignment – checking and adjusting	10
Headlight beam control motor – removal and refitting	11
Horn – renewal	12
Indicator/hazard flasher unit – renewal	6

	Section number
Instrument panel, central information unit and speed sensor – removal and refitting	5
Screenwasher fluid level check	See *Weekly checks*
Speakers – removal and refitting	18
Supplemental Restraint System (SRS) – component renewal	20
Supplemental Restraint System (SRS) – general information and precautions	19
Switches – removal and refitting	4
Tailgate wiper motor – removal and refitting	16
Washer system components – removal and refitting	13
Windscreen wiper motor and linkage – removal and refitting	15
Wiper arms – removal and refitting	14
Wiper blade check	See *Weekly checks*

Degrees of difficulty

Easy, suitable for novice with little experience	Fairly easy, suitable for beginner with some experience	Fairly difficult, suitable for competent DIY mechanic	Difficult, suitable for experienced DIY mechanic	Very difficult, suitable for expert DIY or professional

Specifications

General
System type	12 volt, negative earth
Fuses	See wiring diagrams at end of Chapter and stickers on fusebox lids for specific vehicle details

Bulbs
	Wattage
Brake/tail light	21/5 bayonet
Foglight (front)	55 H3
Foglight (rear)	21 bayonet
Front sidelights	5 wedge
Headlight:	
Models with single headlights	60/55 H4
Models with twin headlights:	
Main beam	60 HB3
Dipped beam	51 HB4
High-level brake light:	
Saloon and Liftback models	21 bayonet
Hatchback models	5 wedge
Estate models	21 wedge
Indicator side repeater lights	5 wedge
Indicators (front and rear)	21 bayonet
Interior light	8 festoon
Luggage compartment light:	
Hatchback and estate	5 festoon
Saloon	3.8 wedge
Number plate light	5 wedge
Reversing light:	
All except Estate	21 bayonet
Estate models	21 wedge

Torque wrench settings
	Nm	lbf ft
Driver's airbag fasteners	9	6
Driver's airbag sensor lock release bolt	9	6
SRS control module	20	15
SRS front crash sensors	20	15
SRS side crash sensors	20	15
Windscreen/tailgate wiper arm nuts	20	15

1 General information and precautions

General information

The electrical system is of 12 volt negative earth type. Power for the lights and all electrical accessories is supplied by a lead/acid type battery, which is charged by the belt-driven alternator.

This Chapter covers repair and service procedures for the various electrical components not associated with the engine. Information on the battery, alternator and starter motor can be found in Chapter 5A.

Precautions

Warning: *Before carrying out any work on the electrical system, read through the precautions given in 'Safety first!' at the beginning of this manual and in Chapter 5A.*

2 Electrical fault finding – general information

Note: *Refer to the precautions given in 'Safety first!' and in Section 1 of this Chapter before starting work. The following tests relate to testing of the main electrical circuits, and should not be used to test delicate electronic circuits, particularly where an electronic control unit is used.*

General

1 A typical electrical circuit consists of an electrical component, any switches, relays, motors, fuses, fusible links or circuit breakers related to that component, and the wiring and connectors which link the component to both the battery and the chassis. To help to pinpoint a problem in an electrical circuit, wiring diagrams are included at the end of this Chapter.

2 Before attempting to diagnose an electrical fault, first study the appropriate wiring diagram, to obtain a complete understanding of the components included in the particular circuit concerned. The possible sources of a fault can be narrowed down by noting if other components related to the circuit are operating properly. If several components or circuits fail at one time, the problem is likely to be related to a shared fuse or earth connection.

3 Electrical problems usually stem from simple causes, such as loose or corroded connections, a faulty earth connection, a blown fuse, a melted fusible link, or a faulty relay. Visually inspect the condition of all fuses, wires and connections in a problem circuit before testing the components. Use the wiring diagrams to determine which terminal connections will need to be checked in order to pinpoint the trouble-spot.

4 The basic tools required for electrical fault finding include a circuit tester or voltmeter (a 12 volt bulb with a set of test leads can also be used for certain tests); an ohmmeter (to measure resistance and check for continuity); a battery and set of test leads; and a jumper wire, preferably with a circuit breaker or fuse incorporated, which can be used to bypass suspect wires or electrical components. Before attempting to locate a problem with test instruments, use the wiring diagram to determine where to make the connections.

Warning: *Under no circumstances may live measuring instruments such as ohmmeters, voltmeters or a bulb and test leads be used to test any of the SRS airbag, SIPS bag, or pyrotechnical seat belt circuitry. Any testing of these components must be left to a Toyota dealer, as there is a danger of activating the system if the correct procedures are not followed.*

5 To find the source of an intermittent wiring fault (usually due to a poor or dirty connection, or damaged wiring insulation), a wiggle test can be performed on the wiring. This involves wiggling the wiring by hand to see if the fault occurs as the wiring is moved. It should be possible to narrow down the source of the fault to a particular section of wiring. This method of testing can be used in conjunction with any of the tests described in the following sub-Sections.

6 Apart from problems due to poor connections, two basic types of fault can occur in an electrical circuit – open-circuit, or short-circuit.

7 Open-circuit faults are caused by a break somewhere in the circuit, which prevents current from flowing. An open-circuit fault will prevent a component from working.

8 Short-circuit faults are caused by a short somewhere in the circuit, which allows the current flowing in the circuit to escape along an alternative route, usually to earth. Short-circuit faults are normally caused by a breakdown in wiring insulation, which allows a feed wire to touch either another wire, or an earthed component such as the bodyshell. A short-circuit fault will normally cause the relevant circuit fuse to blow.

2.20a Earth connection on the front of the transmission housing . . .

Finding an open-circuit

9 To check for an open-circuit, connect one lead of a circuit tester or the negative lead of a voltmeter either to the battery negative terminal or to a known good earth.

10 Connect the other lead to a connector in the circuit being tested, preferably nearest to the battery or fuse. At this point, battery voltage should be present, unless the lead from the battery or the fuse itself is faulty (bearing in mind that some circuits are live only when the ignition switch is moved to a particular position).

11 Switch on the circuit, then connect the tester lead to the connector nearest the circuit switch on the component side.

12 If voltage is present (indicated either by the tester bulb lighting or a voltmeter reading, as applicable), this means that the section of the circuit between the relevant connector and the switch is problem-free.

13 Continue to check the remainder of the circuit in the same fashion.

14 When a point is reached at which no voltage is present, the problem must lie between that point and the previous test point with voltage. Most problems can be traced to a broken, corroded or loose connection.

Finding a short-circuit

15 To check for a short-circuit, first disconnect the load(s) from the circuit (loads are the components which draw current from a circuit, such as bulbs, motors, heating elements, etc).

16 Remove the relevant fuse from the circuit, and connect a circuit tester or voltmeter to the fuse connections.

17 Switch on the circuit, bearing in mind that some circuits are live only when the ignition switch is in a particular position.

18 If voltage is present (indicated either by the tester bulb lighting or a voltmeter reading, as applicable), this means that there is a short-circuit.

19 If no voltage is present during this test, but the fuse still blows with the load(s) reconnected, this indicates an internal fault in the load(s).

Finding an earth fault

20 The battery negative terminal is connected to earth – the metal of the engine/transmission and the vehicle body – and many systems are wired so that they only receive a positive feed, the current returning via the metal of the car body **(see illustrations)**. This means that the component mounting and the body form part of that circuit. Loose or corroded mountings can therefore cause a range of electrical faults, ranging from total failure of a circuit, to a puzzling partial failure. In particular, lights may shine dimly (especially when another circuit sharing the same earth point is in operation), motors (eg, wiper motors or the radiator cooling fan motor) may run slowly, and the operation of one circuit may have an apparently-unrelated effect on another.

Body electrical system 12•3

2.20b ... left-hand end of the cylinder head (arrowed) ...

2.20c ... right-hand engine mounting (arrowed) ...

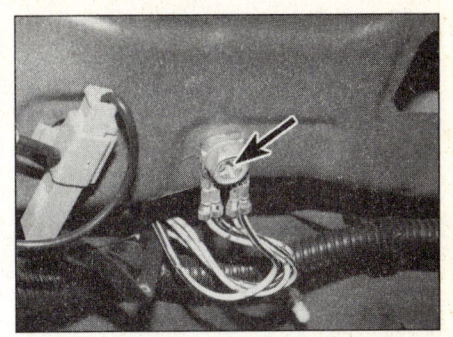

2.20d ... tailgate sill panel (arrowed) ...

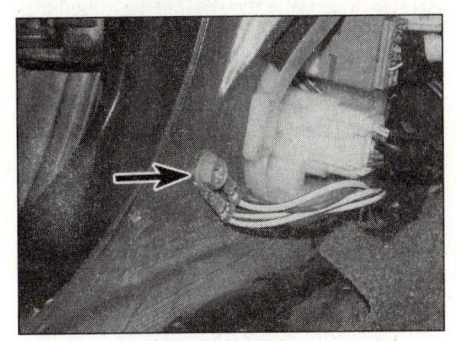

2.20e ... passenger's footwell kick panel (arrowed) ...

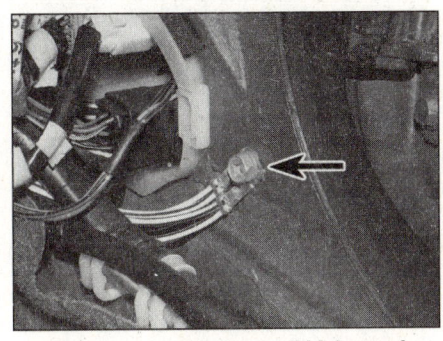

2.20f ... driver's footwell kick panel (arrowed) ...

2.20g ... right-hand rear quarter panel – 3-door Hatchback (arrowed)

21 Note that on many vehicles, earth straps are used between certain components, such as the engine/transmission and the body, usually where there is no metal-to-metal contact between components, due to flexible rubber mountings, etc.
22 To check whether a component is properly earthed, disconnect the battery and connect one lead of an ohmmeter to a known good earth point. Connect the other lead to the wire or earth connection being tested. The resistance reading should be zero; if not, check the connection as follows.
23 If an earth connection is thought to be faulty, dismantle the connection, and clean both the bodyshell and the wire terminal (or the component earth connection mating surface) back to bare metal. Be careful to remove all traces of dirt and corrosion, then use a knife to trim away any paint, so that a clean metal-to-metal joint is made. On reassembly, tighten the joint fasteners securely; if a wire terminal is being refitted, use serrated washers between the terminal and the bodyshell, to ensure a clean and secure connection.
24 When the connection is remade, prevent the onset of corrosion in the future by applying a coat of petroleum jelly or silicone-based grease, or by spraying on (at regular intervals) a proprietary ignition sealer, or a water-dispersant lubricant.

3 Fuses and relays – general information

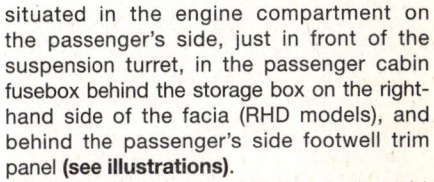

Fuses

1 The fuses are located in the fuseboxes situated in the engine compartment on the passenger's side, just in front of the suspension turret, in the passenger cabin fusebox behind the storage box on the right-hand side of the facia (RHD models), and behind the passenger's side footwell trim panel (see illustrations).
2 If a fuse blows, the electrical circuit(s) protected by that fuse will cease to operate. The fuse positions and the circuits protected depends on vehicle specification, model year and country. Refer to the wiring diagrams at the rear of this manual, and the sticker on the fusebox lid which gives details for the particular vehicle.
3 To remove a fuse, first switch off the ignition. Using the plastic removal tool provided, pull the fuse out of its terminals (see illustrations). The wire within the fuse should be visible; if the fuse is blown, the wire will be broken or melted.

3.1a Engine compartment fuse/relay boxes

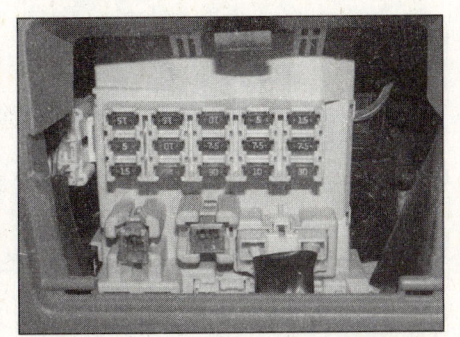

3.1b The driver's side fusebox is located behind the storage compartment

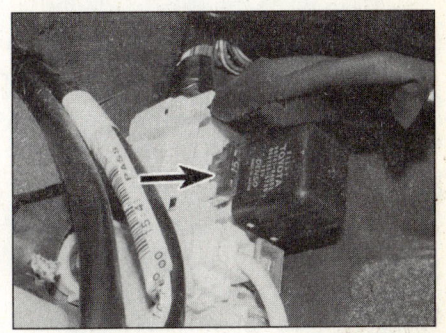

3.1c Passenger's side footwell kick panel fuse (arrowed)

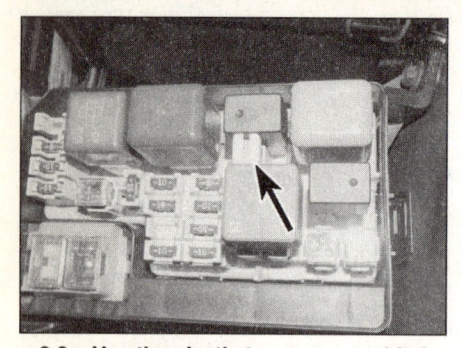

12•4 Body electrical system

3.3a Use the plastic tweezers provided (arrowed) . . .

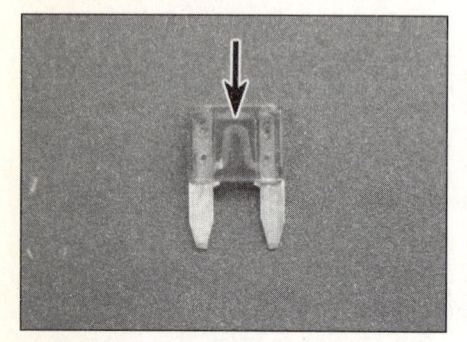

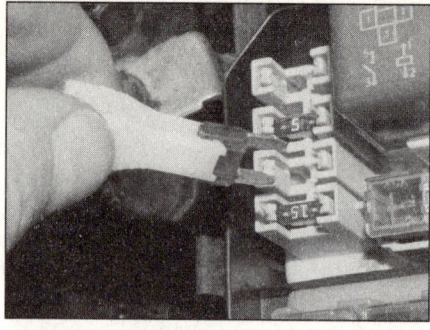

3.3b . . . to pull a fuse from its terminals

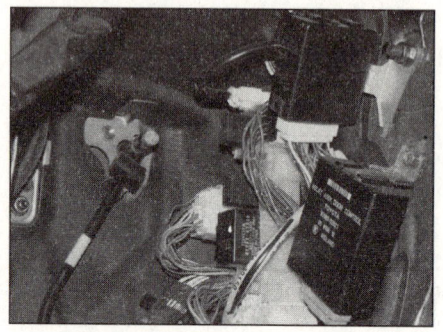

3.3c The wire within the fuse (arrowed) should be visible

3.12 Some relays are located behind the driver's side footwell kick panel

4 Always renew a fuse with one of an identical rating; never use a fuse with a different rating from the original, or substitute anything else, as it may lead to a fire. Never renew a fuse more than once without tracing the source of the trouble. The fuse rating is stamped on top of the fuse; note that fuses are also colour-coded for easy recognition. Spare fuses are provided in the fusebox.
5 Persistent blowing of a particular fuse indicates a fault in the circuit(s) protected. Where more than one circuit is involved, switch on one item at a time until the fuse blows, so showing in which circuit the fault lies.
6 Besides a fault in the electrical component concerned, a blown fuse can also be caused by a short-circuit in the wiring to the component. Look for trapped or frayed wires allowing a live wire to touch vehicle metal, and for loose or damaged connectors.
7 Note that **only** the blade-type fuses should ever be renewed by the DIY mechanic. If one of the large fusible links in the main fusebox blows, this indicates a serious electrical fault, which should be diagnosed by a Toyota dealer or automotive electrical specialist.

Relays – general

8 A relay is an electrically-operated switch, which is used for the following reasons:
a) A relay can switch a heavy current remotely from the circuit in which the current is flowing, allowing the use of lighter-gauge wiring and switch contacts.
b) A relay can receive more than one control input, unlike a mechanical switch.
c) A relay can have a timer function – for example an intermittent wiper delay.
9 If a circuit which includes a relay develops a fault, remember that the relay itself could be faulty. A basic test of relay operation is to have an assistant switch on the item concerned, while you listen for a click from the relay. This would at least determine whether the relay is switching or not, but is not conclusive proof that a relay is working.
10 Most relays have four or five terminals – two terminals supplying current to its solenoid winding to provide the switching, a main current input and either one or two outputs to either supply or isolate the component concerned (depending on its configuration). Using the wiring diagrams at the end of this Chapter, test to ensure that all connections deliver the expected voltage or good earth.
11 Ultimately, testing is by substitution of a known good relay, but be careful – relays which look similar are not necessarily identical for purposes of substitution.
12 The relays are found in the all the fuse-boxes **(see illustrations 3.1a, 3.1b and 3.1c)**. And behind the driver's side footwell kick panel **(see illustration)**.
13 To remove a relay, make sure that the ignition is switched off, then pull the relay from its socket. Push the new relay firmly in to refit.

4 Switches – removal and refitting

Steering column switches

1 Set the steering wheel to the straight-ahead position.
2 Release the steering wheel/column adjuster, and pull the steering wheel away from the facia as far as possible.
3 Remove the steering wheel as described in Chapter 10.
4 Undo the three retaining screws and remove the steering column lower shroud, then undo the single screw and remove the upper shroud **(see illustrations)**.
5 Undo the 3 screws securing the switch assembly to the steering column **(see illustrations)**. Disconnect the wiring plugs, and remove the switch assembly.
6 Each switch is secured by two screws **(see illustration)**. Remove the screws, pull the switch out to the side carefully. Note that if required, each switch can be removed without removing the assembly as described in paragraph 5.

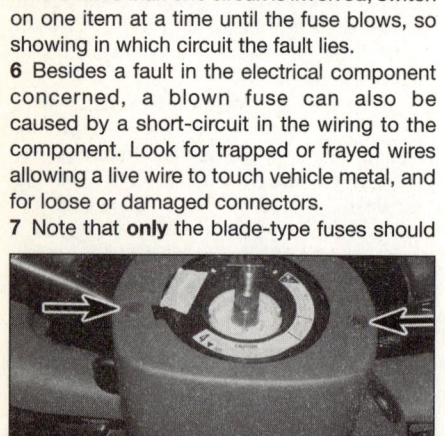

4.4a Undo the lower steering column shroud retaining screws (arrowed)

4.4b Upper steering column shroud retaining screw (arrowed)

4.5a Steering column multi-function switch assembly upper retaining screws (arrowed) . . .

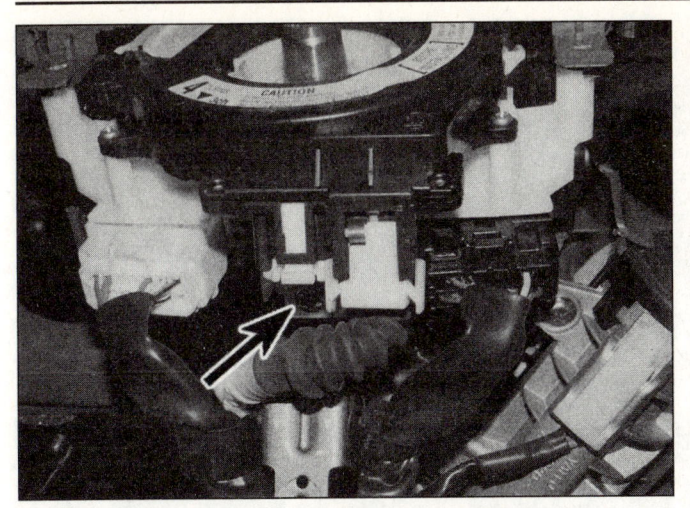

Body electrical system 12•5

4.5b ... and lower retaining screw (arrowed)

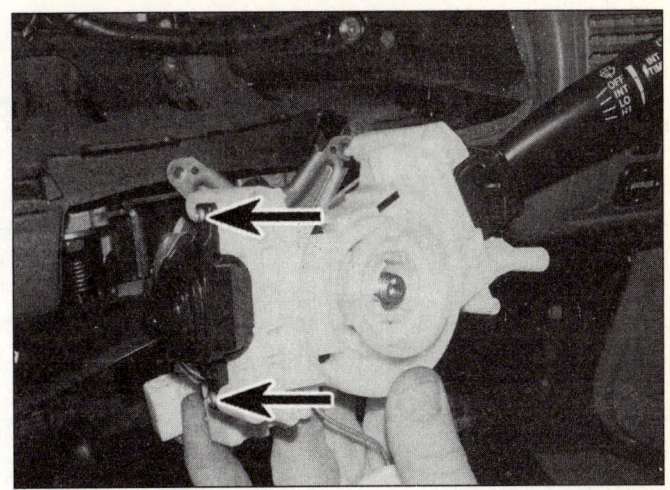

4.6 Switch retaining screws (arrowed)

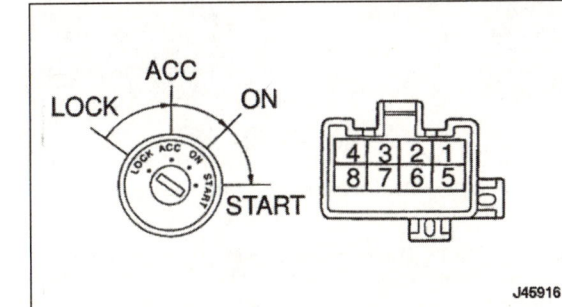

Switch position	Tester connection	Specified condition
LOCK	–	No continuity
ACC	2 – 3	Continuity
ON	2 – 3 – 4 6 – 7	Continuity
START	1 – 2 – 4 6 – 7 – 8	Continuity

4.13a Ignition switch terminal guide and continuity table – up to Aug '98

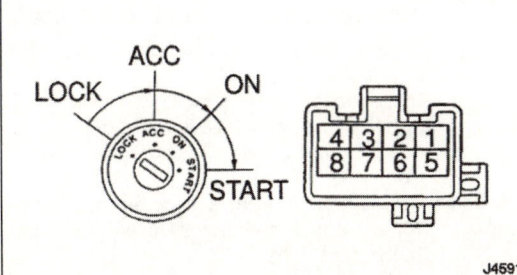

Switch position	Tester connection	Specified condition
LOCK	–	No continuity
ACC	5 – 6	Continuity
ON	1 – 4 5 – 6 – 8	Continuity
START	1 – 3 – 4 5 – 7 – 8	Continuity

4.13b Ignition switch terminal guide and continuity table – from Aug '98

7 Refit the relevant switch using a reversal of removal.

Ignition/starter switch

8 Set the steering wheel to the straight-ahead position.
9 Release the steering wheel/column adjuster, and pull the steering wheel away from the facia as far as possible.
10 Remove the steering wheel as described in Chapter 10.
11 Undo the three retaining screws and remove the steering column lower shroud, then undo the single screw and remove the upper shroud (see illustrations 4.4a and 4.4b).
12 Disconnect the switch wiring plugs.
13 Use an ohmmeter to check for continuity at the indicated terminals with the switch in each indicated position (see illustrations).
14 Renew the switch if continuity is not as specified.
15 Remove the screws retaining the switch to the rear of the lock cylinder housing and remove the switch (see illustration).
16 Installation is the reverse of removal.

Key lock cylinder

17 Set the steering wheel to the straight-ahead position.
18 Release the steering wheel/column

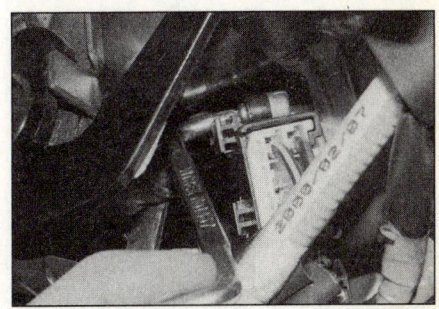

4.15 Undo the screws securing the ignition/starter switch to the rear of the lock cylinder housing

12•6 Body electrical system

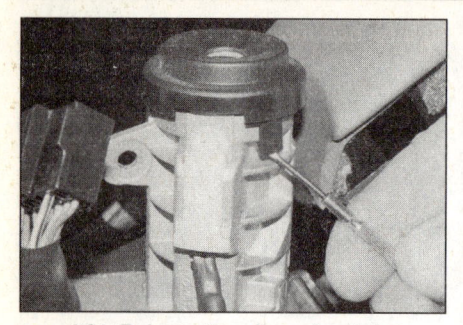

4.21 Release the clip and pull the transponder from the end of the lock cylinder housing

4.22 Depress the release button and pull the lock cylinder from the housing

4.23 Drill out the shear bolts (arrowed) to remove the lock assembly

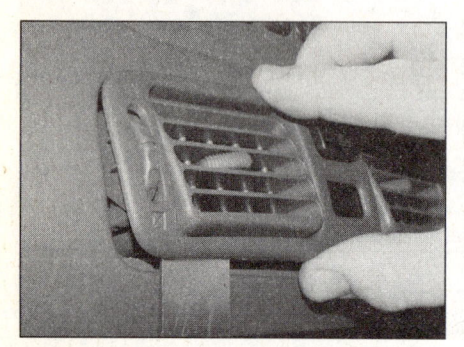

4.25 Carefully prise out the centre air vents

4.26 Release the clip and prise the switch from the vent panel

4.28 Prise up the switch panel from the door

adjuster, and pull the steering wheel away from the facia as far as possible.
19 Remove the steering wheel as described in Chapter 10.
20 Undo the three retaining screws and remove the steering column lower shroud, then undo the single screw and remove the upper shroud **(see illustrations 4.4a and 4.4b)**.
21 Disconnect the wiring plug, then carefully pull the transponder coil from the end of the lock cylinder **(see illustration)**.
22 With the key in the Accessory position, insert a small screwdriver or punch in the hole in the casting and press the release button while pulling the lock cylinder straight out. Remove it from the steering column **(see illustration)**.
23 If required, drill out the shear bolts and remove the steering lock from the column **(see illustration)**. When refitting, tighten the new bolts until the heads shear off.

24 Installation is the reverse of removal.

Hazard warning light switch

25 Carefully prise out the centre air vent assembly **(see illustration)**.
26 Disconnect the wiring connector at the rear of the switch, then release the clip and prise the switch from the vent **(see illustration)**.
27 Refitting is a reversal of removal.

Door panel switches

28 Prise up the switch panel from the door trim **(see illustration)**. Disconnect the wiring plugs as the panel is withdrawn.
29 Undo the screws and remove the switch assembly from the panel **(see illustration)**.
30 Refitting is a reversal of removal.

Door courtesy light switches

31 Undo the screw and pull the switch from the door aperture **(see illustration)**.

32 Disconnect the wiring plug and remove the switch.
33 Refitting is a reversal of removal.

Stop-light switch

34 Refer to Chapter 9.

Handbrake warning light switch

35 Remove the centre console as described in Chapter 11.
36 Undo the screw securing the switch to the handbrake bracket **(see illustration)**.
37 Lift out the switch, disconnect the spade connector and remove it.
38 Refitting is a reversal of removal. Check for correct operation of the switch before refitting the console.

Mirror/foglight switch

39 Using a flat-bladed tool, carefully prise the switch assembly from the right-hand end of

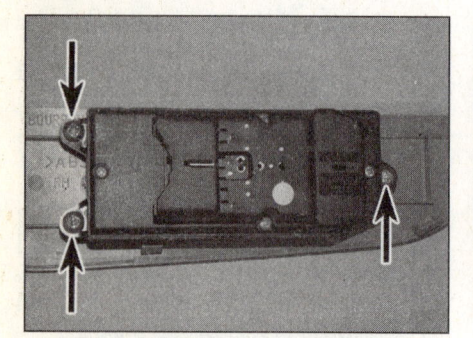

4.29 Undo the screws (arrowed) and separate the switch assembly from the panel

4.31 Undo the screw (arrowed) and pull the courtesy light switch from place

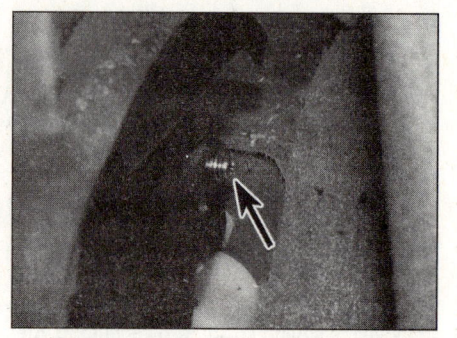

4.36 Handbrake warning light switch retaining screw (arrowed)

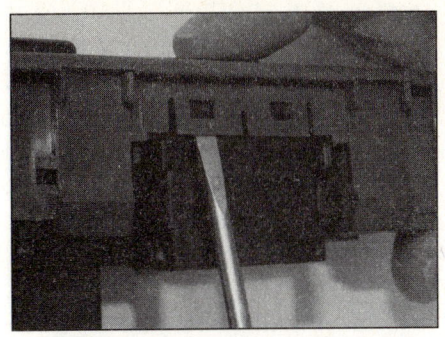

Body electrical system 12•7

4.40a Release the clips and slide the mirror switch from the panel

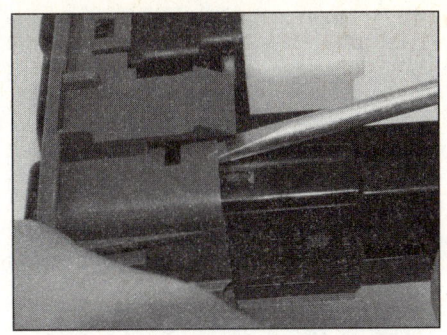

4.40b Foglight switch retaining clip

4.43 Depress the clip and remove the headlight level control switch from the centre console

4.45a Pull the heater control knobs from place . . .

4.45b . . . and undo the screws in the knob recesses (arrowed)

4.46 Prise the centre panel surround trim from place

the facia. Disconnect the wiring plugs as the assembly is removed.
40 Release the clips and slide the relevant switch from the assembly **(see illustrations)**.
41 Refitting is a reversal of removal.

Headlight beam level control

42 Remove the centre console as described in Chapter 11.
43 Release the clips and pull the switch from the console **(see illustration)**.
44 Refitting is a reversal of removal.

Heated rear window switch

45 Pull the rotary heater control knobs from place, and undo the two screws in the knob recesses **(see illustrations)**.
46 Carefully prise the centre panel surround from place **(see illustration)**. Disconnect the wiring plugs as the panel is removed.

47 Use a flat-bladed screwdriver to release the clip and pull the switch from the panel **(see illustration)**.
48 Refitting is a reversal of removal.

Air conditioning switch

49 The procedure for the air conditioning switch is identical to that described above for the heated rear window switch.

Sunroof switch

50 Undo the screw and remove the interior light lens **(see illustration 8.3b)**.
51 Undo the two screws and remove the switch **(see illustration)**. Undo the light unit retaining screw, turn the light unit over and undo the two wiring connections for the switch.
53 Refitting is a reversal of removal.

5 Instrument panel, central information unit and speed sensor – removal and refitting

Removal

Instrument panel

1 Disconnect the cable from the negative battery terminal (Chapter 5A).
2 Move the steering wheel to its lowest position, and fully extended the column (where possible).
3 Undo the two screws and pull instrument panel surround from the facia **(see illustrations)**.
4 Remove the retaining screws and pull the panel rearwards **(see illustration)**.
5 Unplug the electrical connectors and remove the panel **(see illustration)**.

4.47 Release the clip and remove the heated rear window switch

4.51 Undo the two screws (arrowed) and remove the sunroof switch assembly

5.3a Instrument panel surround retaining screws (arrowed)

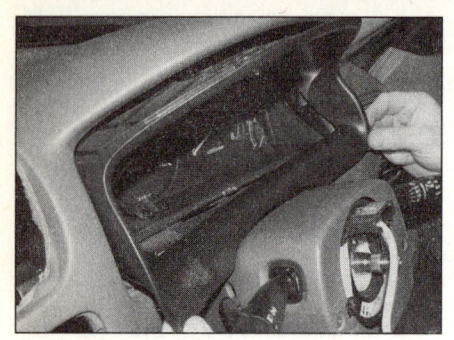

12•8 Body electrical system

5.3b Pull the surround rearwards

5.4 Instrument panel screws (arrowed)

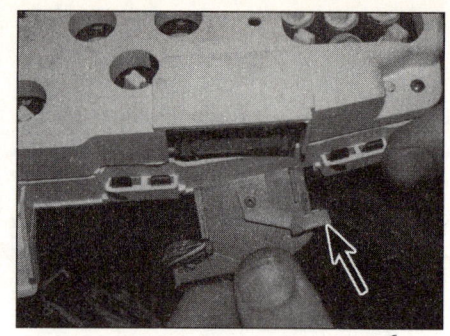

5.5 Lever the locking catch (arrowed) over and disconnect the wiring plug(s)

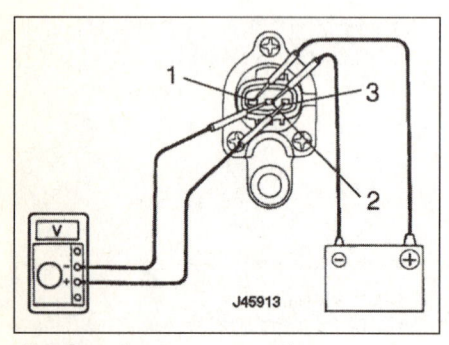

5.8 Speed sensor connections – see text

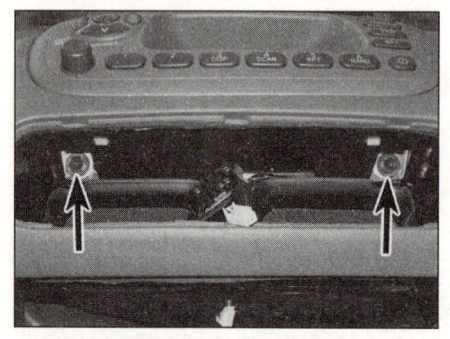

5.11a Undo the screws (arrowed) in the centre air vent aperture

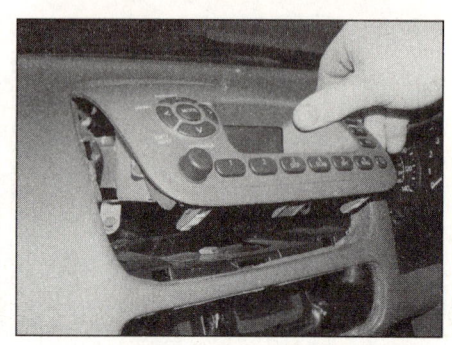

5.11b Pull the central information unit upwards and rearwards

6 Refitting is reversal of removal.

Vehicle speed sensor

7 The vehicle speed sensor is located on the transmission casing. Removal is described in Section 3 of Chapter 7B.

8 To check the sensor, disconnect the speed sensor wiring plug, then connect the positive lead of a voltmeter to the sensor terminal 3 and the negative to terminal 2. Then connect the positive lead from a 12 volt battery to terminal 1 and the negative to terminal 2 **(see illustration)**. Rotate the shaft, and the voltage measured should change from approximately 0V to 11V 4 times per revolution. If the voltage is not as specified, the sensor may be defective.

Central facia information unit

9 Disconnect the battery negative lead as described in Chapter 5A.

10 Remove the centre air vents from the facia by prising out the lower edge, the squeeze the top edge down and pull them from the facia **(see illustration 4.25)**.

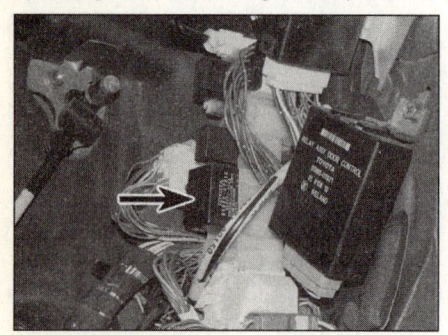

11 Undo the two screws in the air vents aperture, and carefully pull the information unit upwards and rearwards **(see illustrations)**. Disconnect the wiring plugs as the unit is withdrawn.

Refitting

12 Refitting is a reversal of removal.

6 Indicator/hazard flasher unit – renewal

1 The indicator/hazard flasher unit is responsible for controlling the flow of power to directional indicators. The indicators should flash at a rate of 60 to 120 times per minute. The flasher unit is fitted to the relay board behind the driver's side footwell trim panel. Remove the driver's side lower facia panel as described in Chapter 11, Section 27.

2 Pull the relay from the board **(see illustration)**.

3 Push the new relay into place, and refit the trim panel.

6.2 Indicator/hazard flasher unit (arrowed)

7 Bulbs (exterior lights) – renewal

General

1 Whenever a bulb is renewed, note the following points:

a) Remember that if the light has just been in use, the bulb may be extremely hot.
b) Always check the bulb contacts and holder, ensuring that there is clean metal-to-metal contact between the bulb and its live(s) and earth. Clean off any corrosion or dirt before fitting a new bulb.
c) Wherever bayonet-type bulbs are fitted, ensure that the live contact(s) bear firmly against the bulb contact.
d) Always ensure that the new bulb is of the correct rating and that it is completely clean before fitting it; this applies particularly to headlight/foglight bulbs (see below).
e) With quartz halogen bulbs (headlights and similar applications), use a tissue or clean cloth when handling the bulb; do not touch the bulb glass with the fingers. Even small quantities of grease from the fingers will cause blackening and premature failure. If a bulb is accidentally touched, clean it with methylated spirit and a clean rag.

Headlight dipped or main beam

Models with single headlights

2 Remove the front indicator as described in this Section, then undo the 2 remaining bolts securing the headlight unit **(see illustration 9.1a)**. Pull the headlight unit forwards.

3 Pull the wiring plug off the rear of the bulb, and remove the rubber cover from the back of the headlight **(see illustration)**.

4 Release the bulb retaining clip **(see illustration)**.

Body electrical system 12•9

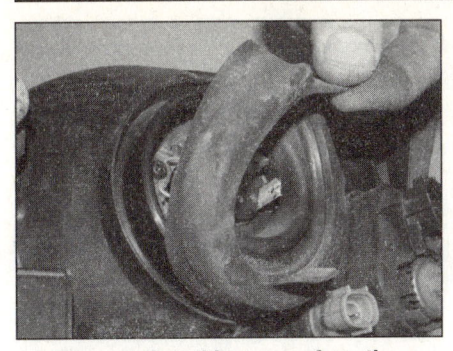

7.3 Remove the rubber cover from the rear of the headlight

7.4 Release the bulb retaining clip

7.5 Note how the bulb flange locates in the slots in the headlight

7.9 Disconnect the headlight wiring plug

7.10 Rotate the bulbholder anti-clockwise and pull it from the headlight

7.12 Rotate the sidelight bulbholder anti-clockwise (arrowed)

5 Lift out the bulb, noting how it fits in the reflector **(see illustration)**.
6 When fitting the new bulb, do not touch the glass (paragraph 1). Make sure that the lugs on the bulb flange engage with the slots in the holder.
7 Refitting is a reversal of removal.

Models with twin headlights

8 Open the bonnet. Undo the 3 bolts securing the headlight unit. The outer bolt also secures the indicator **(see illustration 9.1b)**. Pull the headlight unit forwards.
9 Pull the wiring plug off the rear of the bulb **(see illustration)**.
10 Rotate the bulbholder anti-clockwise, and pull it from the headlight **(see illustration)**. Note that the bulb is integral with the holder.
11 Connect the wiring plug onto the new bulb/holder, then insert the bulb into the back of the headlight, and rotate it clockwise to lock it in place.

Front sidelight
Models with single headlights

12 Open the bonnet. Reach behind the headlight, rotate the bulbholder anti-clockwise and pull the holder from place **(see illustration)**.
13 Pull the wedge type bulb from the holder **(see illustration)**.
14 Refitting is a reversal of removal.

Models with twin headlights

15 Remove the front indicator as described in Section 9.
16 Reach through the indicator aperture, and twist the sidelight bulbholder anti-clockwise, then pull it from the side of the headlight **(see illustration)**.
17 Pull the wedge type bulb from the holder.
18 Refitting is a reversal of removal.

Front foglight

19 Remove the foglight as described in Section 9.
20 Rotate the cover at the rear of the foglight anti-clockwise and remove it. Disconnect the bulbholder wiring plug from the cover **(see illustration)**.
21 Release the retaining clip and pull the bulb from the foglight **(see illustration)**.
22 Insert the new bulb, noting how the cut-out in the bulb flange aligns with the protrusion in the of the mounting.
23 The remainder of refitting is a reversal of removal.

Front direction indicator

24 Remove the indicator as described in Section 9.
25 Rotate the bulbholder anti-clockwise and pull it from the indicator **(see illustration)**.
26 The bulb is a bayonet fitting. Push it in a

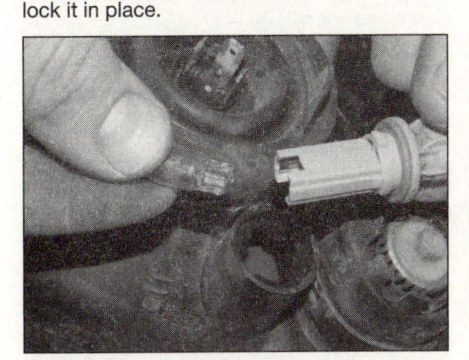

7.13 Pull the sidelight wedge bulb from the holder

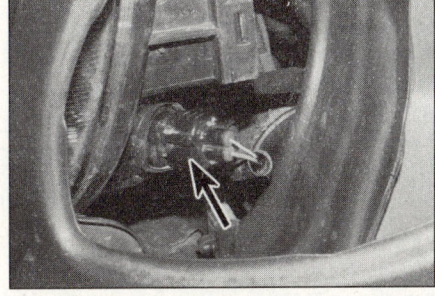

7.16 Reach through the indicator aperture, and twist the sidelight bulbholder anti-clockwise (arrowed)

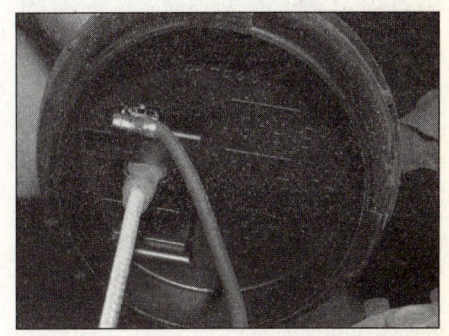

7.20 Disconnect the wiring plug from the inside of the foglight rear cover

12•10 Body electrical system

7.21 Release the foglight bulb retaining clip (arrowed)

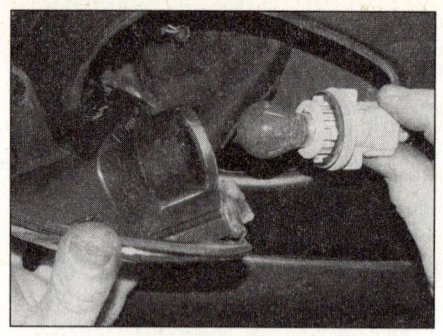

7.25 Rotate the bulbholder anti-clockwise and pull it from the indicator

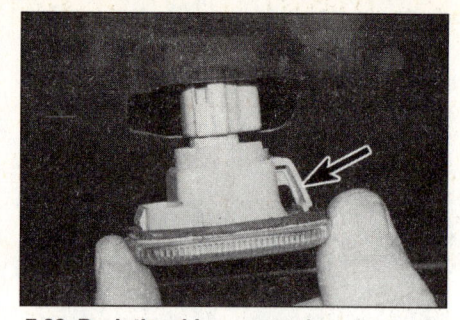

7.28 Push the side repeater lens forwards to compress the clip (arrowed), then pull the other end of the lens from the wing

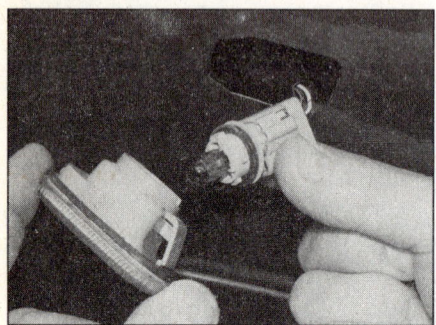

7.29 Twist the side repeater bulbholder anti-clockwise and pull it from place

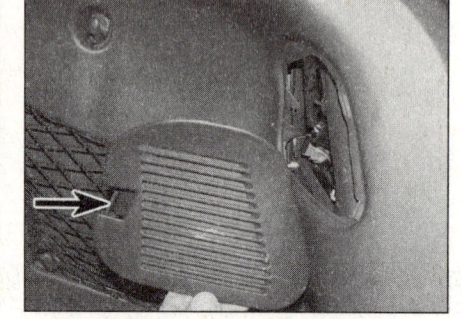

7.35 Release the clip (arrowed) and remove the access panel

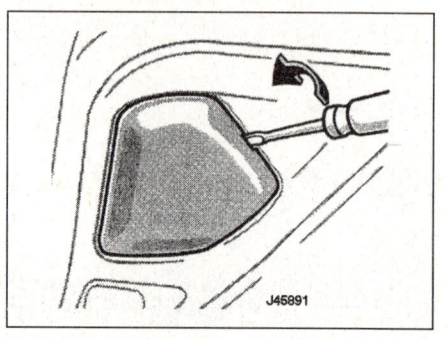

7.45 Prise the access cover from the boot lid

little, rotate it anti-clockwise and pull it from the bulbholder.
27 Refitting is a reversal of removal.

Direction indicator side repeater

28 Use a flat-bladed screwdriver to push the lens forward, and lever the rear edge of the lens from the wing (see illustration). Take great care not to damage the vehicle bodywork – use a piece of card between the screwdriver and the wing.
29 Twist the bulbholder through a quarter-turn anti-clockwise to release it from the light unit, and withdraw the holder (see illustration).
30 Pull the bulb from its holder, and press the new one into position.
31 Refitting is a reversal of removal.

Rear direction indicators, stop-light and tail light

Saloon models

32 Open the boot. Two different types of access cover are fitted. Either prise open the cover with a screwdriver, or undo the three nuts and pull the cover from place.
33 Twist the bulbholder anti-clockwise and pull it from the light unit. Push in and twist the bulb anti-clockwise to remove it from the bulbholder.
34 Refitting is a reversal of removal.

Hatchback and Liftback models

35 From within the luggage compartment, open the access panel on the side concerned (see illustration).
36 Rotate the relevant bulbholder anti-clockwise and pull it from the light unit. Push

in and twist the bulb anti-clockwise to remove it from the bulbholder.
37 Refitting is a reversal of removal.

Estate models

38 Open the tailgate, and undo the two retaining bolts (see illustration 9.30).
39 Pull the light unit from position, noting how the pins on the outside edge of the unit engage with the locating holes in the vehicle body.
40 Rotate the relevant bulbholder anti-clockwise, and pull the bulb from the holder.
41 Refitting is a reversal of removal.

Reversing light

Hatchback and Liftback models

42 From within the luggage compartment, open the access panel on the side concerned (see illustration 7.35).
43 Rotate the relevant bulbholder anti-clockwise and pull it from the light unit. Push in and twist the bulb anti-clockwise to remove it from the bulbholder.
44 Refitting is a reversal of removal.

Saloon models

45 Prise the access cover from the boot lid (see illustration).
46 Rotate the bulbholder anti-clockwise and pull it from the light unit. Push in and twist the bulb anti-clockwise to remove it from the bulbholder.
47 Refitting is a reversal of removal.

Estate models

48 Open the tailgate, and undo the two retaining bolts (see illustration 9.30).

49 Pull the light unit from position, noting how the pins on the outside edge of the unit engage with the locating holes in the vehicle body.
50 Rotate the relevant bulbholder anti-clockwise, and pull the bulb from the holder.
51 Refitting is a reversal of removal.

Rear foglight

Hatchback and Liftback models

52 From within the luggage compartment, open the access panel on the side concerned (see illustration 7.35).
53 Rotate the relevant bulbholder anti-clockwise and pull it from the light unit. Push in and twist the bulb anti-clockwise to remove it from the bulbholder.
54 Refitting is a reversal of removal.

Saloon models

55 Prise the access cover from the boot lid (see illustration 7.45).
56 Rotate the bulbholder anti-clockwise and pull it from the light unit. Push in and twist the bulb anti-clockwise to remove it from the bulbholder.
57 Refitting is a reversal of removal.

Estate models

58 Undo the two retaining screws, and pull the lens from the tailgate.
59 Pull the wedge type bulb from place.
60 Refitting is a reversal of removal.

High-level stop-light

Saloon models

61 Prise up the front edge of the light cover

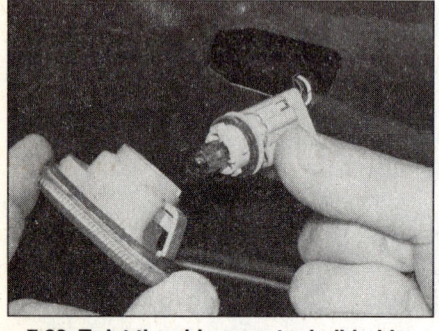

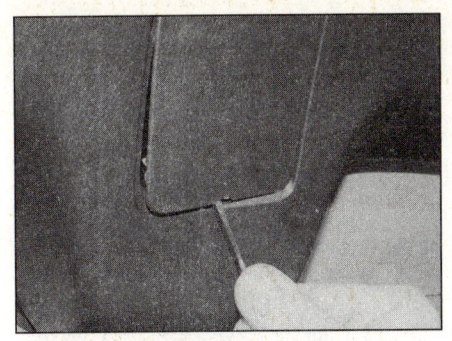

Body electrical system 12•11

7.64 Prise out the lower edge of the access cover

7.65 Twist the bulbholder anti-clockwise

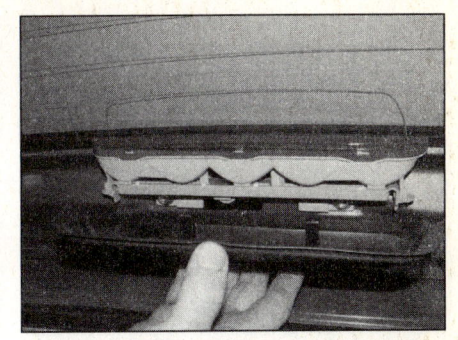

7.67 Carefully prise off the high-level brake light cover

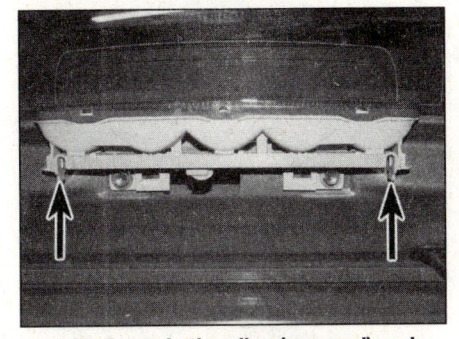

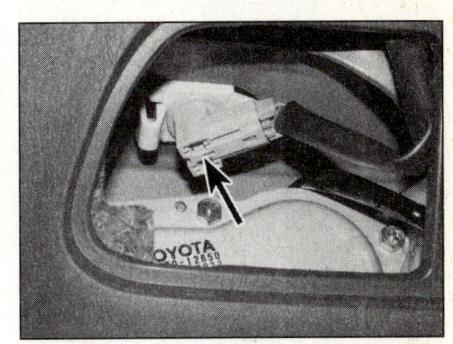

7.68 Press in the clips (arrowed) and remove the bulbholder

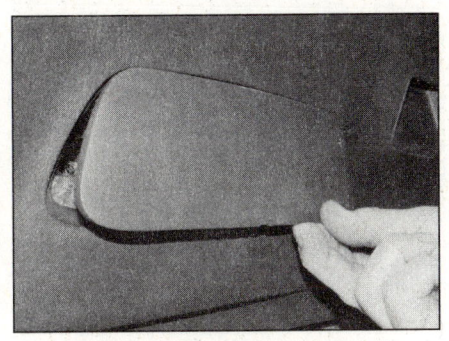

7.79 Prise out the lower edge of the access cover

7.80 Rotate the bulbholder (arrowed) anti-clockwise

from the parcel shelf, then pull the cover forward.
62 Twist the bulbholder anti-clockwise, and pull it from the light unit. Push in and twist the bulb anti-clockwise to remove it.
63 Refitting is a reversal of removal.

Liftback models
64 Prise out the lower edge of the access cover (see illustration).
65 Rotate the bulbholder anti-clockwise, and pull it from the light unit. Push in and twist the bulb anti-clockwise to remove it (see illustration).
66 Refitting is a reversal of removal.

Hatchback models
67 Working at the edge, carefully prise off the light cover (see illustration).
68 Press in the retaining clips and remove the bulbholder assembly (see illustration). Pull the wedge type bulb(s) from the holder.
69 Refitting is a reversal of removal.

Estate models
70 Pull the access cover downwards.
71 Rotate the bulbholder anti-clockwise and remove it from the light unit. Pull the wedge bulb from the holder.
72 Refitting is a reversal of removal.

Number plate light

Saloon models
73 Remove the boot lid inner trim panel.
74 Rotate the bulbholder anti-clockwise and pull it from the light unit. Pull the wedge bulb from the holder.
75 Refitting is a reversal of removal.

Liftback models
76 Prise open the lower edge and remove the access cover (see illustration 7.64).
77 Rotate the bulbholder anti-clockwise and pull it from the light unit. Pull the wedge bulb from the holder.
78 Refitting is a reversal of removal.

Hatchback models
79 Prise open the lower edge and remove the access cover (see illustration).
80 Rotate the bulbholder anti-clockwise and pull it from the light unit (see illustration). Pull the wedge bulb from the holder.
81 Refitting is a reversal of removal.

Estate models
82 Undo the two screws securing the light unit to the tailgate.
83 Rotate the bulbholder anti-clockwise and pull it from the light unit. Pull the wedge bulb from the holder.

8.3a Prise the interior light lens from place

84 Refitting is a reversal of removal.

8 Bulbs (interior lights) – renewal

General
1 Whenever a bulb is renewed, note the following points:
a) Remember that if the light has just been in use, the bulb may be extremely hot.
b) Always check the bulb contacts and holder, ensuring that there is clean metal-to-metal contact between the bulb and its live(s) and earth. Clean off any corrosion or dirt before fitting a new bulb.
c) Wherever bayonet-type bulbs are fitted, ensure that the live contact(s) bear firmly against the bulb contact.
d) Always ensure that the new bulb is of the correct rating and that it is completely clean before fitting it.
2 Some switch illumination/pilot bulbs are integral with their switches, and cannot be renewed separately.

Courtesy/interior light
3 Using a small flat-bladed screwdriver, carefully prise the lens from place. On some models the lens is retained by a screw (see illustrations).
4 Pull the bulb from the contacts (see illustration).
5 Refitting is a reversal of removal.

12•12 Body electrical system

8.3b On some models, the interior light lens is retained by a screw (arrowed)

8.4 Pull the interior light bulb from the contacts

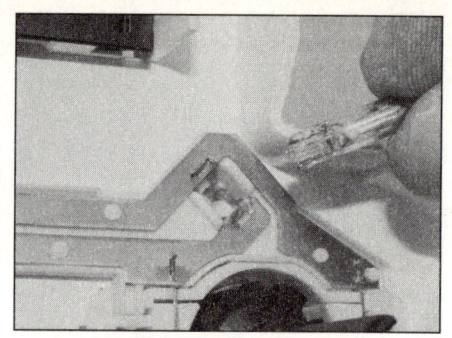

8.8 Pull the heater control panel illumination bulb from place

8.11 Twist the bulbholder anti-clockwise, and pull it from the selector lever panel

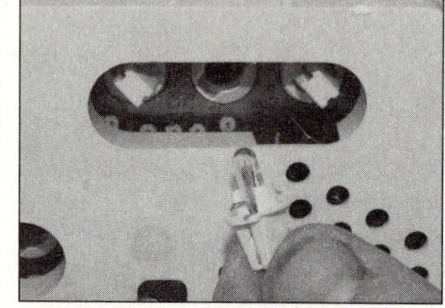

8.15 The instrument panel illumination bulbs are integral with the bulbholders

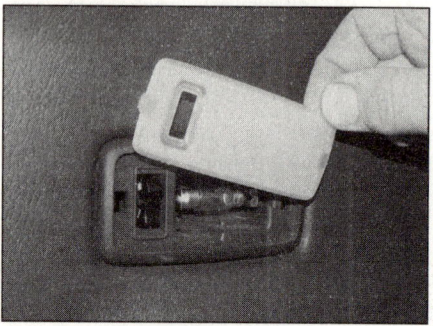

8.17 Prise the luggage compartment light lens from place

Heater control panel illumination

6 Pull the rotary heater control knobs from place, and undo the two screws in the knob recesses **(see illustration 4.45a and 4.45b)**.
7 Carefully prise the centre panel surround from place **(see illustration 4.46)**. Disconnect the wiring plugs as the panel is removed.
8 The wedge-type bulbs simply pull from place **(see illustration)**.
9 Refitting is a reversal of removal.

Automatic transmission selector panel illumination

10 Remove the centre console as described in Chapter 11.
11 Twist the bulbholder anti-clockwise then pull it from the selector housing **(see illustration)**.
12 Pull the wedge type bulb from the holder.
13 Refitting is a reversal of removal.

Instrument panel

14 Remove the instrument panel as described in Section 5.
15 Rotate the bulbholder anti-clockwise and pull it from the rear of the panel **(see illustration)**. The bulbs are integral with the holders.
16 Refitting is a reversal of removal.

Luggage area illumination

17 Carefully prise the light lens from position **(see illustration)**.
18 Remove the bulb from the holder.
19 Refitting is a reversal of removal.

Heated rear window, rear foglight, headlamp levelling and air conditioning switches

20 Remove the relevant switch (see Section 4).
21 Use a screwdriver to rotate the bulbholder anti-clockwise, and remove it **(see illustrations)**. The bulb is integral with the holder.

22 Refitting is a reversal of removal.

Hazard light switch

23 Remove the hazard light switch as described in Section 4.
24 Use a pair of thin-nosed pliers to rotate the bulbholder anti-clockwise and pull it from the switch. The bulb is integral with the holder **(see illustration)**.
25 Refitting is a reversal of removal.

9 Exterior light units – removal and refitting

Caution: Ensure the ignition is turned off before proceeding.

Headlight

1 Open the bonnet, undo the three screws and pull the headlight forwards. Note that

8.21a Use a screwdriver to rotate the bulbholder anti-clockwise

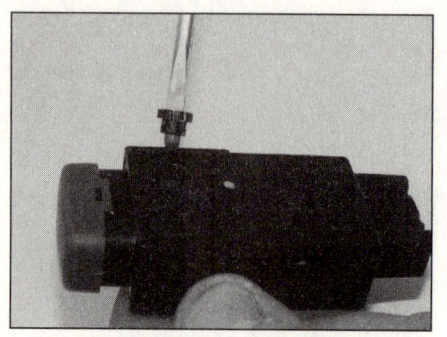

8.21b The switch illumination bulbs are integral with the bulbholders

8.24 Use a pair of thin-nosed pliers to rotate the hazard light illumination bulbholder anti-clockwise

Body electrical system 12•13

9.1a Headlight retaining screws (arrowed) – models with single headlights

9.1b Headlight retaining screws (arrowed) – models with twin headlights

9.4 Remove the front foglight retaining screw (arrowed)

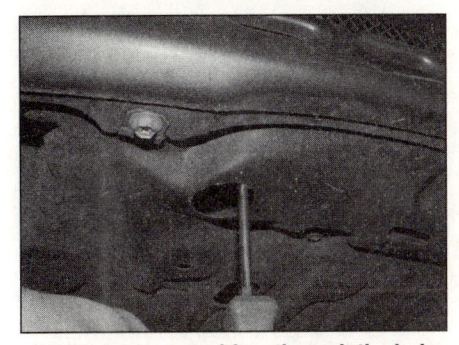

9.7 Insert a screwdriver through the hole in the bumper, and rotate the adjuster

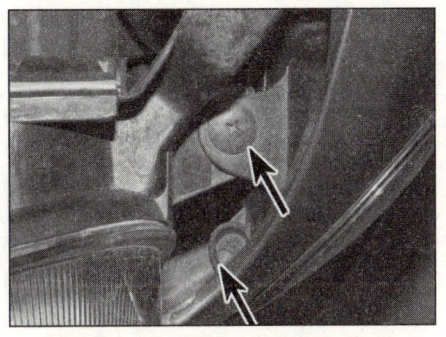

9.8 Front indicator retaining screw and clip (arrowed) – models with single headlights

9.10 Rotate the indicator until the mounting bracket aligns with the notch in the wing

the outer bolt also secures the indicator **(see illustrations)**.
2 Disconnect the wiring plugs and remove the headlight.
3 Refitting is a reversal of removal. Have the headlight beam alignment checked on completion (see Section 10).

Front foglight

4 Undo the screw and pull the foglight from position **(see illustration)**.
5 Disconnect the wiring plug as the foglight is withdrawn.
6 Refitting is a reversal of removal.
7 To adjust the headlight aim, insert a cross-head screwdriver through the hole in the base of the bumper cover, and rotate the adjusting wheel to the desired position **(see illustration)**

Front direction indicator

Models with single headlights

8 Lift the bonnet, and undo the indicator retaining screw **(see illustration)**.
9 Insert a screwdriver down beside the indicator, and release the retaining clip.
10 Rotate the indicator 90° to the outside, and pull the indicator forwards **(see illustration)**.
11 Rotate the bulbholder anti-clockwise and remove it from the indicator unit.
12 Refitting is a reversal of removal.

Models with twin headlights

13 Lift the bonnet, and undo the indicator retaining screw **(see illustration)**.

14 Insert a screwdriver down beside the indicator, and release the retaining clip by pushing it outwards **(see illustration)**.
15 Pull the indicator forwards.
16 Rotate the bulbholder anti-clockwise and remove it from the indicator unit.
17 Refitting is a reversal of removal.

Front indicator side repeater

18 Use a flat-bladed screwdriver to push the lens forward, and lever the rear edge of the lens from the wing **(see illustration 7.28)**. Take great care no to damage the vehicle bodywork – use a piece of card between the screwdriver and the wing.
19 Twist the bulbholder through a quarter-turn anti-clockwise to release it from the light unit, and withdraw the holder.
20 Refitting is a reversal of removal.

9.13 Indicator retaining screw (arrowed) – models with twin headlights

Rear light clusters

Saloon models

21 At the time of writing, no information was available.

Hatchback models

22 From within the luggage compartment, release the light unit access cover.
23 Disconnected the rear light cluster wiring plugs(s).
24 Undo the nuts and remove the cluster from the vehicle **(see illustration)**.
25 Refitting is a reversal of removal.

Liftback models

26 From within the luggage compartment, release the light unit access cover.
27 Disconnected the rear light cluster wiring plugs(s).

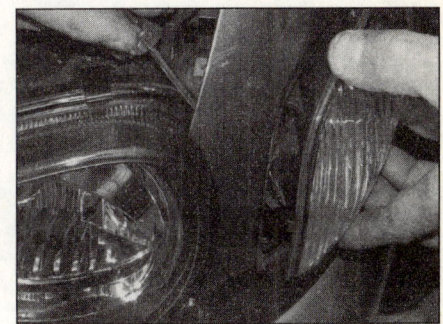

9.14 Release the retaining clip with a screwdriver

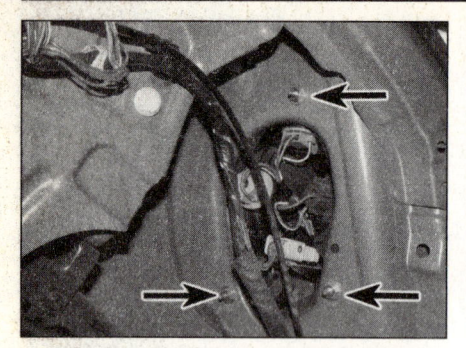

12•14 Body electrical system

9.24 Rear light cluster retaining nuts (arrowed) – Hatchback models

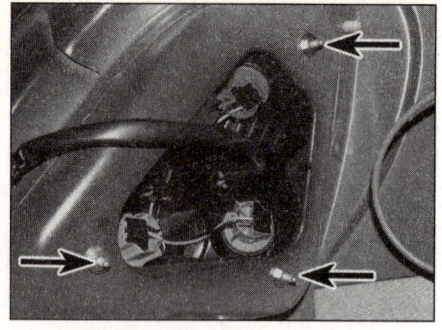

9.28 Rear light cluster retaining nuts (arrowed) – Liftback models

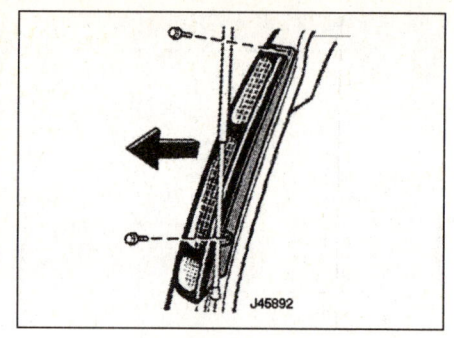

9.30 Undo the rear cluster retaining screws – Estate models

9.35 High-level brake light unit retaining screws (arrowed) – Liftback models

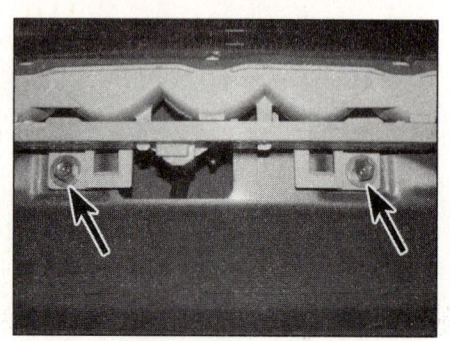

9.39 High-level brake light retaining screws (arrowed) – Hatchback models

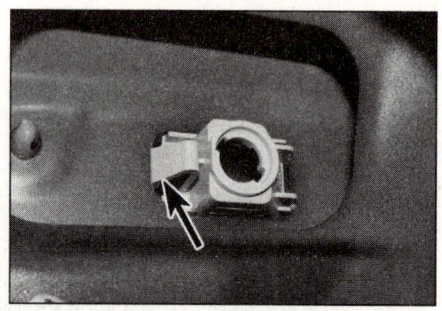

9.46 Depress the clip (arrowed) and remove the number plate light unit – Liftback models

28 Undo the three nuts and remove the cluster from the vehicle (see illustration). It is possible to remove the upper nut although access is limited. If improved access is required, remove the luggage compartment side panel as described in Chapter 11, Section 27.
29 Refitting is a reversal of removal.

Estate models
30 Open the tailgate, and undo the rear light cluster retaining screws (see illustration).
31 Disconnected the rear light cluster wiring plugs(s).
32 Refitting is a reversal of removal.

High-level brake light

Saloon models
33 No information was available at the time of writing.

Liftback models
34 Remove the tailgate interior trim panels as described in Chapter 11, Section 27.
35 Undo the light unit retaining bolts (see illustration).
36 Disconnect the wiring plug as the unit is withdrawn.
37 Refitting is a reversal of removal.

Hatchback models
38 Carefully prise off the plastic cover (see illustration 7.67).
39 Undo the two bolts and pull the light from the tailgate (see illustration).
40 Disconnect the light unit wiring plug as the light unit is removed.
41 Refitting is a reversal of removal.

Estate models
42 No information was available at the time of writing.

Number plate light

Saloon models
43 No information was available at the time of writing.

Liftback models
44 Remove the tailgate trim panel as described in Chapter 11, Section 27.
45 Rotate the bulbholder anti-clockwise and pull it from the light unit.
46 Depress the clip and pull the light unit from the tailgate (see illustration).
47 Refitting is a reversal of removal.

Hatchback models
48 Remove the tailgate trim panel as described in Chapter 11, Section 27.

10.2 Headlight aim adjusting screws (arrowed)

49 Release the fasteners and remove the exterior trim from over the number plate lights.
50 Release the clips and withdraw the number plate light from the tailgate.
51 Refitting is a reversal of removal.

Estate models
52 No information was available at the time of writing.

10 Headlight beam alignment – checking and adjusting

1 Beam alignment should be carried out by a Toyota dealer or other specialist having the necessary optical alignment equipment.
2 For reference, the headlights can be adjusted by means of the vertical and horizontal adjuster controls at the back of the headlight unit (see illustration).
3 Some models are equipped with an electrically-operated headlight beam adjustment system which is controlled through the switch on the facia. On these models, ensure that the switch is set to the off position before adjusting the headlight aim.

11 Headlight beam control motor – removal and refitting

At the time of writing, then beam control motor appears not to be available as a separate part. If faulty, the entire headlamp

Body electrical system 12•15

12.2 Horn retaining bolt (arrowed)

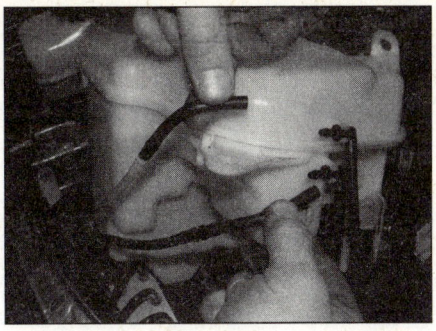

13.2 Pull the rubber washer hoses from the pump

13.4 Pull the pump from the grommet in the washer fluid reservoir

unit must be renewed as described in Section 9. Check with your Toyota dealer or parts specialist.

12 Horn – renewal

1 Undo the three screws and remove the radiator grille.
2 Unbolt the horn complete with its bracket **(see illustration)**. Disconnect the wiring plug as the horn is removed.
3 Refitting is a reversal of removal.

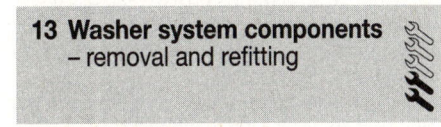

13 Washer system components – removal and refitting

Washer pump
1 Remove the washer reservoir as described in this Section.
2 Note their fitted locations, then pull the hose(s) from the motor **(see illustration)**, and disconnect the motor wiring plug.
3 Place a container under the reservoir, and be prepared for spillage.
4 Grip the washer pump and pull it out of the reservoir **(see illustration)**.
5 Refitting is a reversal of removal.

Washer reservoir
6 From within the engine compartment, undo the retaining screw then lift the reservoir from place **(see illustration)**. Disconnect the washer tubes and wiring plugs as the reservoir is removed.
7 Refitting is a reversal of removal.

Washer jets

Windscreen jet
8 Open the bonnet.
9 Disconnect the jet wiring plug (where applicable) and disconnect the washer hose.
10 Squeeze together the two retaining clips on the underside of the jet using pliers, and remove the jet from the bonnet **(see illustration)**.
11 Push the jet into its location until the clips spring out to lock. Reconnect the fluid hose and wiring plug (where applicable)
12 Adjust the jet nozzle(s) using a pin so that liquid is sprayed onto the centre of the glass.

Rear screen jet
13 Open the tailgate, prise out the rubber grommet, then disconnect the washer jet hose **(see illustration)**.
14 Use a small screwdriver to carefully depress the front or rear retaining clip and pull the jet from the tailgate **(see illustration)**.
15 Push the jet into its location until the clips spring out to lock. Reconnect the fluid hose and wiring plug (where applicable)
16 Adjust the jet nozzle(s) using a pin so that liquid is sprayed onto the centre of the glass.

Non-return check valve
17 To prevent washer fluid running back into the reservoir, a non-return valve is fitted into

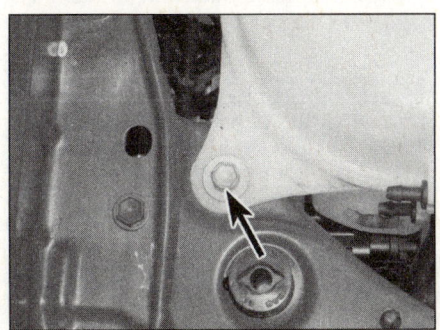

13.6 Washer fluid reservoir retaining bolt (arrowed)

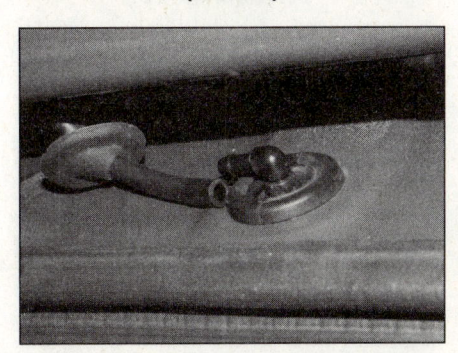

13.11 Prise out the rubber grommet and disconnect the tailgate washer jet hose

the supply hose to each washer jet. Open the bonnet, and release the washer hose from the retaining clips.
18 Carefully pull the hoses from the non-return valve, noting the direction of flow marking on the valve.
19 It should only be possible to blow through the valve in one direction. If faulty, the valve must be renewed.
20 Refitting is a reversal of removal.

14 Wiper arms – removal and refitting

Removal
1 Prise off the cover (where applicable) then slacken the nut at the base of the wiper arm **(see illustrations)**.

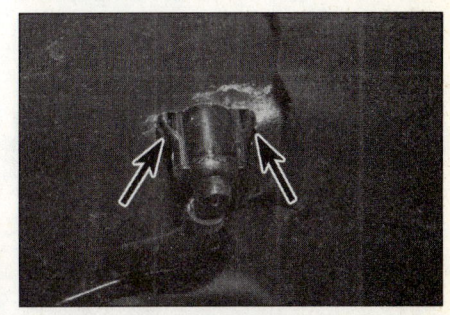

13.10 Squeeze together the clips (arrowed) and pull the windscreen washer jet from the bonnet

13.12 Tailgate washer retaining clips (arrowed)

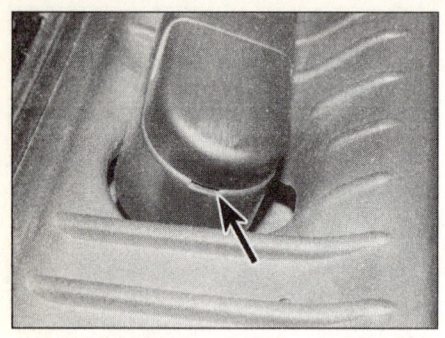

12•16 Body electrical system

14.1a Prise up the windscreen wiper arm cover (arrowed) . . .

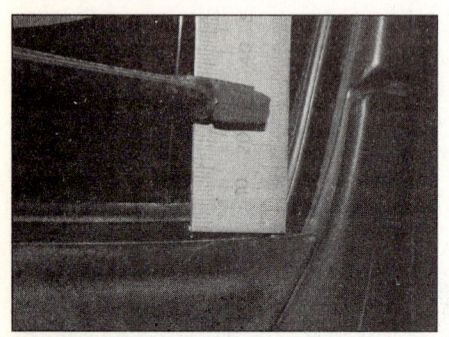

14.1b . . . then undo the retaining nut

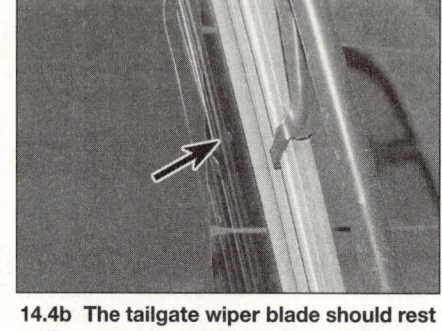

14.3 Tailgate wiper arm retaining nut

off again to ensure that the motor and linkage are parked. Position the windscreen wiper arms so that the end of the wiper blade is 25 mm above the base of the windscreen trim. Position the tailgate wiper arm so that the end of the blade aligns with the mark on the rear screen **(see illustrations)**.

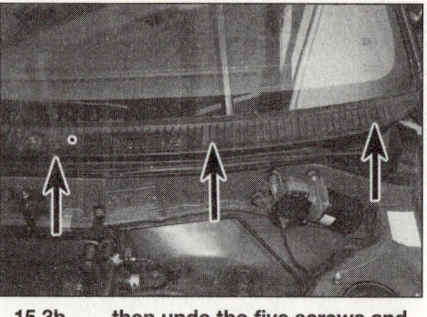

15 Windscreen wiper motor and linkage – removal and refitting

14.4a The end of the windscreen wiper blade should be 25 mm above the base of the windscreen trim

14.4b The tailgate wiper blade should rest adjacent to the mark on the rear screen (arrowed)

2 Using a rocking motion, pull the arms off the splines. If necessary, use a puller to remove the arms.
3 On the tailgate wiper, fold up the cover, and undo the nut securing the arm to the spindle.

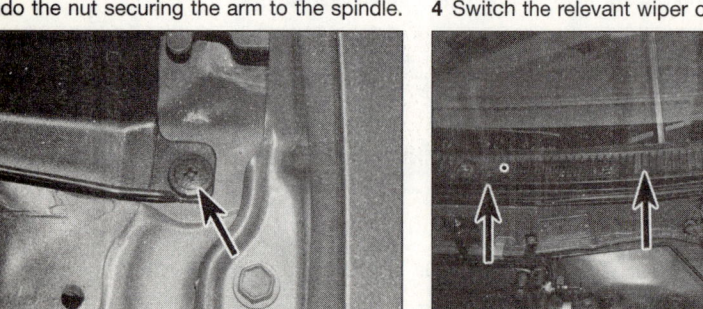

Pull the arm from the spindle using a rocking motion **(see illustration)**.

Refitting

4 Switch the relevant wiper on, then switch it

Removal

1 Switch the wipers on, then off again to ensure that the motor and linkage are parked.
2 Remove the windscreen wiper arms as described in Section 14.
3 Undo the retaining screws and prise out the clip at each end of the scuttle trim, then undo the remaining five screws securing the trim **(see illustrations)**.
4 Prise up the front edge of the scuttle trim from the bulkhead, and remove the trim.
5 Disconnect the wiper motor wiring plug, then undo the four screws and remove the motor. Separate the motor arm from the linkage **(see illustrations)**.
6 If required, undo the six bolts and remove the linkage assembly from position **(see illustration)**.

Refitting

7 Refit the linkage, and tighten the retaining bolts securely
8 Reconnect the linkage to the motor arm ball-

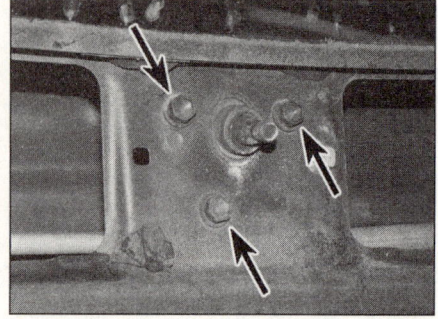

15.3a Undo the screw, and prise out the expanding clip at each end of the scuttle trim (arrowed) . . .

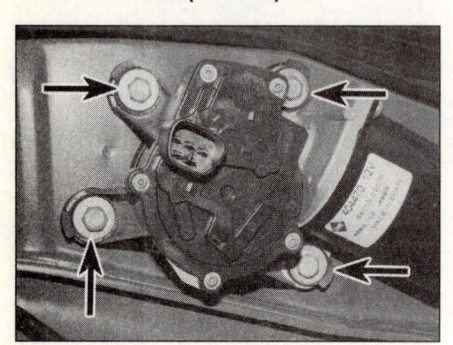

15.3b . . . then undo the five screws and remove the scuttle trim (3 left-hand side screws arrowed)

15.5a Undo the four wiper motor retaining screws (arrowed)

15.5b Prise the motor arm from the wiper linkage

15.6 The wiper linkage is secure by three bolts around each spindle (arrowed)

Body electrical system 12•17

16.5 Tailgate wiper motor bolts (arrowed)

17.2 The console mounted audio unit is retained by four screws (arrowed)

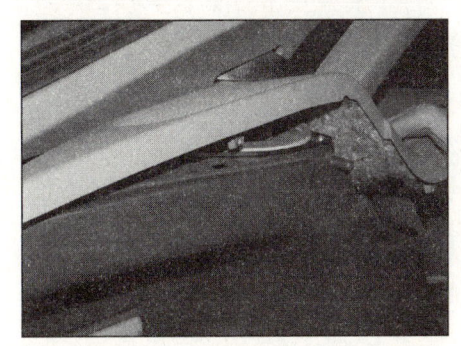

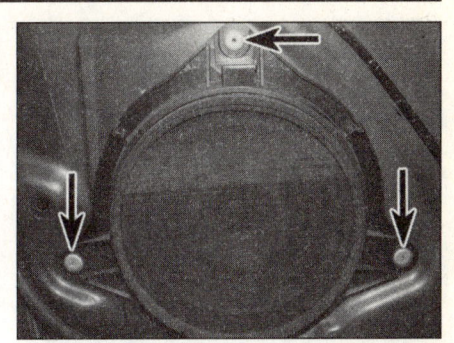

18.2 Drill out the door speaker rivets (arrowed)

joint, then refit the motor and tighten the mounting bolts securely. Reconnect the wiring plug.
9 The remainder of refitting is a reversal of removal.

16 Tailgate wiper motor – removal and refitting

Removal

1 Switch the wiper on then off again to ensure that the motor and linkage are parked.
2 Remove the tailgate wiper arm as described in Section 14. On Estate models, undo the spindle nut.
3 Remove the tailgate interior trim panel as described in Chapter 11, Section 27.
4 Disconnect the motor wiring plug.
5 Undo the motor retaining bolts and withdraw it from the tailgate (see illustration).

Refitting

6 Refit the motor to the tailgate and securely tighten the mounting bolts.
7 If a new motor is being fitted, temporarily connect the wiring connector, switch on the motor then switch it off again to ensure that it is parked.
8 Refitting is a reversal of removal.

17 Audio units – removal and refitting

Centre console mounted unit

Removal

1 Remove the centre console switch panel as described in Chapter 11.
2 Undo the four screws and pull the unit from position (see illustration). Disconnect the wiring plugs as the unit is withdrawn.

Refitting

3 Refitting is a reversal of removal.

Facia mounted unit

4 Removal of the central facia mounted unit is identical to 'Central information unit removal' as described in Section 5 of this Chapter.

18.6 Prise up the trim panel above the rear speaker

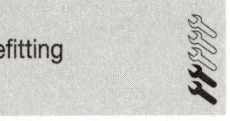

18 Speakers – removal and refitting

Door speaker

1 Remove the door trim panel as described in Chapter 11.
2 Drill out the rivets securing the speaker to the door frame (see illustration).
3 Remove the speaker and disconnect the wiring connector.
4 Refitting is a reversal of removal.

Parcel shelf speaker

5 Remove the parcel shelf
6 Prise up the trim panel above the speaker (see illustration).
7 Disconnect the speaker wiring plug.
8 Undo the screws, then lift the speaker from position (see illustration).
9 Refitting is a reversal of removal.

19 Supplemental Restraint System (SRS) – general information and precautions

General information

A supplemental restraint system is fitted in various forms as standard or optional equipment depending on model and territory.
The main system component is a driver's airbag, which is designed to prevent serious chest and head injuries to the driver during an

18.8 The rear speakers are retained by three screws

accident. There are also airbags for the front seat passenger and side airbags (built into the side of the front seats). Side impact crash sensors are located on the B-pillars of the vehicle, with two frontal sensors fitted on the left- and right-hand side of the engine compartment. A control module is fitted under the front section of the centre console. The module incorporates a deceleration sensor, and a microprocessor ECM, to monitor the severity of the impact and trigger the airbag where necessary. The airbag is inflated by a gas generator, which forces the bag out of the module cover in the centre of the steering wheel, or out of a cover on the passenger's side of the facia/seat cover/headlining. A contact reel behind the steering wheel at the top of the steering column ensures that a good electrical connection is maintained with the airbag at all times, as the steering wheel is turned in each direction.

In addition to the airbag units, the supplemental restraint system also incorporates pyrotechnical seat belt tensioners fitted in the belt inertia reel assembly. The pyrotechnical units are also triggered by the crash sensors, in conjunction with the airbags, to tighten the seat belts and provide additional collision protection.

Precautions

⚠️ *Warning: Any attempt to dismantle the airbag module, SIPS bag, crash sensors, contact reel, seat belt tensioners or any associated wiring or components without dedicated equipment, and the specialist knowledge needed to use it correctly, could result in severe personal injury and/or malfunction of the system.*

12•18 Body electrical system

20.2 Undo the airbag retaining screws with a T30 Torx bit (shown with the airbag removed for clarity)

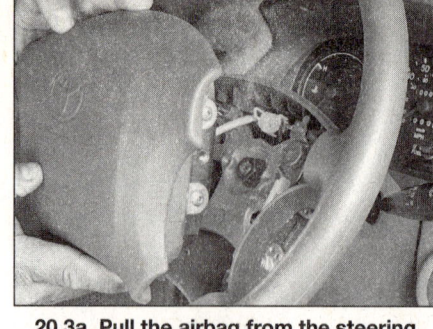

20.3a Pull the airbag from the steering wheel . . .

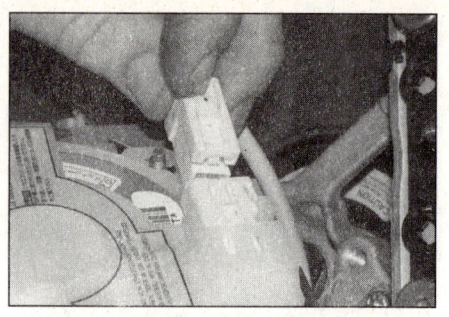

20.3b . . . then depress the clip and disconnect the wiring plug – single headlight models

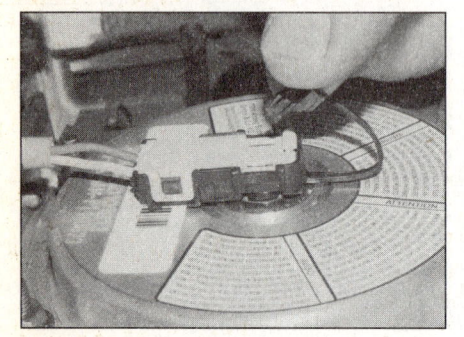

20.3c On twin headlight models, prise out the locking clip . . .

20.3d . . . and disconnect the airbag wiring plug

- Before carrying out any work on the SRS components, disconnect the battery and wait for at least 5 minutes for any residual electrical energy to dissipate before proceeding.
- Handle the airbag unit with extreme care as a precaution against personal injury, and always hold it with the cover facing away from the body. If in doubt concerning any proposed work involving the airbag unit or its control circuitry, consult a Toyota dealer.
- Note that the airbag(s) must not be subjected to temperatures in excess of 90°C (194°F). When the airbag is removed, ensure that it is stored with the pad facing up to prevent possible inflation.
- Do not allow any solvents or cleaning agents to contact the airbag assemblies. They must be cleaned using only a damp cloth.
- The airbag(s) and control unit are both sensitive to impact. If either is dropped or damaged they should be renewed.

- Disconnect the airbag control unit wiring plug prior to using arc-welding equipment on the vehicle.

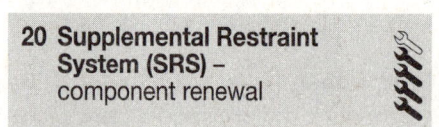

20 Supplemental Restraint System (SRS) – component renewal

Note: Before proceeding, refer to the warnings in Section 19.

Driver's airbag

Removal

1 Turn the ignition key to off, then disconnect the cable from the negative terminal of the battery (see Chapter 5A), then wait at least 5 minutes before proceeding.
2 Turn the steering wheel so the wheels are pointing straight-ahead, and prise out the two plastic plugs either side of the steering wheel (where fitted). Undo the T30 Torx screw each side of the steering wheel boss securing the airbag. There is no need to remove the screws, simply undo them to the 'released' position **(see illustration)**.
3 Pull the airbag module off the steering wheel and disconnect the module electrical connector **(see illustration)**.

⚠ *Warning: Set the airbag module down with the trim side facing up.*

Refitting

4 Reconnect the airbag wiring plug, and position the airbag on the steering wheel.
5 Tighten the airbag retaining screws.
6 Make sure that no-one is inside the car, then reconnect the battery negative lead.

Driver's airbag contact reel

Removal

7 Remove the airbag unit as described above, and the steering wheel and column shrouds as described in Chapter 10.
8 Taking care not to rotate the contact unit, undo the four retaining screws and remove it from the steering column switch assembly. Disconnect the wiring plug **(see illustrations)**.

Refitting

9 If a new contact unit is being fitted, cut the cable-tie which is fitted to prevent the unit accidentally rotating.
10 A new reel should be supplied in the centralised position – if not, or there is a chance the unit is not centralised, proceed as follows. Turn the reel gently clockwise as far as it will go, then turn it back anti-clockwise two turns. The arrow marks on the contact unit should align **(see illustration)**.
11 Fit the unit to the steering column switch assembly and securely tighten its retaining screws.
12 Refit the steering wheel as described in Chapter 10, and the airbag unit as described above.

Passenger's airbag

Removal

13 Disconnect the battery negative lead (see Chapter 5A), and wait 5 minutes before proceeding.

20.8a Disconnect the contact unit wiring plug (arrowed) . . .

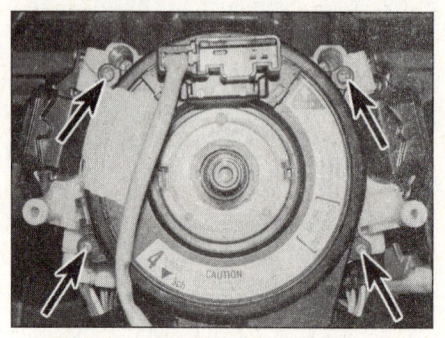

20.8b . . . then undo the contact unit retaining screws (arrowed)

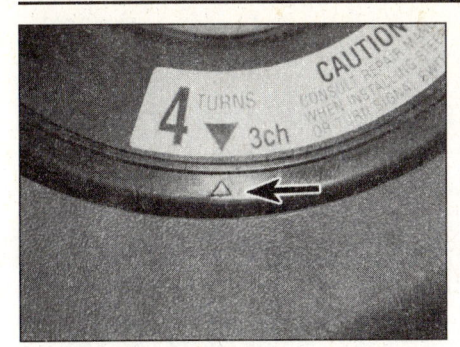

Body electrical system 12•19

20.10 When centralised, the arrows on the contact unit should align (arrowed)

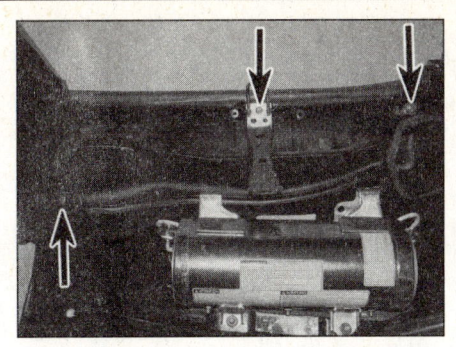

20.15 Undo the centre bracket screw and air duct screws (arrowed)

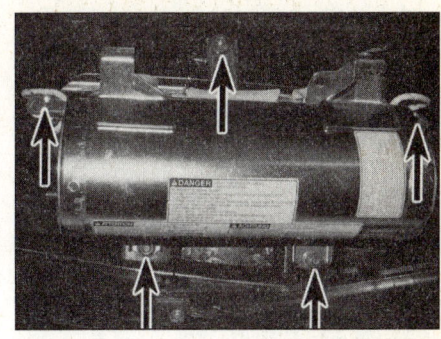

20.16 Undo the three nuts and two bolts, then remove the passenger's airbag

14 Remove the complete facia as described in Chapter 11.
15 Undo the retaining screw, remove the centre bracket, then undo the two screws and unclip and remove the air vent duct from the underside of the facia **(see illustration)**.
16 Undo the three retaining nuts and two bolts, then remove the airbag from the facia **(see illustration)**.

Refitting

17 Refitting is a reversal of removal.
18 On completion, make sure that no-one is inside the car, then reconnect the battery negative lead.

Airbag control module

Removal

19 Disconnect the battery negative lead as described in Chapter 5A. Wait at least 5 minutes before proceeding, to allow any residual electrical energy to dissipate.
20 Remove the engine management ECM as described in Chapter 4A.
21 Unclip the carpet each side, then undo the 3 screws and remove the module to the passenger's side **(see illustration)**. Note that, on some models, it may be necessary to unbolt the wiring loom support bracket from the left-hand side of the module in order to remove it.
22 Depress the retaining clips and disconnect the module wiring plugs **(see illustration)**.

Refitting

23 Refitting is a reversal of removal, ensuring the module is fitted with the arrow on its top surface facing forwards.
24 On completion, make sure that no-one is inside the car, then reconnect the battery negative lead.

Side airbags

25 The side airbag units are built into the front seats, and their removal requires that the seat fabric be removed. This is not considered to be a DIY operation, and should be referred to a Toyota dealer or upholstery specialist.

Side crash sensors

Removal

26 Disconnect the battery negative lead as described in Chapter 5A. Wait at least 5 minutes before proceeding, to allow any residual electrical energy to dissipate.
27 The side crash sensors are fitted to vehicles B-pillar (between the driver's and passenger's doors) only on models equipped with side airbags.
28 Remove the front seat belt inertia reel units as described in Chapter 11.
29 Release the clip and disconnect the wiring plug from the sensor.
30 Undo the four retaining Torx screws and remove the sensor.

Refitting

31 Refit the sensor(s) to the pillar(s) and tighten the retaining screws to the specified torque. Reconnect the wiring plug.

32 The remainder of refitting is a reversal of removal.
33 On completion, make sure that no-one is inside the car, then reconnect the battery negative lead.

Front crash sensors

34 Disconnect the battery negative lead as described in Chapter 5A. Wait at least 5 minutes before proceeding, to allow any residual electrical energy to dissipate.

Left-hand sensor

35 Jack up the front of the vehicle and support it securely on axle stands (see *Jacking and vehicle support*).
36 Release the fasteners and remove the left-hand engine undershield.
37 Disconnect the sensor wiring plug, and undo the two bolts and remove the sensor **(see illustration)**.

Right-hand sensor

38 Remove the right-hand headlight as described in Section 9.
39 Reach through the headlight aperture, disconnect the sensor wiring plug, then undo the two nuts and remove the sensor **(see illustration)**.

Both sensors

40 Refitting is a reversal of removal, tightening the retaining bolts/nuts to the specified torque.
41 On completion, make sure that no-one is inside the car, then reconnect the battery negative lead.

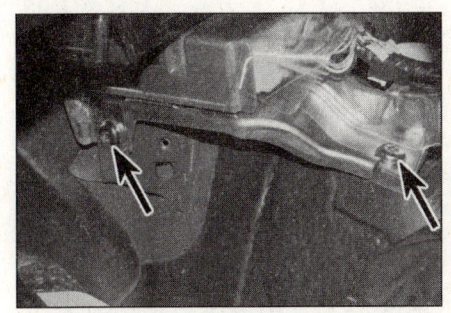

20.21 Undo the airbag control module retaining screws (two left-hand ones arrowed)

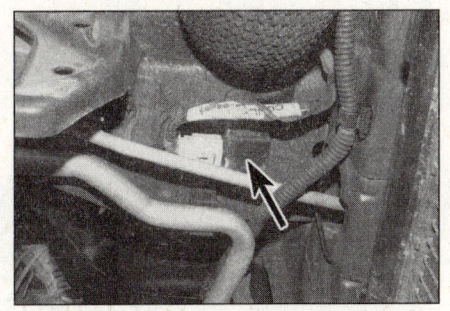

20.37 Left-hand front crash sensor (arrowed – shown with the battery removed for clarity)

20.39 Right-hand front crash sensor (arrowed)

12•20 Wiring diagrams

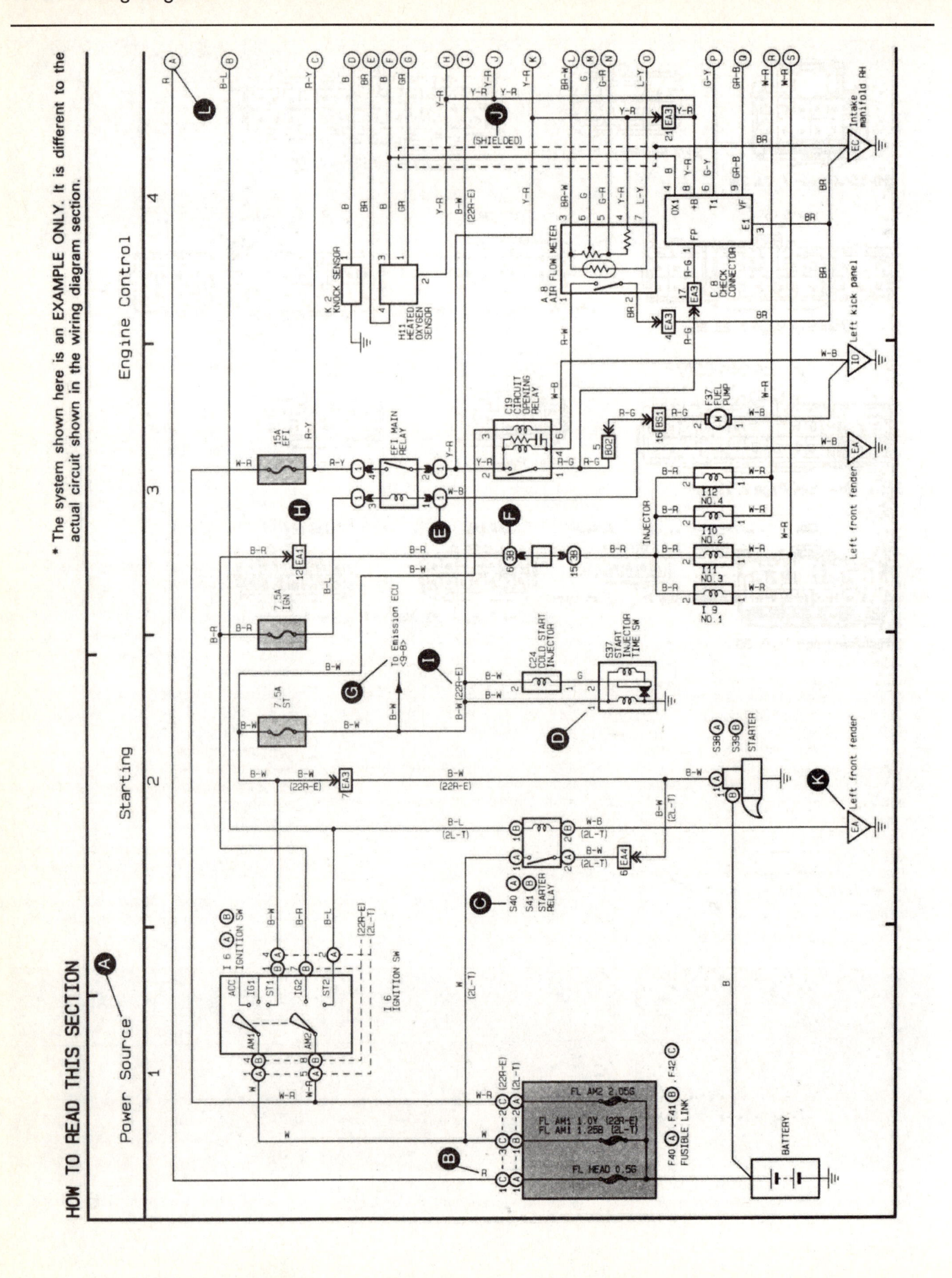

Wiring diagrams 12•21

A: System Title

B: Indicates the wiring color.

Wire colors are indicated by an alphabetical code.

B = Black	L = Blue	R = Red
BR = Brown	LG = Light Green	V = Violet
G = Green	O = Orange	W = White
GR = Gray	P = Pink	Y = Yellow

The first letter indicates the basic wire color and the second letter indicates the color of the stripe.

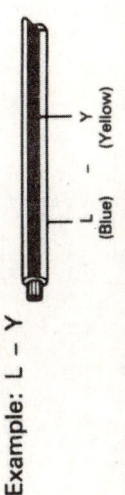

Example: L – Y

(Blue) (Yellow)

C: The position of the parts is the same as shown in the wiring diagram and wire routing.

D: Indicates the pin number of the connector. The numbering system is different for female and male connectors.

Example: Numbered in order from upper left to lower right. Numbered in order from upper right to lower left.

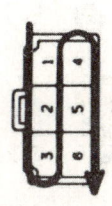

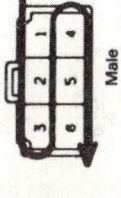

The numbering system for the overall wiring diagram is the same as above.

E: Indicates a Relay Block. No shading is used and only the Relay Block No. is shown to distinguish it from the J/B.

Example: ① Indicates Relay Block No. 1.

F: Junction Block (The number in the circle is the J/B No. and the connector code is shown beside it). Junction Blocks are shaded to clearly separate them from other parts.

Example:

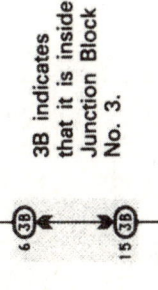

3B indicates that it is inside Junction Block No. 3.

G: Indicates related system.

H: Indicates the wiring harness and wiring harness connector. The wiring harness with male terminal is shown with arrows (➤). Outside numerals are pin numbers.

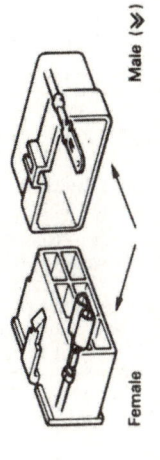

I: ( ) is used to indicate different wiring and connector, etc. when the vehicle model, engine type, or specification is different.

J: Indicates a shielded cable.

K: Indicates and located on ground point.

L: The same code occuring on the next page indicates that the wire harness is continuous.

Note: *Only diagrams relevant to the specific coverage of this manual are included, so these do not follow a complete numerical sequence (non-applicable diagrams have been omitted). Consequently some diagrams contain cross-references to others which are not included here.*

12•22 Wiring diagrams

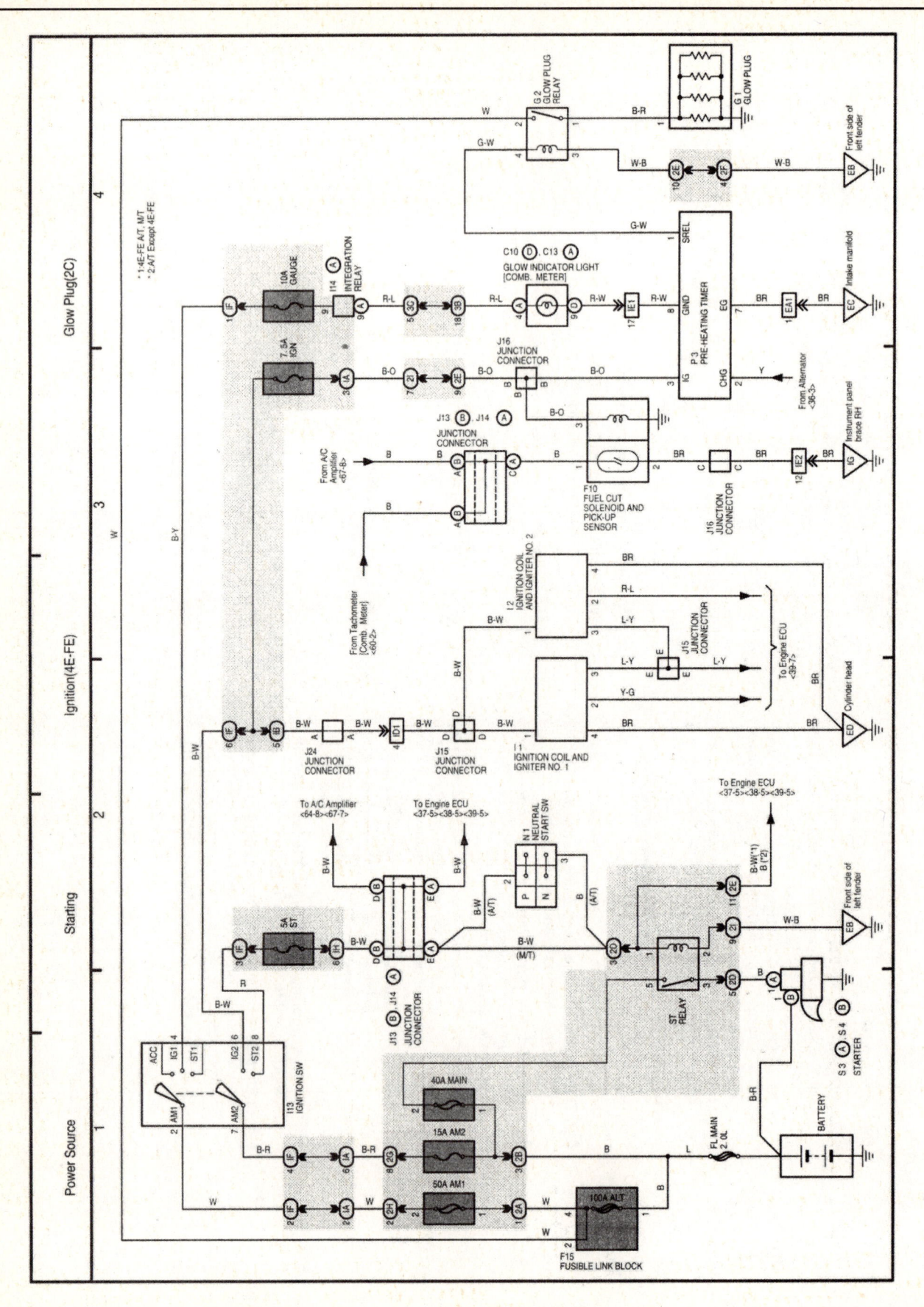

Diagram 34

Wiring diagrams 12•23

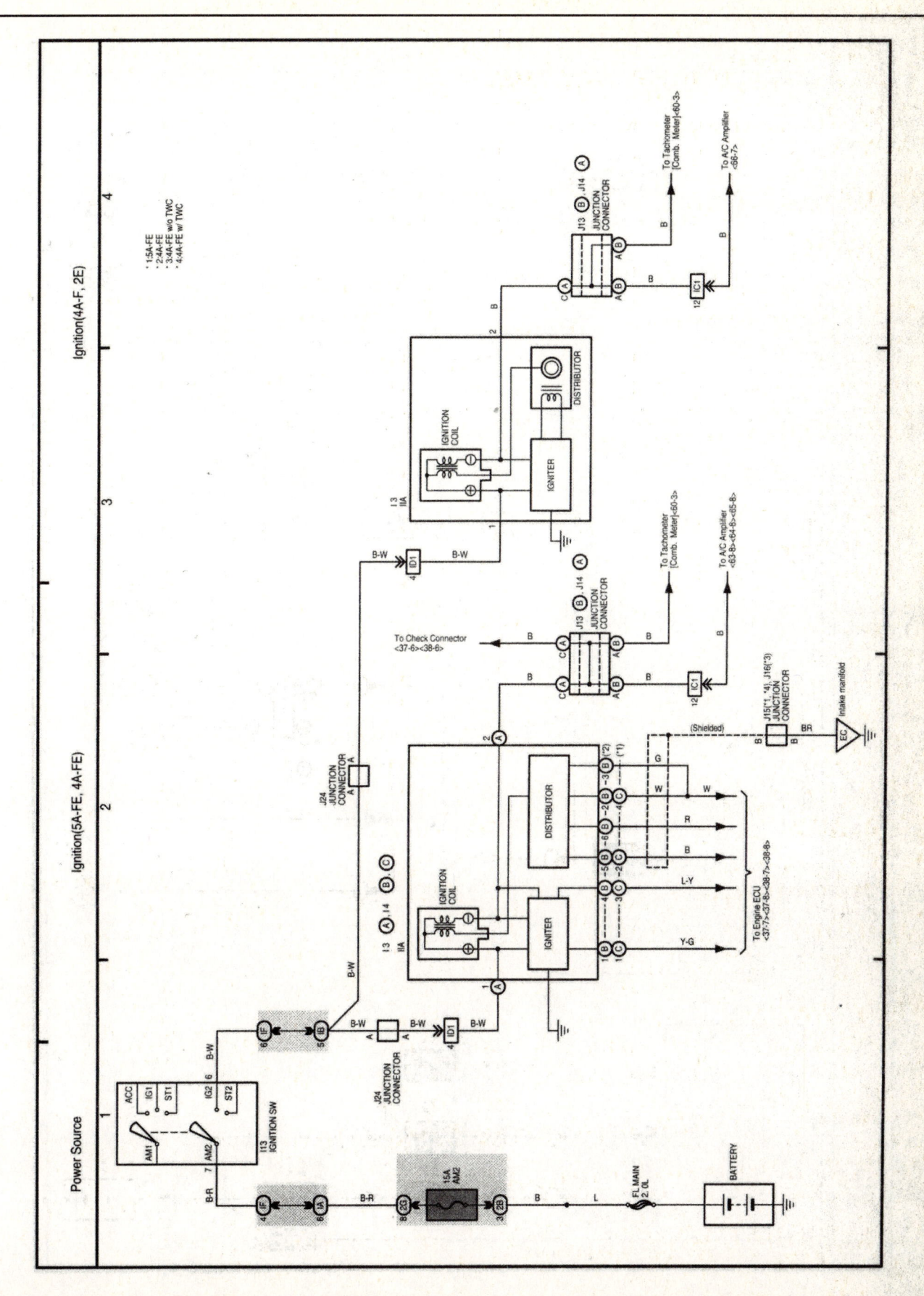

Diagram 35

12•24 Wiring diagrams

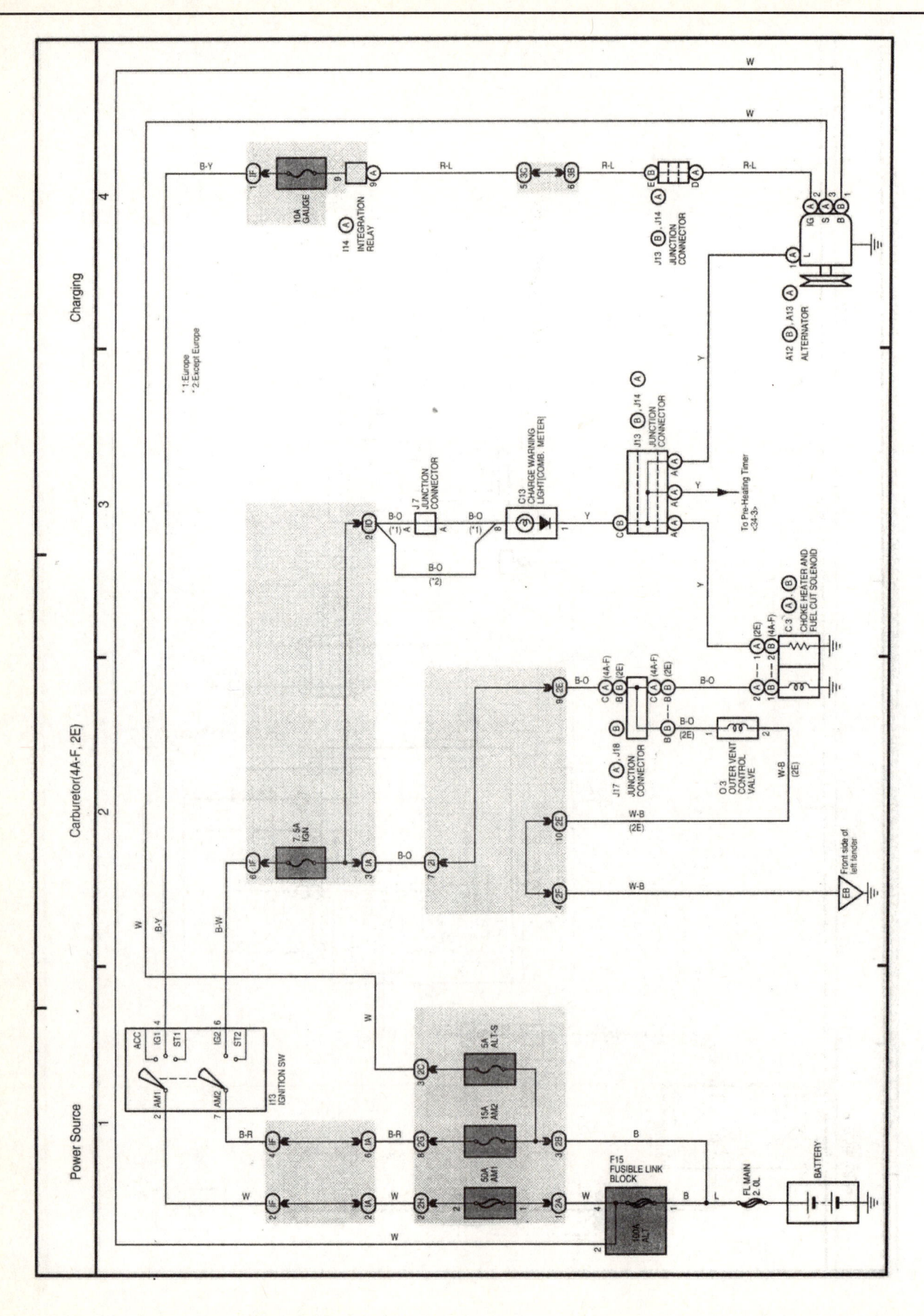

Diagram 36

Wiring diagrams 12•25

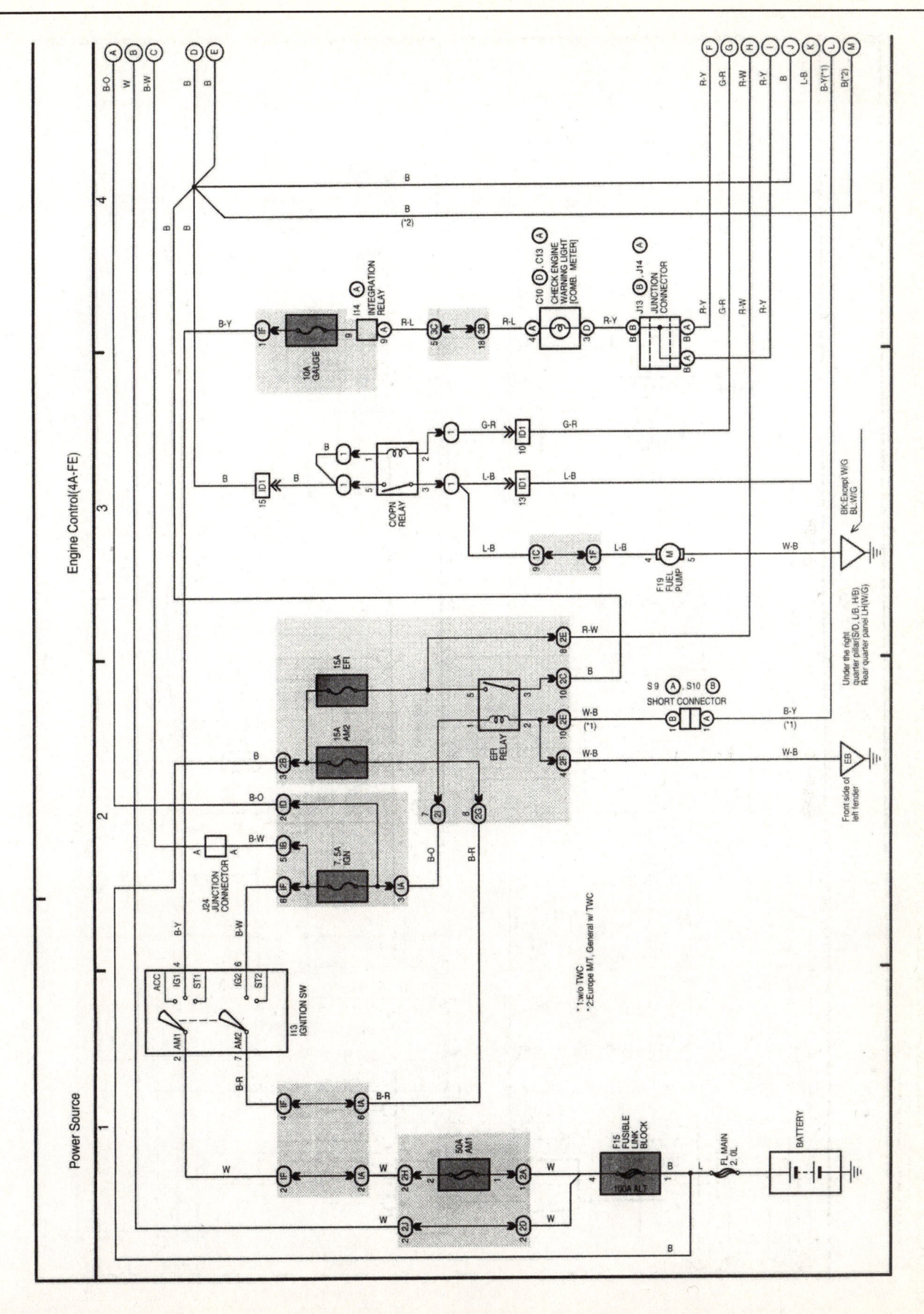

Diagram 38 Part 1

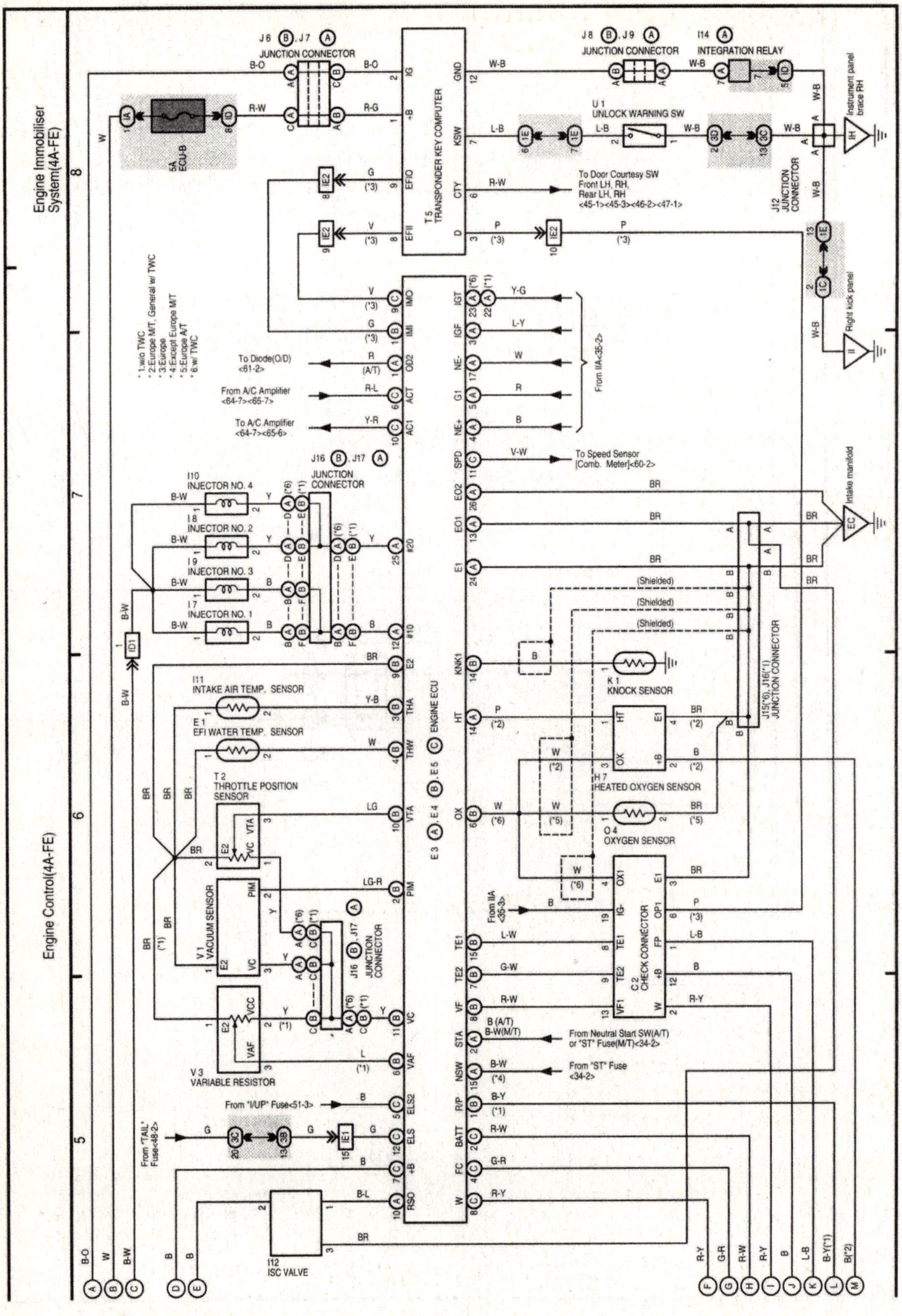

12•26 Wiring diagrams

Diagram 38 Part 2

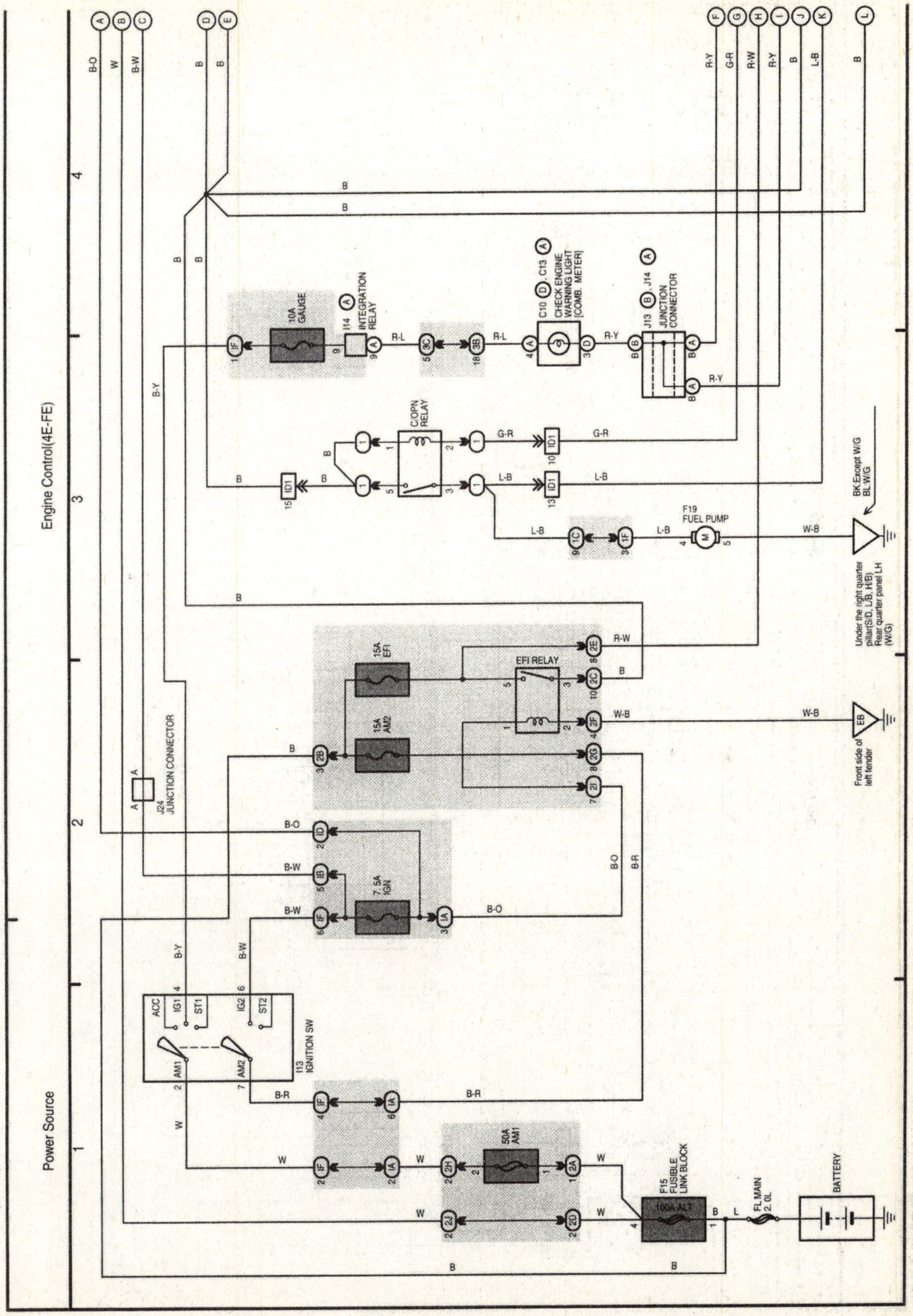

Wiring diagrams 12•27

Diagram 39 Part 1

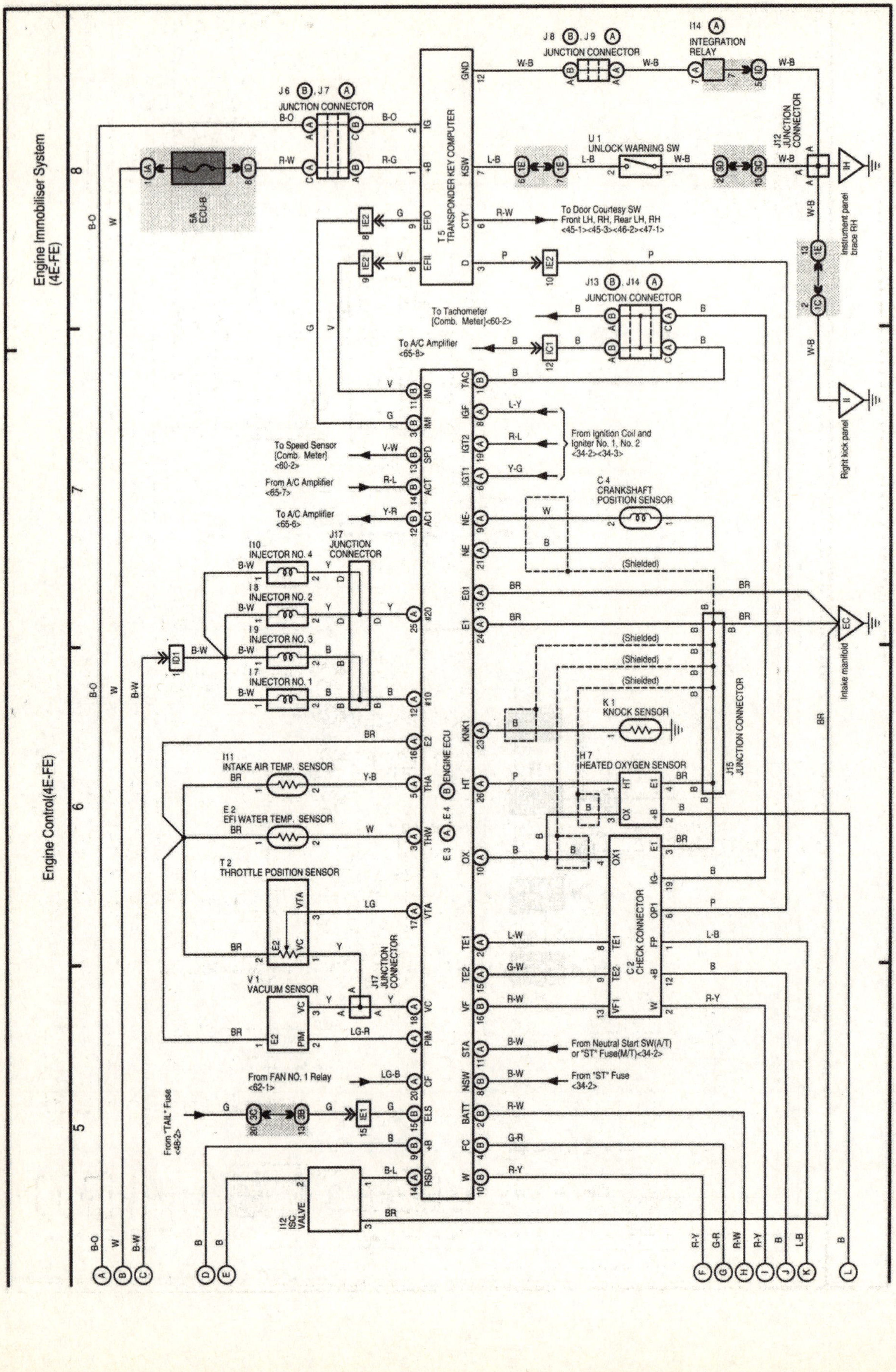

12•28 Wiring diagrams

Diagram 39 Part 2

Wiring diagrams

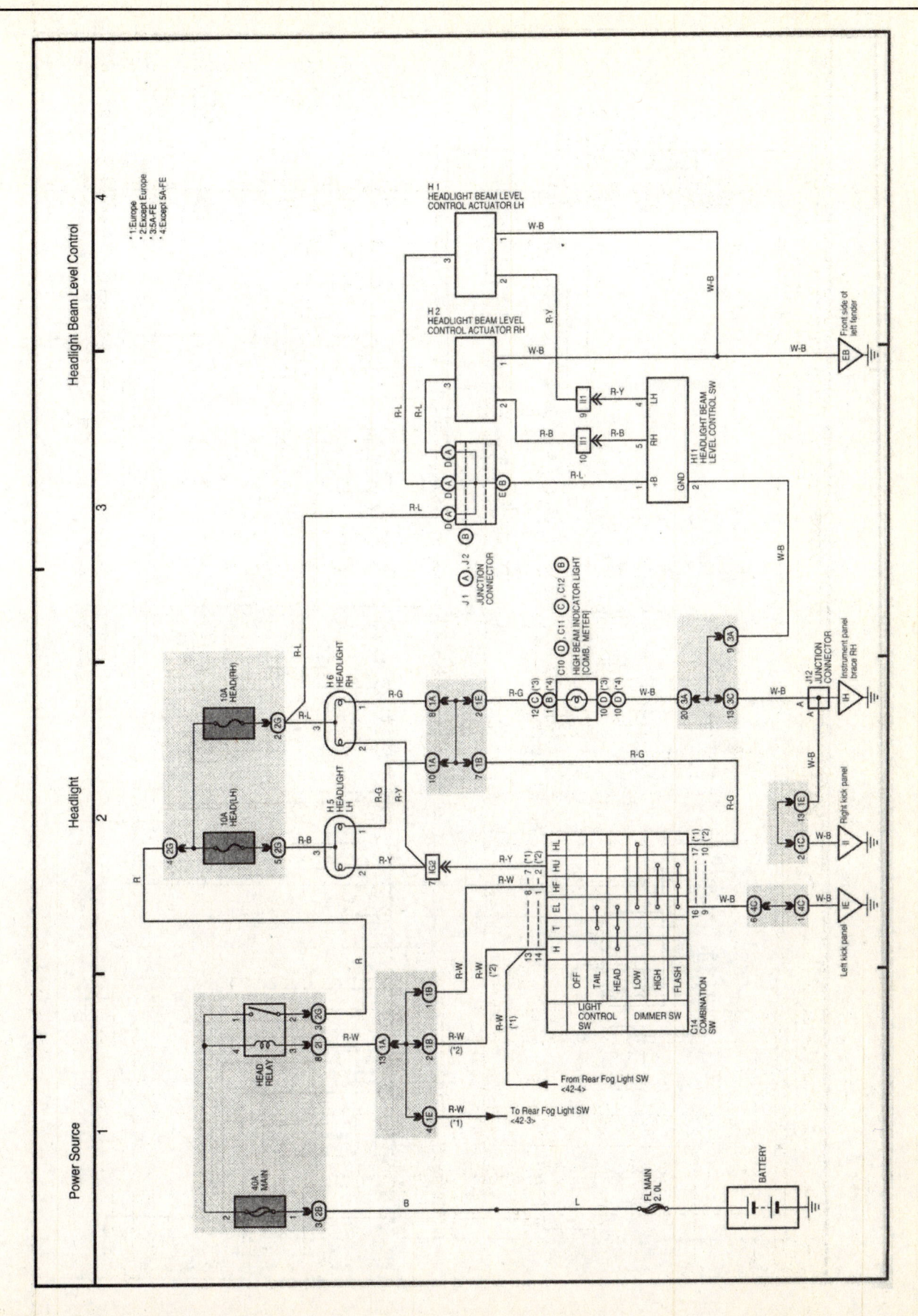

Diagram 41

12•30 Wiring diagrams

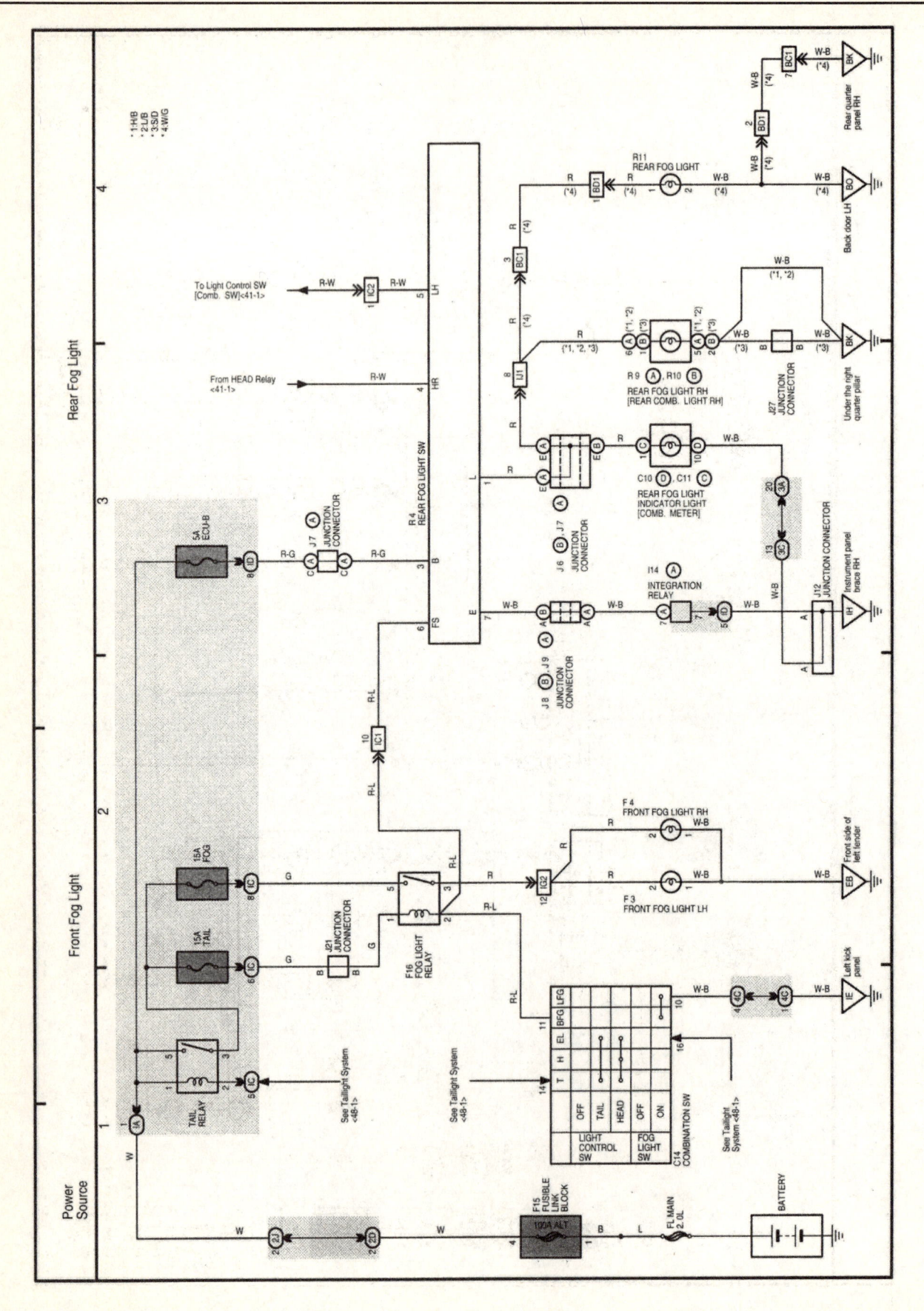

Diagram 42

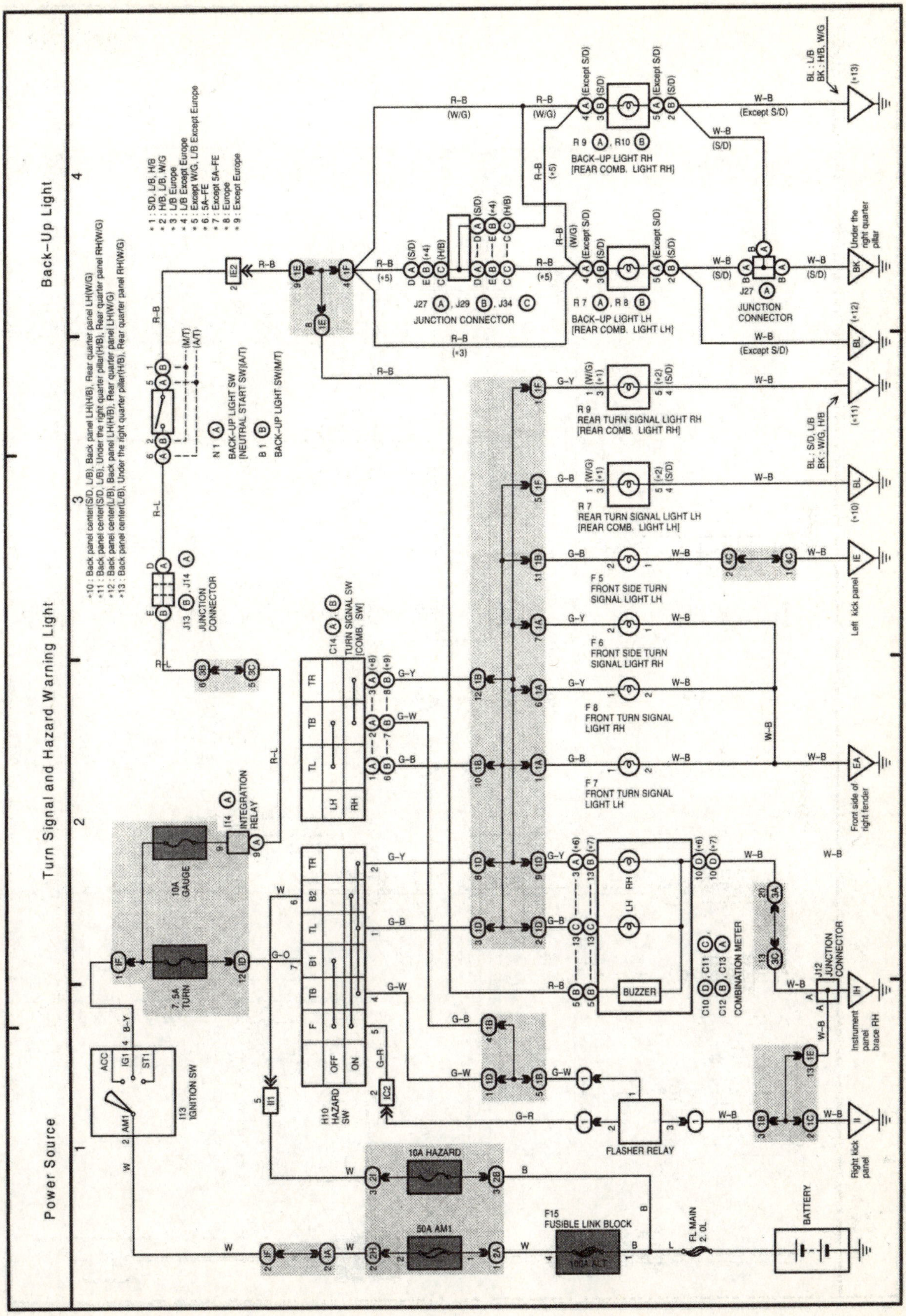

Power Source
Turn Signal and Hazard Warning Light
Back-Up Light
I13 IGNITION SW
H10 HAZARD SW
C14 (A), (B) TURN SIGNAL SW [COMB. SW]
I14 (A) INTEGRATION RELAY
J13 (B), J14 (A) JUNCTION CONNECTOR
N1 (A) BACK-UP LIGHT SW [NEUTRAL START SW](A/T)
B1 (B) BACK-UP LIGHT SW(M/T)
J27 (A), J29 (B), J34 (C) JUNCTION CONNECTOR
R7 (A), R8 (B) BACK-UP LIGHT LH [REAR COMB. LIGHT LH]
R9 (A), R10 (B) BACK-UP LIGHT RH [REAR COMB. LIGHT RH]
R9 REAR TURN SIGNAL LIGHT RH [REAR COMB. LIGHT RH]
R7 REAR TURN SIGNAL LIGHT LH [REAR COMB. LIGHT LH]
F5 FRONT SIDE TURN SIGNAL LIGHT LH
F6 FRONT SIDE TURN SIGNAL LIGHT RH
F8 FRONT TURN SIGNAL LIGHT RH
F7 FRONT TURN SIGNAL LIGHT LH
C10 (D), C11 (C), C12 (B), C13 (A) COMBINATION METER
BUZZER
J12 JUNCTION CONNECTOR
FLASHER RELAY
F15 FUSIBLE LINK BLOCK
100A ALT
FL MAIN 2.0L
BATTERY
10A HAZARD
50A AM1
7.5A TURN
10A GAUGE
Right kick panel
Instrument panel brace RH
Front side of right fender
Left kick panel
Under the right quarter pillar

Diagram 43

12•32 Wiring diagrams

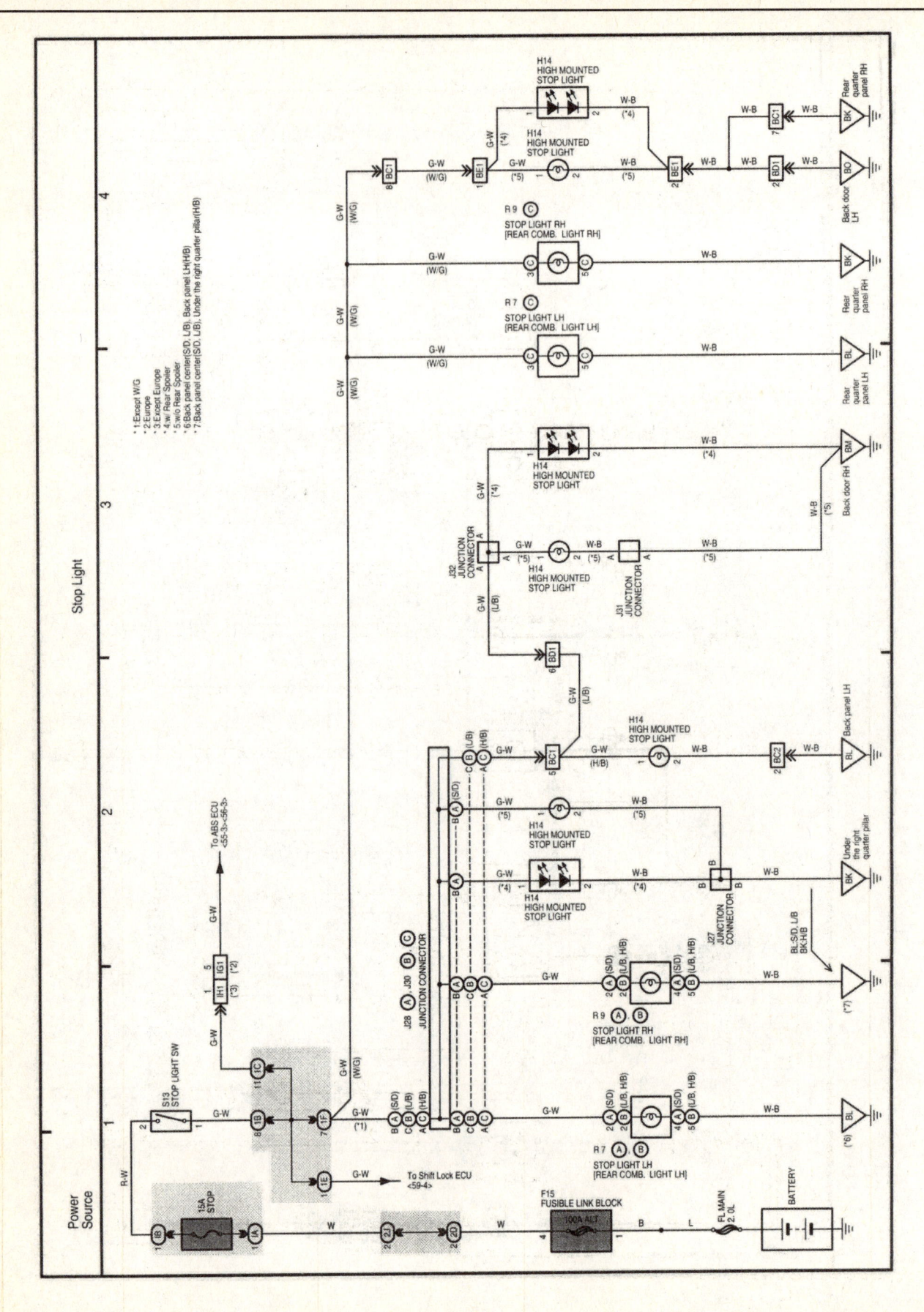

Diagram 44

Wiring diagrams 12•33

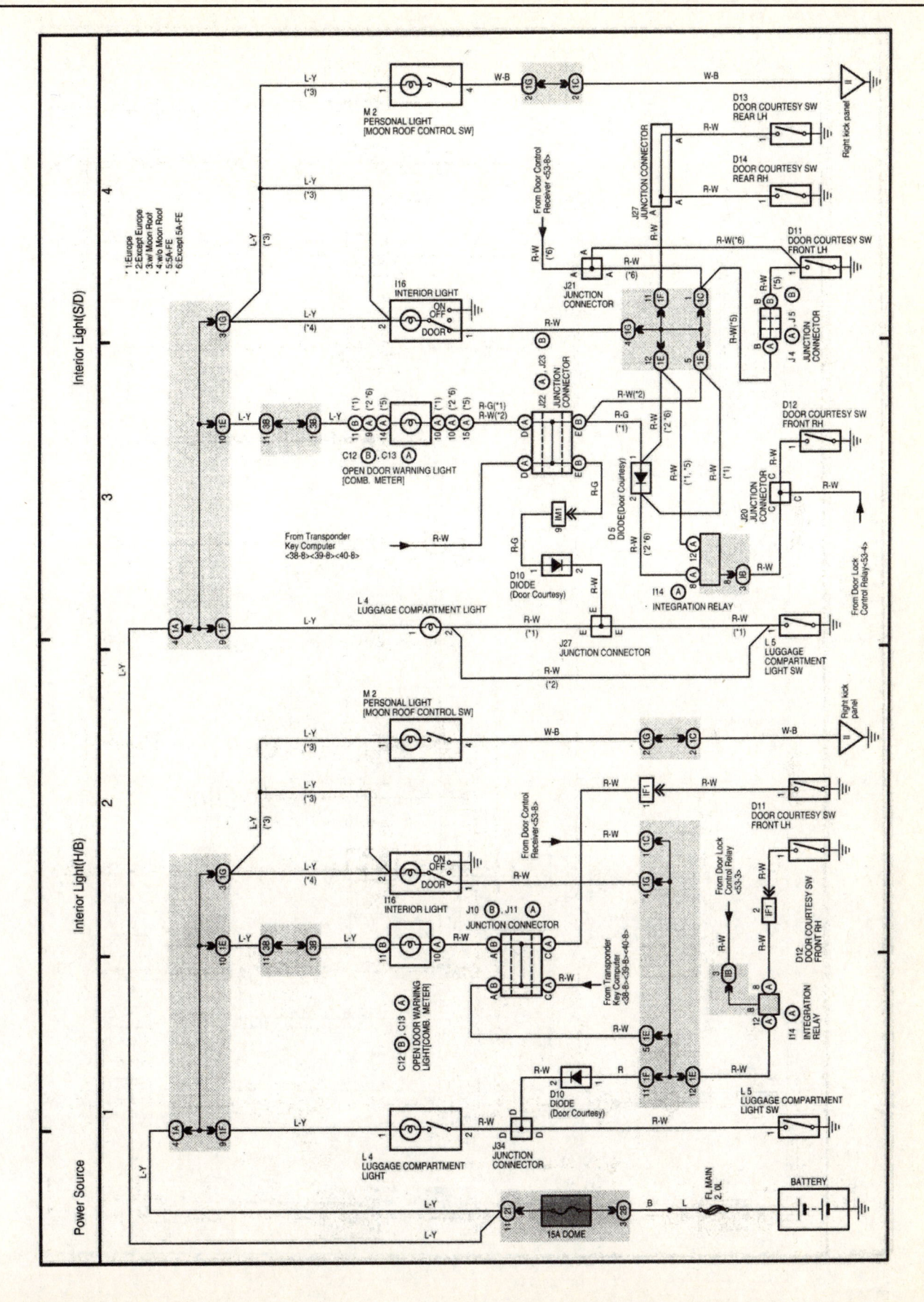

Diagram 45

12•34 Wiring diagrams

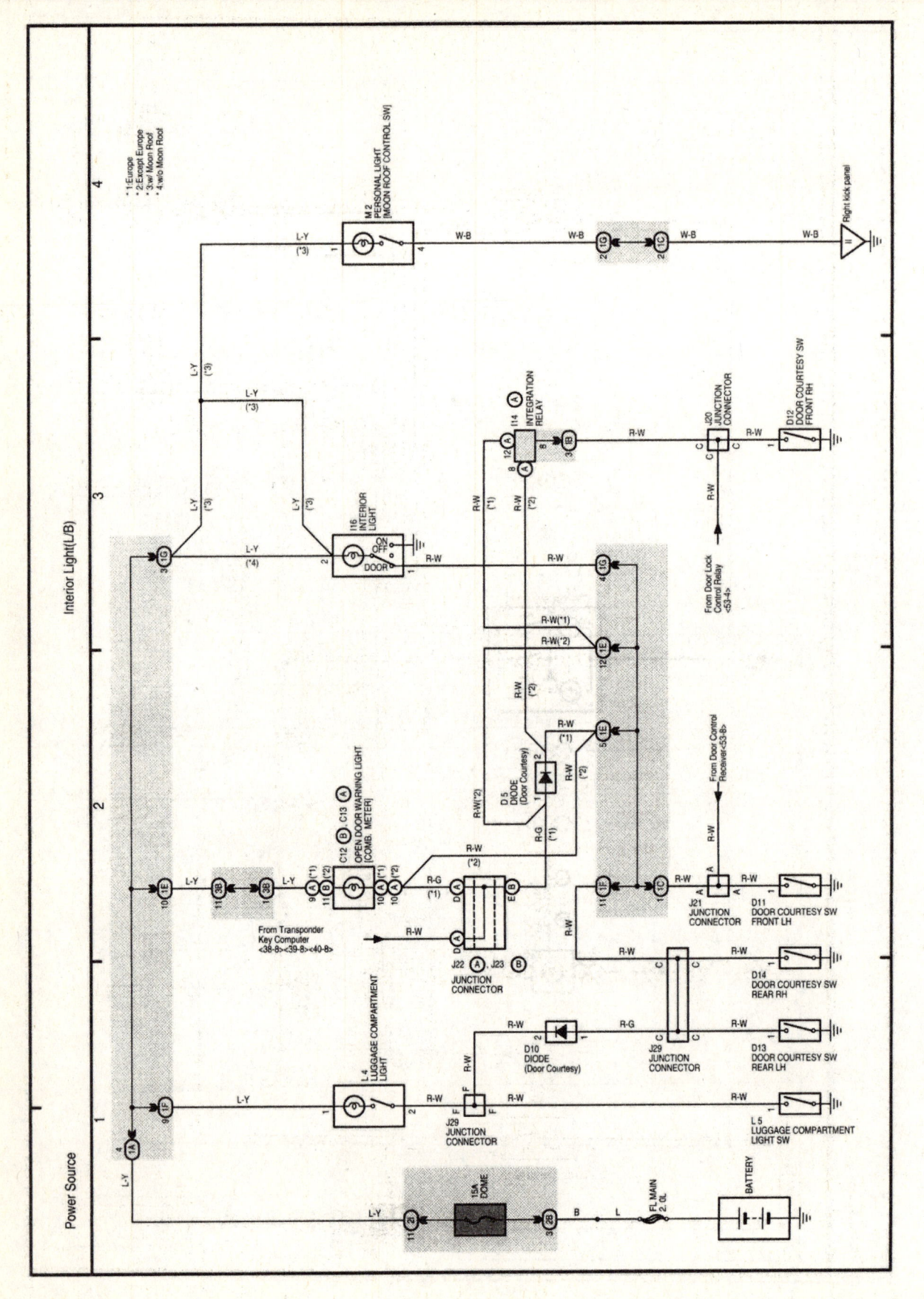

Diagram 46

Wiring diagrams 12•35

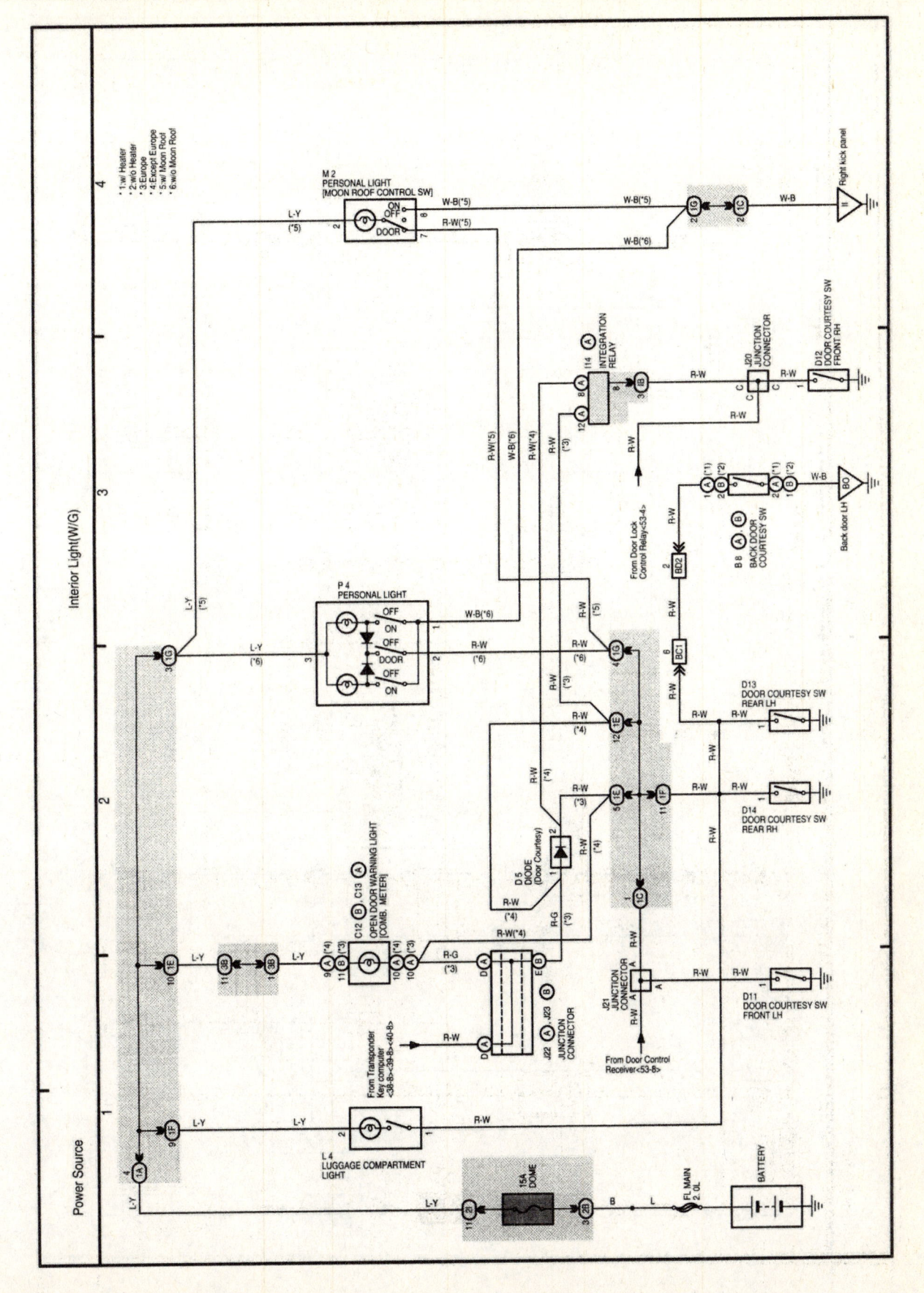

Diagram 47

12•36 Wiring diagrams

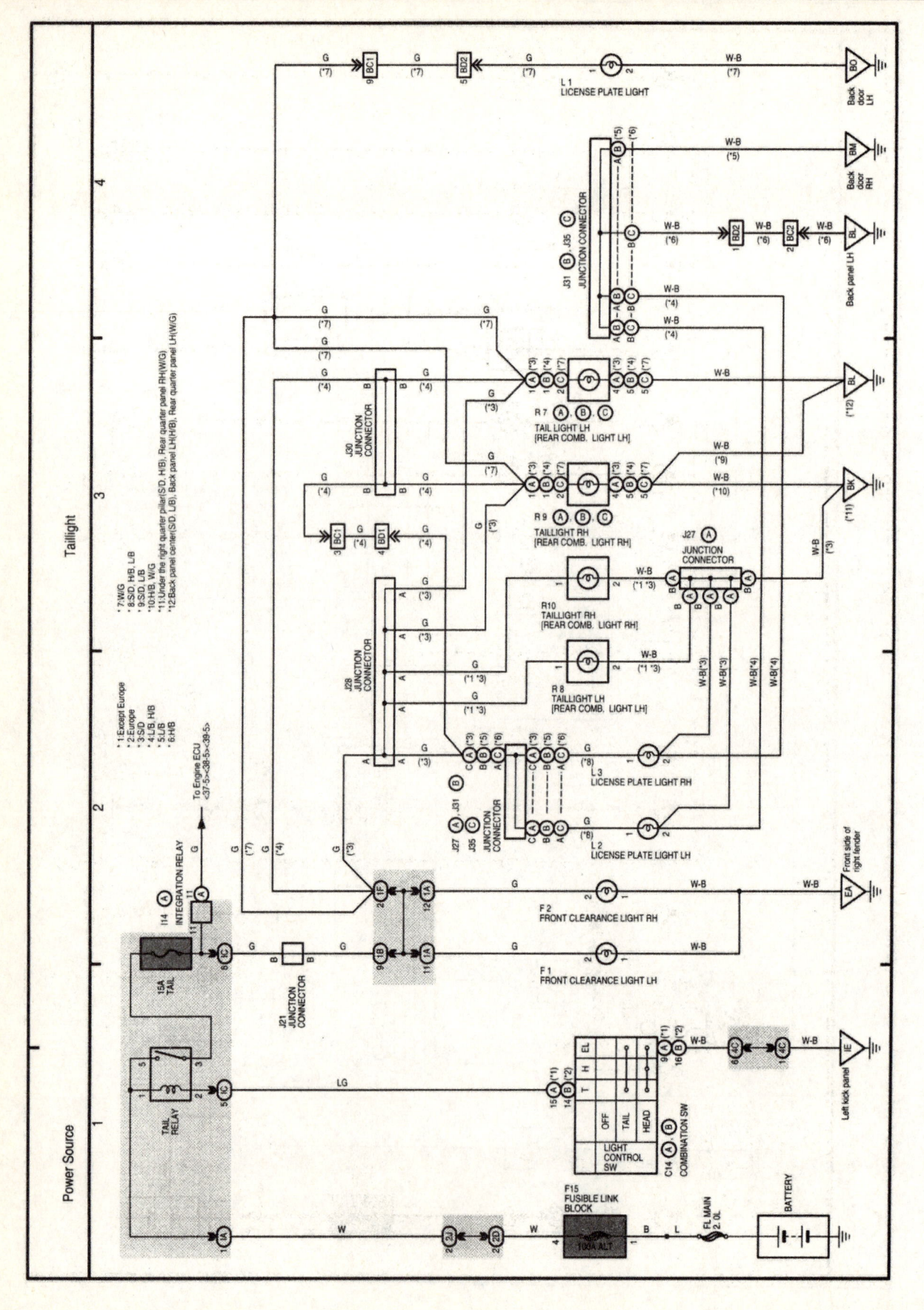

Diagram 48

Wiring diagrams

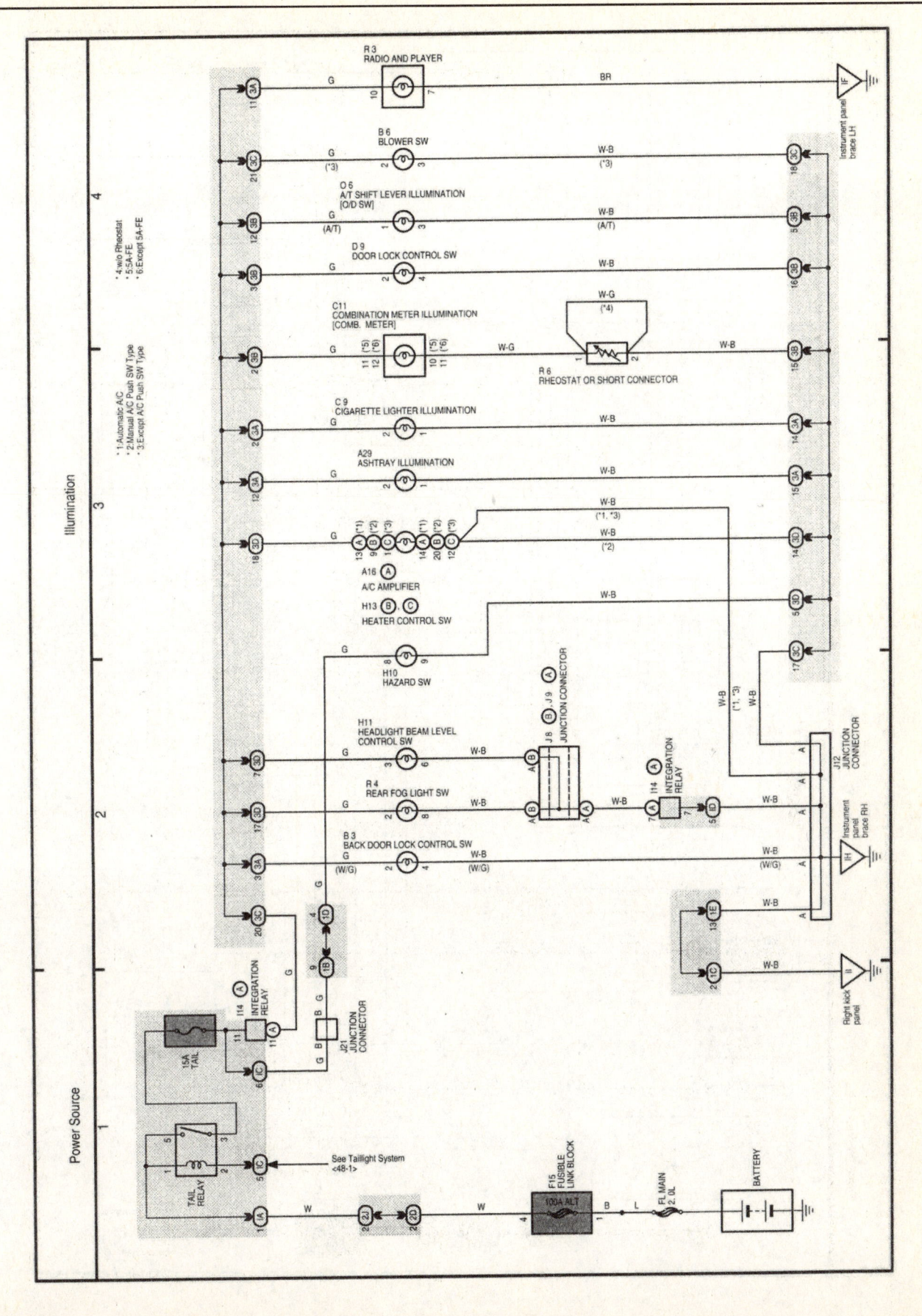

Diagram 49

12•38 Wiring diagrams

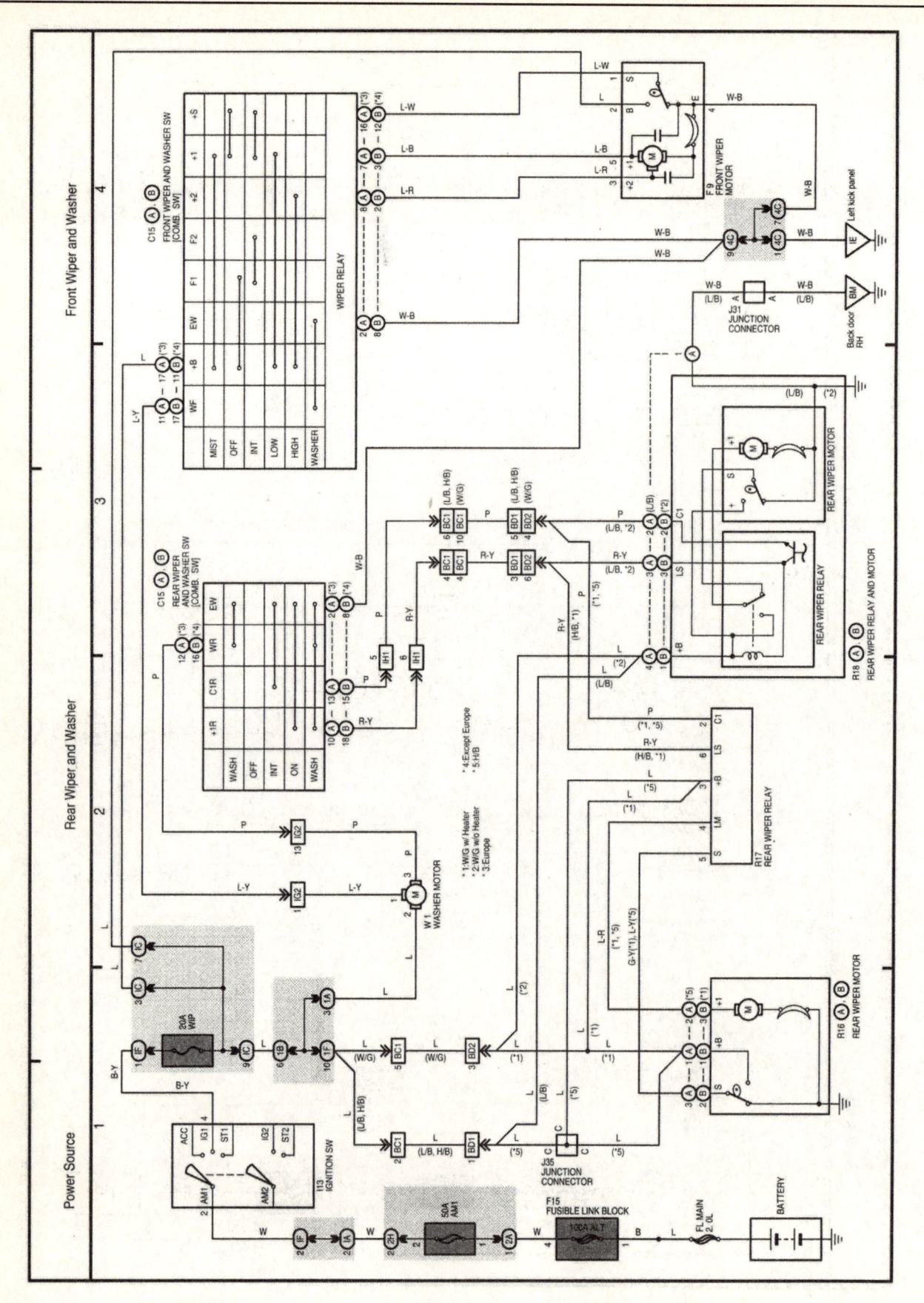

Diagram 50

Wiring diagrams 12•39

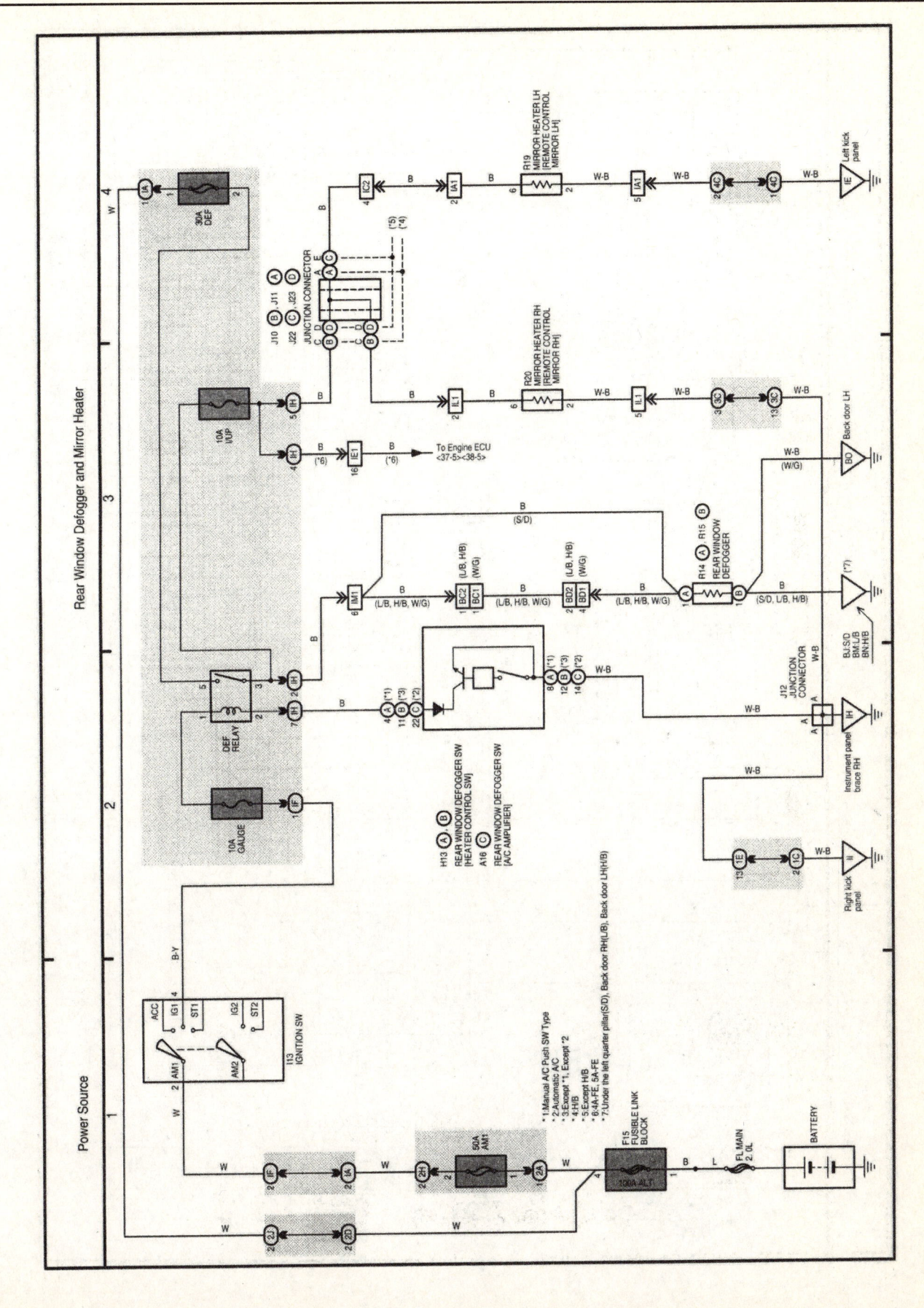

Diagram 51

12•40 Wiring diagrams

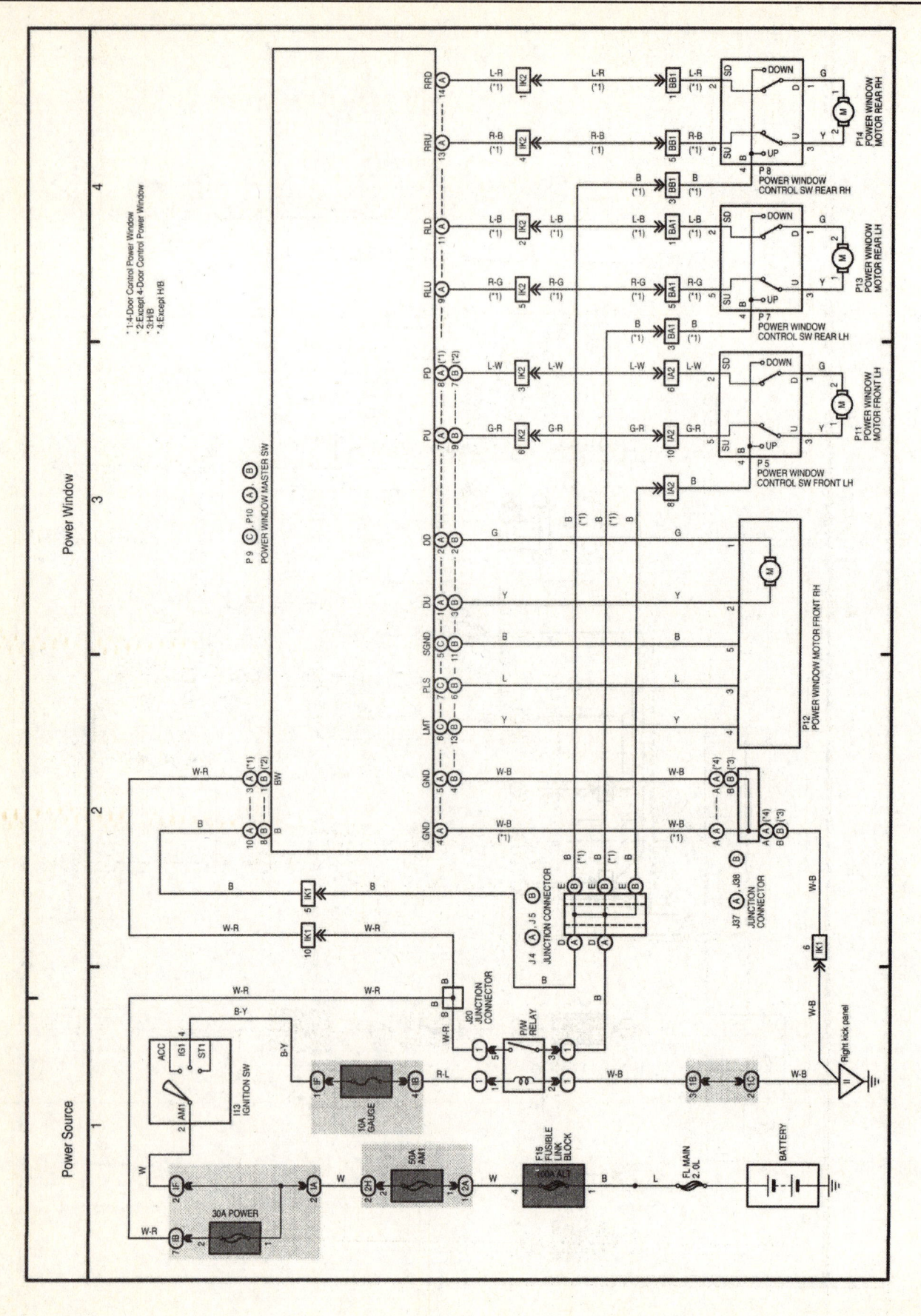

Diagram 52

Wiring diagrams 12•41

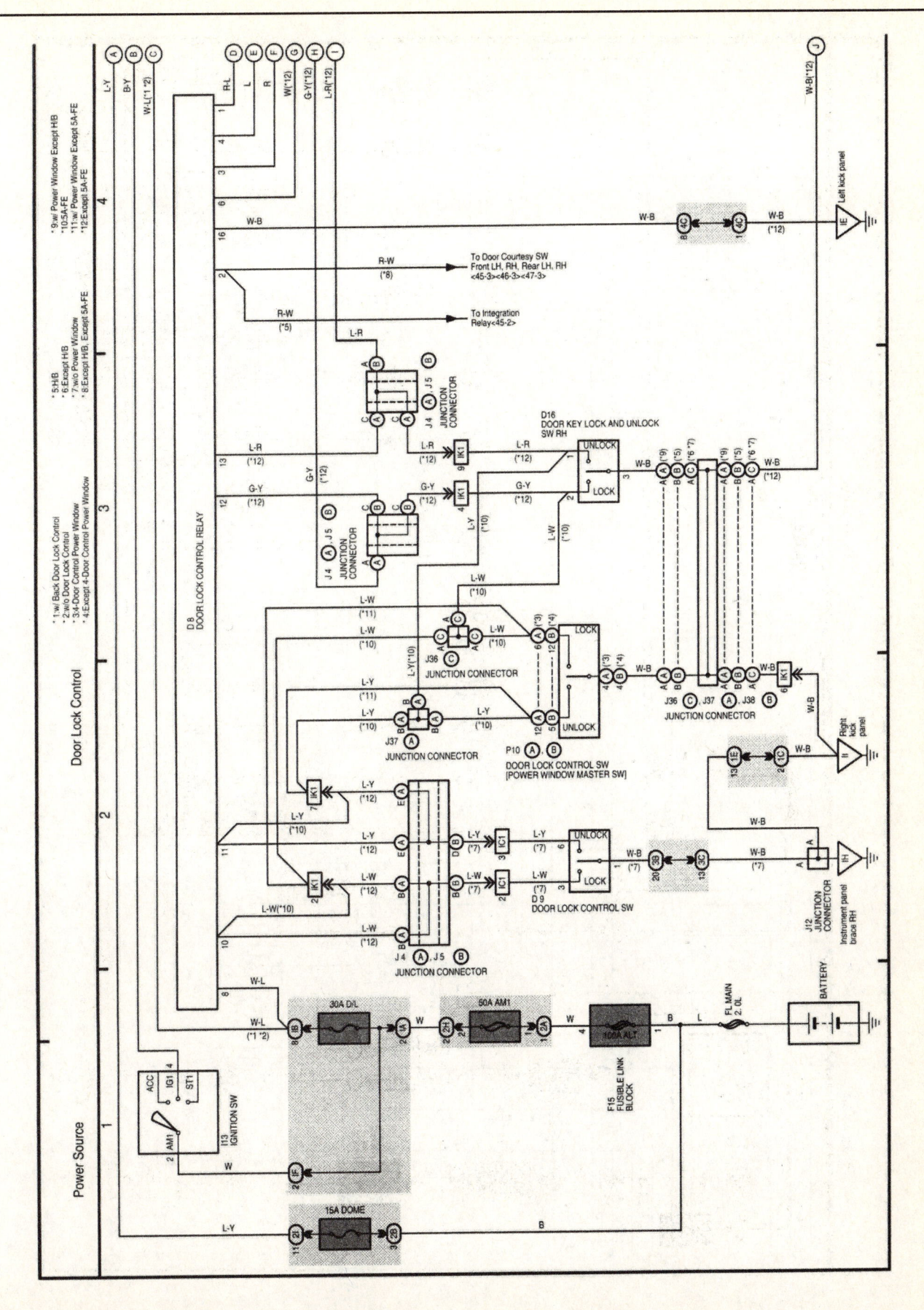

Diagram 53 Part 1

12•42 Wiring diagrams

Diagram 53 Part 2

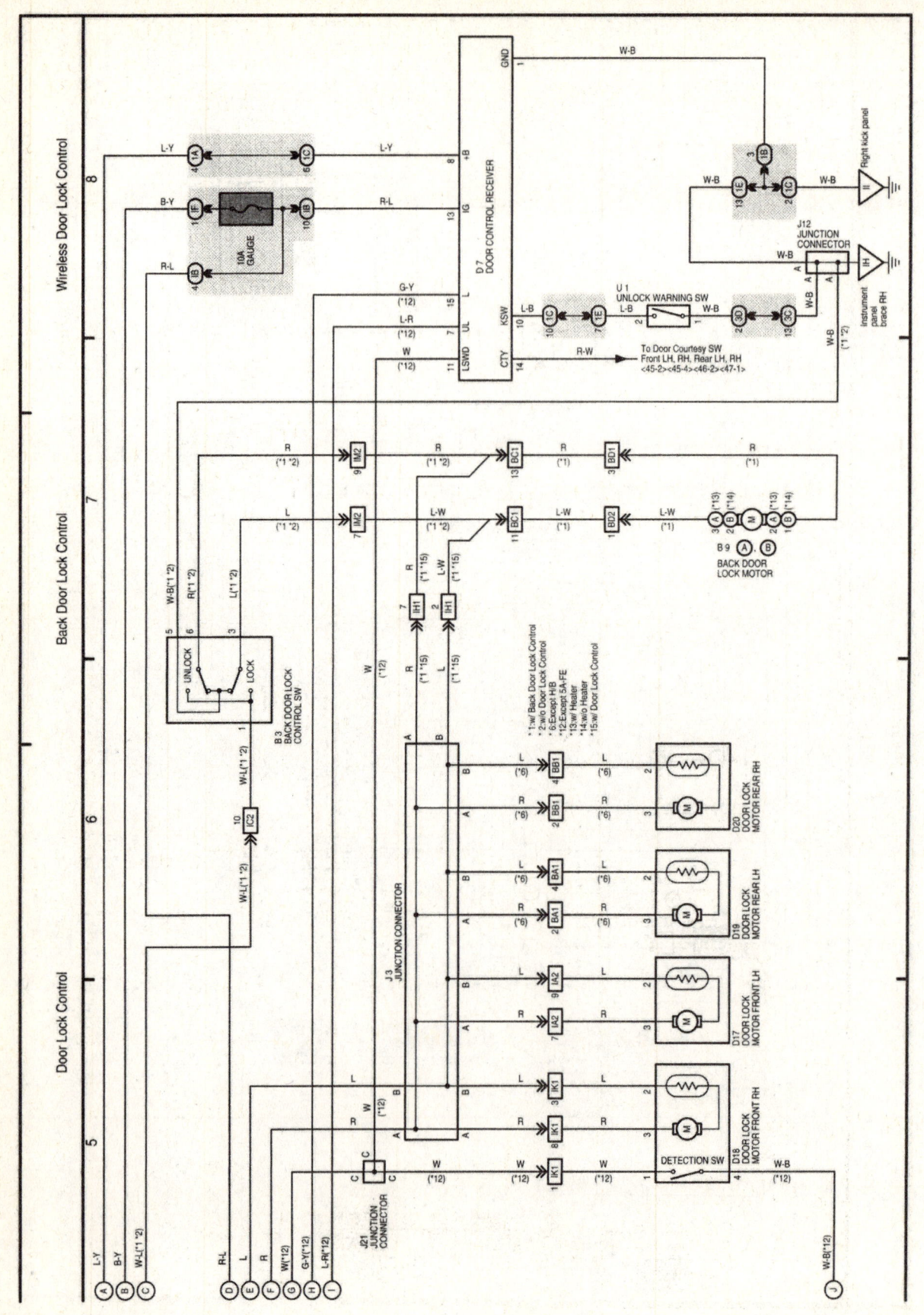

Wiring diagrams 12•43

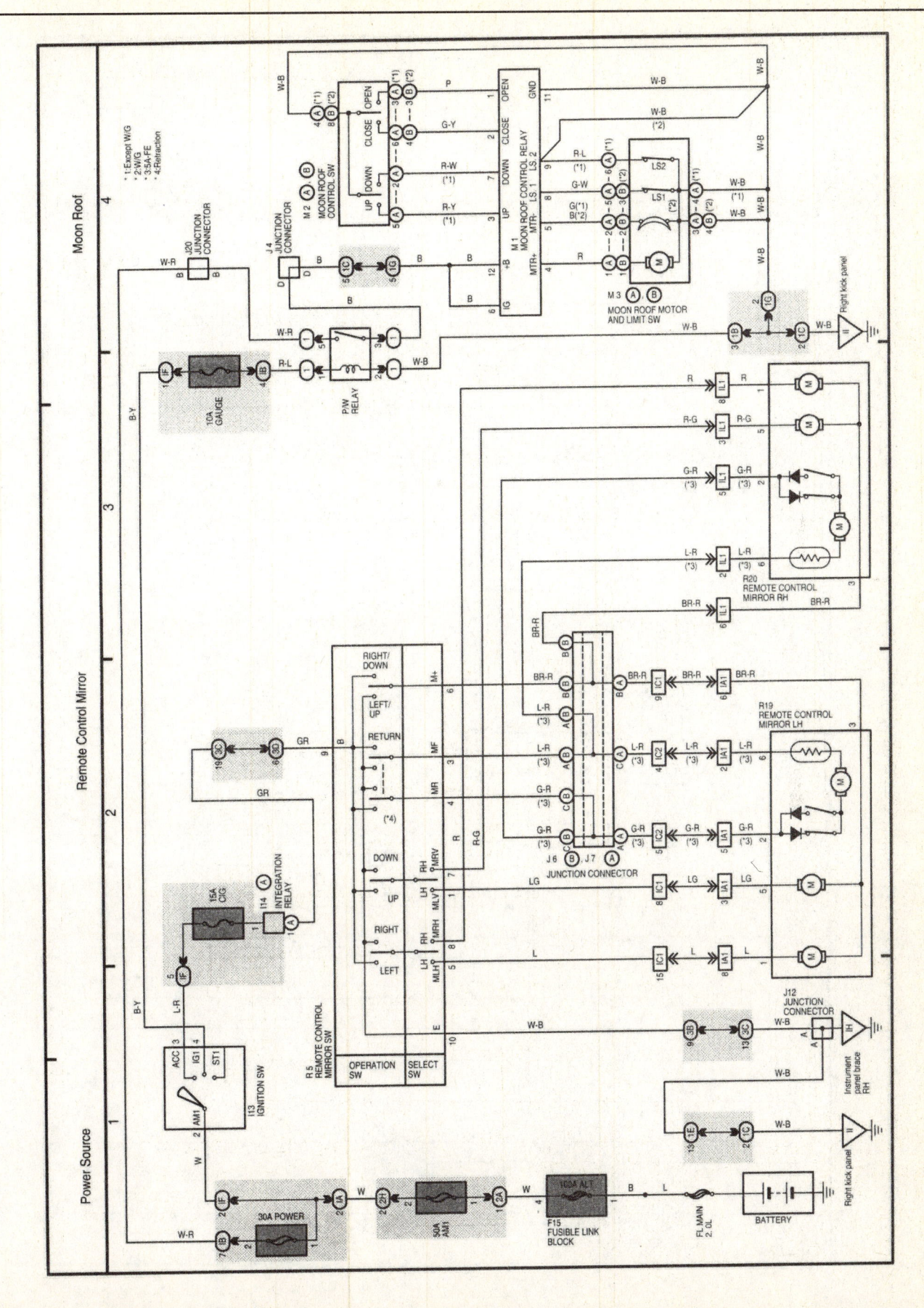

Diagram 54

12•44 Wiring diagrams

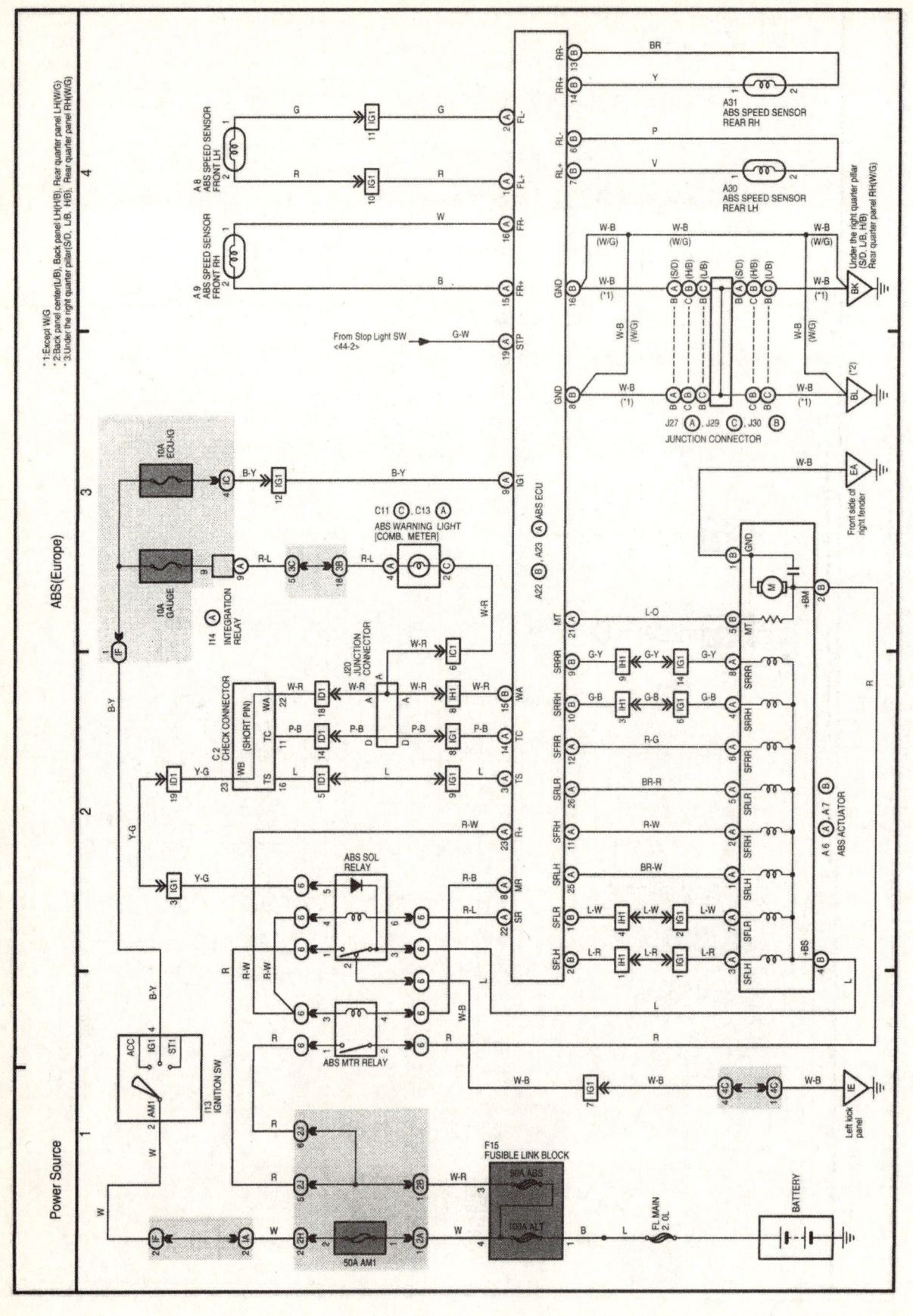

Diagram 55

Wiring diagrams 12•45

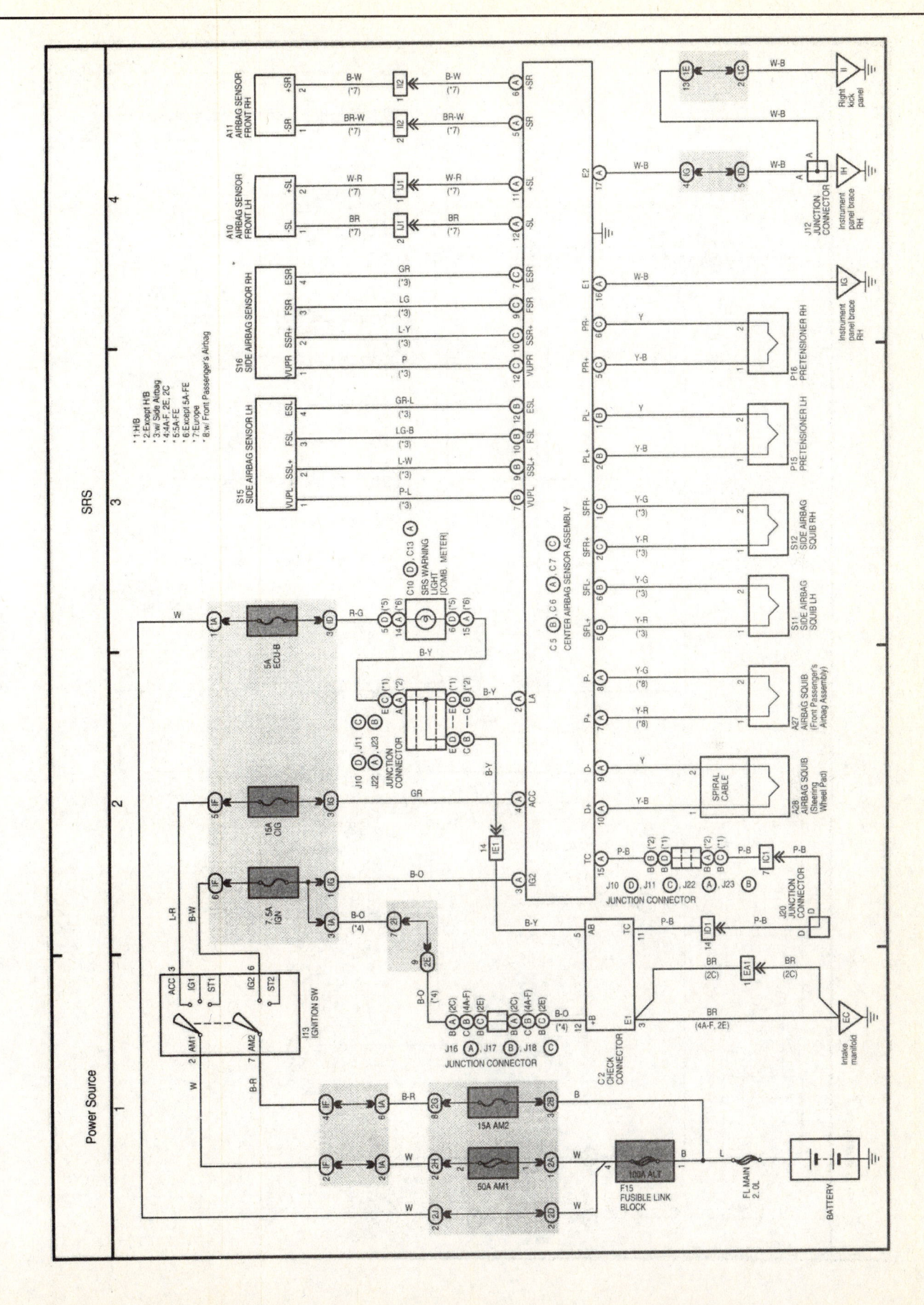

Diagram 57

12•46 Wiring diagrams

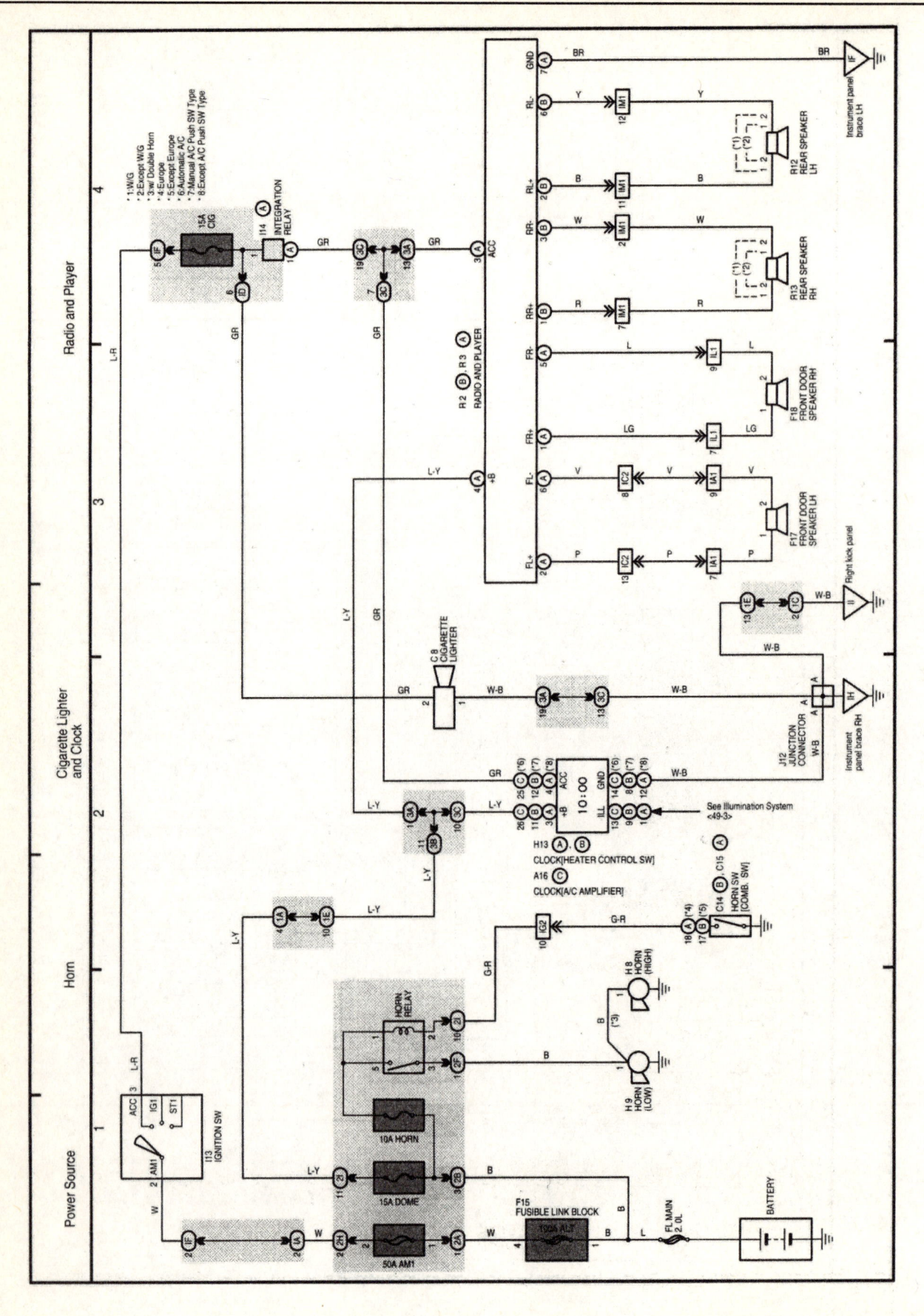

Diagram 58

Wiring diagrams 12•47

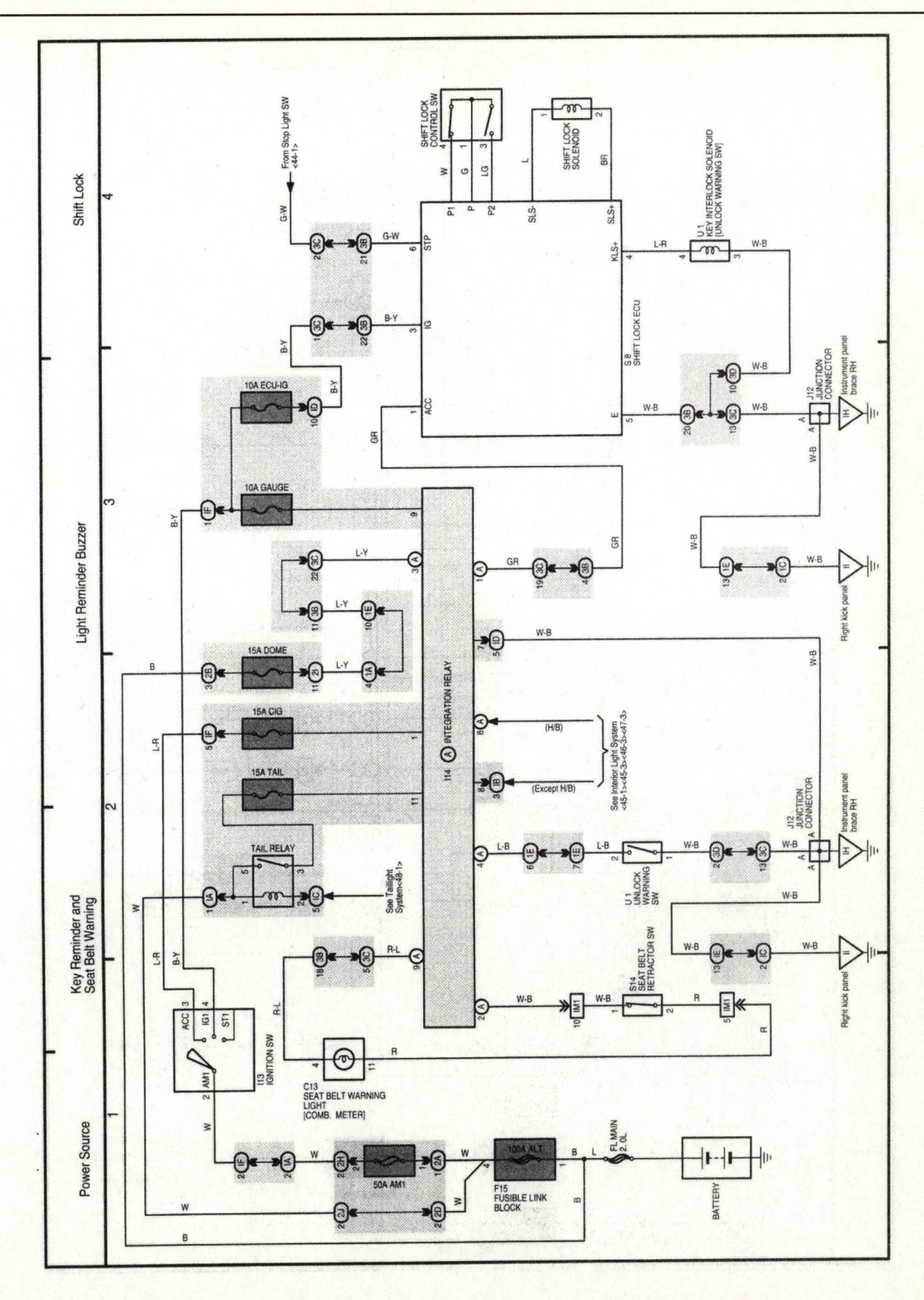

Diagram 59

12•48 Wiring diagrams

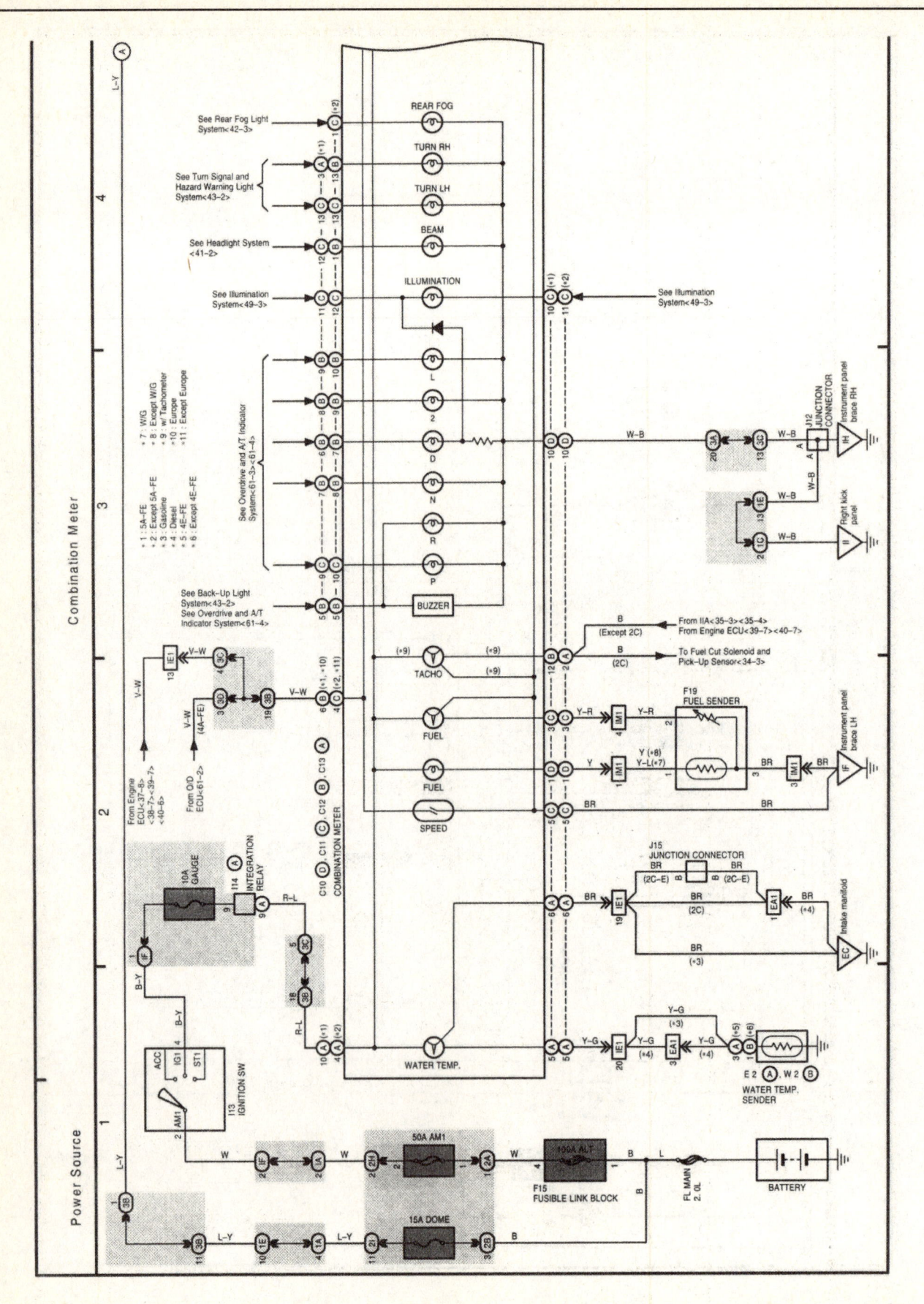

Wiring diagrams 12•49

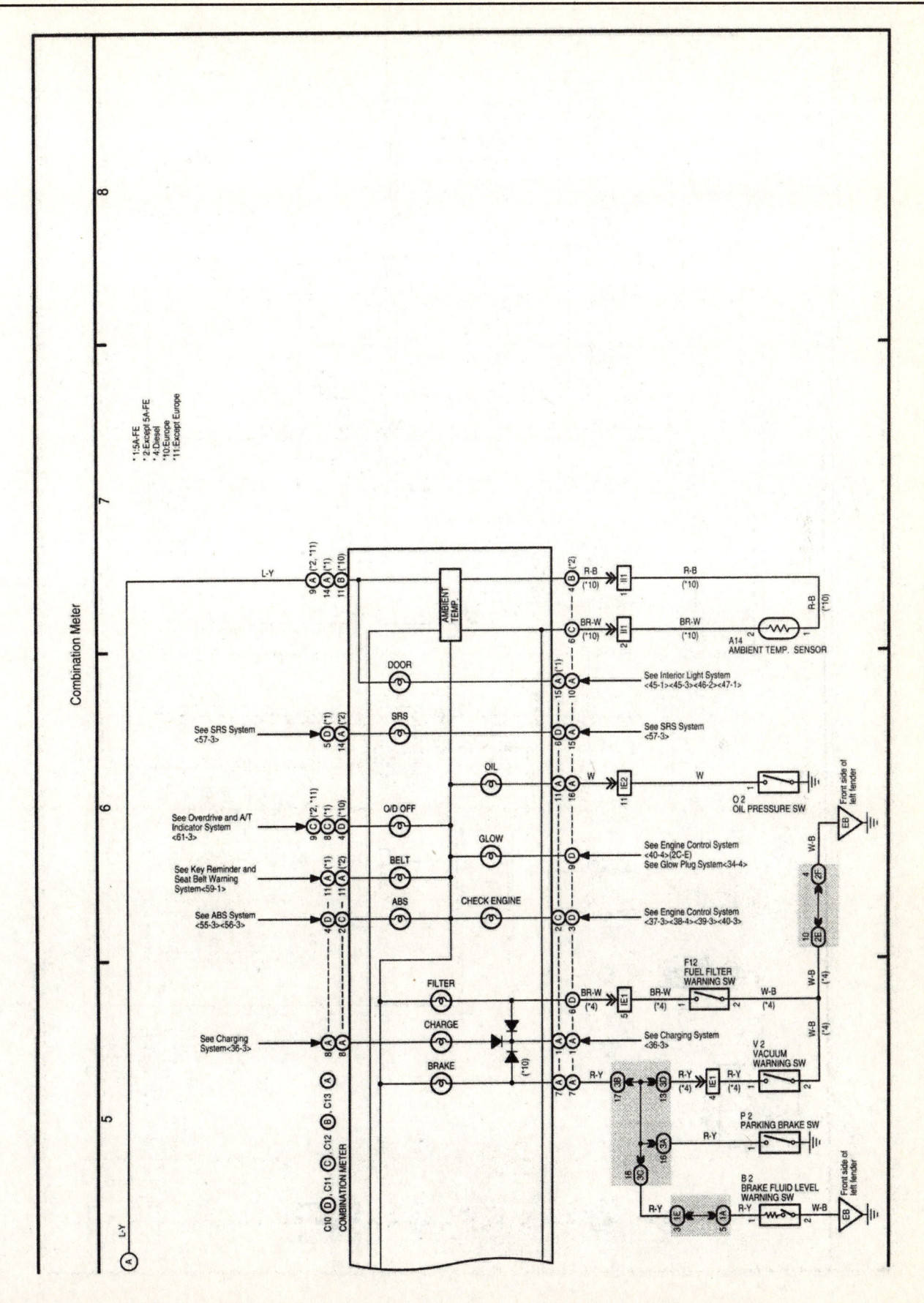

Diagram 60 Part 2

12•50 Wiring diagrams

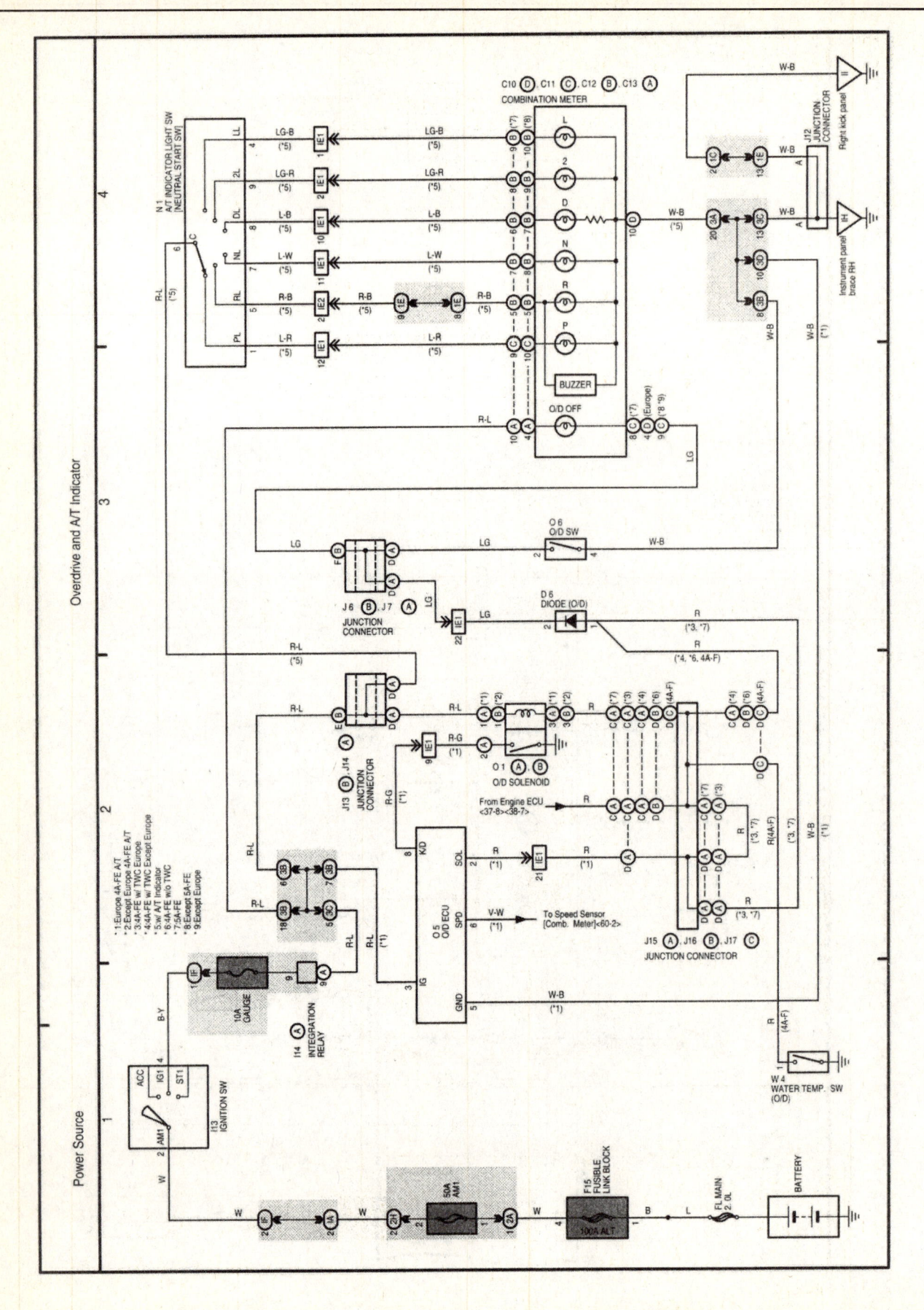

Diagram 61

Wiring diagrams 12•51

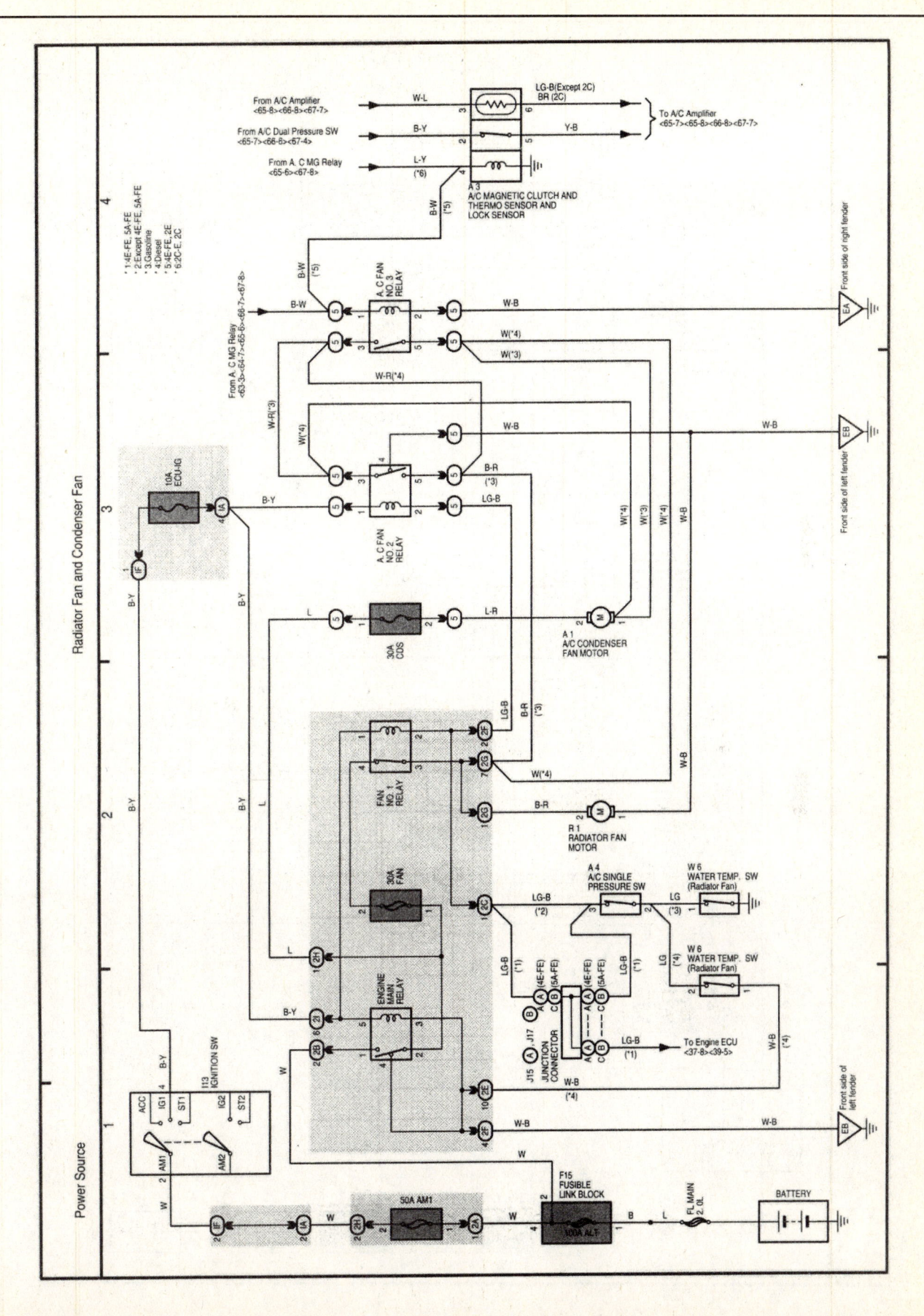

Diagram 62

12•52 Wiring diagrams

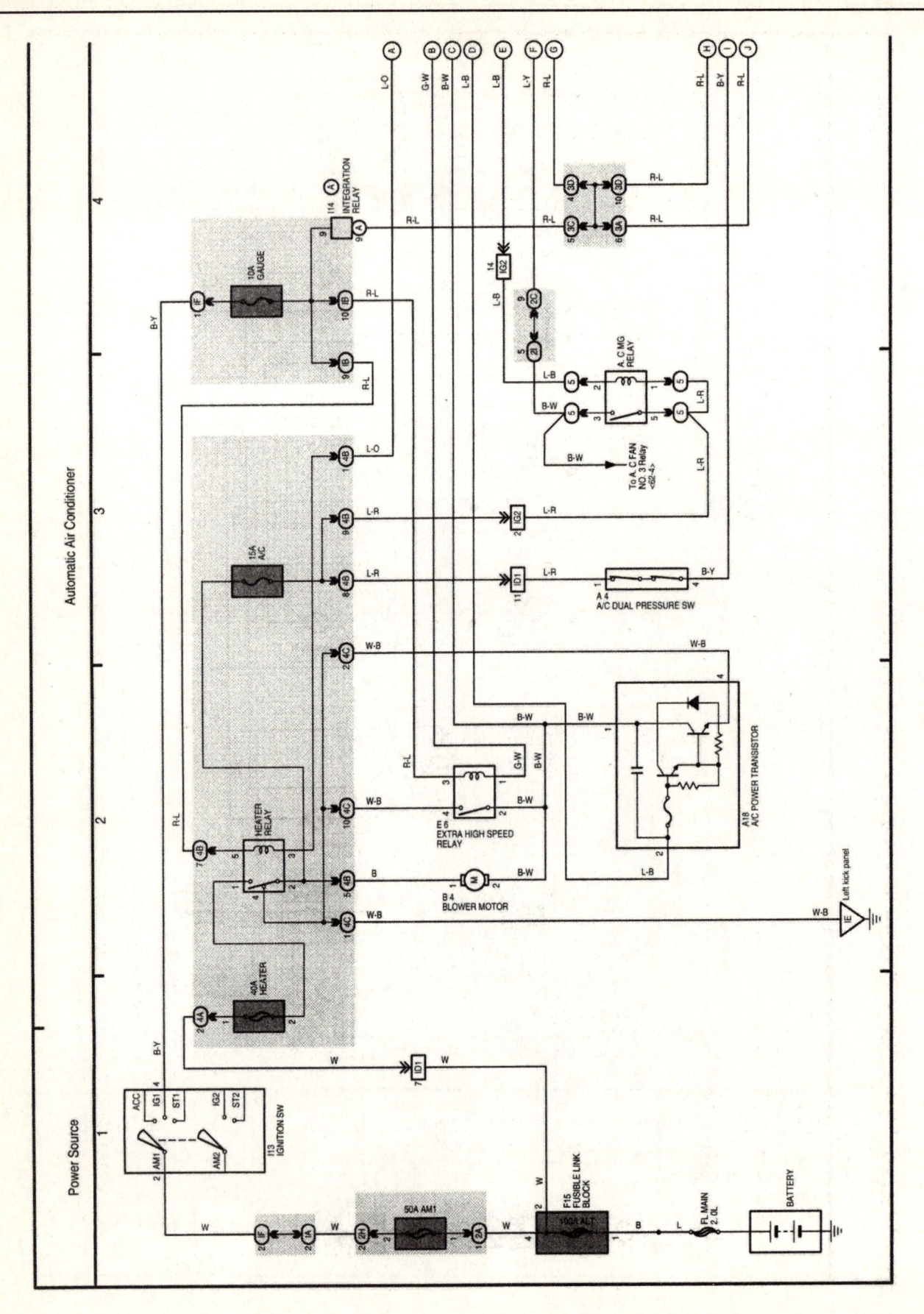

Diagram 63 Part 1

Wiring diagrams

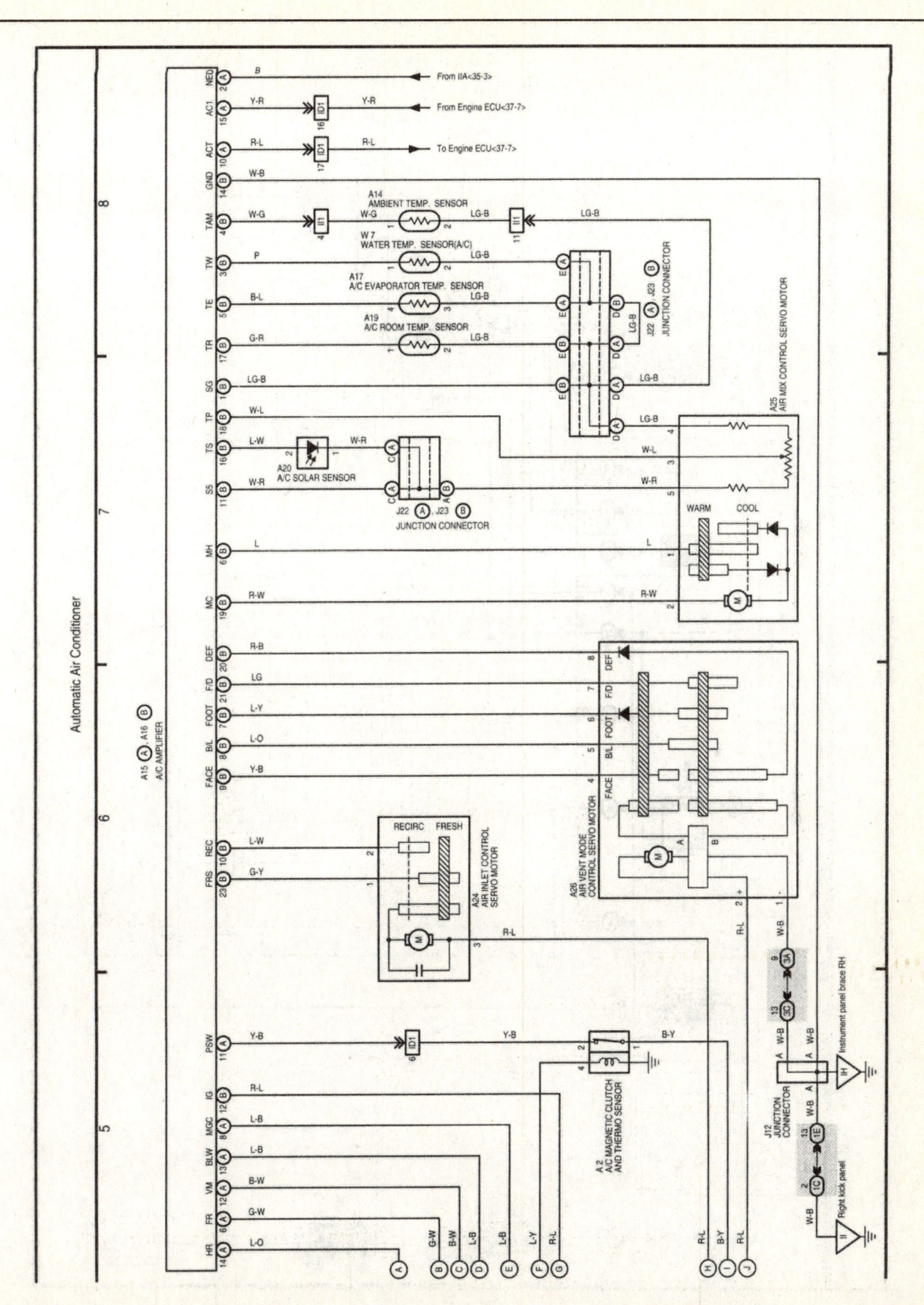

Diagram 63 Part 2

12•54 Wiring diagrams

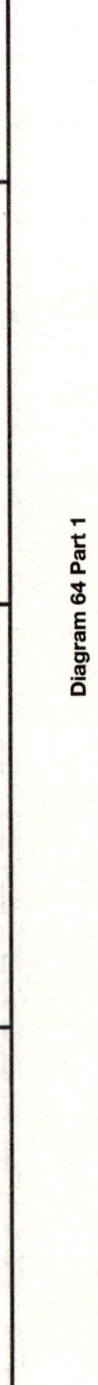

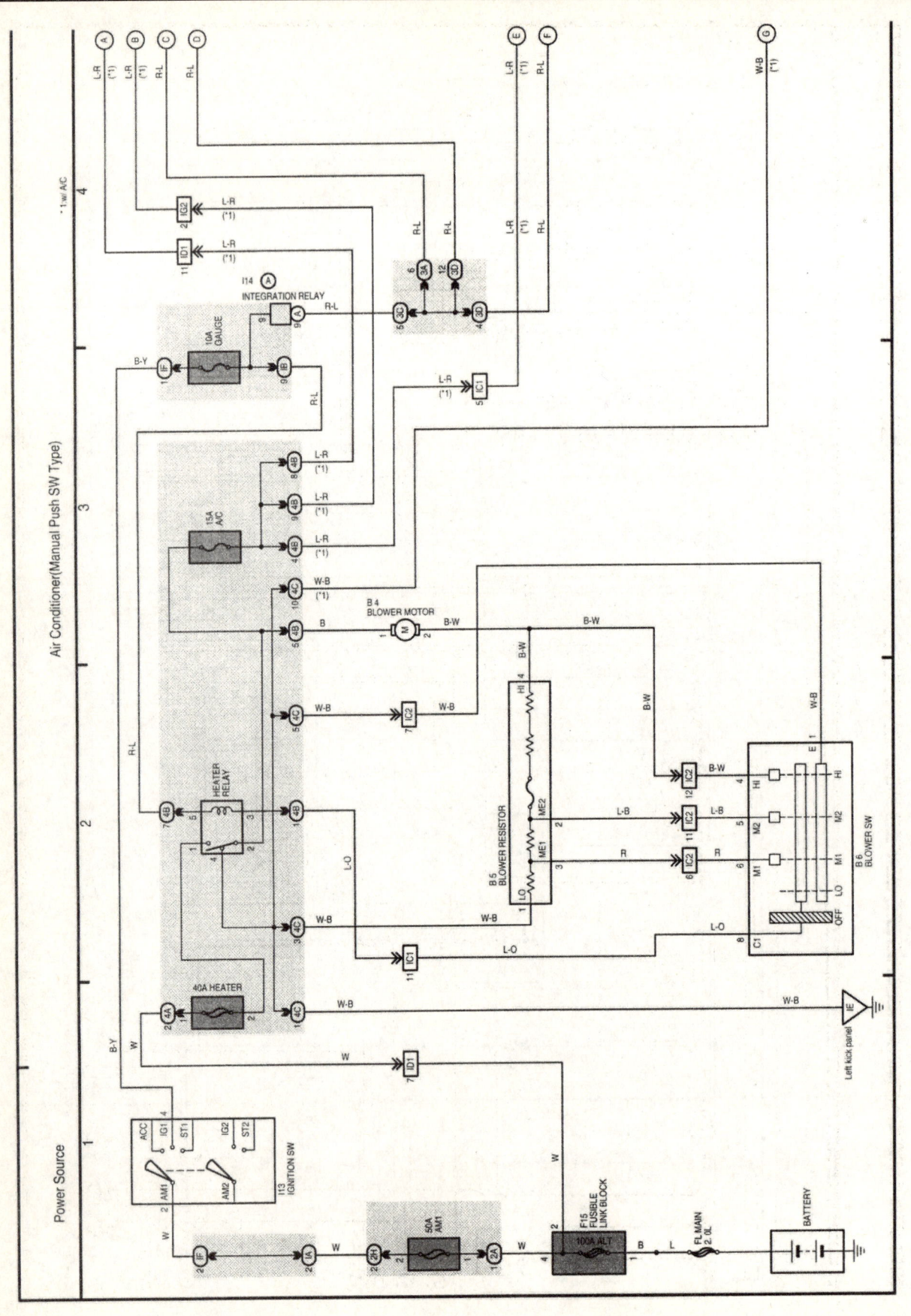

Wiring diagrams

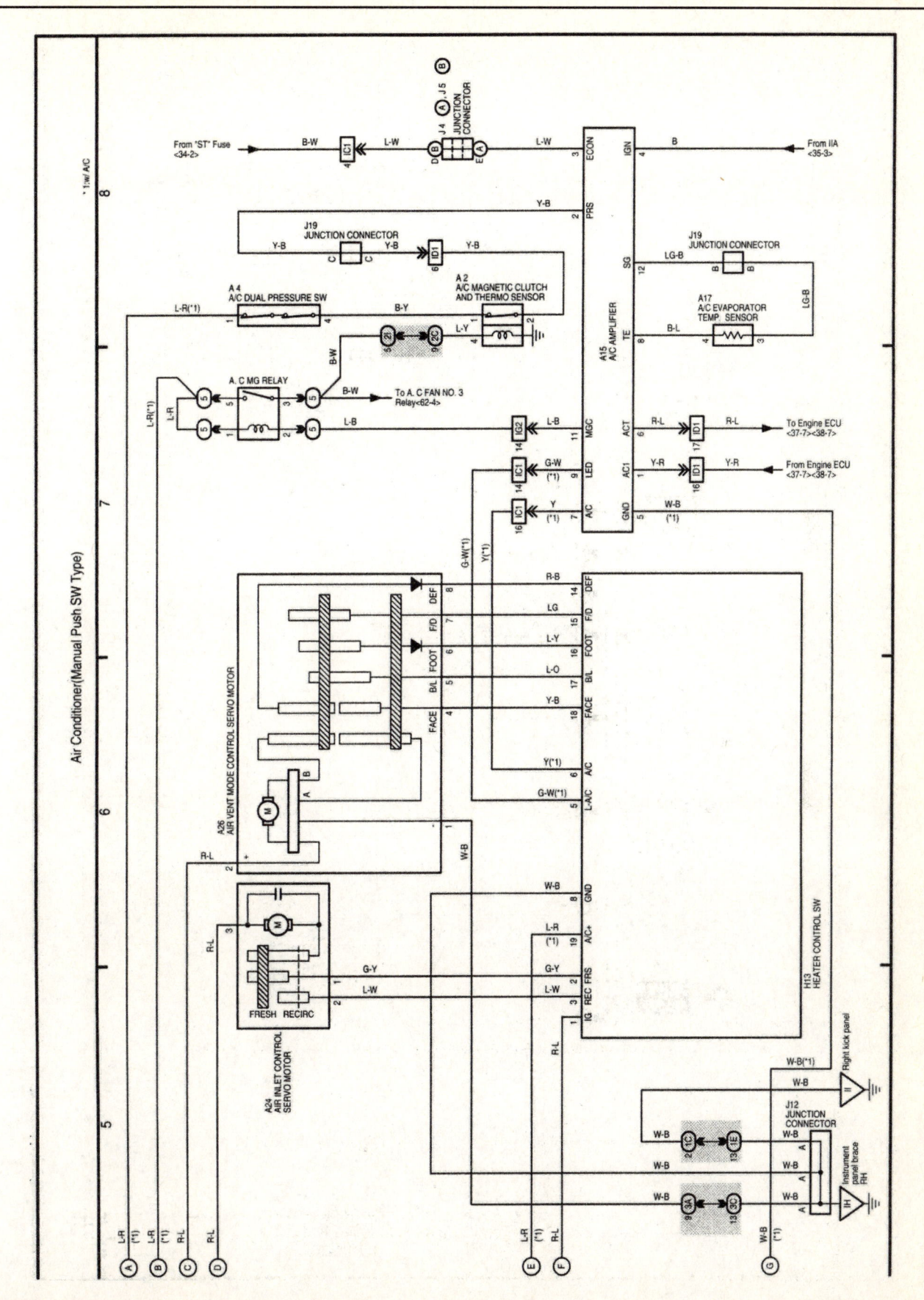

Diagram 64 Part 2

Notes

Reference

Dimensions and weights	**REF•1**	Tools and working facilities	**REF•6**
Conversion factors	**REF•2**	MOT test checks	**REF•8**
Buying spare parts	**REF•3**	Fault finding	**REF•12**
Vehicle identification	**REF•3**	Glossary of technical terms	**REF•22**
General repair procedures	**REF•4**	Index	**REF•27**
Jacking and vehicle support	**REF•5**		

Dimensions and weights

Note: *All figures are approximate, and may vary according to model. Refer to manufacturer's data for exact figures.*

Dimensions
Overall length:
- Hatchback .... 4120 mm
- Liftback .... 4270 mm
- Saloon .... 4315 mm
- Estate .... 4340 mm

Overall width (excluding mirrors) .... 1690 mm

Overall height (unladen):
- Hatchback .... 1385 mm
- Liftback .... 1385 mm
- Saloon .... 1385 mm
- Estate (excluding roof rails) .... 1445 mm

Wheelbase .... 2465 mm

Weights
Maximum gross vehicle weight*:
- 1.3 litre engine .... 1580 kg
- 1.4 litre engine:
  - Except estate .... 1580 kg
  - Estate models .... 1615 kg
- 1.6 litre engine:
  - Except estate .... 1615 kg
  - Estate 1650

Maximum towing weight*:
- Unbraked trailer:
  - 1.3 litre engine .... 450 kg
  - 1.4 litre engine .... 450 kg
  - 1.6 litre engine .... 450 kg
- Braked trailer:
  - 1.3 litre engine .... 1000 kg
  - 1.4 litre engine .... 1000 kg
  - 1.6 litre engine .... 1200 kg

* Refer to the Vehicle Identification Plate for the exact figures for your vehicle – see 'Vehicle identification'

REF•2 Conversion factors

Length (distance)
Inches (in)	x 25.4	= Millimetres (mm)	x 0.0394	= Inches (in)
Feet (ft)	x 0.305	= Metres (m)	x 3.281	= Feet (ft)
Miles	x 1.609	= Kilometres (km)	x 0.621	= Miles

Volume (capacity)
Cubic inches (cu in; in³)	x 16.387	= Cubic centimetres (cc; cm³)	x 0.061	= Cubic inches (cu in; in³)
Imperial pints (Imp pt)	x 0.568	= Litres (l)	x 1.76	= Imperial pints (Imp pt)
Imperial quarts (Imp qt)	x 1.137	= Litres (l)	x 0.88	= Imperial quarts (Imp qt)
Imperial quarts (Imp qt)	x 1.201	= US quarts (US qt)	x 0.833	= Imperial quarts (Imp qt)
US quarts (US qt)	x 0.946	= Litres (l)	x 1.057	= US quarts (US qt)
Imperial gallons (Imp gal)	x 4.546	= Litres (l)	x 0.22	= Imperial gallons (Imp gal)
Imperial gallons (Imp gal)	x 1.201	= US gallons (US gal)	x 0.833	= Imperial gallons (Imp gal)
US gallons (US gal)	x 3.785	= Litres (l)	x 0.264	= US gallons (US gal)

Mass (weight)
Ounces (oz)	x 28.35	= Grams (g)	x 0.035	= Ounces (oz)
Pounds (lb)	x 0.454	= Kilograms (kg)	x 2.205	= Pounds (lb)

Force
Ounces-force (ozf; oz)	x 0.278	= Newtons (N)	x 3.6	= Ounces-force (ozf; oz)
Pounds-force (lbf; lb)	x 4.448	= Newtons (N)	x 0.225	= Pounds-force (lbf; lb)
Newtons (N)	x 0.1	= Kilograms-force (kgf; kg)	x 9.81	= Newtons (N)

Pressure
Pounds-force per square inch (psi; lbf/in²; lb/in²)	x 0.070	= Kilograms-force per square centimetre (kgf/cm²; kg/cm²)	x 14.223	= Pounds-force per square inch (psi; lbf/in²; lb/in²)
Pounds-force per square inch (psi; lbf/in²; lb/in²)	x 0.068	= Atmospheres (atm)	x 14.696	= Pounds-force per square inch (psi; lbf/in²; lb/in²)
Pounds-force per square inch (psi; lbf/in²; lb/in²)	x 0.069	= Bars	x 14.5	= Pounds-force per square inch (psi; lbf/in²; lb/in²)
Pounds-force per square inch (psi; lbf/in²; lb/in²)	x 6.895	= Kilopascals (kPa)	x 0.145	= Pounds-force per square inch (psi; lbf/in²; lb/in²)
Kilopascals (kPa)	x 0.01	= Kilograms-force per square centimetre (kgf/cm²; kg/cm²)	x 98.1	= Kilopascals (kPa)
Millibar (mbar)	x 100	= Pascals (Pa)	x 0.01	= Millibar (mbar)
Millibar (mbar)	x 0.0145	= Pounds-force per square inch (psi; lbf/in²; lb/in²)	x 68.947	= Millibar (mbar)
Millibar (mbar)	x 0.75	= Millimetres of mercury (mmHg)	x 1.333	= Millibar (mbar)
Millibar (mbar)	x 0.401	= Inches of water (inH₂O)	x 2.491	= Millibar (mbar)
Millimetres of mercury (mmHg)	x 0.535	= Inches of water (inH₂O)	x 1.868	= Millimetres of mercury (mmHg)
Inches of water (inH₂O)	x 0.036	= Pounds-force per square inch (psi; lbf/in²; lb/in²)	x 27.68	= Inches of water (inH₂O)

Torque (moment of force)
Pounds-force inches (lbf in; lb in)	x 1.152	= Kilograms-force centimetre (kgf cm; kg cm)	x 0.868	= Pounds-force inches (lbf in; lb in)
Pounds-force inches (lbf in; lb in)	x 0.113	= Newton metres (Nm)	x 8.85	= Pounds-force inches (lbf in; lb in)
Pounds-force inches (lbf in; lb in)	x 0.083	= Pounds-force feet (lbf ft; lb ft)	x 12	= Pounds-force inches (lbf in; lb in)
Pounds-force feet (lbf ft; lb ft)	x 0.138	= Kilograms-force metres (kgf m; kg m)	x 7.233	= Pounds-force feet (lbf ft; lb ft)
Pounds-force feet (lbf ft; lb ft)	x 1.356	= Newton metres (Nm)	x 0.738	= Pounds-force feet (lbf ft; lb ft)
Newton metres (Nm)	x 0.102	= Kilograms-force metres (kgf m; kg m)	x 9.804	= Newton metres (Nm)

Power
Horsepower (hp)	x 745.7	= Watts (W)	x 0.0013	= Horsepower (hp)

Velocity (speed)
Miles per hour (miles/hr; mph)	x 1.609	= Kilometres per hour (km/hr; kph)	x 0.621	= Miles per hour (miles/hr; mph)

Fuel consumption*
Miles per gallon, Imperial (mpg)	x 0.354	= Kilometres per litre (km/l)	x 2.825	= Miles per gallon, Imperial (mpg)
Miles per gallon, US (mpg)	x 0.425	= Kilometres per litre (km/l)	x 2.352	= Miles per gallon, US (mpg)

Temperature
Degrees Fahrenheit = (°C x 1.8) + 32   Degrees Celsius (Degrees Centigrade; °C) = (°F - 32) x 0.56

*It is common practice to convert from miles per gallon (mpg) to litres/100 kilometres (l/100km), where mpg x l/100 km = 282

Buying spare parts REF•3

Spare parts are available from many sources, including maker's appointed garages, accessory shops, and motor factors. To be sure of obtaining the correct parts, it may sometimes be necessary to quote the vehicle identification number. If possible, it can also be useful to take the old parts along for positive identification. Items such as starter motors and alternators maybe available under a service exchange scheme – any parts returned should be clean.

Our advice regarding spare part sources is:

Officially-appointed garages

This is the best source of parts which are peculiar to your car, and are not otherwise generally available (eg, badges, interior trim, certain body panels, etc). It is also the only place at which you should buy parts if the vehicle is still under warranty.

Accessory shops

These are very good places to buy materials and components needed for the maintenance of your car (oil, air and fuel filters, spark plugs, light bulbs, drivebelts, oils and greases, brake pads, touch-up paint, etc). Components of this nature sold by a reputable shop are of the same standard as those used by the car manufacturer.

Besides components, these shops will also sell tools and general accessories, usually have convenient opening hours, charge lower prices, and can often be found close to home. Some accessory shops also have parts counters where components needed for almost any repair job can be purchased or ordered.

Motor factors

Good factors will stock all the more important components which wear out comparatively quickly and can sometimes supply individual components needed for the overhaul of a larger assembly. They may also handle work such as cylinder block reboring, crankshaft regrinding and balancing, etc.

Tyre and exhaust specialists

These outlets may be independent or members of a local or national chain. They frequently offer competitive prices when compared with a main dealer or local garage, but it will pay to obtain several quotes before making a decision. Also ask what 'extras' may be added to the quote – for instance, fitting a new valve and balancing the wheel are both often charged on top of the price of a new tyre.

Other sources

Beware of parts or materials obtained from market stalls, car boot sales or similar outlets. Such items are not invariably sub-standard, but there is little chance of compensation if they do prove unsatisfactory. In the case of safety-critical components such as brake pads there is the risk not only of financial loss but also of an accident causing injury or death.

Vehicle identification

Modifications are a continuing and unpublicised process in vehicle manufacture, quite apart from major model changes. Spare parts manuals and lists are compiled upon a numerical basis, the individual vehicle identification numbers being essential for correct identification of the part concerned.

When ordering spare parts, always give as much information as possible. Quote the car model, year of manufacture, body and engine numbers.

The *vehicle identification number (VIN) plate* is fitted to the bulkhead in the engine compartment. The plate carries the vehicle identification number (VIN) and vehicle weight information **(see illustration)**.

The *vehicle identification number (VIN)* is stamped onto a plate visible through the base of the windscreen, and also stamped into the engine compartment bulkhead **(see illustration)**.

The engine number is situated on the front face of the cylinder block on non-VVT-i models, or on the left-hand end of the cylinder block on VVT-i models **(see illustrations)**

The VIN plate is located at the rear of the engine compartment

The VIN number is also stamped into the bulkhead at the rear of the engine compartment

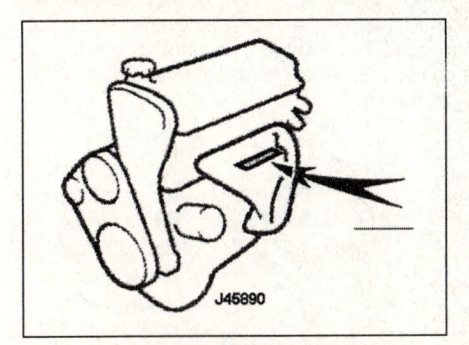

Engine number location – 1.3 litre 4E-FE engine

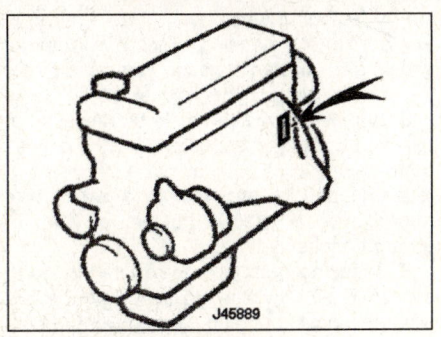

Engine number location – 1.6 litre 4A-FE engine

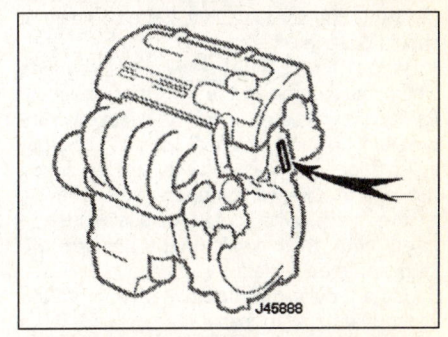

Engine number location – 1.4 litre 4ZZ-FE and 1.6 litre 3ZZ-FE VVT-i engines

General repair procedures

Whenever servicing, repair or overhaul work is carried out on the car or its components, observe the following procedures and instructions. This will assist in carrying out the operation efficiently and to a professional standard of workmanship.

Joint mating faces and gaskets

When separating components at their mating faces, never insert screwdrivers or similar implements into the joint between the faces in order to prise them apart. This can cause severe damage which results in oil leaks, coolant leaks, etc upon reassembly. Separation is usually achieved by tapping along the joint with a soft-faced hammer in order to break the seal. However, note that this method may not be suitable where dowels are used for component location.

Where a gasket is used between the mating faces of two components, a new one must be fitted on reassembly; fit it dry unless otherwise stated in the repair procedure. Make sure that the mating faces are clean and dry, with all traces of old gasket removed. When cleaning a joint face, use a tool which is unlikely to score or damage the face, and remove any burrs or nicks with an oilstone or fine file.

Make sure that tapped holes are cleaned with a pipe cleaner, and keep them free of jointing compound, if this is being used, unless specifically instructed otherwise.

Ensure that all orifices, channels or pipes are clear, and blow through them, preferably using compressed air.

Oil seals

Oil seals can be removed by levering them out with a wide flat-bladed screwdriver or similar implement. Alternatively, a number of self-tapping screws may be screwed into the seal, and these used as a purchase for pliers or some similar device in order to pull the seal free.

Whenever an oil seal is removed from its working location, either individually or as part of an assembly, it should be renewed.

The very fine sealing lip of the seal is easily damaged, and will not seal if the surface it contacts is not completely clean and free from scratches, nicks or grooves. If the original sealing surface of the component cannot be restored, and the manufacturer has not made provision for slight relocation of the seal relative to the sealing surface, the component should be renewed.

Protect the lips of the seal from any surface which may damage them in the course of fitting. Use tape or a conical sleeve where possible. Lubricate the seal lips with oil before fitting and, on dual-lipped seals, fill the space between the lips with grease.

Unless otherwise stated, oil seals must be fitted with their sealing lips toward the lubricant to be sealed.

Use a tubular drift or block of wood of the appropriate size to install the seal and, if the seal housing is shouldered, drive the seal down to the shoulder. If the seal housing is unshouldered, the seal should be fitted with its face flush with the housing top face (unless otherwise instructed).

Screw threads and fastenings

Seized nuts, bolts and screws are quite a common occurrence where corrosion has set in, and the use of penetrating oil or releasing fluid will often overcome this problem if the offending item is soaked for a while before attempting to release it. The use of an impact driver may also provide a means of releasing such stubborn fastening devices, when used in conjunction with the appropriate screwdriver bit or socket. If none of these methods works, it may be necessary to resort to the careful application of heat, or the use of a hacksaw or nut splitter device.

Studs are usually removed by locking two nuts together on the threaded part, and then using a spanner on the lower nut to unscrew the stud. Studs or bolts which have broken off below the surface of the component in which they are mounted can sometimes be removed using a stud extractor. Always ensure that a blind tapped hole is completely free from oil, grease, water or other fluid before installing the bolt or stud. Failure to do this could cause the housing to crack due to the hydraulic action of the bolt or stud as it is screwed in.

When tightening a castellated nut to accept a split pin, tighten the nut to the specified torque, where applicable, and then tighten further to the next split pin hole. Never slacken the nut to align the split pin hole, unless stated in the repair procedure.

When checking or retightening a nut or bolt to a specified torque setting, slacken the nut or bolt by a quarter of a turn, and then retighten to the specified setting. However, this should not be attempted where angular tightening has been used.

For some screw fastenings, notably cylinder head bolts or nuts, torque wrench settings are no longer specified for the latter stages of tightening, "angle-tightening" being called up instead. Typically, a fairly low torque wrench setting will be applied to the bolts/nuts in the correct sequence, followed by one or more stages of tightening through specified angles.

Locknuts, locktabs and washers

Any fastening which will rotate against a component or housing during tightening should always have a washer between it and the relevant component or housing.

Spring or split washers should always be renewed when they are used to lock a critical component such as a big-end bearing retaining bolt or nut. Locktabs which are folded over to retain a nut or bolt should always be renewed.

Self-locking nuts can be re-used in non-critical areas, providing resistance can be felt when the locking portion passes over the bolt or stud thread. However, it should be noted that self-locking stiffnuts tend to lose their effectiveness after long periods of use, and should then be renewed as a matter of course.

Split pins must always be replaced with new ones of the correct size for the hole.

When thread-locking compound is found on the threads of a fastener which is to be re-used, it should be cleaned off with a wire brush and solvent, and fresh compound applied on reassembly.

Special tools

Some repair procedures in this manual entail the use of special tools such as a press, two or three-legged pullers, spring compressors, etc. Wherever possible, suitable readily-available alternatives to the manufacturer's special tools are described, and are shown in use. In some instances, where no alternative is possible, it has been necessary to resort to the use of a manufacturer's tool, and this has been done for reasons of safety as well as the efficient completion of the repair operation. Unless you are highly-skilled and have a thorough understanding of the procedures described, never attempt to bypass the use of any special tool when the procedure described specifies its use. Not only is there a very great risk of personal injury, but expensive damage could be caused to the components involved.

Environmental considerations

When disposing of used engine oil, brake fluid, antifreeze, etc, give due consideration to any detrimental environmental effects. Do not, for instance, pour any of the above liquids down drains into the general sewage system, or onto the ground to soak away. Many local council refuse tips provide a facility for waste oil disposal, as do some garages. If none of these facilities are available, consult your local Environmental Health Department, or the National Rivers Authority, for further advice.

With the universal tightening-up of legislation regarding the emission of environmentally-harmful substances from motor vehicles, most vehicles have tamperproof devices fitted to the main adjustment points of the fuel system. These devices are primarily designed to prevent unqualified persons from adjusting the fuel/air mixture, with the chance of a consequent increase in toxic emissions. If such devices are found during servicing or overhaul, they should, wherever possible, be renewed or refitted in accordance with the manufacturer's requirements or current legislation.

Note: *It is antisocial and illegal to dump oil down the drain. To find the location of your local oil recycling bank, call this number free.*

0800 66 33 66
www.oilbankline.org.uk

Jacking and vehicle support REF•5

The jack supplied with the vehicle should only be used for changing the roadwheels – see *Wheel changing* at the front of this manual. When carrying out any other kind of work, raise the vehicle using a hydraulic (or 'trolley') jack, and always supplement the jack with axle stands at the vehicle jacking points.

When using a hydraulic jack or axle stands, always position the jack head or axle stand head under one of the relevant jacking points; the jacking point is the area marked by two cut-outs in the sill **(see illustration)**. Use a block of wood between a trolley jack or axle stand and the sill – the block of wood should have a groove cut into it, into which the welded flange of the sill will locate.

Do not attempt to jack the vehicle under the front crossmember, the sump, or any of the suspension components.

The jack supplied with the vehicle locates in the jacking points on the underside of the sills – see *Wheel changing*. Ensure that the jack head is correctly engaged before attempting to raise the vehicle.

Never work under, around, or near a raised vehicle, unless it is adequately supported in at least two places.

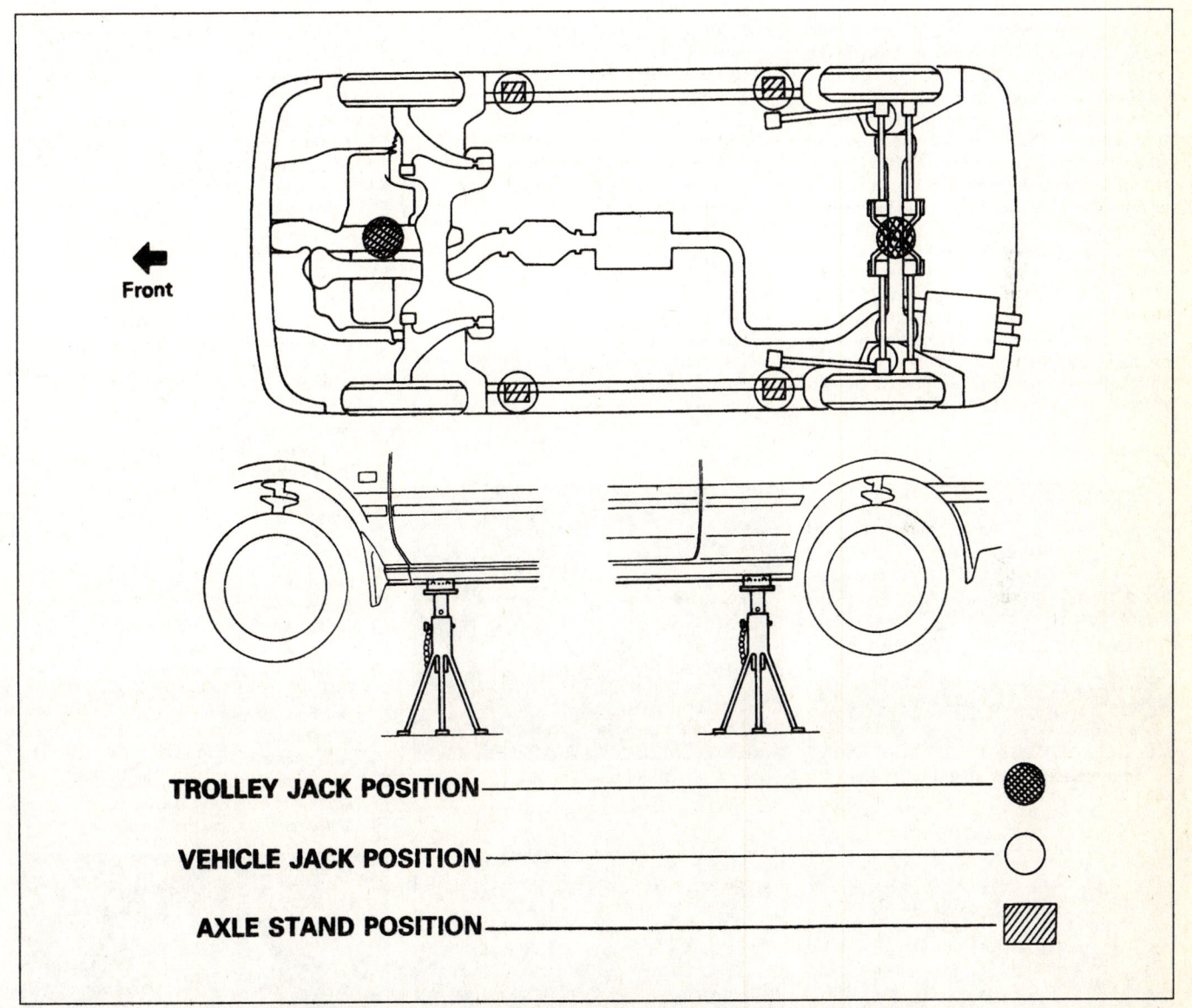

Underside of the vehicle showing the jacking points and axle stand positions

Tools and working facilities

Introduction

A selection of good tools is a fundamental requirement for anyone contemplating the maintenance and repair of a motor vehicle. For the owner who does not possess any, their purchase will prove a considerable expense, offsetting some of the savings made by doing-it-yourself. However, provided that the tools purchased meet the relevant national safety standards and are of good quality, they will last for many years and prove an extremely worthwhile investment.

To help the average owner to decide which tools are needed to carry out the various tasks detailed in this manual, we have compiled three lists of tools under the following headings: *Maintenance and minor repair*, *Repair and overhaul*, and *Special*. Newcomers to practical mechanics should start off with the *Maintenance and minor repair* tool kit, and confine themselves to the simpler jobs around the vehicle. Then, as confidence and experience grow, more difficult tasks can be undertaken, with extra tools being purchased as, and when, they are needed. In this way, a *Maintenance and minor repair* tool kit can be built up into a *Repair and overhaul* tool kit over a considerable period of time, without any major cash outlays. The experienced do-it-yourselfer will have a tool kit good enough for most repair and overhaul procedures, and will add tools from the *Special* category when it is felt that the expense is justified by the amount of use to which these tools will be put.

Maintenance and minor repair tool kit

The tools given in this list should be considered as a minimum requirement if routine maintenance, servicing and minor repair operations are to be undertaken. We recommend the purchase of combination spanners (ring one end, open-ended the other); although more expensive than open-ended ones, they do give the advantages of both types of spanner.

- [ ] *Combination spanners:*
  Metric - 8 to 19 mm inclusive
- [ ] *Adjustable spanner - 35 mm jaw (approx.)*
- [ ] *Spark plug spanner (with rubber insert) - petrol models*
- [ ] *Spark plug gap adjustment tool - petrol models*
- [ ] *Set of feeler gauges*
- [ ] *Brake bleed nipple spanner*
- [ ] *Screwdrivers:*
  Flat blade - 100 mm long x 6 mm dia
  Cross blade - 100 mm long x 6 mm dia
  Torx - various sizes (not all vehicles)
- [ ] *Combination pliers*
- [ ] *Hacksaw (junior)*
- [ ] *Tyre pump*
- [ ] *Tyre pressure gauge*
- [ ] *Oil can*
- [ ] *Oil filter removal tool*
- [ ] *Fine emery cloth*
- [ ] *Wire brush (small)*
- [ ] *Funnel (medium size)*
- [ ] *Sump drain plug key (not all vehicles)*

Repair and overhaul tool kit

These tools are virtually essential for anyone undertaking any major repairs to a motor vehicle, and are additional to those given in the *Maintenance and minor repair* list. Included in this list is a comprehensive set of sockets. Although these are expensive, they will be found invaluable as they are so versatile - particularly if various drives are included in the set. We recommend the half-inch square-drive type, as this can be used with most proprietary torque wrenches.

The tools in this list will sometimes need to be supplemented by tools from the *Special* list:

- [ ] *Sockets (or box spanners) to cover range in previous list (including Torx sockets)*
- [ ] *Reversible ratchet drive (for use with sockets)*
- [ ] *Extension piece, 250 mm (for use with sockets)*
- [ ] *Universal joint (for use with sockets)*
- [ ] *Flexible handle or sliding T "breaker bar" (for use with sockets)*
- [ ] *Torque wrench (for use with sockets)*
- [ ] *Self-locking grips*
- [ ] *Ball pein hammer*
- [ ] *Soft-faced mallet (plastic or rubber)*
- [ ] *Screwdrivers:*
  Flat blade - long & sturdy, short (chubby), and narrow (electrician's) types
  Cross blade – long & sturdy, and short (chubby) types
- [ ] *Pliers:*
  Long-nosed
  Side cutters (electrician's)
  Circlip (internal and external)
- [ ] *Cold chisel - 25 mm*
- [ ] *Scriber*
- [ ] *Scraper*
- [ ] *Centre-punch*
- [ ] *Pin punch*
- [ ] *Hacksaw*
- [ ] *Brake hose clamp*
- [ ] *Brake/clutch bleeding kit*
- [ ] *Selection of twist drills*
- [ ] *Steel rule/straight-edge*
- [ ] *Allen keys (inc. splined/Torx type)*
- [ ] *Selection of files*
- [ ] *Wire brush*
- [ ] *Axle stands*
- [ ] *Jack (strong trolley or hydraulic type)*
- [ ] *Light with extension lead*
- [ ] *Universal electrical multi-meter*

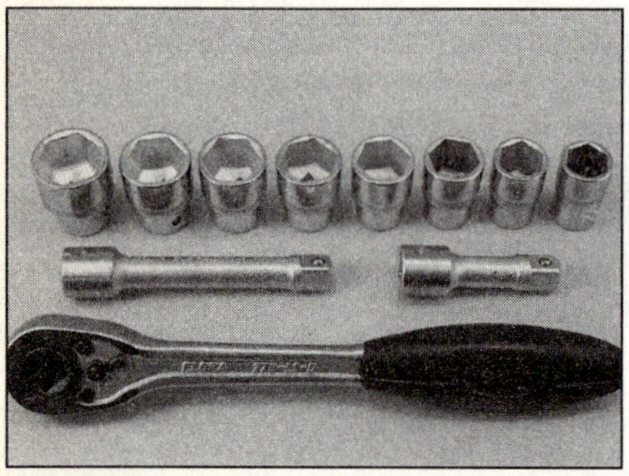

Sockets and reversible ratchet drive

Brake bleeding kit

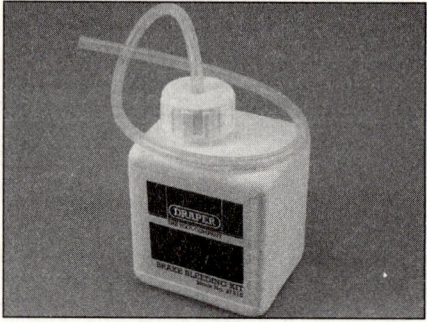

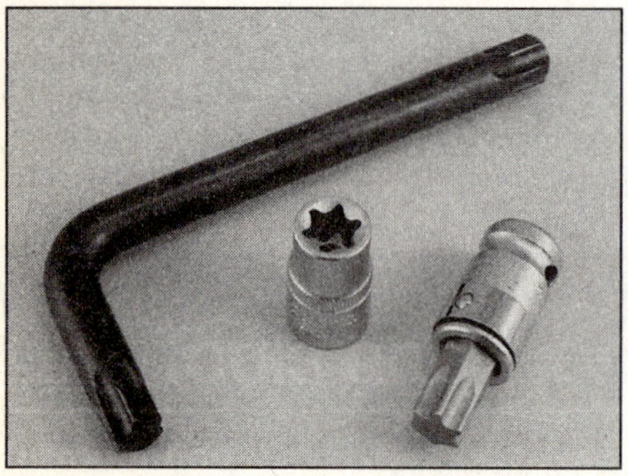

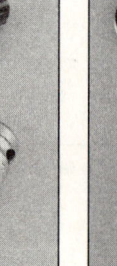

Torx key, socket and bit

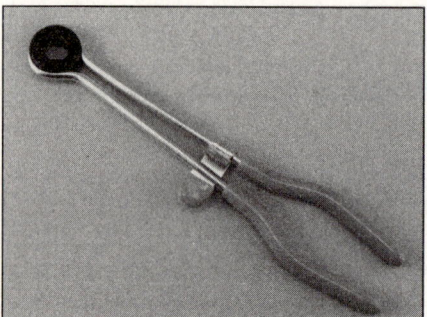

Hose clamp

Angular-tightening gauge

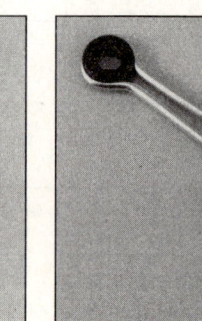

Tools and working facilities REF•7

Special tools

The tools in this list are those which are not used regularly, are expensive to buy, or which need to be used in accordance with their manufacturers' instructions. Unless relatively difficult mechanical jobs are undertaken frequently, it will not be economic to buy many of these tools. Where this is the case, you could consider clubbing together with friends (or joining a motorists' club) to make a joint purchase, or borrowing the tools against a deposit from a local garage or tool hire specialist. It is worth noting that many of the larger DIY superstores now carry a large range of special tools for hire at modest rates.

The following list contains only those tools and instruments freely available to the public, and not those special tools produced by the vehicle manufacturer specifically for its dealer network. You will find occasional references to these manufacturers' special tools in the text of this manual. Generally, an alternative method of doing the job without the vehicle manufacturers' special tool is given. However, sometimes there is no alternative to using them. Where this is the case and the relevant tool cannot be bought or borrowed, you will have to entrust the work to a dealer.

- ☐ Angular-tightening gauge
- ☐ Valve spring compressor
- ☐ Valve grinding tool
- ☐ Piston ring compressor
- ☐ Piston ring removal/installation tool
- ☐ Cylinder bore hone
- ☐ Balljoint separator
- ☐ Coil spring compressors (where applicable)
- ☐ Two/three-legged hub and bearing puller
- ☐ Impact screwdriver
- ☐ Micrometer and/or vernier calipers
- ☐ Dial gauge
- ☐ Stroboscopic timing light
- ☐ Dwell angle meter/tachometer
- ☐ Fault code reader
- ☐ Cylinder compression gauge
- ☐ Hand-operated vacuum pump and gauge
- ☐ Clutch plate alignment set
- ☐ Brake shoe steady spring cup removal tool
- ☐ Bush and bearing removal/installation set
- ☐ Stud extractors
- ☐ Tap and die set
- ☐ Lifting tackle
- ☐ Trolley jack

Buying tools

Reputable motor accessory shops and superstores often offer excellent quality tools at discount prices, so it pays to shop around.

Remember, you don't have to buy the most expensive items on the shelf, but it is always advisable to steer clear of the very cheap tools. Beware of 'bargains' offered on market stalls or at car boot sales. There are plenty of good tools around at reasonable prices, but always aim to purchase items which meet the relevant national safety standards. If in doubt, ask the proprietor or manager of the shop for advice before making a purchase.

Care and maintenance of tools

Having purchased a reasonable tool kit, it is necessary to keep the tools in a clean and serviceable condition. After use, always wipe off any dirt, grease and metal particles using a clean, dry cloth, before putting the tools away. Never leave them lying around after they have been used. A simple tool rack on the garage or workshop wall for items such as screwdrivers and pliers is a good idea. Store all normal spanners and sockets in a metal box. Any measuring instruments, gauges, meters, etc, must be carefully stored where they cannot be damaged or become rusty.

Take a little care when tools are used. Hammer heads inevitably become marked, and screwdrivers lose the keen edge on their blades from time to time. A little timely attention with emery cloth or a file will soon restore items like this to a good finish.

Working facilities

Not to be forgotten when discussing tools is the workshop itself. If anything more than routine maintenance is to be carried out, a suitable working area becomes essential.

It is appreciated that many an owner-mechanic is forced by circumstances to remove an engine or similar item without the benefit of a garage or workshop. Having done this, any repairs should always be done under the cover of a roof.

Wherever possible, any dismantling should be done on a clean, flat workbench or table at a suitable working height.

Any workbench needs a vice; one with a jaw opening of 100 mm is suitable for most jobs. As mentioned previously, some clean dry storage space is also required for tools, as well as for any lubricants, cleaning fluids, touch-up paints etc, which become necessary.

Another item which may be required, and which has a much more general usage, is an electric drill with a chuck capacity of at least 8 mm. This, together with a good range of twist drills, is virtually essential for fitting accessories.

Last, but not least, always keep a supply of old newspapers and clean, lint-free rags available, and try to keep any working area as clean as possible.

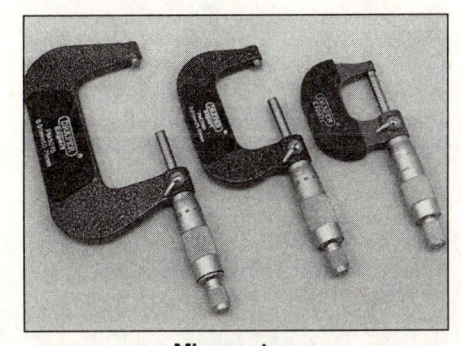

Micrometers

Dial test indicator ("dial gauge")

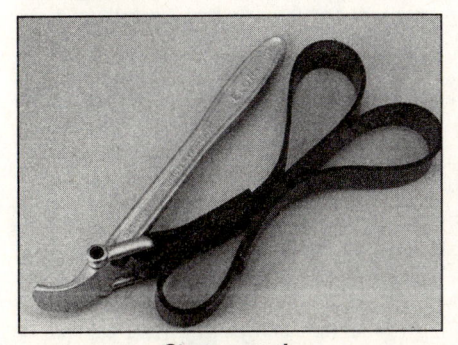

Strap wrench

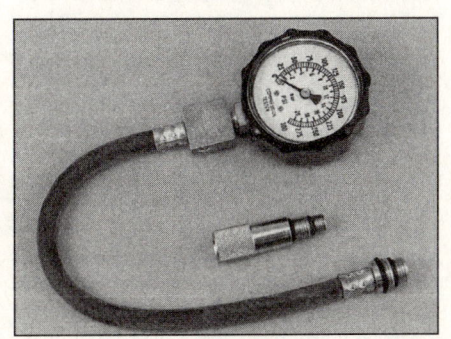

Compression tester

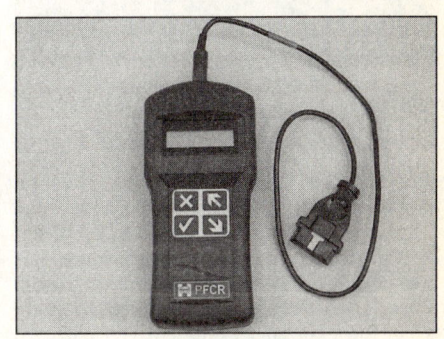

Fault code reader

REF•8 MOT test checks

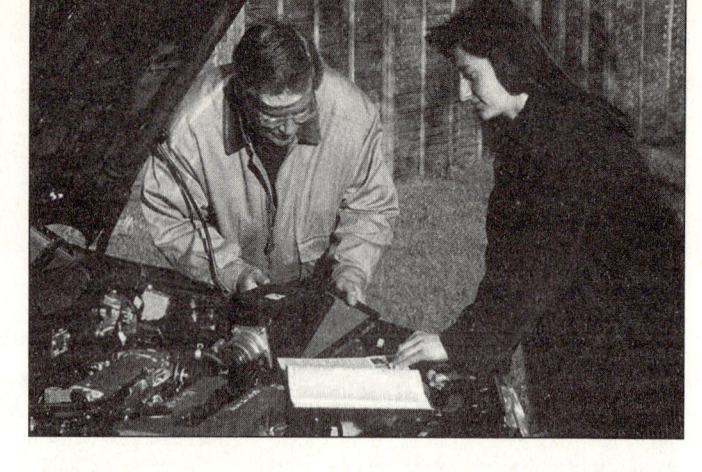

This is a guide to getting your vehicle through the MOT test. Obviously it will not be possible to examine the vehicle to the same standard as the professional MOT tester. However, working through the following checks will enable you to identify any problem areas before submitting the vehicle for the test.

Where a testable component is in borderline condition, the tester has discretion in deciding whether to pass or fail it. The basis of such discretion is whether the tester would be happy for a close relative or friend to use the vehicle with the component in that condition. If the vehicle presented is clean and evidently well cared for, the tester may be more inclined to pass a borderline component than if the vehicle is scruffy and apparently neglected.

It has only been possible to summarise the test requirements here, based on the regulations in force at the time of printing. Test standards are becoming increasingly stringent, although there are some exemptions for older vehicles.

An assistant will be needed to help carry out some of these checks.

The checks have been sub-divided into four categories, as follows:

1 Checks carried out **FROM THE DRIVER'S SEAT**

2 Checks carried out **WITH THE VEHICLE ON THE GROUND**

3 Checks carried out **WITH THE VEHICLE RAISED AND THE WHEELS FREE TO TURN**

4 Checks carried out on **YOUR VEHICLE'S EXHAUST EMISSION SYSTEM**

---

1 Checks carried out **FROM THE DRIVER'S SEAT**

Handbrake

☐ Test the operation of the handbrake. Excessive travel (too many clicks) indicates incorrect brake or cable adjustment.

☐ Check that the handbrake cannot be released by tapping the lever sideways. Check the security of the lever mountings.

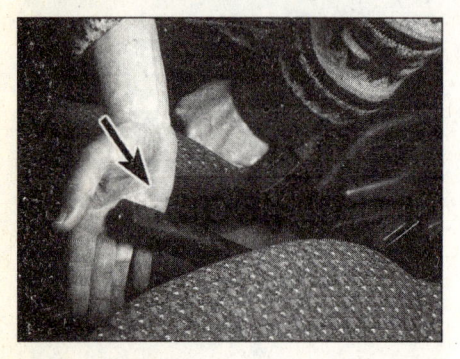

Footbrake

☐ Depress the brake pedal and check that it does not creep down to the floor, indicating a master cylinder fault. Release the pedal, wait a few seconds, then depress it again. If the pedal travels nearly to the floor before firm resistance is felt, brake adjustment or repair is necessary. If the pedal feels spongy, there is air in the hydraulic system which must be removed by bleeding.

☐ Check that the brake pedal is secure and in good condition. Check also for signs of fluid leaks on the pedal, floor or carpets, which would indicate failed seals in the brake master cylinder.

☐ Check the servo unit (when applicable) by operating the brake pedal several times, then keeping the pedal depressed and starting the engine. As the engine starts, the pedal will move down slightly. If not, the vacuum hose or the servo itself may be faulty.

Steering wheel and column

☐ Examine the steering wheel for fractures or looseness of the hub, spokes or rim.

☐ Move the steering wheel from side to side and then up and down. Check that the steering wheel is not loose on the column, indicating wear or a loose retaining nut. Continue moving the steering wheel as before, but also turn it slightly from left to right.

☐ Check that the steering wheel is not loose on the column, and that there is no abnormal movement of the steering wheel, indicating wear in the column support bearings or couplings.

Windscreen, mirrors and sunvisor

☐ The windscreen must be free of cracks or other significant damage within the driver's field of view. (Small stone chips are acceptable.) Rear view mirrors must be secure, intact, and capable of being adjusted.

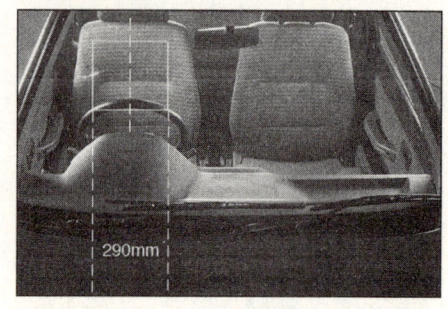

☐ The driver's sunvisor must be capable of being stored in the "up" position.

MOT test checks REF•9

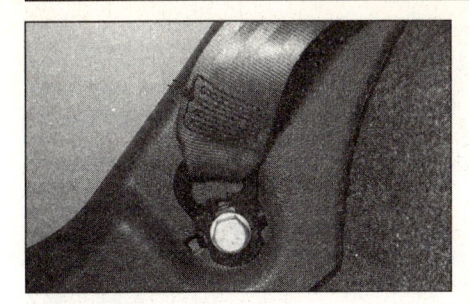

Seat belts and seats

Note: *The following checks are applicable to all seat belts, front and rear.*

☐ Examine the webbing of all the belts (including rear belts if fitted) for cuts, serious fraying or deterioration. Fasten and unfasten each belt to check the buckles. If applicable, check the retracting mechanism. Check the security of all seat belt mountings accessible from inside the vehicle.

☐ Seat belts with pre-tensioners, once activated, have a "flag" or similar showing on the seat belt stalk. This, in itself, is not a reason for test failure.

☐ The front seats themselves must be securely attached and the backrests must lock in the upright position.

Doors

☐ Both front doors must be able to be opened and closed from outside and inside, and must latch securely when closed.

2 Checks carried out WITH THE VEHICLE ON THE GROUND

Vehicle identification

☐ Number plates must be in good condition, secure and legible, with letters and numbers correctly spaced – spacing at (A) should be at least twice that at (B).

☐ The VIN plate and/or homologation plate must be legible.

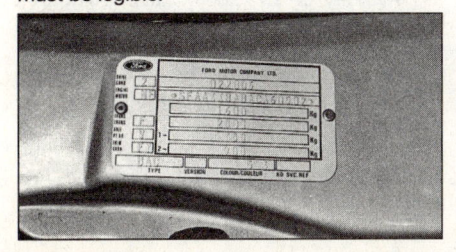

Electrical equipment

☐ Switch on the ignition and check the operation of the horn.

☐ Check the windscreen washers and wipers, examining the wiper blades; renew damaged or perished blades. Also check the operation of the stop-lights.

☐ Check the operation of the sidelights and number plate lights. The lenses and reflectors must be secure, clean and undamaged.

☐ Check the operation and alignment of the headlights. The headlight reflectors must not be tarnished and the lenses must be undamaged.

☐ Switch on the ignition and check the operation of the direction indicators (including the instrument panel tell-tale) and the hazard warning lights. Operation of the sidelights and stop-lights must not affect the indicators - if it does, the cause is usually a bad earth at the rear light cluster.

☐ Check the operation of the rear foglight(s), including the warning light on the instrument panel or in the switch.

☐ The ABS warning light must illuminate in accordance with the manufacturers' design. For most vehicles, the ABS warning light should illuminate when the ignition is switched on, and (if the system is operating properly) extinguish after a few seconds. Refer to the owner's handbook.

Footbrake

☐ Examine the master cylinder, brake pipes and servo unit for leaks, loose mountings, corrosion or other damage.

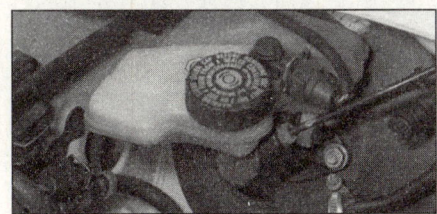

☐ The fluid reservoir must be secure and the fluid level must be between the upper (**A**) and lower (**B**) markings.

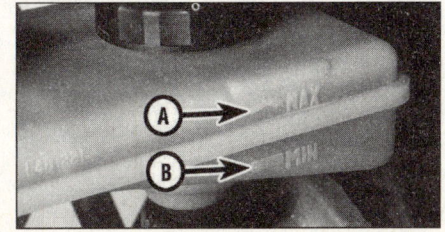

☐ Inspect both front brake flexible hoses for cracks or deterioration of the rubber. Turn the steering from lock to lock, and ensure that the hoses do not contact the wheel, tyre, or any part of the steering or suspension mechanism. With the brake pedal firmly depressed, check the hoses for bulges or leaks under pressure.

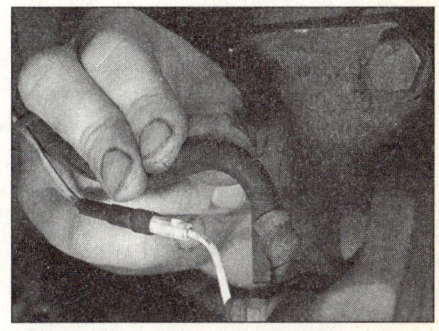

Steering and suspension

☐ Have your assistant turn the steering wheel from side to side slightly, up to the point where the steering gear just begins to transmit this movement to the roadwheels. Check for excessive free play between the steering wheel and the steering gear, indicating wear or insecurity of the steering column joints, the column-to-steering gear coupling, or the steering gear itself.

☐ Have your assistant turn the steering wheel more vigorously in each direction, so that the roadwheels just begin to turn. As this is done, examine all the steering joints, linkages, fittings and attachments. Renew any component that shows signs of wear or damage. On vehicles with power steering, check the security and condition of the steering pump, drivebelt and hoses.

☐ Check that the vehicle is standing level, and at approximately the correct ride height.

Shock absorbers

☐ Depress each corner of the vehicle in turn, then release it. The vehicle should rise and then settle in its normal position. If the vehicle continues to rise and fall, the shock absorber is defective. A shock absorber which has seized will also cause the vehicle to fail.

REF•10 MOT test checks

Exhaust system

☐ Start the engine. With your assistant holding a rag over the tailpipe, check the entire system for leaks. Repair or renew leaking sections.

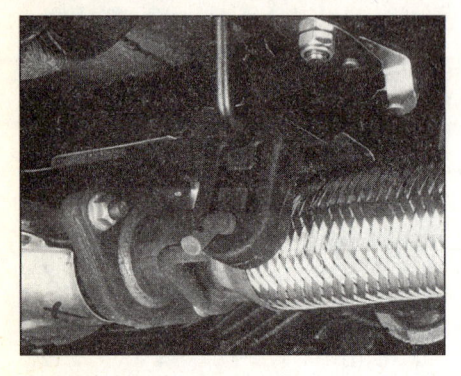

3 Checks carried out WITH THE VEHICLE RAISED AND THE WHEELS FREE TO TURN

Jack up the front and rear of the vehicle, and securely support it on axle stands. Position the stands clear of the suspension assemblies. Ensure that the wheels are clear of the ground and that the steering can be turned from lock to lock.

Steering mechanism

☐ Have your assistant turn the steering from lock to lock. Check that the steering turns smoothly, and that no part of the steering mechanism, including a wheel or tyre, fouls any brake hose or pipe or any part of the body structure.

☐ Examine the steering rack rubber gaiters for damage or insecurity of the retaining clips. If power steering is fitted, check for signs of damage or leakage of the fluid hoses, pipes or connections. Also check for excessive stiffness or binding of the steering, a missing split pin or locking device, or severe corrosion of the body structure within 30 cm of any steering component attachment point.

Front and rear suspension and wheel bearings

☐ Starting at the front right-hand side, grasp the roadwheel at the 3 o'clock and 9 o'clock positions and rock gently but firmly. Check for free play or insecurity at the wheel bearings, suspension balljoints, or suspension mountings, pivots and attachments.

☐ Now grasp the wheel at the 12 o'clock and 6 o'clock positions and repeat the previous inspection. Spin the wheel, and check for roughness or tightness of the front wheel bearing.

☐ If excess free play is suspected at a component pivot point, this can be confirmed by using a large screwdriver or similar tool and levering between the mounting and the component attachment. This will confirm whether the wear is in the pivot bush, its retaining bolt, or in the mounting itself (the bolt holes can often become elongated).

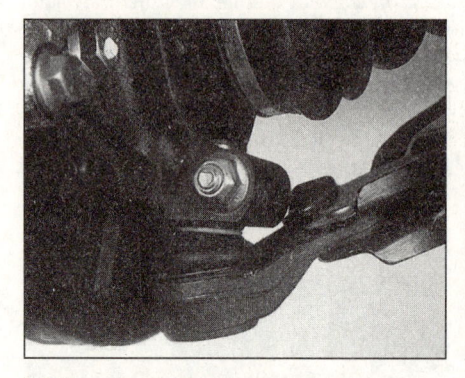

☐ Carry out all the above checks at the other front wheel, and then at both rear wheels.

Springs and shock absorbers

☐ Examine the suspension struts (when applicable) for serious fluid leakage, corrosion, or damage to the casing. Also check the security of the mounting points.

☐ If coil springs are fitted, check that the spring ends locate in their seats, and that the spring is not corroded, cracked or broken.

☐ If leaf springs are fitted, check that all leaves are intact, that the axle is securely attached to each spring, and that there is no deterioration of the spring eye mountings, bushes, and shackles.

☐ The same general checks apply to vehicles fitted with other suspension types, such as torsion bars, hydraulic displacer units, etc. Ensure that all mountings and attachments are secure, that there are no signs of excessive wear, corrosion or damage, and (on hydraulic types) that there are no fluid leaks or damaged pipes.

☐ Inspect the shock absorbers for signs of serious fluid leakage. Check for wear of the mounting bushes or attachments, or damage to the body of the unit.

Driveshafts (fwd vehicles only)

☐ Rotate each front wheel in turn and inspect the constant velocity joint gaiters for splits or damage. Also check that each driveshaft is straight and undamaged.

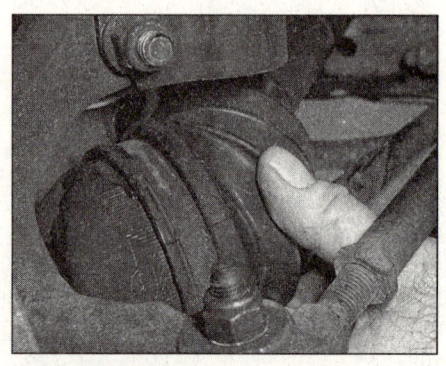

Braking system

☐ If possible without dismantling, check brake pad wear and disc condition. Ensure that the friction lining material has not worn excessively, (A) and that the discs are not fractured, pitted, scored or badly worn (B).

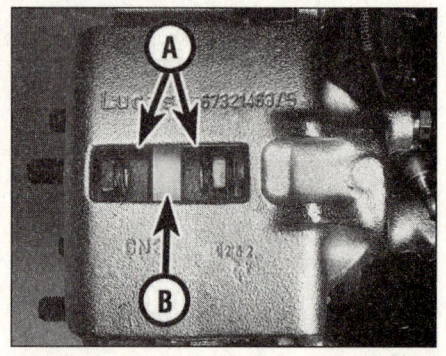

☐ Examine all the rigid brake pipes underneath the vehicle, and the flexible hose(s) at the rear. Look for corrosion, chafing or insecurity of the pipes, and for signs of bulging under pressure, chafing, splits or deterioration of the flexible hoses.

☐ Look for signs of fluid leaks at the brake calipers or on the brake backplates. Repair or renew leaking components.

☐ Slowly spin each wheel, while your assistant depresses and releases the footbrake. Ensure that each brake is operating and does not bind when the pedal is released.

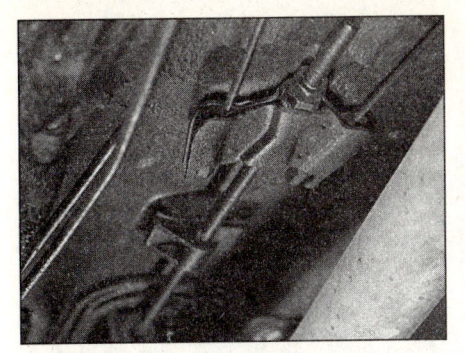

MOT test checks   REF•11

☐ Examine the handbrake mechanism, checking for frayed or broken cables, excessive corrosion, or wear or insecurity of the linkage. Check that the mechanism works on each relevant wheel, and releases fully, without binding.

☐ It is not possible to test brake efficiency without special equipment, but a road test can be carried out later to check that the vehicle pulls up in a straight line.

Fuel and exhaust systems

☐ Inspect the fuel tank (including the filler cap), fuel pipes, hoses and unions. All components must be secure and free from leaks.

☐ Examine the exhaust system over its entire length, checking for any damaged, broken or missing mountings, security of the retaining clamps and rust or corrosion.

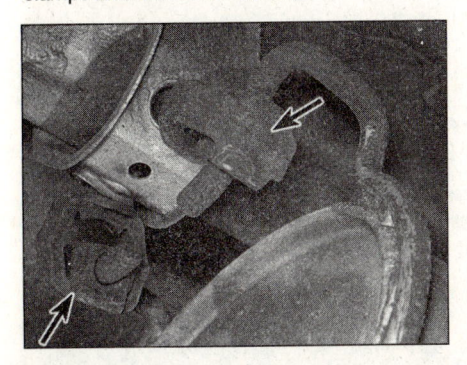

Wheels and tyres

☐ Examine the sidewalls and tread area of each tyre in turn. Check for cuts, tears, lumps, bulges, separation of the tread, and exposure of the ply or cord due to wear or damage. Check that the tyre bead is correctly seated on the wheel rim, that the valve is sound and properly seated, and that the wheel is not distorted or damaged.

☐ Check that the tyres are of the correct size for the vehicle, that they are of the same size and type on each axle, and that the pressures are correct.

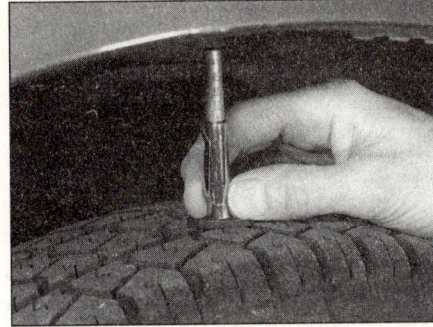

☐ Check the tyre tread depth. The legal minimum at the time of writing is 1.6 mm over at least three-quarters of the tread width. Abnormal tread wear may indicate incorrect front wheel alignment.

Body corrosion

☐ Check the condition of the entire vehicle structure for signs of corrosion in load-bearing areas. (These include chassis box sections, side sills, cross-members, pillars, and all suspension, steering, braking system and seat belt mountings and anchorages.) Any corrosion which has seriously reduced the thickness of a load-bearing area is likely to cause the vehicle to fail. In this case professional repairs are likely to be needed.

☐ Damage or corrosion which causes sharp or otherwise dangerous edges to be exposed will also cause the vehicle to fail.

4 Checks carried out on YOUR VEHICLE'S EXHAUST EMISSION SYSTEM

Petrol models

☐ The engine should be warmed up, and running well (ignition system in good order, air filter element clean, etc).

☐ Before testing, run the engine at around 2500 rpm for 20 seconds. Let the engine drop to idle, and watch for smoke from the exhaust. If the idle speed is too high, or if dense blue or black smoke emerges for more than 5 seconds, the vehicle will fail. Typically, blue smoke signifies oil burning (engine wear); black smoke means unburnt fuel (dirty air cleaner element, or other fuel system fault).

☐ An exhaust gas analyser for measuring carbon monoxide (CO) and hydrocarbons (HC) is now needed. If one cannot be hired or borrowed, have a local garage perform the check.

CO emissions (mixture)

☐ The MOT tester has access to the CO limits for all vehicles. The CO level is measured at idle speed, and at 'fast idle' (2500 to 3000 rpm). The following limits are given as a general guide:
   At idle speed – Less than 0.5% CO
   At 'fast idle' – Less than 0.3% CO
   Lambda reading – 0.97 to 1.03

☐ If the CO level is too high, this may point to poor maintenance, a fuel injection system problem, faulty lambda (oxygen) sensor or catalytic converter. Try an injector cleaning treatment, and check the vehicle's ECU for fault codes.

HC emissions

☐ The MOT tester has access to HC limits for all vehicles. The HC level is measured at 'fast idle' (2500 to 3000 rpm). The following limits are given as a general guide:
   At 'fast idle' – Less then 200 ppm

☐ Excessive HC emissions are typically caused by oil being burnt (worn engine), or by a blocked crankcase ventilation system ('breather'). If the engine oil is old and thin, an oil change may help. If the engine is running badly, check the vehicle's ECU for fault codes.

Diesel models

☐ The only emission test for diesel engines is measuring exhaust smoke density, using a calibrated smoke meter. The test involves accelerating the engine at least 3 times to its maximum unloaded speed.

Note: *On engines with a timing belt, it is VITAL that the belt is in good condition before the test is carried out.*

☐ With the engine warmed up, it is first purged by running at around 2500 rpm for 20 seconds. A governor check is then carried out, by slowly accelerating the engine to its maximum speed. After this, the smoke meter is connected, and the engine is accelerated quickly to maximum speed three times. If the smoke density is less than the limits given below, the vehicle will pass:
   Non-turbo vehicles: 2.5m-1
   Turbocharged vehicles: 3.0m-1

☐ If excess smoke is produced, try fitting a new air cleaner element, or using an injector cleaning treatment. If the engine is running badly, where applicable, check the vehicle's ECU for fault codes. Also check the vehicle's EGR system, where applicable. At high mileages, the injectors may require professional attention.

Fault finding

Engine
- [ ] Engine fails to rotate when attempting to start
- [ ] Engine rotates, but will not start
- [ ] Engine difficult to start when cold
- [ ] Engine difficult to start when hot
- [ ] Starter motor noisy or excessively-rough in engagement
- [ ] Engine starts, but stops immediately
- [ ] Engine idles erratically
- [ ] Engine misfires at idle speed
- [ ] Engine misfires throughout the driving speed range
- [ ] Engine hesitates on acceleration
- [ ] Engine stalls
- [ ] Engine lacks power
- [ ] Engine backfires
- [ ] Oil pressure warning light on with engine running
- [ ] Engine runs-on after switching off
- [ ] Engine noises

Cooling system
- [ ] Overheating
- [ ] Overcooling
- [ ] External coolant leakage
- [ ] Internal coolant leakage
- [ ] Corrosion

Fuel and exhaust systems
- [ ] Excessive fuel consumption
- [ ] Fuel leakage and/or fuel odour
- [ ] Excessive noise or fumes from exhaust system

Clutch
- [ ] Pedal travels to floor – no pressure or very little resistance
- [ ] Clutch fails to disengage (unable to select gears)
- [ ] Clutch slips (engine speed rises, with no increase in vehicle speed)
- [ ] Judder as clutch is engaged
- [ ] Noise when depressing or releasing clutch pedal

Manual transmission
- [ ] Noisy in neutral with engine running
- [ ] Noisy in one particular gear
- [ ] Difficulty engaging gears
- [ ] Jumps out of gear
- [ ] Vibration
- [ ] Lubricant leaks

Automatic transmission
- [ ] Fluid leakage
- [ ] Transmission fluid brown, or has burned smell
- [ ] General gear selection problems
- [ ] Transmission will not downshift (kickdown) on full throttle
- [ ] Engine won't start in any gear, or starts in gears other than P or N
- [ ] Transmission slips, shifts roughly, is noisy, or has no drive in forward or reverse gears

Driveshafts
- [ ] Clicking or knocking noise on turns (at slow speed on full-lock)
- [ ] Vibration when accelerating or decelerating

Braking system
- [ ] Vehicle pulls to one side under braking
- [ ] Noise (grinding or high-pitched squeal) when brakes applied
- [ ] Excessive brake pedal travel
- [ ] Brake pedal feels spongy when depressed
- [ ] Excessive brake pedal effort required to stop vehicle
- [ ] Judder felt through brake pedal or steering wheel when braking
- [ ] Brakes binding
- [ ] Rear wheels locking under normal braking

Suspension and steering systems
- [ ] Vehicle pulls to one side
- [ ] Wheel wobble and vibration
- [ ] Excessive pitching and/or rolling around corners, or during braking
- [ ] Wandering or general instability
- [ ] Excessively-stiff steering
- [ ] Excessive play in steering
- [ ] Lack of power assistance
- [ ] Tyre wear excessive

Electrical system
- [ ] Battery will not hold a charge for more than a few days
- [ ] Ignition/no-charge warning light stays on with engine running
- [ ] Ignition/no-charge warning light fails to come on
- [ ] Lights inoperative
- [ ] Instrument readings inaccurate or erratic
- [ ] Horn inoperative, or unsatisfactory in operation
- [ ] Windscreen/tailgate wipers failed, or unsatisfactory in operation
- [ ] Windscreen/tailgate washers failed, or unsatisfactory in operation
- [ ] Electric windows inoperative, or unsatisfactory in operation
- [ ] Central locking system inoperative, or unsatisfactory in operation

Fault finding

Introduction

The vehicle owner who does his or her own maintenance according to the recommended service schedules should not have to use this section of the manual very often. Modern component reliability is such that, provided those items subject to wear or deterioration are inspected or renewed at the specified intervals, sudden failure is comparatively rare. Faults do not usually just happen as a result of sudden failure, but develop over a period of time. Major mechanical failures in particular are usually preceded by characteristic symptoms over hundreds or even thousands of miles. Those components which do occasionally fail without warning are often small and easily carried in the vehicle.

With any fault-finding, the first step is to decide where to begin investigations. Sometimes this is obvious, but on other occasions, a little detective work will be necessary. The owner who makes half a dozen haphazard adjustments or replacements may be successful in curing a fault (or its symptoms), but will be none the wiser if the fault recurs, and ultimately may have spent more time and money than was necessary. A calm and logical approach will be found to be more satisfactory in the long run. Always take into account any warning signs or abnormalities that may have been noticed in the period preceding the fault – power loss, high or low gauge readings, unusual smells, etc – and remember that failure of components such as fuses or spark plugs may only be pointers to some underlying fault.

The pages which follow provide an easy-reference guide to the more common problems which may occur during the operation of the vehicle. These problems and their possible causes are grouped under headings denoting various components or systems, such as Engine, Cooling system, etc. The general Chapter which deals with the problem is also shown in brackets; refer to the relevant part of that Chapter for system-specific information. Whatever the fault, certain basic principles apply. These are as follows:

Verify the fault. This is simply a matter of being sure that you know what the symptoms are before starting work. This is particularly important if you are investigating a fault for someone else, who may not have described it very accurately.

Don't overlook the obvious. For example, if the vehicle won't start, is there fuel in the tank? (Don't take anyone else's word on this particular point, and don't trust the fuel gauge either!) If an electrical fault is indicated, look for loose or broken wires before digging out the test gear.

Cure the disease, not the symptom. Substituting a flat battery with a fully-charged one will get you off the hard shoulder, but if the underlying cause is not attended to, the new battery will go the same way. Similarly, changing oil-fouled spark plugs (petrol models) for a new set will get you moving again, but remember that the reason for the fouling (if it wasn't simply an incorrect grade of plug) will have to be found and corrected.

Don't take anything for granted. Particularly, don't forget that a 'new' component may itself be defective (especially if it's been rattling around in the boot for months), and don't leave components out of a fault diagnosis sequence just because they are new or recently-fitted. When you do finally diagnose a difficult fault, you'll probably realise that all the evidence was there from the start.

REF•14 Fault finding

Engine

Engine fails to rotate when attempting to start
- [ ] Battery terminal connections loose or corroded (*Weekly checks*).
- [ ] Battery discharged or faulty (Chapter 5A).
- [ ] Broken, loose or disconnected wiring in the starting circuit (Chapter 5A).
- [ ] Defective starter motor (Chapter 5A).
- [ ] Starter pinion or flywheel/driveplate ring gear teeth loose or broken (Chapter 2A and 5A).
- [ ] Engine earth strap broken or disconnected (Chapter 12).

Engine rotates, but will not start
- [ ] Fuel tank empty.
- [ ] Battery discharged (engine rotates slowly) (Chapter 5A).
- [ ] Battery terminal connections loose or corroded (*Weekly checks*).
- [ ] Worn, faulty or incorrectly-gapped spark plugs (Chapter 1).
- [ ] Engine management system fault – petrol models (Chapter 4A).
- [ ] Low cylinder compressions (Chapter 2A).
- [ ] Major mechanical failure (eg camshaft drive) (Chapter 2A).

Engine difficult to start when cold
- [ ] Battery discharged (Chapter 5A).
- [ ] Battery terminal connections loose or corroded (*Weekly checks*).
- [ ] Worn, faulty or incorrectly-gapped spark plugs (Chapter 1).
- [ ] Engine management system fault (Chapter 4A).

Engine difficult to start when hot
- [ ] Engine management system fault (Chapter 4).
- [ ] Low cylinder compressions (Chapter 2A).

Starter motor noisy or excessively-rough in engagement
- [ ] Starter pinion or flywheel/driveplate ring gear teeth loose or broken (Chapters 2A and 5A).
- [ ] Starter motor mounting bolts loose or missing (Chapter 5A).
- [ ] Defective starter motor (Chapter 5A).

Engine starts, but stops immediately
- [ ] Vacuum leak at the throttle housing/inlet manifold (Chapter 4A).
- [ ] Engine management system fault (Chapter 4A).

Engine idles erratically
- [ ] Vacuum leak at the throttle housing/inlet manifold (Chapter 4A).
- [ ] Worn, faulty or incorrectly-gapped spark plugs (Chapter 1).
- [ ] Engine management system fault (Chapter 4A).
- [ ] Uneven or low cylinder compressions (Chapter 2A).
- [ ] Camshaft lobes worn (Chapter 2A).
- [ ] Timing belt/chain incorrectly fitted (Chapter 2A).

Engine misfires at idle speed
- [ ] Worn, faulty or incorrectly-gapped spark plugs (Chapter 1).
- [ ] Vacuum leak at the throttle housing/inlet manifold (Chapter 4A).
- [ ] Engine management system fault (Chapter 4A).
- [ ] Uneven or low cylinder compressions (Chapter 2A).
- [ ] Disconnected, leaking, or perished crankcase ventilation hoses (Chapter 4B).

Engine misfires throughout the driving speed range
- [ ] Fuel filter blocked (Chapter 1).
- [ ] Fuel pump faulty (Chapter 4A).
- [ ] Fuel tank vent blocked, or fuel pipes restricted (Chapter 4A).
- [ ] Worn, faulty or incorrectly-gapped spark plugs (Chapter 1).
- [ ] Vacuum leak at the throttle housing/inlet manifold (Chapter 4A).
- [ ] Engine management system fault (Chapter 4A).
- [ ] Faulty ignition HT coil (Chapter 5B).
- [ ] Uneven or low cylinder compressions (Chapter 2A).

Engine hesitates on acceleration
- [ ] Worn, faulty or incorrectly-gapped spark plugs (Chapter 1).
- [ ] Vacuum leak at the throttle housing/inlet manifold (Chapter 4A).
- [ ] Engine management system fault (Chapter 4A).

Engine stalls
- [ ] Fuel filter blocked (Chapter 1).
- [ ] Fuel pump faulty (Chapter 4A).
- [ ] Fuel tank vent blocked, or fuel pipes restricted (Chapter 4A).
- [ ] Worn, faulty or incorrectly-gapped spark plugs (Chapter 1).
- [ ] Vacuum leak at the throttle housing/inlet manifold (Chapter 4A).
- [ ] Engine management system fault (Chapter 4A).

Engine lacks power
- [ ] Timing belt/chain incorrectly fitted (Chapter 2A).
- [ ] Fuel filter blocked (Chapter 1).
- [ ] Fuel pump faulty (Chapter 4A).
- [ ] Uneven or low cylinder compressions (Chapter 2A).
- [ ] Worn, faulty or incorrectly-gapped spark plugs (Chapter 1).
- [ ] Vacuum leak at the throttle housing/inlet manifold (Chapter 4A).
- [ ] Engine management system fault (Chapter 4A).
- [ ] Brakes binding (Chapters 1 and 9).
- [ ] Clutch slipping (Chapter 6).

Engine backfires
- [ ] Timing belt/chain incorrectly fitted (Chapter 2A).
- [ ] Vacuum leak at the throttle housing/inlet manifold (Chapter 4A).
- [ ] Engine management system fault (Chapter 4A).

Oil pressure warning light on with engine running
- [ ] Low oil level, or incorrect oil grade (*Weekly checks*).
- [ ] Faulty oil pressure warning light switch (Chapter 5A).
- [ ] Worn engine bearings and/or oil pump (Chapter 2B).
- [ ] High engine operating temperature (Chapter 3).
- [ ] Oil pressure relief valve defective (Chapter 2A).
- [ ] Oil pick-up strainer clogged (Chapter 2A).

Engine runs-on after switching off
- [ ] Excessive carbon build-up in engine (Chapter 2B).
- [ ] High engine operating temperature (Chapter 3).
- [ ] Engine management system fault (Chapter 4A).

Fault finding REF•15

Engine (continued)

Engine noises

Pre-ignition (pinking) or knocking during acceleration or under load
- [ ] Engine management system fault (Chapter 4A).
- [ ] Incorrect grade of spark plug (Chapter 1).
- [ ] Incorrect grade of fuel (Chapter 4A).
- [ ] Vacuum leak at the throttle housing/inlet manifold (Chapter 4A).
- [ ] Excessive carbon build-up in engine (Chapter 2B).

Whistling or wheezing noises
- [ ] Leaking inlet manifold or throttle housing gasket (Chapter 4A).
- [ ] Leaking vacuum hose (Chapters 4A and 9).
- [ ] Blowing cylinder head gasket (Chapter 2A).

Tapping or rattling noises
- [ ] Worn valve gear or camshaft (Chapter 2A).
- [ ] Ancillary component fault (coolant pump, alternator, etc) (Chapters 3, 5A, etc).

Knocking or thumping noises
- [ ] Worn big-end bearings (regular heavy knocking, perhaps less under load) (Chapter 2B).
- [ ] Worn main bearings (rumbling and knocking, perhaps worsening under load) (Chapter 2B).
- [ ] Piston slap (most noticeable when cold) (Chapter 2B).
- [ ] Ancillary component fault (coolant pump, alternator, etc) (Chapters 3, 5A, etc).

REF•16 Fault finding

Cooling system

Overheating
- ☐ Insufficient coolant in system (*Weekly checks*).
- ☐ Thermostat faulty (stuck closed) (Chapter 3).
- ☐ Radiator core blocked, or grille restricted (Chapter 3).
- ☐ Electric cooling fan or sensor faulty (Chapter 3).
- ☐ Pressure cap faulty (Chapter 3).
- ☐ Inaccurate temperature gauge/sensor (Chapter 3).
- ☐ Airlock in cooling system (Chapter 1).
- ☐ Engine management system fault (Chapter 4).

Overcooling
- ☐ Thermostat faulty (stuck open) (Chapter 3).
- ☐ Inaccurate temperature gauge/sensor (Chapter 3).

External coolant leakage
- ☐ Deteriorated or damaged hoses or hose clips (Chapter 1).
- ☐ Radiator core or heater matrix leaking (Chapter 3).
- ☐ Pressure cap faulty (Chapter 3).
- ☐ Coolant pump leaking (Chapter 3).
- ☐ Boiling due to overheating (Chapter 3).
- ☐ Core plug leaking (Chapter 2B).

Internal coolant leakage
- ☐ Leaking cylinder head gasket (Chapter 2A).
- ☐ Cracked cylinder head or cylinder bore (Chapter 2A or 2B).

Corrosion
- ☐ Infrequent draining and flushing (Chapter 1).
- ☐ Incorrect coolant mixture or inappropriate coolant type (Chapter 1).

Fuel and exhaust systems

Excessive fuel consumption
- ☐ Air filter element dirty or clogged (Chapter 1).
- ☐ Engine management system fault (Chapter 4).
- ☐ Faulty injector(s) (Chapter 4).
- ☐ Tyres under-inflated (*Weekly checks*).
- ☐ Brakes binding (Chapters 1 and 9).

Fuel leakage and/or fuel odour
- ☐ Damaged or corroded fuel tank, pipes or connections (Chapter 4A).

Excessive noise or fumes from exhaust system
- ☐ Leaking exhaust system or manifold joints (Chapters 1 and 4A).
- ☐ Leaking, corroded or damaged silencers or pipe (Chapters 1 and 4A).
- ☐ Broken mountings causing body or suspension contact (Chapters 1 and 4A).

Fault finding REF•17

Clutch

Pedal travels to floor – no pressure or very little resistance
- [ ] Air in hydraulic system/faulty master or slave cylinder (Chapter 6).
- [ ] Broken clutch release bearing or fork (Chapter 6).
- [ ] Broken diaphragm spring in clutch pressure plate (Chapter 6).

Clutch fails to disengage (unable to select gears)
- [ ] Air in hydraulic system/faulty master or slave cylinder (Chapter 6).
- [ ] Clutch disc sticking on gearbox input shaft splines (Chapter 6).
- [ ] Clutch disc sticking to flywheel or pressure plate (Chapter 6).
- [ ] Faulty pressure plate assembly (Chapter 6).
- [ ] Clutch release mechanism worn or incorrectly assembled (Chapter 6).

Clutch slips (engine speed rises, with no increase in vehicle speed)
- [ ] Faulty hydraulic release system (Chapter 6).
- [ ] Clutch disc linings excessively worn (Chapter 6).
- [ ] Clutch disc linings contaminated with oil or grease (Chapter 6).
- [ ] Faulty pressure plate or weak diaphragm spring (Chapter 6).

Judder as clutch is engaged
- [ ] Clutch disc linings contaminated with oil or grease (Chapter 6).
- [ ] Clutch disc linings excessively worn (Chapter 6).
- [ ] Faulty or distorted pressure plate or diaphragm spring (Chapter 6).
- [ ] Worn or loose engine or gearbox mountings (Chapter 2A or 2B).
- [ ] Clutch disc hub or gearbox input shaft splines worn (Chapter 6).

Noise when depressing or releasing clutch pedal
- [ ] Worn clutch release bearing (Chapter 6).
- [ ] Worn or dry clutch pedal bushes (Chapter 6).
- [ ] Faulty pressure plate assembly (Chapter 6).
- [ ] Pressure plate diaphragm spring broken (Chapter 6).
- [ ] Broken clutch disc cushioning springs (Chapter 6).

Manual transmission

Noisy in neutral with engine running
- [ ] Input shaft bearings worn (noise apparent with clutch pedal released, but not when depressed) (Chapter 7A).*
- [ ] Clutch release bearing worn (noise apparent with clutch pedal depressed, possibly less when released) (Chapter 6).

Noisy in one particular gear
- [ ] Worn, damaged or chipped gear teeth (Chapter 7A).*

Difficulty engaging gears
- [ ] Clutch fault (Chapter 6).
- [ ] Worn or damaged gear selection cables (Chapter 7A).
- [ ] Worn synchroniser units (Chapter 7A).*

Jumps out of gear
- [ ] Worn or damaged gear selection cables (Chapter 7A).
- [ ] Worn synchroniser units (Chapter 7A).*
- [ ] Worn selector forks (Chapter 7A).*

Vibration
- [ ] Lack of oil (Chapters 1 and 7A).
- [ ] Worn bearings (Chapter 7A).*

Lubricant leaks
- [ ] Leaking differential output oil seal (Chapter 7A).
- [ ] Leaking housing joint (Chapter 7A).*
- [ ] Leaking input shaft oil seal (Chapter 7A).

* Although the corrective action necessary to remedy the symptoms described is beyond the scope of the home mechanic, the above information should be helpful in isolating the cause of the condition, so that the owner can communicate clearly with a professional mechanic.

REF•18 Fault finding

Automatic transmission

Note: *Due to the complexity of the automatic transmission, it is difficult for the home mechanic to properly diagnose and service this unit. For problems other than the following, the vehicle should be taken to a Toyota dealer service department or suitably equipped specialist.*

Fluid leakage

☐ Automatic transmission fluid is usually dark in colour. Fluid leaks should not be confused with engine oil, which can easily be blown onto the transmission by airflow.

☐ To determine the source of a leak, first remove all built-up dirt and grime from the transmission housing and surrounding areas using a degreasing agent, or by steam-cleaning. Drive the vehicle at low speed, so airflow will not blow the leak far from its source. Raise and support the vehicle, and determine where the leak is coming from.

Transmission fluid brown, or has burned smell

☐ Transmission fluid level low, or fluid in need of renewal (Chapter 1 and 7B).

General gear selection problems

☐ Chapter 7B deals with checking and adjusting the selector cable on automatic transmissions. The following are common problems which may be caused by a poorly-adjusted cable:

a) Engine starting in gears other than Park or Neutral.
b) Indicator panel showing a gear other than that being used.
c) Vehicle moves when in Park or Neutral.
d) Poor gear shift quality or erratic gear changes.

☐ Refer to Chapter 7B for the selector cable adjustment procedure.

Transmission will not downshift (kickdown) at full throttle

☐ Low transmission fluid level (Chapter 1).
☐ Incorrect selector cable adjustment (Chapter 7B).

Engine won't start in any gear, or starts in gears other than Park or Neutral

☐ Incorrect multi-function switch adjustment (Chapter 7B).
☐ Incorrect selector cable adjustment (Chapter 7B).

Transmission slips, shifts roughly, is noisy, or has no drive in forward or reverse gears

☐ There are many probable causes for the above problems, but the home mechanic should be concerned with only one possibility – fluid level. Before taking the vehicle to a dealer or transmission specialist, check the fluid level as described in Chapter 1. Correct the fluid level as necessary, or change the fluid. If the problem persists, professional help will be necessary.

Driveshafts

Clicking or knocking noise on turns (at slow speed on full-lock)

☐ Lack of constant velocity joint lubricant, possibly due to damaged gaiter (Chapter 8).
☐ Worn outer constant velocity joint (Chapter 8).

Vibration when accelerating or decelerating

☐ Worn inner constant velocity joint (Chapter 8).
☐ Bent or distorted driveshaft (Chapter 8).

Fault finding

Braking system

Note: *Before assuming that a brake problem exists, make sure that the tyres are in good condition and correctly inflated, that the front wheel alignment is correct, and that the vehicle is not loaded with weight in an unequal manner. Apart from checking the condition of all pipe and hose connections, any faults occurring on the anti-lock braking system should be referred to a Toyota dealer for diagnosis.*

Vehicle pulls to one side under braking
- [ ] Worn, defective, damaged or contaminated brake pads/shoes on one side (Chapter 9).
- [ ] Seized or partially-seized brake caliper (Chapter 9).
- [ ] A mixture of brake pad/shoe materials fitted between sides (Chapter 9).
- [ ] Brake caliper mounting bolts loose (Chapter 9).
- [ ] Seized/leaking wheel cylinder (Chapter 9).
- [ ] Worn or damaged steering or suspension components (Chapters 1 and 10).

Noise (grinding or high-pitched squeal) when brakes applied
- [ ] Brake pad/shoe material worn down to metal backing (Chapters 1 and 9).
- [ ] Excessive corrosion of brake disc/drum. May be apparent after the vehicle has been standing for some time (Chapter 9).
- [ ] Foreign object (stone chipping, etc) trapped between brake disc and shield (Chapter 9).

Excessive brake pedal travel
- [ ] Faulty master cylinder (Chapter 9).
- [ ] Air in hydraulic system (Chapter 9).
- [ ] Rear shoes auto adjusters mechanism faulty (Chapter 9).
- [ ] Faulty vacuum servo unit (Chapter 9).

Brake pedal feels spongy when depressed
- [ ] Air in hydraulic system (Chapter 9).
- [ ] Deteriorated flexible rubber brake hoses (Chapters 1 and 9).
- [ ] Master cylinder mounting nuts loose (Chapter 9).
- [ ] Faulty master cylinder (Chapter 9).

Excessive brake pedal effort required to stop vehicle
- [ ] Faulty vacuum servo unit (Chapter 9).
- [ ] Disconnected, damaged or insecure brake servo vacuum hose (Chapter 9).
- [ ] Primary or secondary hydraulic circuit failure (Chapter 9).
- [ ] Seized brake caliper/wheel cylinder (Chapter 9).
- [ ] Brake pads/shoes incorrectly fitted (Chapter 9).
- [ ] Incorrect grade of brake pads fitted (Chapter 9).
- [ ] Brake pads/shoes contaminated (Chapter 9).

Judder felt through brake pedal or steering wheel when braking
- [ ] Excessive run-out or distortion of discs (Chapters 9).
- [ ] Brake pads/shoes worn (Chapters 1 and 9).
- [ ] Brake caliper mounting bolts loose (Chapter 9).
- [ ] Wear in suspension or steering components or mountings (Chapters 1 and 10).

Brakes binding
- [ ] Seized brake caliper/wheel cylinder (Chapter 9).
- [ ] Incorrectly-adjusted handbrake mechanism (Chapter 9).
- [ ] Faulty master cylinder (Chapter 9).

Rear wheels locking under normal braking
- [ ] Rear brake pads/shoes contaminated (Chapters 1 and 9).
- [ ] Load sensing proportioning valve faulty (Chapter 9).
- [ ] ABS system fault (Chapter 9).

REF•20 Fault finding

Suspension and steering

Note: *Before diagnosing suspension or steering faults, be sure that the trouble is not due to incorrect tyre pressures, mixtures of tyre types, or binding brakes.*

Vehicle pulls to one side
- [ ] Defective tyre (*Weekly checks*).
- [ ] Excessive wear in suspension or steering components (Chapters 1 and 10).
- [ ] Incorrect front wheel alignment (Chapter 10).
- [ ] Damage to steering or suspension components (Chapter 1).

Wheel wobble and vibration
- [ ] Front roadwheels out of balance (vibration felt mainly through the steering wheel) (Chapters 1 and 10).
- [ ] Rear roadwheels out of balance (vibration felt throughout the vehicle) (Chapters 1 and 10).
- [ ] Roadwheels damaged or distorted (Chapters 1 and 10).
- [ ] Faulty or damaged tyre (*Weekly checks*).
- [ ] Worn steering or suspension joints, bushes or components (Chapters 1 and 10).
- [ ] Wheel nuts loose (Chapters 1 and 10).

Excessive pitching and/or rolling around corners, or during braking
- [ ] Defective shock absorbers (Chapters 1 and 10).
- [ ] Broken or weak spring and/or suspension part (Chapters 1 and 10).
- [ ] Worn or damaged anti-roll bar or mountings (Chapter 10).

Wandering or general instability
- [ ] Incorrect front wheel alignment (Chapter 10).
- [ ] Worn steering or suspension joints, bushes or components (Chapters 1 and 10).
- [ ] Roadwheels out of balance (Chapters 1 and 10).
- [ ] Faulty or damaged tyre (*Weekly checks*).
- [ ] Wheel nuts loose (Chapters 1 and 10).
- [ ] Defective shock absorbers (Chapters 1 and 10).

Excessively-stiff steering
- [ ] Lack of power steering fluid (Chapter 10).
- [ ] Seized track rod end balljoint or suspension balljoint (Chapters 1 and 10).
- [ ] Incorrect front wheel alignment (Chapter 10).
- [ ] Steering rack or column bent or damaged (Chapter 10).
- [ ] Power steering pump fault (Chapter 10).

Excessive play in steering
- [ ] Worn steering column universal joint (Chapter 10).
- [ ] Worn steering track rod end balljoints (Chapters 1 and 10).
- [ ] Worn steering rack (Chapter 10).
- [ ] Worn steering or suspension joints, bushes or components (Chapters 1 and 10).

Lack of power assistance
- [ ] Incorrect power steering fluid level (*Weekly checks*).
- [ ] Restriction in power steering fluid hoses (Chapter 1).
- [ ] Faulty power steering pump (Chapter 10).
- [ ] Faulty steering rack (Chapter 10).

Tyre wear excessive

Tyre treads exhibit feathered edges
- [ ] Incorrect toe setting (Chapter 10).

Tyres worn in centre of tread
- [ ] Tyres over-inflated (*Weekly checks*).

Tyres worn on inside and outside edges
- [ ] Tyres under-inflated (*Weekly checks*).

Tyres worn on inside or outside edges
- [ ] Incorrect camber/castor angles (wear on one edge only) (Chapter 10).
- [ ] Worn steering or suspension joints, bushes or components (Chapters 1 and 10).
- [ ] Excessively-hard cornering.
- [ ] Accident damage.

Tyres worn unevenly
- [ ] Tyres/wheels out of balance (*Weekly checks*).
- [ ] Excessive wheel or tyre run-out (Chapter 1).
- [ ] Worn shock absorbers (Chapters 1 and 10).
- [ ] Faulty tyre (*Weekly checks*).

Fault finding REF•21

Electrical system

Note: *For problems associated with the starting system, refer to the faults listed under 'Engine' earlier in this Section.*

Battery won't hold a charge for more than a few days
- ☐ Battery defective internally (Chapter 5A).
- ☐ Battery terminal connections loose or corroded (*Weekly checks*).
- ☐ Auxiliary drivebelt broken, worn or incorrectly adjusted (Chapter 1).
- ☐ Alternator not charging at correct output (Chapter 5A).
- ☐ Alternator or voltage regulator faulty (Chapter 5A).
- ☐ Short-circuit causing continual battery drain (Chapters 5A and 12).

Ignition/no-charge warning light stays on with engine running
- ☐ Auxiliary drivebelt broken, worn, or incorrectly adjusted (Chapter 1).
- ☐ Internal fault in alternator or voltage regulator (Chapter 5A).
- ☐ Broken, disconnected, or loose wiring in charging circuit (Chapter 5A).

Ignition/no-charge warning light fails to come on
- ☐ Warning light bulb blown (Chapter 12).
- ☐ Broken, disconnected, or loose wiring in warning light circuit (Chapter 12).
- ☐ Alternator faulty (Chapter 5A).

Lights inoperative
- ☐ Bulb blown (Chapter 12).
- ☐ Corrosion of bulb or bulbholder contacts (Chapter 12).
- ☐ Blown fuse (Chapter 12).
- ☐ Faulty relay (Chapter 12).
- ☐ Broken, loose, or disconnected wiring (Chapter 12).
- ☐ Faulty switch (Chapter 12).

Instrument readings inaccurate or erratic

Fuel or temperature gauges give no reading
- ☐ Faulty gauge sensor unit (Chapter 3 or 4).
- ☐ Wiring open-circuit (Chapter 12).
- ☐ Faulty gauge (Chapter 12).

Fuel or temperature gauges give continuous maximum reading
- ☐ Faulty gauge sensor unit (Chapter 3 or 4).
- ☐ Wiring short-circuit (Chapter 12).
- ☐ Faulty gauge (Chapter 12).

Horn inoperative, or unsatisfactory in operation

Horn operates all the time
- ☐ Horn push either earthed or stuck down (Chapter 12).
- ☐ Horn cable-to-horn push earthed (Chapter 12).

Horn fails to operate
- ☐ Blown fuse (Chapter 12).
- ☐ Cable or cable connections loose, broken or disconnected (Chapter 12).
- ☐ Faulty horn (Chapter 12).

Horn emits intermittent or unsatisfactory sound
- ☐ Cable connections loose (Chapter 12).
- ☐ Horn mountings loose (Chapter 12).
- ☐ Faulty horn (Chapter 12).

Windscreen/tailgate wipers failed, or unsatisfactory in operation

Wipers fail to operate, or operate very slowly
- ☐ Wiper blades stuck to screen, or linkage seized or binding (Chapters 1 and 12).
- ☐ Blown fuse (Chapter 12).
- ☐ Cable or cable connections loose, broken or disconnected (Chapter 12).
- ☐ Faulty built-in system interface (BSI) unit (Chapter 12).
- ☐ Faulty wiper motor (Chapter 12).

Wiper blades sweep over too large or too small an area of the glass
- ☐ Wiper arms incorrectly positioned on spindles (Chapter 12).
- ☐ Excessive wear of wiper linkage (Chapter 12).
- ☐ Wiper motor or linkage mountings loose or insecure (Chapter 12).

Wiper blades fail to clean the glass effectively
- ☐ Wiper blade rubbers worn or perished (*Weekly checks*).
- ☐ Wiper arm tension springs broken, or arm pivots seized (Chapter 12).
- ☐ Insufficient windscreen washer additive to adequately remove road film (*Weekly checks*).

Windscreen/tailgate washers failed, or unsatisfactory in operation

One or more washer jets inoperative
- ☐ Blocked washer jet (*Weekly checks*).
- ☐ Disconnected, kinked or restricted fluid hose (Chapter 12).
- ☐ Insufficient fluid in washer reservoir (*Weekly checks*).

Washer pump fails to operate
- ☐ Broken or disconnected wiring or connections (Chapter 12).
- ☐ Blown fuse (Chapter 12).
- ☐ Faulty washer switch (Chapter 12).
- ☐ Faulty washer pump (Chapter 12).

Electric windows inoperative, or unsatisfactory in operation

Window glass will only move in one direction
- ☐ Faulty switch (Chapter 12).

Window glass slow to move
- ☐ Regulator seized or damaged, or in need of lubricant (Chapter 11).
- ☐ Door internal components or trim fouling regulator (Chapter 11).
- ☐ Faulty motor (Chapter 11).

Window glass fails to move
- ☐ Blown fuse (Chapter 12).
- ☐ Broken or disconnected wiring or connections (Chapter 12).
- ☐ Faulty motor (Chapter 11).

Central locking system inoperative, or unsatisfactory in operation

Complete system failure
- ☐ Blown fuse (Chapter 12).
- ☐ Broken or disconnected wiring or connections (Chapter 12).

Door/tailgate locks but will not unlock, or unlocks but will not lock
- ☐ Broken or disconnected link rod(s) (Chapter 11).
- ☐ Faulty lock motor (Chapter 11).

One lock fails to operate
- ☐ Broken or disconnected wiring or connections (Chapter 12).
- ☐ Faulty lock motor (Chapter 11).
- ☐ Broken, binding or disconnected link rod(s) (Chapter 11).

REF•22 Glossary of technical terms

A

ABS (Anti-lock brake system) A system, usually electronically controlled, that senses incipient wheel lockup during braking and relieves hydraulic pressure at wheels that are about to skid.

Air bag An inflatable bag hidden in the steering wheel (driver's side) or the dash or glovebox (passenger side). In a head-on collision, the bags inflate, preventing the driver and front passenger from being thrown forward into the steering wheel or windscreen.

Air cleaner A metal or plastic housing, containing a filter element, which removes dust and dirt from the air being drawn into the engine.

Air filter element The actual filter in an air cleaner system, usually manufactured from pleated paper and requiring renewal at regular intervals.

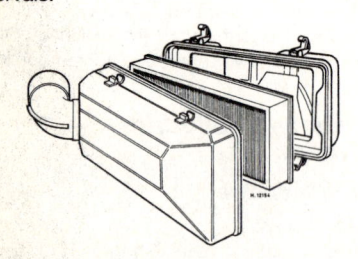

Air filter

Allen key A hexagonal wrench which fits into a recessed hexagonal hole.

Alligator clip A long-nosed spring-loaded metal clip with meshing teeth. Used to make temporary electrical connections.

Alternator A component in the electrical system which converts mechanical energy from a drivebelt into electrical energy to charge the battery and to operate the starting system, ignition system and electrical accessories.

Alternator (exploded view)

Ampere (amp) A unit of measurement for the flow of electric current. One amp is the amount of current produced by one volt acting through a resistance of one ohm.

Anaerobic sealer A substance used to prevent bolts and screws from loosening. Anaerobic means that it does not require oxygen for activation. The Loctite brand is widely used.

Antifreeze A substance (usually ethylene glycol) mixed with water, and added to a vehicle's cooling system, to prevent freezing of the coolant in winter. Antifreeze also contains chemicals to inhibit corrosion and the formation of rust and other deposits that would tend to clog the radiator and coolant passages and reduce cooling efficiency.

Anti-seize compound A coating that reduces the risk of seizing on fasteners that are subjected to high temperatures, such as exhaust manifold bolts and nuts.

Anti-seize compound

Asbestos A natural fibrous mineral with great heat resistance, commonly used in the composition of brake friction materials. Asbestos is a health hazard and the dust created by brake systems should never be inhaled or ingested.

Axle A shaft on which a wheel revolves, or which revolves with a wheel. Also, a solid beam that connects the two wheels at one end of the vehicle. An axle which also transmits power to the wheels is known as a live axle.

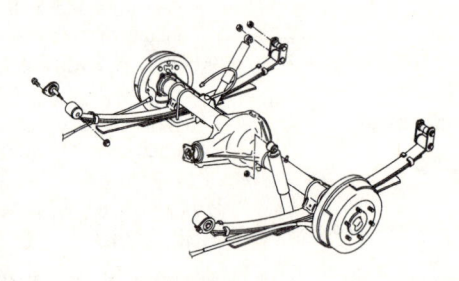

Axle assembly

Axleshaft A single rotating shaft, on either side of the differential, which delivers power from the final drive assembly to the drive wheels. Also called a driveshaft or a halfshaft.

B

Ball bearing An anti-friction bearing consisting of a hardened inner and outer race with hardened steel balls between two races.

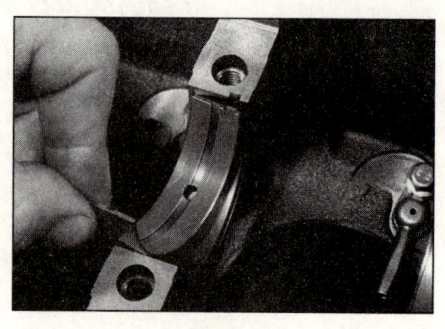

Bearing

Bearing The curved surface on a shaft or in a bore, or the part assembled into either, that permits relative motion between them with minimum wear and friction.

Big-end bearing The bearing in the end of the connecting rod that's attached to the crankshaft.

Bleed nipple A valve on a brake wheel cylinder, caliper or other hydraulic component that is opened to purge the hydraulic system of air. Also called a bleed screw.

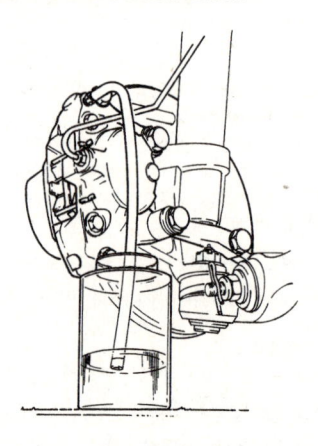

Brake bleeding

Brake bleeding Procedure for removing air from lines of a hydraulic brake system.

Brake disc The component of a disc brake that rotates with the wheels.

Brake drum The component of a drum brake that rotates with the wheels.

Brake linings The friction material which contacts the brake disc or drum to retard the vehicle's speed. The linings are bonded or riveted to the brake pads or shoes.

Brake pads The replaceable friction pads that pinch the brake disc when the brakes are applied. Brake pads consist of a friction material bonded or riveted to a rigid backing plate.

Brake shoe The crescent-shaped carrier to which the brake linings are mounted and which forces the lining against the rotating drum during braking.

Braking systems For more information on braking systems, consult the *Haynes Automotive Brake Manual*.

Breaker bar A long socket wrench handle providing greater leverage.

Bulkhead The insulated partition between the engine and the passenger compartment.

C

Caliper The non-rotating part of a disc-brake assembly that straddles the disc and carries the brake pads. The caliper also contains the hydraulic components that cause the pads to pinch the disc when the brakes are applied. A caliper is also a measuring tool that can be set to measure inside or outside dimensions of an object.

Glossary of technical terms REF•23

Camshaft A rotating shaft on which a series of cam lobes operate the valve mechanisms. The camshaft may be driven by gears, by sprockets and chain or by sprockets and a belt.

Canister A container in an evaporative emission control system; contains activated charcoal granules to trap vapours from the fuel system.

Canister

Carburettor A device which mixes fuel with air in the proper proportions to provide a desired power output from a spark ignition internal combustion engine.

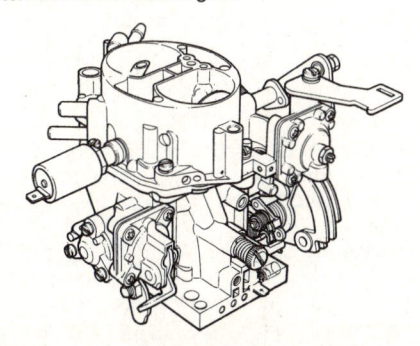

Carburettor

Castellated Resembling the parapets along the top of a castle wall. For example, a castellated balljoint stud nut.

Castellated nut

Castor In wheel alignment, the backward or forward tilt of the steering axis. Castor is positive when the steering axis is inclined rearward at the top.

Catalytic converter A silencer-like device in the exhaust system which converts certain pollutants in the exhaust gases into less harmful substances.

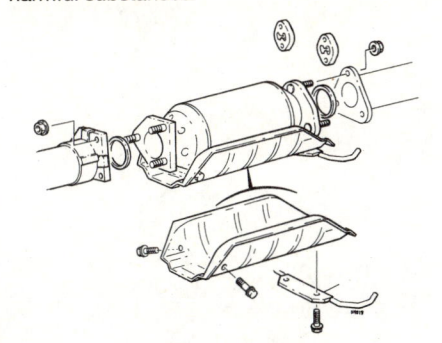

Catalytic converter

Circlip A ring-shaped clip used to prevent endwise movement of cylindrical parts and shafts. An internal circlip is installed in a groove in a housing; an external circlip fits into a groove on the outside of a cylindrical piece such as a shaft.

Clearance The amount of space between two parts. For example, between a piston and a cylinder, between a bearing and a journal, etc.

Coil spring A spiral of elastic steel found in various sizes throughout a vehicle, for example as a springing medium in the suspension and in the valve train.

Compression Reduction in volume, and increase in pressure and temperature, of a gas, caused by squeezing it into a smaller space.

Compression ratio The relationship between cylinder volume when the piston is at top dead centre and cylinder volume when the piston is at bottom dead centre.

Constant velocity (CV) joint A type of universal joint that cancels out vibrations caused by driving power being transmitted through an angle.

Core plug A disc or cup-shaped metal device inserted in a hole in a casting through which core was removed when the casting was formed. Also known as a freeze plug or expansion plug.

Crankcase The lower part of the engine block in which the crankshaft rotates.

Crankshaft The main rotating member, or shaft, running the length of the crankcase, with offset "throws" to which the connecting rods are attached.

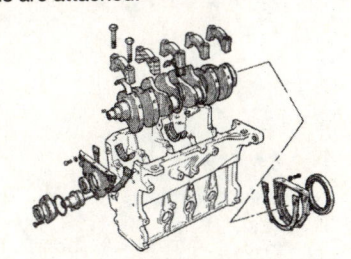

Crankshaft assembly

Crocodile clip See Alligator clip

D

Diagnostic code Code numbers obtained by accessing the diagnostic mode of an engine management computer. This code can be used to determine the area in the system where a malfunction may be located.

Disc brake A brake design incorporating a rotating disc onto which brake pads are squeezed. The resulting friction converts the energy of a moving vehicle into heat.

Double-overhead cam (DOHC) An engine that uses two overhead camshafts, usually one for the intake valves and one for the exhaust valves.

Drivebelt(s) The belt(s) used to drive accessories such as the alternator, water pump, power steering pump, air conditioning compressor, etc. off the crankshaft pulley.

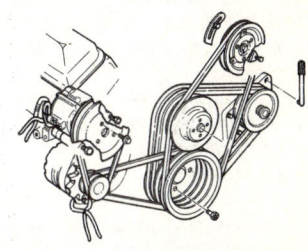

Accessory drivebelts

Driveshaft Any shaft used to transmit motion. Commonly used when referring to the axleshafts on a front wheel drive vehicle.

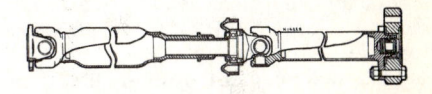

Driveshaft

Drum brake A type of brake using a drum-shaped metal cylinder attached to the inner surface of the wheel. When the brake pedal is pressed, curved brake shoes with friction linings press against the inside of the drum to slow or stop the vehicle.

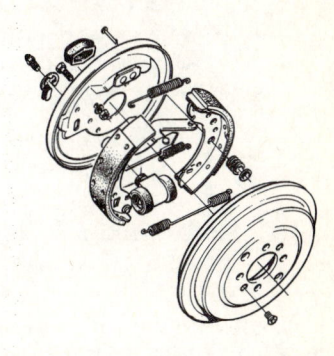

Drum brake assembly

REF•24 Glossary of technical terms

E

EGR valve A valve used to introduce exhaust gases into the intake air stream.

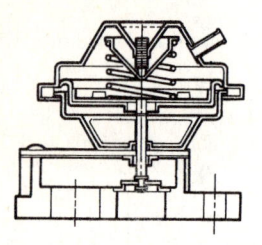

EGR valve

Electronic control unit (ECU) A computer which controls (for instance) ignition and fuel injection systems, or an anti-lock braking system. For more information refer to the *Haynes Automotive Electrical and Electronic Systems Manual*.

Electronic Fuel Injection (EFI) A computer controlled fuel system that distributes fuel through an injector located in each intake port of the engine.

Emergency brake A braking system, independent of the main hydraulic system, that can be used to slow or stop the vehicle if the primary brakes fail, or to hold the vehicle stationary even though the brake pedal isn't depressed. It usually consists of a hand lever that actuates either front or rear brakes mechanically through a series of cables and linkages. Also known as a handbrake or parking brake.

Endfloat The amount of lengthwise movement between two parts. As applied to a crankshaft, the distance that the crankshaft can move forward and back in the cylinder block.

Engine management system (EMS) A computer controlled system which manages the fuel injection and the ignition systems in an integrated fashion.

Exhaust manifold A part with several passages through which exhaust gases leave the engine combustion chambers and enter the exhaust pipe.

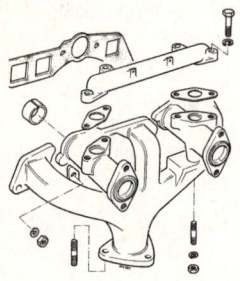

Exhaust manifold

F

Fan clutch A viscous (fluid) drive coupling device which permits variable engine fan speeds in relation to engine speeds.

Feeler blade A thin strip or blade of hardened steel, ground to an exact thickness, used to check or measure clearances between parts.

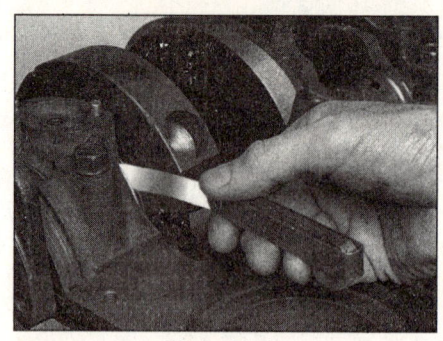

Feeler blade

Firing order The order in which the engine cylinders fire, or deliver their power strokes, beginning with the number one cylinder.

Flywheel A heavy spinning wheel in which energy is absorbed and stored by means of momentum. On cars, the flywheel is attached to the crankshaft to smooth out firing impulses.

Free play The amount of travel before any action takes place. The "looseness" in a linkage, or an assembly of parts, between the initial application of force and actual movement. For example, the distance the brake pedal moves before the pistons in the master cylinder are actuated.

Fuse An electrical device which protects a circuit against accidental overload. The typical fuse contains a soft piece of metal which is calibrated to melt at a predetermined current flow (expressed as amps) and break the circuit.

Fusible link A circuit protection device consisting of a conductor surrounded by heat-resistant insulation. The conductor is smaller than the wire it protects, so it acts as the weakest link in the circuit. Unlike a blown fuse, a failed fusible link must frequently be cut from the wire for replacement.

G

Gap The distance the spark must travel in jumping from the centre electrode to the side electrode in a spark plug. Also refers to the spacing between the points in a contact breaker assembly in a conventional points-type ignition, or to the distance between the reluctor or rotor and the pickup coil in an electronic ignition.

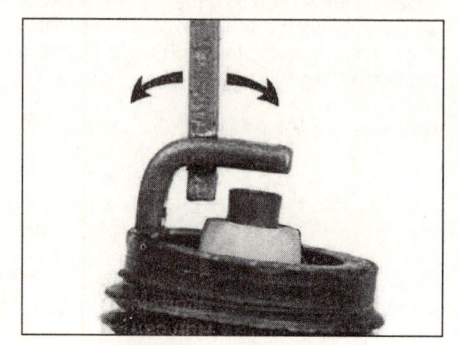

Adjusting spark plug gap

Gasket Any thin, soft material - usually cork, cardboard, asbestos or soft metal - installed between two metal surfaces to ensure a good seal. For instance, the cylinder head gasket seals the joint between the block and the cylinder head.

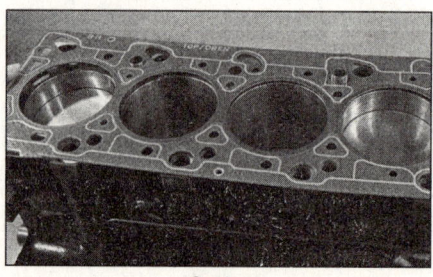

Gasket

Gauge An instrument panel display used to monitor engine conditions. A gauge with a movable pointer on a dial or a fixed scale is an analogue gauge. A gauge with a numerical readout is called a digital gauge.

H

Halfshaft A rotating shaft that transmits power from the final drive unit to a drive wheel, usually when referring to a live rear axle.

Harmonic balancer A device designed to reduce torsion or twisting vibration in the crankshaft. May be incorporated in the crankshaft pulley. Also known as a vibration damper.

Hone An abrasive tool for correcting small irregularities or differences in diameter in an engine cylinder, brake cylinder, etc.

Hydraulic tappet A tappet that utilises hydraulic pressure from the engine's lubrication system to maintain zero clearance (constant contact with both camshaft and valve stem). Automatically adjusts to variation in valve stem length. Hydraulic tappets also reduce valve noise.

I

Ignition timing The moment at which the spark plug fires, usually expressed in the number of crankshaft degrees before the piston reaches the top of its stroke.

Inlet manifold A tube or housing with passages through which flows the air-fuel mixture (carburettor vehicles and vehicles with throttle body injection) or air only (port fuel-injected vehicles) to the port openings in the cylinder head.

Glossary of technical terms REF•25

J
Jump start Starting the engine of a vehicle with a discharged or weak battery by attaching jump leads from the weak battery to a charged or helper battery.

L
Load Sensing Proportioning Valve (LSPV) A brake hydraulic system control valve that works like a proportioning valve, but also takes into consideration the amount of weight carried by the rear axle.
Locknut A nut used to lock an adjustment nut, or other threaded component, in place. For example, a locknut is employed to keep the adjusting nut on the rocker arm in position.
Lockwasher A form of washer designed to prevent an attaching nut from working loose.

M
MacPherson strut A type of front suspension system devised by Earle MacPherson at Ford of England. In its original form, a simple lateral link with the anti-roll bar creates the lower control arm. A long strut - an integral coil spring and shock absorber - is mounted between the body and the steering knuckle. Many modern so-called MacPherson strut systems use a conventional lower A-arm and don't rely on the anti-roll bar for location.
Multimeter An electrical test instrument with the capability to measure voltage, current and resistance.

N
NOx Oxides of Nitrogen. A common toxic pollutant emitted by petrol and diesel engines at higher temperatures.

O
Ohm The unit of electrical resistance. One volt applied to a resistance of one ohm will produce a current of one amp.
Ohmmeter An instrument for measuring electrical resistance.
O-ring A type of sealing ring made of a special rubber-like material; in use, the O-ring is compressed into a groove to provide the sealing action.

O-ring

Overhead cam (ohc) engine An engine with the camshaft(s) located on top of the cylinder head(s).
Overhead valve (ohv) engine An engine with the valves located in the cylinder head, but with the camshaft located in the engine block.
Oxygen sensor A device installed in the engine exhaust manifold, which senses the oxygen content in the exhaust and converts this information into an electric current. Also called a Lambda sensor.

P
Phillips screw A type of screw head having a cross instead of a slot for a corresponding type of screwdriver.
Plastigage A thin strip of plastic thread, available in different sizes, used for measuring clearances. For example, a strip of Plastigage is laid across a bearing journal. The parts are assembled and dismantled; the width of the crushed strip indicates the clearance between journal and bearing.

Plastigage

Propeller shaft The long hollow tube with universal joints at both ends that carries power from the transmission to the differential on front-engined rear wheel drive vehicles.
Proportioning valve A hydraulic control valve which limits the amount of pressure to the rear brakes during panic stops to prevent wheel lock-up.

R
Rack-and-pinion steering A steering system with a pinion gear on the end of the steering shaft that mates with a rack (think of a geared wheel opened up and laid flat). When the steering wheel is turned, the pinion turns, moving the rack to the left or right. This movement is transmitted through the track rods to the steering arms at the wheels.
Radiator A liquid-to-air heat transfer device designed to reduce the temperature of the coolant in an internal combustion engine cooling system.
Refrigerant Any substance used as a heat transfer agent in an air-conditioning system. R-12 has been the principle refrigerant for many years; recently, however, manufacturers have begun using R-134a, a non-CFC substance that is considered less harmful to the ozone in the upper atmosphere.

Rocker arm A lever arm that rocks on a shaft or pivots on a stud. In an overhead valve engine, the rocker arm converts the upward movement of the pushrod into a downward movement to open a valve.
Rotor In a distributor, the rotating device inside the cap that connects the centre electrode and the outer terminals as it turns, distributing the high voltage from the coil secondary winding to the proper spark plug. Also, that part of an alternator which rotates inside the stator. Also, the rotating assembly of a turbocharger, including the compressor wheel, shaft and turbine wheel.
Runout The amount of wobble (in-and-out movement) of a gear or wheel as it's rotated. The amount a shaft rotates "out-of-true." The out-of-round condition of a rotating part.

S
Sealant A liquid or paste used to prevent leakage at a joint. Sometimes used in conjunction with a gasket.
Sealed beam lamp An older headlight design which integrates the reflector, lens and filaments into a hermetically-sealed one-piece unit. When a filament burns out or the lens cracks, the entire unit is simply replaced.
Serpentine drivebelt A single, long, wide accessory drivebelt that's used on some newer vehicles to drive all the accessories, instead of a series of smaller, shorter belts. Serpentine drivebelts are usually tensioned by an automatic tensioner.

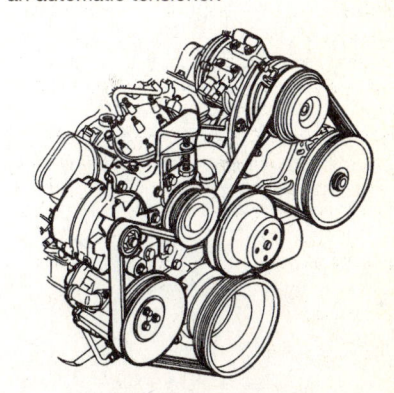

Serpentine drivebelt

Shim Thin spacer, commonly used to adjust the clearance or relative positions between two parts. For example, shims inserted into or under bucket tappets control valve clearances. Clearance is adjusted by changing the thickness of the shim.
Slide hammer A special puller that screws into or hooks onto a component such as a shaft or bearing; a heavy sliding handle on the shaft bottoms against the end of the shaft to knock the component free.
Sprocket A tooth or projection on the periphery of a wheel, shaped to engage with a chain or drivebelt. Commonly used to refer to the sprocket wheel itself.

Glossary of technical terms

Starter inhibitor switch On vehicles with an automatic transmission, a switch that prevents starting if the vehicle is not in Neutral or Park.

Strut See MacPherson strut.

T

Tappet A cylindrical component which transmits motion from the cam to the valve stem, either directly or via a pushrod and rocker arm. Also called a cam follower.

Thermostat A heat-controlled valve that regulates the flow of coolant between the cylinder block and the radiator, so maintaining optimum engine operating temperature. A thermostat is also used in some air cleaners in which the temperature is regulated.

Thrust bearing The bearing in the clutch assembly that is moved in to the release levers by clutch pedal action to disengage the clutch. Also referred to as a release bearing.

Timing belt A toothed belt which drives the camshaft. Serious engine damage may result if it breaks in service.

Timing chain A chain which drives the camshaft.

Toe-in The amount the front wheels are closer together at the front than at the rear. On rear wheel drive vehicles, a slight amount of toe-in is usually specified to keep the front wheels running parallel on the road by offsetting other forces that tend to spread the wheels apart.

Toe-out The amount the front wheels are closer together at the rear than at the front. On front wheel drive vehicles, a slight amount of toe-out is usually specified.

Tools For full information on choosing and using tools, refer to the *Haynes Automotive Tools Manual*.

Tracer A stripe of a second colour applied to a wire insulator to distinguish that wire from another one with the same colour insulator.

Tune-up A process of accurate and careful adjustments and parts replacement to obtain the best possible engine performance.

Turbocharger A centrifugal device, driven by exhaust gases, that pressurises the intake air. Normally used to increase the power output from a given engine displacement, but can also be used primarily to reduce exhaust emissions (as on VW's "Umwelt" Diesel engine).

U

Universal joint or U-joint A double-pivoted connection for transmitting power from a driving to a driven shaft through an angle. A U-joint consists of two Y-shaped yokes and a cross-shaped member called the spider.

V

Valve A device through which the flow of liquid, gas, vacuum, or loose material in bulk may be started, stopped, or regulated by a movable part that opens, shuts, or partially obstructs one or more ports or passageways. A valve is also the movable part of such a device.

Valve clearance The clearance between the valve tip (the end of the valve stem) and the rocker arm or tappet. The valve clearance is measured when the valve is closed.

Vernier caliper A precision measuring instrument that measures inside and outside dimensions. Not quite as accurate as a micrometer, but more convenient.

Viscosity The thickness of a liquid or its resistance to flow.

Volt A unit for expressing electrical "pressure" in a circuit. One volt that will produce a current of one ampere through a resistance of one ohm.

W

Welding Various processes used to join metal items by heating the areas to be joined to a molten state and fusing them together. For more information refer to the *Haynes Automotive Welding Manual*.

Wiring diagram A drawing portraying the components and wires in a vehicle's electrical system, using standardised symbols. For more information refer to the *Haynes Automotive Electrical and Electronic Systems Manual*.

Index

Note: *References throughout this index are in the form* **"Chapter number"** • **"Page number"**. *So, for example, 2C•15 refers to page 15 of Chapter 2C.*

A

A-pillar trim – 11•16
Accessory shops – REF•3
Accelerator cable – 4A•6
Acknowledgements – 0•6
Air conditioning system – 3•2, 3•9
    compressor – 3•11
    condenser – 3•11
    control assembly – 3•9
    control cables – 3•9
    evaporator and expansion valve – 3•12
    receiver/drier – 3•11
    sensors – 3•13
    service ports – 3•10
    switch – 12•7, 12•12
Air filter – 1•12, 4A•6
Air gap – 5B•5
Air induction system – 4A•7
Air temperature sensor – 4A•11
Airbags – 0•5, 12•18
    control module – 12•19
Airflow meter – 4A•11
Alternator – 5A•4, 5A•5
Ambient temperature sensor – 3•13
Antifreeze – 0•12, 0•17, 1•18, 3•2
Anti-lock Braking System (ABS) – 9•21
Anti-roll bar and bushings – 10•6, 10•8
Asbestos – 0•5
Audio units – 12•47
Automatic transmission – 7B•1 *et seq*
    fault finding – 7B•1, REF•18
    fluid – 0•17, 1•10
    selector panel illumination – 12•12
Auxiliary drivebelt – 1•11

B

B/C-pillar trim – 11•17
B-pillar trim – 11•17
Badges – 11•14
Balljoints – 10•7
Battery – 0•5, 0•16, 5A•2, 5A•3
    remote control – 1•14
Big-end bearings – 2B•9
Bleeding
    brake system – 9•2
    clutch hydraulic system – 6•2
    power steering system – 10•15
Block – 2B•8
Blower motor and resistor – 3•7
Body electrical system – 12•1 *et seq*
Body trim strips – 11•14
Body under-panels – 11•14
Bodywork and fittings – 11•1 *et seq*
    corrosion – REF•11
Bonnet – 11•5
    lock – 11•6
    release cable – 11•6
Boot lid – 11•11
    lock – 11•13
Brake fluid – 0•13, 0•17, 1•16
Brake pedal – 9•17
Braking system – 1•16, 9•1 *et seq*, REF•8, REF•9, REF•10
    fault finding – REF•19
Bulbs – 0•16, 12•8, 12•11
Bumpers – 11•4
Burning – 0•5
Buying spare parts – REF•3

Note: *References throughout this index are in the form* **"Chapter number"** • **"Page number"**. *So, for example, 2C•15 refers to page 15 of Chapter 2C.*

C

C/D-pillar trim – 11•18
C-pillar trim – 11•18
Cabin temperature sensor – 3•13
Cables
  accelerator – 4A•6
  automatic transmission selector – 7B•4
  bonnet release – 11•6
  handbrake – 9•18
  heater and air conditioning – 3•9
  manual transmission gearchange – 7A•1
  throttle valve (TV) – 7B•3
Calipers – 9•9, 9•10
Camshafts – 2A•12
  oil seal – 2A•12
  position sensor – 4A•12
  VVT-i unit – 2A•11
Carpets – 11•2, 11•19
Case leaks – 7B•2
Catalytic converter – 4B•4
Central information unit – 12•8
Central locking components – 11•12
Centre console – 11•19
Charcoal canister – 4B•3
Charging – 5A•2, 5A•3
Clutch – 6•1 *et seq*
  fault finding – REF•17
  fluid – 0•13, 0•17
  master cylinder – 6•4
  pedal – 1•15
  release bearing and lever – 6•3
  release cylinder – 6•5
  start switch – 6•6
Coil – 5B•2
Compressor – 3•11
Condenser – 3•11
  cooling fan – 3•5
Connecting rods – 2B•7, 2B•8, 2B•12
  bearings – 2B•9
Console – 11•19
Control arm – 10•7
Conversion factors – REF•2
Coolant – 0•12, 0•17, 1•18, 3•2
  pump – 3•5, 3•6
  reservoir – 3•5
  temperature gauge sender unit – 3•7
Cooling fan and relay – 3•3
Cooling, heating and air conditioning systems – 3•1 *et seq*
  fault finding – REF•16
Courtesy light – 12•11
  switches – 12•6
Crankshaft – 2B•7, 2B•9, 2B•11
  oil seal – 2A•11
  position/speed sensor – 4A•12
Crash sensors – 12•19
Crushing – 0•5
CV joints – 1•10, 8•3
Cylinder compression – 2A•4
Cylinder head – 2A•16, 2B•5, 2B•6
  cover – 2A•5

D

Dents – 11•2
Depressurisation fuel injection system – 4A•2
Diesel injection equipment – 0•5
Differential fluid – 0•17, 1•10
Dimensions – REF•1
Direction indicator – 12•9, 12•10, 12•13
  flasher unit – 12•8
Discs – 9•8, 9•9
Distributor – 5B•3
  pick-up coil – 5B•5
Doors – 11•6, REF•9
  courtesy light switches – 12•6
  glass and regulator – 11•10
  handle and lock components – 11•8
  inner trim panel – 11•7
  lock actuator (central locking) – 11•13
  panel switches – 12•6
  window – 11•11
Drivebelt – 1•11
Driveplate – 2A•21
Driver's side facia lower panel – 11•19
Driveshafts – 8•1 *et seq*, REF•10
  fault finding – REF•18
  gaiter – 1•10, 8•3
  oil seals – 7A•4, 7B•2
Drivetrain – 1•15
Drums – 1•13, 9•10

E

Earth fault – 12•2
Electric shock – 0•5
Electric windows – 11•13
Electrical equipment – 1•15, REF•9
  fault finding – 12•2, REF•21
Electronic control unit (ECU)
  ABS – 9•21
  central locking – 11•12
Emissions and engine control systems – 4B•1 *et seq*, REF•11
Engine block – 2B•8
Engine fault finding – REF•14, REF•15
Engine in-car repair procedures – 2A•1 *et seq*
Engine management ECM – 4A•11
Engine oil – 0•12, 0•17, 1•8
Engine removal and overhaul procedures – 2B•1 *et seq*
Environmental considerations – REF•4
Evaporative Emission Control (EVAP) system – 4B•2
Evaporator – 3•12
  temperature sensor – 3•13
Exhaust manifold – 4A•13
Exhaust specialists – REF•3
Exhaust system – 1•13, 4A•2, 4A•14, REF•10, REF•11
Expansion valve – 3•12

Index

Note: *References throughout this index are in the form* **"Chapter number"** • **"Page number"**. *So, for example, 2C•15 refers to page 15 of Chapter 2C.*

F

Facia panel – 11•20
  lower panel – 11•19
Fan – 3•3
Fault finding – REF•12 et seq
  automatic transmission – 7B•1
  electrical system – 12•2
Filling – 11•3
Filters
  air – 1•12, 4A•6
  fuel – 1•16
  oil – 1•8
  oil control valve – 2A•11
  pollen – 1•15
Fire – 0•5
Fixed window – 11•11, 11•13
Fluids – 0•17
  leak – 1•9, 7B•2
Flywheel – 2A•21
Foglight – 12•9, 12•10, 12•13
  switch – 12•6, 12•12
Followers – 2A•12
Fuel and exhaust systems – 4A•1 et seq, REF•11
  fault finding – REF•16
Fuel filter – 1•16
Fuel injection system – 4A•2, 4A•6, 4A•7
Fuel injectors – 4A•9
Fuel level sender unit – 4A•4
Fuel pipes – 4A•2, 4A•5
Fuel pressure regulator – 4A•8
Fuel pump – 4A•2, 4A•3
Fuel rail – 4A•9
Fuel tank – 4A•5, 4A•6
Fume or gas intoxication – 0•5
Fuses – 0•16, 12•3

G

Gaiter
  driveshaft – 1•10, 8•3
  steering rack – 10•13
Gashes – 11•2
Gaskets – REF•4
  leaks – 7B•2
Gearchange
  cables – 7A•1
  lever – 7A•2
General repair procedures – REF•4
Glossary of technical terms – REF•22 et seq
Glovebox – 11•18
Grille – 11•6

H

Handbrake – 1•13, 9•18, REF•8
  warning light switch – 12•6
Handles – 11•8
Hazard flasher unit – 12•8
  switch – 12•6, 12•12
Headlight – 12•8, 12•12
  beam alignment – 12•14
  beam control motor – 12•14
  beam level control – 12•7
  levelling switch – 12•12
Headlining – 11•19
Heated rear window switch – 12•7, 12•12
Heating system – 3•2, 3•9, 3•10
  control assembly – 3•9
  control cables – 3•9
  control panel illumination – 12•12
  matrix – 3•8
High-level stop-light – 12•10, 12•14
Hinge lubrication – 1•10
Horn – 12•15
Hoses – 1•9, 9•3
Hub and bearing assembly – 10•8, 10•11
Hub carrier – 10•7, 10•11
Hydrofluoric acid – 0•5

I

Identifying leaks – 0•10
Idle speed control (ISC) valve – 4A•9
Igniter – 5B•6
Ignition coil – 5B•2
Ignition switch – 12•5
Ignition systems – 5B•1 et seq
Ignition timing – 5B•4
Indicator – 12•9, 12•10, 12•13
  flasher unit – 12•8
Injectors – 4A•9
Input shaft oil seal – 7A•4
Instruments – 1•15
  instrument panel – 12•7, 12•12
Intake air temperature sensor – 4A•11
Intake manifold – 4A•12
Interior light – 12•11

J

Jacking and vehicle support – REF•5
Joint mating faces – REF•4
Jump starting – 0•8

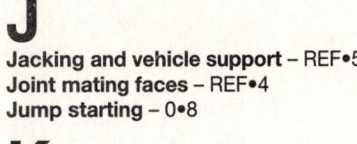

K

Key lock cylinder – 12•5
Knock sensor – 5B•6

Note: *References throughout this index are in the form* **"Chapter number"** • **"Page number"**. *So, for example, 2C•15 refers to page 15 of Chapter 2C.*

L

Leaks – 0•10, 1•9, 7B•2
Load-sensing proportioning valve – 9•19
Lock cylinder – 12•5
Locknuts, locktabs and washers – REF•4
Locks
  bonnet – 11•6
  boot lid – 11•11, 11•13
  door – 11•8, 11•13
  lubrication – 1•10
  tailgate – 11•11, 11•13
Lubricants and fluids – 0•17
Luggage area illumination – 12•12

M

Main bearings – 2B•9
Main oil seal – 2A•21
Manifolds – 4A•12, 4A•13
Manual transmission – 7A•1 *et seq*
  fault finding – REF•17
  oil – 0•17, 1•11
Master cylinder
  brakes – 9•16
  clutch – 6•4
Matrix – 3•8
Mirrors – 11•13, REF•8
  switch – 12•6
MOT test checks – REF•8 *et seq*
Motor factors – REF•3
Mountings – 2A•22, 7B•5
Multi Point Fuel Injection – 4A•2

N

Neutral start switch – 7B•4
Number plate light – 12•11, 12•14

O

Oil control valve – 2A•11
  filter – 2A•11
Oil
  engine – 0•12, 0•17, 1•8
  manual transmission – 0•17, 1•11
Oil filter – 1•8
Oil pressure switch – 2A•20
Oil pump – 2A•19
Oil seals – REF•4
  automatic transmission – 7B•2
  camshaft – 2A•12
  crankshaft – 2A•11, 2A•21
  manual transmission – 7A•4
Oil sump – 2A•18
Open-circuit – 12•2

P

Pads – 1•13, 9•4, 9•7
Parts – REF•3
Pedals
  brake – 9•17
  clutch – 1•15
Pick-up coil – 5B•5
Pipes – 4A•2, 4A•5, 9•3
Piston rings – 2B•10
Pistons – 2B•7, 2B•8, 2B•12
Plastic components – 11•3
Poisonous or irritant substances – 0•5
Pollen filter – 1•15
Positive Crankcase Ventilation (PCV) system – 4B•3
Power steering fluid – 0•15, 0•17
Power steering pump – 10•14
Puncture repair – 0•9

R

Radiator – 1•18, 3•5
  cooling fan – 3•4
  grille – 11•6
Rear light clusters – 12•13
Rear screen – 11•13
Receiver/drier – 3•11
Refrigerant charge – 3•10
Regulator
  alternator – 5A•4
  ABS – 9•21
  window – 11•10, 11•11
Relays – 3•3, 3•4, 12•4
Release bearing and lever (clutch) – 6•3
Release cylinder (clutch) – 6•5
Remote control battery – 1•14
Repair procedures – REF•4
Respraying – 11•3
Reversing light – 12•10
  switch – 7A•2
Road test – 1•15
Roadside repairs – 0•7 *et seq*
Routine maintenance and servicing – 1•1 *et seq*
  bodywork and underframe – 11•1
  upholstery and carpets – 11•2
Rust holes – 11•2

S

Safety first! – 0•5, 0•13, 0•15
Scalding – 0•5
Scratches – 11•2
Screenwasher fluid – 0•13
Screw threads and fastenings – REF•4
Seal leaks – 7B•2
Seat belts – 11•15
Seats – 11•14
Selector cable – 7B•4

Index

Note: *References throughout this index are in the form* **"Chapter number"** • **"Page number"**. *So, for example, 2C•15 refers to page 15 of Chapter 2C.*

Sensors (air conditioning system) – 3•13
Service ports – 3•10
Servo unit – 9•17, 9•18
Shock absorber – 1•14, REF•9, REF•10
Shoes – 1•13, 9•11
Short-circuit – 12•2
Side airbags – 12•19
Sidelight – 12•9
Spare parts – REF•3
Spark plug – 1•16
Speakers – 12•47
Speed sensor – 12•8
    O-ring – 7B•2
Spring assembly – 10•4, REF•10
Sprockets – 2A•6, 2A•8
Starter motor – 5A•6
Starter switch – 12•5
Starting and charging systems – 5A•1 *et seq*
Start-up after overhaul – 2B•13
Steering – 1•14, 1•15, 10•12, REF•9, REF•10
Steering column – REF•8
    switches – 12•4
Steering rack – 10•13
Steering wheel – 10•12, REF•8
Stop-light – 12•10, 12•14
    switch – 9•19
Strut
    suspension – 1•14, 10•3, 10•4, 10•9, 10•10
    tailgate – 11•12
Sunlight sensor – 3•13
Sunroof – 11•14
    switch – 12•7
Sunvisors – 11•19
Supplemental Restraint System (SRS) – 12•17, 12•18
Suspension and steering systems – 1•14, 1•15, 10•1 *et seq*, REF•9, REF•10
    fault finding – REF•20
Suspension arms – 10•10
Suspension strut – 10•3, 10•4, 10•9, 10•10
Switches – 12•4
    automatic transmission neutral start – 7B•4
    clutch start – 6•6
    oil pressure – 2A•20
    reversing light – 7A•2
    stop-light – 9•19
    sunroof – 11•14

T

Tail light – 12•10
Tailgate – 11•11
    glass – 11•13
    lock actuator (central locking) – 11•13
    support struts – 11•12
    trim panel – 11•18
    wiper motor – 12•17
Tappets – 2A•12
Temperature gauge sender unit – 3•7
Temperature sensor – 3•13, 4A•11

Thermostat – 3•3
Throttle body – 4A•8
Throttle position sensor (TPS) – 4A•8
Throttle valve (TV) cable – 7B•3
Timing belt and sprockets – 2A•6
Timing chain and sprockets – 2A•8
Timing ignition – 5B•4
Tools and working facilities – REF•4, REF•6 *et seq*
Top Dead Centre (TDC) for number one piston location – 2A•4
Towing – 0•10
Toyota manual – 0•6
Track rod ends – 10•13
Trim panels – 11•7, 11•14, 11•16
Tyres – 10•15, REF•11
    condition and pressure – 0•14
    pressures – 0•17
    specialists – REF•3

U

Underbonnet check points – 0•11
Underframe – 11•1
Under-panels – 11•14
Upholstery – 11•2

V

Vacuum (MAP) sensor – 4A•11
Vacuum servo unit – 9•17, 9•18
Valve clearances – 1•19
Valves – 2B•6
Variable Valve Timing (VVT-i) – 2A•11
Vehicle identification – REF•3, REF•9
Vehicle speed sensor – 12•8
Vehicle support – REF•5

W

Washer system – 12•15
Weekly checks – 0•11 *et seq*
Weights – REF•1
Wheel arch liners – 11•14
Wheel bearing assembly – 10•8, 10•11, REF•10
Wheel cylinder – 9•15
Wheel speed sensors ABS – 9•21
Wheels – 10•15, REF•11
    alignment – 10•16
    changing – 0•9
Windows – 11•13
    door – 11•10
    fixed – 11•11, 11•13
Windscreen – 11•13, REF•8
Windscreen wiper motor – 12•16
Wiper arms – 12•15
Wiper blades – 0•15
Wiper motor
    tailgate – 12•17
    windscreen – 12•16
Wiring diagrams – 12•20 *et seq*
Working facilities – REF•7

Haynes Manuals – The Complete List

Title	Book No.
ALFA ROMEO Alfasud/Sprint (74 - 88) up to F *	0292
Alfa Romeo Alfetta (73 - 87) up to E *	0531
AUDI 80, 90 & Coupe Petrol (79 - Nov 88) up to F	0605
Audi 80,-90 & Coupe Petrol (Oct 86 - 90) D to H	1491
Audi 100 & 200 Petrol (Oct 82 - 90) up to H	0907
Audi 100 & A6 Petrol & Diesel (May 91 - May 97) H to P	3504
Audi A3 Petrol & Diesel (96 - May 03) P to 03	4253
Audi A4 Petrol & Diesel (95 - Feb 00) M to V	3575
AUSTIN A35 & A40 (56 - 67) up to F *	0118
Austin/MG/Rover Maestro 1.3 & 1.6 Petrol (83 - 95) up to M	0922
Austin/MG Metro (80 - May 90) up to G	0718
Austin/Rover Montego 1.3 & 1.6 Petrol (84 - 94) A to L	1066
Austin/MG/Rover Montego 2.0 Petrol (84 - 95) A to M	1067
Mini (59 - 69) up to H *	0527
Mini (69 - 01) up to X	0646
Austin/Rover 2.0 litre Diesel Engine (86 - 93) C to L	1857
Austin Healey 100/6 & 3000 (56 - 68) up to G *	0049
BEDFORD CF Petrol (69 - 87) up to E	0163
Bedford/Vauxhall Rascal & Suzuki Supercarry (86 - Oct 94) C to M	3015
BMW 316, 320 & 320i (4-cyl) (75 - Feb 83) up to Y*	0276
BMW 320, 320i, 323i & 325i (6-cyl) (Oct 77 - Sept 87) up to E	0815
BMW 3- & 5-Series Petrol (81 - 91) up to J	1948
BMW 3-Series Petrol (Apr 91 - 96) H to N	3210
BMW 3-Series Petrol (Sept 98 - 03) S to 53	4067
BMW 520i & 525e (Oct 81 - June 88) up to E	1560
BMW 525, 528 & 528i (73 - Sept 81) up to X *	0632
BMW 5-Series 6-cyl Petrol (April 96 - Aug 03) N to 03	4151
BMW 1500, 1502, 1600, 1602, 2000 & 2002 (59 - 77) up to S *	0240
CHRYSLER PT Cruiser Petrol (00 - 03) W to 53	4058
CITROËN 2CV, Ami & Dyane (67 - 90) up to H	0196
Citroën AX Petrol & Diesel (87 - 97) D to P	3014
Citroën Berlingo & Peugeot Partner Petrol & Diesel (96 - 05) P to 55	4281
Citroën BX Petrol (83 - 94) A to L	0908
Citroën C15 Van Petrol & Diesel (89 - Oct 98) F to S	3509
Citroën C3 Petrol & Diesel (02 - 05) 51 to 05	4197
Citroën CX Petrol (75 - 88) up to F	0528
Citroën Saxo Petrol & Diesel (96 - 04) N to 54	3506
Citroën Visa Petrol (79 - 88) up to F	0620
Citroën Xantia Petrol & Diesel (93 - 01) K to Y	3082
Citroën XM Petrol & Diesel (89 - 00) G to X	3451
Citroën Xsara Petrol & Diesel (97 - Sept 00) R to W	3751
Citroën Xsara Picasso Petrol & Diesel (00 - 02) W to 52	3944
Citroën ZX Diesel (91 - 98) J to S	1922
Citroën ZX Petrol (91 - 98) H to S	1881
Citroën 1.7 & 1.9 litre Diesel Engine (84 - 96) A to N	1379
FIAT 126 (73 - 87) up to E *	0305
Fiat 500 (57 - 73) up to M *	0090
Fiat Bravo & Brava Petrol (95 - 00) N to W	3572
Fiat Cinquecento (93 - 98) K to R	3501
Fiat Panda (81 - 95) up to M	0793
Fiat Punto Petrol & Diesel (94 - Oct 99) L to V	3251
Fiat Punto Petrol (Oct 99 - July 03) V to 03	4066
Fiat Regata Petrol (84 - 88) A to F	1167
Fiat Tipo Petrol (88 - 91) E to J	1625
Fiat Uno Petrol (83 - 95) up to M	0923
Fiat X1/9 (74 - 89) up to G *	0273
FORD Anglia (59 - 68) up to G *	0001

Title	Book No.
Ford Capri II (& III) 1.6 & 2.0 (74 - 87) up to E *	0283
Ford Capri II (& III) 2.8 & 3.0 V6 (74 - 87) up to E	1309
Ford Cortina Mk III 1300 & 1600 (70 - 76) up to P *	0070
Ford Escort Mk I 1100 & 1300 (68 - 74) up to N *	0171
Ford Escort Mk I Mexico, RS 1600 & RS 2000 (70 - 74) up to N *	0139
Ford Escort Mk II Mexico, RS 1800 & RS 2000 (75 - 80) up to W *	0735
Ford Escort (75 - Aug 80) up to V *	0280
Ford Escort Petrol (Sept 80 - Sept 90) up to H	0686
Ford Escort & Orion Petrol (Sept 90 - 00) H to X	1737
Ford Escort & Orion Diesel (Sept 90 - 00) H to X	4081
Ford Fiesta (76 - Aug 83) up to Y	0334
Ford Fiesta Petrol (Aug 83 - Feb 89) A to F	1030
Ford Fiesta Petrol (Feb 89 - Oct 95) F to N	1595
Ford Fiesta Petrol & Diesel (Oct 95 - Mar 02) N to 02	3397
Ford Fiesta Petrol & Diesel (Apr 02 - 05) 02 to 54	4170
Ford Focus Petrol & Diesel (98 - 01) S to Y	3759
Ford Focus Petrol & Diesel (Oct 01 - 04) 51 to 54	4167
Ford Galaxy Petrol & Diesel (95 - Aug 00) M to W	3984
Ford Granada Petrol (Sept 77 - Feb 85) up to B *	0481
Ford Granada & Scorpio Petrol (Mar 85 - 94) B to M	1245
Ford Ka (96 - 02) P to 52	3570
Ford Mondeo Petrol (93 - Sept 00) K to X	1923
Ford Mondeo Petrol & Diesel (Oct 00 - Jul 03) X to 03	3990
Ford Mondeo Diesel (93 - 96) L to N	3465
Ford Orion Petrol (83 - Sept 90) up to H	1009
Ford Sierra 4-cyl Petrol (82 - 93) up to K	0903
Ford Sierra V6 Petrol (82 - 91) up to J	0904
Ford Transit Petrol (Mk 2) (78 - Jan 86) up to C	0719
Ford Transit Petrol (Mk 3) (Feb 86 - 89) C to G	1468
Ford Transit Diesel (Feb 86 - 99) C to T	3019
Ford 1.6 & 1.8 litre Diesel Engine (84 - 96) A to N	1172
Ford 2.1, 2.3 & 2.5 litre Diesel Engine (77 - 90) up to H	1606
FREIGHT ROVER Sherpa Petrol (74 - 87) up to E	0463
HILLMAN Avenger (70 - 82) up to Y	0037
Hillman Imp (63 - 76) up to R *	0022
HONDA Civic (Feb 84 - Oct 87) A to E	1226
Honda Civic (Nov 91 - 96) J to N	3199
Honda Civic Petrol (Mar 95 - 00) M to X	4050
HYUNDAI Pony (85 - 94) C to M	3398
JAGUAR E Type (61 - 72) up to L *	0140
Jaguar MkI & II, 240 & 340 (55 - 69) up to H *	0098
Jaguar XJ6, XJ & Sovereign; Daimler Sovereign (68 - Oct 86) up to D	0242
Jaguar XJ6 & Sovereign (Oct 86 - Sept 94) D to M	3261
Jaguar XJ12, XJS & Sovereign; Daimler Double Six (72 - 88) up to F	0478
JEEP Cherokee Petrol (93 - 96) K to N	1943
LADA 1200, 1300, 1500 & 1600 (74 - 91) up to J	0413
Lada Samara (87 - 91) D to J	1610
LAND ROVER 90, 110 & Defender Diesel (83 - 95) up to M	3017
Land Rover Discovery Petrol & Diesel (89 - 98) G to S	3016
Land Rover Freelander Petrol & Diesel (97 - 02) R to 52	3929
Land Rover Series IIA & III Diesel (58 - 85) up to C	0529
Land Rover Series II, IIA & III 4-cyl Petrol (58 - 85) up to C	0314
MAZDA 323 (Mar 81 - Oct 89) up to G	1608
Mazda 323 (Oct 89 - 98) G to R	3455
Mazda 626 (May 83 - Sept 87) up to E	0929
Mazda B1600, B1800 & B2000 Pick-up Petrol (72 - 88) up to F	0267

Title	Book No.
Mazda RX-7 (79 - 85) up to C *	0460
MERCEDES-BENZ 190, 190E & 190D Petrol & Diesel (83 - 93) A to L	3450
Mercedes-Benz 200D, 240D, 240TD, 300D & 300TD 123 Series Diesel (Oct 76 - 85) up	1114
Mercedes-Benz 250 & 280 (68 - 72) up to L *	0346
Mercedes-Benz 250 & 280 123 Series Petrol (Oct 76 - 84) up to B *	0677
Mercedes-Benz 124 Series Petrol & Diesel (85 - Aug 93) C to K	3253
Mercedes-Benz C-Class Petrol & Diesel (93 - Aug 00) L to W	3511
MGA (55 - 62) *	0475
MGB (62 - 80) up to W	0111
MG Midget & Austin-Healey Sprite (58 - 80) up to W *	0265
MINI Petrol (July 01 - 05) Y to 05	4273
MITSUBISHI Shogun & L200 Pick-Ups Petrol (83 - 94) up to M	1944
MORRIS Ital 1.3 (80 - 84) up to B	0705
Morris Minor 1000 (56 - 71) up to K	0024
NISSAN Almera Petrol (95 - Feb 00) N to V	4053
Nissan Bluebird (May 84 - Mar 86) A to C	1223
Nissan Bluebird Petrol (Mar 86 - 90) C to H	1473
Nissan Cherry (Sept 82 - 86) up to D	1031
Nissan Micra (83 - Jan 93) up to K	0931
Nissan Micra (93 - 02) K to 52	3254
Nissan Primera Petrol (90 - Aug 99) H to T	1851
Nissan Stanza (82 - 86) up to D	0824
Nissan Sunny Petrol (May 82 - Oct 86) up to D	0895
Nissan Sunny Petrol (Oct 86 - Mar 91) D to H	1378
Nissan Sunny Petrol (Apr 91 - 95) H to N	3219
OPEL Ascona & Manta (B Series) (Sept 75 - 88) up to F *	0316
Opel Ascona Petrol (81 - 88)	3215
Opel Astra Petrol (Oct 91 - Feb 98)	3156
Opel Corsa Petrol (83 - Mar 93)	3160
Opel Corsa Petrol (Mar 93 - 97)	3159
Opel Kadett Petrol (Nov 79 - Oct 84) up to B	0634
Opel Kadett Petrol (Oct 84 - Oct 91)	3196
Opel Omega & Senator Petrol (Nov 86 - 94)	3157
Opel Rekord Petrol (Feb 78 - Oct 86) up to D	0543
Opel Vectra Petrol (Oct 88 - Oct 95)	3158
PEUGEOT 106 Petrol & Diesel (91 - 04) J to 53	1882
Peugeot 205 Petrol (83 - 97) A to P	0932
Peugeot 206 Petrol & Diesel (98 - 01) S to X	3757
Peugeot 306 Petrol & Diesel (93 - 02) K to 02	3073
Peugeot 307 Petrol & Diesel (01 - 04) Y to 54	4147
Peugeot 309 Petrol (86 - 93) C to K	1266
Peugeot 405 Petrol (88 - 97) E to P	1559
Peugeot 405 Diesel (88 - 97) E to P	3198
Peugeot 406 Petrol & Diesel (96 - Mar 99) N to T	3394
Peugeot 406 Petrol & Diesel (Mar 99 - 02) T to 52	3982
Peugeot 505 Petrol (79 - 89) up to G	0762
Peugeot 1.7/1.8 & 1.9 litre Diesel Engine (82 - 96) up to N	0950
Peugeot 2.0, 2.1, 2.3 & 2.5 litre Diesel Engines (74 - 90) up to H	1607
PORSCHE 911 (65 - 85) up to C	0264
Porsche 924 & 924 Turbo (76 - 85) up to C	0397
PROTON (89 - 97) F to P	3255
RANGE ROVER V8 Petrol (70 - Oct 92) up to K	0606
RELIANT Robin & Kitten (73 - 83) up to A *	0436
RENAULT 4 (61 - 86) up to D *	0072

* Classic reprint

Title	Book No.
Renault 5 Petrol (Feb 85 - 96) B to N	1219
Renault 9 & 11 Petrol (82 - 89) up to F	0822
Renault 18 Petrol (79 - 86) up to D	0598
Renault 19 Petrol (89 - 96) F to N	1646
Renault 19 Diesel (89 - 96) F to N	1946
Renault 21 Petrol (86 - 94) C to M	1397
Renault 25 Petrol & Diesel (84 - 92) B to K	1228
Renault Clio Petrol (91 - May 98) H to R	1853
Renault Clio Diesel (91 - June 96) H to N	3031
Renault Clio Petrol & Diesel (May 98 - May 01) R to Y	3906
Renault Clio Petrol & Diesel (June 01 - 04) Y to 54	4168
Renault Espace Petrol & Diesel (85 - 96) C to N	3197
Renault Laguna Petrol & Diesel (94 - 00) L to W	3252
Renault Laguna Petrol & Diesel (01 - 05) X to 05	4283
Renault Mégane & Scénic Petrol & Diesel (96 - 98) N to R	3395
Renault Mégane & Scénic Petrol & Diesel (Apr 99 - 02) T to 52	3916
Renault Megane Petrol & Diesel (Oct 02 - 05) 52 to 55	4284
Renault Scenic Petrol & Diesel (Sept 03 - 06) 53 to 06	4297
ROVER 213 & 216 (84 - 89) A to G	1116
Rover 214 & 414 Petrol (89 - 96) G to N	1689
Rover 216 & 416 Petrol (89 - 96) G to N	1830
Rover 211, 214, 216, 218 & 220 Petrol & Diesel (Dec 95 - 99) N to V	3399
Rover 25 & MG ZR Petrol & Diesel (Oct 99 - 04) V to 54	4145
Rover 414, 416 & 420 Petrol & Diesel (May 95 - 98) M to R	3453
Rover 45 / MG ZS	4384
Rover 618, 620 & 623 Petrol (93 - 97) K to P	3257
Rover 75 / MG ZT Petrol & Diesel (Feb 99 - 05) T to 05	4292
Rover 820, 825 & 827 Petrol (86 - 95) D to N	1380
Rover 3500 (76 - 87) up to E *	0365
Rover Metro, 111 & 114 Petrol (May 90 - 98) G to S	1711
SAAB 95 & 96 (66 - 76) up to R *	0198
Saab 90, 99 & 900 (79 - Oct 93) up to L	0765
Saab 900 (Oct 93 - 98) L to R	3512
Saab 9000 (4-cyl) (85 - 98) C to S	1686
Saab 9-5 4-cyl Petrol (97 - 04) R to 54	4156
SEAT Ibiza & Cordoba Petrol & Diesel (Oct 93 - Oct 99) L to V	3571
Seat Ibiza & Malaga Petrol (85 - 92) B to K	1609
SKODA Estelle (77 - 89) up to G	0604
Skoda Fabia (00 - 06) W to 06	4376
Skoda Favorit (89 - 96) F to N	1801
Skoda Felicia Petrol & Diesel (95 - 01) M to X	3505
Skoda Octavia Petrol & Diesel (98 - Apr 04) R to 04	4285
SUBARU 1600 & 1800 (Nov 79 - 90) up to H *	0995
SUNBEAM Alpine, Rapier & H120 (67 - 74) up to N *	0051
SUZUKI SJ Series, Samurai & Vitara (4-cyl) Petrol (82 - 97) up to P	1942
Suzuki Supercarry & Bedford/Vauxhall Rascal (86 - Oct 94) C to M	3015
TALBOT Alpine, Solara, Minx & Rapier (75 - 86) up to D	0337
Talbot Horizon Petrol (78 - 86) up to D	0473
Talbot Samba (82 - 86) up to D	0823
TOYOTA Avensis Petrol (Nov 97 - Jan 03) R to 52	4264
Toyota Carina E Petrol (May 92 - 97) J to P	3256
Toyota Corolla (80 - 85) up to C	0683

Title	Book No.
Toyota Corolla (Sept 83 - Sept 87) A to E	1024
Toyota Corolla (Sept 87 - Aug 92) E to K	1683
Toyota Corolla Petrol (Aug 92 - 97) K to P	3259
Toyota Corolla Petrol (June 97 - 01) P to 51	4286
Toyota Hi-Ace & Hi-Lux Petrol (69 - Oct 83) up to A	0304
Toyota Yaris Petrol (99 - 05) T to 05	4265
TRIUMPH GT6 & Vitesse (62 - 74) up to N *	0112
Triumph Herald (59 - 71) up to K *	0010
Triumph Spitfire (62 - 81) up to X	0113
Triumph Stag (70 - 78) up to T *	0441
Triumph TR2, TR3, TR3A, TR4 & TR4A (52 - 67) up to F *	0028
Triumph TR5 & 6 (67 - 75) up to P *	0031
Triumph TR7 (75 - 82) up to Y *	0322
VAUXHALL Astra Petrol (80 - Oct 84) up to B	0635
Vauxhall Astra & Belmont Petrol (Oct 84 - Oct 91) B to J	1136
Vauxhall Astra Petrol (Oct 91 - Feb 98) J to R	1832
Vauxhall/Opel Astra & Zafira Petrol (Feb 98 - Apr 04) R to 04	3758
Vauxhall/Opel Astra & Zafira Diesel (Feb 98 - Apr 04) R to 04	3797
Vauxhall/Opel Calibra (90 - 98) G to S	3502
Vauxhall Carlton Petrol (Oct 78 - Oct 86) up to D	0480
Vauxhall Carlton & Senator Petrol (Nov 86 - 94) D to L	1469
Vauxhall Cavalier Petrol (81 - Oct 88) up to F	0812
Vauxhall Cavalier Petrol (Oct 88 - 95) F to N	1570
Vauxhall Chevette (75 - 84) up to B	0285
Vauxhall/Opel Corsa Diesel (Mar 93 - Oct 00) K to X	4087
Vauxhall Corsa Petrol (Mar 93 - 97) K to R	1985
Vauxhall/Opel Corsa Petrol (Apr 97 - Oct 00) P to X	3921
Vauxhall/Opel Corsa Petrol & Diesel (Oct 00 - Sept 03) X to 53	4079
Vauxhall/Opel Frontera Petrol & Diesel (91 - Sept 98) J to S	3454
Vauxhall Nova Petrol (83 - 93) up to K	0909
Vauxhall/Opel Omega Petrol (94 - 99) L to T	3510
Vauxhall/Opel Vectra Petrol & Diesel (95 - Feb 99) N to S	3396
Vauxhall/Opel Vectra Petrol & Diesel (Mar 99 - May 02) T to 02	3930
Vauxhall/Opel 1.5, 1.6 & 1.7 litre Diesel Engine (82 - 96) up to N	1222
VOLKSWAGEN 411 & 412 (68 - 75) up to P *	0091
Volkswagen Beetle 1200 (54 - 77) up to S	0036
Volkswagen Beetle 1300 & 1500 (65 - 75) up to P	0039
Volkswagen Beetle 1302 & 1302S (70 - 72) up to L *	0110
Volkswagen Beetle 1303, 1303S & GT (72 - 75) up to P	0159
Volkswagen Beetle Petrol & Diesel (Apr 99 - 01) T to 51	3798
Volkswagen Golf & Jetta Mk 1 Petrol 1.1 & 1.3 (74 - 84) up to A	0716
Volkswagen Golf, Jetta & Scirocco Mk 1 Petrol 1.5, 1.6 & 1.8 (74 - 84) up to A	0726
Volkswagen Golf & Jetta Mk 1 Diesel (78 - 84) up to A	0451
Volkswagen Golf & Jetta Mk 2 Petrol (Mar 84 - Feb 92) A to J	1081
Volkswagen Golf & Vento Petrol & Diesel (Feb 92 - Mar 98) J to R	3097
Volkswagen Golf & Bora Petrol & Diesel (April 98 - 00) R to X	3727
Volkswagen Golf & Bora 4-cyl Petrol & Diesel (01 - 03) X to 53	4169

Title	Book No.
Volkswagen LT Petrol Vans & Light Trucks (76 - 87) up to E	0637
Volkswagen Passat & Santana Petrol (Sept 81 - May 88) up to E	0814
Volkswagen Passat 4-cyl Petrol & Diesel (May 88 - 96) E to P	3498
Volkswagen Passat 4-cyl Petrol & Diesel (Dec 96 - Nov 00) P to X	3917
Volkswagen Passat Petrol & Diesel (Dec 00 - May 05) X to 05	4279
Volkswagen Polo & Derby (76 - Jan 82) up to X	0335
Volkswagen Polo (82 - Oct 90) up to H	0813
Volkswagen Polo Petrol (Nov 90 - Aug 94) H to L	3245
Volkswagen Polo Hatchback Petrol & Diesel (94 - 99) M to S	3500
Volkswagen Polo Hatchback Petrol (00 - Jan 02) V to 51	4150
Volkswagen Scirocco (82 - 90) up to H *	1224
Volkswagen Transporter 1600 (68 - 79) up to V	0082
Volkswagen Transporter 1700, 1800 & 2000 (72 - 79) up to V *	0226
Volkswagen Transporter (air-cooled) Petrol (79 - 82) up to Y *	0638
Volkswagen Transporter (water-cooled) Petrol (82 - 90) up to H	3452
Volkswagen Type 3 (63 - 73) up to M *	0084
VOLVO 120 & 130 Series (& P1800) (61 - 73) up to M *	0203
Volvo 142, 144 & 145 (66 - 74) up to N *	0129
Volvo 240 Series Petrol (74 - 93) up to K	0270
Volvo 262, 264 & 260/265 (75 - 85) up to C *	0400
Volvo 340, 343, 345 & 360 (76 - 91) up to J	0715
Volvo 440, 460 & 480 Petrol (87 - 97) D to P	1691
Volvo 740 & 760 Petrol (82 - 91) up to J	1258
Volvo 850 Petrol (92 - 96) J to P	3260
Volvo 940 Petrol (90 - 96) H to N	3249
Volvo S40 & V40 Petrol (96 - Mar 04) N to 04	3569
Volvo S70, V70 & C70 Petrol (96 - 99) P to V	3573
Volvo V70 / S80 Petrol & Diesel (98 - 05) S to 55	4263

AUTOMOTIVE TECHBOOKS

Title	Book No.
Automotive Air Conditioning Systems	3740
Automotive Electrical and Electronic Systems Manual	3049
Automotive Gearbox Overhaul Manual	3473
Automotive Service Summaries Manual	3475
Automotive Timing Belts Manual – Austin/Rover	3549
Automotive Timing Belts Manual – Ford	3474
Automotive Timing Belts Manual – Peugeot/Citroën	3568
Automotive Timing Belts Manual – Vauxhall/Opel	3577

DIY MANUAL SERIES

Title	Book No.
The Haynes Air Conditioning Manual	4192
The Haynes Manual on Bodywork	4198
The Haynes Manual on Brakes	4178
The Haynes Manual on Carburettors	4177
The Haynes Car Electrical Systems Manual	4251
The Haynes Manual on Diesel Engines	4174
The Haynes Manual on Engine Management	4199
The Haynes Manual on Fault Codes	4175
The Haynes Manual on Practical Electrical Systems	4267
The Haynes Manual on Small Engines	4250
The Haynes Manual on Welding	4176

* Classic reprint

All the products featured on this page are available through most motor accessory shops, cycle shops and book stores. Our policy of continuous updating and development means that titles are being constantly added to the range. For up-to-date information on our complete list of titles, please telephone: (UK) +44 1963 442030 • (USA) +1 805 498 6703 • (France) +33 1 47 17 66 29 • (Sweden) +46 18 124016 • (Australia) +61 3 9763 8100

Preserving Our Motoring Heritage

The Model J Duesenberg Derham Tourster. Only eight of these magnificent cars were ever built – this is the only example to be found outside the United States of America

Almost every car you've ever loved, loathed or desired is gathered under one roof at the Haynes Motor Museum. Over 300 immaculately presented cars and motorbikes represent every aspect of our motoring heritage, from elegant reminders of bygone days, such as the superb Model J Duesenberg to curiosities like the bug-eyed BMW Isetta. There are also many old friends and flames. Perhaps you remember the 1959 Ford Popular that you did your courting in? The magnificent 'Red Collection' is a spectacle of classic sports cars including AC, Alfa Romeo, Austin Healey, Ferrari, Lamborghini, Maserati, MG, Riley, Porsche and Triumph.

A Perfect Day Out

Each and every vehicle at the Haynes Motor Museum has played its part in the history and culture of Motoring. Today, they make a wonderful spectacle and a great day out for all the family. Bring the kids, bring Mum and Dad, but above all bring your camera to capture those golden memories for ever. You will also find an impressive array of motoring memorabilia, a comfortable 70 seat video cinema and one of the most extensive transport book shops in Britain. The Pit Stop Cafe serves everything from a cup of tea to wholesome, home-made meals or, if you prefer, you can enjoy the large picnic area nestled in the beautiful rural surroundings of Somerset.

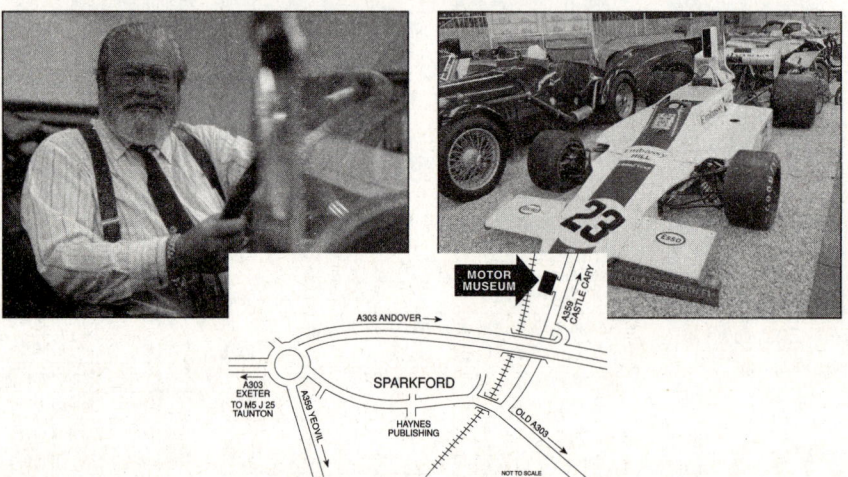

John Haynes O.B.E., Founder and Chairman of the museum at the wheel of a Haynes Light 12.

Graham Hill's Lola Cosworth Formula 1 car next to a 1934 Riley Sports.

The Museum is situated on the A359 Yeovil to Frome road at Sparkford, just off the A303 in Somerset. It is about 40 miles south of Bristol, and 25 minutes drive from the M5 intersection at Taunton.
Open 9.30am - 5.30pm (10.00am - 4.00pm Winter) 7 days a week, *except Christmas Day, Boxing Day and New Years Day*
Special rates available for schools, coach parties and outings Charitable Trust No. 292048